The Interdisciplinary Reader

A COLLECTION OF STUDENT WRITING

James D. Williams
University of North Carolina—Chapel Hill

David Huntley
Appalachian State University

Christine Hanks
University of North Carolina—Chapel Hill

■ HarperCollins*Publishers*

Sponsoring Editor: Patricia Rossi
Project Editor: David Nickol
Design Supervisor: Mary Archondes
Text Design: Lisa Douglis
Cover Art/Design: Molly Heron
Production Administrator: Kathleen Donnelly/Beth Maglione
Compositor: American-Stratford Graphic Services, Inc.
Printer and Binder: R. R. Donnelley & Sons Company
Cover Printer: The Lehigh Press, Inc.

The Interdisciplinary Reader: A Collection of Student Writing

Copyright © 1992 by HarperCollins Publishers Inc.

All rights reserved. Printed in the United States of America. No part of this book may be used or reproduced in any manner whatsoever without written permission, except in the case of brief quotations embodied in critical articles and reviews. For information address HarperCollins Publishers Inc., 10 East 53rd Street, New York, NY 10022.

Library of Congress Cataloging-in-Publication Data
Williams, James D. (James Dale), 1949–
    The interdisciplinary reader / James D. Williams, David Huntley, Christine Hanks.
       p.   cm.
    ISBN 0-673-38575-2
    1. College readers.   2. English language—Rhetoric.
3. Interdisciplinary approach in education.   I. Huntley, David.
II. Hanks, Christine.   III. Title.
PE1417.W49   1992
808'.0427—dc20   91-18253
                                                        CIP

91 92 93 94 9 8 7 6 5 4 3 2 1

Dedications

This book is dedicated to my sisters—Betty, Barbara, and Joan—and to W. Ross Winterowd, my teacher and friend.

JDW

I want to dedicate this book to my wife, Edelma, who through the three years it took to complete was always kind, considerate, and, above all, patient.

DEH

In appreciation of his love and encouragement, this book is dedicated to my father, Jerome M. Fesperman.

CFH

Contents

Rhetorical Table of Contents ix
Preface xii
Introduction for Students xxi

Part One **LIFE AND APPLIED SCIENCES**
Writing in Life and Applied Sciences 1

1 Chemistry 9
Introduction to Writing in Chemistry 9
CHEMISTRY ASSIGNMENT 1 10
CHEMISTRY ASSIGNMENT 2 31
CHEMISTRY ASSIGNMENT 3 41

2 Mathematics 53
Introduction to Writing in Math 53
MATH ASSIGNMENT 1 55
MATH ASSIGNMENT 2 71
MATH ASSIGNMENT 3 77

3 Biology — 85
Introduction to Writing in Biology — 85
BIOLOGY ASSIGNMENT 1 — 87
BIOLOGY ASSIGNMENT 2 — 93
BIOLOGY ASSIGNMENT 3 — 97

4 Physics — 110
Introduction to Writing in Physics — 110
PHYSICS ASSIGNMENT 1 — 113
PHYSICS ASSIGNMENT 2 — 156
PHYSICS ASSIGNMENT 3 — 179

Part Two SOCIAL SCIENCES
Writing in the Social Sciences — 195

5 Psychology — 208
Introduction to Writing in Psychology — 208
PSYCHOLOGY ASSIGNMENT 1 — 209
PSYCHOLOGY ASSIGNMENT 2 — 222
PSYCHOLOGY ASSIGNMENT 3 — 248

6 Political Science — 267
Introduction to Writing in Political Science — 267
POLITICAL SCIENCE ASSIGNMENT 1 — 268
POLITICAL SCIENCE ASSIGNMENT 2 — 292
POLITICAL SCIENCE ASSIGNMENT 3 — 307

7 Anthropology — 345

Introduction to Writing in Anthropology — 345

ANTHROPOLOGY ASSIGNMENT 1 — 347

ANTHROPOLOGY ASSIGNMENT 2 — 360

ANTHROPOLOGY ASSIGNMENT 3 — 381

Part Three HUMANITIES

Writing in the Humanities — 389

8 English — 402

Introduction to Writing in English — 402

ENGLISH ASSIGNMENT 1 — 404

ENGLISH ASSIGNMENT 2 — 429

ENGLISH ASSIGNMENT 3 — 456

9 History — 469

Introduction to Writing in History — 469

HISTORY ASSIGNMENT 1 — 471

HISTORY ASSIGNMENT 2 — 491

HISTORY ASSIGNMENT 3 — 506

10 Philosophy — 538

Introduction to Writing in Philosophy — 538

PHILOSOPHY ASSIGNMENT 1 — 539

PHILOSOPHY ASSIGNMENT 2 — 558

PHILOSOPHY ASSIGNMENT 3 — 590

11 Fine and Applied Arts — 618

Introduction to Writing in the
Fine and Applied Arts — 618

ART ASSIGNMENT 1 — 620
ART ASSIGNMENT 2 — 625
DRAMA ASSIGNMENT 1 — 632
DRAMA ASSIGNMENT 2 — 645
FILM ASSIGNMENT 1 — 653
FILM ASSIGNMENT 2 — 665
MUSIC ASSIGNMENT 1 — 675
MUSIC ASSIGNMENT 2 — 682

Part Four BUSINESS

Writing in Business — 697

12 Business Writing — 701

Introduction to Writing in Business — 701
BUSINESS ASSIGNMENT 1 — 708
BUSINESS ASSIGNMENT 2 — 728
BUSINESS ASSIGNMENT 3 — 737

Rhetorical Table of Contents

The Research Paper

CHEMISTRY ASSIGNMENT 1	10
PHYSICS ASSIGNMENT 1	113
PHYSICS ASSIGNMENT 3	179
ANTHROPOLOGY ASSIGNMENT 1	347
ANTHROPOLOGY ASSIGNMENT 2	360
HISTORY ASSIGNMENT 3	506

The Abstract

CHEMISTRY ASSIGNMENT 2	31

The Lab Report

CHEMISTRY ASSIGNMENT 3	41
PHYSICS ASSIGNMENT 2	156

The Essay Exam

BIOLOGY ASSIGNMENT 1	87
BIOLOGY ASSIGNMENT 2	93
ANTHROPOLOGY ASSIGNMENT 3	381
ENGLISH ASSIGNMENT 3	456

The Critical Review

PSYCHOLOGY ASSIGNMENT 2	222
POLITICAL SCIENCE ASSIGNMENT 2	292
HISTORY ASSIGNMENT 1	471
ART ASSIGNMENT 2	625
DRAMA ASSIGNMENT 2	645
FILM ASSIGNMENT 1	653
MUSIC ASSIGNMENT 1	675

Analysis and Argument

ENGLISH ASSIGNMENT 1	404
ENGLISH ASSIGNMENT 2	429
DRAMA ASSIGNMENT 1	632
FILM ASSIGNMENT 2	665
MUSIC ASSIGNMENT 2	682

Integration and Summary

BIOLOGY ASSIGNMENT 3	97
POLITICAL SCIENCE ASSIGNMENT 1	268
ART ASSIGNMENT 1	620
BUSINESS ASSIGNMENT 2	728

The Case Study

PSYCHOLOGY ASSIGNMENT 3	248
POLITICAL SCIENCE ASSIGNMENT 3	307
BUSINESS ASSIGNMENT 1	708

Exposition and Argument

MATH ASSIGNMENT 1	55
MATH ASSIGNMENT 2	71
MATH ASSIGNMENT 3	77
PSYCHOLOGY ASSIGNMENT 1	209
HISTORY ASSIGNMENT 2	491
PHILOSOPHY ASSIGNMENT 1	539
PHILOSOPHY ASSIGNMENT 2	558
PHILOSOPHY ASSIGNMENT 3	590

Preface

WHAT IS THIS BOOK ABOUT?

The Interdisciplinary Reader is a real writing-across-the-curriculum text. Unlike other books, it does not emphasize professional samples, which by their nature seldom reflect the concerns undergraduates have when asked to respond to a teacher's assignment. Instead, it accurately models the kinds of writing activities students perform during their undergraduate years, particularly at the lower-division level, by drawing on what teachers and students actually do in their classes. The result is a rich collection of faculty writing assignments and student responses to those assignments, including sample essay exams. The assignments and the responses are authentic, not artifacts attempting to mimic composing in the disciplines. They have an immediacy and a presence that professional models rarely attain.

We don't want to suggest, however, that professional writing is useless in composition classes. When well integrated with composing activities, it can provide important "genre familiarity" that leads to improved skills. *The Interdisciplinary Reader* therefore complements its student models with a significant array of professional writing. For numerous assignments, if professional writing was related to the paper students had to produce, we included the piece or a representative excerpt from it. The professional writing is thus embedded in the context of the assignment and the response, making it far more relevant and meaningful to students than it would be otherwise.

The Interdisciplinary Reader is designed for writing-across-the-curriculum courses that introduce nonmajors to composing in a range of subject areas. The majority of the assignments and responses come from freshman and sophomore classes. We believe, however, that lower-division students can gain important insights into writing through exposure to the more rigorous demands faced by majors at the upper-division level. As a result, we have included some assignments and responses that reflect these demands. Wherever practical, we sequenced the selections so that they move from the freshman, nonmajor level to the senior, major level. A significant consequence of this approach is that *The Interdisciplinary Reader* lends itself well to writing-across-the-curriculum (WAC) programs that include courses for more advanced students.

Ultimately, this book is about literacy, in the broadest sense. It aims to help students acquire the academic literacy skills they need not only to "survive" the undergraduate curriculum but to thrive in it. We believe that developing the skills needed for academic achievement is correlated with success in the American socioeconomic system. In our view, however, such practical outcomes cannot be divorced from intellectual and cultural development, or from personal growth and expression. Therefore, while we regularly stress the pragmatic aspects of certain rhetorical strategies and writing techniques, the underlying premise of *The Interdisciplinary Reader* is that studying this text will enhance students' critical faculties, with consequences that extend far beyond the merely pragmatic.

ORGANIZATION

The Interdisciplinary Reader is divided into four broad categories: Life and Applied Sciences, Social Sciences, Humanities, and Business. Each major division begins with an overview that addresses how the goals of *explaining, exploring, arguing,* and so forth, often govern the kind of writing that gets done in related disciplines. Equally important, they also consider how related disciplines define adequate evidence for assertions and how they share standards of proof. The purpose is to offer general strategies that students can transfer from one writing task to another.

In addition, the overviews introduce the perception that writers do not have unlimited freedom when composing a paper for others to read. They set the framework for weighing the influence communities or groups of readers exert on writers and writing. In this respect, the over-

Preface

views are informed by the perception that writing is a social action and that texts are social and cultural artifacts. The purpose is to help students master the particular strategies appropriate to specific contexts. Consequently, the overviews address some of the specific conventions of style and form that are critical to writing in every discipline. In many cases, they show how related disciplines may differ in regard to organization, format, or goals. In our view, however, the fundamental characteristic of writing across the curriculum is similarity, not difference, so the introductions stress underlying commonalties. They conclude with brief notes on documentation, offering examples of some standard documentation formats that students can use as references.

All of the teachers who contributed assignments to this text use writing as a way of learning. Their assignments immerse students in subject matter, as one would expect, but that does not appear to be the principal goal. Rather, they consistently use writing to help students develop the ability to interpret facts. In the process, students are learning how to view the world from the perspective of individual disciplines, but they are also learning how to construct their own view as critical thinkers. The act of interpreting is the rhetorical thread that winds through all the disciplines and binds them together; it is fundamentally argumentative. Our analyses build on this thread, using it as a teaching device to help students better understand reading and writing in the disciplines.

The sample assignments that follow the introductions are presented unedited and are shown exactly as they were given to students. As one might expect, some are better than others. Our aim, however, is not to offer "ideal" assignments but to provide real ones. The assignments are analyzed in detail, and when one is not well constructed, we note as much, to help students in developing strategies to cope with less-than-ideal writing prompts.

In each chapter, the student papers that accompany the first assignment are analyzed in depth. Generally, these papers range from the successful to the unsuccessful and, like the faculty assignments, are presented unedited. With the aim of helping students discover just how intrusive surface errors can be, we have indicated errors by underlining the text where the error occurs. We also hope that students will be able to detect in the errors patterns that they can use to improve their own work. If a word is misspelled, the entire word is underlined. If the problem is capitalization, just the first letter is marked. When a phrase is flawed or misplaced, the whole construction is underlined, and the same is true for fragments. Punctuation problems are noted with a single underline, and when a word is missing, as occurs often with faulty parallelism, we opened a space in the sentence and marked it. We italicized items that were underlined in the students' original papers, and in cases where students failed to signify italicization, we underlined the items to indicate the error. This situation occurs frequently in those papers that refer to books.

It is worth noting that deciding what to label a surface error and what to ignore was no small task. For example, formal usage dictates that *since* must function as a temporal subordinator, but even among highly educated people it is commonly used to indicate causality. Formal usage also dictates that *which* be used with nonrestrictive relative clauses, but even well-educated writers generally use it interchangeably with *that*. In British English, *due to* is used as a preposition, but standard American usage accepts it only as a predicate adjective. Should we have marked these and similar problems in the student papers as surface errors? Perhaps, but we chose not to, because we believe that it is the teacher's duty to discuss these fine points of standard usage with students. Consequently, we have marked only what we believe constitute serious surface errors. Many others were left untouched. Chances are that some teachers will be disturbed both by what we marked and what we didn't, but we hope that the majority will look kindly on our effort, understanding the difficulties involved.

Our use of unedited papers with marked surface errors was guided throughout by our desire to help students understand why some approaches are better than others, while simultaneously pointing out some of the structural and rhetorical features that are commonly associated with success or failure. Although *The Interdisciplinary Reader* is not explicitly a rhetoric and anthology, a significant amount of writing instruction is inherent in these analyses, and it forms an important part of the text.

Additional writing assignments are provided throughout the text with each assignment. These are commonly built around the sample assignments and extend them in various ways. Wherever feasible, the additional assignments are sequenced to balance rhetorical and cognitive demands. In every instance, the sequence is informed by our understanding that rhetorical complexity is fundamentally different from cognitive complexity. The assignments engage students in progressively more challenging *intellectual* tasks while simultaneously engaging them in progressively more challenging *writing* tasks.

Preface

RATIONALE FOR THIS BOOK

Twenty years of literacy research has shown that students become more engaged in reading and writing when they work with their own texts or those generated by peers. Teachers generally seem to find professional models more interesting than students do, yet these models do not seem to enhance performance in any measurable way over the short term. Over the long term, however, they provide an underlying familiarity with different genres of writing, such as poetry, argumentation, analysis, editorials, and so on. Without this genre familiarity, success at writing is overwhelmingly difficult, if not impossible.

On this account, *The Interdisciplinary Reader* is designed to engage students with student texts. Professional writing is secondary. The book is grounded on the notion that, if models are going to be effective, they must resemble the kinds of writing people are actually going to produce.

UNIQUE FEATURES

This book is unlike other WAC texts in that it deals directly with the kinds of writing tasks undergraduates are asked to perform. Among its unique features are

- Real faculty assignments from 14 different departments
- Essay exam questions and responses
- Detailed analyses of each assignment
- A range of student papers, from successful to unsuccessful
- Professional samples integrated with faculty assignments and student responses
- Detailed analyses of selected responses, explaining why some approaches are more successful than others
- Introductions that examine the commonalties in writing, providing strategies that can be transferred to numerous composing situations
- Writing instruction integrated into analyses of assignments and student papers

HOW TO USE THIS BOOK

The Interdisciplinary Reader is designed for a broad-based writing-across-the-curriculum course that introduces students to the goals and conventions of writing in a range of disciplines. It will work best in a classroom workshop, where the focus is on students' writing and where the teacher provides appropriate feedback as students develop their texts in groups.

When we tested the materials we've included here, we found that the more effective classes were structured around the four major divisions of the undergraduate curriculum. Teachers divided the fifteen-week semester evenly, devoting just over three weeks to writing and reading in the life and applied sciences, just over three weeks to writing and reading in the social sciences, and so forth. They selected the individual chapters in each division according to their own preferences. We recommend using *The Interdisciplinary Reader* in this way, although we recognize that the ideal situation would provide for two terms to cover all the material in the text. Because some teachers will be able to take advantage of this ideal approach, we have included materials that will make *The Interdisciplinary Reader* an excellent text for students' second, as well as their first, term of composition.

If the text is used for one term, the class will be fast-paced, but teachers will nevertheless be able to improve students' writing and reading abilities while simultaneously acquainting them with the conventions that characterize different kinds of writing. Students will have the added benefit of working with more faculty writing assignments in a single term than they would otherwise encounter over a couple of years or more. Rather than becoming confused by the multiple expectations, goals, and requirements inherent in such an array of assignments, students begin to make a significant discovery. Beneath the seeming diversity is a fundamental rhetorical similarity: The majority of the assignments, regardless of discipline, ask students to analyze and interpret data. As we have already noted, these tasks are argumentative, and in our view, argumentation subsumes most other rhetorical modes. Consequently, the teacher in the chapter on English who asks for an "expository" essay is asking for an analytical argument.

The Interdisciplinary Reader contains a wealth of information about successful writing at the undergraduate level. As a result, it can be used without an accompanying rhetoric, although teachers will want to complement the discussions of writing during their interactions with students. Some teachers may feel more comfortable supplementing the text with a rhetoric, and certainly *The Interdisciplinary Reader* lends itself well to this approach.

The faculty writing assignments are the real starting points for using this book, but the overviews and introductions offer critical background material that informs each task. Students should therefore read the overviews and introductions with the goal of subsequently placing the faculty assignments and analyses into the context of that background information. The "Introduction for Students" section at the beginning of the book will help them do this.

The student responses become opportunities to engage in critical reading, with the analyses serving as models to help train students to be effective readers and ultimately effective writers. In every instance, the additional writing assignments have some relation to the responses, so students should be encouraged to refer to the sample papers frequently as they are producing their drafts.

We can predict that students using this book (or any other, for that matter) will encounter various difficulties as they are composing. When they do, teachers can in many cases direct them to the better student responses, helping them use these models to see how other writers dealt with the same problem or a similar one. There will be times, however, when the students who produced the models were unable to overcome some difficulty, when their rhetorical or structural skill was insufficient to solve a given problem. It is in these situations that the professional samples will function best. They therefore should be used as rhetorical models when students' drafts are well under way, *not before the writing begins*. Using them rhetorically (rather than conceptually) on an as-needed basis allows students to match their writing with the work of professionals far more readily, because the textual problem is more immediate and the motivation to achieve a match is more intense.

Finally, teachers should remember that their students' papers are important models in their own right. Whenever the opportunity arises to use these papers to illustrate specific techniques or to share with the class what individual students are doing well, teachers should seize the moment. Quite simply, no book is a substitute for the dynamic interaction that exists among students and teachers in well-planned writing classes, and the true source of that dynamism is students' own work. We encourage teachers to focus on their students' writing first and foremost, even if it means setting *The Interdisciplinary Reader* aside from time to time.

ACKNOWLEDGMENTS

Many people figured significantly in our effort to complete this book. We would like to thank the many faculty members at colleges and universities around the country who were kind enough to respond to our request for student papers. We would also like to thank the students who contributed their papers to this collection. In addition, we want to thank Anne Smith, Patricia Rossi, Constance Rajala, Ted Simpson, Byron Hopkins, Kathleen Spaltro, and Cindy Yates for their help and encouragement.

James D. Williams
David Huntley
Christine Hanks

Introduction for Students

WHAT IS THIS BOOK ABOUT?

The Interdisciplinary Reader is a book about writing and reading in the many disciplines that make up the undergraduate curriculum. It is also a book about interpreting facts.

If you're like most people, you aren't particularly interested in either. Most people believe facts speak for themselves and don't need interpreting. Also, you've taken other writing classes in the past, and if you did well, you most likely think you're a pretty good writer already. If you didn't do well, you probably think you just don't have a talent for writing or English, and no course is going to give you what you weren't born with.

We believe this book and the course you're using it in, however, aren't like anything you've experienced before. They offer a different approach to learning about language. One of their major goals is a bit more practical than what we find in most composition courses: to help you develop the "survival" skills you need to write clear, interesting, and successful papers for the various courses you will take during your years as an undergraduate. In addition, this book is based on our understanding that, contrary to popular opinion, facts *don't* speak for themselves. They must be interpreted. Those people who learn to interpret them well and convincingly shape the realities we all live by.

This book focuses on student writing produced by people just like you. From professors across the country, we collected numerous writing assignments and students' responses to those assignments. They are completely genuine. We've even kept the errors; you'll find that we underlined the more serious ones in each student paper to help you become more aware of correctness. We have analyzed assignments and responses to give you some insight into what teachers expect from their students and some advice on different ways to approach writing tasks. A few of the student papers we've included aren't very good (and some of the faculty assignments aren't either). Others are quite well written. We want to help you recognize the difference between a successful paper and an unsuccessful one. Frankly, many students aren't sure what distinguishes success from failure, why they received a *D* on a paper whereas a person sitting nearby received an *A*.

We have also provided an important range of professional samples. They should be used as references to provide a context for the student samples and to help you whenever you have a writing problem you can't solve. There's a good chance that you will find a solution in the professional work.

WRITING ACROSS THE CURRICULUM

Writing across the curriculum is an expression used to describe an effort to emphasize composing in all disciplines, not just English. Over the last few years, numerous teachers have come to recognize that success in nearly every academic endeavor is linked to language. Writing happens to be the most characteristic form of language in school, so these teachers have developed and continue to develop many ways to include more writing in various subjects. Many math teachers, for example, are now asking students to write papers, and teachers in such other subjects as economics, political science, and chemistry have increased the amount of writing they ask students to produce.

The shift toward viewing writing as something important to everyone in every field is likely to have personal consequences for you. You may have to "unlearn" much of what you were taught in high school so you can master a broader, more widely applicable range of skills. You may have to become more *flexible* in regard to the way you approach writing tasks. For example, if the composition class you took in high school dealt only with the sort of papers generally found in older handbooks on writing, you were probably taught the "five-paragraph" essay. The introductory paragraph in this essay is supposed to resemble a funnel, with the thesis statement—that is, the claim you are going to argue—lodged comfortably at the end. The next three paragraphs, or body, are supposed to "prove" the thesis statement. The concluding paragraph is supposed to rephrase the thesis. You may have been taught and may believe that a paper without these characteristics is a failure. Does any of this sound familiar?

You were also probably taught that, along the way, from the introduction to the conclusion, you were supposed to avoid the passive voice (Rita kicked Fritz, *not* Fritz was kicked by Rita), use "strong" rather than "weak" verbs (the door *stood* open, *not* The door *was* open), never begin a sentence with a word like *and* or *but,* and never end a sentence with a preposition.

But if you've ever taken an essay exam, or if you've ever written a research paper, perhaps you already know that the five-paragraph essay exists only in handbooks and in someone's imagination. Real writing tasks usually require longer or shorter responses. If you've paid careful attention to the books and articles you've read, perhaps you also know that many writers don't put a thesis statement at the end of the first paragraph. Sometimes it appears in the second paragraph, sometimes in the middle of a paper, and sometimes at the end. Certain types of writing, such as letters, descriptions, and manuals, don't even have thesis statements. Moreover, in the sciences and social sciences, passive voice is a long-standing convention. Using the active voice in many cases isn't very acceptable. And as for the injunction against beginning sentences with *and* or *but,* it has absolutely no foundation, as the first and the last sentences in this paragraph show.

The point here is not to try to give you a mini-lesson on writing, merely to demonstrate that there is a great deal more to successful composing than you may have considered. Every fall for years we have worked with freshmen who bring the above "rules" to college, and we have seen their dismay as they struggle to apply them to writing tasks that aren't amenable to such rules. Most students aren't very successful in that struggle. We therefore want to stress that good writers are generally flexible, having developed the ability to adapt easily to the particular expectations and conventions of different fields. To develop this ability, you may have to discount much of what you've been told about writing.

WRITING TO LEARN

Writing across the curriculum has become very popular over the last several years, in part because writing improves learning. When people write about a subject, particularly in conjunction with reading about it, they learn more and retain that knowledge longer than they would otherwise. In addition, they understand the subject better, perceiving details and complexities than reading alone, for example, cannot provide. Thus, writing offers tangible benefits for students interested in academic achievement.

Yet you may have been taught that writing is fundamentally a form of self-expression, in which case these largely utilitarian benefits may seem antithetical to the reasons you would like to have for writing. If one views writing purely as a means of self-expression, composing a history paper on the War of the Roses may seem pretty trying. There's not much room for "self" in such a paper, which in a real situation would no doubt be assigned by a professor who has relatively little concern for a given student's personal interests. The topic is simply part of what the course is about.

It is certainly true that teachers who study writing often talk about another kind of learning different from the practical sort outlined above, one that is related to self-discovery. Some of these teachers propose that writing activities can function significantly to help people understand themselves and who they are. In this view, writing to learn means writing to learn about *oneself*. Many teachers who accept this view consequently have students produce papers deemed personally expressive. Writing assignments that ask "What do you feel about XYZ?" or "What is your reaction to EFG?" reflect this emphasis, as do assignments that call for autobiography.

Too frequently, these two types of learning are held to be mutually exclusive. If you accept one, that is, you must reject the other. There is really no reason why they should be exclusive. Learning more about different subjects is an effective way of learning about yourself. In fact, the liberal arts education provided by most colleges is based on this premise. All those general education requirements you have to complete in literature, math, social science, life science, and so on are designed to help you discover more about yourself and your culture. It's therefore quite appropriate that large numbers of entering freshmen don't declare a major until their junior year, because they need time to explore several areas to determine what suits them. Many others who enter with a declared major discover they would rather study something else. In these cases, subject knowledge and self-knowledge are clearly intertwined.

Recently, writing has come to be recognized as a vital part of this learning process. Consider that with very few exceptions, writing is meant to be read by someone other than the writer. Like language in general, it is a *social activity*. We don't mean that a person may not produce a piece of writing alone in his or her room, but that *what* is produced, *why* it is produced, and what it *does* is significantly influenced by society. The first requirement for good writing, of course, is that writers must decide they want others to take their work seriously. Once

Introduction for Students

they do, they find they must abide by a range of different conventions that are accepted and expected by readers. If they refuse or fail to abide by these conventions, their effort generally won't be taken seriously but will be dismissed—perhaps it won't even be read completely.

For the sake of illustration, let's set aside for a moment the question of why a piece of writing is being produced. We can then look at some examples to see how this process works. Suppose you want to write a poem, one good enough for others to want to read in a "published" form, which simply means it becomes *public* in some way, such as posted on a bulletin board, read in a class, printed in a school paper, or circulated among friends. The very term *poem* evokes a set of characteristics generally associated with what a poem *is*. As a result, there is a high probability that you will include in your poem such features as sound effects (rhyme and alliteration), irregular line divisions, figurative language, and so forth. You would include them because you are aware that they function to define poetry, in a sense, and because you are aware that without them readers may not recognize your effort for what you intend it to be.

If you don't know much about these features of poetry, your desire to "publish" would motivate you to learn about them. You might read a book about the mechanics of poetry, a book about the history of poetry, and a collection of representative poems. In the process, you learn a great deal more about poetry than you set out to learn, and you may come to realize that the work you produce is linked in a significant way to all the other poems that have ever been published. You may also begin to see that, as a writer and reader of poetry, you are equally linked to the broad community of all the other people who have ever written or read about poems.

This process replicates itself for every act of writing. Thus, if you wanted to write a legal brief, a financial statement, a business letter, a scientific report, or a recipe, you would be compelled to include the various features that serve to define each of these types of writing. Likewise, if you knew little about these kinds of writing, you would be compelled to learn about them and the disciplines they are associated with.

Obviously, there are factors other than form that define different kinds of writing. Poems are about different things than, say, business letters. Lab reports are about different things than political science papers. So what a piece of writing is about also functions to define it. By implication, you must know a subject to write about it successfully. In addition, different kinds of writing hold different assumptions regarding how writers may communicate their ideas to readers convincingly. Some types of writing, for example, require well-documented proof for every assertion, whereas other types don't. It depends on the discipline and the audience.

We can see, then, that serious writing involves a significant degree of learning across a range of dimensions, including subject matter, conventions of form, audience, and standards of proof. By association, learning about subject matter also includes coming to know something about the significant questions in different fields, how people have answered them in the past, and how people are attempting to answer them now and in the future. There is a point at which writing, and the reading and thinking and talking that accompany it, so immerse people in a subject that they become experts. Doctoral dissertations are excellent examples of how this process works.

Still, if learning about different subjects were the only kind of learning connected to writing, we might question its importance. But there is more. Writing can indeed function to help people learn about themselves and how they relate to others. In exploring subjects in college, for example, you discover your interests and talents. What you learn about those subjects tells you many things about yourself. There is a sense in which writing, as part of language, actually functions to help you define who you are and what role you will play in society or in a range of communities.

Without having to go to great lengths, we can see how this process works when we consider that attorneys write legal briefs, accountants write financial statements, professors write scholarly books, and so forth. In each case, the act of engaging in a specified kind of writing serves to define *who we are*. On the other hand, the writing you do in a given field, to the extent that it makes a contribution or has an influence, serves to define that field and the people in it. In the end, writing and learning are reciprocal processes involving writers, subjects, and the communities they exist in. Each shapes and influences the others.

INTERPRETING FACTS

Many writing teachers tell classes, "I'm not here to teach you how to write but how to think." Students are commonly put off by such statements, because they believe they already know how to think and because they are enrolled in composition, after all, and expect to learn about writing.

Writing classes, however, have a history that goes back to ancient

Introduction for Students

Greece, where people like Isocrates and Aristotle studied and taught language as *rhetoric*. In their view, the world was full of uncertainties, and "facts" were seldom much help in facing life with conviction. Rhetoric was seen in part as a means of sorting through these uncertainties by separating the probable from the improbable, which necessarily involves the ability to interpret facts, events, and experiences.

In this respect, your writing class is a class in rhetoric. Clearly, it's important that you know how to meet readers' expectations regarding formal writing—its conventions, in other words—such as correct spelling and punctuation. But most writing teachers are far more interested in helping you develop your ability to interpret the world around you. They want you to be able to explain *what it all means*. The ability is deemed fundamental in an educated person.

Some people are confused by the idea that facts can mean different things. They believe that facts must be immutable and above interpretation, because they want facts to represent indisputable truths. As a result, they often become angry when facts are interpreted. For example, Charles Darwin, after years of collecting specimens and analyzing them, compiled a list of facts related to how plants and animals adapt to their environment. On the basis of these facts, he proposed that life evolves into many different and increasingly complex forms in an effort to interact with the environment more effectively. Over the last two decades, some scientists have reexamined these facts and made a different interpretation: The number of different life forms (species) on the planet has indeed been increasing for hundreds of millions of years, but the number of anatomical designs for life has been *decreasing*.

Notice that facts here are the same, but what they mean is quite different. Predictably, the reaction among some people has ranged from assertions that evolution has been proved false to claims that scientists can't agree on anything, so they must not know what they're talking about. In this view, Darwin was either right or wrong; he either had his facts right or he didn't. Similarly, if scientists have to interpret facts, which speak for themselves, why do they bother calling themselves scientists and putting on the airs associated with fancy titles? If it's all merely a matter of opinion, the postman or barber will be just as reliable.

In other arenas, however, we usually accept as a given that people routinely disagree on what facts mean. Our law courts are places where judges and juries are asked to make impartial interpretations of facts called "evidence." Movie critics never disagree on who starred in a film, who wrote the script, or who directed it, but they frequently disagree on what a film is "really" about.

MAKING A WITHDRAWAL FROM THE KNOWLEDGE BANK

Probably all students come to college or university with a set of expectations regarding what the experience is supposed to be, and most appear to believe that college is a kind of knowledge bank. Students attend their classes and do their assignments because that's how they transfer knowledge from the bank into their intellectual wallets. In other words, teachers and colleges are places where students go to get the "right answers." Teachers are the tellers who process the withdrawals, the people with the keys to the strongbox.

If you have this view of what college is about, you will probably be surprised when you start to discover that teachers generally don't profess to have many "right answers" and that the majority see themselves as lifelong students ever in search of more information. Certainly, every discipline has its core of knowledge, and teachers are concerned that students master part of this core. There are things they want you to learn.

This knowledge, however, is indeterminate. People in each discipline are always adding to the core through research, and new information inevitably and gradually displaces the old. Moreover, most teachers don't perceive such additive research as being their sole professional task. They must also interpret what that knowledge means. In the sense that a "theory" is a way of describing (interpreting) some aspect of reality, teachers are actively involved in theory making. Many disciplines actually value theory making more than research that adds to the core of knowledge. Indeed, as a society we tend to value theory more than research, because, as stated above, interpretation shapes the realities we all live by. Consider that Einstein, for example, was a theoretical, not an experimental, physicist.

For these reasons, you will frequently be examined on your mastery of core knowledge, where memorization is a significant factor. But you will also encounter the "open-ended" writing assignment. These assignments appear in practically every course that has any writing, and characteristically they do not allow you to make a withdrawal from the knowledge bank. Instead, they ask you to read a book or an article, visit a museum, perform an experiment, or see a play; describe what you've experienced; and then write about what it all means. The writing task is not simply an exercise in repeating what the teacher has told you or what you have read. It is not an opportunity to demonstrate that you've got the "right answer."

Introduction for Students

Students commonly dislike these assignments and often become angry when they have to complete them. They seem to feel betrayed by teachers who refuse to tell them what to say and who ask them to discover things to say on their own through an interpretation of facts. Like those people ready to dismiss Darwin, evolution, and science as so much hokum, such students dismiss open-ended assignments and the teachers who give them as "dumb," "irrelevant," "a waste of time," and so forth.

Teachers give such assignments for several reasons; many are too complex to analyze in detail here. But we can say that most teachers understand that asking students to memorize a list of terms or a list of dates is not what education is really about. Training minds to think about the world and make sense of it is.

THE FACULTY ASSIGNMENTS IN THIS BOOK

When we set out to produce this book, we had no preconceived ideas of what kinds of assignments we were going to collect. We simply contacted faculty in departments around the country and asked them to send us what they used in their classes. We expected, if anything, to see great diversity in the kinds of tasks teachers in different disciplines give their students.

As the materials began arriving and we started analyzing them, we perceived a pattern of similarity that we hadn't anticipated. We knew from earlier work in writing across the curriculum that most of the assignments teachers give require analysis and argumentation, but this knowledge didn't prepare us for what we found. We discovered that, with few exceptions, the samples of writing across the curriculum we received correspond to everything we've been talking about. We could not have written the first part of this introduction without the insights gained from studying the materials we collected.

In sample after sample, we saw teachers asking students to interpret facts, to explain what they mean either to someone in a particular discipline or to someone outside it. This feature is fundamental. It links the many different types of writing in the disciplines and is one of the more important messages of this book. Students who understand it will be able to see beyond the superficial differences in their writing assignments to the central task at hand: analyzing a piece of information and explaining what it means to readers. The explanation, the interpretation, is always a personal one in the best papers, not one cooked up from published sources. It is inherently argumentative in that writers must substantiate why their interpretation is reasonable.

On the basis of our analysis of the numerous assignments we sorted through to produce *The Interdisciplinary Reader,* we have concluded that writing across the curriculum, which is often characterized by attention to the differences that exist in various types of writing, is better characterized by the similarities. Throughout our analyses, we will return again and again to this point.

Generally, there are three types of assignments that appear dominant in writing across the curriculum: the lab report, the essay/research paper, and the exam. Their formats are quite different, but they almost invariably ask for a brief description of an event, object, or experience and an evaluation of what it means. They are essentially activities designed to engage students in writing as learning.

The criteria for success in the papers that follow differ significantly in one respect: Some teachers were more explicit than others when stating expectations. For example, a teacher might ask students to write a research paper without saying anything about references. Those students who neglected to include references in their papers were marked down, because the teacher assumed that the need for proper documentation was a given all students were aware of. A teacher might say nothing about the need for mechanical correctness or might even go so far as to say that spelling errors, punctuation mistakes, and so on, won't matter. Nevertheless, he or she proceeded to grade mechanically correct papers higher than those with flaws. The same holds true for those teachers who neglected to mention whether a paper should be typed. Students who turned in handwritten papers more often received lower grades than those who typed their work. In fact, those who used word processors and laser printers tended to receive higher grades than those who used typewriters, even though the content of their papers was approximately the same.

It would be easy to criticize these assignments and the teachers who produced them if we didn't recognize how extremely difficult it is to put together good writing assignments. Don't take this statement as an attempt to rationalize poor assignments, because it isn't intended to be. It is meant to help direct your attention away from a real source of frustration for you and everyone who teaches toward what can be a learning experience. Because you can anticipate many writing assignments that are less than they could be, you need to understand what features your teachers look for, *both consciously and unconsciously,* in successful papers.

We will address these features in detail throughout the book, but we

Introduction for Students xxxi

can list the more important ones here for easy reference, pointing out, of course, that in practice these features are inevitably so intertwined as to make the listing a bit artificial:

1. Does the paper do what the teacher asked?
2. Does the paper describe the event, object, or experience in enough detail to indicate that the student knows what he or she is talking about?
3. Does the paper offer an interpretation of the event, object, or experience that is well supported and reasonable in the context of how reality is shaped in the discipline?
4. Is the paper free of annoying errors in spelling, punctuation, and usage?
5. Does the paper suggest that the writer learned anything about the topic and about the discipline?

The difficulty in presenting such a list is that the features appear far more straightforward than they actually are. Number 1, for example, probably strikes you as obvious. If a teacher asks you to write a research paper on the sociopolitical reforms in Eastern Europe, you aren't likely to turn in a short story. But how many research papers have you written before? How similar were they to the sort of research paper expected in college? *More specifically, how similar were they to the sort of research paper expected in a college political science course?*

Many high school research papers are designed primarily to introduce students to using the library and some form of documentation. As a result, the teachers who assign them are likely to focus on helping students transfer to their papers what others had to say about a topic. Not much analysis and interpretation is involved. At the college level, however, teachers will be more inclined to expect students to analyze the information they collect about the topic in a way that enables them to draw conclusions from it. They won't want students simply to report what others say about the events associated with, in our example, recent sociopolitical reforms. Moreover, on the basis of these conclusions, they will expect students to interpret the information they present to forge an acceptable argument.

The other features in our list can be equally subtle. In some departments and with some teachers, turning in a paper with mechanical errors may be seen as plain ignorance of standard conventions. In others, it may be seen as a student's unwillingness to take the task, the course, and the teacher seriously. Few teachers are likely to appreciate that message. Particularly interesting is Number 3, which suggests that teachers view writing as an opportunity for students to display how well they grasp the way a discipline looks at the world. Students convinced that subjects are principally domains of knowledge rather than different ways of seeing the human experience will be stymied by this feature. In fact, they may find the whole liberal arts curriculum baffling and irrelevant to what they want to do with their lives, missing the point entirely that the curriculum is designed to be personally enriching and defining.

DOCUMENTATION

Providing readers with references to published texts is an important part of just about every kind of academic writing. Whenever you use someone else's words or ideas in a paper, you must document the sources. Failure to do so constitutes plagiarism. Nevertheless, many students don't understand why they have to bother. At best, these students may assume that their teachers simply want them to repeat what "the masters" have to say on a given topic. This assumption is false, of course, because most teachers have good reasons for asking students to examine published works as part of the writing process and for asking them to provide accurate documentation in their papers.

One important reason is that reviewing such works often furnishes an effective way for students to get to know a topic better. The knowledge gained from reading what others have said can enrich your own work, making it more informed and more interesting. Many times, reading related materials will actually stimulate you in such a way that you think of new things to say about your topic because through the reading you're asked to look at it from different perspectives. Most teachers are aware of how this process works and take advantage of it to help their students learn more. *Documenting* the references is a means of allowing readers (in most cases, your teacher) to distinguish clearly what you have to say from what others have to say. For teachers particularly concerned about helping students become thinkers—and we believe that the majority are in this category—being able to make this distinction is quite important.

Another reason for asking students to provide references is related to one of the more important goals of academic writing mentioned earlier—convincing readers that your interpretation of an event, a text, or a body of data is well reasoned. There are several ways to go about this task, and a large number of them involve projecting a certain sense of character, or what is sometimes called a *persona*, to readers through your writing. For example, most people are more likely to listen to someone's

Introduction for Students

interpretation if it is presented in an even, objective voice than if it is presented in a shrill, emotional one.

Demonstrating your knowledge and awareness of a topic is another way to be more convincing, and an effective and long-standing means of making such a demonstration is to turn to "authorities" who support your particular interpretation. References, in other words, function as pieces of evidence that make your point of view more credible. If a published expert shares your interpretation of, say, a political event, your perception moves out of the realm of mere opinion and into the realm of critical analysis. Thinking people tend to be unswayed by opinion, but they will attend to an analysis that is carefully supported.

No doubt you can see now how the quality of your references—that is, the stature of the authorities you mention in your writing—reflects your character by a process of association. Are you aware of who is important in the area of your topic? Then your references will include their work. Are you aware of current information about your topic? Then your references will be recent—say, published within the last five years. Likewise, documentation is related to the image you want to project. Accurate documentation is, to a significant degree, a reflection of how seriously you value the role authorities play in convincing readers. It is also a reflection of how seriously you want others to take you as a writer and thinker.

Most teachers believe that being able to document references accurately is a significant skill that students should learn. Ironically, however, few students document their references properly. Because they tend to view this skill as relatively unimportant, students generally produce sloppy bibliographic entries that seldom conform to any published style guide. Ample evidence exists in the student papers presented in this book!

In each of the overviews that accompany the division sections, we present the most widely used documentation formats. They are provided as references, which means that you shouldn't study them or try to memorize them. Instead, you should use them on an "as-needed" basis, when you have to write a paper with documentation. At that point, ask your teacher which format he or she prefers. All formats offer approximately the same information about a publication, but they present it in different ways. Once you've collected the information, your task is to record it *exactly* as the format specifies. That means every comma and period must be in the correct place. Capitalization must be perfect. You should even note the spacing between words. Admittedly, documenting references is boring and tedious for most of us, and it requires a fairly high level of concentration, but these factors can't excuse sloppiness.

We hope that this introduction will motivate you to think about the goals and intentions that underlie your writing class. Without question, the work ahead is challenging, not only because it will demand your full attention if you are to do the job right, but also because it will require you to set aside much of what you have come to believe writing and learning to write are about. Throughout this text, we have provided a wide range of suggestions and advice that can help you become a better writer, reader, and thinker, but we have been careful to avoid as much as possible lists and rules to follow. We don't believe that lists and rules lead to better writing. Instead, we have integrated what you need to know about good writing in our discussions of assignments and student papers. If you work at understanding this information as well as applying it, your writing will improve.

JDW
DH
CH

Part One | # LIFE AND APPLIED SCIENCES

WRITING IN THE LIFE AND APPLIED SCIENCES

Overview

Intellectual disciplines may be defined as different ways of looking at and trying to reach an understanding of the human experience. Each brings a set of goals, assumptions, critical tools, standards of proof, and methodologies to the enterprise. In related fields, certain commonalities exist, and such is the case for chemistry, math, biology, and physics —the disciplines in this text that together are classified under the life and applied sciences.

Scientific writing, in the minds of most people, calls up images of highly technical prose that only other scientists can understand. Certainly, it can be that. Much scientific writing, the sort that we will call "professional," is designed to report the results of research to a small group of experts in a discipline. These readers already know a great deal about the subject, and they are usually more concerned with content than with style.

The goals of professional scientific writing are related to the primary goal of science—to discover the nature of the world around us. Scientists are in the business of asking questions about life and its mechanisms, and these questions motivate their research. The writing they produce provides answers to the questions they ask, and it also communicates those answers to others who hold similar interests.

Although science, like every other field, has its share of personalities, scientific writing generally attempts to present information and conclusions in a neutral manner. It is based on the principle of close, objective observation of natural events, or phenomena, which constitute the "facts" that writers then interpret. This reliance on observation allows us to call the disciplines of science and their work *empirical*, from the Greek word for "experience." (Some scholars argue that mathematics is a possible exception, because it tends to focus on theoretical concerns that don't lend themselves to observation.)

It's a well-known fact that personal biases and emotions influence people's perceptions, so the sciences strive to eliminate these factors as much as possible. One way to accomplish this goal is to construct studies in such a way that research biases can't influence the outcome of any investigation. In medicine, the so-called "double-blind" experiments, which you may have heard about, represent one way to reduce biases. The effects of drugs are tested by selecting a group of patients and giving half of them a drug, giving the other half some harmless substance like sugar, and measuring the results. No one directly associated with the testing knows which patients received the drug and which received the placebo, until after all the data are collected.

It's also a well-known fact that the language one uses to report an event or, in this case, research findings, can convey personal biases. The sciences have therefore adopted conventions regarding how data are reported and interpreted as another way of making work more objective. Scientific papers generally begin with an abstract that summarizes the report; then the body is divided into sections, commonly labeled "introduction," "methods," "results," and "conclusions." The aim is to standardize features in order to reduce personal touches that can detract from the straightforward presentation of content.

Each of these sections performs a purpose that reveals something about the nature of scientific writing and the various conventions writers must work with. In the introduction, for example, writers offer a brief review of studies that are related to the research being reported, describing what has been done before and sometimes what hasn't. They also present the research question, or hypothesis, that motivated the current study, usually showing how it emerged out of the previous work in the review. The link between past and present research reveals an important operating assumption in the sciences—that progress occurs incrementally as new knowledge builds upon old.

Part One   LIFE AND APPLIED SCIENCES

In the process of reviewing previous work, the introduction establishes the theoretical rationale for the current study. This rationale is a model that attempts to explain in a simplified way how the world, or some small part of it, operates. For example, perhaps you've seen depictions of the structure of an atom that show electrons orbiting the nucleus, much like planets orbiting the sun. Atoms don't really have the structure that is depicted, yet the model allows us to understand some of their important characteristics and to interpret certain atomic behaviors. If you were writing a paper about ionic bonding, which is the chemical bond formed by transferring electrons from one kind of atom to another, you might first describe the orbiting model. Then you could explain how in ionic bonding an electron breaks out of its orbit around the nucleus of one atom to enter orbit around another.

In scientific writing, providing a theoretical framework is crucial, because writers must interpret their results in the conclusion section through the filter of the model. Thus, an investigation doesn't merely answer the research question, doesn't merely confirm or disconfirm the hypothesis that motivated the work. It must also explain what the findings mean. You can provide a viable explanation only if you have the necessary tools: in this case, the theoretical framework.

As the name indicates, the methods section describes the procedures a writer used to collect information. Key characteristics of this section are how closely the researcher followed established procedures for certain types of tasks and how reliable they are. Anyone should be able to use the methods section to collect data similar to those reported. If other researchers are not able to reproduce the data, the report is deemed to have a serious flaw, and the findings are usually rejected. One notable case of just such an occurrence made the national news in 1989, when a pair of chemists reported that they had achieved cold nuclear fusion through a simple electrochemical process. The potential here is staggering, because it opens the door to unlimited, cheap, clean power. Such a discovery would be as important to mankind as the discovery of fire. Previously, researchers had rejected the possibility of cold nuclear fusion—the reaction that powers the sun—because of their understanding of the tremendous pressures and temperatures required to force atoms together. Sadly, when other scientists attempted to reproduce the data the two chemists reported, they had no success. When asked for more detailed procedures, the chemists refused to provide them. Predictably, the scientific community now sees the entire episode as either a wild fraud or gross ignorance.

There is no question that professional scientific writing is very important. But most people probably don't consider its inherent value. Instead, they are motivated by its inaccessibility to believe that science is unrelated to their lives, the flurry of new reports about cold fusion notwithstanding. We would suggest that few beliefs are farther from the truth of everyday experience. Science, and therefore scientific writing, is provocative exactly because it does indeed touch us all. Vast and not always obvious, its influence extends from the quality of the food we eat and of the air we breathe to the ways we think about ourselves and our place in the cosmos.

There have always been efforts to bridge the knowledge gap between those in science and those outside. For example, Charles Darwin took great pains to make his *Journal of Researches into the Geology and Natural History of the Various Countries Visited by the H.M.S. Beagle, 1832–1836* and his *Origin of Species* accessible to nonscientists. In our own time, scientists like Carl Sagan, an astronomer, and Stephen Jay Gould, a geologist and paleontologist, have likewise worked to make science more accessible to the general public through what we may call "nonprofessional" writing.

Professional and nonprofessional scientific writing should not be viewed as being distinctly different in ways other than audiences and readability. Both are fundamentally argumentative and governed by similar goals, assumptions, standards of proof, and critical tools. The empirical nature of the life and applied sciences establishes standards of proof that are related to the procedures used to observe phenomena. The way facts or data are collected, in other words, is one of the most important measures in determining whether the subsequent interpretation of those facts is valid. When reading a piece of scientific writing, whether it be professional or nonprofessional, knowledgeable readers will apply these standards by asking how well the reported procedures match those used in the past for other, similar studies. They will look closely for possible sources of error or "artifacts" in the data. They will assess the level of objectivity the writer brings to the topic. And they will evaluate whether the procedures, if repeated by another researcher, are likely to produce similar results. The report of cold fusion mentioned above provides a good example of work that failed to meet the accepted standards of proof in the sciences.

Undergraduate students have relatively few opportunities to produce professional scientific writing. Many disciplines, such as engineering, don't even allow students to enroll in core classes until their junior year, so the freshman and sophomore years are spent meeting prerequisites in science and math. When students are allowed to enroll in core classes, they spend their time learning the methods of scientific research, not exploring new areas. Activities in the laboratory and in the field are designed to train them to be careful observers, detailed note-takers, and logical interpreters of scientific information. They perform work that has been done before so they and their teachers can compare their performance against a known standard. As a result, much of the writing students produce in the sciences is in the form of lab reports and general-audience papers that talk about the importance of science to daily life.

Nevertheless, such nonprofessional writing is subject to the conventions and expectations defined by the disciplines. For example, it should be argumentative in that it makes a claim that must then be supported. It should be rational rather than emotional. It should clearly differentiate between what is known and what isn't. And it should provide clear, reasonable interpretation of facts.

Documentation

If you use someone else's words or *ideas* to support your writing, you are obligated to provide accurate references for them, giving credit to the originators. Failure to do so constitutes plagiarism.

A wide range of documentation styles exists in the life and applied sciences, with separate formats for chemistry, physics, math, and biology. Within each discipline, there are additional formats. In chemistry, for example, two of the more widely used are the *Handbook for Authors of Papers in American Chemical Society Publications,* issued by the American Chemical Society, and *Style Guide for Chemists,* written by L. F. Fieser and Mary Fieser. More often than not, however, writers in the sciences follow the documentation format dictated by a specific journal in which they hope to publish a report. Consequently, many professionals in the sciences rarely refer to published documentation guides, because such texts can't cover all the specific requirements of the various journals.

In biology, for example, several people troubled by the lack of standardized documentation in the field decided to attempt a reform. Calling themselves the Council of Biology Editors, they published the *CBE Style Manual.* This reference comments on the wide variety of formats used in the field and then offers two general approaches for documentation: a numerical system and a parenthetical system.

The efforts of the CBE are admirable, but they don't really solve the problem presented by a lack of standardization in the sciences. Unlike the authoritative guides that govern work in the social sciences and the humanities, the *CBE Style Manual* provides, at best, a sense of what one can do with documentation when writing in the sciences. The number of available formats makes it crucial that you talk with your teachers to find out which you should use.

The parenthetical citation system used in the sciences is very similar to the one formulated by the American Psychological Association (APA), which will be described later in this book. We have therefore decided to introduce at this point the numeric system. Students interested in the parenthetical system should refer to the Social Sciences section.

The Numeric Format

This format uses a numbering system in the text to refer readers to a list of sources titled "References" at the end of the paper. The numbers appear consecutively, so the sources are listed by order of appearance rather than alphabetically or chronologically by publication date. Example 1 below illustrates how the numbers appear in the text, and Example 2 illustrates how the sources appear in the list of references. (A variation of this format superscripts reference numbers without the parentheses.)

Example 1

Theophylline, an alkaloid of the xanthine group, is a drug commonly used as a smooth muscle relaxant of bronchi constriction. It is an important drug in treating acute bronchial asthma and other bronchial disorders. Theophylline is present in small quantities in the leaves of the tea plant, and it was from this source that Kossel first isolated the drug in 1888 (1). The original synthesis was performed by Traube in 1900 (2). Traube's work involved the general use of 4,5-diaminopyrimidines to form purines, but within a few years, formic acid, ethyl chloroformate, urea, and thiourea were employed for the preparation of 8-oxo- and 8-thiopurine (3). As characterized by Garcia and Campuzano (4, p. 73), this advance "represented a significant breakthrough in treating asthma."

Example 2

1. Brown, D. J. The chemistry of heterocyclic compounds. Interscience 34:175–189; 1971.
2. Traube, S. Theophylline. Ber. 33:303–305; 1901.
3. Speer, D. K.; Raymond, E. Formulation of 8-thiopurine. J. Amer. Chem. Soc. 75:115–120; 1953.

4. Garcia. Y; Campuzano, P. Treatment of bronchial asthma. New York: Columbia University Press; 1975.

Please note that all documentation guides in the sciences recommend that writers use quotations sparely in their work. We therefore don't provide an example that illustrates how to incorporate long quotations (more than three lines) into your text. In the event that circumstances compel you to include a long quotation, called a "block quotation," use the procedure in Example 1 above, in which the quoted material is introduced with the authors' names followed by the reference number and page number in parentheses. Also, the numeric format requires double spacing throughout the manuscript, including any block quotations.

The examples that follow illustrate how to document various sources using the numeric format.

BOOKS

A Book by One Author

1. Kumoda, J. L. Analysis of CFCs in holons. Washington, D.C.: U.S. Government Printing Office; 1989.

Two or More Books by the Same Author

2. Wolff, K. Electromagnetic interference. New York: Academic Press; 1990.
3. Wolff, K. Nonlinear dynamic systems. New York: Academic Press; 1991.

A Book with More than One Author

4. Winston, S.; Clark, I.; Juthrey, M.T. Chemical analysis of VOCs released during operation of municipal waste incinerators. Washington, D.C.: U.S. Government Printing Office; 1989.

A Book with an Editor

5. Chang, J., Fractual functions in mathematical topology. Los Angeles: Scientific Press; 1992.

A Work in an Edited Volume

6. McDuffy, V. Splitting prime numbers. Mathias, C. R., Elementary functions. Chicago: Utica; 1990: 97–110.

A Multivolume Work

7. Feigenbaum, M. Strange attractors: the mathematics of phase space arrays. 2 vols. Sante Fe: Los Alamos Press; 1985.

A Translation

8. Oxaca, T. T. Mesons. Trans. Newman, N. San Diego: Physica; 1988.

ARTICLES

Journals and Periodicals

9. Miller, L.; Rudder, C. Reduction of NO_x and SO_2 emissions through a dry-spray injection process. J. Envir. Tech. 17:189–211.
10. Simpson, F. Climatic change and ozone depletion. Atm. Sci. 15(3):17–25; 1989.

1 Chemistry

INTRODUCTION TO WRITING IN CHEMISTRY

Most undergraduates enrolled in chemistry classes are there to meet general education requirements. They are not majoring in science or engineering, so the classes are not designed to provide a particularly rigorous program in chemistry. Instead, they aim at giving students an overview of how chemistry is part of their daily lives and at introducing them to simple chemical reactions through laboratory experience.

The writing students produce, therefore, has fairly limited goals, and perhaps the most common is demonstrating knowledge to the teacher. In the case of papers that address the importance of chemistry in daily life, students may expect to show they can appropriately use special terms or concepts covered in either the text or lectures. That is, the papers are opportunities to demonstrate what you have learned in class. Equally important, they often ask you to do some library work to discover even more about the topic, which allows you to demonstrate what you are capable of learning outside of class. In the case of lab reports, students demonstrate knowledge by following the guidelines for the experiment they perform.

At times, lab reports may seem like mindless exercises, because students are merely replicating what someone else has already done. No new knowledge results from this replication, so the work often appears meaningless. To make matters worse, the results don't always match those found in the lab manual, which leads many students to believe that they have made an error in the procedure, an error that they must mask.

When writing a lab report, you need to be aware of two factors. First, the procedures for even simple experiments are sufficiently complex that any number of variables can influence the results. Arriving at results that are different from those expected doesn't necessarily mean that you've made a mistake. Second, few chemistry teachers are particularly concerned about whether your results match the expected ones exactly. Their interest is not in the results per se but rather in the procedures, in your attempt to comprehend how a chemistry experiment proceeds. It is this knowledge that they want to convey.

With these two points in mind, you should be able to see the undesirability of any attempt to mask an apparent error, to dismiss it as trivial, or to leave out mentioning it. In fact, you should strive for the opposite, focusing attention on analyzing why your results differ from those you expected, tracing the steps you took during the experiment to find possible errors or artifacts or variables that could have influenced the results. We would suggest that this sort of analysis is an implicit part of any laboratory work, one seldom mentioned when students are introduced to the lab. The report allows students the opportunity to learn from their "mistakes" and can serve as a means for them to demonstrate their willingness to do so, which is indeed part of the scientific method.

The sample papers below illustrate the two different types of writing assignments most commonly found in general chemistry classes for undergraduates. You should use them to familiarize yourself with both the conventions and expectations chemistry teachers are likely to have when they ask you to write a paper.

CHEMISTRY ASSIGNMENT 1

Course: **Introduction to Chemistry for Non-Chemistry Majors**

> Each student will complete a research paper. It must be at least 1500 words and must include a bibliography listing at least three sources besides the textbook. The topic of the paper must relate in some way to chemistry. Thus topics such as energy, air or

Chemistry

water pollution, polymers, food and additives, nutrition, and synthetic fabrics are acceptable. The paper will be graded on the basis of content. Style will not be considered unless it is atrocious.

Analysis of Chemistry Assignment I

This assignment is interesting for two reasons. First, it suggests several topics to give students some idea of the range of acceptable papers. In such cases, many in the class will select the easiest or most well-known topic, which in this instance is pollution. Ambitious students always keep this tendency in mind and should spend a few extra moments considering possible topics. After all, even the most conscientious teacher will have a hard time being enthusiastic about a paper after reading 50 others on exactly the same topic. A little more thought, leading to an uncommon topic, will usually result in a better assessment.

The second reason this assignment is interesting is that it explicitly subordinates form to content. It tells students the teacher is concerned that they get their facts right and that the way they present those facts is not particularly important.

Many students will take a statement like this at face value, having frequently encountered the attitude toward writing it exemplifies, and perhaps even believing it themselves. Without regard to the manner of presentation, they will be certain to fill their papers with terminology and will engage in a form of flattery by stating several times that chemistry is vital to modern life. Their bibliographies will have exactly the minimum number of books, and it isn't uncommon to find that the impressive terminology comes directly from the references.

Such students are usually puzzled when they receive a C on their papers, and conferences with their teachers often do not prove enlightening because the major criticism may be "lack of detail," "failure to relate topic to everyday experiences," or something along these lines. A more accurate analysis of these C papers would have to include a conflict between the teacher's stated expectations and the unstated ones. Quite simply, few educated readers can prevent themselves from considering organization, coherence, tone, support, and so forth as part of their assessment criteria; indeed, these may be *unconscious* elements in any evaluation, as the following sample papers will show. Therefore, students should disregard apparent devaluations of style.

Moreover, it's common for teachers to have in mind a set of success criteria for each assignment, criteria that influence their evaluation of student responses. For example, if you look closely at this first assignment, you'll realize that it describes the *minimal* requirements: the paper "must be at least 1500 words," the topic "must relate in some way to chemistry," and so on. Students who follow this description faithfully will inevitably produce, at the very best, a C paper.

The teacher says nothing in the assignment about what characteristics an A paper will have. Consequently, students aren't likely to do very well on the assignment, unless they already know a great deal about writing in general, writing in chemistry in particular, and the teacher's criteria for success.

On a more personal level, even though you may have been an A student in high school, in college you may not be able to rely much on your previous experiences. We therefore suggest that when confronted with an assignment like this one, which offers no clue as to what an outstanding paper will look like, you should talk to your teacher. Ask about his or her criteria for an A response and ask if there are any sample papers that you may use for models.

It's also worth mentioning that the assignment above assumes that students know how to write research papers. Yet a large number of freshmen have never written a research paper, and even more have never written one that meets the standards and expectations of university discourse. As we will see when examining the following responses to the assignment, students' failure to address this assumption leads to failure on the task.

We can draw some important conclusions from this analysis. Although this assignment initially appears to be very straightforward, calling for a simple assessment of how some area of chemistry affects our daily lives, there are unstated factors that will significantly influence a student's success or failure.

Guide for Reading

The following paper is a better-than-average response to the assignment, in part because Juanita's content and organization show that she is trying to inform readers; she isn't just trying to demonstrate to her teacher that she has done the necessary research. As you read, pay attention to how Juanita organizes her paper. How does she move smoothly from one point to the next? What are some specific ways she tries to inform readers?

SAMPLE CHEMISTRY PAPER 1

Present and Future Uses of Plastics

Juanita M. (a freshman)

Our civilization has passed through the Stone Age, the Bronze Age, the Iron Age, and now we are in the midst of a plastics age. From the discovery of plastics in the 19th century, to the forming of The Society of the Plastics Industry in 1937, until now, plastics have made an indescribable impact on our lives that will not soon diminish. In fact, quite the opposite is expected. The plastics industry is growing, and will continue to grow, as it serves to make our lives better and easier.

Although there are some disadvantages in the use of plastics, they are far outweighed by the advantages. For example, the toxicity of fumes emitted from burning plastics has raised some questions and concerns. It is however, far less likely that plastics will cause a fire than wood or other materials. Also, plastic requires only one-tenth of the energy required to produce aluminum, and the basic resin-manufacturing process is much cleaner than a steel mill; little smoke and soot are produced. There are many other advantages to plastics that can be seen in individual products. For example, several manufacturers now make biodegradable forms of plastics; some six-pack rings gradually decompose when exposed to sunlight. Researchers are also developing ways to make plastics as recyclable as metal or glass.

Plastics can be both lighter and stronger than steel. Composites—plastics reinforced with fibers of graphite or other compounds—made the round-the-world flight of the Voyager possible. The latest jet fighters are about 25% composite, and the top-secret Stealth bomber is believed to have and all-composite skin to help avoid radar.

Graphite tennis raquets introduced composites to the public, and now high-performance bicycles are made of them as well. Composites have been proved in combat; a helmet saved an infantryman's life by deflecting two bullets in the Grenada invasion.

The 21st century is likely to see the emergence of a completely new way of making polymers: biologically produced polymers. The first hints are already here, with the development and commercialization of bacterial polyhydrobutyrate valerate (PHBV). Large companies have made investments in biotechnology, mainly focusing on pharmaceuticals and agricultural products.

Biotechnology will bring a number of changes to polymer production. More than likely, polymers will be produced by genetically altered bacteria or yeast in large fermentation vats, similar to the way that beer is made today. The feedstocks will be renewable sources, probably plants. For example, bacteria-made PHBV from corn syrup or molasses.

The polymers produced by living organisms may be quite similar to what we synthesize today, or they may be far more complex than we are capable of making economically on a mass scale. Polymer chemists are happy to be able to combine two or three substances into a copolymer, but even the simplest life forms regularly combine twenty different amino acids into an almost infinite variety of proteins.

Copolymers and terpolymers are likely to be superseded by multipolymers. Such complexity may bring unique functionability, such as compatibility with human tissue, or unusual permeability characteristics for packaging. Or it may bring combinations or properties that do not exist in simpler polymers.

Another area of extreme interest is the emergence of plastics into the auto industry. Already many advancements have been made in this area. For example, a plastic automobile engine is already a reality. The Polimotor, 200 pounds lighter than its metal counterparts, and plastic right down to its block and connecting rods, started running on the racing circuit last year. Such an engine could power luxury cars in the near future, with the agility of a small sports car.

Du Pont is working on material called Bexloy C that it hopes will replace exterior sheet metal on most cars after 1995. This would cut the cost of producing exterior parts by 20%. Volkswagen is working on a plastic fuel tank, and plastic drive shafts are already a reality. Plastic bumpers will soon be commonplace in new cars. Other possibilities are windshields that tint with the flip of a switch, friction-free truck engines that require no radiator and get 100 miles to the gallon, and cars that never rust—running on highways without potholes.

Another area in which plastics are becoming increasingly popular is the medical field. Plastics have simplified patient care, reduced contamination, made possible new prostheses and treatment techniques, and cut medical costs. Medical cost-containment pressures, and aging population, artificial organ implant research, proliferation of medical-device producers, and a growing number of private clinics and diagnostic facilities will create greater opportunities for plastics well into the next century.

Polyvinyl choloride, polystyrene, polyethylene, and polypropylene are the high-volume plastics for medical applications. Much of this volume goes into disposable products and devices—syringes, intravenous (I.V.) and blood bags, tubing, labware, instrument trays, and surgical drapes. These materials will continue to dominate the market, while the pressure for materials with a wider performance range and cost options will continue to build.

Although cost-containment pressures revived the issue of reusable versus disposable devices, the risk of contamination (high-lighted by the spread of AIDS) will expand the use of disposables and the plastics that go into them.

Cost-containment also will accelerate the transition from metals to plastics in durable medical goods. Everything from mobile analyzers and monitors, to wheelchairs, crutches, and walkers will be made of engineering plastics and composites.

Along with economic benefits, a switch to plastics will bring a reduction in weight and more durability over metal. For example, the control console of a cardiodiagnostic ultrasound scanner is molded of a glass-fiber reinforced PC structural foam from Mobay Corporation. This material saves 25% in weight over other plastics considered, and 30% in tooling costs.

Home health care is the fastest-growing segment of the medical care industry, primarily because of the aging population and the push to reduce medical costs. This market segment has the potential for the complete spectrum of plastics. Disposable products will generate increased volume for the commodity-type resins, while monitor and scanner housing will boost volume for engineering thermoplastics and their blends.

Many of the home-care monitoring and treatment devices are being simplified and down-sized for ease of use and portability. Among these devices are glucose monitors, blood-pressure screening systems, and internal feeding systems for delivering liquid food products directly into the stomach.

Controlled delivery of drugs directly to the organs requiring the medication is another growth area. The critical device for this technique is the catheter; a small-diameter elastomeric tube that is inserted into the body and pushed to the desired site. Catheters are classed as diagnostic or intraventional; the former are used to determine the source of the problem, the latter are used to treat it.

Until recently drug-delivery catheters protruded from the patient, providing an avenue for contamination and restricting the patient's mobility. Now an infusion port has been developed that eliminates these problems.

The infusion port is implanted under the skin so that a connection can be made to in-dwelling catheters. The device has an elastomeric button through which the medication is infused. A flange anchors the implant beneath the skin.

Transdermal controlled-release drug-delivery systems that combine pharmaceutical science and polymer chemistry are a medical application in its infancy. As the name indicates, the drug, which is contained with an adhesive patch, is administered through the skin at a pre-determined rate. Transdermal delivery enables drugs to bypass the digestive system and circulate once through the body before reaching the liver, which deactivates many drugs.

Essentially the transdermal patch consists of the drug, a drug-permeable, non-biodegradable plastic backing, and a compatible adhesive. In the simplest construction, the drug is dispersed in adhesive polymer matrix and cast onto a flat impermeable plastic backing over which a protective liner is placed. The polymer in the matrix controls the drug-release rate. Silicone, ethylene-vinyl

Chemistry

acetate copolymer, and polyurethane are commonly used in transdermal membranes.

The ultimate frontier of medical plastics is implantable artificial organs. The major focus is the cardiovascular system, including artificial hearts and heart-assist devices. Presently, for coronary artery by-passers, the saphenous vein is taken from the leg and used to by-pass the occluded coronaries. Because this involves additional surgical procedure, the search is on for a plastic material to make an artificial artery. Polymers that are implanted must be inert and blood-compatible. The major hurdle is to develop a material that does not promote blood clotting.

For artificial hearts and ventricular assist devices (VADS), the search goes on for bio-elastomers to make the ultimate pumping diaphram. Flex life, resistance to clot formation, high tear and tensile strength, low moisture absorption, and creep resistance are needed.

By the year 2000, three billion pounds of plastic will be used in the medical market. Improved plastics will make possible artificial kidneys, urinary bladders, artificial skin, and replacement hip joints that meld with natural bone.

In talking about composites, biologically produced polymers, and plastics in the automotive and medical industries, I have barely scratched the surface of present and future uses of plastics. I have not even mentioned plastics in the building and construction industries, or in packaging. As you can see, plastics are a major part of our world today, and will continue to be in the future. As one plastics optimist put it, "The next fifty years promises to be every bit as spectacular as the last fifty!"

Bibliography

"The Age of Superstuff", *Newsweek,* May 25, 1987, p. 73.

"On Land, At Sea, and In the Air, Those Polymer Invaders Are Here", *Smithsonian,* November 1985, p. 76.

"Plastic Skyscrapers", *Omni,* March 1985, p. 45.

"Plastics in the 21st Century", *Plastic World,* September 1987.

Analysis of Sample Chemistry Paper 1

Juanita begins with an introductory paragraph that clearly states the aim of her paper. It will explain why plastics are going to play a greater role in our lives in the future. Such a statement of aim is an important characteristic of any well-written paper. Notice, however, that Juanita also provides a *framework* for the paper by setting the discussion in a historical context. In two sentences, she notes the discovery of plastics in the nineteenth century and comments on their importance today and in the future. Providing this quick background helps orient readers and lets them know why the topic is worth writing about—and worth reading about. As a technique, it reflects another characteristic of good writing.

In the second paragraph, Juanita acknowledges current concerns about plastics, although failing to provide much detail. She mentions the toxic fumes emitted when plastic burns and then simply hints at the problem caused by the difficulty we have in disposing of plastic. Nevertheless, the acknowledgment, modest as it is, goes a long way toward making her appear objective when in the third paragraph she moves into a detailed analysis of the benefits of plastics. From a rhetorical perspective, Juanita is working well: It's important to recognize early a point of view that differs from the one advocated in the paper.

Although this is not a technical paper, Juanita demonstrates to the reader (in this case, her teacher) that she can use the terminology of chemistry; in our analysis of the assignment, we recognized terminology as being a significant criterion for success. Terms such as "polyhydrobutyrate valerate" (p. 14), "transdermal controlled-release drug-delivery systems" (p. 16), and "bio-elastomers" (p. 17) suggest familiarity with the subject.

We should note in this regard, however, that at no point does Juanita refer to her sources. Simply tacking a bibliography onto the end of the paper is insufficient (also notice that Juanita improperly punctuates the bibliography, putting commas *outside* the quotation marks when they should be *inside*). Careful readers must question where these terms, and indeed the information throughout the paper, came from; they certainly aren't everyday expressions, and it's doubtful that they were part of the chemistry lectures. Lack of proper documentation is always a serious weakness in any writing and can lead to charges of plagiarism.

Throughout the body of the paper, Juanita shows good attention to detail, moving skillfully from the general to the specific. For example, rather than simply stating that "Plastics are a major part of medical research," she shows us *how* they are being used and how researchers are trying to devise new ways to use them. Note the first full paragraph on page 15 in this regard. This sort of paragraph structure greatly contributes to a paper's coherence.

Juanita's concluding paragraph is quite interesting, because it violates the model that most undergraduates have acquired at some point: That is, the final paragraph should summarize everything discussed in the paper. In reality, concluding paragraphs of short papers (anything less than 25 pages) do not summarize but look forward. A summary is useful only when a paper is so long that readers need help synthesizing the important points. For most of the papers you will write in college and out, the last paragraph should resemble the one in this response.

Notice how Juanita admits that the topic is much larger than she could hope to address, but she does so without any air of apology. Instead, the tone is upbeat, optimistic, and in this sense is a reflection of the discussion of the wide-ranging research in the body, where we found the suggestion that new discoveries and applications are being made on a daily basis. This forward-looking perspective is reinforced by the quotation (again not referenced) in the final sentence: "The next fifty years promises to be every bit as spectacular as the last fifty!"

Guide for Reading

Cindy's paper has the promise of being interesting simply because of her topic. Biographies of notable people are naturally fascinating, provided the writer avoids getting immersed in trivia. Cindy avoided this problem, but she ran into another—she couldn't decide what she wanted to focus on. As you read her paper, you may sense that she has, in a sense, produced two overlapping essays: one on the life of Dmitri Ivanovich Mendeleyev and the other on the importance of the periodic table. What advice would you have given Cindy about how to make the paper more focused, without writing two separate essays? Would visuals make the paper more understandable?

> **SAMPLE CHEMISTRY PAPER 2**

The Life of Dmitri Ivanovich Mendeleyev

Cindy C. (a freshman)

Dmitri Ivanovich Mendeleyev, a Russian chemist, developed the periodic table of elements. This accomplishment has remained the most important organizing principle of chemical knowledge since its first appearance in 1869. Dmitri was born on Feb. 8, 1834, the fourteenth and last child of the Mendeleyev family in Tobolsk, Siberia, where his father was a teacher of arts and literature in the local gymnasium. In later years, his father became blinded and Mendeleyev's mother supported the family by running a local glass factory that was owned by her brother, Dmitri's uncle. When Dmitri was fourteen, his father died and also at this same time their factory caught fire and burned. His mother took Dmitri to Moscow and then to St. Petersburg to obtain a good education for her son. He enrolled (1850) in the Faculty of the Physics and Mathematics of the Main Pedagogical Institute in Saint Petersburg. He graduated from the Pedagogical Institute in 1855 and received a master's degree and doctor's degree from the University of Saint Petersburg. He then started a long academic teaching career. From 1855 to 1856 he taught at the Odessa lyceum, where he continued his work on the relationships between the crystal forms and the chemical composition of substances. In addition to his theoretical research, the application of science to industry and economics remained one of his primary concerns of study. He then worked from 1859 to 1860 at the University of Heidelberg, where he first collaborated with Rovert Bunsen and studied capillary phenomena and the deviations of gases and vapors from the ideal gas laws. In 1860, Mendeleyev discovered the concept of critical temperature. He then attended the International Chemical Congress at Karlsruhe, where Cannizzario's views on atomic weights planted the seeds for the concept of the periodic table.

Mendeleyev then served as a professor of chemistry at the Saint Petersburg Technological Institute from 1864 to 1866. He later took a job as a professor of chemistry at the University of St. Petersburg from 1867 to 1890. He resigned from this position because of the administrations treatment of the students petitions for reform. Since he could find no suitable text for his students, he wrote his own text. It was called the Principles of Chemistry (1868–1870), which appeared in eight Russian versions, three English versions (the first one printed in 1905, then reprinted in 1969), and several French and German editions. The systematization of ideas required for this book led Mendeleyev to formulate the periodic law in March 1869.

When Mendeleyev began teaching, he felt the need to bring to inorganic chemistry the same degree of order that organic chemistry was then gaining through the theory of molecular structure. Just like many other chemists, he was convinced that the answer lay somewhere in the ordering of the atomic weights of the elements. Our modern periodic chart is different from Mendeleyev's in that the elements in ours are arranged according to atomic number. The atomic number gives the number of protons in the nucleus and—for a neutral atom—the number of extranuclear electrons. (Atoms of most elements have varying numbers of neutrons in their nucleus. That is why, we have isotopes, which are atoms of the same element that have different weights). The modern periodic table is divided into vertical columns called groups or families. Each group includes elements with similar properties. Each element within a group also have the exact same number of electrons in their highest energy levels. The horizontal rows of the periodic table are called periods. Each element in a given period has outer electrons in the same main energy level.

Certain groupings of elements on the periodic table are each designated by special names. The heavy stair-stepped diagonal line on the table divides the elements into two major classes. The ones to the left of the line are known as metals, the ones to the right are nonmetals. The Group IA elements are known as alkali metals; Group IIA are alkaline earth metals; and Group VIIA are the halogens. On the extreme right of the chart is a group containing the noble gases. All the Group B elements on the periodic table are called transition metals.

In subsequent years Mendeleyev refined and modified his law, even so it was received with considerable skepticism. But after Paul Emile Lecoq de Boisbaudran, Lars Fredrik Nilson, and Clemens Winkler discovered the elements gallium in 1875, scandium in 1879, and germanium in 1886, respectively, whose existence was predicted by Mendeleyev in 1871. From that point on the standard periodic law was universally accepted as correct among the scientific community. This accomplishment made Mendeleyev gain great fame and respect and then hen was showered with many academic honors.

His table provided and still provides a useful guide to many areas of scientific and chemical research. When the first two inert fases argon and helium, were discovered in the 1890's, it was evident that there should be two or three more to fill and entire family. This justified William Ramsay's successful search for xenon and krypton. The periodic table also guided the working out of radioactive decay series for uranium and radium in the early twentieth century.

With the development of the nuclear atom by Ernest Rutherford and Niels Bohr, came theoretical explanations for the periodicity of elemental properties in the twentieth century. Theoretical elaboration required only a few minor changes in Mendeleyev's periodic table. This standard table is still the basic organization for the teaching of general chemistry.

In addition to his academic activities, Mendeleyev was involved throughout his life in technical applications of science and in public affairs. He participated in the early development of oil fields in southern Russia and in 1876, he visited the United States in order to investigate petroleum industry. He made similar studies on the production and utilization of coal. His interest later turned to commercial matters concerned with the national economy. He then worked on the liquefication of gases and the expansion of liquids. Other intense studies included a theory of solutions, a theory of the inorganic origin of petroleum, the chemistry of coal, Russian weights and measurements and the universal ether. In 1868 he helped found the Russian Chemical Society. And in 1887 he undertook a solo balloon ascension to study a solar eclipse.

In 1890, he resigned from the university. This was brought about by his active support of the students in their unrest against conservative academic policies. He then quickly gained an important position as director of the Bureau of Weights and Measures in St. Petersburg and in various government bureaus, becoming involved with tariff policys for Russian industry, the development of smokeless powder, the establishment of uniform weights and measures, and promotion of shipbuilding. He held these positions until he died on February 2, 1907, in Saint Petersburg. In 1906, a few months before his death, he missed winning the Nobel Prize for chemistry by one vote.

Bibliography

"Dmitri Ivanovich Mendeleyev." *Encyclopedia Americana.* Danbury, Connecticut: Grolier Incorporated, 1983, Volume 18, p. 687.

"Dmitri Ivanovich Mendeleyev." *Academic American Encyclopedia.* Danbury, Connecticut: Grolier Incorporated, 1986, p. 294.

"Dmitri Ivanovich Mendeleyev." *Funk and Wagnall's New Encyclopedia.* New York, New York: The Dun and Bradstreet Corporation, 1985, Volume 17, p. 173.

"Dmitri Ivanovich Mendeleyev." *Chemistry for Changing Times.* Minneapolis, Minnesota: Gurgess Publishing Company, pp. 45, 46.

Analysis of Sample Chemistry Paper 2

The most positive feature of this paper is the subject matter. Biographical information of the sort presented here is interesting to most readers, and the teacher is likely to find it especially so after having read a large stack of papers about air and water pollution. Our analysis of Cindy's work is that the subject prevents a fairly weak paper from slipping out of the average category into a lower one.

Probably the first thing that strikes readers is that the beginning paragraph goes on for almost a full page. Failure to control paragraph length is a characteristic of weak writing. This long paragraph would be far more readable and better organized if it were broken into five shorter ones. We would have recommended paragraph breaks at the following sentences: "Dmitri was born," "His mother took Dmitri," "From 1855 to 1856," and "He then worked from 1859 to 1860." Notice that each one introduces slightly different information, a slightly different focus on the life of Mendeleyev. Consequently, each may be thought of as a "topic sentence." Topic sentences, when they appear in paragraphs, generally determine what information the sentences immediately following will convey. In Cindy's case, the sentences that immediately follow the topic sentences above elaborate on them.

After you have made these recommended paragraph breaks mentally, you can learn an important lesson by comparing the introduction of this paper (the first two sentences) to the introduction of Paper 1. Cindy begins by telling us that Mendeleyev developed the periodic table. In the next sentences, she tells us that the periodic table is an important part of chemistry. The difficulty is that these sentences work against each other and ultimately against the paper because we don't know after reading the introduction just what the paper will focus on. The first suggests that the paper will be about Mendeleyev, whereas the second suggests that the paper will be about the importance of the periodic table.

Because focus is an important criterion for successful writing in any area, Cindy could have greatly improved the paper if she had limited her focus to one topic or the other. Instead, she develops it in two parts, the first a brief biography of Mendeleyev, the second a discussion of the periodic table. Although these two topics are certainly related, they are not so closely related that they make for a coherent paper. For example, it's difficult to understand how the fact that Mendeleyev's mother took him to St. Petersburg for a good education (paragraph 1) has any bearing on the importance of the periodic table to chemistry. By the same token, the importance of the table to chemistry seems to have no connection to the fact that he resigned a teaching position out of sympathy for students demanding educational reform (paragraph 2). To create a stronger relationship between the two topics, Cindy might have highlighted those aspects of Mendeleyev's education and career that directed his attention to and helped him develop the periodic table.

Notice also that Cindy isn't quite sure who her audience is. Overall, her writing is not particularly technical, and she supplies much general information, as though she is writing for a general audience. Certainly there is no indication that her audience is limited to her teacher, who of course knows more about the periodic table than she does. In paragraphs 3 and 4, however, we begin to suspect that perhaps her audience isn't quite so general, but instead is made up of people who know enough about chemistry to have seen and perhaps even used a periodic chart before. Her description of the chart will be clear only to someone with this knowledge. With a better sense of audience, and with a bit more ambition, she would have supplied a photocopy of the periodic table to enhance her description.

Another difficulty with this paper is the lack of documentation. It has a bibliography, but at no point does Cindy attribute any of her information to her sources. We have no way of knowing where she obtained the information on Mendeleyev and the periodic table. As already noted in regard to Paper 1, the lack of proper documentation is a serious weakness in any paper and can lead to charges of plagiarism. At some universities, students guilty of plagiarism receive an F for the course and are suspended from school.

The concluding paragraph is very good toward the end, where Cindy tells us that Mendeleyev died shortly after failing to win the Nobel Prize by one vote. In any narrative (and certainly a biography is a narrative), death usually brings matters to an end, so Cindy made a good choice here. Unfortunately, the first part of that paragraph attempts to reiterate points already made, such as the fact that Mendeleyev resigned his university post in 1890. Given the shortness of the paper, this summary approach would have involved some discussion of how Mendeleyev was recognized for his contribution to chemistry by being nominated for the Nobel Prize, which is an honor in itself. Stating the date of his death and how he missed winning the Prize would then follow naturally, providing an appropriate conclusion.

Guide for Reading

The following paper is a clear example of plagiarism. Most, if not all, of the paper was taken verbatim from the sources listed under Works Cited and is included without proper documentation. Even if Amy had used quotation marks to show that she copied from her sources, the paper would not be acceptable; it doesn't develop a topic—it merely presents facts without interpreting them. As you read, you may want to make notes on how Amy's work affects you. What is your reaction to her paper? What would you have told Amy if she had asked you to look over her work before turning it in?

SAMPLE CHEMISTRY PAPER 3

Fetal Alcohol Syndrome

Amy S. (a freshman)

..... a 40-month-old black female was born 7/1/69 to a gravida 1-0-0-1, 37-year-old unwed mother who was an alcoholic and died of cirrhosis of the liver in October 1970. During the pregnancy the mother had an unspecified venereal disease with generalized rash. The mother also was known to have irregular menstruation, menorrhagia and dysmenorrhea for years (Bergsma, pg 459).

The patient was born at term but her birthweight was 4 pounds 5½ ounces, length 18 inches and head circumference 32 cm. On physical examination she was found to have bilateral ptosis with blepharophimosos, large amount of scalp hair, weakness of the neck muscles, peculiar looking face with right esotropia and nystagmus on lateral gaze; she was unable to gaze upwards. The right ear was larger and more protuberant and both ears were borderline low-set. The mouth was somewhat cupid bow-shaped with downturning of the lips. The palate was broad and high. She had clinocamptobrachydactyly of the 5th finger bilaterally with a single flexion crease. The left 4th tow underlapped the 3rd. The neonatal period was uneventful apart from the unspecified conjunctivitis and low birthweight, which kept her in the nursery 33 days (Bergsma pg. 459).

During the first 3 years of her life she showed mildly delayed motor landmarks: walking at 16–18 months, running at 2–2½ years, spoon feeding at 27 months; first word at 24 months, 3–4 words at 26 months, 2-word phrases at 34 months. She is still not toilet trained. The family history was inadequate, but there was no apparent consanguinity (Bergsma, pg. 459).

Babies born to alcoholic mothers often are small, deformed, and mentally retarded. Some investigators believe that this fetal alcohol syndrome can occur even if the mothers drink only moderately. Alcohol is by far the most abused drug in the United States (Hill, pg. 188).

Some women should not drink any alcohol during pregnancy.

Foremost are those with vulnerability to addictive behavior. All women who report consuming 5 or more drinks on an occasion should be advised to stop drinking. Supportive counseling should be focused on abstaining for the remainder of the pregnancy (Rosette, pg. 149).

How much can a women drink during pregnancy without having an effect on her child? Both moderate and high levels of alcohol may result in alterations of growth and morphogenesis (Hanson et al., 1978), and there appears to be a definite risk with six drinks a day (Morrison and Maykut, 1979). Beyond these pronouncements, there is disagreement. One statement emerging from studies thus far is that no safe drinking level has been established for pregnant women (Schardein, pg. 786–787).

..... the most conservative advice is to abstain from all alcohol consumption from conception through delivery and lactation. It appears that daily intake of 28.5ml of alcohol or more presents a risk to the fetus and this risk rises progressively with increased intake during pregnancy (Newman and Correy, pg. 80). This risk has been cited as about 2.5% for the alcoholic women to give birth to a child with the cluster of defects identifiable as FAS (Sokol, 1981). However the danger form light drinking (= 1 oz absolute alcohol daily) has not been demonstrated and should not be overstated, since exagerbation could decrease credibility about the adverse effects of heavy drinking and may cause parents of abnormal children to feel guilty that ___ small amount of alcoholic beverages caused abnormalities that were actually due to other factors (Rosett, 1980) (Schardein, pg. 788).

Between 5% and 10% of pregnant women drink heavily, consuming far more than other pregnant women. Alcohol in high concentrations has the potential to adversely affect every maternal organ system and to disturb the maternal-placental-fetal system. Lower doses can alter moods but have no pesistant effects. Of particular concern in pregnancy are changes in the liver and other parts of the gastrointestinal system, the immune system, the CNS, the cardiovascular system, and the endocrine and reproductive system. (Rosett, pg. 29).

The initial publications that identified and described the fetal alcohol syndrome stimulated case reports from around the world. Findings from 65 patients evaluated in Seattle and 180 cases reported from other centers helped establish minimal criteria for the diagnosis of FAS (Clarren and Smith, 1978). The routine use of these criteria was recommended by the Fetal Alcohol Study Group of the Research Society on Alcoholism (Rosett, 1980a): "The diagnosis of FAS should be made only when the patient has signs in each of these three categories:

1. Prenatal and/or postnatal growth retardation (weight, length, and/or head circumference below the tenth percentile when corrected for gestational age).

2. Central nervous system involvement (signs of neurological abnormality, developmental delay, or intellectual impairment).

3. Characteristics facial dysmorphology with at least two of these three signs: (a) microcephaly (head circumference below the third percentile), (b) micro-ophthalmia and/or short palperbral fissures, (c) poorly developed philtrum, thin upper lip, and/or flattening of the maxillary area."

Retarded growth in weight, length, and head circumference both before and after birth is the most common sign of FAS. While some studies have associated prematurity with maternal alcohol use, the observed growth retardation is not merely a reflection of prematurity. FAS infants are significantly smaller than nonaffected infants after adjustment for gestational age. Postnatally, growth retardation persists even though nutrition is adequate and the environment is stable. In contrast, most children who fail to thrive for nutritional or environmental reasons respond with a growth spurt when provided with adequate nutrition in a stable environment. Catch-up growth has been demonstrated only in children with milder forms of FAS (Rosett, pp. 6–7).

During the years following the identification and description of the fetal alcohol syndrome, there has been growing recognition of the adverse effects on offspring of heavy drinking during pregnancy. Within a relatively brief period, a body of new research findings has developed that is consistent with research and clinical observations dating back to the 18th Century. The scientific attitude toward these data has shifted from skepticism to recognition of a major health problem. In our society people have intense feelings about alcohol abuse, maternal responsibility, and child welfare. Consequently there has been a tendency for research findings to be seized upon, interpreted, and used by well-intentioned groups and a variety of social goals. By carefully examining the data first, the historical cycle of acceptance and rejection of findings about alcohol's effects on fetal development can be avoided. Only with scientific objectivity can we untangle the interacting metabolic, environmental, and social variables. (Rosett, pg. 12).

Given the total evidence available at this time, pregnant women should be particularly conscious of the extent of their drinking. While safe levels of drinking are unknown, it appears that a risk is established with ingestion above 3 ounces of absolute alcohol or 6 drinks per day. Between 1 ounce and 3 ounces, there is still uncertainty but caution is advised. Therefore, pregnant women and those likely to become pregnant should discuss their drinking habits and the potential dangers with their physicians (Rosett, pg. viii).

Works Cited

Bergsma, Daniel, M.D. *Malformation Syndrome.* The National Foundation-March of Dimes, New York, 1975.

Hill, John W. *Chemistry for Changing Times.* Burgess Publishing Company, Minneapolis, Minnesota, 1984.

Rosett, Henry L. M.D. and Lyn Weiner, M.P.H. *Alcohol and the Fetus.* Oxford University Press, New York, 1984.

Schardein, James L. *Chemically Induced Birth Defects.* Marcel Dekker, Inc., New York and Basel, 1985.

Analysis of Sample Chemistry Paper 3

This response is interesting because it illustrates what can happen when a student does not understand what is expected in a research paper. By the second or third sentence, it is clear that this isn't student writing and that Amy has simply copied various paragraphs from her sources.

Her concern for terminology, which you'll remember is a feature of the assignment, leads to unpleasant extremes: "She was found to have bilateral ptosis with blepharophimosis . . . , with esotropia and nystagmus on lateral gaze. . . . She had clinocamptobrachydactyly of the 5th finger bilaterally with a single flexion crease" (paragraph 2). We expect such terminology in a professional medical publication, not in an undergraduate chemistry class. All it demonstrates is that the writer is capable of copying paragraphs verbatim out of a text.

We must credit Amy, however, with supplying the sources of her information, something we didn't see in the other responses to this assignment we've examined. But the problem is fourfold. First, a research paper uses sources to substantiate a position that the writers want to argue; it does not consist solely of quotations from sources. Second, the material isn't shown as quoted material; it is shown as text with a reference at the end of each paragraph. Third, the citations don't follow any standard documentation guide. The format appears to be one that Amy put together from her past experiences with documentation. Fourth, Amy includes several references in the text but fails to include them under works cited, which strengthens the perception of plagiarism.

From every perspective, this paper is a failure. Amy has not *written* anything but has merely copied other writers' work. She would have performed far better had she conferred with her teacher before starting the project. The teacher could have clarified the procedures for academic research.

Writing Assignments

The following assignments ask you to investigate some aspect of chemistry as it relates to our lives. Your responses can therefore be guided by our analyses of the sample papers above. You should note that the assignments are sequenced from the least to the most demanding. Each assignment will require some library research. Allow ample time to produce one or more preliminary drafts. Set up a conference with your writing teacher to discuss how to make the draft better. You can also benefit from feedback supplied by your classmates. Exchange drafts and help one another with revision.

1. Most people rarely think about how chemistry affects their lives on a daily basis, yet the products of chemistry are all around us. In a

3- to 5-page paper, identify three objects in your room that would not exist were it not for work in chemistry and then provide a summary of the chemical processes involved in their manufacture. Successful papers will provide significant detail without becoming burdened with terminology; they will be informative, interesting, and free of surface errors. Direct the paper to your classmates.
2. Our understanding of chemical mechanisms has increased greatly over the last three decades. In a 4- to 7-page paper, identify two products that you use on a regular basis and explain how increased knowledge of chemistry has led to improvements in them. Successful responses will include an analysis of how the products were manufactured in the past and how they are manufactured today. They will be informative, interesting, and free of surface errors. Direct the paper to your classmates.
3. The Montreal Protocol went into effect January 1, 1989, and was designed to reduce the level of ozone-altering chemicals being released into the atmosphere. In a 5- to 7-page paper, trace the events that led to the protocol and evaluate its short-term (say over the next 50 years) effect on atmospheric and climatic changes. Successful papers will provide a detailed analysis of the history of the treaty and will draw on a number of sources not only to assess its consequences but also to predict the possible state of the atmosphere and climate 50 years from now. They will also be informative, interesting, and free of surface errors. Direct the paper to readers of your campus or local newspaper.

CHEMISTRY ASSIGNMENT 2

Course: **Beginning Chemistry, Honors Section**

An important part of chemistry consists of being able to read and write abstracts of research. Below you will find the abstract of a published article. Your tasks for this assignment are the following:

1. *Rewrite the abstract in a way that makes it more readable. The resulting abstract should be appropriate for a scientific audience.*

2. Write an article about this work which would be appropriate for the science page of the New York Times. Assume that your audience is reasonably intelligent and somewhat informed about chemistry. You can assume that your readers know what isotopes are (although they may need reminding) but that they are unfamiliar with natural enrichment processes.

CLASS ARTICLE 1

"Life History of Symbiont-Bearing Giant Clams from Stable Isotope Profiles," by Douglas S. Jones, Douglas F. Williams, & Christopher S. Ronmanek

Stable isotopic and shell-growth banding studies of the symbiont-bearing giant clam *Tridacna maxima* reveal the existence of two growth phases related to sexual maturity that can be discerned in the shells of extinct and extant mollusks. The changeover from the first to the second growth phase at an age of approximately 10 years is accompanied by a decrease in rate of calcification and suggests a reordering of energy priorities between biomineralization and reproduction. The carbon-13 to carbon-12 ratio of *Tridacna maxima* is systematically depleted relative to symbiont-barren mollusks, making it possible to determine the importance of algalmolluscan symbiosis to the functional morphology and paleoecology of mollusks in the geologic record.

Analysis of Chemistry Assignment 2

This assignment is another that focuses on relating chemistry to the everyday world, but it differs from the first sample assignment in some significant ways. In Assignment 1, the emphasis seemed to be on providing students with a vehicle for demonstrating that they were able to use concepts and terminology from chemistry in an appropriate manner. As we saw in our analyses, some of the writers appear to have simply copied terms from their sources, and there is no way to determine from the papers whether the students really understood the terms or not.

In this assignment, however, the instructor is setting a more challenging task by asking students not only to rewrite an abstract but to produce a paper on the basis of that abstract. The reason this task is more challenging should be clear. To perform the assignment successfully students must know a great deal about the topic; otherwise, they won't be able to explain it to an audience that knows very little.

The instructor evidently constructed the assignment on the basis of a very old principle: Someone who really knows the subject should be able to explain even quite complicated material to an average person. Thus, where accurate use of jargon was a measure of success in Assignment 1, it would be a sign of failure here. In fact, the better papers will avoid the academic tone of the original article and adopt one more appropriate for a general audience.

Obviously, the abstract will not provide enough information to write the paper, but notice that the instructor says nothing about locating the original article and studying it. The teacher implicitly assumes that students will do so, and we would suggest that the more conscientious students will locate related articles and synthesize several as background for their responses. They will use the assignment as a learning activity. Weaker papers, written by students aiming at a minimal response, will merely paraphrase the original article.

Finally, when scholars write for a professional audience, they usually relate their findings to the field in some way, emphasizing why the research is important. Indicating the importance of a study is always a requirement, but different audiences will have different values. Thus a general audience is not likely to value the same things as a professional audience. We can therefore expect more successful responses to attempt to relate the research on giant clams to the concerns of everyday readers. Papers that stick to the purely scholarly value of the study are not paying sufficient attention to the stated audience. They are confusing the goals of professional and nonprofessional writing.

Guide for Reading

Overall, Ester's paper is not an adequate response to the assignment. Even though her abstract is very good, her article is only a slight expansion of this abstract. As you read, try to relate the paper to the purpose or use of the research. Ask yourself if Ester succeeds in this regard or if she simply describes the process of the research in a little more detail. Do you get the impression that Ester has read the original article thoroughly?

SAMPLE CHEMISTRY PAPER 4

Abstract

Ester M. (a sophomore)

Studies have recently been made of the isotopes and the growth bands in the shells of the giant clam Triacna maxima. The studies reveal that these clams, which support symbiont algae, have two distinct growth phases in their life cycles. In the first phase, the clam is basically interested in reinforcing its calcified shell. This is evident because the rate of calcitration in the first phase is very high. After its tenth year, the mollusk makes a transition to its second growth phase, where it is more interested in reproduction than calcitration. The isotopic and growth-banding studies also show that levels of carbon-13 are much lower in symbiont-bearing mollusks than in independent ones. This information makes it possible to determine, through fossils, the evolutional role of algal-molluscan symbiosis.

Article

Tridacnidae is a family of giant clams which live in the shallow waters of the Indo-Pacific coral reef. These clams harbor a symbiotic algae called *zooxanthellae,* in the grooves of their outer shell.

Samples of *Tridacna maxima* were taken from Rose Atoll, which is located in American Samoa. The average water temperature and salinity of the ocean water were calculated, and samples were taken from different stages of the shells' lives. These samples revealed the amounts of ^{13}C and ^{18}O (isotopes of the elements carbon and oxygen) in different stages of the shells' growth.

These samples also showed that calcification was fairly rapid up until the tenth year of the shells' lives. After ten years, calcification occurred at a slower rate, and mostly during the cold seasons.

By plotting a graph of ^{13}C and ^{18}O against the age of the shell, scientists have concluded that there are two different rates of growth in the life of *Tridacnidae* clams: rapid growth during the first ten years, and slower growth after that time. They have also concluded that the beginning of sexual maturity is noted by the records of ^{13}C and ^{18}O in the shell growth bands. The *zooxanthellae* in the grooves accounts for the depletion in the ^{13}C record in the skeletal carbonate of the shell.

> **STUDY QUESTIONS**
>
> 1. Point out the characteristics of Ester's abstract that make it easily understood and complete.
>
> 2. What information contained in the abstract needs to be more completely explained in the article?
>
> 3. Given the discussions of interpretation in the section "To the Students" and the overview to writing in the sciences, what is one very significant feature missing from Ester's article?

Guide for Reading

Paul's abstract doesn't provide a good overview of the article or the research, but his article gives a good description of the research. He also attempts, but does not quite succeed, in showing the relevance of the research on giant clams to a general audience. You should pay special attention to the last few paragraphs to determine where Paul's paper exhibits its most visible weaknesses. What are they?

SAMPLE CHEMISTRY PAPER 5

Abstract

Paul K. (a junior)

This work explores the influence of symbiotic algae, zooxanthellae, on the giant clams *Tridacna maxima*. Specimens of the clams were studied using stable oxygen and carbon analyses of the shell carbonate. Changes in oxygen values of the shells reflect seasonal changes in water temperature. When compared to those of mollusks without the algae, Tridacna maxima's carbon values are more depleted. Profiles of oxygen and carbon values change significantly after about 110 mm., of shell growth. This change occurs at sexual maturity at about 10 years of age.

Article

Scientists have recently concluded studies on the shell of the giant clam *Tridacna maxima.* This study involved measuring the isotope ratios of carbon and oxygen in the shell.

Isotopes are atoms of an element which due to differently structured nucleus (differing numbers of neutrons while the number of protons remain the same) have different masses. Isotopes of an element are almost chemically identical; however, heavier isotopes have a slight chemical preference for compounds with stronger bonds. As this preference is related to temperature, measuring ratios of isotopes can give an indication of the temperature at the time the sample was isolated from interacting with the environment.

Clams do this isolating when they form their shells. The compounds bound into the shell are stabilized and their isotope ratios will not change regardless of changing conditions. By sampling a shell from its center to its edge and finding the ratios of isotopes, a graph can be developed showing the ratio vs. time.

The Oxygen-18 to Oxygen-16 ratio shows definite yearly cycles. These cycles are due to the changing seasonal temperatures. The cycles also show the growth rate of the clam. Before nine years the frequency of the cycle indicates most of the clam's energy went into producing the shell. After nine years, when the clan is sexually mature, much less shell formation occurs as energy is devoted to reproduction. By counting the cycles the age of the clam can be determined—some subjects live almost three decades.

The Carbon-12 to Carbon-13 ratios also contains information. *Tridacana maxima* has an algae (zooxanthellae) living in its tissues. This symbiotic relationship, while not fully understood, does have a noticeable effect on the carbon ratio.

Chemistry

By comparing the shell of *T. maxima* to the shell of *T. areolata* (a simular clam with out zooxanthellae) it can be shown that *T. maxima's* shell is much lower in Carbon-13.

This relationship can be used on fossil records to determine when and possibly how the relationship between zooxanthellae and *T. maxima* started.

The knowledge of changing oxygen ratios can be used to improve our interpretation of early conditions by studying the shells of clams. This may have possible consequences on the current greenhouse—ice age debates as well as helping improve knowledge of times past.

STUDY QUESTIONS

1. What specific information does Paul's abstract need before it can provide a good overview of the research?

2. At what points in the article do you feel you need more information to fully appreciate the significance of this research?

3. The concluding paragraph of Paul's paper mentions that studying the growth rate of these giant clam shells may provide information about the greenhouse effect. What is the strength and weakness inherent in this paragraph?

Guide for Reading

Overall, Joan's abstract and article do the best job in relating the research on *Tridacna maxima* to a general audience. She organizes the technical information around the purposes and uses of this research, a method that takes readers' needs into account. As you read, try to identify how she achieves this organization. Although you may not feel that studying the growth phases of the giant clam has any relevance to you (and from this perspective you may deem Joan's article less than completely successful), this paper should give you a clearer picture of the research and its uses than the previous two papers. In this respect, her paper is more successful than the others.

SAMPLE CHEMISTRY PAPER 6

Abstract

Joan B. (a sophomore)

Stable isotopic and shell-growth banding studies of the symbiont-bearing giant clam *Tridacna maxima* reveal two growth phases in the shells of extinct and extant mollusks. The shift between the phases is related to sexual maturity. It occurs around 10 years of age. The changeover is accompanied by a decrease in rate of calcification. This suggests a reordering of energy priorities between biomineralization and reproduction. The ratio of carbon-13 to carbon-12 is systematically depleted relative to symbiont-barren mollusks. This depletion makes possible the determination of the importance of algal-molluscan symbiosis to the functional morphology and paleoecology of mollusks in the geologic record.

Article

Giant clams of the family *Tridacnidae* are prominent members of the Indo-Pacific coral reef community. They are among the largest bivalves to have existed. The giant clams live in shallow waters where they point their wave-like shell edges upward so that symbiotic algae (*zooxanthellae*) which live in the enlarged, tube-like tissues, receive maximum sunlight. There is disagreement as to the true nature of the symbiotic relation between the algae and the giant clams. Similar relations are common in other calcifying groups, but they are rare among the mollusks.

Stable oxygen and carbon analyses of shell carbonate combined with shell growth increment studies (scherochronology) of one species of giant clam, *Tridacna maxima,* can be used to determine the influence of *zooxanthellae* on both calcification processes and the unusual shell growth rates of this group of giant clams. During growth, the algae aid in the deposit of carbon and oxygen. Integration of these analyses of living and fossil mollusks provides information on life histories and the environment which conventional approaches cannot yield. For example, changes in the oxygen isotopes occurring in the molluscan shells accurately reflect the annual seasonal changes in water temperature. The correlation of isotopic records with shell structural changes allows for determination of age, growth rate, season of calcification, and season of death. These analyses can also potentially be used to estimate changes in productivity and nutrient concentrations in both modern and ancient marine environments as well as to monitor the pathways of calcification.

The objective of this study was to find out whether the presence of *zooxanthellae* has a systematic effect on the ^{18}O or ^{13}C values of shell carbonate in modern mollusks. Work on other groups of calcifying animals has shown that the presence of *zooxanthellae* has an effect on the calcification rate, use of metabolic CO_2, inorganic carbon pool, nutritional requirements of the host, and possibly the removal of metabolic waste products.

This study also investigated the relative effects of the environment on the isotopic composition of the shells and the life history of *Tridacna maxima*. This genus is the subject of much research as a potential food source for further experiments. It is also useful in determining the magnitude and timing of sea-level fluctuations because of its similarity with larger mollusks.

Shells of *T. maxima* were taken from live specimens collected in 3 to 10 m of water at Rose Atoll, American Samoa. The ^{18}O profile of one mature *T. maxima* shows systematic cycles of large amplitude throughout the first 100 mm of shell growth. The cyclical peaks are consistent with changes observed in annual water temperature. Nine years of shell growth are thus recorded between 0 and 110 mm. From 110 to 195 mm of shell, higher frequency and lower amplitude fluctuations occur. This indicates that little calcification occurs during the warmer parts of the year. The total age of the mollusc can thus be estimated by the cyclical nature of the amount of oxygen isotope deposited during calcification.

^{13}C analysis also revealed significant changes at approximately 110 mm, dividing the shell isotopic record into two distinct growth phases. It has been observed previously that *T. maxima* reaches sexual maturity at this size, implying that this maturity occurs around 10 years of age (110 mm).

Thus the isotopic evidence reveals the existence of two distinct growth phases in a molluscan species that are associated with the onset of sexual maturity. It also shows that the onset of sexual maturity is reflected in the character of both the ^{18}O and ^{13}C records. Such pronounced changes have not been described before in mollusks, perhaps because specimens in previous studies reached sexual maturity at a relatively early age. It appears that *Tridacne* change their energy priorities upon maturity, using energy which was previously expended on calcification for the production of gametes.

The methods used in this study may be useful in interpreting the age, longevity, growth rate, and time of onset of sexual maturity of other fossil shells. Analysis may also prove useful in determination of sea-level movement, as the mollusks must live in a prescribed depth zone in order to survive.

STUDY QUESTIONS

1. Underline the sentences in Joan's article that explain the purpose and use of the clam research. Which of these are effective and which need more information?

2. Reread Joan's paper as though she were in your writing class and has asked you to give her some feedback on this draft of her work. As you reread, jot down questions that will guide her in making this article more interesting and relevant to you. Then write Joan a paragraph of helpful advice that she could use to make her paper better.

Writing Assignments

A significant part of what it means to be knowledgeable about chemistry involves the ability to comprehend writing in the field at a level that allows you to explain the ideas to someone less knowledgeable. The preceding papers were attempting to grapple with this fact. The following assignments provide additional opportunities to practice this skill.

Chemistry

1. Select an article dealing with chemistry from a recent (less than four years old) issue of *Science*. In a 3-page paper, summarize the article in such a way that it would be suitable for publication in your local newspaper. Successful responses will not only be clear and readable but will stress the same points that the original stresses. They will be informative and free of surface errors. Please include a photocopy of the original article with your completed paper.
2. Knowing something about a field like chemistry means that one is able to identify its significant issues, the problems that researchers are most interested in. In a 4- to 7-page paper, describe two of the significant issues in chemistry and explain how they are being researched. As in the previous assignment, your paper should be suitable for publication in your local newspaper. Successful responses will be clear, informative, and interesting, with specific details that illustrate the nature of the problem and the nature of the research.
3. Many writing assignments in science are collaborative efforts. As an option for assignment 2, team up with a classmate and produce the paper as a joint project. After finishing your first draft, confer with your teacher about ways to make the collaboration more successful.

CHEMISTRY ASSIGNMENT 3

Course: **Elementary Physical Chemistry Laboratory**

In this lab session, you will use an atomic absorption spectrometer to determine the percentage of copper present in a sample of copper oxide. Be certain to show all calculations and to use the proper format in presenting findings.

Analysis of Chemistry Assignment 3

This assignment is fairly typical in chemistry labs. It involves preparing a solution and then performing the analytical procedure. The process appears to be very straightforward, especially considering that, before the lab started, the instructor gave students a handout that explained the procedures they should use when operating the spectrometer. Nevertheless, there is substantial room for variation and error: Students can improperly prepare their solution, they can misread the data supplied by the spectrometer, they can miscalculate the results, or they can misinterpret their findings.

In addition, the instructor asks students to prepare their lab reports using the "proper format." It isn't uncommon for instructors simply to provide a handout that lists the various sections of a lab report, without any explanation of what each section contains. As a result, students may make errors in presentation that detract from their success.

Generally, a chemistry lab report will have an introduction that outlines the principles involved in the measurement, a procedures section that details the steps performed to generate the data, a results section that often presents any mathematical operations performed on the data as well as the results of the measurement (sometimes this section is referred to as *analysis*), and a conclusion that interprets the findings, relating them to previous work or a theoretical principle.

Because so many factors prevent students from obtaining exactly the results predicted on their procedure handout, they are often in the uncomfortable position of having to account for errors. The conclusion is the place to do this. Our experience suggests that instructors value the ability to trace errors just as much as they value the ability to replicate the procedures under study. Paper 8 offers an example of how students can redeem their lab reports when their findings are far off what they should have obtained.

Guide for Reading

Too often, students in a chemistry lab don't give writing much importance, and, as a result, their reports are simple recitations of facts with little or no interpretation. Part of the problem, of course, is that lab work involves repeating what has been done before, so students have a hard time understanding the need for interpreting data. The lack of interpretation and an overreliance on presenting data are two major problems in the following lab reports.

Harry, for example, uses his conclusion to tell his teacher that he "enjoyed using" the lab apparatus. We're certain that his teacher was delighted to hear it. But does Harry demonstrate that he has learned much about the nature and goals of scientific writing? Ricky doesn't even bother to provide a conclusion. Of the three, Barbara's report is the best, because she comes closest to meeting the implicit requirements of lab reports to provide an interpretation of results. Her teacher praised her conclusion, even though her data were not very accurate. You should therefore try to determine what she does to warrant her teacher's praise.

Although none of the reports below is outstanding, we feel that studying the three together will provide you with the means to write a lab report better than any of these. As you read them, mark sections that are clear and sections that are confusing and see if you can identify the features of each report that could be used to write something better.

SAMPLE CHEMISTRY PAPER 7

Untitled

Harry J. (a sophomore)

Introduction

Flame Atomic Absorption uses a flame to turn liquids and solids into gases and to change the molecules into their atomic components. By measuring the absorbance at a specific wavelength, produced by a lamp made from the element your analyzing for, you can determine the concentration of that element present in the sample. An easy way to do this is by preparing a calibration curve of Absorbance vs Concentration of Standards, by extrapolation of the data for the Absorbances of the Standards and the Absorbance of the unknown(s) you can calculate the concentration of that element in the unknown sample.

Purpose

The purpose of this lab is to use an AA spectrometer in the determination of the percentage of copper present in a sample of copper oxide. Standard solutions of known copper concentration were prepared in the range from 0.1, 0.5, 1.0, 2.5, 5.0, 7.5, and 10.0 ppm copper. From the Absorbance readings for these solutions a calibration curve (A vs Concentration) can be developed. From this curve and the absorbance reading of the unknown you can read the concentration of copper in the unknown sample solution in parts per million.

Procedure

Standard solutions are prepared in the concentration ranges (0.1, 0.5, 1.0, 2.5, 5.0, 7.5, and 10.0 ppm copper) and analyzed using the AA to find their absorbances. An unknown sample is prepared based on the assumption that it contains 15% copper and should wind up in the middle portion of the Calibration Curve. The unknown was dried in an oven. The solution was prepared that gave in unknown sample 1 a concentration of 34.30 mg/l of unknown and in unknown sample 2 a concentration of 35.90 mg/l of unknown. These samples were then run on the AA spectrometer.

Data

Sample	Weight	Absorbance 1st run	Absorbance 2nd run
—	—	0.000	0.000
10.0 ppm	—	0.430	0.389
7.5 ppm	—	0.332	0.302
5.0 ppm	—	0.169	0.168
2.5 ppm	—	0.086	0.085
1.0 ppm	—	0.035	0.034
0.5 ppm	—	0.016	0.015
0.1 ppm	—	0.002	0.002
unknown S1	0.034 g	0.225	0.203
unknown S2	0.035 g	0.240	0.217

AA Spectrometer Settings:

Energy 74%
lambda 324.8 uv range
Absorbance Mode
Repeat Mode
Damping 2

Flowmeter
Fuel 36
Pressure 7.9 lb/in^2
Oxidant 53
Pressure 29.9 lb/in^2

Chemistry

Linear Regression Calculation Data

	1st Run	2nd Run
y intercept	−0.013	−0.008
Slope	0.044	0.039
Correlation	0.994	0.997
x intercept	0.298	0.206
Unknown S1	0.225	0.203
	ppm 5.453	ppm 5.338
Unknown S2	0.240	0.217
	ppm 5.796	ppm 5.692

Calculations

Sample unknown 1   1st Run = 5.339 ppm
                    2nd run = 5.453 ppm
         Average   = 5.396

% Cu = $\dfrac{5.396 \text{ mg/l}}{34.306 \text{ mg/l}}$ × 100 = 15.73% Cu in CuO of sample 1 made from unknown 1

Sample unknown 2   1st run = 5.796
                    2nd run = 5.693
         Average   = 5.744

% Cu = $\dfrac{5.744 \text{ mg/l}}{35.900 \text{ mg/l}}$ × 100 = 16.00% Cu in CuO of sample 2 made from unknown 1

Conclusion

I enjoyed using the AA especially since I have never used it before. As for the results of testing unknown #1, I have that the Copper concentration was 15.87% + or − 1.20%.

SAMPLE CHEMISTRY PAPER 8

Untitled

Barbara H. (a junior)

Principle

In this experiment we are to determine the amount of copper in a copper, brass solution. This will be obtained by using the method of standard additions. Several standards of copper solution will be prepared, and each solution will contain the same concentration of unknown. The solutions should be prepared within a linear range for Atomic Absorption. Data collected should be graphed to determine the unknown concentration.

Procedure

Standard solutions of copper are prepared, which will fall into the linear range for atomic absorption. The standard concentrations are (.1, .5, 1.0, 2.5, 5.0, 7.5, 10.0) ppm. The unknowns are prepared assuming 90% copper in brass. A 1:1 mixture of HNO_3 is used to dissolve the copper and unknowns. These solutions are then diluted to contain a 1% by volume of HNO_3. A set volume of unknown, corresponding to approximately 2.5 ppm is added to each standard solution. The volume of the diluted unknown added was 10.0 ml which was pipetted into each standard. Since two unknowns are to be determined, one set of standards is prepared for each unknown. Once the solutions are prepared you can collect two determination for each unknown by atomic absorption. Atomic absorption is carried out using acetylene as the fuel and air as the oxidant. The AA instrument was set at lambda 324.2 uv and slit -4.

Data

Atomic Absorption Readings

Standard conc. (ppm)	1st determination	2nd determination	average
0.0	.130	.130	.130
0.1	.135	.134	.135
0.5	.130	.130	.130
1.0	.178	.177	.178
2.5	.236	.248	.242
5.0	.363	.360	.362
7.5	.465	.465	.465
10.0	.565	.558	.562

Standard conc. (ppm)	1st determination	2nd determination	average
0.0	.128	.129	.129
0.1	.135	.134	.135
0.5	.155	.154	.155
1.0	.178	.178	.178
2.5	.249	.250	.250
5.0	.357	.357	.357
7.5	.465	.465	.465
10.0	.557	.557	.557

Standard wt. Cu = 1.0009 g

Unknown x = .0311 g

Unknown #3 = .0301 g

Fuel acetylene pressure = 7.9 lbs/in^2 flow = 38

Oxidant pressure = 30 lbs/in^2 flow = 53 79%

Repeat Absorption Reading: lambda = 324.4 uv
slit = 4

Calculations

Unknown x

C_x = 2.69 mg/l

(2.69 mg/l)(100/10)(1.00 1) = 26.9 mg = .0269 g

% Cu = (.0269/.0311)(100) = 86.5 Cu

% Cu with error between 84.6–88.4

Unknown #3

C_x = 2.60 mg/l

(2.60 mg/l)(100/10)(1.00 1) = 26.0 mg = .0260 g

% Cu = (.0260/.0301)(100) = 86.4%

% Cu with error between 84.4–88.4

Conclusion

The preparation of this lab went very well until I discovered my partner prepared the wrong concentration of unknowns. Since I had no free time to redue the lab with my partner, I had to rely on his data. The major error found in the data is the absorbance of .130 for unknown x, and .5 ppm standard. This absorbance is the same as the absorbance of unknown x, without any standard add. The only conclusion I can come to is that no standard was add, so I did not use it to determine the unknown conc. Their is also a substantial negative deviation for both unknowns. I calculated the possible percents of copper in the unknowns to be between 84.6–88.4% for unknown x and 84.6–88.4% for unknown #3. I don't have much faith in the accuracy of these results, but I can say that the concentration of copper for both unknowns is very close.

SAMPLE CHEMISTRY PAPER 9

Untitled

Ricky T. (a junior)

The purpose of this lab is to determine the amount of Cu in an unknown that has no impurities. A standard solution of Cu of known concentration is prepared and absorbance measurements are taken using Atomic Absorption. Absorbance measurements are taken of the unknown using the A.A. and compared against the standards. If the concentration of Cu in this solution is between the least and highest concentration of the standard Cu solution, then the concentration of Cu in ____ unknown can be calculated.

1.0 g of copper metal was dissolved in a minimum value of (1 + 1) HNO_3 and diluted to 1 liter with 1% HNO_3. The standard of different concentrations were derived from this 1000 ppm standard Cu solution.

10 ml/100 m. × (1000 ppm) = 100 ppm (A)

10 ml/100 ml × A = 10 ppm

75 ml/1000 m. × A = 7.5 ppm

50 ml/100 ml × 10 ppm = 5 ppm

1.0 g Cu was weighed out and dissolved with the (1 + 1) HNO_3 and diluted to 1000 ml with 1% HNO_3. The dilutions were then carried out.

The unknown was weighed out but not by "weight by difference." I then proceeded to dry the unknown for 45 minutes and then let the unknown cool off in a desiccator. Then, the unknown was weighed out (2nd try). Both of these unknown samples were diluted to 1 liter using 1% HNO_3.

0.0343 g UNK (1st try)

0.0359 g UNK (2nd try)

The standard solutions as well as the unknowns were run on the AA measuring the absorbance of each seperate solution twice. An average of the two data points corresponding to each solution was calculated. The points were plotted. Those that didn't correlate were dropped and the correlation coeficient of the other points were calculated giving a result of 0.9999. The two unknown solutions measurements were used to determine a corresponding concentration for each.

Unknown (1st try) = 6.34 ppm Cu

Unknown (2nd try) = 6.75 ppm Cu

6.34 ppm/34.3 ppm × 100 = 18.48% Cu (1st try)

6.75 ppm/35.9 ppm × 100 = 18.80% Cu (2nd try)

The 2nd try is probably more accurate because it was weighed by difference and the participation of H_2O in the weighing of the unknown was not as big a factor. Water must have played a big part in the 1st try because the percent of Cu in____ unknown went up because the H_2O did not interfere with the weighing of the unknown.

This is very similar to the lab that was done at the first of the semester titled "Spectrophotometric Determination of Iron." This is a good method to use if the unknown does not have any impurities that absorb at that wavelength. The applications are not as broad as in Standard Additions Method.

Settings of AA:

Energy—73%

Wavelength—324.8

Slit—4

Absorbance Mode

Repeat Mode

Damping—2

Fuel Pressure Gauge—7.9 lbs/in^2

Fuel flow meter—36

Oxygen flow meter—54

Chemistry

Sentence Lesson

English sentences can be written in either the active or the passive voice, although active predominates. One of the primary factors that distinguish the two forms is structure. An active sentence has the subject or agent at the beginning, promptly followed by the verb that indicates the action or state of being of the subject:

1. Rita kicked Fred.

In this sentence, "Rita" is the subject or agent, and "kicked" is the action the subject performs. "Fred," on the other hand, *receives* the action.

Passive sentences change this structure significantly:

1a. Fred was kicked by Rita.

The recipient of the action is shifted to the subject position of the sentence. The agent is moved to the end and follows the word "by." The verb is now attached to "was."

Consider these other active/passive pairs to become more familiar with the structural pattern:

2. A feminist wrote the book.
2a. The book was written by a feminist.
3. The subjects increased the electric current.
3a. The electric current was increased by the subjects.

A significant feature of passive construction is that in many instances the agent at the end can be dropped. This option has the effect of separating actions from those who perform them, which is often viewed as a way of making writing more "objective." Below are examples of sentences with a dropped agent:

4. The legislators raised taxes.
4a. Taxes were raised.

5. The factory workers installed the brakes improperly.
5a. The brakes were installed improperly.

6. Our governor declared martial law.
6a. Martial law was declared.

7. I diluted the solution with 5 mL H_2O.
7a. The solution was diluted with 5 mL H_2O.

STUDY QUESTIONS

1. Which of the three reports gives you the best picture of the experiment? Identify the characteristics of this report that make it the easiest to understand.

2. Harry is the most careful about separating the report into conventional sections, yet his conclusion is very weak. What is inappropriate about his conclusion? What could he have said in this section to make it a strong ending to his report?

3. Barbara's conclusion is an account of how she handled a mistake. Do you feel that this discussion, even though it indicates a shortcoming in the process of performing the experiment, indicates a greater or lesser understanding of the experiment than either Harry's or Ricky's conclusion?

4. In Paper 9, Ricky does not provide subheadings to divide the report. If you were to supply subheadings, where would you put them?

5. You should notice that each report uses—although inconsistently—the passive voice ("Measurements were made" rather than "The investigator measured"). This is an accepted convention in scientific writing, but it sometimes makes sentences hard to read. Examine the reports carefully and find four instances where the writers use passive constructions that are difficult to read.

6. Which of the three reports analyzes its own errors most minutely?

2 Mathematics

INTRODUCTION TO WRITING IN MATH

You will probably not encounter many writing assignments in most general math classes, although instructors are becoming more interested in making writing a part of their courses, especially in computer courses where students are often faced with explaining a programming procedure. Teachers are realizing that the act of writing about tasks helps students better understand course material. Writing prompts students to express in words what they understand and forces them to confront what they do not yet understand well enough to explain in writing.

We predict that math teachers will ask their students to write even more in the future, in part because computer science classes now make up a large percentage of the undergraduate course offerings in mathematics, and in part because many educators are reevaluating traditional methods of instruction. The reevaluation is related to the fact that most people who enroll in a math course work with practice problems over and over again. For example, students in a beginning algebra class will solve equations like the following:

$$2x - 3y = 3(2-y)$$

The aim is to teach the principles involved so that students can then work through similar problems.

A major snag in this approach, however, is the lack of any practical application. This shortcoming has increasingly been associated with the difficulties students experience when they face "word problems." Among engineering students, the situation has become so severe—with students who have performed very well in their math courses being unable to use their mathematical skills to solve even simple engineering problems—that several schools of engineering have changed the way calculus is taught. The new methodology involves writing activities that require students not only to explain mathematical principles and techniques but also to explain how those principles and techniques may be applied.

The typical math/computer science writing assignment, as evidenced by the examples below, requires relatively short papers that translate a mechanical process into essay form. The language of math is explained in the language of English, usually for the benefit of someone who is not familiar with math language. Instructors want their students to accomplish three things in papers: (1) to show that they understand the procedure they are writing about, (2) to instruct or inform an intelligent reader, and (3) to write in a pleasing, error-free manner. The implication is clear: You need to know the material well enough to explain it to someone else. Because your audience is someone who is not especially knowledgeable in math or computers, you should be able to put this explanation into a broad perspective relevant to what you expect an intelligent reader to know.

Although you will rarely receive writing instruction in a math class, teachers will usually expect you to write well and will recognize and appreciate informative, engaging writing. It is to your benefit to approach math writing assignments with the same care you would show were you writing for an English class.

The following papers exemplify how some students responded to characteristic assignments in math/computer science. By reading them and the accompanying analyses carefully, you'll be able to gain a clearer sense of how to write for this specific audience.

MATH ASSIGNMENT 1

Course: **Introduction to Computer Programming**

You have been given a handout of excerpts from books on programming:

1. Dock, Structured Fortran Programming
2. Van Tassel, Program Style, Design, Efficiency, Debugging, and Testing
3. Linger, Mills, Witt (IBM Corp.), Structured Programming: Theory and Practice

Editors' Note: Because of space limitations, we've included only three of the excerpts students received. Some of the following papers refer to those we excluded.

1. DOCK, *STRUCTURED FORTRAN PROGRAMMING* : MODULE A (WEST)

Top-Down Design and Structured Programming

In recent years, data processing personnel have been searching for ways to improve program design techniques to reduce the costs of program development and maintenance. Using traditional methods of program design, programming costs have continued to rise in relation to computer hardware and software costs. Many programmers consider programs to be a personal creation. Programmers with this viewpoint often write programs that are complex and obscure. These programs are hard for other programmers to understand. Even the original programmer may find it difficult to understand months later. Such programs are also difficult to maintain, especially if they become the responsibility of another programmer. One new approach to program design and coding that is receiving widespread attention is called top-down design. It can provide the following benefits:

1. Program standardization is improved because program design is emphasized.

2. Programmers are more productive; they write more program instructions per day and make fewer errors.
3. Program complexity is reduced; as a result programs are easier to read, write, debug, and maintain.

Top-Down Program Design

Top-down program design differs from traditional methods of program design. Instead of being concerned about details through flowcharting, top-down design attempts to primarily focus on the major functional modules of a program. After these modules have been planned, the programmer can decide on the next level of modules, and so on. When this method of program design is used, many details of the solution plan can be put off until the lowest-level modules are designed.

2. DENNIE VAN TASSEL, *PROGRAM STYLE, DESIGN, EFFICIENCY, DEBUGGING, AND TESTING:* CHAPTER II: PROGRAM DESIGN (PRENTICE-HALL)

Program design permeates program style, efficiency, debugging, testing, and maintainability. Thus it is a very important part of any program development. But it is also an area where recommendations for one project or one programmer do not always work for a different project or programmer.

One obvious suggestion for better program design is: Design before coding. In the rush to get "something" started, the tendency is to start coding before the design stage is completed or sometimes even started.

Small programs do not offer the difficulty of large programs. Small programs can be easily coded and comprehended by one person. But how can we intellectually organize programs which are so large that they can't be comprehended by one person? Much work is being done on this problem, but at this time we are all amateurs when it comes to building *large* programs. Here are a few thoughts on program design.

Structured Programming

One method suggested to produce better programs is structured programming. The goal of structured programming is to organize and discipline the program design and coding process in order to prevent most logic errors and to detect those remaining errors. Structured programming has two important characteristics:

1. Top-down design
2. Modular design

These two characteristics are discussed next.

Top-Down Design

Top-down program design is similar to top-down report-writing. Reports are structured hierarchically and written from the top of the hierarchy, that is, starting with a brief synopsis.

Thus the first thing to be done is to write a synopsis of what the program is supposed to be doing. Each module can have one sentence describing the action to take place. As soon as a module takes more than a line or a short paragraph to explain, redesign it.

Next, the data should be described, indicating the essential structures and the major processes to which the data will be subjected. This description should include carefully selected examples to illustrate the functions and their most important variations. These will be useful later as test cases. Each module should have the test data described when the module is described.

One major advantage of this method of working is that it guarantees that the documentation is produced. It should also lead to better programs. The programmer is forced to think about the structure, the data, and the testing of his program more carefully than otherwise in order to describe it on paper.

Much of the work on structured programming has suggested that program correctness is more likely simply because of the way the program is developed.

Coding. The first coding is best done with skeleton coding. Rather than aiming at finished code, the first steps should be aimed at exploring sizes of critical modules, and the complexity and adequacy of modules. Some of the critical modules should be further checked out.

The skeleton coding technique helps avoid the problem of large rewriting effort. For example, most large programs are modified extensively as they are coded and certain problems, restrictions, and desired changes become apparent. By doing a skeleton coding first, some of the problems may be discovered before a great deal of effort has been put into the programming.

Modular Design

In order for the structured programming to succeed, the program must be planned in a modular fashion. Modular programming is the dividing of your program into logical parts called modules, and the successive programming of each part. Once a large monolithic problem is divided into smaller logical, more workable units it is easier to understand and read.

3. LINGER, MILLS, WITT, IBM CORP., *STRUCTURED PROGRAMMING: THEORY AND PRACTICE* (ADDISON-WESLEY)

Mental Weight Lifting

Fifty years ago swimming champions were products of long hours of swimming practice—swimming and swimming and swimming. But these days, when the varsity swimming team assembles in the fall, emphasis is also placed on running and weight lifting to build stamina and muscles more effectively.

There is a similar lesson to learn in programming. A previous generation of programmers learned by programming and programming and programming—sometimes this led to one year of experience repeated ten times, rather than ten years of experience. For this reason, we will stress mental weight lifting for programming that develops capabilities for precise logical expression. Precise logical expression requires a discipline of thought that is invaluable in programming but that is easily bypassed in simple programming problems through ignorance or intent. In either case, the result is frustration and inability in more complex programming problems because of simple lessons bypassed.

We all learned in elementary mathematics courses that it wasn't enough just to get the right answers if we couldn't show how we got them. There was good reason: Though we might guess the answers on simple problems, we won't be able to do so on complex ones. Structured programming provides a systematic process for creating correct programs, but the steps require mental precision rather than clever guesses. There is still room and reason for insight and ingenuity, but they should be addressed to the strategy of programming and not to its mechanics.

Structured Programs and Good Design

Structured programs are written for people to read and understand. At first, they may seem a little more difficult to write than unstructured programs. But a typical program uses up much more human effort being read than being written (including being read by its author), so there is great value indeed in producing readable structured programs. Readable programs are beneficiaries of good design and good style—of good precise logical expression.

Good design means finding a good solution to a problem that is often ill-defined. Therefore, there are usually two steps: 1) define a right problem, and 2) invent a good solution. A few problems (very few) are so well known and universal that a simple phrase will define them; for example, sort a linear table; find the sum of a list of numbers. Most problems need to be formulated more precisely, with respect to both what is to be done and what logical resources are available. For example, finding a sum of a list of numbers is one thing if an adder is available, and still another if only character operations are available.

A structured program does not guarantee a good design. Structured programming introduces the possibility of good design but not the necessity. A good design provides a solution that is no more complex than the problem it solves. A good design is based on deep simplicities, not on simplemindedness. Usually, a good design is the last thing you think of, not the first thing. A familiar example of an overcomplicated solution is the earth-centered description of the solar system. Two thousand years ago humans attempted to explain the motion of the planets with epicycles. It took another thousand years and much personal pain for people to put the sun at the center and make the explanation much simpler thereby. The moral is that if it took a thousand years for mankind's best and brightest to solve this problem, one shouldn't feel badly about taking an extra hour to think harder about a program design.

Good program design—finding deep simplicities in a complex logical task—leads to work reduction. It can reduce a 500-line program that makes sense line-by-line to 100 lines that make sense as a whole. Good design can reduce a 50,000-line program impossible to code correctly to a 20,000-line program that runs error free.

The Difference Between Detailing and Design

A computer program doesn't need its design—all it needs is its code. No matter what lofty ideas went into the program, if the code is right, the computer runs right. Since these facts are indisputable, it is small wonder that program designs are usually regarded as stepping stones to executing code—and throwaway stepping stones at that. There is only one difficulty with this argument; although the logic is absolutely correct, no one is smart enough to build large and complex programs that way without untold trouble and frustration.

In fact, even though the term *design* is used in programming, the term *detailing* is often more accurate. Detailing is writing a lot of details about what programs have to do, what data formats are, how program parts interact, and so on. Detailing is characterized by a preoccupation with particulars, to the exclusion of overall program structure and design. In contrast, designing is a step-by-step expansion of a set of well-defined requirement specifications into high-level, then successively lower-level, programs and subspecifications, until the level of code is reached. A program design has a hierarchical structure; it can be viewed both vertically, from requirements down to code, and horizontally, across the design at each level of detail.

Designing produces details, but detailing does not produce design.

One symptom of detailing, as opposed to design, is inflexibility. When details reveal that a project schedule and budget are jeopardized, how easy is it to subset requirements and assign new priorities to meet the challenge? When details reveal that performance is jeopardized, how easily is reanalysis undertaken? Are programming projects managed by working out mountains of details and just seeing how things come out? Or is systematic redesign used to make development means and ends meet?

Another symptom of detailing, as opposed to design, is the system-integration crunch—the frustration of program parts not going together as planned, along with the "last error" problem (a new "last error" every test run). Program parts written from detailings are based on faith in human infallibility, a notably risky proposition. The fixes undertaken in the integration crunch bring new details and new idiosyncrasies not imagined in the detailing. The more fixes, the more idiosyncratic and accidental the final result becomes.

The final symptom of detailing is the maintenance of an idiosyncratic system. The merit of the program is that it works most of the time. But discovering why it doesn't work is a major detective story. In fact, one way to solve difficult corrective maintenance is to stop using the unreliable function—the ultimate solution is to stop using the program.

You are to read these excerpts and prepare a writing assignment, described in detail below.
The writing assignment:

Mathematics

Write a paper using the ideas from the excerpts to explain to beginning programmers the difficulties top-down structured programming is intended to relieve; a general idea of what the method involves (not the details of how to do it); and the extent to which, according to the references, it seems to be successful.

The paper can probably be done in about two double-spaced typewritten pages, which is about four double-spaced handwritten pages. More or less than that is okay if it does the job. Do at least some revision, so that the version you hand in is clearer than your first attempt.

Any claims you make in the paper should be based on the readings. You don't have to footnote or explain where in the readings each point comes from. Don't try to teach top-down structured programming, but to explain its purpose and how and to what extent it succeeds.

Some of the selections speak directly to the questions your paper is to address, and some of them are more in the nature of background for you, so don't feel you have to include everything. Some of them go into more detail than you would need for your paper.

Except for "top-down structured programming," either avoid technical terms or include some explanation of them. Remember, you are writing for people who, while intelligent and reasonably well-educated (like you and me), don't know very much about this subject yet.

Analysis of Math Assignment 1

This assignment provides clear, thorough, and specific directions, including references to sources, approximate length, and audience. It asks students to cover three specific topics: (1) the problems this programming procedure will help programmers avoid, (2) a general outline of top-down structured programming, and (3) the success of the method.

Because it lists the sources and the information required, an assignment of this nature may seem to leave no room for individual approaches. Too often students may feel that all the instructor wants is an assembly of the required information, just to show that they have read and understood the material. And many students will do just this and nothing more, and then wonder why they receive a grade of C on the assignment.

If you want to do better than average, though, you must realize that your paper needs to offer something more than the minimal requirement.

You may wonder what more can be done, given that the assignment is quite limiting. The difference between an outstanding paper and an average one in this case is not the amount of technical information the writers produce but the way they present it. At issue, in other words, is the style of presentation. In an assignment like this one, style is especially important because the instructor will read essentially the same information in each paper. Better writers will demonstrate their involvement with the topic, but not by repeating themselves and stating the obvious. Instead, they will make an effort to inform readers by putting the material in a broader perspective. In the process, they obviously demonstrate what they know and have learned, which is important to teachers.

The assignment clearly identifies readers as people who are intelligent and well-educated but who are not familiar with the topic. This means that the writer must explain top-down structured programming in such a way that someone who is not familiar with computer programming can understand it. In this case, the steps must be carefully separated and explained, and the language used should not be unique to the world of computers. A paper written this way will enable readers to understand the topic well enough to become involved with it.

Better students will also take seriously the suggestion that they "do at least some revision." Here again, minimal effort will probably result in no better than a C paper. Writers who want to communicate with their readers and to engage them in the topic will probably work through two or three revisions. As part of this process, students should plan on getting suggestions for improvement from other members of the class and from the teacher. Basing a revision on the helpful comments of classmates and the teacher is central to improving one's writing.

Guide for Reading

The following paper is a very good description of top-down structured programming. Readers of Mark's paper who have never programmed a computer can understand the principles behind this method and recognize its advantages. As you read the paper you should feel that Mark wants you to understand his topic; he isn't trying to impress you with what he knows, but at the same time he has done much more than show his teacher he has done this assignment. You might want to try to identify those parts of the paper that create this impression.

SAMPLE MATH PAPER 1

Top-Down Structured Programming

Mark N. (a freshman)

The task of writing a computer program can be extremely complicated, depending on the requirements dictated by the task at hand. Some applications, for example, might require that data files of several types be manipulated to perform a desired function. Obviously, one cannot expect to sit down at a terminal and begin entering code to perform such a task without some amount of preparation. There needs to be an organized method which emphasizes pre-planning and design before actual coding takes place. Such a method does exist, and it's called "top-down structured programming" (TDSP). TDSP attempts to simplify the task of programming by encouraging the practice of careful program design as opposed to "intuitive programming."

There appear to be three main aims of TDSP: program standardization, increased programmer productivity, and reduced program complexity. These goals can be attained if careful program design is carried out prior to producing machine code.

Program standardization helps to reduce the influence of personal creativity introduced by each programmer. A program based on one's creativity is often very hard for another person to understand. The original programmer himself may become confused when attempting to edit the program at a later date.

An increase in programmer productivity is realized, because if TDSP is practiced regularly, a programmer will produce fewer mistakes than he once did when haphazardly rushing to begin code production. The complexity of programs can be reduced because TDSP calls for a given task to be divided into main components of operation. Each component can be more easily understood by itself than if one tries to comprehend the program as a whole.

The purpose of this paper is not to teach the TDSP technique. However, the main steps of the system can be briefly summarized. The first step of the process involves <u>careful</u> studying the problem at hand by asking these questions: What is the program supposed to do? What types of input are present? What types of output are desired?

Once this has been done, the programmer tries to divide the task into several generic components which will link the input to the output. After these main components have been identified, each one is expanded into more specific subcomponents. When the programmer feels that all of the main components have been adequately subdivided, he concentrates on the specific calculations or operations to be performed within each subcomponent and may begin to deal with formal statements of the target language. These statements are then debugged and revised until the completed code in the target language is reached.

As there has been some amount of data published expressing the effectiveness of TDSP, support for it is continually growing. If utilized properly, it has been found that TDSP can reduce a 500-line program that makes sense line-by-line to a 100-line program that makes sense as a whole. Good design can also make a 50,000-line program, which is nearly impossible to code correctly, become a 20,000 line program that runs error free. In one report it was claimed that productivity was increased five to six times over unstructured programs, and the error frequency in programs has been reduced from one bug per 200 lines of code to one bug per 3000 lines of code.

It appears that TDSP does indeed have the potential to produce many benefits and improvements. However, many people believe that TDSP is all too often described in vague and general terms, which are open to individual interpretation. In all, the effectiveness of TDSP is very dependent on the individual. Each programmer must realize that TDSP represents a tool that must be properly used in order to achieve satisfactory results.

Analysis of Sample Math Paper 1

Mark's paper is a very good response to the assignment. It includes all that the assignment requires in a well-organized form. It is written for an intelligent audience that may not be familiar with the process of programming computers, and it is free of problems that can distract readers.

Mathematics

You probably noticed that his paper contains all the information that is required and no more, so we need to discover what makes it a better-than-average response.

The most important feature is that Mark, throughout the paper, communicates with readers and engages them with his writing. He does this by knowing a great deal about the topic, which enables him to talk about computers and top-down structured programming intelligently without limiting the discussion to a simple report of the assigned sources. Instead of trying to impress readers with his knowledge, Mark works to present a lucid explanation of the topic so they can understand top-down structured programming in relation to computer programming and complex tasks in general. The quality of the explanation is sufficient demonstration of knowledge.

The introductory paragraph is a good example of how Mark has managed to communicate effectively with readers. He begins with general statements about programming that focus on the specific problem TDSP is designed to alleviate: that is, managing the complexity of writing certain programs. Moving from the general to the specific puts the problem in a reasonable perspective. Mark briefly explains the relationship of TDSP to these problems, using such common expressions as "pre-planning," "design," and "intuitive programming" to help make the topic readable. Throughout the paper, Mark explains, clarifies, and offers specifics; he never asks readers to interpret or make assumptions.

A good example of his careful explanation occurs in paragraph 3, concerning program standardization. Here Mark supports the need for standardization when he states that it allows more than one person to understand the program and that it enables the programmer to better understand his own work later. The specifics in paragraph 7, easily interpreted numbers, show the results of TDSP clearly.

Note that the concluding paragraph doesn't summarize the paper. In a paper this short, readers do not need to be told what they have just read. A summary of information at the end of this paper would both insult readers and make Mark seem disorganized and redundant. Instead, he has taken his topic one step further by explaining how the programmer must approach TDSP for it to be a valuable method.

Guide for Reading

Jennifer's paper demonstrates that she understands top-down structured programming well enough to explain it to readers who are already somewhat familiar with computer programming. Unfortunately, she fails to put the topic into a broader context, focusing instead on individual steps that are relevant only when the overall process is well understood. As you read, see if you can find additional difficulties that work to make Jennifer's paper an average response to the assignment.

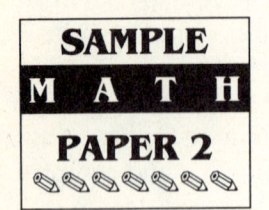

SAMPLE MATH PAPER 2

Top-Down Structured Programming

Jennifer S. (a freshman)

Top-down structured programming is a method of designing programs which has come about in recent years. It is an interesting method of designing a program by which users and programmers alike can benefit.

Top-down problem analysis consists of taking a problem for computer programming and transposing it into an algorithm. This is done in three steps. The first step is to study the problem, especially the expected input and output. In the second step, the programmer subdivides the problem into pieces, and designs and rechecks the logic for each step. In the final step, the programmer re-evaluates the sections of his program and repeats steps one and two for any segment not simple enough. The programmer then writes an NS chart, or modified flowchart, which is a sort of "map," using symbols and statements showing a step-by-step procedure the program will perform. When doing this chart, the programmer starts at the top and works down, hence the name "top-down structured programming."

There are three major advantages of top-down structured programming. The first of these is the improvement of program standardization. It is improved because of the emphasis this system places on program design. A second advantage is the increase in productivity and efficiency programmers get from top-down structuring. Due to the systematic planning of this system, programmers can plan programs faster and make fewer errors. The third major advantage (and probably the greatest) is the reduction in program complexity top-down structuring provides. This makes programs easier to read, write, debug, and maintain, which are the major problems most beginning programmers experience in programming.

The efficiency of top-down structuring in helping programmers alleviate problems was clearly demonstrated in studies done on projects by *The New York Times* and other notable sources.

Analysis of Sample Math Paper 2

This paper falls into the middle of the grade range because it does what the assignment asks for, but no more. It is an average response, competent but not especially informative or engaging. It gives the impression that Jennifer was making an effort to fulfill the requirements of the assignment rather than to inform readers. From the beginning, we sense that she is not fully involved with the topic and has not made a serious effort to communicate with readers.

Note how the introduction presents two ideas that aren't very concrete: top-down structured programming is of recent origin, and it provides benefits to users and programmers. The paper lacks focus at this point, and the statement, "It is an interesting method," indicates that Jennifer is searching for something to say and trying to catch readers' attention. In fact, we can conclude that whenever writers use labels such as *interesting, fantastic, unique, great,* and *amazing,* they are at a loss for something more detailed to say. Telling readers that a topic is interesting rather than showing them may be quicker and faster, but it isn't very convincing, because the writer's task is to make a topic interesting to readers.

We should also note that when in paragraphs 2 and 3 Jennifer lists the steps involved in TDSP, she does it as though readers are already familiar with computer programming. The description is too brief to provide any perspective on the task, and as a result many readers will feel that the subject is irrelevant to their interests. The advantages in paragraph 4 are presented with the same brevity, as are the "proofs" in the last paragraph. Although there is nothing essentially wrong with this approach, the final result is a paper that has a narrow purpose (to show that the assignment has been completed), suitable for a limited audience (in this case, the teacher). Admittedly, the teacher will, in most instances, be the sole reader of student papers, but usually papers should be written as though they will be read by many people.

The paper does have some strong points that keep it from being a failure. It is organized and clear, even if not well developed. As a whole, it is relatively free of surface difficulties that could distract readers: There aren't any spelling problems, the punctuation is correct, and so on. Although these characteristics are necessary ingredients of good writing, they do not automatically guarantee that a paper will be good, as this composition proves. A well-organized paper can be simply a mechanical response to an assignment—sound in structure but deficient in information.

Jennifer seems to have revised her work at least once, and maybe a second time, because it is put together in a logical order. But in this case the order is a weakness rather than a strength: It is mechanical and repetitive. In paragraph 2, Jennifer tells us there are three steps in top-down problem analysis, and then she proceeds to list them—1, 2, 3. In the next paragraph, she uses the same organization, stating that there are three advantages to TDSP and then listing them—1, 2, 3. Such repetition is easy on the writer, but readers usually find it monotonous.

More revising might have helped Jennifer's organization, but it might not have helped the paper overall, because the writer seems uninvolved with her topic. Evidence for this conclusion lies in the last paragraph: The paper ends on a weak note. Jennifer merely directs readers to other sources that support the success of TDSP rather than demonstrating this claim in the paper. She is, in other words, avoiding the whole premise of the assignment, which is that she should demonstrate the effectiveness of TDSP. She tells readers that it's a good approach and if they don't believe it, they can go do the research themselves—not a very agreeable tone to take with an audience!

Guide for Reading

William's paper is below average because he never really deals with the topic in a specific manner. In addition, the order and development of his paragraphs are haphazard and incomplete. Had you not already read the first two papers on this topic, William's would be confusing because he doesn't focus enough on the purpose, methods, and success of top-down structured programming. As you read, pay particular attention to paragraph 4. See if you can identify a topic sentence in that paragraph and then assess how well the individual sentences work together.

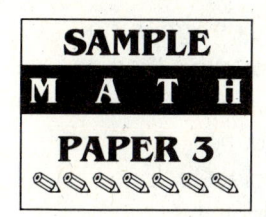

Top-Down Structured Programming

William T. (a freshman)

Since the 1960's, it became apparent that the difficulty of programming had been grossly underestimated. Generally, programs were complex. They were difficult to design, difficult to write and to test, and virtually impossible to understand and maintain. In recent years, we have been searching for ways to improve program design technique to reduce the costs of program development and maintenance. Top-down structured programming was introduced as a partial answer to these programming problems.

Let's look at the cost. The cost of hardware was decreasing, but the cost of software (programs) was steadily increasing. However, the cost of hardware did not stop with its development. Maintaining software was also a problem. The cost of maintenance could be as great as 40% of the total cost of originally developing the software.

The maintenance history of a production program has been characterized by an error frequency of one bug per 200 lines of code. This rate was reduced to approximately one production error per 3000 lines of code. It is this potential benefit of top-down structured programming that should be emphasized.

Another benefit of this method of working is that it guarantees the documentation it produced. It should also lead to better programs. The programmer is forced to think about the structure, the data, and the testing of his program more carefully than otherwise in order to describe it on paper.

Top-down structured programming provides a systematic process for creating correct programs. Structured programs are written for people to read and understand. A typical program uses up much more human effort being read than being written, so there is a great value in producing readable structured programs. Readable programs are beneficiaries of good design and good style. A structured program does not guarantee a good design, mind you, but introduces the possibility of a good design. A good design provides a solution that is no more complex than the problem it solves. Good program design leads to work reduction. It can reduce a 500-line program, which makes sense line-by-line, to a 100-line program that makes sense as a whole. Good design can reduce a 50,000-line program, which is impossible to code correctly, to a 20,000-line program that can run free of error. In conclusion, top-down design can provide the following benefits:

1. Program standardization is improved because program design is emphasized.

2. Programmers are more productive; they write more program instructions per day and make fewer errors.

3. Program complexity is reduced; as a result programs are easier to read, write, debug, and maintain.

As you can see top-down structured programming is an essential part of your programming techniques.

Analysis of Sample Math Paper 3

This paper begins with a clear, specific introduction, particularly in sentences 3 and 4, where William mentions the difficulty involved in writing complex programs and how programmers have been looking for a way to improve program design. Given this introduction, readers expect the paper to explain how top-down structured programming helps alleviate the difficulties of designing, writing, testing, understanding, and maintaining programs. The paragraphs that follow, however, fail to live up to these expectations; the writing is often vague or nonspecific, and the topics relevant to TDSP are scattered.

Note that the order and the development of the paragraphs are faulty. For example, both paragraph 3 and the latter part of paragraph 5 contain facts about the efficiency of top-down structured programming, information that should be in one paragraph devoted to this topic. Paragraphs 2 and 4 and the first part of paragraph 5 begin with a specific idea, but this idea is not developed or explained in a manner that will inform readers.

Although the sentences in these paragraphs are connected, they don't work together well to expand the topic. In paragraph 4, the first sentence

Mathematics

mentions documentation, the second mentions better programs, and the third mentions the structure, data, and testing of the program. Here, as elsewhere in the paper, it seems as if William is tossing out information from the readings, with no concept of what it means as a whole. A paper put together this way makes William seem to have been searching for what to say next, resulting in an assembly of tenuously related facts and information.

The conclusion is a summary of what has been hinted at (not necessary in such a short paper) but never convincingly presented. His list indicates that William knows what should be covered, but for some reason he never actually discusses it in the paper.

Note also how the final sentence shifts the point of view. For the first time in the paper, William addresses his readers. A writer who wants to use second person as a means of involving readers should do it throughout the paper. This shift in point of view seems a desperate plea to readers to accept what has been written and is another example of the "what next" approach to writing.

MATH ASSIGNMENT 2

Course: **Introduction to Computer Programming**

> Write a paragraph explaining to someone who knows nothing of programming (maybe that's you, last week) what a variable is good for in a program. Use the sample program from class as an example. Your paragraph should address the following questions, but in some natural order, and not just as a list. What is a variable? Why is it called a "variable"? What are the things a program can do with a variable? What are the important properties of variables that one should know? Try to convey the information clearly and pleasantly. About 100 words or so could probably do it.

Analysis of Math Assignment 2

Assignments like this one usually motivate students to prepare a simple list of answers to the teacher's questions. The finished paragraph certainly demonstrates that the student knows the information, but this alone is insufficient to satisfy the requirements of the assignment.

If you look very carefully at what the assignment has to say about presenting the information in a "natural order" that is both clear and pleasant to read, you understand that the instructor wants more than just a presentation of the material; he or she wants some demonstration of writing skill.

The better responses to this assignment will be those that explain variables by placing the discussion in a broad context that helps readers associate variables in programming with other, similar types of variables. Keeping the paragraph to "about 100 words" won't be easy, but the teacher does allow some flexibility on length. Two hundred words may be more suitable to the task, but you wouldn't want to go beyond 200 without conferring with your teacher.

Guide for Reading

Andy's paragraph gives a good general idea of variables without becoming tedious. If you feel that this explanation is confusing at first reading, it may be because the topic is irrelevant or uninteresting to you. Read this paragraph carefully and thoughtfully and you should begin to understand the general purpose of variables in a computer's memory. A good test of your comprehension would involve paraphrasing Andy's work. As you read, consider how you might rewrite the paper to put it into your own words.

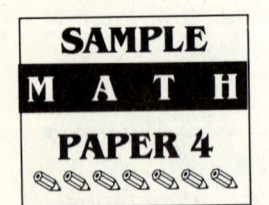

SAMPLE MATH PAPER 4

Untitled

Andy W. (a freshman)

A variable can be considered to represent a location in the memory of the computer. Each variable has a name and value associated with it. The value associated with a given variable can change throughout the program. This is why the term "variable" is used. Variables are very versatile and thus, are an important programming tool. They can be used to store numeric values as well as character strings (other information such as names, addresses, or phone numbers). The value of a variable can be altered by the results of operations on other variables. These operations may be mathematical in nature or may involve handling portions of character strings. Important properties of variables include how they are initialized, altered, and used throughout the program. Different languages have different rules regarding these properties and one must study the requirements of a given language to become proficient in the utilization of variables.

Guide for Reading

Even though Ruth's explanation is longer than Andy's, it doesn't explain variables quite as well. Instead of defining variables, she focuses more on how to use them, information relevant only to someone who already knows what they are. She overlooks the list of questions in the assignment and answers her own: "How should variables be used?" How could you combine definition with use? How would such a combination affect the quality of the paper?

SAMPLE MATH PAPER 5

Untitled

Ruth P. (a freshman)

A variable is a representation of something.
It can stand for either a number or another quantity. It is very different than a constant because the value of a variable can easily be changed through the program—it "varies."

Many things can be done with a variable. There are basically three different ways to fill a variable: it can be initialized up at the top of the program where it is declared; it can be filled by an assignment statement in the middle of the program (Age = 19); or it can be done by using a read statement that reads the information from the data that you put at the end of the program.

You can do a mathematical calculation with either a variable or by a constant and store the answer into a variable. The answer can either be stored into the same variable (changing the value of it) or it can be placed into a new variable.

A programmer should use "meaningful" names. If he is calculating the area of a square, he should call that variable "area"—not a name such as "x" or "y." <u>This</u> is done to make the program easy to understand. If at a later time he wants to look back at the program—or if someone else wants to look at it—he will understand what the variable is supposed to represent.

A variable name can be from one to six letters. The first one must be a letter (A–Z) or the dollar sign ($). The other ones can be either a letter (A–Z), a number (0–9), or the dollar sign ($).

All variables must be declared in the program before they can be used. To do so, you must tell the computer what type of variable it is. Four common types of variables are real, integer, character (* ?), and logical. Declaring the variable, though, does not put a value on it. It will have "garbage" or "junk"—numbers left over from the last programmer that used the same location in memory.

Guide for Reading

After reading this response, you may feel that Joe doesn't inform you about variables. What he says is correct, but he doesn't provide a good explanation of what a variable is. His first two sentences need to be expanded with examples relevant to people who use (but don't program) computers. Can you determine what major problem Joe's paragraph has because it lacks these examples? In addition, his sentences don't have much variation. Of the eleven in the paragraph, six begin with "A variable." Four begin with "The" plus a noun. Joe could have increased his variety by combining some of these sentences, as we illustrate in the following Sentence Lesson.

Sentence Lesson

Effective writing can be characterized as using a variety of different sentence patterns. For example, some sentences will be short, some long, and some medium. Most people tend to write short sentences of under 12 words, so a useful technique to begin making your sentences longer is "sentence combining." It involves taking short sentences and joining them to produce medium (about 20 words) and long (over 30 words) ones. The technique is illustrated below:

1. A variable in a Fortran program is used to identify an unknown value. A variable designates the location in the computer's memory.

Mathematics

1a. A variable in a Fortran program is used to identify an unknown value and its location in the computer's memory.
2. A variable has two components. One is constant. The other can change during the course of a program.
2a. A variable has two components, one that is constant and one that can change during the program's operation.

SAMPLE MATH PAPER 6

Untitled

Joe F. (a freshman)

A variable in a fortran program is used to identify an unknown value. A variable designates the location in the computer's memory. A variable has two components. One is constant. The other can change during the course of a program. The constant component of a variable is the name it is assigned. The name assigned never changes during the run of the program. The value assigned to a variable can change during the course or run of a program. A variable may contain the letters of the alphabet, the dollar symbol, and numbers zero through nine. A variable must always begin with a letter or the dollar symbol. A variable can only be one to six characters long.

STUDY QUESTIONS

1. Which of the three papers answers all of the questions listed in the assignment?

2. The assignment stated that the information should be expressed clearly and pleasantly and that it should not read like a list. In which of the papers (if any) do you feel that the writer is truly trying to communicate information to readers and not simply to show the instructor that he or she has learned something about variables?

Writing Assignments

The following assignments require no knowledge of computer programming. They do, however, require that you know something about some of the more common functions of computers other than word processing. Unless you already use the programs below, you will have to do some research before you can explain their purpose, uses, advantages, and so on.

Assume that your reader knows only that computers can perform many complicated functions but is not aware of any of the specific ones. A good paper will explain each of these in terms that an intelligent person can understand without having to know technical jargon. A good paper will also show a complete understanding of the topic, will provide examples that readers can identify with, and will be free of surface errors.

1. Rewrite each student's paragraph for Math Assignment 2, using sentence combining to increase sentence variety.
2. Imagine that your boss wants to purchase a new spreadsheet software program for the firm, but she doesn't have the time to evaluate the most popular packages. Consequently, she asks you to evaluate three spreadsheet software programs, providing her with a 2- to 3-page report that includes an overview of the usefulness of spreadsheets, a comparison and contrast of the three leading packages, and your recommendations.
3. Your teacher wants the university to buy a database program that he can use in his research on the drinking habits of undergraduates, but he doesn't have time to assess what's available. He asks you to visit computer stores and to examine computer magazines so you can write a proposal that advises him of the relative advantages of the two most popular programs. Your proposal should be 2–3 pages.
4. Your mother just bought a personal computer, and she's having a hard time learning how to use it. She knows that she has to load DOS (Disk Operating System) before she can do anything with the computer, but she doesn't really understand what DOS is, so she turns to you for help. In a 2- to 3-page letter, describe and explain the purpose of DOS. Include in your explanation examples of the more common functions of DOS.

Mathematics

MATH ASSIGNMENT 3

Course: **Selected Topics in Mathematics**

You are to collect a set of data that will make an interesting graph, graph it, and then explain the results in essay form. Your audience is someone with no special knowledge of math, but who can understand the mathematical relationship after reading your explanation and examining your graphs. The writing should explain what relationship you worked with, how you collected the data, and anything else necessary to explain what you have done.

Analysis of Sample Math Assignment 3

This assignment allows students to choose their topic. The only specific requirement is that they graph information. Because the instructor has not stated anything about the paper except the information it should include, some students may feel that the quality of the writing is of small importance. For this type of assignment, though, students who spend time making the writing informative, well organized, and interesting will do better than those who assume that the verbal part of a math assignment takes second place to the figures and graphs.

The better papers are likely to treat a topic that lends itself to a graphic representation and to a verbal explanation. To make the paper informative, you would want to include what is stated in the assignment and then consider what is necessary "to explain what you have done." As the following papers show, it is easy to wander off the topic and to discuss an issue that is not relevant to the assignment.

(Please note that the graphs students generated are not included here because they were not germane to our analysis of the papers.)

Guide for Reading

None of the responses to this assignment is better than average, probably because the students spent most of their effort collecting and graphing data. Sherry's paper is the most clearly expressed, although she should have elaborated her comments about the drop in the town's population and its nonlinear growth. As you read her work, consider what relationship (if any) should exist between the writing and the graph. Stan has failed to give the results on one of his focal points—the comparison of rates among different types of crime. His description of the different types of crime seems superfluous without a comparison of the rates of these crimes. Why do you think he took the time to define each category? Neal's paper is the most informative of the three, and he seems to have become involved enough in his topic to argue a specific point. Some teachers may commend him for this; others may fault him for doing more than explaining. Look closely at the assignment. What suggestions would you make to Neal regarding this aspect of his paper?

These papers can be effective models if you realize they all need to be revised extensively. They should be as informative as the graphs (without including all the numbers) and should explain how the data were collected and what factors influenced the results.

SAMPLE MATH PAPER 7

A Comparison of Population Growth and University Enrollment

Sherry R. (a freshman)

Using U.S. census statistics dating back to 1940 I found the population of B____ at ten year intervals. The population between 1940 and 1950 dropped from 4500 to 3000. This may be, although it's only personal speculation, attributed to WWII. The town has grown during every census since then.

Using statistics from the Office of Institutional Research I found the university's enrollment since 1971. Enrollment data before then was taken in a different manner so it could not be included in my graph. Overlaying the 1970–1980 portion of the B data onto the university data (both graphs are on the same scale) shows a similarity in growth rates. This is just a general comparison because the town probably does not grow linearly, as has been shown. This discrepancy can be overlooked however for the purpose of the comparison.

Mathematics

SAMPLE MATH PAPER 8

Crime Rate in N.C.

Stan K. (a freshman)

When I first started gathering data on the number of crimes committed in N.C. over the past several years, I wanted to show the variations in the crime rate as it appeared over a period of several years. After a while, however, I decided that I wanted to compare the crime rates among the various different types of crime, as well. This is what I gave more attention to in my graph, although it is possible to see the varying rates over the years, particularly in the crimes with a very high incident rate.

One interesting fact to note on the graph is that the rate of crime dropped in almost every area in the years 1983 and 1984 before rising again to previous numbers. It is also interesting to see that there isn't so much variation between the crime rate in 1980 and the crime rate in 1986. Most numbers from 1980 are only slightly lower in 1980 than they are in 1986 and, in a couple of cases, the numbers are even higher—such as the murder rate and burglary rate.

All information was taken from uniform crime reports, "Crime in the United States," which are published yearly by the FBI's U.S. Department of Justice. I found these journals in the university library. I would have liked to have included figures from 1987 but, unfortunately, that volume has not yet been released for publication, although it should be out soon.

I have included, so as to avoid all possible confusion, the definitions of all the crimes listed. This will help clarify what exactly has been included in the counts of incidents per year.

Murder and Non-negligent Manslaughter: The willful (non-negligent) killing of one human being by another.

Forcible Rape: The carnal knowledge of a female forcibly and against her will. Assaults or attempts to commit forcible rape by force or threat of force are included. Statutory rape (without force) is not included.

Robbery: The taking or attempting to take anything of value

from the care, custody, or control of a person or persons by force or threat of force or violence and/or by putting the victim in fear.

Burglary: The unlawful entry of a structure to commit a felony or theft. The use of force to gain entry is not required to classify an offense as burglary.

Larceny-theft: The unlawful taking, carrying, leading or riding away of property from the possession or constructive possession of another. Includes crimes such as shoplifting, pick-pocketing, purse-snatching, thefts from motor vehicles, thefts of motor vehicle parts, bicycle thefts, etc. in which no use of force, violence, or fear occurs. Does not include embezzlement, "con" games, forgery, or worthless checks.

Motor Vehicle Theft: The theft or attempted theft of a motor vehicle.

Aggravated Assault: The unlawful attack by one person upon another for the purpose of inflicting severe or aggravated bodily injury. This type of assault is usually accompanied by the use of a weapon or by means likely to produce death or great bodily harm.

This information has been taken directly from "Crime in the United States," uniform crime reports published by the FBI, U.S. Department of Justice.

SAMPLE MATH PAPER 9

S.A.T.—Data

Neil B. (a freshman)

Whether one talks to an educator, a high school student, and/or a parent, these kinds of people have mixed feelings about the SAT especially the validity of this multiple choice test. The College Entrance Examination Board who sponsors the SAT, says that high school grades are better than SAT scores at predicting how a student will fare in college. This examination board also claims that a combination of grade point averages and SAT scores are better. There is no question about colleges continuing to use these SAT scores for entrances but the importance of these scores should

Mathematics

be lessoned compared to student's high school grades. I will discuss the SAT, its validity, its minority validity, and the national SAT averages over the past fifteen years.

The SAT is a multiple choice test which is divided into a verbal section with 85 questions and a math section with 65 questions. It is scored on a scale of 200 to 800 for each section or a combined scale of 400 to 1600. Some students say that the SAT is not worthy of its importance because students have guessed 100% of it where as some answered only a portion of the test and also did real well. Others say they got worked up over it and could not concentrate, thus, scoring poorly. Therefore, the test does not measure everyone's potential equally thus, its validity is questionable.

The SAT exam was created in 1926 to measure a student's academic ability, regardless of whether he attended an expensive private school or a rural school. The fact remains that the test does not fairly measure the abilities of women and minorities. While females consistently score higher grades than males in high school and again in college, they averaged sixty-one points lower than males on the combines SAT scores in 1986. In addition, Blacks, Mexican-Americans, and students from low-income families usually score below the national average SAT score. Therefore, the SAT's validity is not fair among minorities.

The national averages among SAT scores each year are quite variable. The exam scores are dated from 1972 to 1987. The scores range from 960 down to 919 for men, however, for women, it ranges from 918 down to 858. The higher of the scores were achieved in the early 70's where as the lower scores were in 1980 and 1981. Since the slump in scores of the early 80's, the averages have risen slowly. The improvements in these scores could be contributed to better prepared students like those that attend SAT classes, read books, and master SAT programs, also the fact that students retake the test at least once or twice. The national averages of the SAT:

⟨M⟩ale, ⟨F⟩emale

yr.—72, 73, 74, 75, 76, 77, 78, 79, 80, 81, 82, 83, 84, 85, 86
M—960 - 949 - 950 - 935 - 930 - 930 - 928 - 924 - 919 - 920 - 923
920 - 930-935-938

F—918 - 903 - 900 - 880 - 875 - 870 - 865 - 862 - 860 - 858 - 860 - 860 - 865-875-875

In 1987, 1988 it was 906, 904 respectively including both sexes.

Even though the SAT data is not the highlight of this paper, I did want to explain some reasons why the test should not be looked upon so heavily for admissions into college and universities. Finally, the graphs of the SAT averages explains the data quite well.

Bibliography

Autry, Jenette. "Current freshman class called 'brightest' in university history." *The Daily Voice,* 30 August 1988.

Graves, Bill. "Testing the powerful SAT." *Raleigh Journal,* 15 November 1987, sec. D1–D5.

"SAT Scores Rise for Fourth Straight Year." *Phi Delta Kappan.* November 1985: pg 238, vol. 67.

Mathematics

> ## STUDY QUESTIONS
>
> 1. Which of the three papers contains what is required in the assignment: an explanation of the relationship and how the data were collected?
>
> 2. Which of the three papers contains information irrelevant to the purpose of the assignment? You may need to make a distinction between what is interesting and what is relevant.
>
> 3. What special information included in the paper will help you understand the relationship described in Sherry's analysis?
>
> 4. What additional data are necessary in Sherry's paper to make the relationship a valid one?
>
> 5. Explain what might be a problem with the section of definitions in Stan's paper.
>
> 6. Comment on the development of the topic of paragraph 2 in Neil's paper.
>
> 7. In the last paragraph of Neil's paper, he writes, "Even though the SAT data is not the highlight of this paper, . . ." What do you think the highlight is, and where is it stated in the paper?

Writing Assignments

The following writing assignments are similar to the one above in that they require basic math skills and some research. The increase in difficulty results from the increased complication of the relationship and the research involved. Your reader is someone who has no special knowledge of math but is intelligent enough to understand the relationship you have discovered after seeing your graph and reading your explanation.

1. Collect data on the relationship between cost and weight of a specific item in a number of fast food restaurants in your home or college town. In a 2-page paper, explain how you measured and collected the data and explain what the relationship means.
2. Collect data on one of the following relationships (or one of a similar

nature). Graph the data, and in a 2-page paper explain what you focused on in the relationship and what the data mean.
   a. GPA of students in one of your classes and the amount of time they spend on their homework
   b. GPA of students in one of your classes and the average number of hours they sleep at night
   c. GPA of a sample of students and the number of hours they work during the week
3. Collect data on one of the following (or a similar relationship). Graph it and in a 2-page paper explain how you collected the data and what the results mean.
   a. Take a specific sport from a number of colleges or universities (five to ten) and plot the winning percentage of the team against the percentage of players who graduate from that institution.
   b. Take the salaries of coaches in a number of colleges or universities (minimum of ten) and plot these against the winning percentages of the coaches.
   c. Take the winning percentages of coaches at a number of colleges or universities (minimum of ten) and plot these against the number of years each coach has been at that institution.

3 Biology

INTRODUCTION TO WRITING IN BIOLOGY

As we noted in the overview, two formalized structures dominate writing in the life and applied sciences: the lab report and the research paper. The lab reports students are asked to write in a biology course will probably follow the outline we provided in the overview. That is, they will begin with an abstract and an introduction, followed by methods and results sections, and ending with a conclusion section where the results are interpreted. This organization is designed to help make the various parts of the report easily accessible. The tone students use in a lab report is also important; it should be objective, free of personal bias or subjectivity. The goal is to create a tone that seems rational rather than emotional, because emotions are thought to cloud "facts." A widely accepted convention in this regard is the use of passive-voice rather than active-voice constructions, particularly in the methods and results sections.

The research paper, although having a less formalized structure than the lab report, nevertheless has its own organization, and it requires careful integration and interpretation of a variety of published materials, which are usually the "facts" that you will interpret. Research papers fall into the category of nonprofessional writing, meaning that they address a general audience rather than a special one. Their tone is not informal, but it isn't completely formal, either; it is comfortably in between. A significant difference between the research paper and the lab report is that the former is expected to be intrinsically more interesting to most readers, given that the lab report will be a replication of a routine task.

Your teacher may ask you to follow a particular documentation format rigorously for all the citations you include in the research paper. The CBE format, for example, which we described in the overview to writing in the life and applied sciences, is a method of documentation that biology instructors sometimes require students to use. Proper documentation that allows readers to easily identify sources used in a paper is an important part of substantiating your interpretation.

It would be misleading to suggest, however, that the writing students do in science courses is limited to these two types. More and more instructors in science have become convinced of the link between writing and thinking. As a result, science teachers increasingly are requiring more writing assignments of a variety of lengths and forms, assignments that ask students to provide immediate feedback and response to the material covered in the course. These writing assignments may take the form of short, in-class paragraphs, brief summaries of outside reading, or even journal entries. Many teachers are also moving away from the objective, multiple-choice examination and are instead testing their students' knowledge of material through short-essay exams. These changes in the ways biology teachers structure their classes and assess students' learning are inspired by a growing conviction that students best absorb the complexities of a subject when they are required to grapple with it during the writing process—that is, that students can use writing to learn more about the subject. The sample assignments in this chapter reflect this recent trend in biology and other science courses.

You may feel, as do many students, that the most harrowing writing experience you face in college is the in-class essay exam. When the exam happens to be in a science course, in which teachers are looking for correctness as well as depth of thought, the experience becomes even more excruciating for large numbers of students. To help alleviate some of the stress associated with writing an essay exam in biology (and by extrapolation in other science courses), we included as our first two assignments sample questions from a midterm exam in an introductory biology course. In our analyses of these questions, we provide strategies for responding to in-class essay questions that may allow you to approach this difficult writing experience with more confidence and ease. The final assignment in this chapter is a response to an out-of-class reading and is typical of the short papers many biology instructors require of their students.

BIOLOGY ASSIGNMENT 1

Course: **Introduction to Biology**

Midterm Examination

Directions: Answer the following question as clearly and concisely as you can.
   Define and describe the process of natural selection. Include in your answer a discussion of how the lab experiment with fruit flies illustrated evolution in action.

Analysis of Biology Assignment 1

The above question was part of a one-hour midterm exam that included several other short-essay questions. The time factor, then, demanded that students think and write quickly and did not allow for extensive revision.

When you encounter an essay exam of this nature, you will be able to write with the precision and speed necessary only if you have prepared properly in advance. The following questions my be helpful to consider when studying for such an exam:

What terms will my instructor expect me to know?
What processes should I understand and be able to explain clearly?
What topics has my instructor emphasized in class?
What connections can I make between the various activities taking place in the course: lab work, lectures, readings, class discussions, and so on?

Answering such questions before an essay exam is important because, unlike objective tests, essay exams require that you *synthesize* material rather than memorize it. In other words, preparing for an essay exam means thinking about the material you have studied in the course, determining what is important and why. In our view, writing and thinking are integrally linked, and we would encourage you to make writing part of your studying process. You might even want to make up practice essay questions and write out answers to them, which will provide you with practice using key terms in context and will, in general, make you more comfortable with the material.

No matter how conscientiously you prepare for a written exam, your success still depends on how wisely you use your time during the test itself. Most essay exams do not allow time for more than minor surface revision, so you should always take at least a minute or two to organize your thoughts before responding even to the shortest essay question. Once again, it may be helpful to consider certain questions before you begin to write your answer.

What key terms does the instructor use to define my task?
Can the questions be broken down into parts?
What form should my answer take? Will I be able to answer this question sufficiently in one paragraph?
What one organizing thought can I use to give my response a coherent form?
What important terms will my teacher expect me to use in answering this question?
What examples from class, readings, and my own knowledge will help me develop my response quickly and concisely?

Reflecting briefly on each of these questions before you begin to write will save you from the panic that besets many students who plunge into an exam question without thinking it through first. Writing in a blind fury may be a natural response to the frustrations of time restrictions in an essay exam, but resisting this impulse will result in clearer and more concise writing. It will also allow you to work quickly and efficiently when you do begin to write.

Guide for Reading

Mary's response represents a well-organized, unified answer to what initially seems like a very difficult question. Notice that she doesn't formally define natural selection. That is, she doesn't write something along the lines of: "Natural selection is. . . ." Instead, she defines it by describing the process, logically making connections as she moves through each step. She then goes on to smoothly relate the lab work with fruit flies to the process she has just described; as you read, try to identify

Mary's transitional sentence. Her answer shows how an organized approach can make even a hard question like this one relatively easy.

Mary R. (a freshman)

SAMPLE BIOLOGY PAPER 1

Natural selection takes place through the changes in gene frequencies in a population. The organisms in an environment interact with it and each other. There are limiting factors in the environment which cause some organisms to survive better than others. There is a natural tendency for organisms to reproduce, so the surviving organisms leave more offspring than those who aren't well-equipped to survive. The offspring will have the traits which enabled their parents to survive, and so they will pass them on to their own offspring. This changes the allele frequencies of the population. Eventually this can cause the evolution of a new species.

The fruit flies showed how natural selection can take place. The limiting factor in the environment was the fly paper. The flies who could fly stuck to the paper and died. The ones who couldn't fly now had a reproductive advantage. They survived better in the environment and so were able to produce more offspring. The expected gene frequency had been 75% to 25%, but because of the reproductive advantage of the vestigial flies, it was actually closer to 50% to 50%.

Analysis of Sample Biology Paper 1

As instructed, Mary wrote a clear, concise response to the question. The most notable features of her answer are its sense of organization and unity.

She understood that the question has two parts, and she devotes a paragraph to each. In the first, Mary outlines the process of natural selection, simultaneously defining it, whereas in the second she focuses on the significance of her findings from the lab. A transition sentence, "The fruit flies showed how natural selection can take place," connects the two paragraphs. This simple organization may not seem remarkable, but it is surprising how, in the rush of an essay exam, students completely abandon paragraph structure (the long one-paragraph response is familiar to many instructors) and transitional phrases.

In addition to providing a neat, unobtrusive organization for her response, Mary logically orders her thoughts within each paragraph. The question requires that students "define and describe the process of natural selection." Describing a process requires a careful, step-by-step analysis. Note how Mary's consistent use of language—words such as "organism," "environment," "offspring," from previous sentences—weaves the sentences of the paragraph together. Thus the process is easy to follow and each step is easily recognizable. Once again using consistent terminology, Mary successfully links her discussion of the specific process of natural selection seen in the fruit fly lab with her general discussion of the process in the first paragraph.

Guide for Reading

Robert's response is good because it has some degree of organization and is coherent, but his rough and uneven sentences make it harder to read than Mary's. We sense he has his facts right, but he just doesn't seem able to express them very well. As a result, Robert's teacher gave this response a lower grade than he gave Mary's.

SAMPLE BIOLOGY PAPER 2

Robert F. (a freshman)

Natural selection is the process of the genes of one generation, being passed to the gene pool of the next, providing the structural, physiological, and behavioral alleles for that generation, and the individual reacting to the environment; Thus providing limiting factors (fly paper for example) in the environment, making the species with the less adaptive traits less abundant.

In the fruit fly experiment, there were more flies with the vestigial wings than the "wild" type wings. This can be further studied by the fly paper "cage". The "wild winged" flies would fly around the cage and get stuck to the flypaper, while the vestigial flies with small wings stayed close to the bottom.

Here we see survival of the fittest. The limiting factor is the fly paper, and the "less adaptive" trait (allele) is the wild wings. It would be safe to <u>concur</u> that the wild wing flies are not safe in the flypaper environment. Therefore, the vestigial will survive, thus passing on the more adaptive trait (small wings) to the next generation.

Analysis of Sample Biology Paper 2

The three-paragraph structure suggests that Robert took time to organize his thoughts before putting them down on paper. The first paragraph defines natural selection and demonstrates that he has mastered some of the key terms relevant to the process. In the second, he describes the lab experiment. He uses the third paragraph to make connections between the general discussion of natural selection and the specific example of the fruit fly lab and to repeat the key terms used earlier. This repetition helps connect the three parts of the response.

The weaknesses in Robert's writing are representative of those found in many student essay exams. For example, the answer seems rushed, as evidenced by the fact that the first paragraph is a single sentence, poorly punctuated though it be. The statement in the second paragraph, "This can be further studied by the fly paper 'cage' " has no clear referent or meaning. Readers have to work to discover what "this" refers to. Although instructors rarely expect error-free writing in an essay exam, they do demand clarity. Essay exam situations don't allow for much rewriting, but Robert might have made his writing clearer by spot-checking his work and quickly changing a word or two and a mark of punctuation. For example, fixing the punctuation in the first sentence would have improved the response significantly.

Guide for Reading

KayKeo has her facts right, but she doesn't express them very well. Notice that she has no clear paragraph structure but jumbles everything together into a string of sentences. Her response could be improved by supplying a transition between sentences 3 and 4: "The desirable beneficial genes help make the species better able to cope or survive in its particular environment. *For example,* the fly box experiment showed a high number of vestigial flies alive." She also fails to provide much detail to elaborate her bare facts. These features contribute to making KayKeo's answer below average.

SAMPLE BIOLOGY PAPER 3

KayKeo S. (a freshman)

Natural selection is the passing of genes to offspring thus, increasing allele frequency in the gene pool. These alleles passed to the offspring help continue the species. The desirable beneficial genes help make the species better able to cope or survive in its particular environment. The fly box experiment showed a high number of vestigial flies alive. The number of wild (winged) type flies had decreased. Thus, the winged flies were all caught on the fly paper. Therefore, the genes passed on aren't always good genes.

Analysis of Sample Biology Paper 3

Comparing this paper to Mary's shows the range of responses that a teacher can receive on any given essay question. One of two problems might be operating here. Either KayKeo did not study sufficiently, or she ran out of time during the test.

You should note how insufficiently KayKeo's single paragraph responds to the question. The task here—defining and describing a process, summarizing a lab experiment, and relating the experiment to the process described—is simply too involved to be contained in one short paragraph. For example, natural selection is not merely the passing of genes to offspring; what KayKeo defines is heredity. Moreover, the connections that we saw working in the previous two papers are lacking here, so readers are forced to rely on their own understanding and awareness to "fill in" what is missing, as in the case of the "fly box" experiment.

Most readers are generous enough to perform a writer's job on occasion, although usually not for very long. Teachers, however, especially those giving an essay exam, can't afford to be so generous. Because they are measuring how well a student can express what he or she knows, they can't fill in what is missing. It is a situation in which the facts don't speak for themselves, one in which writers must explain what they mean.

BIOLOGY ASSIGNMENT 2

Course: **Introduction to Biology**

Midterm Exam

Answer the following as clearly and concisely as you can:
From a genetic-evolutionary point of view, why is it undesirable to let a population of endangered animals become very small before acting to protect them in order to save that species?

Analysis of Biology Assignment 2

If you noticed that the instructions here are exactly the same as those for the first assignment, you might recall that, in our earlier analysis, we mentioned that students should consider a number of questions before beginning to write a response to an essay exam.

In this case, "What key terms does the instructor use to define my task?" is a question especially useful in preparing an answer. The key term here is *why:* "Why is it undesirable to let a population of endangered animals become very small before acting to protect them?" In other words, what will be the effect or effects if this is allowed to happen?

The word *why* signals that the teacher expects you to formulate a *causal relationship* regarding the diminution of a population of endangered animals. Your task is to explore the effects of such an event. These effects will either take the form of a causal chain—one effect in turn causes another in a kind of snowball process—or will be separate and random. If the effects are separate and random, you will need to find some way of ordering them in a logical fashion, perhaps moving from least to most significant. We would mention that many students have a tendency to view *all* events as being part of a causal chain, perhaps because the notion of randomness seems too chaotic. You may therefore want to think carefully about your initial response to questions such as the one above if you immediately begin seeing causal relationships lurking everywhere.

Guide for Reading

Bobbi's response is tight and concise. She provides a logically ordered chain of causal events, and she effectively uses the scientific language and terms related to the subject. As you read, consider her use of *this* at the beginning of sentences 1, 2 and 3. Do you quickly understand what the word refers to? If using *this* is a problem, how could Bobbi have avoided it?

SAMPLE BIOLOGY PAPER 4

Bobbi B. (a freshman)

This is important because as a species' population becomes very small, the amount of alleles in the gene pool becomes limited. This causes a "bottleneck" when the population begins to grow again and the result is very little genetic material for evolution to work with. This will hamper the adaptive ability of the species and may cause it to have difficulty in surviving as its environment changes. If, for example, a population of animals is drawn close to the edge of extinction, traits which provide resistance to certain diseases might disappear. If the new population is exposed to one of those diseases, then it may become extinct despite human effort.

STUDY QUESTIONS

1. Read our discussion of subordinate clauses in the *Guide for Reading* below. List sentences in which Bobbi uses subordinate clauses to express a causal relationship.

2. Rewrite the first sentence of Bobbi's response, using the exam question in a way that introduces the answer and that avoids the use of *this*.

Guide for Reading

Wandisha begins her response with a better opening sentence than Bobbi used, but the quality quickly drops from that point. She exhibits famil-

Biology 95

iarity with the material, using specific terms and a concrete example, but she does not organize her ideas into a clear causal analysis. The biggest problem lies in her sentences, which tend to be simple assertions. Here's a useful tip: Causal analyses require writing that uses subordinate clauses, constructions that begin with such words as *although, if, because,* and *until*. Subordinate clauses by their nature *give reasons* for things (as in Wandisha's first sentence), so they are an inherent part of explaining causes.

SAMPLE BIOLOGY PAPER 5

Wandisha U. (a freshman)

It is undesirable to let a population of already endangered animals become small, because they will become extinct. <u>This</u> happens when there <u>is</u> too many homozygous traits for genes. <u>This</u> is caused by inbreeding. Inbreeding causes homozygous genes, which affect the offspring. <u>Too much</u> homozygous and not enough heterozygous can be fatal. <u>This</u> can lead to extinction. This process is happening in the cheetah today. Most of the <u>babies</u> have too many homozygous genes, which leads to death. 70% of cheetah cubs die early.

STUDY QUESTIONS

1. What terms that seem specific to a discussion of natural selection and evolution does Wandisha use?

2. Several of Wandisha's sentences have the reference word *this* as subject. Mark those sentences where it is difficult to determine what "this" refers to.

3. Most of Wandisha's sentences are simple assertions, which means that she doesn't really provide a causal analysis. Using the description of subordinate clauses above, how could you rewrite her answer to make it a causal analysis?

Guide for Reading

As articulate and as heartfelt as this response to the question is, Skippy's efforts are misdirected. He focuses on the undesirability of a species' extinction rather than the undesirability of allowing a population of endangered species to become small. The difference is subtle, but in this case it's significant. The shift ahead to the ultimate effect, extinction, leaves the intermediary effects unexplained. Thus the response is deprived of its most important details, and the teacher felt that Skippy failed to answer the question.

SAMPLE BIOLOGY PAPER 6

Skippy A. (a freshman)

It is very undesirable to allow a species to become extinct. With each living thing on earth, we learn more and more about our meaning of life and why we are here. It is very important to keep each species alive (or at least try) because through breeding we can save the favorable characteristics within future species (forming new species). Many people believe that because of "Natural Selection" certain species die out because they can no longer adapt to their surrounding environment. With our help we can save them. Once they become extinct, we will never see them again—therefore limiting our knowledge of their life and how they survived and why they died out.

STUDY QUESTIONS

1. Look carefully at Bobbi's response in Sample Paper 4. What details from that paper would you have wanted Skippy to include?

2. How would you describe the tone of Skippy's paragraph—objective and factual, or subjective and emotional?

3. Does Skippy's paragraph have a unifying idea? If so, what is it?

Biology

Writing Assignments

The following assignments are designed to give you some practice in studying for, planning, and writing an in-class essay exam. You'll need a watch or a clock to time yourself, and you should follow the time limitations closely to mimic an exam situation. Use the questions in the analysis of Assignment 1 as a guide for effectively organizing and developing your writing.

1. Locate in the library a freshman biology textbook that includes a chapter on natural selection. Read the chapter, taking notes as though preparing for an exam on the material. Make a list of important terms and possible exam questions. Go have a sandwich. When you're finished, write for 15 minutes on one of your essay exam questions.
2. In an encyclopedia or biology textbook, read about the process of photosynthesis, taking notes as you read. Study these notes and then put them aside for an hour or so. Take 15 minutes to write an essay that outlines the process of photosynthesis step by step.
3. Using an encyclopedia or biology textbook, take notes on the following terms: *divergent evolution*, *convergent evolution*, and *coevolution*. Put your notes aside. Limiting yourself to 20 minutes, compare and contrast these three terms. Provide as much detail as the time allows.

SAMPLE BIOLOGY ASSIGNMENT 3

A friend of yours has brought you the newspaper article which is attached and has asked you to explain it, using your understanding of evolution and ecology. Your goal is to discuss this article and the important biological principles which it illustrates or addresses. Before you write your essay, discuss (in your journal) the following questions. Doing so will help you write a good explanation for your curious friend.

1. *Where did the DS sparrow live? Why was it endangered in the first place?*
2. *What can be learned from comparisons of mitochondrial DNA? How does this relate to the taxonomic status of the*

sparrows? How does this relate to their inclusion in the list of endangered species?
3. Why might the Audubon Society consider the isolation of the DS sparrow an important criterion in support of the effort to save the DS sparrows?
4. Why were the last six DS sparrows crossed with other sparrows?
5. Why can't the hybrids be released? Why is hybridization of DS sparrows with Gulf Coast sparrows more of a problem than hybridization with Atlantic Coast sparrows?

As part of your essay, after you have explained the background which applies to the dusky seaside sparrow's extinction, your friend says—"Well, the dusky seaside sparrow is extinct. How important is that to you?" Respond to this reasonable question.

DUSKY SPARROW: SURPRISE ENDING TO 'EXTINCT' BIRD

By Mike Toner
Science/Medicine Editor

Two Georgia geneticists have written an unusual postscript to the short, tragic story of Florida's dusky seaside sparrow.

The last dusky seaside sparrow died in a cage at Disney World in June 1987. Naturalists mourned the loss—and lamented the failure of a 21-year effort to save the rare bird from extinction.

That might have been the end of the story—except for the fact that the sparrow's frozen remains were sent to a University of Georgia genetics laboratory for further study.

Now, after carefully comparing the bird's mitochondrial DNA to that of other seaside sparrows, Drs. John C. Avise and William S. Nelson have concluded that the dusky was genetically "indistinguishable" from the other seaside sparrows that inhabit coastal salt marshes from Florida to Massachusetts.

"The dusky seaside sparrow is certainly extinct, but it wasn't as

"Dusky Sparrow: Surprise Ending to 'Extinct Bird'" by Mike Toner, *The Atlanta Journal and Constitution*, February 7, 1989. Copyright © 1989 The Atlanta Journal and Constitution. Reprinted by permission.

Biology

distinct as we thought," Dr. Avise said. "There is little basis for calling this bird a distinct subspecies."

In a report published in the current issue of the journal *Science*, the Georgia researchers call the 21-year effort to save the bird a "well-intentioned but misdirected effort in endangered species management."

Part of that effort included the U.S. Fish and Wildlife Service's acquisition—at the cost of more than $1 million—of 3,500 acres of wetlands in Brevard County, Fla., to help ensure the bird's survival.

"In the absence of a formal species or subspecies designation for the 'dusky seaside sparrow,' the exceptional preservation efforts mandated by the Endangered Species Act would never have applied," Dr. Avise said.

Dr. Herbert W. Kale, a Florida Audubon Society ornithologist who helped coordinate efforts to save the sparrow, says the dusky's distinctive plumage, darker than that of its cousins, and its isolation from other seaside sparrows justified trying to protect it.

Even ornithologists, however, have sometimes had trouble making up their minds about the bird. In 1973, a century after its discovery, it was "demoted" to subspecies status but remained under federal protection.

Taxonomic errors have confused the definitions of species before. A few years ago, similar genetic analysis showed that a "rare" pocket gopher once thought to occur only in Camden County, Ga., was no different than thousands of other common gophers scattered throughout the Southeast.

In the case of the dusky seaside sparrow, however, the erroneous classification has also led to a handful of problematic progeny.

In 1980, when it became clear that drainage and development would destroy the sparrow's marshy habitat, wildlife officials decided to capture all of the remaining birds and breed them in captivity. They found only six birds—all of them males. Undaunted, they crossed the endangered males with the females of another seaside sparrow species from Florida's Gulf Coast, hoping to produce a flock of hybrid sparrows that would perpetuate some of the dusky's genes.

The descendants of that experiment—five hybrids resulting from a cross between the last duskies and Scott's seaside sparrow—remain in captivity at the Disney zoological park near Orlando. They may never know another home. Since the hybrid strain doesn't exist in nature, the U.S. Fish and Wildlife Service won't allow them to be released into the wild.

The latest research, in fact, suggests that the Disney breeding program may have unwittingly bridged an evolutionary chasm that nature had maintained for at least 250,000 years.

Because mitochondrial DNA—genetic material contained in the energy-producing structures of every cell—evolves rapidly, comparing differences between populations makes it possible to use the DNA as an "evolutionary clock" to approximate the time since wild populations diverged from each other.

The genetic similarity among seaside sparrows on the Atlantic Coast is a sign that they have mingled and bred with each other in comparatively recent times. Gulf Coast sparrows are also genetically similar to each other—but not to the birds from the Atlantic Coast.

Dr. Avise says the sharp differences from coast to coast suggest that the evolution of the two groups diverged between 250,000 and 500,000 years ago, probably when the Florida Peninsula rose from the sea to create two distinct coasts.

"If the goal of the captive breeding program has been to establish nativelike seaside sparrows in the wild, it was ill-advised," he said. "They should have crossed one of the remaining duskies with one of the other populations from the Atlantic Coast."

Analysis of Biology Assignment 3

The instructor of this course has given students a clear context for the writing task assigned: A friend who doesn't know much about biology needs a newspaper article explained. This friend also wants to know what implications the article has for the biology student. Why is the extinction of the dusky seaside sparrow important? The context of the writing, then, is informal and personal. The audience is someone who reflects the interests and needs of a general audience. Unlike the teacher or any other member of the scientific community, the friend needs to be convinced that the fate of the dusky seaside sparrow matters.

The assignment implicitly requires two different kinds of writing—exposition and persuasion—and some students may find this dual task disconcerting. It seems clear, however, that the emphasis is on exposition, or explaining. Through a series of questions, the teacher directs students to those aspects of the article most in need of clarification. Answering these questions, using language accessible to a general reader, is the students' primary responsibility. The teacher expects that exploring *why* these questions are important in the first place will enable students to conclude their exposition in a meaningful way.

Notice that the assignment requires students to go beyond merely summarizing the article. The language and structure of the student's paper should follow that of the original article as little as possible. It's also important to note that the teacher has not asked students to write a research paper on the dusky seaside sparrow; he does not encourage the use of any sources other than the article. Students are asked to present the facts available in the article, but—and this is most important—they must filter these facts through their own understanding and knowledge of ecology and environment. The primary goal of the assignment, therefore, is to test students' ability to use the general principles they have learned in the course to interpret real-world events. It is this act of interpretation that links exposition with persuasion.

Guide for Reading

In this average response, Duong works hard to use class material in a way that clarifies the article for his audience. In fact, he works a bit too hard, because the first part of his paper seems only marginally related to the assignment. As you read, see if you can determine what the problem is. Here's a hint: Readers of short papers like this one expect to know very quickly what the topic is and where the writer will take them. Also, look carefully at paragraph organization. What is the topic sentence in paragraph one? How are the sentences in that paragraph interrelated?

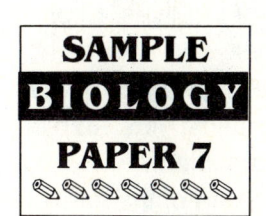

SAMPLE BIOLOGY PAPER 7

Extinction of the Duskies

Duong Y. (a freshman)

The dusky seaside sparrow has a long history in front of it, just like every other organism living today. It all begins with the famous biological theory of evolution by Charles Darwin, who was an English naturalist. Evolution is the genetic change of organisms which leads to progressive change from simple to complex. An example of an animal that has undergone evolution is the horse. Many years ago, a horse looked more or less like a dog of today. Over the years, really centuries, the neck has gotten longer because of the constant feeding on grass. The legs got longer eventually because of continuous running for exercise. The genetic process of this is when a horse stretches its neck constantly for food, the offspring gets the parents' genes for the longer neck. This causes the offspring to be a little bit more accustomed to its style of life. After thousands of years, with much reproduction, the 'dog' has grown to be the horse of today. This process has occurred with all the organisms that are living today, and also ones that have become extinct.

Darwin did not just come up with this theory, but has gone on a long journey as a study for evolution. He found six evidences supporting the theory that evolution occurs. From the journey, Darwin concluded that: 1) extinct species closely resemble living ones in the same area, 2) progressive changes can be seen in fossils from rock strata, 3) lands having similar climate have unrelated plants and animals, showing that diversity is not parallel to environments, 4) the plants and animals of each continent are very distinctive, 5) oceanic islands show relatedness of species indicating their ancestors reached these islands, and 6) species on oceanic islands show strong affinities to those on the nearest mainland, showing they could be directly related to one another. Fossils are the main evidence today showing us that evolution has actually occurred. Evolution is a constant process, which will continue for thousands even millions of years more.

Unlike evolution, ecology is seen every day of our lives. Ecology is how organisms interact with one another, and with their physical environment. Each organism has its own niche, or profession, growing in a suitable habitat. Each habitat has many different kinds of the same species of an animal/plant. For example, all the different breeds of dogs are members of the same species. Species are groups of organisms that differ in one or more characteristic and do not interbreed extensively. Collies and German Shepherds are two different breeds of dogs and are considered to be subspecies. If interbreeding occurs constantly between these two types of dogs, a new subspecies may occur. There are also many subspecies of birds which can be indistinguishable. For example, in this newspaper article, the dusky seaside sparrows were obscure from others.

The reason the duskies from Brevard, Fla. were endangered is because there are so many different species of seaside sparrows. There were not many actual duskies to begin with, therefore their mitochondrial DNA was also indistinguishable. Also be-

Biology

cause of so much interbreeding, there is not a clear-cut taxonomic status of these birds, this results in endangerment later becoming extinct. It was a good idea that the Audubon Society isolated the dusky so that the original genes will increase in numbers. Since there were only six males left, it was necessary to breed them with other seasides just so the original genes well be perpetuated. It was also important to keep the hybrids of this interbreeding so at least the original genes of the dusky will continue to pass on, if they are kept to breed with only seasides. Having too many similarities of genes can easily cause deficiencies in offspring, that is the reason the duskies were bred with other seasides from the Atlantic Coast. Living in the same environment can cause too many likenesses in genes, but going to a further environment is safer because of less similarites.

It is very important to me that the duskies became extinct, because of the diversity. If there is not much diversity among subspecies of these birds, this will result in even more extinction. A decrease in birds will definitely cause an increase in insects. Birds keep a firm control on the insect population, and the loss of this niche could be harmful to our society. This extinction should also teach the entire human population a good lesson because the main reason these birds became extinct was because of our drainage in their environments. This drainage problem can cause much more extinction to other animals, later resulting in our extinction, if it is not kept under control. This lesson tells us that we are careless of our beautiful environment, which we have to remember is not only shared by us!

> **STUDY QUESTIONS**
>
> 1. According to Duong, Darwin found "six evidences" supporting the theory of evolution. Which of the six come into play in his discussion of the fate of the dusky sparrow?
>
> 2. In addition to the dusky sparrow, what other animals does Duong refer to when explaining basic principles of ecology and environment? Why are these additional examples useful?
>
> 3. In the next to the last paragraph, Duong misstates a key fact from the dusky sparrow article. What fact does he get wrong? What effect does this mistake have on your impression of Duong as a writer?

Guide for Reading

Patricia's phrasing often parallels that used in the source article, making the first part of her paper seem like an abstract of the original work rather than an explanation of it. Why would this be a problem? In the concluding paragraph, where she explains why the dusky's extinction is important to her, Patricia's writing is detailed and allows her to conclude in a voice more fully her own. Her teacher saw this feature as an important strength, one that made Patricia's paper slightly above average. See if you can determine why it is a strength. Do you think it compensates for the high number of surface errors throughout the paper?

SAMPLE BIOLOGY PAPER 8

Dusky Seaside Sparrow

Patricia C. (a freshman)

The Dusky Seaside Sparrow was once a wild bird in a population of nearly 6,000. Now due to the mosquito abatement efforts near the Kennedy Space Center, which was heavy spraying with insecticides, then flooding the marshes, and other development in their region the DS sparrow

Biology

faced extinction. In the late 1960's it was evident that the DS sparrow did face extinction. In 1980 efforts were made to help save these birds from extinction. The last six remaining were captured and held in captivity. Then the six remaining were back-crossed with other types of seaside sparrow of the Gulf Coast. This was done in order to save some of the birds genetic constitution. The last seaside sparrow died in June 1987 with many believing it was a distinct species.

However with further studies by two Georgia geneticists they found the bird really wasn't that distinct. The reason so much effort was put on saving these birds was because many believe they were a one of a kind. The geneticists studied the birds mitochondral DNA to other seaside sparrows and found that genetically the DS sparrow was "indistinguishable" from other seaside sparrows that inhabit the coastal marshes. With these observations they find that the endangered species management was misdirected.

With these finding we are able to see that the species of the DS sparrow was becoming extinct, but they weren't as distinct as many thought. The DS sparrow ___ related to other seaside sparrows which made them not very distinct. The species of the DS sparrow is now gone but its genes were left behind because of backcrossing them with other seaside sparrows. They also made a mistake there. Scientists have figured out that the DS sparrow resemble the Atlantic Coast sparrow more than the Gulf Coast sparrows. If they were trying to breed native like sparrows they should have breeded them with the Atlantic Coast sparrows. Instead they breeded with the Gulf Coast sparrows and may have "unwittingly bridged an evolutionary chasm that nature has maintained for at least 250,000 years." This breeding through evolutionary time may produce a new type of species. They already have 5 hybrids from the backcrossing, but are not able to be released. This is because the hybrid strain doesn't exist in nature.

This article effects us in may ways. first of all the fact that the DS sparrow is extinct and now gone effects us. Its death takes away possibilities of us learning more about them and there genetic make-up. It also effects the ecology. The species which lived off them will need to have another type of prey. Also the prey which the DS sparrow lived on will also change. The other effect which is the most important is how the DS sparrow became extinct. If they have become extinct because of our doings, what is going to stop other species from becoming extinct in time. The genetic make-up of each species is of importance to us, because of evolution. The more genes there are the possibility is there for new ones to develop. That chance won't happen if we don't stop and take a look around and see what is happening. We need to find a better way to protect species that need it, and ___ let the ecosystem take care of the others. I really don't know how it could be done, but someone needs to find a way. If not there is a chance that we will become extinct before our time.

> ## STUDY QUESTIONS
>
> 1. Quickly reread Patricia's paper and the dusky sparrow article. What key phrases from the original article does she rely on to develop her analysis?
>
> 2. Does Patricia provide general information about ecology and the environment to help the audience better comprehend the dusky sparrow article? If so, where is this information?
>
> 3. Patricia states that there are two main effects of the dusky's extinction. What are these effects? Does this paper move from least important effect to most important, or vice versa?

Sentence Lesson

One of the more common structural problems in writing involves indefiniteness and the word *this*. Sometimes *this* functions as a pronoun, as in the sentences below:

1. This was the moment she had been waiting for.
2. This is his finest hour.

More often, however, *this* functions as an adjective, which means that it must work with a noun, as in the sentences below:

Biology

3. This report should have been submitted Friday.
4. This question has come up in previous meetings.
5. This test is the worst I've ever seen.

Many inexperienced writers mistakenly assume that *this* can function as a pronoun for entire constructions. The papers above illustrate this mistake. Look carefully at the following sentences, taken from papers 7 and 8:

6. *This* causes the offspring to be a little bit more accustomed to its style of life.
7. Also because of so much interbreeding, there is not a clear-cut taxonomic status of these birds, *this* results in endangerment later becoming extinct.
8. If there is not much diversity among the subspecies of these birds, *this* will result in even more extinction.
9. *This* was done in order to save some of the birds genetic constitution.

You should note that in 1 and 2, *this* refers to "the moment" and "finest hour," respectively. In 6–9, however, it is unclear what *this* refers to. In 7, we can assume that it refers to the entire first part of the sentence, but in this case the proper word to use would be *which*.

Generally, there are two ways to solve this problem. The first consists of placing an appropriate noun after *this* to produce structures similar to those in 3–5. The second solution consists of rewriting the sentence to delete the word altogether. In most cases, the revision is fairly easy. Consider the following version of 8:

8a. If there is not much diversity among subspecies of these birds, the result will be even more extinction.

Guide for Reading

Brad's paper isn't easy to read because it isn't very well organized and because it had numerous surface errors. In addition, Brad has tried to convey everything he has to say about the dusky sparrow in a single paragraph. Admittedly, he doesn't have much to say about the topic, but he still has too much for one paragraph.

One consequence of the single-paragraph approach is that the writing doesn't seem to have any logical order. Brad places too much emphasis on the question of whether the extinction of the dusky is important rather than on the main purpose of the assignment: explaining and clarifying the article assigned. Together, these factors make Brad's paper a below-average response. As you read, try to determine why.

SAMPLE BIOLOGY PAPER 9

The Dusky Seaside Sparrow

Brad J. (a freshman)

The Dusky Seaside Sparrow that use to live in the marshy areas of Central Florida is now extinct. It's extinction is a result from population pressures such as spraying with insecticides, flooding and draining the marshes, and development of the area. The extinction of the Dusky Seaside Sparrow isn't as important to me in the fact that we lost that particular species. It is important to me in showing how population pressure can make a species extinct. The pressures of man that is put on the environment and certain species ecologies can and does effect many species not just this one. The loss of this bird isn't that big of an ordeal compared to other extinction that have happened, because there are many sparrows in the area that resemble the Dusky Seaside Sparrow. The Dusky Seaside Sparrow was genetically "indistinguishable" from the other seaside sparrows in the area, it and the Atlantic Coast sparrow were very much alike. Scientist tried interbreeding the dusky with the Gulf Coast Sparrow which characteristics aren't quite as similar. They hope to come out with a hybrid that carries many of the same traits as the dusky. The experiment seemed not to work as one scientists said that it was ill-advised and that they should have crossed the dusky with an Atlantic Coast Sparrow.

STUDY QUESTIONS

1. Brad's one paragraph has no focus and needs to be divided. Where would you put new paragraph breaks? Can you explain your decisions?

2. Why do you think Brad discusses the importance of the dusky's extinction at the beginning of the paper? Can you determine what brings him to this subject? Does he return to this subject at the conclusion? How exactly does he conclude his paper?

3. Return to the list of questions provided in the instructor's assignments. How many of these questions does Brad address? How fully, in your opinion, does he address these questions?

4. Does Brad supplement his discussion of the article with general information about ecology and the environment?

Writing Assignments

The following assignments are designed as follow-ups to our discussion of Assignments 2 and 3:

1. Call your local Sierra Club chapter and get information about endangered species particular to your area. Locate articles and newspaper clippings concerning one of these endangered species. Using this published material, write a researched causal analysis of the problem. Why is this species endangered? What do you believe will be the consequences, if any, of its extinction?

2. Go to your campus library and find Lewis Thomas' *The Lives of a Cell: Notes of a Biology Watcher*. Read his essay entitled "Natural Science," taking notes as you do. How does Thomas define and describe scientific behavior? What kind of metaphors does he use to illustrate this behavior? Write an essay about research and exploration in the natural sciences using both his essay and your knowledge of the subject from class discussions, the life and applied sciences overview in this book, and your own experience in science courses.

4 Physics

INTRODUCTION TO WRITING IN PHYSICS

Physics is concerned with the way things work—not primarily machines, but rather the natural world. Physics classes therefore deal with such topics as energy, electricity and magnetism, relativity, sound, optics, and astronomy.

Physics departments, like so many others in the sciences, generally offer two types of courses. One is for nonscience majors and is designed to give students a broad overview of what physics is about. Teachers sometimes refer lightheartedly to these introductory courses as "Physics for Poets." Commonly, students chart the study of physics from the Greeks to Copernicus, Galileo, Newton, and Einstein. They gain a general understanding of major theories such as thermodynamics and relativity but do minimal lab work, if any. Students often have at least one writing assignment, characteristically a research paper that either relates physics to the everyday world or investigates some historical aspect of the field.

Students majoring in science, on the other hand, take physics courses that require numerous hours of lab work. Chemistry and calculus are usually prerequisites for enrollment, and it isn't unusual for students to have 10 to 20 complicated calculus problems every week. The labor is intense, and writing activities typically consist of lab reports.

The criteria for success on these two types of assignments differ in some obvious ways. Research assignments are designed to help students become more familiar with a given topic and to help them better understand the relationship between work in physics and their own lives. Given these general aims, few teachers ask for or expect students to engage in any in-depth investigations that would involve scholarly journals. They prefer students to stick to sources readily accessible to the nonprofessional. Moreover, they don't want a lengthy recitation of facts about a topic but prefer instead to see a thoughtful analysis in which writers interpret or assess work in a particular area. For example, students researching nuclear energy could find huge amounts of information about the topic in specialized journals, and they could perhaps even make some of that information understandable to a general audience, but in most cases they would be missing the point of the assignment unless they focused on how developments in nuclear research have influenced the way people live.

Although this sort of interpretation of facts is central to research papers in physics, there are other concerns. Many teachers, for example, use this type of assignment to acquaint students with the library and formal documentation. They may stress accuracy in citations and bibliographies, and some students may wonder what all the concern is about, unwisely believing that if the content of the paper is good, then something as mechanical as documentation should be largely irrelevant. Few teachers agree, however, viewing the ability to attend to details as a reflection of understanding physics well enough to talk about it.

These research assignments are in the category of "nonprofessional" writing, and the papers students produce are expected to follow the general conventions associated with formal academic work. The papers will begin, for example, with a paragraph that "sets the scene" for the discussion, one that provides some background for the paper. If the topic is, say, Galileo's contribution to modern science, the introduction might begin by describing his early work with telescopes or his treatise on the orbits of the planets around the sun, a novel idea during the late sixteenth and early seventeenth centuries. Then it would offer a claim, or thesis, that the writer is going to defend. The remainder of the paper will consist of the presentation of facts and an interpretation of them.

Because these papers are designed for a general audience, writers should use little jargon, and what they do use they should explain. Also, the papers should be well documented, and writers will need to make a clear distinction between the facts they have collected from published sources and their own analysis and interpretation of those facts. (The most popular documentation guides are mentioned in the overview to writing in the sciences.) Documentation in this instance should be performed as carefully as a lab experiment. The facts collected from published sources are the equivalent of data collected in the laboratory, and in both cases you should strive for accuracy.

The stylistic features of nonprofessional papers in physics are identical to those in other disciplines. Teachers expect the writing to be free of surface errors, clear, and readable. They want students to provide rich details and thoughtful interpretations, and they expect the tone to be somewhere between formal and informal. Above all, they appreciate papers that are interesting and that show students learned something from the assignment.

Lab reports, on the other hand, fall more closely into the category of "professional writing." They present the results of experiments assigned in a manual of some sort. They rarely involve library research or documentation, and they are commonly written for a specialized audience rather than a general one. Unlike the research paper, the lab report is divided into sections, with subheadings that identify the focus of the writing. It begins with an "introduction" section that is usually followed by "procedures," "data analysis," "results," and "conclusions." (Some minor variations exist, of course, as the following lab reports demonstrate.)

In addition to these features, lab reports use more of the conventions associated with scientific writing. Unlike the research paper, for example, lab reports commonly use passive voice, a sentence pattern in which the agent of any action is not readily identifiable. Teachers would be more likely to expect students to write the passive voice, "The material was scanned with the electron microscope," than the active voice, "I scanned the material with the electron microscope." The passive voice allows writers to suppress the personal "I" and to give a more detached, and presumably more objective, account of the lab work. The style of the lab report is also likely to be more terse than the research paper, with shorter sentences and paragraphs.

Underlying these obvious differences, however, are some fundamental similarities between the two types of writing in physics. It isn't unusual for undergraduate science students to begin their work in physics with the belief that lab work is designed primarily to test their ability to conduct experiments with sufficient accuracy to obtain the results predicted in their lab manual. Actually, successful lab reports, like successful research papers, devote far less attention to "facts" or "results" than to interpretations of those results. That is, in the minds of most physics teachers, it isn't enough for students to be able to get an experiment to run correctly; they also want to see some discussion of what the results *mean*.

In addition, attention to details is important in both kinds of writing. Students who leave subheadings out of their lab reports, like students who fail to document a research paper properly, are likely to receive a lower grade than those who put them in.

PHYSICS ASSIGNMENT 1

Course: Physics from a Historical Perspective

Write a paper—2,000 words, besides footnotes and bibliography—on the history of a physical concept. The paper should include footnotes and bibliography at the end. Unconventional forms (e.g., creative writing) may be allowed with prior permission.

Though the subject of the paper is the history of the development *of a concept in physics, the concept itself should be explained in its various stages. The paper should also address at least the following questions (not necessarily explicitly):*

How did the concept develop from precursors to successors?
What did it replace/improve/answer?
When did it arise? Who was/were responsible?
Through what stages did it progress?
If appropriate, how was it overthrown?
What is and was its importance?
Did the new concept appear suddenly (revolution), develop gradually, or part and part?
How was its rise (and fall?) influenced by the thought of the times?
How did it influence the thought of the times and thereafter?

Research need not be exhaustive, but should be more than minimal. Do not rely on a single source. Acknowledge all your sources. You will probably find an encyclopedia (or dictionary of science) the best starting point, but will probably need to go on to a more specialized source for some details.

Your paper will be graded according to the following criteria:

Understanding. *Did you understand the subject? Are the statements and explanations basically correct? Was enough effort put into figuring out the meaning of technical words and ideas? Were words and phrases echoed without understanding?*

Content. *Were the questions asked on the assignment addressed? Was the paper sufficiently meaty, or was it stuffed with filling? Were the topics discussed relevant and to the point of the subject, or were there excessive side excursions?*

Thought and Effort. *Did you* think *about the topic? Did you raise at least the more obvious questions? Was a reasonable amount of effort put into finding out or thinking about the topic? Was enough research done, using several sources? Did you express your own views, take a position, or find an interesting angle?*

Organization. *Was the paper well-organized, with a well-connected flow of paragraphs? Was it just fact, fact, fact, or was it more interesting? Was there a central theme, thesis, or focus to tie the ideas together? Was the first paragraph a good introduction, overview, or thesis statement? Did the last paragraph have some form of conclusion or summary? Were the topics approached in an appropriate order? Were figures or tables or appendices used if appropriate?*

English and Style. *Was the paper well-written? Did it flow well? Were there many mistakes of grammar, semantics, punctuation or spelling? Was it in the specified form, with footnotes and bibliography?*

Analysis of Physics Assignment 1

It is clear that the teacher who wrote the above assignment appreciates good writing and knows something about the specific qualities that characterize well-written papers. Because the teacher provides precise guidelines for the paper, most students will probably believe they know exactly what to do. One aspect of the assignment, however, may prove troubling: Who is the audience supposed to be? Although the assignment does not say explicitly, there are indications that the teacher expects students to write for a general audience. For example, the instructions encourage students to avoid "words and phrases echoed without understanding." The implication is that students should define technical terms in everyday language. Such definitions would not only help the teacher measure how well students understand the words they are using but would also allow a general audience to read the paper easily.

In addition, the instructions encourage students to avoid "just fact, fact, fact," which may be fascinating to members of the scientific community but tiresome to a general audience. Writing for anything other than a general audience requires a background and a knowledge of the subject that most undergraduates just don't have in a course for nonmajors. Thus, students who try to impress their teachers by borrowing too liberally from specialized sources may not only be guilty of plagiarism but may also be missing the point of the assignment.

The important question for students, therefore, becomes what information they should include in the paper if they aren't supposed to dwell on facts. We've already mentioned explanations of terms, but several pages of definitions will make for a most boring paper. No—the central part of this paper will be *interpretations* of facts and ideas. Look again at the third criterion, thought and effort. The teacher asks students to "express your own views, take a position, or find an interesting angle."

If you have been studying the range of assignments presented in this text, you will note that the majority of them ask for interpretations of the topics students are writing about. Very few teachers want you to repeat information you've acquired from reading or lab work; they want to know what the information means to you. Understanding this point is central to success on the assignment above and on most other writing assignments you will encounter.

Guide for Reading

Nancy's paper is an above-average response to the assignment. She narrates an interesting history of inventors and schemers who have attempted to build a perpetual motion device. Her organization is effective because she groups similar devices together. But her success is based on more than good organization of an interesting topic. She also takes care to explain some important laws of physics that are relevant to her paper and that demonstrate how much she knows about the subject.

As good as Nancy's paper is, it isn't outstanding for three reasons.

First, she relies too heavily on a single source for her information. Second, her paper is simply too long. As you read, you will notice places where Nancy seems determined to provide more details than are necessary to get her point across. The length of the paper is related to the third reason, which is that her paragraphs are too long. Some are a full typed page or more, making the paper harder to read than it should be. As you read, mark your text where you believe Nancy should have made paragraph breaks.

SAMPLE PHYSICS PAPER 1

Perpetual Motion

Nancy W. (a freshman)

When one mentions the term perpetual motion, most people envision a machine that will run forever. For the physics student, however, a perpetual motion machine is one that does useful work without drawing on an external force. In other words, it is a machine in which the output is greater than the input, ultimately leading to a machine which can create energy. Historically, perpetual motion arose in connection with the search for a machine or mechanism which would continue to do useful work once set in motion, or would give more energy than it absorbed in a cycle of operation. The early perpetual motionists saw what they perceived to be perpetual motion on a large scale everyday—the sun rising and setting, the moon waxing and waning, and the tides ebbing and flowing. Nature's forces surrounded the perpetual motionists, and harnessing these ever-present forces in order to make work easier was seen as a natural and necessary thing to do. To these early people, who concentrated on supplying everyone with the basic necessities, automatic machinery was not a goal to be achieved but rather another aspect of the work to be done. It is not surprising, then, to discover that all of the early perpetual motion machines concerned the craft of the miller, who used either water or wind to grind his corn. However, efforts to create perpetual motion machines were not limited to wind and water propulsion, and for the most part, the perpetual motionists kept up with the technological advances of the times, such that a sort of perpetuity was established between the perpetual motionist and technology itself—any advance in technology seeming to spark a new idea for perpetual motion in the mind of some inventor. It seemed that perpetual motion was always close, but the ineluctable laws of motion and energy conservation, of which these early inventors had no knowledge, thwarted their success every time. Looking back on these early inventors with the knowledge that we have gained up to the twentieth century, it would be easy to judge these people as foolish or place them among the alchemists in the sense that they were seeking for the impossible. But to look at them in this manner would be to sell oneself short, because it was their failure in many cases that became the foundation from which theories were developed—theories that still stand today and ___ have become the basis of our laws of thermodynamics.

In order to fully appreciate what the perpetual motionist were attempting to create, it is perhaps helpful to know the odds that they were up against. Simon Stevinus, a great mathematician of the sixteenth century, proved the law of equilibrium on an inclined plane by showing that perpetual motion could not exist. This is one of the earliest examples of a theory still in use today that came about, in part, as an attempt to disprove the notion that a perpetual motion machine could be made. Stevinus proved his theory of equilibrium on an inclined plane by taking a cord of uniform density on which were strung fourteen balls of equal mass and at equal distance apart. He then hung the connected balls on a triangular-shaped support made up of two unequally inclined planes with a common horizontal base, such that the following picture was formed.

In determining the conditions for equilibrium, one of two things must be true: either the balls are in equilibrium when so arranged or they are not. If they are not in equilibrium and motion ensues, the motion can't change the condition of the system because there will always be eight balls in the part AEB, four on AC, and two on CB. Therefore, once the system starts to move it must continue, or more specifically, it must demonstrate perpetual motion. Since the system does not move, the law for equilibrium on an inclined plane is proved, whereby the acting force CB (as opposed to the resisting force AC) is parallel to the inclined plane.[1] Despite this attack on the possibility of perpetual motion, people continued looking for machines which could create inexhaustible supplies of energy.

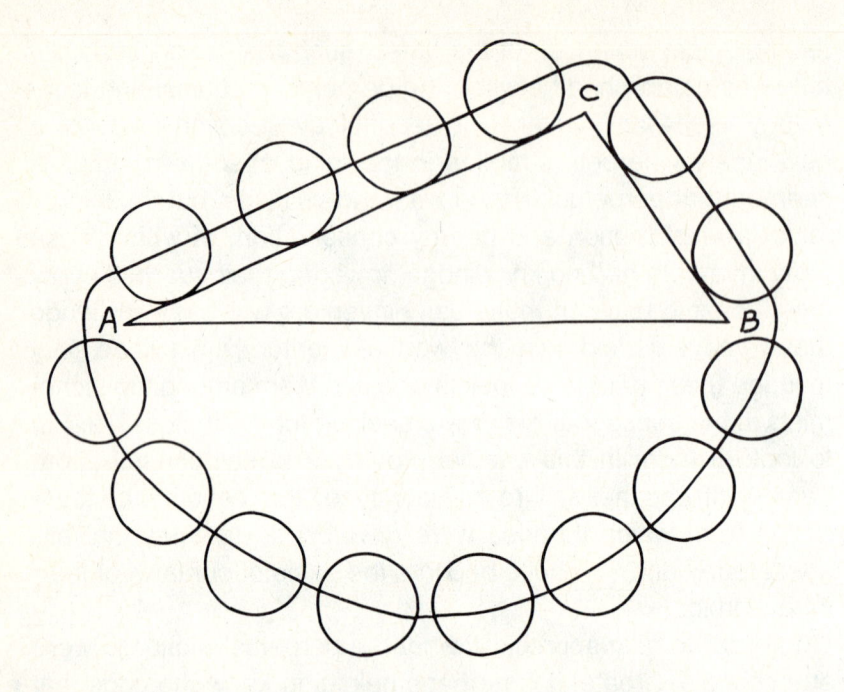

While their quest ensued, physicists continued to turn their attention toward finding relationships between heat and other forms of energy. These relationships were finally experimented with and theorized about until finally, in 1842, the German physicist Julius Robert Mayer (1814–1878) formally stated that "Once in existence, force cannot be annihilated; it can only change its form."[2] This statement, known as the foundation of the First Law of Thermodynamics, has been expanded, such that the law now states, in simplified terms that "a fixed amount of mechanical work always produces the equivalent amount of heat, and thus energy can be converted from work into heat, but it can neither be created nor can it be destroyed."[3]

This latter part of the First Law, concerning the creation and destruction of energy, is referred to as the Principle of the Conservation of Energy. This principle is the primary reason why it is now believed that a perpetual motion machine cannot exist. If, as stated earlier, a perpetual motion machine is one whose efficiency exceeds 100%, then energy would have to be created somewhere during the cycle of operation, and it is this fact that violates the Principle of the Conservation of Energy. Just from a practical point of view, if one chose to invalidate the First Law of Thermodynamics, (as many perpetual motionists did) creating a perpetual motion machine would still be impossible because in the world of man, all motion involves some rubbing of one material over another. At the point of rubbing, opposing forces, called friction, tend to stop the machine, requiring energy to keep the machine going. Even if friction could be reduced, as with a pendulum hanging in a vaccuum, not all friction is lost because at the string, where the fibers rub up against one another, friction will still exist. Even if hung on a string of quartz glass, one of the best materials for reducing internal rubbing friction, the pendulum would swing for a long time but not forever. Despite this argument, some perpetual motionists say that the friction does not destroy the energy of motion; it merely converts some mechanical kinetic energy into heat energy. In this regard they are correct, but if these inventors go one step further to suggest that the heat energy can be converted back into mechanical energy to be returned to the machine, then they lack understanding of one of the fundamental laws of heat engines that states that no heat engine can ever exceed 100% efficiency.

Interestingly enough, an experiment was done with heat engines by Nicolas Leonard Sadi Carnot (1796–1832), a French physicist and theoretician on the steam engine which proved the law about 100% efficiency. The First Law of Thermodynamics states that a fixed amount of mechanical work can be converted into an equal amount of heat, but based on experience, Carnot did not feel that this held true for a heat engine such as a steam engine. Carnot experimented with the steam engine as a "closed circuit" in which water was heated until it changed into steam, the steam moved the piston, was exhausted, condensed back into water and fell back into the boiler. From this experiment, he concluded that there was an unavoidable loss of thermal energy in the process of condensation. Therefore, the transformation of heat into useful power was "fixed solely by the temperature of the bodies between which (was) effected . . . the transfer of the caloric."[4] Later, Carnot's findings were formally presented by Rudolf J. E. Clausius (1822–1888) in the form of the Second Law of Thermodynamics. This law states that to do work, heat acts like a water-mill; it must run "downhill" to do work, and the more it goes downhill, the more work it will do. In other words, heat goes from a higher temperature to a lower temperature to do work and cannot be increased without the expenditure of more work. If a hot body is placed with a colder one, the tendency is to equalize their temperatures—not increase their difference. Coincidentally, designs for perpetual motion machines were presented in which neither friction nor electrical resistance were significant problems in the design of the machine, but a problem arose in that these machines were, in effect, trying to circumvent the Second Law of Thermodynamics. For example, it was proposed that an oceanliner could extract the heat from the ocean and use it for propulsion. This violates the Second Law of Thermodynamics in that heat does not naturally run "uphill,"[5] which is to say that heat won't of its own accord flow from a cooler body to a warmer body. The First and Second Laws of Thermodynamics and the Principle of Conservation of Energy were firmly established and accepted into the scientific community by the mid-nineteenth century. Unfortunately, these scientific advancements seemed to remain within the scientific community, falling on deaf ears whenever announced to the public, such that many people went on searching for the miracle machine which would provide them with a constant source of energy and make them instantly wealthy.

The first recorded account of a perpetual motion machine dates back to 1518 with a man named Mark Antony Zimara, an Italian philosopher, physician, astrologer, and alchemist. He was born in Galatino about the year 1460, and died in Padua in 1523. Zimara left directions for constructing a perpetual motion machine, but never left an illustration of it anywhere. His description went as follows:

Directions for Constructing a Perpetual Motion Machine without the Use of Water or a Weight

Construct a raised wheel of four or more sides, like the wheel of a windmill, and opposite it two or more powerful bellows, so arranged that their wind will turn the wheel swiftly. Connect to the periphery of the wheel, or to its centre (whichever the builder may think better), an instrument which will operate the bellows as the wheel itself turns (this will be an honour to the ingenuity of the maker). It will happen that the wind which comes from the bellows and blows against the vanes of the wheel will cause the wheel to rotate, and that the bellows themselves, operated by the rotating wheel, will blow perpetually. This, perchance, is not absurd, but is the starting point for investigating and discovering that sublime thing, perpetual motion, a starting point which I have not read of anywhere, neither do I know of any one who has worked it out.[6]

Zimara practically claims that the idea of perpetual motion originated with him. From his description, drawings have been made of what his machine would have looked like, but it would not have worked because the forces needed to compress the bellows was far more than that which could possibly be achieved by blowing, with the available amount of wind and its pressure, upon the windmill. Given the time period and the belief in magic and sorcery that were prevalent during this age, it is not surprising that many accounts which followed Zimara's were mystical in nature. For example, according to the writings of Thomas Tymme, Cornelius Drebble (1572-1634), the Dutch chemist and natural philosopher, devised a machine in 1612 that revolved of itself, for it was a wheel about an axis, and was actuated by a fiery spirit within the axis of the wheel. With both Zimara and Drebble, water power was used, and as more perpetual motionists come to the picture it seems that water power was particularly prone to implant the idea of perpetual motion into the human mind. This phenomenon can most probably be attributed to the assumption that water comes from nowhere in particular and costs man nothing. This deludes the miller into thinking that his power costs him nothing by concealing the fact that his power is bought and paid for in terms of energy units and can only be brought to him once. It seems logical that any mill operator, whose driving stream was subject to seasonal diminutions of flow, would try to make the water go back uphill and work for him twice. There was only one way that the early perpetual motionists were aware of to make water run uphill and that was through the use of the Archimedean screw, named after its discoverer, Archimedes. Although called a screw, this device was really a pipe coiled like the end of a screw. When immersed in water and rotated, the water would climb up the pipe until the screw stopped rotating. This screw, once it was discovered by Archimedes, became a part of many intricate schemes to create perpetual motion. These perpetual motionists thought nothing could be simpler than to connect an Archimedean screw with the waterwheel of the mill and make the mill run the screw and the screw run the mill. They failed to realize, however, that the Archimedean screw worked because it was turned by some outside agency.[7] Since they overlooked this small detail, none of the plans for perpetual motion based on the Archimedean screw were successful—not to mention the Laws of Thermodynamics they violated.

The perpetual motionists were a stubborn breed, and after all of the attempts at perpetual motion with the Archimedean screw had been exhausted, the perpetual motionists didn't give up. They simply moved on to another method, namely overbalancing weights. Early perpetual motionists who tried to make use of overbalancing weights seemed to have an idea that friction was a constant to be dealt with in any machine, and the way to overcome friction was to make everything that much larger so that the effect of friction would be almost negligible. The bigger the machine, the more wheels it had, the nearer one came to producing a machine which had no friction. Once this stage was reached, friction was overcome by adding yet another wheel such that, in terms of friction, you move over on to the credit side of the system and your wheels turn of themselves. This may seem rather far-fetched to the twentieth century reader, but without the knowledge that we have today it is easy to see how perpetual motion could be seen as something to be used to its fullest potential instead of something to be striven for. One of the first examples of the overbalancing wheel attempt was by the Frenchman Wilars de Honecort. Accompanied by this bold statement, "Many a time have skilful [sic] workmen tried to contrive a wheel that shall turn of itself; here is a way to make such by means of an uneven number of mallets of quicksilver [mercury],"[8] de Honecort's model consisted of four mallets on the descending side of a wheel, and three mallets on the other side. To get the mallets into this desirable position, the top mallet on the descending side must be made to fall before its shaft becomes vertical. As long as this occurs with every mallet on the ascending side of the wheel, then the wheel will continue to turn until it wears out. Unfortunately, the only way to do this is to move the mallet by external force, thereby removing the device as a candidate for perpetual motion.

Other schemes using overbalancing weights for perpetual motion were of this same order, some slightly more elaborate than de Honecort's, but all resulting in failure. One particularly interesting case needs to be mentioned at this time, because it was an overbalanced wheel built as a fraud by a man named E. P. Willis of Conneticut. The device designed by Mr. Willis was a large gearwheel mounted at an angle to the horizontal and fitted with a series of rods and weights. This whole system supposedly drove a small flywheel.[9] Mr. Willis placed the entire contraption inside of a glass case and displayed the exhibit in New Haven where it attracted a great deal of attention. After his successful debut in New Haven, Mr. Willis took his device to New York where the truth was unveiled. Mr. Willis had constructed his device in such a way that a steady flow of compressed air kept the flywheel turning, and it was the flywheel that turned the larger wheel, not the other way around as Mr. Willis had claimed.

At about the same time that some perpetual motionists were experimenting with wheels, others decided to try magnetic substances. It had long been known by man that some substances had magnetic properties, most specifically the "lodestone" as it was called, which was a mix of two different ores of iron. Many accounts have been written by those claiming to have seen such models, but very few actually left illustrations of these models.

The earliest model for which an illustration can be found is the one made by the Jesuit priest Johannes Taisneirus in 1570. Taisneirus's idea was to place a lodestone on top of a pillar to which was attached an inclined plane. Iron balls were to be placed at the bottom of the inclined plane and drawn up the incline by the lodestone. Before the iron balls can reach the lodestone, however, they were to fall through a hole in the plane and thus reach their initial starting place whereby the process could be repeated. In a book entitled *Continual Motions*, published in 1579, Taisneirus left this account:

> But amongst all these kinds of invention, that is most likely, wherein a lodestone is so dispersed that it shall draw unto it on a reclined plane a bullet of steel, which steel as it ascends near the lodestone, may be contrived to fall down through some hole in the plane, and so return unto the place from whence at first it began to move; and, being there, the lodestone will again attract it upwards till coming to this hole, it will fall down again; and so the motion shall be perpetual, as may be more easily conceivable by this figure.[10]

Not long after the natural magnets came designs using the electro-magnet, because science had progressed a long way since the watermill, and the perpetual motionists weren't about to be undone. With the electro-magnet, most designs came in the form of clocks that were supposed to run forever without being rewound. One of these clocks actually ran for forty years in England's Leicester Museum without attention. The power came from two underground electrodes about a foot apart. One was made of zinc and the other was made of copper, and between the

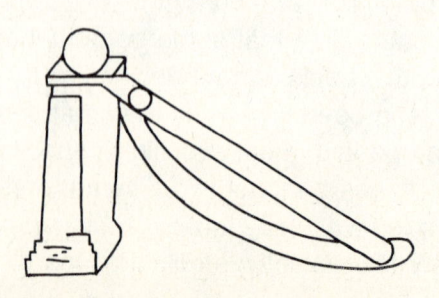

Physics

two of them approximately one volt was produced. This type of clock cannot be called a perpetual motion machine because the electrodes eventually need replacing. Therefore, they are generally called extended motion clocks.

Although the attempts at perpetual motion through the use of overbalancing weights, lodestones, or electro-magnets may not be familiar to most people the attempt at perpetual motion through the use of hydrostatic paradox is probably the most well-known attempt in the history of perpetual motion. When a very large quantity of liquid is apparently balanced by a very small quantity of liquid, the situation is referred to as the hydrostatic paradox. The most familiar scheme in this category is Robert Boyle's device which looks like this:

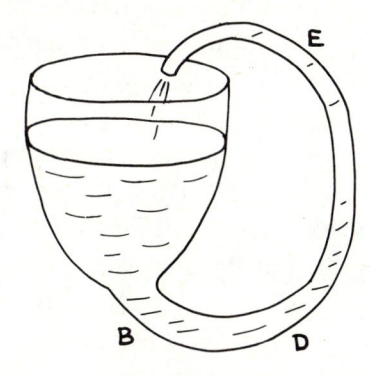

Boyle thought that since the water in the basin was heavier than that in the tube, the liquid would be forced upward and ___ continue to flow out of the tube, thus repeating the cycle forever as long as the water didn't evaporate.[11] The problem with this proposed perpetual motion machine is that should the water rise as high as E, the pressure at the bottom of ED would be greater than the pressure at B and the water would flow back from D towards B. Here again, some knowledge of the basic laws of motion and physics would have saved this inventor a lot of time and energy.

While most perpetual motionists were honest people trying to make significant contributions to science through the use of their discovery, many others, after trying in vain to create perpetual motion, turned to trickery and deceit in order to prove that they had created what no one else could. Of all the frauds concerning perpetual motion, the story of John W. Keely's scheme must be the most amazing and therefore needs to be included in this paper. Without this account, perhaps the feverish excitement which took over both the inventor and the public may not be fully conveyed to the reader. John Keely, in 1873, claimed to have discovered a new motive power, and this claim was strengthened by the knowledge that many scientists who saw Keely's experiments couldn't discover any fraud. Soon the newspapers were reporting about Keely's amazing new power source and how if perfected, it would replace all previous forms of energy used. With this sort of propaganda circulating, Keely was able to start the Keely Motor Company, designed to perfect this new power, with a capital of five million dollars. People from all walks of life became shareholders, from the poor farmer to the wealthy scientist. When people began to lose faith in Mr. Keely's company because it was taking him too long to produce the evidence, a sympathetic wealthy widow, named Mrs. Moore, came to Keely's aid and endorsed his project. Mrs. Moore invited the leading physicists in the United States and Europe to examine and report on Keely's discovery, but the few who accepted the invitation weren't allowed to touch the apparatus by reason of Keely's orders. Many of the physicists went away puzzled and others formed theories about how the machine actually worked. Nothing that they said, however, could convince Mrs. Moore that Keely was a fraud. Keely died in 1898, and after his death the machine was thoroughly examined. It was discovered that Keely's so-called solid wires were really small tubes which delivered compressed air to the system. Further examination revealed that under Keely's floor were rubber bulbs which yielded to foot pressure, and the pressure created by stepping on these bulbs really ran the entire system.

It may seem that all these accounts were matters that basically concerned one area or one state, but this is not the case. There was actually one case that involved the entire country and almost made a mockery out of the United States Congress. Garabed Giragossian was an Armenian immigrant who claimed to have discovered how to create free energy. All of America was at his attention, and Giragossian went to Congress stating that the machine could be used to power all of America, and he wanted the Congress to assume its development for the benefit of the nation as a whole. He admitted that his project wasn't yet in the form where it could be used to power all of America, but he assured Congress that this was but a small detail and taxpayers would be sure to fund the project. Giragossian never mentioned what his project was for fear of someone stealing his idea, but in 1918, a Congressional committee made a preliminary investigation and passed a special act of Congress whereby the President could appoint a team of five scientists to look into the machine and report what they found. The project known as the Garabed Commission, held America's undivided attention. Finally, the Commission reported on what they found. It was a flywheel, the same type used in other types of perpetual motion schemes. Giragossian measured the power that he got from the invention by a brake loaded with weights until the flywheel stopped. From this he calculated the horsepower, and since it took more horsepower to stop the machine than it did to keep it going, Giragossian thought that he was actually making energy. Giragossian was not out to defraud anyone, so America soon forgot about Girabed Giragossian and his perpetual motion machine.

Perhaps had Giragossian gone through the Patent Office, he and the rest of the country would have been spared that embarrassing chapter in our history. Inventors throughout history have secured patents in order to work on their inventions without the fear of infringement by hungry entrepreneurs, and perpetual motionists were no exception. The earliest record of a patent for a perpetual motion machine was in England in 1635, twelve years after an act was passed securing the rights of inventors in arts and manufactures by a letters patent. During the early stage of patent requirements, no illustrations or working models were required to secure a patent. Patent-seeking wasn't confined to England, however, because U.S. attempts to secure patents for the impossible were made at the United States Patent Office in Washington D.C. As early as 1828, the journal of the Franklin Institute in Philadelphia published an account of why perpetual motion was not possible. Even with this evidence and the established belief of the scientists in the Laws of Thermodynamics and the Conservation of Energy, the United States Patent Office failed to act. To make matters worse, almost one hundred years earlier, in 1775, the Parisian Academy of Sciences refused to accept any scheme for perpetual motion.

The general procedure in the United States was to give an inventor a patent and then allow the inventor one year to prove his or her idea with a working model. Since the perpetual motionists usually never returned with a working model but still continued to flock to the Patent Office to secure a patent, the Commissioner decided in 1911 that for all perpetual motionists, a working model had to be presented even before an application could be filed. From that point on, every person coming to the Patent Office trying to secure a patent for perpetual motion was greeted with this circular:

> The views of the Patent Office are in accord with those of the scientists who have investigated this subject and are to the effect that such devices are physical impossibilities. The position of the office can be rebutted only by the exhibition of a working model. Were the application to be taken to the Examiner for consideration, he would make no examination as to the merits, but his first action would be the requirement that a working model be filed. In view of all the circumstances, the Commissioner has instructed that applications for patent on Perpetual Motion, complete in all other particulars, shall be held in the Applications Room as incomplete until a working model has been filed. Such model must be filed within one year from the date of application, or the application will be abandoned. The Office hesitates to accept the filing fees from applicants who believe they have discovered Perpetual Motion, and deems it only fair to give such applicants a word of warning that the fees paid cannot be recovered after the case has been considered by the Examiner. For these reasons it has been thought best to meet the inventor at the threshold of the Office, and give him an opportunity to recover the moneys paid into the Office, in the event of his failure to comply with the requirement.[12]

Physics

Clearly, the quest for perpetual motion has been a long one indeed. From the simple devices contrived in the minds of inventors to ease daily life to the fraudulent schemes of desperate men trying to ease their daily expenses, all perpetual motion machines have one thing in common despite the inventor, and that is their inability to work. Whether the attempt is made with overbalancing weights, magnets, or electricity, none of the devices can get around the laws of Thermodynamics which are thoroughly accepted today as the most accurate laws we have governing the properties of heat and other forms of energy. The perpetual motionists who appeared over the centuries in order to take their place in history were of varied types—some were creative, honest people who became disheartened, some were visionaries who theorized, and some were tricksters who could separate fools and innocent believers from their money in no time. No matter what category the perpetual motionists fall into, however, they must be valued because proven, accepted, theories have resulted in part from their failure, and they are a representation of the intellectual curiosity and creativity of which humans are capable.

Bibliography

1. Blackwood, Oswald. *General Physics.* London: John Wiley & Sons, Inc., 1955. pg. 18.
2. Cajori, Florian. *A History of Physics.* London: The Macmillan C., 1899. pg. 91.
3. Chase, Carl Trueblood. *The Evolution of Modern Physics.* New York: D. Van Nostrand Co. Inc., 1947. pg. 48.
4. Fraser, Charles G. *Half-Hours with Great Scientists: The Story of an Obsession.* New York: Reinhold Publishing Corporation, 1948. pgs. 70, 77, 358, 380.
5. Gamow, George. *Biography of Physics.* New York: Harper & Brothers Publishers, 1961. pgs. 104, 106, 286.
6. Haar, D. der. *Elements of Thermodynamics.* Massachusetts: Wesley Publishing Company, 1966. pg. 9.

7. Koslow, Arnold. *The Changeless Order: The Physics of Space, Time, and Motion.* New York: George Brazeller Publishing Co., 1967. pgs. 230–234.
8. Mach, Ernst. *The Science of Mechanics.* Chicago: The Open Court Publishing Company, 1915. pg. 25.
9. Ord-Hume, Arthur W. J. G. *Perpetual Motion.* New York: St. Martin's press, 1977.
10. Stewart, Alec T. *Perpetual Motion: electrons and atoms in crystals.* New York: Anchor Books, Doubleday & Company, Inc., 1965. pgs. 1–4.
11. Stewart, Oscar. *Physics.* Boston: Ginn & Company, 1931. pg 112.
12. Wilson, William. *A Hundred Years of Physics.* London: Gerald Duckworth & Company, Ltd., 1950. pgs. 20, 32, 39, 45.

Analysis of Sample Physics Paper 1

The assignment asks students to present the history of a physical concept in an interesting, engaging manner. Nancy chose a topic, perpetual motion, that lends itself well to this goal. She narrates an often amusing history of hard-luck inventors and money-hungry schemers whose efforts to build a perpetual motion machine continually come to nought. But Nancy's task involves more than entertaining her audience with this tale: She must also supply her readers with sufficient technical information to enable them to understand the physical concept of perpetual motion and the laws of physics operating against it.

Nancy does a good job of attending to both aims in this paper. The history she presents involves a sizeable cast of characters and numerous schemes for attaining perpetual motion. In her introduction, she provides a unifying theme for this assortment of material when she states that though all efforts at perpetual motion were unsuccessful, and often seem to us foolish or misguided, they provided important lessons in the laws of physics. She organizes her discussion by grouping together those machines that involved water power, those that worked on a system of weights, and so on. In addition, through effective transitions, she continues to connect the many parts of her narrative. In these ways, Nancy allows her readers to follow the narrative with relative ease and enjoyment as she charts the varied paths taken by scientists in the search for perpetual motion.

Much of what she presents would be lost on the general reader if Nancy had not taken care to explain important laws of physics at the outset of her paper. It might be off-putting to some readers that Nancy delays discussing the first attempt at perpetual motion for several paragraphs. But Nancy realizes she must introduce readers to the laws of thermodynamics and the principle of the conservation of energy before they can understand the failings of the individual perpetual motion machines. In addition, she demonstrates in these opening paragraphs her understanding of physical concepts discussed in the course and their relationship to the particular history she narrates.

All in all, Nancy succeeds in this paper because she is aware of the needs of her reader. She defines all technical terms clearly and, in general, speaks in a language accessible to the average reader. To aid readers who may have difficulty visualizing some of the machines she describes, she includes drawings.

Nancy has followed the dictates of the assignment carefully, with two exceptions. Her paper is much longer than the suggested length. Although the history she chose to present is complex and involved, the extreme length of her paper is unnecessary and no doubt produced an audible groan from the teacher who had to read it. She could easily condense her narration of particular events—for example, the Keely scheme and the Giragossian fiasco. In fact, most of Nancy's paragraphs run far too long and would benefit significantly from further editing. Notice also that her block quotations are at least three times longer than they should be. By convention, writers are expected to limit such quotations to about a hundred words, at most. Anything over that should be paraphrased.

In addition, Nancy relies too heavily on a single source—Ord-Hume's *Perpetual Motion*. A quick check of her sources indicates that Nancy has paraphrased a great deal of information from this book and neglected to document it. This failure in documentation is a problem. Moreover, over-reliance on a single source might suggest to her teacher that Nancy naively fails to realize that in her paper she could reflect a particular source's bias. Note also that all her sources are dated; she seemed unable to locate any information published recently. Although this characteristic isn't necessarily a flaw in this type of paper, most readers appreciate knowing that sources represent current views on a topic, not views of 15, 20, or even more years ago.

Guide for Reading

Elizabeth's paper, like Nancy's, offers an interesting narrative full of details about her topic. She addresses many of the assignment questions in a thoughtful way, and in her conclusion she looks forward to possible studies of color in the future. Nevertheless, Elizabeth's paper is only an average response to the assignment. As you read, look carefully at how well Elizabeth connects her explanation of physical principles with her historical narrative. Are all the important terms in the introduction carried forward into the body of the paper? Also note places in the paper where a figure or a graph would have helped you better understand the point Elizabeth was explaining.

SAMPLE PHYSICS PAPER 2

"Color"

Elizabeth G. (a freshman)

Human interest in color is as old as the hills. Well, at least as old as recorded history. Man's oldest recorded symbols, Cro-magnon cave paintings in Spain and France, display a sophistication of color preparation and use that seems wildly out of character for the thick-skulled, slope-shouldered simpleton many of us still imagine our European ancestors were. Indeed, though he may not have been linguistically competent or agriculturally sophisticated, he was at times a profound speculator quite sensitive to his surroundings. We know this from his beautifully rendered and subtly colored paintings. This is merely evidence for the proposition that vision is the most important sense for mankind, and that man has been fascinated by light and color from the beginning of time.[1] This paper will pick up the history of man's preoccupation with color in the fifth century B.C. with Plato and will trace the history of the science of color through the mid-1800's.

First it is necessary to examine our present understanding of the relationship between light and color, so as to have a groundwork for appreciating developments in the history of color. Color is used to describe three different but related aspects of the world we live in. Most commonly color is used to describe a property of an object, as in "the book is red." More scientifically color can be used to describe a characteristic of light rays, such as "the book reflects red light while absorbing light of other colors more or less completely." Finally, psychologists and philosophers in their quest for ontological accuracy might say that color describes a class of sensations; for example, "the brains interpretation of the specific manner in which the eye perceives light selectively reflected from the book results in the perception of red."[2]

In everyday usage these distinctions are not particularly meaningful, but in some cases they are crucial. For instance, in talking about the color black. If an object is described as being black, what is meant is not that the object is black, but that the surface of the object has zero reflectivity. In other words, all light is absorbed with none reflected for us to perceive. As a property of a light wave or ray, "black" has no meaning at all. Black is not a part of the spectrum of component colors that light can be broken down into. Thirdly, in describing a perception, "black" means the total absence of sensation or visual stimuli.[3]

In any usage, color is considered to have three attributes: hue, saturation, and brightness. These are called attributes because they describe a visual perception, not physical properties of the light itself (hence Newton's statement "the rays are not coloured"). "Hue" is the attribute implied in the naming of colors, such as red, blue, green, etc. Hue is a feature of monochromatic, or indivisible, light, and varies with wavelength. Blue denotes a part of the spectrum of color with rays of longer wavelength than red. "Saturation" is a measure of the lack of whiteness in a color, or how much a color differs from white. For example, pink is an unsaturated form of red. "Brightness" is the perceived intensity of light in a color. The yellow of the sun at noon has a high degree of brightness, while the yellow of the late afternoon sun is low in brightness. It is easy to illustrate these definitions in describing gray. Any shade of gray is devoid of hue and completely unsaturated. Various grays can only be described in terms of brightness. Black, therefore, when describing light, means devoid of hue, saturation, and brightness.[4]

The spectrum of colors in light is generally broken down into seven hues; red, orange, yellow, green, blue, indigo, and violet.

These hues are considered monochromatic. In other words, when light shines through a prism these colors are indivisible. White light can be broken down into these hues but no further. Colored light has special characteristics that differ from the characteristics of pigments (inks, dyes, paints, etc.). One of these characteristics is additive color mixing, or adding one light to another. The more lights that are added, the brighter the net effect. The rules of additive color mixing apply to all light, not just monochromatic light. Virtually all colors can be produced from a set of three lights whose colors are found in the short, medium, and long wavelength regions of the spectrum. If the three colors can be added together to produce white light, the three colors are considered primary colors. There are different sets of primary colors, but the most common are red, green, and blue (note that the primarys are different for pigments). Any two colors that produce white light when mixed are called complementary colors. A secondary color is one which complements a primary.[5] Take an equation of any set of primarys, such as blue + green + red = white light. Two components mixed together will be the complement of the third (e.g. green + red = yellow, the complement of blue). This complement is also a secondary color.

Now we turn to pigments. The phenomenon of color in pigments comes from fine particles suspended in a clear liquid. The particles of pigment reflect the light of certain wavelengths. The wavelength of light reflected gives the pigment its hue (i.e. its name; blue green, etc.). The rest of the light is absorbed or transmitted by the pigment.[6]

The laws of additive color mixing do not hold for mixing pigments. The primary colors for pigments are magenta, yellow, and cyan. They are not called primarys because they can be mixed to make white, but because all other colors can be made by mixing these three pigments together in different ratios. When complementary pigments are mixed, once again white is not created, but black is. Another important distinction between colored light and colored pigment is that when you mix lights, the net effect is brighter, but when you mix pigments the net effect is less bright. This is known as subtractive color mixing.[7]

The Impressionist painters of the nineteenth century had a

good understanding of the difference between subtractive color effects produced by mixing paints and additive effects achieved when colored dots are placed side by side on a white reflecting surface. With additive color effects, the eye produces the color mixing, with each part of the painting reflecting more light than if the paints were mixed. This is because only one pigment is present, which gives maximum reflectance and brightness to convey the effect of intense sunlight. In conventional painting, colors are achieved by mixing paints or applying them in successive layers. This causes a diminution of brightness as absorption of light occurs over a broader span of the spectrum within each small part of the painting.[8]

Texture of surfaces also has a profound effect on the production of color. The color of a surface seen by reflected light is affected by the color and nature of the illumination and the nature of the surface. Whenever light passes from one media to another, be it liquid or solid, part of it is reflected immediately and the rest of it is refracted (bent) when entering the second medium, where it will be transmitted and absorbed in accordance with the optical properties of the medium.[9]

If the surface of the second medium is smooth, light is reflected from it in a specific direction, determined by the angle at which the incident light struck the medium. The light is reflected specularly, which means that the angle of the reflected light is identical to the angle of the incident light (with respect to the medium). The characteristics of the color of specularly reflected light (i.e. hue, saturation, and brightness) are generally very similar to the color characteristics of the incident light; the light has not penetrated deeply into the medium nor has it been reflected many times by pigment particles.[10]

On the other hand, if the surface of the second medium has a pronounced or irregular texture, light is reflected diffusely. If the light penetrates the medium and is affected by irregularities in the structure such as pigment particles or fractures, it emerges in multiple directions and contributes to a diffuse reflection. Diffusely reflected light is more strongly influenced by selective absorption of light rays at the surface of the media than is specularly reflected light. It should be noted that reflection of light from any surface is partly diffuse and partly specular, since only idealized surfaces are perfectly smooth. The proportion of diffuse versus specular reflection change with the direction of illumination and viewing angle.[11]

The above description of properties of color as they are understood today should be sufficient to illustrate the proceeding examination of the history of the science of color. Though, as stated earlier, the history of color can be traced back in time almost indefinitely, it is evident that the possibility of a science of color was still doubted in the time of Plato (428–347 B.C.). Plato held a very pessimistic view of the possibility of a science of color. In his own words.

> There will be difficulty in seeing how and by what mixtures the colors are made . . . He, however, who should attempt to verify all of this by experiment would forget the difference of the human and the divine nature. For God only has the knowledge and also the power which are able to combine many things into one and again resolve the one into many. But no man either is or ever will be able to accomplish either the one or the other operation.[12]

Aristotle followed in Plato's footsteps in that he did not experiment with light and color, but he did not devote a substantial amount of thought to the issue. Aristotle did not distinguish between color and light. He believed that "whatever is visible is color and color is what lies upon what is in its own nature visible." He also noted that sunlight always became less intense in its interaction with objects. Since such interaction seemed to produce color, he viewed color as some sort of mixture of black and white. "Thus pure light, such as that from the sun has no color, but is made colored by its degradation when interacting with objects having specific properties which then produce color."[13] This theory lasted until Newton explained the spectrum in the 1600's.

Aristotle also distinguished between apparent (emphatical) and real (true) colors. Real colors were qualities of bodies, and apparent colors were transient phenomena, produced in some way by the modification of incident light. In this way, a rainbow was explained as a weakening of light as it passed through or was reflected from an adjacent cloud. Real colors, however, existed in objects but required the presence of light to illuminate them. Some Aristotelians therefore associated colors with the four earthly elements. If a body contained an abundance of earth, then it was green. Similarly, water was black, air was red, and fire was white.[14] This is particularly interesting because it is counter-intuitive in the Western tradition, in which water is associated with blue, and fire with red.

The next step in the development of a science of color came from Ptolemy, ca. 150 A.D. Ptolemy lived in an era of increased emphasis on experimentation, which led him to several important discoveries. He is credited with the rules of additive light mixtures, knowledge of the effect of spinning a disc with sectors of different colors, and an understanding of certain aspects of refraction, whereby a beam of light is bent when entering a piece of glass at an angle.[15] Aside from these discoveries though, the science of color remained essentially aristotelian for the next 1400 years.

In the early 1600's a glimmer of the revolution to come was seen in the work of Rene Descartes, 1596–1650. Descartes tried to explain color in terms of a spin. When particles of light struck a body they were either absorbed or reflected. If they were absorbed then the body was black. If they were reflected then they might acquire a rotary motion on reflection. If the spin was more rapid than the particle's forward motion, the body appeared red. If the spin was less rapid, then the body appeared green.[16] Descartes' work coincided with the development of the philosophy of mechanics. The real colors of aristotelians were no longer qualities of bodies, but modifications of light rays as they were reflected and refracted by various bodies.[17] This new belief set the stage for Newton.

Isaac Newton, 1642–1727, is the father of our modern conception of light and color. Though many people previously had noted the effects Newton studied in his experiments on light, it took him to provide explanations for the observed phenomena that could stand the test of time. In 1666 Newton noticed that passing white light through a prism will reveal differently colored components of the original light. This had been observed before, but had been ignored because there was no explanation for the phenomen and the ideas of Aristotle were firmly entrenched.[18] The crucial step though was that Newton was the first to note the oblong image of the spectrum produced by a prism. Before Newton, apparently, observers had placed the prism too close to a white wall to get a good image of the spectrum (i.e. a good dispersion of the beam). This discovery led Newton to the idea that light consists of rays that are refrangible in different ways. Newton defined refrangibility as the ability to be refracted (bent) by a prism.[18a] Before Newton, a popular explanation for the spectrum was that as the prism refraced light it must also have affected the color of the light by staining it in various amounts. Newton overturned this theory by a further experiment with his newly discovered oblong spectrum. He took a window shade with a small hole in it to gather a small beam of light to pass through his prism. This produced the spectrum on a wall. Newton substituted a second shade with a small hole in it for the white wall. He allowed only the yellow band of light through the hole and directed it through another prism. The second prism did not affect the yellow color of the light. This meant that the components of light of various colors revealed by the first prism were originally components of the incident white light. The first prism served to separate the white light into its component colors. This second experiment also showed that light could only be broken down into a limited number of components; components could not be further divided. This idea that light from a narrow part of the spectrum could not be divided further led Newton to call the light homogeneal (now called monochromatic).[18b] Newton combined all his discoveries in his work "New Theory about Light and Colors," which was published in the "Philosophical Transactions" of the Royal Society of London in 1672. The essential points included the ideas that (quote):

> 1) Colors are not qualifications of light derived from refractions or reflections of natural bodies ... but original and connate properties (of light).
> 2) To the same degree of refrangibility ever belongs the

same color and to the same color ever belongs the same refrangibility.[19]

3) Blue homogeneal light is more refrangible than red light because it is refracted more. Blue also has a shorter wavelength than red. Therefore, light of shorter wavelengths is refracted more by a prism than light of longer wavelengths.

4) All the colors in the universe which are made by light and which do not depend on the power of imagination, are either the colors of homogeneal light or are compounded of these.[20]

Newton was very careful to distinguish between the physical stimulus and the perception it produces. Though he said that "the rays of smallest refrangibility are all disposed to exhibit a red color . . . " he noted that rays, properly expressed, are not colored. There is nothing else in them but a certain power . . . to produce in us . . . the sensation of this or that color."[21] Unfortunately, Newton's followers were frequently less careful to make this distinction, which left Newton's work open to attack from many directions.

One of Newton's critics was a monk by the name of Franciscus Linus, 1596–1675. His complaint against Newton's work was that he could not reproduce the spectrum except on cloudy days. He tried several times, after much correspondence, to produce the spectrum on a sunny day, but was unsuccessful and went to his grave believing that Newton's spectrum was a meteorological oddity.[22] Most of Newton's critics were not so amusing.

One of these annoying critics was Newton's colleague in the Royal Society, Robert Hooke, 1635–1703. As curator of the Royal Society, Hooke's job was to "peruse and consider" papers submitted by members. After a week's deliberation he reported back to the Society that though he agreed with Newton's observations, he found his conclusions unsubstantiated. He restated his belief from his own work Micrographia that light is nothing but a pulse or motion, propagated through a homogenous, uniform, and transparent medium. Color was not "an original and connate" property of light, but a modification of light as it was reflected and refracted by various bodies.[23]

Newton's most famous critic is bound to have been Johannes Wolfgang von Goethe, 1749–1832. Goethe was a lawyer, playwright, celebrated poet, and scientist. He uttered the last gasp of Aristotle's approach to color.[24] Goethe believed that light, the most elementary of all phenomena, could not possibly be composed of anything more basic (such as waves, particles, or rays). He contended that white light is the purest light, and when light appears colored it has been contaminated.[24a] He claimed color when seen through a prism (he only saw color at such dark boundaries of a wall as window frames) was the result of a tension between light and dark. His objections to Newton appear to have been mostly romantic and aesthetic, backed up with little if any evidence. Indeed, he immortalised his objections to Newton's New Theory about Light and Color in a poem in which he condemned Newton's prism experiments as "the epoch of a decomposed ray of light."[24b]

Despite his critics, Newton's ideas endured, and remain nearly intact to this day. In the early 1800's the English physicist Thomas Young expanded Newton's theories to explain primary colors of light and the laws of additive color mixing.[25] At the same time there was an artistic acceptance of the scientific theory of color. The development of pre-mixed paints and dyes and the introduction of mass-produced textiles, printing ink, and papers produced a need for an objectively correct color theory.[26] This insured the vindication of Newton.

Since the 1800's, the emphasis of the study of color science seems to be focused on perception. Though many have tried, it has become apparent that there is no way to effectively specify color in an absolute or quantitative sense. Though books full of color chips exist, there are even more subtle distinctions to be made. So perhaps it is true that color can only be communicated comparatively—by comparing the attributes of one color with those of another (i.e. in terms of hue, saturation, and brightness).

Writings of psychologists and other scientists on the ontological status of color, have specified that colors are the property of the brain or central nervous system, and not of physical objects. Semir Zeki, a leading researcher on the coding of colors in the brain, has proposed that "the nervous system, rather than analyze colors, takes what information there is in the external environment . . . and transforms that information to construct colors, using its own algorithms to do so. In other words, it constructs something which is a property of the brain, not the world outside."[26a] This argument exists in several forms, the bottom line being that colors are properties not of ordinary material things but of items more intimately associated with the minds of human beings. In other words, what would be perceivable of color without human eyes to perceive it? Most mammals, except the higher-order primates, are color-blind.[27] Therefore, the question can be raised is color-blindness an aberration, a defect, or is color distinction the aberration—is the human eye/brain an essential link in the physical system of color?

This is as far as the history of color has brought us. Perhaps the next topic of study in color science will be the physiology of the human brain. Regardless, we have seen in this paper that the sciences are not isolated, being subject to the strength of religion and the whims of weather, and the truth is ever changing. Any way you look at it though, man's fascination with light and color endure.

Notes

1. from Dr. Elwyn Simon's Visual Predation Theory
2. Nassau, pg. 3
3. Ibid.
4. Williamson, pg. 16.
5. Williamson, pg. 17.
6. Nassau, pg. 28–29.
7. Nassau, pg 12.
8. Williamson, pg. 30
9. Williamson, pg. 40
10. Ibid.
11. Williamson, pg. 41.
12. Nassau, pg. 4

13. Ibid.
14. Gjertsen, pg. 123.
15. Williamson, pg. 2–3.
16. Gjertsen, pg. 123.
17. Ibid.
18. Williamson, pg. 4
18a. Gjertsen, pg 123.
18b. Williamson, pg. 4.
19. Gjertsen, pg. 124.
20. Williamson, pg. 14.
21. Williamson, pg. 5.
22. Gjertsen, pg. 320.
23. Gjertsen, pg. 257.
24. Nassau, pg. 257.
24a. Williamson, pg. 5
24b. Gjertsen, pg. 234.
25. Williamson, pg. 19.
26. Williamson, pg. 6.
26a. Hilbert, pg 1.
27. Anthro 93 class notes

Bibliography

Gjertsen, Derek, *The Newton Handbook*. New York: Rutledge and Kegan Paul, 1986

Hilbert, David R. *Color and Color Perception—A Study in Anthropocentric Realism.* California: Center for the Study of Language and Information, 1987.

Nassau, Kurt. *The Physics and Chemistry of Color.* New York: John Wiley and Sons, 1983.

Williamson, Samuel J. *Light and Color in Nature and Art.* New York: John Wiley and Sons, 1983.

Analysis of Sample Physics Paper 2

Elizabeth does a good job narrating the history of research into the nature of color. Her introduction creatively traces mankind's interest in color back to Cro-Magnon cavemen, and her concluding remarks concerning possible experiments involving color and the physiology of the brain project the study of color into the future.

Elizabeth responds to several of the questions in the "Subject" section of the assignment. For example, in response to the question, "Did the new concept appear suddenly (revolution), develop gradually, or part and part?" she gives a detailed and interesting account of the revolution in color theory that Newton introduced and the resistance to his notions that followed. In response to the question, "How was its rise (and fall) influenced by the thought of the times?" she examines the role religion often played in the course of color research. Wisely, Elizabeth does not answer these questions explicitly or in any formal fashion—the answers arise naturally from her narration.

As Nancy did in Sample Paper 1, Elizabeth chose to preface her history with extensive explanation of the concept itself. Unfortunately, this explanatory material is never fully integrated with the history that follows. Many of the details about color that she discusses in her opening paragraphs play no role, or a very small one, in the history she presents. For example, she discusses pigments in depth in her prefatory remarks, but the term is never used again in the paper. Moreover, she never explains clearly the physical concept of color.

This lack of integration between the first half of the paper and the second makes it difficult for readers to follow easily the purpose and direction of the response. Readers are also likely to find some of the concepts discussed in the paper difficult to grasp, a problem that could have been remedied in part through the use of graphs, figures, or charts that would help readers visualize what she is describing.

Finally, there are a number of surface errors and stylistic problems throughout the paper that are distracting. For example, her paragraph on Newton goes on for a page and a half of typed manuscript. She uses far too many prepositional phrases. Consider the following consecutive sentences: "So perhaps it is true that color can only be communicated comparatively—**by** comparing the attributes **of** one color **with** those **of** another (i.e. **in** terms **of** hue, saturation, and brightness). Writings **of** psychologists and other scientists **on** the ontological status **of** color, have specified that colors are the property **of** the brain or central nervous system, and not **of** physical objects." Reducing the number of prepositions by half would make for a better style.

Sentence Lesson

Prepositions are among the most widely used words in English. The prepositions in boldface type above are part of a long list. Other prepositions and prepositional constructions include:

abroad	below	like	with	in front of
about	beneath	near	within	in place of
above	beside	off	without	in spite of
across	between	on	ahead of	inside of
after	beyond	onto	apart from	instead of
against	but	opposite	as well	on account of
along	by	outside	aside from	out of
alongside	despite	over	because of	owing to
amid	down	since	by means of	rather than
among	during	through	by way of	up at
around	for	throughout	contrary to	up on
as	from	toward	for the sake of	up to
at	inside	under	in addition to	with regard to
before	into	until	in back of	
behind	less	up	in case of	

A preposition plus a noun phrase (e.g., in the morning) is called a prepositional phrase. Too often, writers load sentences with prepositional phrases because they mistakenly believe that the result somehow sounds more impressive. Consequently, we commonly encounter:

1. The researcher was involved in the determination of the effects of sorbent dry-duct injection on SO_2 removal.

An important way to improve your writing is to reduce the number of prepositional phrases you have in each sentence. To accomplish this task, you first have to be able to identify a preposition, and the list above should help in this regard. The next step is to delete a preposition and to turn the noun attached to it into a verb. Writers can apply this procedure in various ways, depending on what they want the focus of a sentence to be. Watch what we can do to sentence (1). If the researcher is part of a team, we might simply produce:

Physics

2a. The researcher was involved in determining the effects of sorbent dry-duct injection on SO_2 removal.

In this case, we want to emphasize the researcher's participation in the team effort; hence we keep "was involved" and several prepositional phrases. If the researcher is not part of a team, we can produce:

2b. The researcher determined the SO_2 removal effects of sorbent dry-duct injection.

or

2c. The researcher used sorbent dry-duct injection to determine its effect on SO_2 removal.

In 2b and 2c, we've reduced the prepositional phrases from four to one. In the process, we've given the subject, "The researcher," a verb that more clearly designates action, which makes the sentences seem more direct and more readable.

Using the information in this Sentence Lesson, go back to the series of sentences above that were extracted from Elizabeth's paper and rewrite them to reduce the prepositional phrases.

Guide for Reading

One of the strengths of Sandra's paper is its topic. Environmental damage and change are of great interest to most intelligent readers because the consequences of such change will affect everyone. Therefore, providing a brief history of the greenhouse effect allows Sandra to enjoy an advantage immediately—her readers are already predisposed to find out what she has to say.

Sandra encounters several problems, however, that lose her this advantage. The audience for this assignment is a general one, so writing that addresses *only* the teacher will be inappropriate. Yet Sandra repeatedly gives the impression that she is writing to no one other than her teacher (look at the fifth paragraph from the end, for example). In addition, her writing is often extremely vague, which will cause most readers to wonder what point she is trying to make. As you read this below-average response, try to identify places where her writing is vague and try to find additional sections that suggest she is writing only to her teacher.

SAMPLE PHYSICS PAPER 3

The Greenhouse Effect

Sandra J. (a freshman)

The greenhouse effect is a worldwide warming trend that is the result of the accumulation of gases in the atmosphere which admit sunlight but trap heat, much like the windows of a real greenhouse. These gases are emitted from the immense consumption of fossil fuels. Surprisingly, the earth has long been experiencing a mild greenhouse effect which is caused by a naturally occurring flow of carbon dioxide and water vapor. Without this natural warming effect the earth would be about sixty degrees Fahrenheit cooler than it is now, and life on earth as we know it, would not be possible (MacKenzie 4). As the years have passed by, the accumulation of these gases have allowed for more heat to be trapped in than desirable, thus raising the global temperature by several degrees. Yet some scientists do not believe in the existing warming trend of the greenhouse effect. Contrary to their beliefs, there is a growing body of evidence which shows that the greenhouse effect is indeed taking place, and that its effect will be detrimental to the well being of the human race.

The concept of the greenhouse effect has developed gradually. The idea of this concept arose in the 17th century, and continues to develop into the 20th century. From the precursors to the successors, each has added their own theory and explanations to the concept of the greenhouse effect.

The "effect" part of the greenhouse effect was first described by British physicist, John Tyndall, as early as in 1861. The actual greenhouse analogy was not attached until a much later date. The "effect" was "among the earliest discoveries resulting from the rapid development of quantitative spectroscopy in the 1850's" (Kaplan 226). Tyndall discovered the "effect" while working on the transparency of gases and the absorption of gases and liquids. He showed through experimentation that water vapor was the major contributor to the "effect" because of its "absorption magnitude" which is greater than that of carbon dioxide. This property is important for the process of trapping the carbon dioxide in the clouds. Clouds are mainly composed of water vapor. Tyndall considered the "effect" as "the role [that] the whole atmosphere, (mainly water vapor and clouds) [plays] in keeping the surface of the earth warm" (Kaplan 226). It seems as though Tyndall's concept of the "effect" did not immensely offend anyone—particularly the Church. So, it is assumed that his ideas were probably accepted as scientific theory. This assumption is based on the fact that in 1867 he was appointed as the superintendent at the Royal Institution of London.

In 1896, Svante Arrehenius noticed that the increase in the temperature of the earth's surface is directly related to the production of carbon dioxide by industrial combustion of fossil fuel (Kaplan 227).

Then about four decades later, G. S. Callendar also supported the idea that the industrial production of carbon dioxide (since the 1860's) could account for the continental rise in surface temperature, despite the fact that there was a continental increase in the levels of atmospheric carbon dioxide (Kaplan 227). This discrepancy aroused the people's suspicions that carbon dioxide was not the cause of the greenhouse effect and that Callendar's prediction was false.

After many tedious years of wondering about the causes of global warming, V. Ramanathan (1975) pointed out that the greenhouse effect is enhanced by the continued release of chlorofluorocarbons into the atmosphere. Even though their concentration in the "big picture" is minute, their effect is extreme because of their corrosive effect on the earth's stratospheric ozone layer (Kaplan 227).

Today, the theory of the greenhouse effect is very complex. There has been much input from scientists worldwide to the configuration of an almost accurate theory. The many concerns of the people and the government about the effects of global warming, along with the introduction of sophisticated computers and machinery, has tremendously increased interest and investigation into this field. There are, as there always will be, some skeptics who do not believe that the earth is experiencing the greenhouse effect. But the majority of the people believe it is.

The greenhouse effect is on the minds of many people when they think of the energy crisis, or maybe when their grocery bill increases due to severe droughts in the agricultural zones, or perhaps even when they are in the doctor's office after a week at the beach, only to find out that their massive consumption of ultraviolet rays have stricken them with cancer.

The greenhouse effect is accurately described in the following passage:

> As with a glass-walled terrarium, literally all of the planet's energy comes from the sun. As this shortwave radiation—raw sunshine—heads earthward, it passes through the ozone layer which absorbs most of the ultraviolet rays. Atmospheric water vapor absorbs the infrared rays, and the sun's energy is transformed into long-wave energy, or heat, and eventually radiated back into space. Since carbon dioxide at the earth's surface absorbs long-wave radiation, the more carbon dioxide in the air the more heat the planetary atmosphere can retain and the warmer our living space can become (Ayensu 134).

The greenhouse effect is developed from the build-up in the atmosphere of carbon dioxide, ozone, methane, chlorofluorocar-

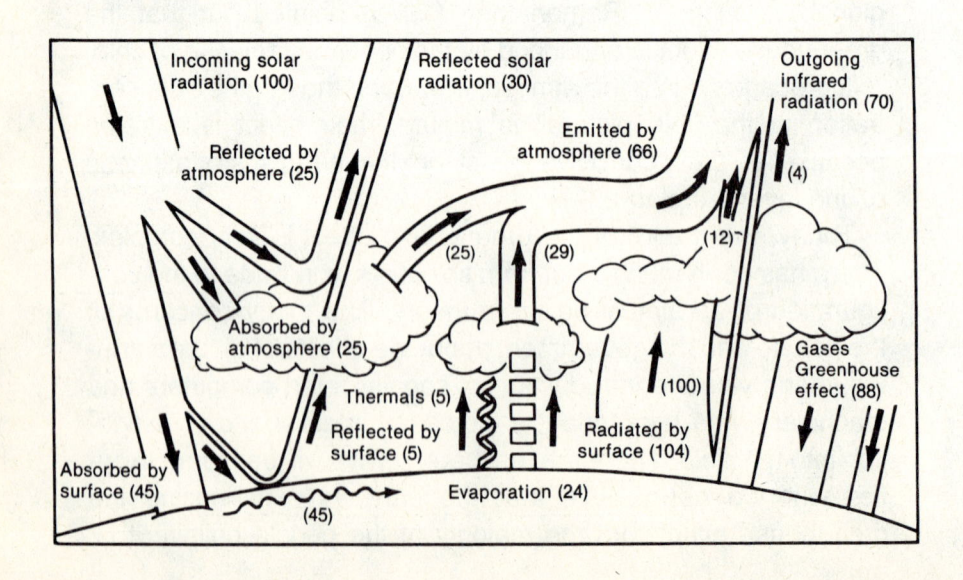

Physics

bons, nitrous oxide, and other heat-trapping gases. All these gases except for the chlorofluorocarbons are produced from the consumption of fossil fuels—nitrous oxide, methane and carbon dioxide also have other sources.

Thus far carbon dioxide seems to be the main culprit of the greenhouse effect (actually, the main culprit is fossil fuel, but gas-wise it is carbon dioxide), it deserves sixty percent of the blame. Carbon dioxide emissions have risen steadily with the increased fossil fuel consumption and the massive deforestation (MacKenzie 5). Deforestation destroys the plants that would have otherwise converted thousands of tons of carbon dioxide into oxygen. Also, the burning of trees triggers the release of the carbon dioxide that the tree has in its storage. Since the 19th century, the increase of atmospheric carbon dioxide has increased about 50 parts per million (ppm). The majority of the carbon dioxide emissions have been absorbed by the oceans, which act as a sort of sponge. Richard A. Kerr notes that the

SEVERAL TRACE GASES CONTRIBUTE
TO GREENHOUSE WARMING
Temperature rise, in °F

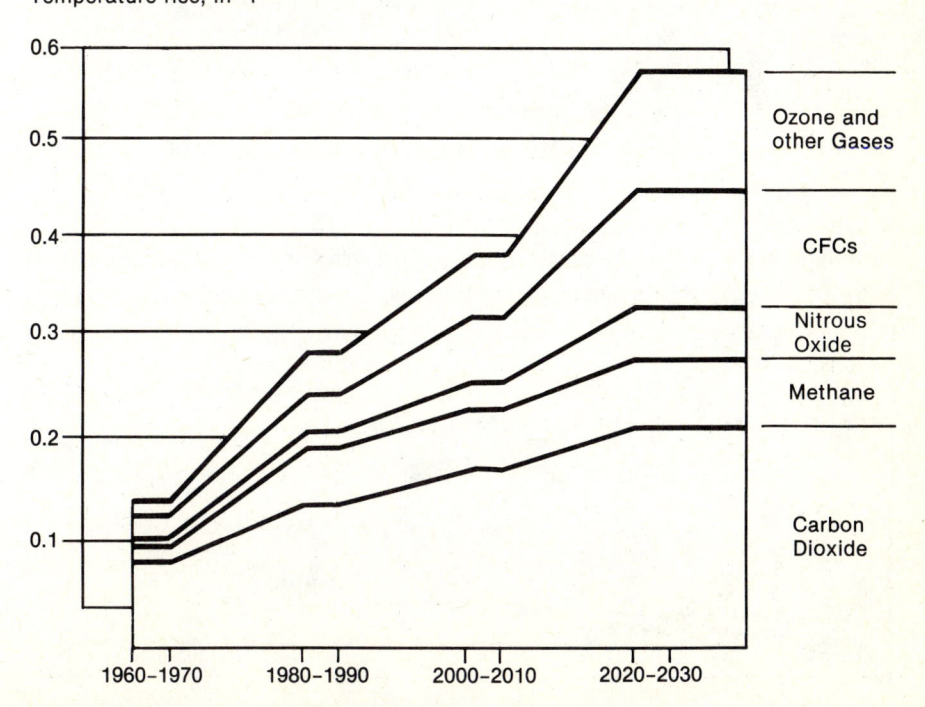

microscopic plants and animals in the oceans use the carbon dioxide to frame their skeletons and to build their tissues (1053). Roger Revelle estimates that about 42 trillion tons of carbon dioxide reside in the oceans, atmosphere, and soil, the majority being in the oceans. Currently, the atmospheric carbon dioxide content stands at about 700 billion tons (Revelle 35). "Total CO_2 emissions from energy systems, for example, can be expressed by a formula termed 'the population multiplie' by Erich and Holden" (Schneider 772).

Methane gas is the second largest contributor to the greenhouse effect. During the past few years, methane concentrations have been increasing by about one percent per year. This increase closely parallels population growth (MacKenzie 6). Judith Stone states that "the planet is about to be cowed into submission" (38). Her statement is supported by the facts that cows belch mightily every minute and a half, and these burps happen to dispense methane gas. A cow can burp up approximately 400 liters of methane a day; imagine that multiplied by the world's more than 1.2 × 10 to the ninth power cows. Methane can be found in 1.7 parts per million (38). Termites, flooded rice paddies, biomass burning, and landfills are also important sources of methane. Indirectly, motor vehicles contribute to the growth of atmospheric methane because carbon monoxide, mostly from vehicle exhaust, slows down processes that normally remove methane from the atmosphere (MacKenzie 6).

The next gaseous contributor to the greenhouse effect is the ground-level concentrations of ozone, a highly reactive form of oxygen which forms "urban smog" as it reacts to the combus-

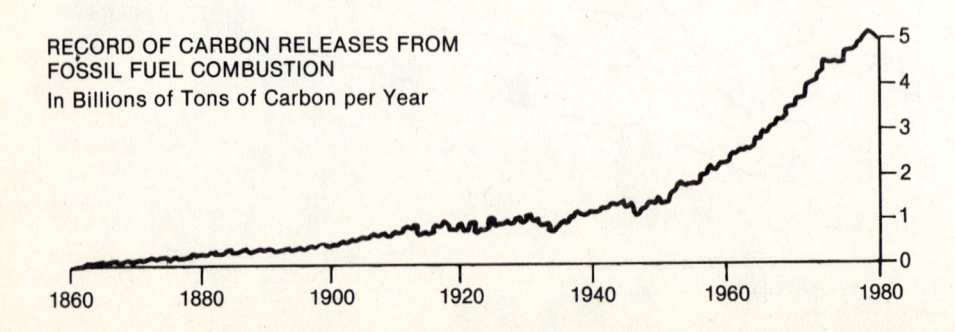

RECORD OF CARBON RELEASES FROM
FOSSIL FUEL COMBUSTION
In Billions of Tons of Carbon per Year

tion of fossil fuels and biomass. This greenhouse gas has doubled over the past century and the amounts now found are damaging trees, crops, materials, and human health (MacKenzie 5).

Nitrous oxide is another one of these potent greenhouse gases. This gas arises as soil microbes release the gas from the nitrogen based fertilizer that farmers apply. It can also arise from the burning of timber, crop residues, and fossil fuels. Nitrous oxide has the ability to destroy the ozone layer in the stratosphere (MacKenzie 6). Other gases that are known to destroy the ozone layer in the stratosphere are chlorofluorocarbons and halons. These gases are frequently used in refrigeration, air conditioning, and fire extinguishers. They can also be found in aerosol propellants, solvents, and foam blowing agents. Each year the amount of these gases increase approximately 5 percent (MacKenzie 6).

One possible explanation for the increase in temperature in the Southern Hemisphere may be sunspot cycles. Sunspots are blemishes on the sun, says Robert W. Noyes, generated by magnetic fields beneath its surface (83). Two separate cycles have been plotted, an 11 year cycle and a 22 year cycle, also known as a double cycle (107–109). "Recent research on sunspot cycles conducted by John Eddy seems to indicate a correlation between active sunspot production and warmer temperatures could be the result of an increase of solar radiation to the troposphere near sunspot maximum giving rise to warm air" (Noyes 223). As the temperature increases, the greenhouse effect traps more gas; it is inevitable that the earth will reach temperatures higher than ever before.

An area that seems to be getting the full thermal effect of the greenhouse effect are the cities. Cities are simply hotter than the country. For example, "in the fall frost warnings go out first to the suburbs and only later to center city" (Kerr 603). This is because concrete, asphalt, and rooftops are not the same as trees, bushes, and grass. Vegetation can cool the surface by evaporating water through its leaves. Contrarily, concrete absorbs and stores heat far more efficiently than does vegetation (Kerr 603). This so-called "urban heat island" effect is not considered a factor to the global warming because it makes no difference to long-term temperature trends. But the deforestation part in the making of a city is an important factor of the greenhouse effect.

As hot as it has been getting these past few years the influence of the greenhouse gases on the earth's temperature and climate have not yet been felt as most of the warmth has been captured by the oceans (MacKenzie 8). Current estimates show that the gases already emitted through 1985 will eventually lead to an increase of 1.8 to 4.5 degrees Fahrenheit. "At current rates of growth, each decade will add another 0.4 to 0.9 degrees Fahrenheit to the earth's long-term temperature rise" (MacKenzie 8). The results of the greenhouse effect have started to get intense. Statistics show that the five warmest years in the past century have all occurred in this decade, in the years 1980, 1981, 1983, 1987, and 1988 (MacKenzie 8).

Some scientists contend that the warming trend will not be all that bad. They predict that an increase in atmospheric carbon dioxide will be beneficial to plant life. Sylvan Wittwer, director of the Michigan State University agricultural station, points out that increased amounts of carbon dioxide will stimulate plant growth and enhance leaf, root, fruit, and flower growth (Revelle 40). Sherwood Idso, a research physicist at the United States Conservation Laboratory in Phoenix, Arizona, also agrees with Wittwer. Furthermore, he goes so far as to say that the doubling of carbon dioxide only causes a temperature increase of about 0.26 degrees Centigrade (Meredith 64).

Unlike these optimists, the majority of climatologists believe that the doubling of carbon dioxide causes a change of 2 degrees Centigrade. Judith Stone states that "A rise in global mean temperature of a mere 3 to 4 degrees could melt the polar ice caps and thereby swell our seas, drown coastal cities, and dramatically change worldwide weather patterns." The rising of ocean levels would jeopardize the well-being of such low-lying U.S. cities as Miami, New Orleans, Galveston, and Charleston. Protecting a medium-sized U.S. coastal city against a three foot sea rise could cost up to $1.5 billion (MacKenzie 8).

Computer simulations predict that by the year 2050 there will indeed be a three foot rise in the oceans. Also for that year they indicate that surface temperatures will rise significantly. Summer temperatures in many U.S. cities will top 100 degrees Fahrenheit far more often than they do today (MacKenzie 8). Along with these warmer temperatures we can expect less precipitation and lower soil moisture. This parched situation will affect the midwest agricultural areas the most.

An increase in temperatures will also take an ecological toll. Many plants, animals, and insects will have to migrate to adapt to new climactic changes. "Given a doubling of carbon dioxide in the next century, Davis found that the four species of trees (beech, birch, hemlock, and sugar maple) would have to shift approximately 500 kilometers north to remain in suitable climate and habitat" (Cohen 142). Among these trees, animals, and insects a "survival of the fittest" will occur and thus some species will become extinct from the face of this earth.

Therefore, on the basis of a review of the literature published thus far, it seems apparent that as atmospheric carbon dioxide increases, so will the earth's temperature. Even if fossil fuel consumption and forest clearing were to cease completely within the next 50 or 60 years, the oceans and forests will not be able to absorb the carbon dioxide fast enough to prevent any further greenhouse effect. Apparently though a significant reduction in atmospheric carbon dioxide is not practical at this time, fossil fuels seem to be the predominant source of energy as they are the predominant source of the greenhouse effect. The use of an alternative energy source such as nuclear power has been condemned. Solar power, yet another alternative, is still in its infancy. As of yet, there are no reasonable energy substitutes and thus fossil fuels are the number one source of energy. With the levels of carbon dioxide in the atmosphere as they are today, it is inevitable that the greenhouse effect will take its toll. There are great uncertainties as to the exact consequences of the extra global warming from the build-up of greenhouse gases, but it could well pose as the greatest environmental threat in the history of mankind.

Works Cited

Ayensu, Edward S. *Fire of Life.* Smithsonian Exposition Books. 1st edition. New York: Norton, 1981.

Cohn J. P. "Gauging the Biological Impacts of the Greenhouse Effect." *Bioscience.* March, 1989: 142–6.

Kaplan, Lewis D. "The Greenhouse Effect." *McGraw Hill Encyclopedia of Science & Technology.* 1987 edition.

Kerr, Richard A. "Carbon Dioxide and the Control of Ice Ages." *Science.* 9 March 1984: 1053–1054.

Kerr, Richard A. "The Global Warming is Real." *Science.* 3 Feb. 1980: 603.

MacKenzie, James. "Breathing Easier: Taking Action on Climate Change, Air Pollution, and Energy Insecurity." *W. R. I. Pamphlet*, 1988.

Meredith, Dennis. "Greenhouse Advantage." *Science Digest.* Sept. 1982: 64.

Revelle, Roger. "Carbon Dioxide and World Climate." *Scientific American.* August 1982: 35–43.

Schneider, Stephen. "the Greenhouse Effect: Science and Policy." *Science.* 10 Feb., 1989: 771–81.

Stone, Judith. "Bovine Madness." *Discover.* Feb. 1989: 38.

Analysis of Sample Physics Paper 3

Sandra has chosen a timely subject for her paper, and you may find it inherently more interesting than the previous two. As she points out, the greenhouse effect is a subject of increasing interest to environmentalists and concerned citizens alike. The fact that a few scientists question the potential threat of increased global warming gives her another rhetorical advantage—controversy—that should help produce an exceptional paper.

 A cursory reading suggests that Sandra is doing what she should do for such a paper. She notes the two sides to the topic, and then, as the assignment encourages, she takes her own stand as well, agreeing with those who argue that the greenhouse effect is indeed a serious threat. A more careful reading, however, begins to reveal some problems.

The language is often uneven, shifting from precise statements to vague generalities. For example, in paragraph 6, Sandra says that "the greenhouse effect is enhanced by the continued release of chlorofluorocarbons into the atmosphere." But in paragraph 7, she writes, "Today, the theory of the greenhouse effect is very complex. There has been much input from scientists worldwide to the configuration of an almost accurate theory." Can you see how the language differs? A cautious teacher may be inclined at this point to suspect plagiarism simply on the basis of the language, especially in view of Sandra's failure to document all her sources properly.

Furthermore, in the third paragraph, Sandra states that "Tyndall's concept of the 'effect' did not immensely offend anyone—particularly the Church." Readers are likely to respond by asking immediately: "Why should it?" There is nothing remotely offensive in Tyndall's theories. Could Sandra be trying too hard to address the question, "How was [the concept's] rise (and fall) influenced by the thought of the times?"

Sandra shows good judgment in providing graphs and diagrams to illustrate her paper. Unfortunately, these visuals don't help readers much because she neglects to explain or even refer to them in the text of her paper. A similar weakness appears in her discussion of concepts that a general audience can't be assumed to know a great deal about. She talks about the nature of the ozone layer and the relationship between sunspot cycles and the greenhouse effect as though readers have a solid background in atmospheric chemistry. A better approach would have included some explanation of these topics and the terms associated with them.

Finally, a very careful reading suggests that Sandra would not have succeeded on this assignment even if she had revised her work to solve the problems above. The source of the difficulty is the topic, which we indeed noted is an inherent strength—for a general purpose essay, but not necessarily for this particular assignment. Usually, atmospheric change is deemed to be in the domain of chemistry, not physics. In fact, over the last few years, many universities have started offering advanced degrees in "environmental chemistry," which includes the climatic factors Sandra is discussing. The overwhelming majority of those working in the area of climatic change are chemists, not physicists. Thus the low grade she received on her paper could reflect her teacher's judgment that she did not adequately understand the assignment and that she does not clearly comprehend the domain of physics.

Writing Assignments

1. Using the assignment above as a guide, write a paper on the history of a physical concept. Choose one of the following topics: gravity, force, resonance, quarks, fusion, fields, neutrons, big bang, luminiferous ether, entropy, radioactivity, fission, or electromagnetic waves. Remember to explain the concept and to provide its history. To begin thinking about your subject, make use of the list of questions included in the "Subject" section of the assignment.
2. Over the last few years, popular news magazines such as *Time* have reported that the number of American high school students majoring in physics is declining, and they predict dire consequences for America's standing in the scientific community. In a 4- to 5-page paper, analyze the shortage of physics majors and argue for your own conclusions about its consequences for the nation. As part of your research on the topic, you may want to interview students on your campus to gauge their views on physics (or science), or you may want to determine what motivated some but not others to select physics as a major.

PHYSICS ASSIGNMENT 2

Course: **Intermediate Physics for Sophomore Majors**

In this lab, you will investigate the efficiency of a photovoltaic cell as it varies with illumination. Use a Panlux illumination meter to measure input illumination and a Fluke 77 multimeter to measure output of voltage and current. Write up your report using the proper format, including a sketch of the apparatus set-up, graphs, and data tables.

Analysis of Physics Assignment 2

This lab session is challenging for two reasons: It requires rather involved apparatus and procedures, and it produces an abundance of data. Writing up a clear and exact report of this session should prove equally challenging.

With some variation, students responding to this assignment divided their reports into the following categories: Introduction and Theory, Setup and Procedure, Data and Error Analysis, and Conclusion. The Introduction should briefly summarize what students know about the subject of their experiment *before* the experiment begins. The Setup and Procedure section should describe the apparatus used and steps taken in the lab in sufficient detail to allow readers to duplicate the experiment. In addition, students want to explain in this section *why* the experiment was set up and carried out in this manner. For example, why must a small fan be included in the apparatus? Why should the low-wattage light sources be tested first and the high-wattage light sources last? In the Data and Error Analysis section, students will look for meaning within the mass of data collected. What do the data suggest about the efficiency of a solar cell as it varies with illumination? Can patterns be found in the data, or are the data inconsistent and erratic? What errors in the experiment might account for these inconsistencies? In the Conclusion, students should evaluate the experiment and suggest how it might be improved in the future.

This assignment is linked with a lab manual that describes the steps students must perform with each instrument, so one could reasonably expect the task to be relatively straightforward. One might even predict that students' lab reports would be monotonously similar. Lab experiments rarely run as smoothly as a manual suggests, however. Meters will behave erratically. Few undergraduate labs offer an ideal research environment, so measurements may be unreliable, making subsequent conversions quite difficult.

An implicit criterion for success on this assignment must therefore be how well students were able to handle the frustrations inherent in the task. The better reports not only acknowledge the difficulties but attempt to analyze them as part of an overall learning experience. Tonda, in Sample Paper 4 below, for example, gives an exact account of the lab's difficulties and the discrepancies in her data, and then she provides detailed suggestions aimed at improving the outcome of future experiments. David, in Sample Paper 6, however, seems to throw his hands up in the air in disgust: He provides a brief and general run-down of the experiment and in the conclusion declares it a "mess."

Guide for Reading

Tonda's paper represents a very good response to the assignment. She uses the conventional subheadings associated with lab reports to organize her paper in a way that is easy to read. Each section presents the appropriate information clearly and concisely.

In addition to performing the experiment successfully, a minimal requirement, Tonda analayzes each aspect of the work, from procedures to results. In the Error Analysis section, she doesn't hesitate to address possible sources of error, which demonstrates to readers (specifically, her teacher) that she is capable of critically assessing her work. Many students responding to this assignment will be inclined to say very little about sources of error, mistakenly believing that admitting the presence of errors is a sign of failure. Note, for example, David's report, the third in this series.

SAMPLE PHYSICS PAPER 4

The Response of a Photovoltaic Cell as A Function of Illumination

Tonda M. (a sophomore)

Introduction and Theory

Photovoltaic cells convert energy from photons of light directly to electrical energy. Photovoltaic cells are made of a number of different semi-conducting materials such as silicon, cadmium sulfide, and gallium arsenide. Incoming photons separate electrons from the atoms of the semi-conductor. If the sight of this reaction is near the electric field created by a p-n junction, the positively charged electron and the negatively charged "hole" will drift apart. If the p-type and n-type junctions are connected by a circuit, a current will be generated, and electric power produced.

This experiment examines the output of a solar cell as a function of input illumination. The output data was voltage and current. The input was illuminance, which is luminous flux per unit area. Luminous flux is simply the time rate of change of luminous energy. Luminous energy, however, is the time rate of change of "that aspect of radiant energy that is light, i.e. visually evaluated radiant energy," according to the *Handbook of Optics*, sponsored by the Optical Society of America. A problem arises in this ex-

Physics

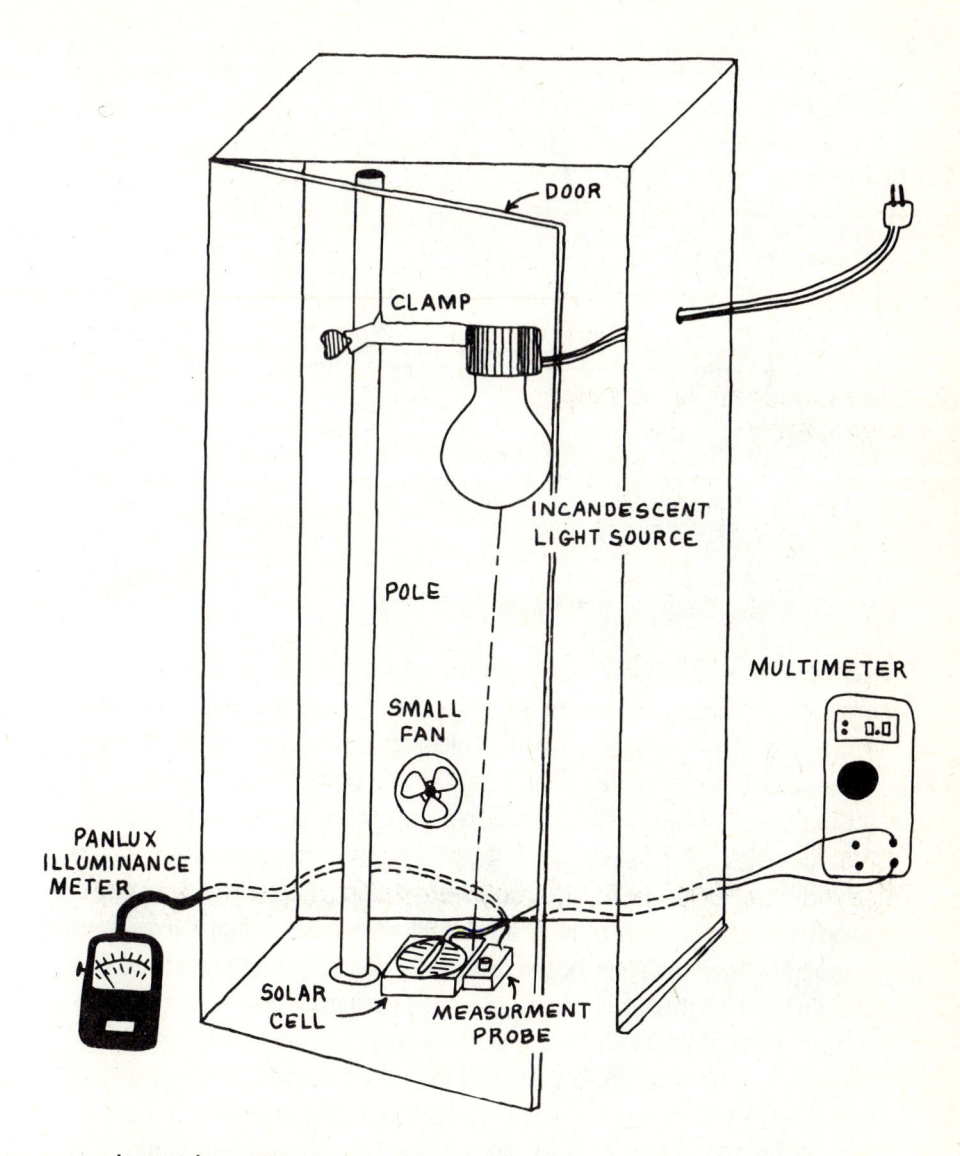

periment because solar cells absorb energy not only from radiation in the visible spectrum, but also from the ultra-violet and infra-red radiation. Silicon solar cells, for example, have the peak conversion of photons to electrical energy in the infra-red range, (figure 2).

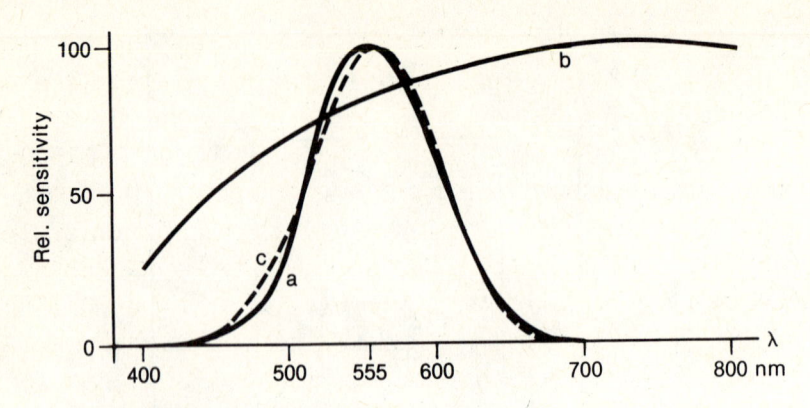

Relative spectral sensitivity (mean values)
a. Eye V(λ)
b. Silicon photo-cell without filter
c. Meter's measuring probe

Instrumentation and Calibration

To measure the input illumination, a Panlux illumination meter was used. The light reaching the meter's silicon cell is internally filtered and adjusted so that it closely corresponds___the response of the human eye, peaking at 555 nanometers. It also has a built in cosine function that corrects light at an oblique angle of incidence by the cosine rule. Therefore no corrections because of an oblique angle of incidence were made. The filter did cause problems, though. It only read the illuminance of light, which is associated with wavelengths in the visible range. We needed the irradiance of light, which takes into account the energy of all wavelengths of light reaching the meter, in order to determine efficiency (figure 2). There is no simple way to correct for this. Qualitatively, however, if the photon source emits wavelengths only in the visible range illumination and irradiance are equivalent, but if the source also emits radiation outside the visible range the illumination reading will be less that the actual irradiance.

To calibrate the illuminance meter, we adjusted the instrument so that the scale read zero when off, then we placed the measuring probe in the dark to find that it also read zero. there are measuring ranges on the illuminance meter. The user is able to select a range, then after reading the appropriate scale, the reading is multiplied by the order of magnitude of the selected range. The range of uncertainty, therefore, changes as the range is changed.

To measure output we used a Fluke 77 multimeter. Two quantities were measured with this meter; output voltage, in milli-Volts, and output current, in milli-Amps. The resolution of the meter when set on 330mV is 0.1 mV. To check the calibration of the meter, the no load voltage was checked and the meter read 0.0 mV. Due to the difficulty of taking data, because the voltage reading continually decreased as the meter was being read, and we do not know how the final digit was rounded off by the meter, the range of uncertainty of the measurement was chosen to be + 0.05 mV. The resolution of the meter when reading from 0 to 32 milli-Amps is 0.01 mA, and when reading from 32 to 320 mA, it is 0.1 mA. When checked with no load, the meter read 0.00 mA, but fluctuated above and below 0.00 in the hundredths digit before settling on 0.00 mA. The uncertainty in the measurement was evaluated to be less that 0.005 mA for readings between 0 and 32 mA, and 0.05 between 32 and 320 mA. All our data readings were less than 60 mA.

A vernier caliper was used to measure the diameter of the solar cell, and the dimensions of the contact grid on the surface of the cell. The least count on the vernier caliper used is 0.01 cm. The difficulty in measuring the diameter of the cell lies in correctly determining the maximum width of the cell. To measure the diameter, the cell was carefully passed through the jaws of the vernier caliper, not allowing any rotational motion. The point at which the cell just barely passed through was measured as the diameter. A table of the trials and the measurements is included (table 1). The measurement varied, this may have been because of the method used or the cell may not have been perfectly round. The average of these values is used in calculations. Due to these problems, the uncertainty in the measurement was determined to be within + 0.005 cm, half of the least-count. The measurement of the dimensions of the contact grid were less complicated, and their accuracy was determined to be within + 0.002 cm; one-fifth of the least count.

Table 1: Diameter of Cell

Trial	Diameter
1	8.79 + 0.05
2	8.78
3	8.74
4	8.81
5	8.76
AVE	8.78

Set Up and Procedure

A sketch of the set up for this experiment is included (figure 1). A light source was centered above the solar cell and the measurement probe using a pole and a clamp so the distance from the cell could be varied. the set up was placed inside a closed white box; to decrease the variation caused by other light sources being turned on and off and to act as a reflector to increase illuminance from low wattage bulbs. A small DC fan was used to blow in cool air from the outside, to help decrease changes in the data due to increase resistance in the cell as temperatures rose. The leads from the solar cell and the measurement probe were passed through the wall of the box so the multimeter and illuminance meter could be read.

Six different incandescent bulbs were used; 7.5, 25, 40, 60, 100, and 200 watts, to increase the range of illumination. The distance from the solar cell was then varied to get several illuminance readings from each bulb. We avoided placing the source close to the meter because we did not want the resistance in the cell to increase due to heating; we wanted the wave front from the light to be approximately planar so the light incident on the entire cell and on the meter would be equal, and we wanted to decrease the infra-red radiation, which travels poorly in air, when compared with visible light.

Data was collected for a range of illuminations varying from 200 watts to 560 footcandles. readings for voltage and current were recorded. The readings for the 200 watt bulb were taken

Physics

with the door of the box left open, so heat within the box could disapate easily. All other experimenters had left by that point, so we turned off the lights and used the box as a reflector only. This procedure was only used for the 200 watt bulb.

Analysis and Conclusions

Two graphs were obtained from plots of the data

The first, Power vs. Irradiance, is a plot of output power as a function of input radiance (graph I). A curve fitted to the data ___ that the power at first rises rapidly as input irradiance is increased, then becomes constant. The horizontal asymptote to the curve is the maximum theoretical efficiency. For this cell under an incandescent bulb, the maximum theoretical efficiency is about 1.41×10 to the second power W. There are some points that deviated from the fitted curve. These occur using the 100-

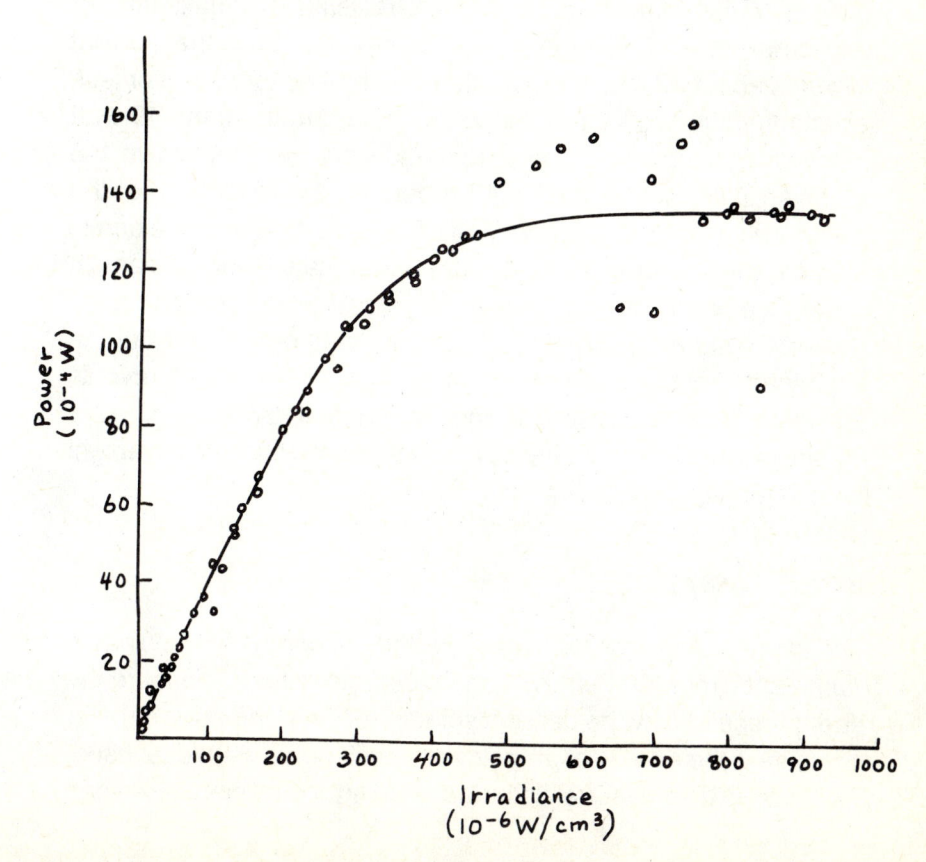

watt bulb. The deviations about the curve are probably caused by large amounts of infra-red radiation given off by the 100-watt bulb, but not recorded by the illuminance meter. This seems to be the best explanation, since the 200-watt bulb fits the curve. The set-up changed in such a way that the effect____ excess infra-red radiation was reduced. The deviations below the curve may be caused by increased resistance in the cell when the temperature rose in the box. Data taking was difficult for the 100-watt bulb because the voltage dropped a readings were being taken, and the current behaved erratically. For example, at one point the current first read over 50 mA, then dropped rapidly to less than 20 mA. When the meter was turned off, then back on and the data re-taken, the meter read a constant current in the upper 40's. There were similar difficulties at several points in the 100-watt bulb series.

A graph of Voltage vs. Current was also made to help analyze the change in resistance (graph II). The resistance is the slope tangent to the curve at any point. The resistance is maximum for low currents and voltages, then decreases until the current reaches about 33 mA, then suddenly increases to a more or less constant value. This change occurs in the data from the 40-watt bulb, so it is probably not associated with the problem in the 100-watt data, but rather____ a property of the resistance of the cell when a current is applied. The resistance may become ohmic as the current increases. This plot also indicates that increase in resistance due to heating may not be a source of error, since the resistance appears to be constant for that range of data. An examination of the plot over that range of data, however, reveals that there is too much scatter and too many discontinuous points to conclude that with finality. Further study on this property might be interesting and informative.

Error Analysis

The main source of error in this experiment comes from using an illuminance meter rather than an irradiance meter to measure the energy received by the cell. On subsequent experiments, a meter measuring the energy of all incident wavelengths should be used. This would give a more accurate reading for efficiency. At one point the efficiency of our cell appeared to be 101% because the input energy was greater than measured.

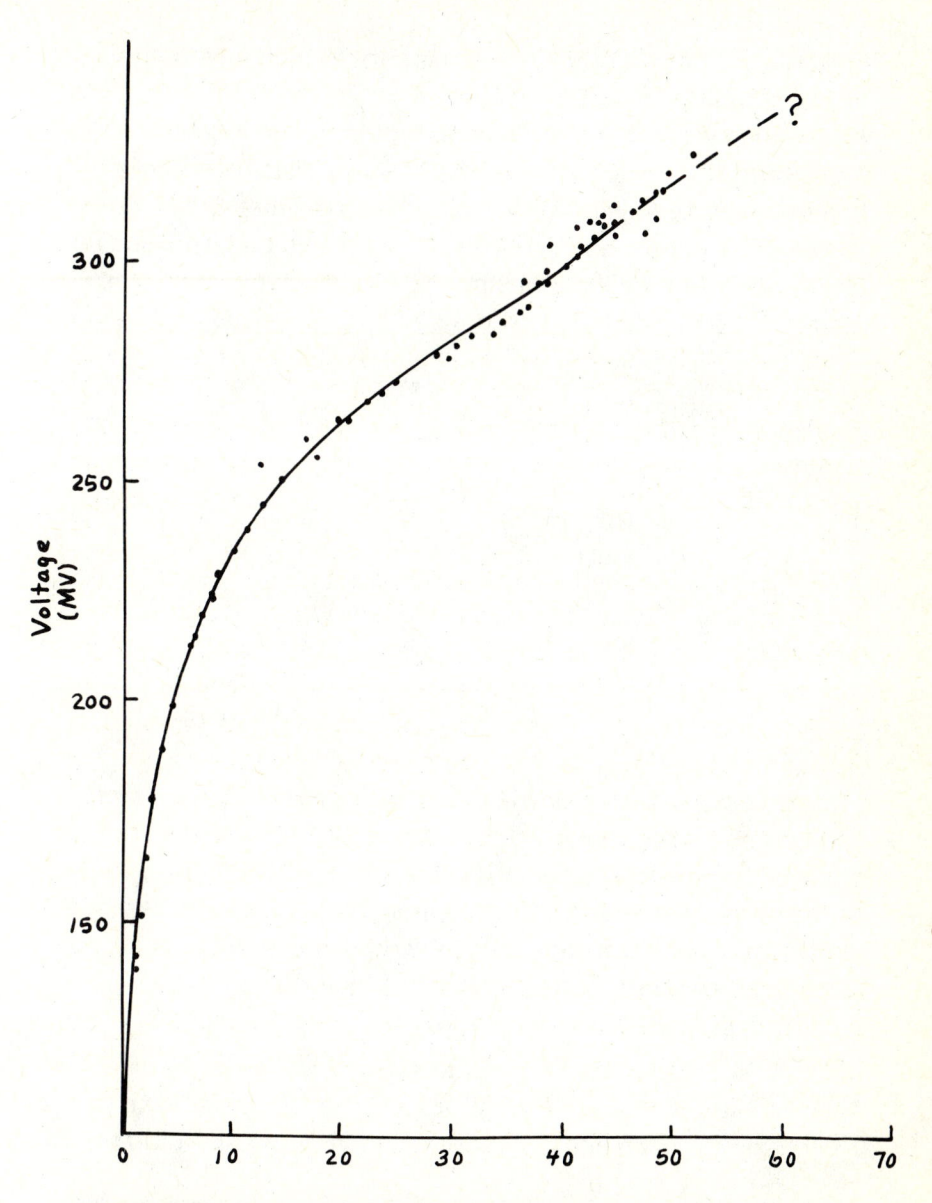

Another source of error is the assumptions we had to make in order to convert from luminous to radiant measurements. The spectral response curve of the meter did not peak exactly at 555, and the graph in the instruction book is slightly skewed. Without the equation of the spectral response curve for the incandescent bulb, we cannot accurately determine the illuminance of the visible light emitted by the bulb.

Another source of error is enclosing the set-up in a box. While this is appropriate for small bulbs at large distances, for larger bulbs the infra-red is reflected rather than radiated out. A possible solution is to use a black enclosure, and longer distances. Using a light source that does not give off much heat and closely approximates white light would also improve results.

> ## STUDY QUESTIONS
>
> 1. From time to time, Tonda's paragraphs become so long that they are hard to read. Identify which paragraphs cause this difficulty and then show where you would break them up into shorter ones.
>
> 2. Tonda consistently uses "data" as a singular noun rather than a plural one. What message do you think this usage could send to a knowledgeable reader?
>
> 3. Tonda's teacher identified her Error Analysis section as being one of the best parts of her report. There is no question that it works very well in regard to the information it presents, but stylistically, it has some problems. How would you rewrite these three paragraphs to make them better?
>
> 4. Identify places in Tonda's report where she inconsistently uses active and passive voice. If Tonda had asked you for advice on how to use active and passive constructions more effectively, what would you have told her?

Guide for Reading

Eric does many of the same things that Tonda does in her report, although not quite as well. His paper is an average response to the assignment. He doesn't provide as much detail as Tonda, and his terse style and numerous sentence errors make the report harder to read. One of his strengths is organization, and the paper proceeds in an orderly fashion that you may find appealing. Note, however, that at times the organization becomes mechanical, as when he talks about error analysis: He tells us there were three sources of error, and then he lists them, one, two, three. As you read, find places where Eric repeats this pattern. What effect does such repetition have on your assessment of the paper?

SAMPLE PHYSICS PAPER 5

The Eficiency of a Solar Cell as It Varies with Illumination

Eric S. (a sophomore)

Introduction

The solar cell, a thin film p-n junction device, can be used to convert light into electricity. This device is becoming more and more common in every day applications. In this lab we will attempt to determine the power conversion efficiency of this device. By measuring the light incident on the cell and testing the voltage and current produced by the cell we will be able to determine the overall efficiency of the cell.

Theory

The basic theory behind solar cells is based on the energy level principle of electron bands. The electron energy levels are altered by doping an element, such as silicon, with impurities that either have more or less electrons that the original element. This creates a p- or n- type material. A p-type material is deficient of electrons and is sometimes called a hole conductor. The material is positively biased. An n-type material is the bearer of an extra electron and is called an electron conductor. This material is negatively biased.

Normally placing these two materials in close proximity to one another would not result in a current flowing however when a photon, a particle of light, strikes this combination the extra electron in the n-type conductor receives enough energy to be able to jump the energy gap and flow to a collector creating a current. This is due to the energy of the photon being transferred to the electron and exciting it from the valence energy band to the conduction energy band. When the conduction of current is due only to those electrons excited up from the valance band to the conduction band the material is called an intrinsic semiconductor. When the conduction is due to impurities, or dopants, the material is called an extrinsic semiconductor. Since extra electrons due to dopants are held in place only by the nuclear attraction to the nucleus, it can be removed and made a conduction electron with far less energy than that required to move a valance electron across the energy gap.

The current then caused by the electrons jumping the gap and flowing to a grid of receptors on the surface of the cell can be used as a potential difference to generate an electromotive force in a circuit.

Procedure

 I. Design of Apparatus
 II. Variation and Data Taking
 III. Taking of Error Related Data

I. The apparatus design for this laboratory was of the utmost importance. First a nearly light-free environment was created using posterboard and tape. A sketch of the apparatus may be found in figure 1. Next we tested our environment by placing our light meters' receptor inside of our environment and took a reading of zero footcandles.

After verifying a nearly light-free environment a platform rest for the solar cell was designed that would support the cell at the same height as the meters' receptor. Then two leads were soldered to the cells electron collectors.

Next our light source was connected to the end of a rod and lowered through the top of our environment. The orifice around the rod was sealed with tape.

Finally a fan and ventilation port were added as indicated in figure 1. The fan and vent were placed on opposite sides of the

Physics

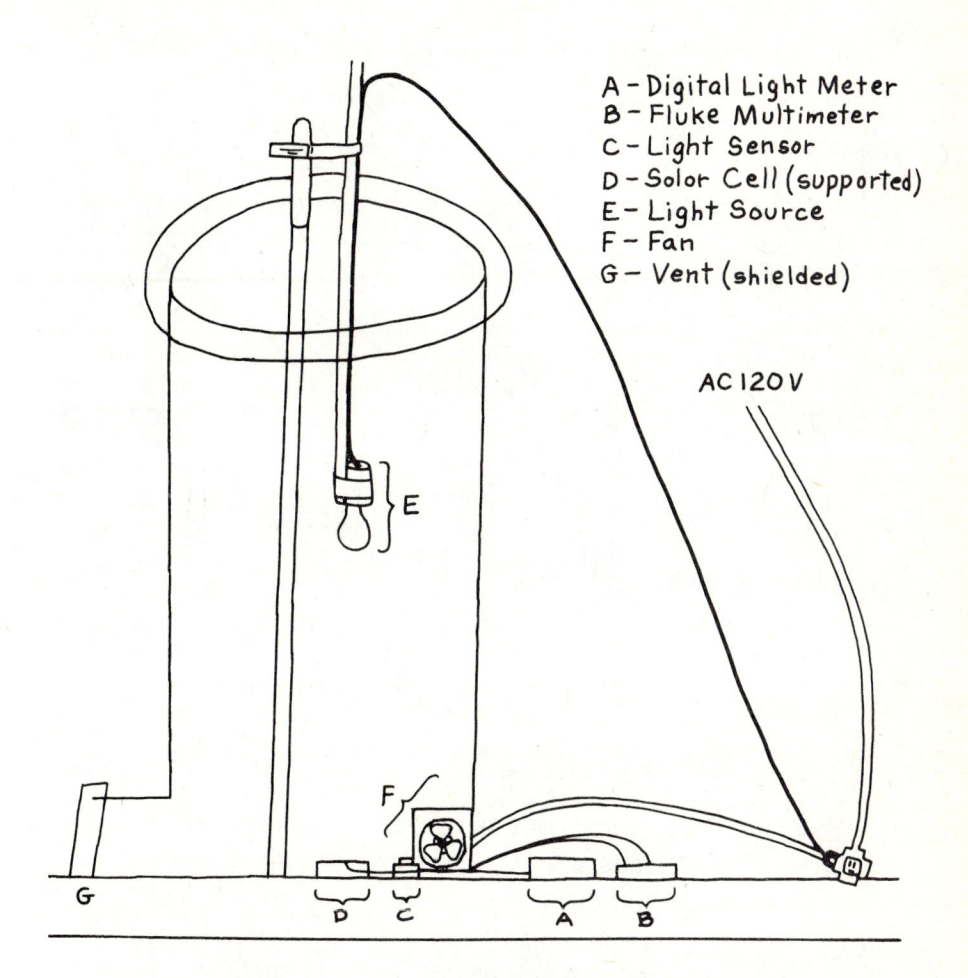

A – Digital Light Meter
B – Fluke Multimeter
C – Light Sensor
D – Solor Cell (supported)
E – Light Source
F – Fan
G – Vent (shielded)

AC 120 V

cell to cause maximum air flow across the cell. The fan and the vent were then shielded to block out any strong or direct light from entering. After all the instalations were accomplished another lightmeter reading was taken and read to be zero footcandles.

II. The first light source used was a seven watt bulb. Starting at the top of our environment we took readings of all our meters as the light source was lowered toward the cell. This sequence was repeated until our source was approximately four inches from our cell.

After a full range of data had been compiled for one source, that source was removed and replaced alternately with fifteen,

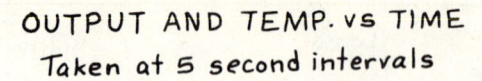

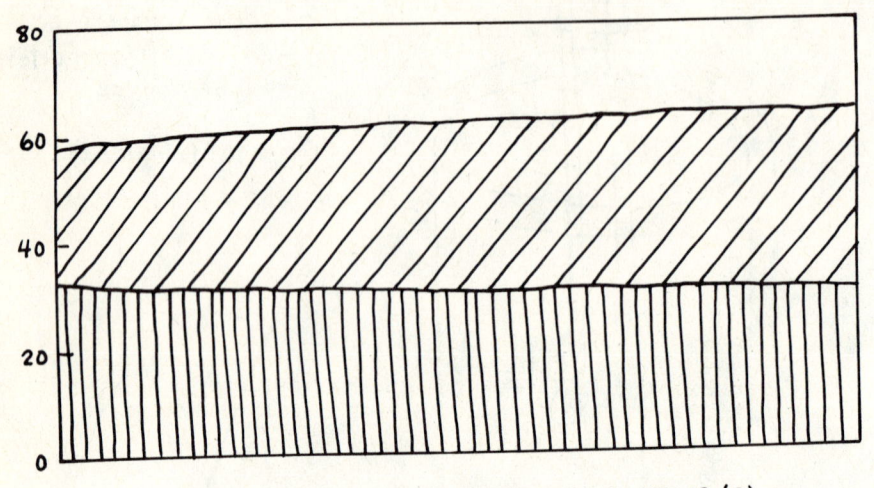

OUTPUT AND TEMP. vs TIME
Taken at 5 second intervals

SERIES A: VOLTAGE(V)   SERIES B: TEMP.(C)

▭ Series A   ▨ Series B

Voltage measured in V X .01

twenty-five, fifty, sixty, one-hundred and two-hundred watt sources. The previous sequence was then repeated. This data is located in tables one through seven for bulbs as indicated. [Editors' note: Eric provided only table 3 in the paper he gave us.]

For the last two sources it was necessary to unplug the source between readings and allow the fan to cool the cell before taking another reading.

III. The final step in our lab procedure consisted of taking data of the efficiency as a function of temperature. A graphical representation of this data can be located in figure 2. As indicated by the data in table 1, the efficiency is extremely temperature sensitive. This data was obtained by disconnecting our fan and closing off the ventallation. The one-hundred watt source was placed a constant distance from the cell and the readings were taken at five second intervals.

Physics

Conversions

Since the pan-lux meter reads the light in footcandles we find it nessissary to convert this to watts in order to calculate efficiency.

This conversion was done as follows:

1 Footcandle = 1 Lumen per square foot

To convert to spectral lunimous efficacy in Lumens per Watt, multiply V} in table 2 by 683. [Editors' note: Eric failed to include Table 2.] Therefore:

1 Watt per square foot = 1 Lumen per square foot/683 × V}
1 W = (1 FC per sq. ft./683 − v})(AREA) 683 × V} = 235.311
1 W = (1 FC/235.311)(AREA)

Data Analysis

The data taken in this experiment did not indicate a constant efficiency throughout all ranges. The efficiencies calculated varied from 9.4% to 8.9% throughout the entire range.

The seven watt source held essentially constant at 9.4% as long as the bulb was at a greater distance than 1 foot. Under this limit the efficiency fell to 9.3%. The other sources exhibited this same behavior with larger and larger distances needed to maintain maximum efficiency.

This series of correlations led us to believe there could be a link between temperature and efficiency. This belief is supported by the relation represented in figure 2. As evidenced by the data in table 1, the voltage dropped significantly as the temperature increased.

Finally the results of this experiment show that the efficiency of our cell dropped considerably with the increase of wattage in our source. This correlation can be examined in table 3.

Error Analysis

Three sources of error are immediately apparent in this experiment.

TABLE 3

Light Bulb	Average Input	Average Output	Cell Efficiency
7-Watt	0.0043 W	0.00040 W	9.24%
15-Watt	0.0189	0.00175	9.26%
25-Watt	0.0263	0.00242	9.23%
40-Watt	0.0536	0.00494	9.22%
60-Watt	0.0957	0.00878	9.17%
100-Watt	0.1718	0.01566	9.12%
200-Watt	0.4336	0.03921	9.04%

First, and probably greatest, the pan-lux manual indicates that the meter is equipped with a filter that restricts the meters measurement to the sensitivity of the human eye. Since the visible spectrum is only about half of the range usable by our solar cell and since a tuntsen filament is capable of emitting light from approximately 200nM to 900nM, our efficiency is likely to be to high. This would be due to the meter reading less light than was actually incident on the cell.

Second, as mentioned before, the temperature of the solar cell plays a large part in the cells efficiency. Since the increase in incident wattage was always accompanied by an increase in temperature this factor is a little difficult to quatitize. Nonetheless this must be considered a major source of error.

Lastly there were likely several forms of instrumental error. The error standard with meter readings must be considered as well as the difficulty of reading an analog meter consistantly. These errors were reduced as much as possible by attempting to adjust the intensity of the incident light to even lightmeter readings.

Conclusion

In conclusion it should be stated that several changes to this experiment would possibly increase its accuracy greatly.

First, the removal of the filter from the light meter probe would help in determining correct efficiencies. Second, isolating the solar cell from direct heat of the bulb should result in less fluctuation in efficiency due to distance or wattage.

The solar cell may one day achieve a significant place in the

Physics

power producing devices of history but for right now it is far too vulnerable to conditions to be relied on extensively.

> ### STUDY QUESTIONS
>
> 1. Pretend for a moment that you are Eric's physics teacher, and then look carefully at his first paragraph. What additional information would you want Eric to provide there?
>
> 2. If you were asked to help edit this report, what changes would you make to paragraph 3?
>
> 3. Look closely at the Theory section of the report. What is a theory? What is the difference between theory and experimentation?
>
> 4. Can you identify where Eric describes a theory for solar cells? What has Eric failed to do in regard to theory and application?

Guide for Reading

David's paper doesn't succeed for several reasons, but the more significant have to do with the lack of sufficient detail and the inappropriate and inconsistent tone. At times, David's writing is very formal, so formal, in fact, that it suggests he may have copied some sentences directly out of a lab manual or some other source. At other times, it is almost conversational. Tone may seem a trivial criterion for success on an assignment, until one considers that for a lab report it can suggest how well a student has adopted the particular way of thinking characteristic of a given discipline. As you read, try to identify places where David's tone shifts.

SAMPLE PHYSICS PAPER 6

The Measurement of Voltage Output from a Solar Cell as a Function of the Intensity of Incident Light

David M. (a sophomore)

Introduction

It is possible to measure the voltage output of a solar cell as a function of the intensity of incident light. Solar cells convert light into energy by absorbing photons from the light rays and converting this reaction onto direct current. The voltage output can be monitored by hooking up a multimeter to a solar cell. To observe how this voltage changes as a function of the intensity of light, a device called a light meter (that measures the intensity of light) is placed next to the solar cell so that they both get the same amount of incident light. To control the intensity of the light, the light meter/solar cell combination is placed in a container (figure 1) that blocks outside light but that has a place in the top to hold different sizes of light bulbs that shine down through a hole onto the light meter/solar cell combination. The intensity can be controlled even more through changing the size of the hole by placing filters with different size holes over the big hole. Before the experiment is run, the intensity of light must be distributed as evenly as possible over the light meter and the solar cell. This distribution is accomplished by a cone in the cylindrical container in figure 1. This cone is directly below the hole that lets the light in. Not only does this cone stop the light from shining directly on the light meter/solar cell combination but it also diffuses the light so that it is evenly distributed over the bottom of the cylinder. To check the effect of temperature from the light bulbs on the solar cell, the voltage is monitored at a constant intensity through a range of temperatures with a temperature probe. It is noted that the voltage changes significantly with the temperature. So a temperature probe is placed, along with the solar cell and the light meter, on the bottom of the container in figure 1 and when the temperature in the container rises by one degree Celcius, the

Physics 175

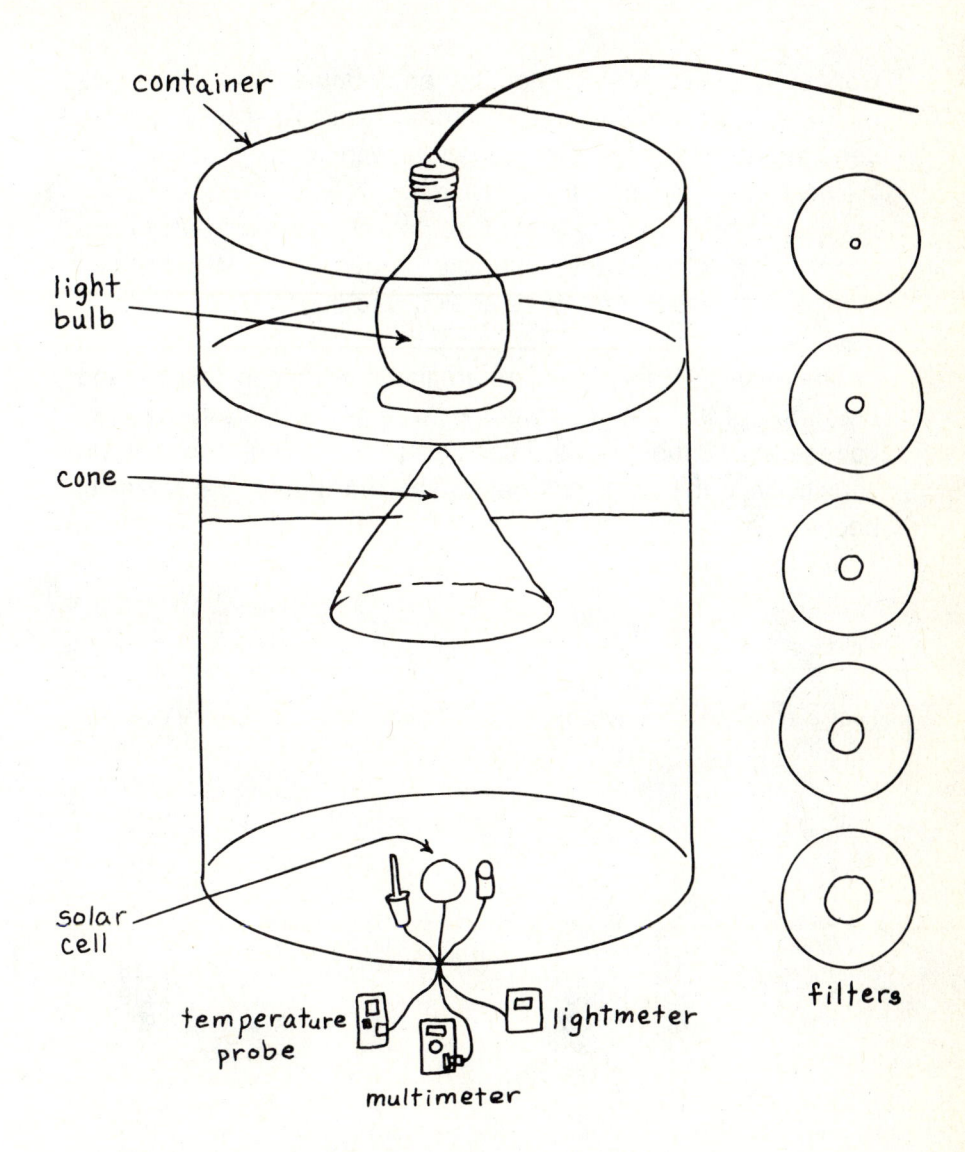

[Diagram showing a container with a light bulb suspended inside, a cone below it, and a solar cell at the bottom. The solar cell connects to a temperature probe, multimeter, and lightmeter. Five circular filters are shown to the right.]

procedure is stopped and the temperature is allowed to <u>cool back</u> to its initial value. Once all of this is set up, it is time to run the procedure.

Procedure

The procedure consisted of putting in different size bulbs and filters and taking the voltage/intensity data, keeping an eye on the temperature making sure that it did not rise by one degree. The best way to do this was to start with the lowest watt bulb and work up to the biggest to keep the temperature down as long as possible. The filters were used from the smallest to largest to keep the data in order. The procedure went: place the filter over the hole, cover the top, take the readings, record the data, change the filters, and repeat the procedure until all filters and bulbs were used. If the temperature rose one degree the procedure was stopped until the temperature cooled one degree.

Results

The results of this procedure are listed as data in Table A and the graph of this data is on graph A. The graph is a function of voltage as it changes with intensity. This graph shows that the sensitivity of the solar cell decreases the greater the intensity becomes.

TABLE A

Intensity (footcandle) ±3%	Voltage (Volts) ±0.03%+.001	Intensity (footcandle) ±3%	Voltage (Volts) ±0.3%+.001
0.40	0.095	5.50	0.191
0.50	0.102	6.00	0.193
0.55	0.105	6.50	0.197
0.60	0.108	6.50	0.207
0.65	0.110	9.00	0.210
0.75	0.118	10.0	0.214
0.90	0.121	11.0	0.216
1.00	0.132	12.0	0.218
1.10	0.135	12.5	0.219
1.20	0.130	14.0	0.227
1.30	0.140	15.0	0.229
1.40	0.143	16.0	0.231
1.50	0.145	17.0	0.232
1.60	0.147	18.0	0.233
1.70	0.149	19.0	0.234
1.80	0.150	22.0	0.241
1.90	0.151	25.0	0.248
2.00	0.152	30.0	0.254
3.00	0.170	33.0	0.258
3.50	0.175	35.0	0.263
4.00	0.180	40.0	0.267
4.10	0.180	45.0	0.270
4.50	0.183	50.0	0.280
4.90	0.185	55.0	0.282
5.00	0.189	60.0	0.285
		70.0	0.291

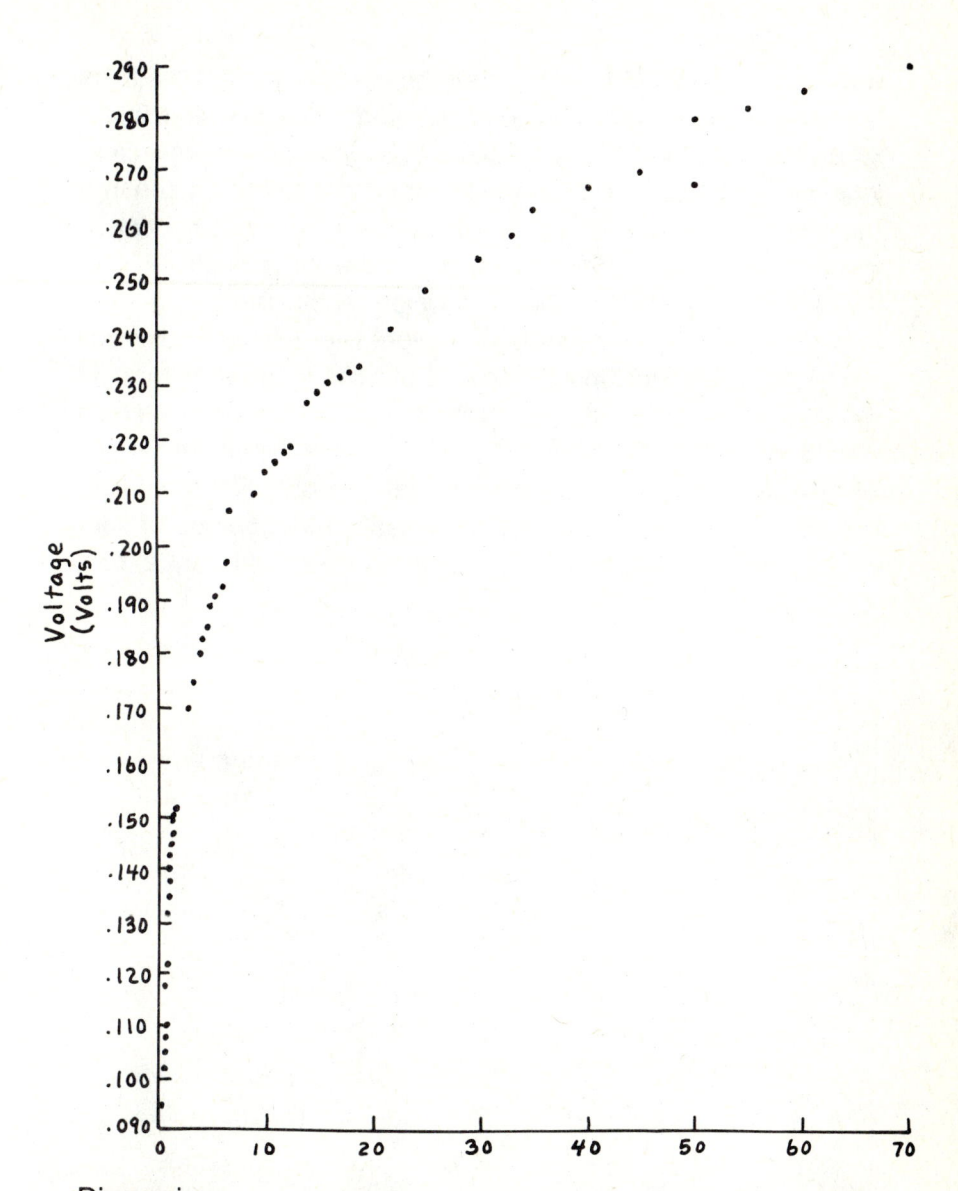

Discussion

The accuracies of the intensity and voltage readings on table A are from the multimeter and lightmeter booklets.

At the same time that the voltage and intensity readings were made a current reading was also made. This was so the voltage could be multiplied by the current to get energy, then to convert ergs to examine the characteristics of the solar cell in ergs per square centimeter. But the current readings were so erratic that they were not used. The reason for the irregular current readings is not known as they were taken at the same time therefore in the same conditions as the voltage/intensity readings were made. Another idea was to convert the intensity in footcandle to energy to compare input to output but this also became a mess because of the fact that at different intensities, the wavelength of light changes, thus changing the conversion factor of energy. What could have been done was to put a light filter over the solar cell light/light meter combination so that only one wavelength could get through. Then a conversion factor for that wavelength could have been used. Other ways to improve on the experiment would be to make the container better so that it would keep more light out and/or run it in a darker room. A less crude method of controlling the intensity could make the experiment run a little smoother.

STUDY QUESTIONS

1. Although it is usually a mistake to equate the length of a paper to how successfully it addressed the assignment, in the case of David's report the equation seems valid. What information do Tonda and Eric provide in their reports that David fails to provide?

2. Identify three places in the report where the language shifts in tone from formal to informal.

3. If you were helping David revise this paper, what would you encourage him to do with paragraph 1?

4. David doesn't seem to know how to punctuate correctly. How would you alter the punctuation in his last paragraph?

PHYSICS ASSIGNMENT 3

Course: **Intermediate Physics for Sophomore Majors**

> *Research and write a paper on solar cell technology. Your paper should cover the following areas: basic physical theory, history and development, structure and materials, types and characteristics, practical uses, state of the art, and future prospects. Include a list of references cited and a bibliography of both cited and uncited sources.*

Analysis of Physics Assignment 3

The goal of this assignment is to give students an overview of solar cell technology and to familiarize them with source material on the subject. The papers that students write will necessarily have broad viewpoints. Because the instructor has required the students to cover several different facets of the solar cell, students must resist focusing on only one.

If you were confronted with this assignment, you might wonder how you could make your paper distinctive when everyone else in the class will be writing on the same subject, covering similar points in the analysis and discussion. The answer is twofold. First, the more detailed your initial research, the more you will have to say. Students who do less research will have correspondingly less to say. Second, a key to this assignment is the last part, "future prospects." It is in this section that you would engage in interpreting the information you've collected, and your interpretation will be unique and therefore individual if you make it sufficiently thoughtful. In this regard, by avoiding the temptation to express what first comes to mind (which is what some students will do), you would be able to state something interesting and readable that will make your paper stand out.

It seems worth noting that the assignment says nothing about the kind of sources students should use. Consequently, students could draw on popular publications such as *Time* and *Newsweek*, because there is no explicit prohibition against them. There is, however, an implicit prohibition that the teacher is likely to take as a given. Solar cell technology has been discussed in *Time* as well as scholarly science journals, but because this is an intermediate course, students will be on safer ground if they refer to published scientific scholarship whenever possible. Simply quoting these specialized sources, however, will lead to a dull paper, one that won't adequately reflect what students have learned about the topic. They will therefore want to summarize complex material and to define technical terms specific to the field. The summaries and the definitions will provide revealing clues as to how well students grasp the material, which is what the teacher wants to know. The finished product will be a paper midway between a popular magazine article and a piece of scholarly research.

This assignment has an inherent danger because of the way the teacher has listed the various parts to address in the paper. That is, it could easily lead students to produce disjointed writing as they move from one section to the next. On assignments like this, students can best avoid disjointed writing by first developing a thesis or argument that ties the various parts together. For example, students could argue that solar power was a dream that appears to have died, which would allow them to discuss each of the required sections in detail while always relating the discussion to the thesis. In addition, effective transitions throughout will further help tie the paper together.

Most important, students will want to illustrate to their teacher—clearly the audience for this paper—that they can use the language of physics with ease.

Guide for Reading

Steve's paper is slightly above average because it includes ample details and because it is easy to read. We don't have to struggle, for example, with numerous surface errors, although you may find his faulty punctuation distracting. As you read, ask yourself if Steve adequately addresses the last part of the assignment, future prospects of solar cells, even though he identifies future prospects as one of the focuses of the paper. In addition, pay particular attention to Steve's references.

A General Discussion of Solar Cells

Steve W. (a sophomore)

SAMPLE PHYSICS PAPER 7

    The purpose of this essay is to give a general background of the history and development of solar cells; and to discuss some of their characteristics, uses, and future prospects. Solar cells work by a principle called the photoelectric effect. In this process, sunlight is converted directly into electricity. This effect was first discovered by Becquerel in selenium in 1839.[1] The process by which the photoelectric effect takes place occurs when a sufficiently energetic photon of light energy is absorbed causing the release of an electron in certain materials. The freed electron moves away from its parent atom, leaving a hole in its previous position.[2] After a time the electron loses its extra energy and falls back into a hole. In order to prevent this recombination, photovoltaic materials have junctions of modified semiconductor PV materials that produce an electrical potential across the cell.[3] A junction is produced when single crystal silicon of ultra-high purity is doped through its bulbs with arsenic to produce n-type silicon. The surface of a wafer is subsequently doped with boron to produce p-type silicon. This forms a pn-junction solar cell.[4] Another type of solar cell is called a pin-junction. In this cell, one layer is made "n-type" by introducing atoms that contain one more valence electron than do the silicon atoms. The other side is made "p-type" by doping the silicon with atoms having one fewer electron. When doped the layers are assembled around an undoped or "i-type" layer, whose excess electrons____ on the p side, which gives the p region a net negative charge. Excess holes move in the opposite direction, making the n side positively charged.[5]

    The first photovoltaic cells were produced at Bell Laboratories in 1958 and were only a laboratory curiosity—superfluous when compared to cheap and plentiful fossil fuels. They didn't find real use until the 1960 space program was established. Weight, not cost, loomed as the major concern.[6] The main problems that made solar cells uneconomical were the expensive production procedures and the low energy output which made for an uncompetitively high cost for the energy produced by the cells. Also a poor method of storing excess electricity has kept photovoltaic energy at a relatively high cost per watt compared to fossil fuels.

However, with the space program, the problem was in finding an energy source that didn't take up much space or weigh a large amount. With solar cells, satellites could be powered by a virtually endless amount of power. And the sun's energy is alot stronger outside of the earth's atmosphere (about 1000 W on earth and 1400 in outer space).[7]

Of the solar cells being used, Silicon is the most widely used material. Single-crystal silicon solar cells are created by growing a single silicon crystal of ultra-pure silicon. The crystal is thin cut into thin wafers; impurities are then diffused into the top of each cell to provide a junction that separates the electrical charges. Electrical contacts attached to the top and bottom of the cell provide a circuit through which the electrons can flow. An antireflecting coating is added to the top layer to minimize the energy lost due to reflected light.[8]

Gallium arsenide is another hopeful photovoltaic, but it is far more expensive than silicon and it also has a far greater theoretical efficiency, especially when coupled with concentrating collectors. Its efficiencies of 19 percent remain constant even at 1700 X the sun. These cells also maintain high efficiencies even at the high temperatures generated in concentrating systems. Gallium arsenide is something of a rare material, and is also toxic.[9]

Another form of silicon solar cell is the amorphous solar cell. The amorphous cells don't have the crystalline structure of single crystal cells; their atom structure is disorganized. Amorphous materials can be much thinner and absorb more light than crystalline silicon; production is far easier too.[10]

Some work is on modifications of the standard silicon solar cell. A joint project of National Patent development Corp and MIT involves a vertical juncture cell. The vertical juncture cell has many junctions sandwiched together. The junctions are parallel to incoming light—output from each multi-junction cell can be as great as 10 volts.[11]

Solar cells have a lot of practical applications. Their main use on earth is to supply energy to equipment that requires a self-contained, long-lasting supply of power (for example buoys and remote signalling and data gathering devices). Also solar cells, when used in large panels can supply power to run homes and other electrical equipment. The main problem with solar cells is that they work very poorly when concentrated in large numbers. They work best when applied at the site where the electricity is needed. One of the more popular home uses of solar cells is in combination with solar heating systems which cool the cells and heat water by running pipes along the solar panels.

At this time, however, the most common use of photovoltaic cells is in outerspace. Because of the restraints on weight, solar cells play a major role in the space program. Solar cells are used by the hundreds of thousands to provide power for satellites. Even without any technological breakthrough solar cells became a major part of the space industry because they could supply electricity for long periods of time and were relatively light-weight as compared to the number of batteries that would be needed to supply the same amount of power.

Some of the more current developments in solar cell technology include the use of stacked solar cells to absorb a greater proportion of the light spectrum. By adjusting the placement of the junction a solar cell can be adapted to absorb different spectra of light. In the stack method, amorphous cells are adjusted to absorb different spectra of light and then stacked on one another so that the light reaching each one was the wavelength it was adapted to absorb. Another form of stacked solar cell uses a combination of amorphous silicon and gallium arsenide. This type of cell was reported to have reached an efficiency of 31 percent.[12]

Also the use of lenses to concentrate sunlight onto solar cells is one that holds high prospects. In an experiment at Stanford University, an efficiency of 27.5 percent was reached using concentrated sunlight.[13] This process, when used with stacked solar cells allows for efficiencies that are well above the theoretical efficiencies of single solar cells. Still, the obstacle that remains to impede solar cells being used on a competitive scale with other sources of energy is the cost. When a means to produce solar cells cheaply is developed, they will certainly become the energy source of the major power users of the world.

Bibliography

Ashley, Steven. "New Life for Solar?" *Popular Science.* May 1989, pp. 117–121, 155–158.

Best, D. W. "Solar Cells: Still a Tough Sell," *Sierra.* May/June 1988, pp. 27–29.

Boer, K. *Photovoltaics and Materials.* (The American Section of the International Solar Energy Society: Cape Canaveral, Florida, 1976).

Halacy, D. S. *The Coming Age of Solar Energy* (Harper & Row: New York, 1973).

Hanakawa, Y. "Photovoltaic Power." *Scientific American.* April 1987, pp. 80–92.

McDermott, J. "What Ever Happened to Solar Cells?" *Popular Science.* January 1984, pp. 60–61.

Meinel, Aden B. and Marjorie P. *Applied Solar Energy: An Introduction.* (Addison-Wesley: Reading, Mass., 1977).

Nordwell, B. D. "Efficient Thin-Film Solar Cells Revive Interest in Space Uses," *Aviation Weekly and Space Technology.* June, 1987, p. 106.

Norman, C. "A Cloudy Forecast for Solar Cells," *Science.* October 19, 1984 pp. 319–320.

Peterson, I. "Pinpointing Solar-cell Efficiency" *Science News.* April 26, 1986, p. 261.

Kassler, Helen S . "Photovoltaics: Readying a Technology," *The Solar Age Resources Book,* ed. Martin MacPhillips (Everest House Publishers: New York, 1979).

Physics   185

> **STUDY QUESTIONS**
>
> 1. Compare Steve's discussion of solar cells in paragraph 1 with Eric's discussion of theory in Sample Paper 6. What similarities and differences do you detect? On the basis of your analysis, what conclusion can you reach in regard to this part of the students' presentations?
>
> 2. In some types of writing, it is appropriate to state at the outset the purpose of a paper, as Steve does in his first sentence. What are some advantages and disadvantages of this approach?
>
> 3. A measure of success for a paper like this one is to ask yourself how much you learned from reading it and then to try to apply that knowledge. Given that Steve did not provide a discussion of future prospects, can you provide it for him, using what you learned from reading his paper?
>
> 4. One of the more serious problems with Steve's paper is the way he presents his documentation. Using the style guide provided in "Writing in the Life and Applied Sciences," describe what is wrong with Steve's documentation.

Guide for Reading

David's paper is interesting for a number of reasons, and it is clearly a very good, although not quite outstanding, response to the assignment. One of its strongest features is the way it weaves numerous technical details into a thoroughly interesting narrative, a characteristic that suggests David knows his material so well that he doesn't have to spend much energy trying to juggle these two components of the paper.

The writing is clear and readable, even though David could have improved it by doing a better proofreading job to eliminate the numerous punctuation errors. In fact, these errors are one factor that keep the paper from being outstanding. Another is the way David approached the future prospects of solar cells. He spends much more time on this topic than Steve did, but he drifts in and out of a discussion of the future and the present. An outstanding paper would more clearly differentiate the two. Can you see why?

SAMPLE PHYSICS PAPER 8

The History and Advancement of the Solar Cell

David C. (a sophomore)

In the early 1970's the Organization of Petroleum ___ Countries, intent on boosting prices and winning political concessions, drastically raised the price for a barrel of crude oil. At the same time these countries reduced the amount of oil shipped to the Western World. Following these decisions by OPEC the affected countries began searching for other means to produce energy. The solar cell, which had been developed in the 1950's, underwent a revival in the Western World. "Almost overnight, the solar cell was embraced by politicians and corporate planners, ballyhooed by the media, and burdened with impossible expectations."[1] As previously stated the solar cell had been developed in the 1950's, but due to the seemingly inexhaustible amount of crude oil the solar cell was reduced to service on the space craft used by nations for exploration.

In the following paragraphs the development of the solar cell will be explored. Other areas to be explored in this paper will be advances made in the production and use of the solar cell, and the way solar cells work. The brunt of the paper will deal with advances made in solar cells.

Basically, a photovoltaic cell converts sunlight into electrical power. This cell is unique in that it generates a voltage and current under the action of light. No battery is required to produce the voltage or current. The solar cell is made primarily of silicon, which is the most abundant element on earth. Unfortunately, in its naturally occuring state, silicon contains a number of contaminants that would seriously reduce solar cell performance. Because of the contaminants the ore must be refined extensively before it can be used. In fact, by the time the processed mineral reaches the manufacturing plant, in the form of polysilicon rocks, it must be at least 99.9% pure. It is then necessary to convert the polysilicon rocks into a perfectly structured crystal. A major problem arises when the crystal has to be enlarged to be used in the photovoltaic cell. The solution to this problem is to grow the crystal.

The main problem with solar cells is efficiency. In the 1960's an efficiency of 14% was thought to be very good. In fact, many of the industry's pioneers proclaimed that by the year 2000 America would have 30,000 megawatts of clean, reliable and inexpensive photovoltaic power in place, which is the equivalent of twenty-seven Seabrook nuclear power plants.[2]

The 1980's have been very tough on the solar cell industry within our society. Many factors have contributed to the downfall of our country's solar cell industry. The first reason has to do with the unstable atmosphere in the Middle East. This instability lead to the demise of OPEC. Oil was sold at cut rate prices that created a glut of oil in this country. Another reason, which is directly connected to the instability in the Middle East, is the conservation of fuel by the public. After the "oil crisis" of the 1970's Americans began to cut back on the consumption of oil. Industry, especially automobile manufacturers, began to introduce products that did not use as much fuel. A third reason for the demise of the solar cell industry was the Reagan administration's decision to stop funding the solar cell industry. Many renewable-energy businesses suffered during the Reagan years. Due to these obstacles other countries took the lead in solar cell production and development. "From 1983 to 1986 U.S. sales slipped six percent, while Japan quietly took over as the world's largest solar cell producer."[3]

During the turbulent 1980's the solar cell industry within our country suffered greatly in size. What the industry lost in size though it gained in technology. Andrew Krantz, the Department of Energy's photovoltaic branch chief, says technological advances have enabled the industry to keep its footing despite the slump. "We made as much progress in 1987 as we did any year in the last ten."[4]

What does the future hold for the solar cell industry? Prices for solar cells have dropped twenty-nine percent over the last five years, and there is no need to anticipate that this trend will change any time in the near future. In the future new markets will be opened for the industry. Ray Watts, a research engineer at Battelle Pacific Northwest Laboratory, says photovoltaics has become the system of choice where hookup to a utility grid is impossible or prohibitively expensive.[5] The future also looks bright for the industry when expansion is mentioned. Many solar cell optimists envision a 100-megawatt or larger photovoltaic systems being used for utility peak power.

The development of the solar cell has grown dramatically since their introduction in the 1950's. Today solar cells have an efficiency exceeding 30%. This was simply a dream one decade ago. The future looks even brighter for the industry, and even though there are many hurdles for the American industry to overcome the technological advances promise a source of energy that no other can match.

Developments and advances in the solar cell industry occur at a pace that is quite unbelievable. Research done in this enthusiastic field could easily fill the shelves of the library. As previously stated this paper is mainly about the development and advances made in photovoltaics. Therefore the remainder of this paper will explore such avenues as thin film solar cells, 30% efficiency of the solar cell, the use of laser blasts to speed up solar cell production, the development of a Gallium Arsenide solar cell, and a photovoltaic panel that could make solar power economical by 1990.

The most intriguing advent in solar cell development is the production of thin-film photovoltaics. One of these thin-film solar cells offers high reliability, low cost, and low weight electrical power generation for space applications by the early 1990's. This particular solar cell was developed by the Boeing Airspace Company. Thus far the ploycrystalline cell has shown an efficiency of almost 12% in tests under simulated terrestrial sunlight. Under simulated space conditions the cell showed an efficiency of 10.4%. The one square centimeter cell produced an open voltage of 440 millivolts and a short-circuit current of about 39 milliamperes at 25 degrees Celsius under xenon-light illumination.[6] The cost of this thin-film solar cell has been estimated to be as low as fifty cents per watt. Solar cells produced for space based power systems however would cost much more. According to Boeing the radiation tolerance of this particular cell is considerably greater than the silicon and gallium-arsenide solar cells.

Another thin-film solar cell has been developed by ARCO Solar Inc. This solar cell, which has just recently been developed, has been billed as one of the biggest breakthroughs in the history of solar energy. The efficiency of this solar cell is at least three percentage points better than any other solar cell produced just a few months ago. This leap in solar cell development came about because of the use of a relatively new material. "ARCO Solar reached 11.2% efficiency in a one-square-foot copper-indium-diselenide cell."[7]

The CIS cell has one more significant feature. A solar cell made of silicon will degrade when exposed to sunlight, thus losing 10 to 20% of their efficiency. The CIS cell will remain stable when exposed to sunlight however. "This means that the best available thin-film silicon cells can be expected to perform at 8% efficiency or less, as compared to a stable 11.2% for CIS.

Five layers make up the CIS solar cells. There is a layer of molybdenum which serves as an electrical conduction layer. Next comes a layer of copper-indium-diselenide and a 0.03 micrometer film of cadmium sulfide. The top layer is comprised of zinc oxide that is transparent to sunlight, so that light can pass through to the cadmium sulfide and the copper-indium-diselenide layers, but that is electrically conductive to serve as the second electrical contact layer.[8]

An advancement that has been widely publicized is an efficiency rating of over 30% for a solar cell. Scientists, stacking two different solar cells, achieved an efficiency of 31%, a full 2% better than the previous best solar cell. One of the solar cells was produced by Varian Associates Inc., and the other was produced by Stanford University. Unfortunately, the 30% efficiency rating is not economically feasible. The cost of solar power depends on two factors. The first is the efficiency of the solar cell. The higher the efficiency, the fewer solar cells are necessary to produce the same amount of electricity.[9] The second factor is the cost of the solar cell, and the cost to put them into operation. The main problem is that the two factors work against each other. The higher the efficiency, the more expensive the solar cell. At this point the solar cell that produced the 30% efficiency rating is impracticable. The Department of Energy estimates that the cost per kilowatt must come down from the 30 to 40 cents per kilowatt-hour to 12 cents per kilowatt-hour before utilities turn to solar power.

Conventionally, solar cells have been produced by "doping" the silicon surface with chemical impurities to form two different, adjacent semiconductor layers. There is a problem with this process in that the "doping" degrades the critical surface structure of the cell. "A problem with polysilicon is that it cannot stand high temperatures. It develops serious structural faults when heated by the diffusion process commonly used for doping."[10] Researchers are using a laser to by-pass the problem. This technique is faster, cheaper, an it avoids heating the polysilicon which would spoil its crystalline structure. The laser has an energy of one or two joules, pulsed to last for only 25 billionths of a second. The researchers in Amsterdam are trying to work on screen printing. This process could improve current collection from polysilicon cells, which would be an important step in bringing solar cells closer to low cost mass production.[11]

In 1985, the development of a solar cell by Varian Associates Inc., offered high-performance for space applications. The 2X2 centimeter cell produced an efficiency of 21%. The maximum efficiency of that time attainable in space was 14.5%. The solar cell also offered more resistance to heat. It was estimated that the efficiency of the cell, when exposed to sunlight, would drop to 19%. Silicon cells under the same conditions decrease to an efficiency of 9%. The gallium-arsenide cell would enable the cells to operate at higher orbits in space.[12]

The gallium-arsenide cell would also have a higher tolerance to radiation in space. In addition to this ability, the cell has the potential to be thinner and lighter. With an increased power output this would allow the reduction in the solar array.

Also in 1985, the Atlantic Richfield Company began the production of a solar cell that would enable solar electricity to compete with kilowatts from fossil and nuclear power stations as early as 1990. The ARCO Solar lab sprays silicon in a gaseous state directly onto a sheet of glass. Little silicon is needed in this process, thus ARCO proclaimed that the new solar cell would be less expensive to make, yet retain the same generating capacity. ARCO, in 1985, planned to use tinted photovoltaic modules in skyscraper windows that would help power lights and office equipment.[13]

In summation, the solar cell industry has grown by leaps and bounds in the past decade. Monumental discoveries five years ago are of little importance today. Efficiency ratings of 20% have been surpassed by 10% today. In this paper the development and history of the solar cell was explored. The solar cell industry is wide open in this country, as well as every other advanced nation in the world. Andrew Krantz, the Department of Energy's photovoltaics branch chief, may have put it best when he said, "Decision-makers sense there's an enormous payoff down the road."[14]

Endnotes

1) *Sierra;* 73:27–29. May/June 1988

2) *Sierra;* 73:27–29. May/June 1988

3) *Sierra;* 73:27–29. May/June 1988

4) *Sierra;* 73:27–29. May/June 1988

5) *Sierra;* 73:27–29. May/June 1988

5a) *Aviation and Space Technology;* Page 159. January 13, 1986

6) *Aviation and Space Technology;* Page 159. January 13, 1986

7) *Scientific American;* 259: 98–99. August 19, 1988

8) *Scientific American;* 259: 98–99. August 19, 1988

9) *Science;* Page 900. August 19, 1987

10) *Popular Science;* 220:93. April 1982

11) *Popular Science;* 220:93. April 1982

12) *Aviation and Space Technology;* 133: 199. December 2, 1985.

13) *Fortune;* 111:74. February 4, 1985

14) *Sierra;* 73:27–29. May/June 1988

STUDY QUESTIONS

1. Some readers might object that David's paper is written exclusively for a general audience, that it isn't sufficiently professional. Assuming this criticism to be valid, what changes would you make to give the paper a more professional tone?

2. David attributes much of the slump in solar-cell research and application to lower oil prices and "the demise" of OPEC. Based on the information he presents, is another interpretation possible? If so, what is it?

3. David's paper has some organizational difficulties that occasionally make it difficult to follow. Look first, for example, at paragraphs 6 and 7, and then look at the paragraphs that follow. Can you identify the organizational problem here? How would you propose fixing it?

4. Compare David's list of references to the style guide provided in "Writing in the Life and Applied Sciences." Identify the problems you see in David's paper and then describe what effect these problems are likely to have on a reader.

Writing Assignments

1. Assume you've been asked to help one of your professors write a study guide for undergraduate physics majors. Your task is to write an overview of nuclear energy technology. Use the subheadings suggested in the assignment above: Basic Physical Theory, History and

Physics

Development, Structure and Materials, Types and Characteristics, Practical Uses, State of the Art, and Future Prospects. Your overview should be no more than 7 pages.

2. After rereading Sample Paper 7 and Sample Paper 8, write a position paper arguing *for* increased funding for solar cell research. To make your argument more effective, provide research data that support your position. Assume your audience is a group of undergraduate science majors.

3. After rereading Sample Paper 7 and Sample Paper 8, write a position paper arguing *against* increased funding for solar cell research. To make your argument more effective, provide research data that support your position. Assume your audience is your local representative, who has introduced a bill to fund such research.

Part Two: SOCIAL SCIENCES

WRITING IN THE SOCIAL SCIENCES

Overview

Intellectual disciplines may be defined as different ways of looking at and trying to reach an understanding of the human experience. Each brings a set of goals, assumptions, critical tools, standards of proof, and methodologies to the enterprise. In related fields, certain commonalities exist, and such is the case for psychology, political science, and anthropology—the disciplines in this text that together are classified under the social sciences. These disciplines all interpret facts to better understand the world, facts that come primarily from direct observations of people, institutions, and cultures. For this reason, the social sciences are called empirical disciplines.

Because there are so many ways to look at human experience, and because one's perspective influences what one understands an experience to be, social scientists are much concerned with "generalizability." They place great emphasis on removing possible sources of bias, in an effort to differentiate between knowledge of how people in general behave and knowledge of how a single person behaves. One result of this emphasis is that the majority of the research in the social sciences has traditionally dealt with groups of people rather than with individuals. It is widely assumed that studying individuals may tell us very much about a person but very little about people. Another result is that many social scientists make serious use of statistics, which depersonalize data, thereby helping eliminate emotions and personal values—strong sources of bias—associated with behavior. Statistics also provide some estimate of how generalizable certain quantifiable behaviors may be.

We don't want to suggest, however, that only quantifiable work is accepted in these disciplines. The social sciences have a long tradition of qualitative research that relies on keen observations of behaviors that can't be converted into numbers. Most beginning college courses actually focus first on training students to be accurate observers rather than skillful statisticians. Teachers understand that quantitative skills aren't particularly useful unless they are informed by qualitative ones.

In the social sciences, *validity* and *reliability* are important considerations in any interpretation process. Validity issues are concerned with whether the facts at hand are indeed representative and with whether they have been measured or observed accurately. Reliability issues are concerned with the degree of consistency inherent in measuring, observing, or analyzing facts. In other words, if ten different people measure a particular feature of human experience the same way, will they get similar results? If they do, then the measurement is reliable.

We can differentiate between two kinds of activities in the social sciences: theoretical and empirical. Theoretical activities are most easily described as efforts to build models of how the world operates. Theoreticians recognize that the world is too complex for any of us to understand very well until we have an appropriate metaphor that allows us to translate complicated behaviors into simpler ones. Their models provide the metaphors. For example, you may have heard or read about how the human brain is like a computer. It stores and retrieves information in certain ways, has "on-off" switches called neurotransmitters, and so forth. In reality, there is very little similarity between a computer and a human brain, but the comparison nevertheless fits our needs and helps us understand something of how the brain works. It is a simplifying metaphor. Before the development of computers, other metaphors were used throughout history, including those comparing the brain to clocks and oranges.

Empirical activities commonly are efforts to substantiate a given theoretical model. For this reason, compositions in the social sciences tend to begin with a summary of the model the writer is using. Analysis and interpretation take place within the framework of the model. Suppose, for example, that you are taking a psychology class in which you learn about "behaviorism," a model that describes human behavior largely in terms of stimulus/response mechanisms. That is, a person receives a stimulus of some sort that evokes a specific response. You decide to test the model, so you go to the campus quad to make an observation. There you see a student sitting under an apple tree. An apple falls from the tree and hits the student on the head, and then the student says "Ouch" and rubs the spot where the apple struck. On the basis of your theoretical model, you would be inclined to interpret your observation as indeed substantiating the stimulus/response mechanisms of behaviorism: the stimulus (the apple) evoked a response ("Ouch").

One observation, of course, involving a single person, isn't enough to validate a model, so a goal of social scientists is to perform numerous observations with many people in an effort to make a thorough assessment. Matters are complicated by the existence of other, often competing, models. In most cases, researchers eventually encounter some phenomenon that a given model can't account for but that an alternative can. At that point, the model is either modified or abandoned as part of the ongoing effort to reach a broad understanding of the human experience.

As you can see, there is a definite *method* to writing in the social sciences. It involves selecting a theoretical framework and then asking a question about human behavior that you believe can be answered in terms of that framework. This step is known as "formulating a hypothesis." To answer your question, you observe, test, measure, and so on, to generate "facts," or data, that are then interpreted in the context of the framework. The more questions you try to answer in a given project, the more difficult it is to control all the many variables that can bias your information, so most researchers limit the scope of their individual studies. As a result, work in the social sciences is usually very focused, evaluating relatively small sets of information. Through careful analyses, writers make interpretations to add to a larger picture that models reality.

You should also be able to recognize in this overview some clear (and intertwined) assumptions and standards of proof that govern much of what you can do as a writer in the social sciences. For example, it is evident that emotions, or what we might think of as personal involvement, should not play a part in this kind of writing. Indeed, the effort to eliminate such involvement in every way possible led to the convention of passive voice in social science writing, where actions, and therefore sentences, often have no obvious agent: "The subjects were prepared for electrode placement" rather than "I prepared the subjects for electrode placement." Other conventions regarding language include a preference for such words as "suggest," "indicate," and "demonstrate," when explaining what data tell us about human behavior. The word "proves" isn't accepted because it's assumed in the social sciences that no interpretations of or conclusions about behavior are perfectly generalizable. Thus, conclusions must always be deemed tentative. Words such as "extremely" and "very" that intensify analyses or conclusions ("The correlations were *extremely* positive") are also considered unacceptable, because they reflect the personal element.

Even though social science writing may be depersonalized in an effort to make it *neutral*, it is nevertheless argumentative. It requires proofs that substantiate the claims you will make as part of the interpretation process. In advanced writing, such proofs come from the design of a project—that is, from the methods used to collect information. As we suggested above, some methods are more acceptable than others; for example, information gathered from a large group of people is generally viewed as being a more credible source of facts for interpretation than information gathered from a case study of one person. Proofs can also come from the specific procedures used to analyze data. If a writer uses a statistical procedure inappropriate for a given body of facts, his or her subsequent interpretation of those facts may well be dismissed.

In the writing assignments you are likely to encounter during your first couple of years as a college student, the usual standard of proof will be how effectively you can interpret facts through the filter of a given theoretical model. Your knowledge of the model is being tested, in other words. Another standard of proof, however, will be your ability to adopt the neutral language of the social sciences and to distance yourself from your facts and the subsequent interpretations. Your teachers will view this ability as a significant first step in understanding what writing in the social sciences is about and are likely to view your papers more positively than they might otherwise. Generally, the information available through library research is not something you can rely on exclusively to support your claims, although it is usually crucial to describing the model or theory that governs your interpretations. That is, information gathered from library research should complement your own words, not replace them.

Documentation

If you use someone else's words or *ideas* to support your writing, you are obligated to provide accurate references for them, giving credit to the originators. Failure to do so constitutes plagiarism.

The documentation format used most widely in the social sciences is that found in the *Publication Manual of the American Psychological Association*

(APA). Although most teachers in sociology, anthropology, and political science ask students to use the APA or a set of very similar guidelines, a few ask students to use the Chicago style, which is also known as "Turabian," after its author. We sense that teachers are moving away from the Chicago format, however, because of its complexity. In addition, some teachers are now using the Modern Language Association (MLA) format, which we describe in Part Three. Although we drew on these published guides to offer a brief summary of the APA and Chicago formats, the summary is far from being comprehensive. We therefore recommend that you buy the guides and keep them as references. Both are published in book form and are available in most book stores.

In addition to specifying how to present references in the text of a paper and in a bibliography, the guides discuss a range of stylistic information, such as how to format quotations, when to write out a number and when to use the Arabic numeral, what to include on the title page, what size margins to use, and so forth. Note that this information is not the same in the two guides, so make certain you know which style your social science teacher expects to see in your papers.

APA

The APA style uses parenthetical citations in the text to refer readers to a list of sources at the end of the paper. This list is titled "References." Citations appear in the text as author's last name and the date of publication. On the reference page, they are in alphabetical order. All lines are double spaced, including long quotations and reference entries. Whether you are providing a direct quotation or simply a paraphrase, place the citation in parentheses. Direct quotations will include page numbers, whereas paraphrases will not.

Another characteristic of this style is that it mandates the use of the past tense, rather than the present, when reporting results of earlier studies. In this respect, the APA guidelines are very different from those most students have practiced in their writing courses, where usually only the Modern Language Association (MLA) guidelines are taught. There are significant implications in this difference that are related to the ways of knowing inherent in each discipline. Implicit in the requirement that students writing in the social sciences use the past tense is the goal of limiting universal claims. To say on the basis of a study that students *demonstrated* a particular behavior is vastly different from saying that students *demonstrate* a particular behavior. Tense therefore seems to be linked to the scientific method.

Example 1

Harris' (1990) investigation revealed strong correlations between belief systems and household artifacts. He found, for example, that people who believed in any one of the following were likely to believe in all the others: astrology, pyramid power, crystal power, reincarnation, palm reading, near-death experiences, the power of positive thinking, UFOs, karma, and the idea that humans may be the descendants of marooned aliens. Moreover, people who held these beliefs were likely to have two or more of the following in their homes: incense, candles, New Age music, ion generators, *The Prophet* by Kahlil Gibran, tofu, or a picture of Shirley MacLaine.

Example 2

Harris (1990, p. 22) reported that "the predictive power of these correlations reached .89 for this population." In this case, it would be possible to assess the beliefs, and therefore the values, of people by simply examining the contents of their living rooms.

When you have already cited a reference by name and date and then go on to provide a direct quotation afterwards, place the page number in parentheses following the quoted material. The same applies to long quotations, which are called block quotations.

Example 3

Kessler (1991) elaborated on Harris' (1990) research in an effort to determine what other factors correlated with these belief systems. She found that "intelligence did not show any correlation" (p. 98), but that level of self-confidence did. She reported, for example:

All subjects with a self-confidence rating of 10 or lower on the 20-point scale indicated moderate-to-strong belief in a range of topics generally associated with pseudo-science. This finding suggests that pseudo-scientific beliefs function to alleviate any need among the subjects to assume responsibility for their own successes and, primarily, failures. If they are not promoted, for example, it is a matter the stars decided, not their own on-the-job performance. If they are out of shape, it is a condition that can be remedied through the power of positive thinking or sitting in front of a crystal, without the demands of a regimen of exercise. In other words, their belief systems are mechanisms by which they perpetuate a denial of reality. (pp. 99–100)

Finally, if you have provided a parenthetical citation and make another reference to the same work in such a way that the connection is clear, you need not repeat the citation.

Example 4

Kessler's findings confirmed, in many respects, what van Allen (1987) reported in this study of self-confidence among religious fundamentalists and cult followers.

The examples that follow illustrate how to make entries in your list of references, which will appear at the end of your paper:

BOOKS

A Book by One Author

Hernandez, J. (1991). *Social psychology among immigrant Hispanics.* Los Angeles: Marlow House.

Two or More Books by the Same Author

Wilson, F. A. (1989a). *Death by violence: A study of apartheid in South Africa.* London: World.
Wilson, F.A. (1989b). *Racism in Israel: The sociological dimensions of institutionalized exclusion.* New York: Erlbaum.
Wilson, F. A. (1990). *The sociology of racism.* New York: Academic Press.

A Book by Two or More Authors

Fields, A., & Juarez, R. M. (1992). *Education and cognitive pathology.* Chapel Hill: University of North Carolina Press.
Waters, L. A., Fahder, J., & Campuzano, P. (1975). *Maturation rituals among Amazonia's Indians.* Berkeley: University of California Press.

A Book with an Editor

Bernbaum-Miller, E. (Ed.). (1989). *Cross-cultural eroticism*. New York: Wiley.

A Work in an Edited Volume

Goodenough, B. (1965). The isolation syndrome: Growing up in small-town America. In D. Ragasa & J. Nunez (Eds.), *Contemporary cultures* (pp. 123–178). Boston: Houghton.

A Multivolume Work

Smith, J. A. (1989). *The art of deception: Studies in abnormal psychology* (K. Swinney, Ed.). (Vol. 2). New York: Holt.

A Translation

Luria, A. (1962). *The working brain*. (F. G. Grjnjowski, Trans.). San Francisco: Jossey-Bass.

ARTICLES

Journals

Kronk, L. A. (1992). Reliability of exit polls as indicators of voter preference. *Journal of Political Science, 23*, 415–428.

Villa, J., & Small, L. (1989). Cultural variation among Mexico's Indian population. *American Anthropologist, 17*(4), 71–89.

Periodicals

Ogami, Y. Y. (1989, July). Fathers and sons. *Psychology Today*, pp. 23–26.

FILMS AND TELEVISION PROGRAMS

Weiskopf, D. (Director), & Prucha, L. (Producer). (1966). *Escape from Moscow*. [Film]. Los Angeles: Crown International Pictures.

Smith, J. (Director), & Oppenheimenn, R. (Producer). (1989). Starlight. Los Angeles: KCET.

Part Two SOCIAL SCIENCES

CHICAGO

The Chicago style is different from the APA style in some significant ways. For example, it doesn't provide in-text, parenthetical citations, and it requires two entries for each reference. The first appears as a reference footnote, and the second appears as a bibliographic entry at the end of the paper. In each case, the information conveyed is very similar; what varies is the format. In Example 1 below, you can see how the reference footnote appears at the bottom of a page of text. In Example 2, you will find the corresponding bibliographic entry:

Example 1

The move to establish a national high school curriculum has been hampered by the fact that, historically, states and in many cases local districts have been responsible for deciding what students learn in school.[1] As a consequence, the quality of education differs radically from one state to the next, even from one district to the next. It is a situation that Chester Finn, President of the National Association of Educational Progress, describes as being "a hodgepodge of texts, content, and standards that must be viewed as a complete disaster."[2]

[1]Rita Moreno Smith. *Educating America* (Los Angeles: Westwood Books, 1989), pp. 18–20.
[2]Chester Finn. "Creating a National Standard for Education," *Harvard Educational Review* 30 (May 1989): 159.

Example 2

Finn, Chester. "Creating a National Standard for Education." *Harvard Educational Review* 30 (May 1989): 159–174.
Smith, Rita Moreno. *Educating America.* Los Angeles: Westwood Books, 1989.

The Chicago style differs from the APA style in several other respects. Block quotations, for instance, are single, not double, spaced. Bibliographic entries are on a separate page, but they are titled "List of References" rather than "References."
One of the more difficult features of this format is the common use of

Latin abbreviations to direct readers to sources cited more than once. These are

> ibid. = *ibidem*, in the same place
> loc. cit. = *loco citato*, in the place cited
> op. cit. = *opere citato*, in the work cited

You should notice that the abbreviations are not italicized, and you should not underline them in your text. In addition to the above, this format uses the Latin term "idem," meaning "the same person," when referring to multiple works by the same author, as we will show below.

The rationale for using these abbreviations can be confusing, and the entire process can be most taxing and frustrating. The system is based on the *order of repeated references*. Suppose, for example, that the writer of the paper above has another reference to Chester Finn's article that immediately follows the one indicated in note 2. In this case, the second reference would be indicated by the abbreviation "ibid." If the citation is from a page different from the one first indicated, "ibid." is followed by the appropriate page number. If the writer follows that reference with one from another source, which is in turn followed by the reference to Finn's work, he or she would provide the author's last name, Finn, followed by either "loc. cit." or "op. cit." If the reference is to the same page used previously, "loc. cit." is correct. If the reference is to a different page, "op. cit." is correct and should be followed by the appropriate page number. This procedure is illustrated in the example below:

Example 3

> There is no question that reaching agreement on what a national curriculum should consist of will be a major challenge. Special interest groups abound that will try to block or influence any proposals. One of the largest of these is the National Education Association (NEA), a group that Finn says is "interested only in the next cost of living increase for its members, who don't give a fig for improving education."[3] NEA Under-Secretary Jane Gabor has recently labeled Finn's assertion "ridiculous and beneath contempt,"[4] but Finn has not wavered in his condemnation of special interest groups like the NEA, calling them a "clear and present danger to American education."[5]

---

[3]Ibid.

Part Two SOCIAL SCIENCES

[4]Jane Gabor, "The Problem with a National Curriculum," *The American Educator* 10 (October 1989): 15.
[5]Op. cit., Finn, p. 164.

The examples below illustrate how to document various sources using the Chicago style. In each instance, we give the reference footnote first, as indicated by reference number, and the bibliographic entry second.

BOOKS

A Book by One Author

[1]Rita Moreno Smith, *Educating America* (Los Angeles: Westwood Books, 1989), pp. 18–20.
Smith, Rita Moreno, *Educating America*. Los Angeles: Westwood Books, 1989.

Two or More Books by the Same Author

[2]Martin Martinez, *The American Presidency, 1900–1960* (Cambridge, MA: Harvard University Press, 1990), p. 211.
Martinez, Martin, *The American Presidency*. Cambridge, MA: Harvard University Press, 1990.
[3]Idem, *America in Transition, 1960–1975* (Cambridge, MA: Harvard University Press, 1991), p. 57.
Martinez, Martin, *America in Transition, 1960–1975*. Cambridge, MA: Harvard University Press, 1991.

A Book by Two or Three Authors

[4]Jesus Winegate and Mary McIntry, *Change in Society* (Boston: Houghton Mifflin Co., 1989), pp. 45–47.
Winegate, Jesus, and McIntry, Mary. *Change in Society*. Boston: Houghton Mifflin Co., 1989.
[5]Fred MacMurry, Edward H. Horse, and Freda Roberts, *Studies in Communication* (New York: Lawrence Erlbaum, 1990), p. 123.
MacMurry, Fred; Horse, Edward H.; and Roberts, Freda. *Studies in Communication*. New York: Lawrence Erlbaum, 1990.

A Book by More than Three Authors

[6]Mary A. Popins, et al., *Umbrellas in Nineteenth Century England* (Chicago: Waterhouse Press, 1987), pp. 22–23.

Popins, Mary A.; Mental, Jonathan; Wilson, Ted C.; Glenn, Cheryl. *Umbrellas in Nineteenth Century England*. Chicago: Waterhouse Press, 1987.

A Book with an Editor

[7]Roberto Duran, ed., *Boxing as Social Commentary* (Panama City, Panama: Republica, 1988), p. 323.

Duran, Roberto, ed. *Boxing as Social Commentary*. Panama City, Panama: Republica, 1988.

A Work in an Edited Volume

[8]Raisa Gorbachev, "Affairs of State: Affairs of Fashion," in *Significant Statements of the Twentieth Century*, ed. Edward M. Koch (New York: Scandalous Press, 1992), pp. 169–170.

Gorbachev, Raisa, "Affairs of State: Affairs of Fashion." In *Significant Statements of the Twentieth Century*, edited by Edward M. Koch. New York: Scandalous Press, 1992.

A Multivolume Work

[9]Willard Scott, *How to Make a Fortune by Being a Clown*, 10 vols. (New York: CBS Books 1988–1989), vol. 2: *From Bozo to Ronald McDonald: The Lean Years*, p. 643.

Scott, Willard. *How to Make a Fortune by Being a Clown*, 10 vols. (New York: CBS Books, 1988–1989), vol. 2: *From Bozo to Ronald McDonald: The Lean Years*, p. 643.

A Translation

[10]Boris Spassky, *Chess and Politics*, trans. Bobbi Fisher (New York: Bantam Books, 1978), p. 36.

Spassky, Boris. *Chess and Politics*. Translated by Bobbi Fisher. New York: Bantam Books, 1978.

ARTICLES

Journals

[11]Edward J. H. K. Simpson, "Latin America: Revolving Dictators," *South* 58 (May 1990): 178–180.

Simpson, Edward J. H. K. "Latin America: Revolving Dictators," *South* 58 (May 1990): 178–180.

Periodicals

[12]Linda Reed-Johnson-Greely-Hope, "The Good Earth: Death of a Rain Forest," *National Review*, June 1991, pp. 75–91.

Reed-Johnson-Greely-Hope, Linda. "The Good Earth: Death of a Rain Forest," *National Review*, June 1991.

FILMS AND TELEVISION PROGRAMS

[13]*Escape from Moscow*, dir. Douglas Weiskopf. Crown International Pictures, 1966.

Escape from Moscow. Directed by Douglas Weiskopf. Crown International Pictures, 1966.

[14]PBS, "The Universe," 31 May 1989, "Starlight," Austin Williams, narrator.

PBS, "The Universe," 31 May 1989, "Starlight," Austin Williams, narrator.

5 Psychology

INTRODUCTION TO WRITING IN PSYCHOLOGY

Most undergraduate students enroll in an introductory psychology course at some point in their college study. Many of these courses require extensive writing, in forms ranging from the familiar essay exam to perhaps an in-depth analysis of a psychological case study. Instructors of undergraduate psychology courses use these writing assignments to introduce students to the subjects the discipline studies—individual personality and behavior—and the methods psychologists use to investigate these subjects. In addition, many teachers hope to familiarize students with some of the conventions associated with writing in psychology, which are often quite different from the conventions used in humanistic disciplines such as English, history, and philosophy.

In an introductory psychology course, students learn in a variety of ways about the methods psychologists use. Many instructors require students to participate in experiments run by the department; others allow students to construct their own experiments and to write up the results. In addition, instructors may ask students to summarize and evaluate an experimental research report published in one of the field's scholarly journals. All of these tasks acquaint students with the procedures psychologists use to collect data, and they allow students to comprehend more forcefully the importance of observation, analysis, and the exact use of evidence to support a hypothesis. In every respect, they allow students to use writing as a means of learning more about psychology.

You will note that the assignments included in this chapter ask students to use different source materials and different forms to shape this material. In the case of the first assignment, the instructor asks the students to watch a videotape and then to draw on class readings, lectures, and discussions to compose an essay on the use of objective language in reporting observations. The second assignment requires students to summarize and evaluate an experiment in group dynamics that was reported in the *Journal of Applied Psychology*. The third assignment provides students with an individual psychological case study to summarize and diagnose.

Purpose and audience dictate the form that writing takes. The first assignment encourages students to use personal experience and asks them to direct their writing to an audience of high school students. The writing produced from this assignment is informal and accessible to a general audience. The second and third assignments engage writers in activities common to professionals in the field and require them to use two different formal structures particular to scholars in the social sciences.

PSYCHOLOGY ASSIGNMENT 1

Course: **Introduction to Psychology**

Aim: *Observation lies at the core of psychological research and practice. Yet objective observation is not easy, as you will see in the process of preparing a short paper. The aim of this initial assignment is thus to permit you to analyze the process of behavioral observation. You will learn about the difficulties of making observations that are devoid of interpretations and evaluations. Moreover, you will learn to describe your evaluations in "neutral" language, thereby minimizing interpretive bias and maximizing objectivity.*

Overview: *There are three phases to this project: observation, discussion, written report.*

Observation: *To supplement our in-class discussion of research methods, you will make a behavioral observation of an infant interacting first with her mother and then with a stranger. We have placed a videotape (approximately 6 minutes per interaction) of these interactions on reserve in the Non-Print Materials Collection in the Undergraduate Library. Your job in the next two weeks is to check out this tape, watch it several times, and record what you observe. Specifically, for each of the two interactions (infant-mother; infant-stranger) you are to use the first two minutes as a "warm-up period" and then to describe the interaction that takes place in the next three minutes. You may transform your raw observations into paragraph form, but do not embellish them or add to them in any way.*

Discussion: *Bring your notes to your Psychology 10 discussion section. At that time, we will break down into smaller groups to note similarities and differences in observations.*

Written report: *Based upon the class discussion of the observations, write a 3–5 page typewritten paper in which you describe what you have learned about observation. You may supplement class discussion by drawing upon what you have learned from the lectures, reading assignments, and your own personal experience in viewing the tape. In the paper, you should reflect on the difficulties of making an observation, comparing objective and interpretive reporting. Assume that you are writing for high school seniors who are thinking about enrolling in a psychology class next year.*

Analysis of Psychology Assignment 1

This assignment, given in the early weeks of an introductory psychology course, asks students to consider a writing task typical to the field: reporting an observation.

Note that the assignment requires students to participate in a variety of prewriting activities before sitting down to compose the paper. The degree to which students engage in these activities—observing videotaped material, listening to class lectures, participating in class discussion, and reading outside sources—will significantly affect the quality of the final product, the written report. Students who participate fully in these prewriting activities should have at their disposal a healthy store of supporting material and the makings of a richly detailed paper.

Unlike some of the assignments we examine in other chapters, such as political science, this one does not specify how to organize the paper. Some students are likely to find the lack of guidance troublesome and may be at a loss in trying to make their papers coherent. A more challenging aspect of the assignment, however, is that most students will probably have no experience with objective observation. Most of their high school teachers will probably have stressed just the opposite, personal interpretation devoid of objectivity. We can therefore begin to perceive an important aim of this assignment: helping students overcome their tendency to color their observations with subjective interpretation. With this insight, we can predict that the more successful responses will be those in which students recognize how difficult it is to be "objective" when reporting behavior.

Although the assignment allows students to choose their own organizational strategy, it clearly stipulates the audience: high school seniors considering enrolling in a college psychology course. The instructor expects, then, that students will write papers that use clear, jargon-free language and certainly hopes that they will present what they have learned about observation in a lively, engaging manner. Moreover, the teacher wants students to distinguish between the expectations that high schoolers have become familiar with and the demands of this college psychology course.

Guide for Reading

Angie's paper is a carefully written, well-organized response to the assignment. Her paper shows that she understood the requirements of the assignment and then incorporated these into an informative paper appropriately styled for its intended audience. Look, for example, at the first two paragraphs. Angie's paper could have been better if she had included more details and separated more clearly her writing from the information in the article. (You should try identifying places where you wish she had offered more information.) Even so, her work can be used as a model for a good paper.

SAMPLE PSYCHOLOGY PAPER 1

Observation vs. Interpretation

Angie V. (a freshman)

There is a *great* drastic difference between observation and interpretation. Observation is the factual account of something that actually happened. Interpretation is an account by the observer of how the actions impressed him or her (Isaksen,1986,p.17). Since observation is the basis for interpretation it is often hard to distinguish between the two (Isaksen,1986,p.3). "It takes a lot of practice to distinguish between what actually happened (observed fact) from how the action impressed you (interpretation or meaning of the fact.)" (Isaksen,1986,p.17).

As high school seniors you are probably unaware of the difficulties involved in making objective observations. This paper will help you in determining the difference between observation and interpretation.

It is easy to confuse what actually happened with what you think actually happened. I was first made aware of the difficulties through the combination of our classroom lectures, discussion groups, viewing the parent/child interaction film, and reading an article "Observation or Interpretation."

I watched a twelve minute film on the interaction between a mother and her child and the same child's interaction with a stranger. I then took down notes which I thought were basically good research. Later it became apparent to me that the notes that I had made were not objective observations at all. They were merely the interpretations of what I had seen.

The first way I became aware of my mistakes was through reading the article. This article was very informative and carefully explained the differences between observation and interpretation. It explained that two people should make the same observations of a situation but that their interpretations may vary greatly (Isaksen,1986,p.16). This is due to the fact that observation is completely unbiased while interpretation may be biased or someone's opinion. The article also pointed out that it is okay to make interpretations but only after objective observations are made and it is made clear that an interpretation is being made (Isaksen,1986). Any interpretation we make should be clearly distinguished from the facts, and its tentative nature made clear." (Isaksen, 1986, p. 19).

I further realized the extent of my interpretation during the classroom discussion. Though all of the students viewed the same film, each one seemed to have different reports of what had taken place. No two observations were exactly the same. For example, one student in our group stated that the child sighed as if it were content. Another student stated that during the same time period the child seemed anxious and restless. The contrasts with statements such as these made it evident that we had been interpreting the data rather than viewing it objectively. A point that was brought out that I felt was well worth remembering was that we cannot make attributions to another person's thoughts or feelings. If this is done, it is no longer objective observation but an interpretation. An observer needs to be factual in order for their information to be classified as observation.

Through the lecture I learned that there are different kinds of observation. One is called a narrative. It is written in paragraph form and describes exactly what is seen second to second. Another type of observation is called time sequence observation. Here the observer gives the details of certain segments of time. Yet another form of observation is event sampling. Here the details are given by the number of times something happens. One example of this would have been to record the number of times the child smiled in the parent/child interaction film. Any of these types of observation may be used at any time. The decision of which type to use is made by the observer according to what type of evidence is being looked for. One point that should be remembered no matter which method is used is that the observer's appraisal of a situation should be avoided (Isaksen,1986,p.21).

Interpretation of data is not always bad. It can, in fact, be very useful but only after the observer has researched his or her objective observations. Observers must remember to make a clear distinction between their observations and their interpretations of an experiment or situation.

While it is often hard to recognize the difference between interpretation and objectivity it is not impossible. A researcher need only be careful to use factual evidence for what he calls his observation. This can be done if the researcher makes himself aware of the possible difficulties involved, records only the events that actually happened, and avoids reading his own thoughts into the actions. A researcher that uses observation and interpretation wisely is a responsible researcher.

Analysis of Sample Psychology Paper 1

In the first three paragraphs of her paper, Angie efficiently prepares readers for the discussion to follow: In the first paragraph, she defines "observation" and "interpretation"; in the second, she speaks directly to her audience and states the purpose of her paper; and in the third she establishes her organization. Her approach admittedly lacks subtlety, but her awareness of audience is commendable.

Angie uses personal narrative effectively. She narrates chronologically the events that led her to a more enlightened view of her subject. She uses first person, but not to the extent that *she* becomes the subject of her paper rather than the issue of objective language in observation. Most of her use of first person takes place in the opening sentences of her paragraph: she uses personal narrative as a means for organizing and unifying the material she wishes to work through.

The paper, then, is clear, coherent, and fairly well organized. For the most part, it is also well developed. Angie develops her paragraphs on classroom discussion and lectures in a detailed and logical fashion. For instance, in the classroom paragraph, she makes an assertion ("No two observations were exactly the same") and then provides an example to support the assertion. This technique is characteristic of effective development. She is less specific, however, when addressing what she learned from observing the videotaped material. She never states exactly what interpretations she let slip into her note-taking during the observation. Had she been more specific here, she would have had a better paper.

There are other things she could have done to improve her writing. For example, she could have clarified her documentation by using attribution within the text to cue readers as to where her use of a source begins. Paragraph 7 is especially problematic in this regard; we have no way of knowing how much of the information offered there came from class lectures and how much came from the Isaksen text. Moreover, she neglected to include a list of references at the end of her paper, and she should have followed the commas in her parenthetical citations with spaces. She could also have combined paragraphs 8 and 9, her final paragraphs, because she makes her point about clear distinctions between observation and interpretation in both. They therefore seem to go together as a single unit. These improvements would provide further polish to an otherwise thoughtful paper.

Guide for Reading

Kim avoided the two major problems that affect Angie's paper, and, as a result, her paper contains good detail and her writing is clearly separate from her source. But, overall, her response is not as good. The assignment states that the intended audience is composed of high school students planning to take college psychology, but Kim doesn't clearly address this audience. As you read, see if you can figure out whom Kim's audience includes. You may also find that it is difficult to grasp the subject as firmly as you would like to, especially if you haven't just read Angie's paper. These difficulties make Kim's paper an average response that fulfills the requirements of the assignment but does nothing more.

Observation

Kim S. (a freshman)

Many high school seniors have a misconception about the difficulties of making an observation without using interpretation. Through class discussions, lectures, and reading assignments the difference between the two became more evident and even I realized my own misconceptions about the process.

In performing observations, many try to interpret rather than just state the facts. Observation consists of gathering information without using any emotional factors. For example, in an experiment we were assigned to observe parent/child interaction followed by stranger/child interaction. As we watched these short segments we were to write down what we observed. This consisted of facts only. For instance, "the baby cried" "the baby moved her arm" and we were not to interpret using phrases such as "the baby is happy" or "the baby is sad." In order to record results accurately, one should know the difference between observation and interpretation. As stated by Isaksen, "Observation, which comes first, is the basis of interpretation, so it is important to be able to distinguish between the two" (1986, p.27). As I viewed the tapes, I interpreted what I saw rather than observed what I saw. I described the baby's moods and reactions rather than her actual movements. However, I did not find what I thought observation to be difficult because I did not have a clear understanding of the definition.

During class discussions, however, I realized my mistakes and my misunderstood preconceptions of observation. It is a much more careful technique which actually takes great thought. In order to become an expert on the subject it takes much time and practice. It is very difficult to try not to include such interpretive words as, "appeared to be," "became interested," and "responded." Nevertheless, in my discussion group I cleared up those misconceptions and it became more evident through lectures and reading assignments.

The lectures revealed the different settings in which an observation might take place. The experiment which we observed was a controlled observation in which the baby had no outside interference. These experiments are regulated by the experimenter. Therefore the results of one's observation might be manipulated and inaccurate in comparison with real-life situations.

The reading assignments revealed a lot about the differences between observation and interpretation. When people interpret something instead of just observing, they usually draw premature conclusions (Wortman and Loftus, 1988). This can lead to inaccurate results and therefore a useless experiment. As stated by Isaksen, "The facts cannot be known unless they are reported as a dependable record in observation notes" (1986, p.32). To make an accurate observation, there are a number of questions to be answered. This line of questioning is referred to as systematic observation. The questions, according to Saslow, include what, whom, when, where, how, and in what form (1982, p. 10). These questions aid in the achievement of an accurate observation without any interpretation.

The objective observation process is one which is easily misconstrued. It is often confused and conflicts with the process of interpretation. However, <u>hopefully</u> I have cleared up any misconceptions that you rising college freshmen might have <u>in</u> hopes that you will be able to make a <u>more clear</u> observation.

Analysis of Sample Psychology Paper 2

You may have noted the similarities in approach between Angie's paper and this one. Both use personal narrative as an organizational strategy, and both speak directly to their audience of high school students. This paper improves on the first in some areas: It uses attribution within the text to make documentation more accurate, and it provides more details about the writer's observation of videotaped material. But, in general, Angie's paper is better than Kim's.

A quick comparison will show why. Consider how each student introduces her material. As we mentioned earlier, Angie begins by defining observation and interpretation. In her next paragraph, she directly addresses her audience when she states: "As high school seniors you are probably unaware of the difficulties involved in making objective observations." The effect is twofold. First, readers know immediately something of the substance of the paper, an important concern in any writing. Second, by speaking directly to her audience, she draws them into the paper quite successfully.

Kim, on the other hand, begins her paper with this statement: "Many high school seniors have a misconception about the difficulties of making an observation without using interpretation." Starting the paper with this statement gives it an abrupt beginning, one that seems out of touch with the audience because, in truth, most high school seniors have probably never thought much about observation and have probably thought even less about such distinctions as objectivity and subjectivity. Moreover, the tone strikes a negative note that might prevent real high school students from reading further.

The differences between the two papers also extend to such mechanical considerations as sentence structure. Angie gives her sentences real subjects that function as agents. We can see who or what performs the action of the verb in each sentence. Kim uses few real subjects other than the pronoun *I*. That is, the agent in her writing tends to be herself. We can see the difference this factor makes in the quality of the writing if we compare the paragraphs below. The first comes from Angie's paper, the second from Kim's:

(1)

> Though all the students viewed the same film, each one seemed to have different reports of what had taken place. No two observations were exactly the same. For example, one student in our group stated that the child sighed as if it were content. Another student stated that during the same time period the child seemed anxious and restless.

(2)

> During class discussions, however, I realized my mistakes and my misunderstood preconceptions of observation. It is a much more careful technique which actually takes great thought. In order to become an expert on the subject it takes much time and practice. It is very difficult to try not to include such interpretive words as "appeared to be," "became interested," and "responded."

What can we conclude about Kim's paper? Primarily that it suffers from both organizational and stylistic difficulties. We get the impression that Kim hasn't thought much about *how* best to present her information, but has probably focused her attention simply on *what* she wanted to say. The problem, of course, is that successful writing at this level requires students to attend to both.

Sentence Lesson

People generally judge sentences with "real" subjects (people or things) easier to read than those with what are called "functional" subjects. Consequently, you should try to write sentences that reflect people or things performing actions, much as Angie does in the example above. We suspect that Kim used the functional subject "it" in an effort to make her writing sound more "objective," but objectivity isn't always a matter of eliminating people from one's work. Writers often achieve an objective tone by examining their topics openly and logically, recognizing differing points of view. In Kim's case, changing the sentence structure to provide real subjects wouldn't have made her prose more "subjective."

Try to rewrite the excerpt above from Kim's paper, supplying each sentence with a real subject.

Guide for Reading

Heather's paper is the most personable of the three. She speaks directly to her audience (high school students) and gets them involved in her situation—that of a college student who has just learned something important. For this reason, many readers will be tempted to call Heather's paper the best of the three. Her use of the parable will reinforce this assessment. A careful analysis, however, shows that Heather avoids the topic of the assignment and deals only vaguely with observation and interpretation. As a result, her response is inadequate, even though parts of it are worth incorporating in a good response. While reading the paper, note those elements that work and those that do not.

SAMPLE PSYCHOLOGY PAPER 3

Observation vs. Interpretation

Heather N. (a freshman)

As a high school senior and a future University of North Carolina at Chapel Hill student, one of the most popular courses on campus may be of great interest to you. I am presently a Psychology major and I am taking Psychology 10. I have always had visions of what psychology class would be like. I would learn about the theories of Sigmund Freud, human interaction, psychoanalysis of dreams, and the class would relate great works of poetry and art to real life. I have received so much more than I expected. I have learned that things are not always as they seem in literary works, in class, and also in life itself.

The most important thing that I have learned is how difficult it is to make an observation without interpreting or being judgemental. Sometimes making interpretations based on one's feelings about a certain issue or observation makes the conclusion false. People observe and make judgements instead of taking the raw facts and drawing the many possibilities from the observation made. For example, a baby smiling may be said to be happy or content. But what are the other possibilities? "The smiling baby may have gas" (Ornstein, 1988). The assumption cannot be taken as an observation. The assumption is an interpretation of what one may see or feel. Relying on common sense, one's own experience and feelings is wrong because it excludes the alternatives.

The parable known as "The Blind Man and the Elephant" is a good example of why interpretation is wrong. Three blind men each feel a different part of the elephant. One of the men thinks the elephant is a wall, another thinks it is a fan, and still another thinks it is a snake. This parable reveals that what we observe is not always wrong but it is always only partially right because one does not see things clearly and objectively. Each man only reached out for a small part of the elephant and that is all they received and interpreted, no more, no less. Each was stagnant in his own views and all were wrong because of it. These men were blind, but sometimes people with sight are also blind because they only see what they want to see. This is where observing without interpreting is crucial when searching for the truth.

One observes with interpretation even without realizing it. Interpreting is natural because people are made up of feelings, morals, and values. Observations need to be composed of the raw facts, to exact precision, without judging, and this is difficult for one to achieve.

In conclusion, observations need to be made without assuming or interpreting. Making interpretations can cause one to lose sight of the facts and make the conclusion of the idea false. Just remember, things are not always as they seem. So think about the guy sitting next to you in English class, your teachers, and your principal. They sure do smile alot!

Analysis of Sample Psychology Paper 3

Of these three responses to the assignment, Heather's attempts to be the most personable. She tells us something about herself and expresses enthusiasm for psychology. Unfortunately, personal revelations and enthusiasm aren't part of the assignment on either an explicit or implicit level, and they are unrelated to what makes a paper successful.

Something that stands out immediately is the five-paragraph structure of the paper, which leads us to suspect that Heather may be under the false impression that if she writes a "five-paragraph theme," then she has written a well-organized paper. This sort of formulaic approach to writing doesn't work, and no organizational pattern can mask a severe lack of substance.

Heather's inability to say much worthwhile is the most damaging feature of her paper. She gives us five paragraphs, but they are empty. She attempts to develop her subject specifically through the use of the parable of the "Blind Men and the Elephant," but she fails to recognize that it isn't really applicable here. Heather doesn't seem to comprehend that not observing completely or accurately is *not* the same as interpreting.

Given the nature of the assignment, it's most surprising that Heather never makes reference to her observation of the videotaped material, attendance at lectures, or participation in class discussions. She does provide a quote from one of the outside sources, but she tucks it away in her second paragraph without making direct reference to what she has learned through these readings. Perhaps she was overwhelmed by the amount of material that these activities produced and was at a loss as to how it all could be incorporated in the paper. Unfortunately, her instructor may assume that she did not participate in these activities and may mark her accordingly.

Writing Assignments

The following three assignments require no specific knowledge of psychology. They do, however, duplicate in some form parts of the assignment above.

1. Write a personal narrative that recounts a learning experience you have had in this class. For example, you might narrate your growing understanding of the importance of revision. What events contributed to your understanding—practical experience? Class discussions? Conferences with your instructor? Class readings? Your audience is composed of people who are planning to take the class you are writing about, and you want to prepare them for a specific feature of the experience. Successful responses will be well organized, presenting information in a chronological manner.
2. Observe a familiar activity: a friend studying in the library, your roommate talking on the telephone, a classmate conferring with your instructor, and so forth. Write a subjective observation, interpreting the event. Compare your interpretation with the way the person felt about the activity. Write a 2- to 3-page paper explaining

what you have learned about this type of interpretation. Your audience is someone who has not considered the differences between observing and interpreting.
3. Team up with a classmate and decide on an unfamiliar activity to observe (one member of a construction crew, a salesperson in a busy store, a police officer directing traffic, and so forth). Take careful notes and try to be as objective as possible. Compare lists so each of you will have all of the relevant actions covered. One of you write your observations in narrative and the other as event sampling (details given by the number of times something happens). Compare the two forms. Write a 2- to 3-page paper analyzing the appropriateness of the two forms for your chosen activity. Your audience is someone who is already familiar with objective observation.

PSYCHOLOGY ASSIGNMENT 2

Course: **Introduction to Psychology**

Aim: *Long before research findings make their way into textbooks and onto the airwaves (e.g., Oprah Winfrey, Phil Donahue, or maybe even NPR), they appear as articles in the psychological literature. Once published in a psychology journal, an article can be read by a large professional audience, as well as by others interested in applying the findings to current problems of society. Learning to read articles in the journal literature is a skill worth cultivating, because one is able to critically evaluate original research and reach personal conclusions about the worth of any particular study. Therefore, the aim of this assignment is to make you more intelligent "consumers" of psychological research by bringing you face to face with an actual experiment. You will summarize and critique an interesting article on "brainstorming" techniques that was published in the* Journal of Applied Psychology. *In the process, you will learn that even published papers can be flawed, and you will come to grips with whether the problems you identify outweigh the positive contributions of the article you review.*

Overview: *Through lectures, discussions, and readings, you will learn a fair amount about how research is designed and executed. You will learn the strength of any research contribution is determined in part by the adequacy of methods and procedures employed. This assignment will give you an opportunity to apply this newly acquired knowledge to a specific research report:*

Bouchard, T. J., Jr. (1972). A comparison of two brainstorming procedures. Journal of Applied Psychology, 56, *418–421.*

There will be two parts to this assignment: a summary and an evaluation. These segments are indicated below and will be illustrated by a sample critique that will be distributed in class.

Summary: *In the first part of your paper, you will concisely summarize each section of the article: Introduction, Method (with its various subsections dealing with Subjects, Design, Procedure, etc.), Results, Discussion. You will identify the author's hypothesis, specify the procedures followed, the data obtained, and the conclusions reached.*

Evaluation: *In the second part of your paper, you will evaluate the article, addressing issues concerning the adequacy of the author's logic, the strength of his methods, the clarity of the obtained data, and the reasonableness of the conclusions. Although you are free to comment on any aspect of the study, you should pay particular attention to the following issues:*

1. *Does the experimenter adequately define his independent and dependent variables?*
2. *Are the independent variables manipulated so as to yield information related to the author's hypothesis?*
3. *Were the subjects sampled in a proper manner? Are the subjects in the different groups established by the experimenter comparable to each other?*
4. *Are the methods employed described adequately so that the reader can evaluate their appropriateness?*
5. *Do the experimenter's conclusions follow directly from the results that were reported?*
6. *Would follow-up experiments be desirable? What issues should be examined?*

The entire summary and evaluation should require no more than 5–7 typewritten pages. In preparing your papers, assume that you have been asked to evaluate this article for possible inclusion in a book of readings for undergraduates. The professors who are assembling the book want to know if students feel that the Bouchard experiment is good enough to be reprinted.

Analysis of Psychology Assignment 2

The overall structure of the paper assigned here—summary followed by evaluation—is familiar to scholars, whether they work in the humanities, natural sciences, or social sciences. The educational process involves not only producing original work, but also digesting and critiquing the work of others.

Part of the challenge of such a structure is keeping the two parts distinct yet related. The summary of the material should be presented objectively; all comments on it should be reserved until the evaluation section. Likewise, the evaluation should present no new facts; it should evaluate only facts included in the summary. This approach ensures unified organization and coherent development.

When constructing the summary, students should note that the instructor asks that they "concisely summarize" Bouchard's article. The summary should be significantly shorter than the original (the sample papers included here are rather lengthy in their summaries). To obtain this brevity, students must put the ideas of the original into their own words and delete extraneous details, while remaining true to the spirit of the original.

When constructing the evaluation, students should consider a comment the instructor makes when explaining the aims of the assignment: that students "will learn that even published papers can be flawed." The instructor is giving students a broad hint that this experimental research report should not receive an exclusively positive evaluation; the report has its weaknesses, and the astute student will note them.

The assignment explicitly states the form that the summary and evaluation should take. The summary should follow the experimental research report and provide sections labeled Introduction, Method, Results, and Discussion. (Most experimental research reports also include an Abstract and References.) The evaluation should focus on issues the instructor has listed and numbered, but it should also respond to the statement that students should determine whether the article to the statement that students should determine whether the article ought to be included in a book of readings for undergraduates. Hence, students are being asked not only to evaluate the quality of the article but to assess its appropriateness for a given audience. The assignment, then, provides students with both valuable practice in adhering to a formal structure and experience in the critical procedures employed by scholars.

Class Article 1

A Comparison of Two Group Brainstorming Procedures:[1]

Thomas J. Bouchard, Jr.[2]
University of Minnesota

> A modified brainstorming procedure that required the Ss to identify psychologically with significant components of the task (called synectics) was compared to standard brainstorming over three sessions and nine different problems. Each treatment condition was also divided into high- and low-interpersonal-effectiveness groups. The synectics groups were superior to the brainstorming groups on all nine problems, but the differences were statistically significant for only four. There were no significant main effects due to group composition, nor were there any interactions. It was concluded that synectics was a more effective group-problem-solving strategy than brainstorming.

Previous research on group-problem-solving procedures suggests that brainstorming is only slightly superior to critical problem solving (Bouchard, 1969), at least with respect to fluency of idea production.

---

[1] This investigation was supported entirely by a grant from the Graduate School of the University of Minnesota. Manuscript revision was supported by PHS Grant No. 1 RO1 HDO5600-01 to the author. The author wishes to acknowledge the valuable assistance of Ronald Page and Joseph Stankus who ran the Ss, and Jean Barsaloux who was responsible for the data analysis.

[2] Request for reprints should be sent to Thomas J. Bouchard, Jr., Elliott Hall, Department of Psychology, University of Minnesota, Minneapolis, Minnesota 55455.

"A Comparison of of Two Group Brainstorming Procedures" by Thomas J. Bouchard, Jr., *Journal of Applied Psychology*, 1972, Vol. 56, No. 5, 418-421. Copyright © 1972 by the American Psychological Association. Reprinted by permission of the American Psychological Association and the author.

Furthermore, since individual brainstorming has been shown consistently to be superior to group brainstorming (Bouchard, 1969; Bouchard & Hare, 1970; Campbell, 1968; Dunnette, Campbell, & Jastaad, 1963; Taylor, Berry, & Block, 1958), it has been advocated over group procedures (Dunnette, 1964). However, Bouchard (in press) recently demonstrated that a structured brainstorming procedure will yield group performances that are comparable to individual or nominal group performances. Structure in that experiment consisted of requiring Ss to follow the standard brainstorming procedure, but in a sequence rather than in an unconstrained fashion. The result was a more equalitarian interaction of group members and a great deal more output.

The study suggested that group procedures that force greater involvement of the participants in a systematic way might be even more productive. A group-problem-solving procedure that attempts to do this is the synectics procedure described by Gordon (1961) and Prince (1969). One of the tactics of synectics groups is "psychological identification" with an object or concept central to the problem being worked on. This tactic is called "personal analogy." A well-known example of a thinker identifying with a component of the problem in order to solve it is that of Archimedes. His problem was to measure the volume of a rather complicated crown in order to check its specific gravity against that of gold. Archimedes, like most of us, knew that the water level in his tub would rise when he got in, but only by recognizing an equivalence between himself and the crown was he able to generalize the relationship and generate a solution.

The purpose of this study is to assess the effectiveness of the mechanism—personal analogy—when it is used as an adjunct to brainstorming. The new procedure is called synectics. It is possible that the synectics procedure might lead to a concertizing mode of thought which in turn may restrict the range of ideas available to the Ss. The brainstorming procedure, on the other hand, is more abstract and may not impose such a restriction.

The present study compares the effectiveness of brainstorming and synectics across nine different problems for groups of different compositions.

METHOD

Subjects

The Ss in the brainstorming groups were the same ones as those used in Bouchard's (in press) Experiment 1.[3] They were male students from an introductory psychology course, recruited to the experiment by offering them points for experimental participation (required of all introductory students), and $2.50 per hr. for up to 2 hrs. over the time necessary to earn their points.

The Ss who performed in the synectics groups were chosen from the same S pool, but much later during the course.

Design

The experiment is a 2 × 2 analysis of variance (ANOVA). There were three four-man groups in each of the synectics cells and eight four-man groups in the brainstorming cells, except in session 3 where one brainstorming, high-interpersonal-effectiveness group was lost due to the failure of a tape recorder.

The two levels of the group composition factor were high and low on the sum of the first five scales of the California Psychological Inventory (Gough, 1957). The scales are Dominance, Capacity for Status, Sociability, Social-Presence, and Self-Acceptance. They define the first factor of the CPI called Interpersonal Effectiveness. In a previous analysis (Bouchard, 1969), this factor was found to be highly predictive of performance in brainstorming groups.

Procedure

Two male Es ran all the groups, and they were partially counterbalanced across conditions. All instructions were presented by tape recorder and all Ss performed in a room monitored by closed circuit television.

All groups worked on three sets of problems during three different sessions. Two sessions were held one wk. and the third during the beginning of the next wk. Each S had a written copy of the rules of brainstorming to examine while he listened to them on the tape re-

---

[3] The brainstorming groups in this study are from the three training sessions of the trained, low- and high-motivation brainstorming groups. The low- and high-motivation groups in that study did not receive different treatments until the fourth session. Only the criterion data gathered in session 4 were analyzed in that study.

corder. A brief summary of the instructions for each session is given below.[4]

Session 1 instructions. The Ss were told that the E was interested in how much a group's performance improved over time as the Ss got to know each other and practiced with the procedure. They were told their performance would be tape-recorded and compared to groups who did not practice.

The brainstorming instructions were identical to those used by Bouchard and Hare (1970) except that the procedural rule described below was added. The procedures proscribed criticism and emphasized freewheeling, quantity, and the combination and improvement of ideas.

This procedural rule required ideas to be contributed by participants in sequence. Each S had to say "Pass" if he had nothing to say. Each was also encouraged not to get bogged down in long discussions about trivial points. The S had a copy of the instructions in front of him. The instructions were repeated at each training session.

The following paragraph appeared in all synectics group instructions, but did not appear in the brainstorming group instructions. Each set of problem instructions was modified to fit this procedure.

Identification with the task. Each of you in turn gets to play a central part of the problem while the group works on it. For example, if the problem were "Think up as many brand names as you can for a new spray deodorant" one of you would get up on the table, sit down, close your eyes, and play the can of deodorant. The amount of time each of you will play the role or part of the problem will vary from task to task and will be indicated on your instruction sheets. The procedure here is simple. Ideas should be contributed in sequence. Note that each of your instruction sheets is numbered. S number one should begin, followed by S number two, etc. This includes the person who is playing the part of the problem object. Don't let this task throw you. An easy way to conceptualize it is to imagine that you are doing an animated cartoon or commercial for television.

Session 2 and 3 instructions. For session 2, the instructions were repeated in full. For session 3, the Ss were told that they were working on the final set of problems, and they were asked to do their best while following the instructions on the sheet in front of them.

Problems

The Ss worked on three problems during each of the three sessions. Each S had a copy of the problem. When the time allotted for a problem

---

[4] All instructions, problems, and ANOVA tables are available directly from the author (see address in Footnote 2).

was up, the *E* simply entered the room, collected the problem that the *S*s had just finished, and handed them a new problem sheet. He simply said, "Here is the next problem for you to work on." The problems were administered in the order shown in Table 1. The first problem of each set was worked on for 5 min., the second for 10 min., and the third for 20. Both the brainstorming and synectics versions of the first problem are given below. The remaining problems were structured in the same way and are described only briefly.

Brand names for a cigar. There are a number of cigars on the table. Each of you please take one. Don't smoke it because there is no ventilation in this room.

One of the factors involved in marketing a product is the brand name. The purpose behind a brand name is to sell the product. Assume a new cigar is to be put on the market. Create as many brand names for this cigar as you can. You will have 5 min. to work on this task. We will tell you when to stop.

Brand names for a cigar. For the synectics condition, the following additional instructions were given.

S number 1 should get up, lie on his back on the table, and play the part of the cigar for 1 min. As the instructions indicated, you should contribute ideas in sequence beginning with *S* number 1. At the end of a minute, we will ring a buzzer and *S* number 2 should take the part of the cigar, then *S* number 3, and then 4.

At the end of the four, 1-min. sessions, you will have 1 additional min. to suggest more names. We will tell you when to stop.

The remaining problems were *brick uses* (Think of as many uses as you can for old bricks), *people problem* (*S*s enumerate the consequences of all children doubling in height over the next 20 yrs.), *brand names for a bra; newspaper uses; tourist problem* (How do you get more tourists to come to the United States?), *brand names for an automobile, uses for old coat hangers,* and *sudden blindness problem* (*S*s enumerate the consequences if suddenly everyone went blind).

Scoring

The analyzed dependent variable was number of different ideas generated. Previous work (Bouchard, 1969; in press) has shown that total number of ideas is the most sensitive indicator of treatment effects and correlates highly with quality scores. The magnitude of effects is generally attenuated somewhat when quality scores are used.

All overlapping ideas within a group were deleted from transcribed tapes. The total number of ideas remaining constituted the criterion total number of ideas (fluency score) applied to all problems. Interjudge

TABLE 1 Means and Standard Deviations for Number of Ideas Produced for all Problems for Procedure and Selection

Session and problem	Procedure					Selection			
	Synectics		Brainstorming		High-interpersonal effectiveness		Low-interpersonal effectiveness	
	M	SD	M	SD	M	SD	M	SD
Session 1								
Cigars	35.3**	16.1	11.9	8.2	15.8	11.1	20.7	17.9
Bricks	62.0*	19.4	43.1	10.5	49.7	15.2	46.7	16.4
People	98.3*	30.5	67.9	15.2	77.0	18.1	75.5	29.7
All three problems	195.7*	62.8	122.6	22.3	142.2	38.4	142.8	59.3
Session 2								
Bras	36.2	17.9	29.1	14.7	29.4	16.4	32.7	15.3
Newspaper	66.5	25.0	58.0	15.2	58.5	18.5	62.2	18.9
Tourist	73.2	27.8	65.8	17.5	70.6	23.8	64.9	17.3
All three problems	175.8	66.6	152.9	41.3	158.5	55.7	159.8	44.8
Session 3								
Autos	48.2	31.2	34.3	19.2	40.3	25.9	36.5	22.2
Coat hangers	55.5	21.8	55.4	16.6	58.9	17.3	52.3	18.6
Blindness	110.5*	25.3	84.7	18.0	96.4	15.6	88.2	28.2
All three problems	214.2	70.1	174.5	40.9	195.6	46.7	176.9	58.5

*$p<.05$.
**$p<.01$.

reliability of the deletion procedure is generally about .95 (Bouchard & Hare, 1970), and only one judge was used.

RESULTS

The data were analyzed as a 2 × 2 ANOVA using an unweighted means analysis (Winer, 1962). The means and standard deviations for the main effects are summarized in Table 1.

The only significant effects in session 1 were due to procedure (synectics vs. brainstorming). There were no significant effects due to selection, nor were there any interactions. The synectics groups performed significantly better than the brainstorming groups on all three problems individually and on all three problems combined.

In session 2, there were no significant main effects or interactions, although the means in Table 1 show that the scores for the synectics groups are higher on all problems than the scores for the brainstorming groups.

In session 3, the only significant effect was for procedure on the blindness problem, where the synectics groups outperformed the brainstorming groups although, as before, the trends are for higher "synectic group means" on all problems.

DISCUSSION

Where significant differences were found, the indication was that the synectics procedure increases the productivity of brainstorming rather than detracting from it. There is no way to determine from this experiment if the increased productivity of the synectics groups is due specifically to the process of "personal identification" as a cognitive strategy or whether the relative uniqueness of the procedure served as a generalized motivator or means of creating greater involvement. Groups seldom engage in as much physical activity as that required by the synectics procedure, and this simply may have involved them in the task to a greater degree. Nevertheless, the time it took the Ss in the synectics groups to change roles, particularly on the briefer tasks, severely cut into the total amount of problem-solving time; this may make their relative superiority over the brainstorming groups even more impressive.

The results suggest that the strategy of personal analogy may be a useful problem-solving tool, and it, as well as other synectic procedures, deserves more investigation.

REFERENCES

Bouchard, T. J., Jr. Personality, problem-solving procedure, and performance in small groups. *Journal of Applied Psychology*, 1969, 53, 1–29.

Bouchard, T. J., Jr. Training, motivation, and personality as determinants of the effectiveness of brainstorming groups and individuals. *Journal of Applied Psychology*, in press.

Bouchard, T. J., Jr., & Hare, M. Size, performance, and potential in brainstorming groups. *Journal of Applied Psychology*, 1970, 54, 51–55.

Campbell, J. Individual versus group problem-solving in an industrial sample. *Journal of Applied Psychology*, 1968, 52, 205–210.

Dunnette, M. D. Are meetings any good for solving problems? *Personnel Administration*, 1964, 27, 12–29.

Dunnette, M. D., Campbell, J., & Jaastad, K. The effects of group participation on brainstorming effectiveness for two industrial samples. *Journal of Applied Psychology*, 1963, 47, 30–37.

Gordon, W. J. *Synectics: The development of creative capacity.* New York: Harper & Row, 1961.

Gough, H. G. *Manual for the California Psychology Inventory.* Palo Alto, Calif.: Consulting Psychologist Press, 1957.

Prince, G. M. *The practice of creativity.* Cambridge: Synectics, 1969.

Taylor, D. W., Berry, P. C., & Block, C. H. Does group participation when using brainstorming facilitate or inhibit creative thinking? *Administrative Science Quarterly*, 1958, 3, 23–47.

Winer, B. J. *Statistical principles in experimental design.* New York: McGraw-Hill, 1962.

Guide for Reading

The following three papers are adequate responses to the assignment. None is outstanding, but they can be ranked in overall quality. We believe that the best way for you to use these samples as guides for writing an outstanding paper is to compare all three and then draw on the strengths of each. Study questions follow the third paper and focus both on individual papers and on ways to compare the three.

The papers are presented in order of descending quality. Mary's is the most complete, both in summary and evaluation, but her attention to detail makes reading it a tedious process in places. You should try to identify those places. David's paper is the most readable, but his summary isn't as informative as it should be, and his evaluation is superficial. Consider what David should have included in his summary. Sonya shows a good understanding of the important points of the article, and in places her writing is lucid and concise. In other parts of her paper, though, her careless word choices and phrasing, as well as her numerous errors, distract and confuse readers. As you go through her response, identify some of the words Sonya uses carelessly.

SAMPLE PSYCHOLOGY PAPER 4

Analysis of Two Brainstorming Procedures

Mary D. (a freshman)

Summary
I. Introduction

The author of this article was trying to prove that synectics is more effective than simple brainstorming. The experimenter had already concluded that systematic brainstorming was more productive than brainstorming that followed no format. Therefore, both groups followed a format which allowed each participant the opportunity to give opinions in an equal fashion. The difference between the two groups, the independent variable, was the personal analogy performed by those of the synectics group. In the synectics group, each member was required to play the part of the object under consideration while the others offered suggestions via the formatted fashion. The brainstorming group and the synectics group were also divided into subgroups, high-interpersonal effectiveness and low-interpersonal effectiveness. The purpose of forming the subgroups was to determine if degree of personal interaction was a factor in the success of one group over the other. The experimenter perceived that synectics would provide greater involvement than brainstorming because the subjects were relating to the problem in a more personal manner. The hypothesis was that the use of a personal analogy in brainstorming would be more effective than brainstorming in which no analogy was used.

II. Method
Subjects

The subjects who participated in the Bouchard experiment were male students from an introductory psychology course. The course required the students to participate in an experiment for a minimum of two hours. For participation over the two hours, each received $2.50 per hour for an additional two hours. The subjects used in the brainstorming group had previously worked together as partners in brainstorming for an earlier experiment. Those participating in the synectics group were chosen from the same group of subjects, but at a much later time.

Design

The experiment consisted of three four-man groups that participated using synectics and eight four-man groups which used simple brainstorming. In the third session there were only seven brainstorming groups evaluated because of a tape recorder failure. The unevaluated group was also a member of the subgroup high-interpersonal effectiveness.

The California Psychological Inventory Scales were used to rank the subjects as either high or low-interpersonal effectiveness. The five factors taken into consideration were Dominance, Capacity for Status, Sociability, Social-Presence, and Self-Acceptance. The experimenter had already concluded that such factors were determinative of whether people were highly interactive and personable (high-interpersonal effectiveness) or not (low-interpersonal effectiveness).

Procedure

During each of the three sessions all groups were given three basically similar problems to answer. The sessions took place over the period of approximately one and one half weeks. Monitored by a closed circuit television, the groups received all instructions via tape recorder. They were also given a printed copy.

Psychology

The subjects were informed that the experimenter was interested in whether their group performance would increase as a result of practicing and getting to know one another better. They were told that their performance would be compared to groups which had not yet practiced.

The brainstorming groups received instructions promoting "freewheeling, quantity, and the combination and improvement of ideas" (Bouchard, 1972, 419). They were also encouraged to participate in sequence, but could pass when they had no response. The directions were repeated on each day of the experiment.

The synectics group received instructions describing how they were to act as the personal analogy given in each problem. Also, they were asked to express their ideas in a particular order. These same instructions were repeated for session two. Before the third session, the subjects were asked to do their best and to follow the instructions on the sheet which they had received.

Problems

During each session the subjects worked on a five minute problem, a ten minute problem, and a twenty minute problem. The time was kept by an individual who ran the group. When time was up, the same individual would collect the completed problem and hand the subjects a new one. Both groups were given the same problems, but the synectics groups received different versions than the brainstorming groups. For example, in the first problem the brainstorming groups were given cigars and asked to create brand names for them. The subjects in the synectics groups were given different instructions. They were asked to alternately take one minute turns lying on the table, while pretending to be a cigar. Each participant was to make suggestions in the given order until the minute was completed. Subject number two then took over as the cigar. The same routine was followed until each subject played the part of a cigar. The remaining minute was used to gather additional ideas.

The other problems had a similar format, but the topics varied slightly. They were based on the following: brick uses, problems resulting in children's height doubling over the next two decades, bra brand names, newspaper uses, how to increase tourism in the United States, automobile brand names, old coat hanger uses, problems resulting from sudden blindness of ___ entire population.

Scoring

The experimenter used the quantity of different ideas <u>contrived</u> as the dependent variable. He had previously come to the conclusion that a high correlation exists between quantity and quality responses; therefore, he justified using the quantity instead of the quality of answers. Identical answers within the same groups were excluded from the count. In the deletion procedure the experimenter used only one judge in order to keep the study accurate.

III. Results

After session one there were no significant effects found between the high and low-interpersonal groups. On the other hand, a significant effect was evident between the synectics and brainstorming groups for the first three problems.

Although the scores for session two of the synectics groups were higher than those of the brainstorming group in all three problems, the effects were insignificant. The difference between the interpersonal groups was found to be irrelevant also.

In section three there was a significant effect which suggested synectics <u>as</u> better for solving the blindness problem. Although the synectics groups outperformed the brainstorming groups on all three problems, all other scores remained inconsequential. There continued to be no comparable difference between the interpersonal divisions.

IV. Discussion

The author concludes from his results that "the synectics procedure increases the productivity of brainstorming rather than detracting from it" (Bouchard, 1972, 421). He remains unsure about the factors which possibly contributed to the synectics groups' better performance, but attributes it to their greater degree of involvement. He also infers that the synectics groups were more impressive because they had less time to actually contribute answers due to their changing of roles. The author also raises the possibility that use of a personal analogy may have a positive influence on problem solving.

Evaluation

1. Although the overall format of the experiment seems to be well designed and executed, a few places appear to contain flaws. Because of the nature of the problems, it is possible that some subjects may have found it easier than others to respond due to their previous experience or knowledge. Such prior exposure would yield results based on intelligence rather than on the brainstorming procedure used. Also, the experimenter seems to ignore the failure of a tape recorder and assumes it does not effect the results. If he accounts for this failure in the statistics, he neglects explaining about it. Another possible error that may influence the results is the time miscalculation. Each group was given the same amount of time to work the problems, but the synectics groups ended up with sufficiently less time to actually work on the problems due to role-changing. An addition of time may have rendered the synectic brainstorming groups as definitely more effective. The independent and dependent variables are very clear. The author directly defines the dependent variables while the independent variable is obvious.

2. All in all, the experimenter manipulates the variables well. By using the same questions for all groups, he keeps the study parallel. He also manipulates one factor; the groups are either given a cigar or play the role of a cigar. A question can be raised as to whether quantity was actually as accurate as a quality measure would have been. It seems necessary that there be criteria to judge whether an answer was applicable to the question or not. Because there was no screening system, nonsense answers were possibly accepted.

3. The sampling procedure used by the experimenter could

have been improved. Although he selected subjects from the same introductory psychology class, the experimenter failed to select all "new" subjects. Because the brainstorming groups had previously worked together, they had an unfair advantage over the synectics groups. If all new subjects had been chosen, the results might have differed. In addition, the experimenter gives no explanation for using three synectics groups as compared to eight brainstorming groups. He cannot justify comparing the unequal number of groups. In contrast, the experimenter's development of interpersonal efectiveness subgroups is intelligent. He makes a logical assumption that personality may affect how individuals react in any group situation. By forming such groups he was able to account for this factor.

4. The experimenter defined his methods accurately. There was only one vague point. In the beginning it was hard to distinguish that there were two groups involved with different methods of brainstorming called *synectics* and *brainstorming*. The experiment was easy to understand as soon as the reader was able to identify these two groups and their function.

5. The experimenter assumes his hypothesis correct although he lacks convincing evidence. Due to the discrepancies in his methods and rather unconvincing results, his assumption cannot be justified. The results conclude synectics was responsible for better performance for only four out of nine problems. In the remaining five the synectics group gave more responses, but failed to produce a significant effect; therefore, such findings may have occured by chance. Because he claims to have proven synectics is the better method, he jumps to the conclusion that the synectic procedure was unique and thus, created motivation and increased the involvement of the participants.

6. Before any conclusions are made, it is imperative that follow-up experiments be performed. The preceding experiment should be reworked considering any necessary changes already mentioned. Further information and creativity should be researched regarding synectics alone. Also, the possible tie between personal analogies and creativity should be investigated. In addition, it might be a good idea to double-check the accuracy of the California Psychological Inventory scales.

Article Critique

David N. (a freshman)

Summary
I. Introduction

The author of this article, Thomas J. Brouchard Jr., was interested with the degree to which different brainstorming techniques would influence the quantity of ideas produced. Previous tests have shown that group brainstorming is less effective than individual brainstorming. Bouchard is testing his hypothesis that *structured* group brainstorming produces more ideas than individual and normal group brainstorming. Structured group brainstorming meaning that subjects were to follow the experiment in a controlled sequence. The process under hypothesis, called synectics, is one that deals with "psychological identification" with the idea or concept during brainstorming.

II. Method
Subjects

The subjects under experimentation were all male, and were taken form an introductory psychology course. They were given points for their participation, needed to meet a requirement in the class.

Design

The subjects (abbreviated as Ss) in the experiment were broken into two groups, and then into two subgroups. The two larger groups were labeled "Synectics" and "Brainstorming." The large groups were then broken into smaller groups of high and low interpersonal effectiveness. Each Synectic subgroup consisted of three four-man groups while each Brainstorming group was made up of eight four-man groups. The subgroups of high and low interpersonal effectiveness were determined by levels of

"Dominance", "Capacity for Status", "Sociability", "Social Presence", and "Self-Acceptance".

Procedure

The Ss were each given nine problems to work on, during which two male Es monitored their work. Each group worked on three sets of problems during each of the three sessions. Each group was given a set of instructions to aid them. The instructions told the Ss that they were being watched for their improvement as they got to know each other. Each must present his idea in sequence. If he drew a blank then he must say "pass". Both sets of instructions were the same except that the Synectic group was given one additional rule:

Each member must get on a table and act out the part of the brainstorming subject. For example, if the problem was to come up with new names for a cigar, each S would have to act out the part of the cigar.

Problems

The nine brainstorming problems were given in three sessions. The Ss were given five, ten, and twenty minutes for the problems respectively. After the time alloted had expired, an E would enter, collect the data and present to them a new problem. The problems ranged from product names for a cigar to the use of old coathangers.

Scoring

Earlier work has shown the total number of ideas produced is a good measure of score. The S's ideas were therefore examined on that basis, with overlapping ideas deleted.

III. Results
The Ratings

The results were analyzed and presented in a table. A clear distinction could be seen in that the synectics group performed much better than the brainstorming group. In all cases, the synectic group mean was higher than that of the brainstorming.

Discussion

The author comes to the conclusion that his hypothesis is correct due to the fact that the synectic group outperformed the standard brainstorming group. The author admits that there is no way to determine if the increase in output is due directly to his "personal identification" theory or to the fact that the "relative uniqueness" of the experiment caused the subjects to be more motivated and therefore produce more ideas. The author adds however that the time taken to change subject roles cuts deeply into the synectics time, making the results for synectics even more impressive.

Evaluation

1. The experiment appears to be well done. The author's hypothesis is stated and proved somewhat clearly. By using the difference in brainstorming techniques as the independent variable, the proof for the hypothesis is seen clearly through the table.

2. There is great ambiguity and confusion in the high and low interpersonal idea. The author does not fully explain this area. What does the high/low interpersonal effectiveness category have to do with brainstorming? Was the author's point in the article to prove that "synectics" is a better brainstorming technique than the present one, or was it to prove whether high or low interpersonal effectiveness made a difference on brainstorming? The author's ideas of brainstorming are good, but his confusing the reader by throwing in this category definately are not.

3. We were told in the Subjects section that only males were chosen. Why weren't any females used? Does this article prove that synectics works in all of society or just by males? The author should have picked a balance of males and females.

4. The author states in the Design section that in session three, one brainstorming high-interpersonal group was lost due

to the failure of a tape recorder. Did this have any effect on the outcome of session three? On the experiment as a whole?

5. In closing, the experiment is a good one, but is made confusing when other factors are thrown in. If these factors can be clarified or overlooked, the results of the exact experiment can definately be confirmed. Therefore, I would recommend that this study be included for a purposed book of readings for undergraduate students in psychology. This experiment gives an example of an idea that can be further researched and investigated.

SAMPLE PSYCHOLOGY PAPER 6

Summary and Evaluation of "A comparison of two brainstorming techniques"

Sonya G. (a freshman)

Summary
I. Introduction

Bouchard compared the effectiveness of two group-problem-solving techniques-standard brainstorming and a type of brainstorming called synectics-over nine different problems for different groups. The hypothesis of the study suggested that synectics was far more effective in the group-problem-solving process than a standard brainstorming procedure (1972, 418).

II. Method
Subjects

The participants or subjects in this particular experiment who were identified by (Ss) involved male students who were enrolled in an introductory psychology course. Experimental participation, which was required of all introductory students, rewarded them with a certain number of points as well as $2.50 per hour for up to two hours over the time that it was necessary for them to earn their points (Bouchard, 1972, 419).

Experimental Design and Materials

Bouchard's experiment is classified as a 2 × 2 analysis of variance (ANOVA). He used two levels of independent variables-synectics and brainstorming - in which he calls the procedure, and two levels of interpersonal effectiveness-high and low-interpersonal. Malfunctioning of a tape recorder, however, refrained one of the brainstorming, high interpersonal effectiveness groups from further progress during the third session.

The student male participants were divided into three four-man groups in each of the synectics groups and eight four-man groups in each of the brainstorming cells. Scales used by the California Psychological Inventory (CPI) in which Bouchard thinks are related to interpersonal effectiveness gave highlight to the conclusion that interpersonal effectiveness was more predictable in performance by brainstorming groups as opposed to synectics groups (1972, 419).

Procedure

The Ss were presented with tape recorder instructions as well as a written hand-out while placed in a monitored room. Each group worked on three sets of problems during three different sessions in which two of the sessions were held in the same week and the third held at the beginning of the next week. During the first session, the Ss were observed as to how well they became acquainted with each other as opposed to groups who had had no practice. The brainstorming rules were identical, however, the synectics included a procedural task of contributing ideas in sequence for several problems while an individual played the role of the problem. In session two, the instructions were repeated however, in session three the Ss were beginning to work on the final set of problems for both the brainstorming and synectic procedures (Bouchard, 1972, 419).

Problems

Each group was given a certain time to work on the problems and then they would be collected by the experimenter (E). The E would then provide the Ss with another problem. The Ss worked on the first problem from each set for five minutes, the second for ten minutes and the third for twenty minutes. The problems included the sequential number of ideas the Ss were to contribute for brand names for a cigar for a total of one minute. Four different subjects took turns playing the role of the cigar. The remaining problems included ideas for the use of a brick, brand names for a bra, and the consequences if everyone would suddenly go blind (Bouchard, 1972, 419–420).

Scoring

The dependent variable was the number of different ideas the Ss came up with for each problem. One of Bouchard's previous studies had indicated that there was a direct correlation between the total number of ideas and quality scores. The total number of ideas left constituted the fluency score which applies to all problems (Bouchard, 1972, 420).

III. Results

From the experiment, analysis of the data was a 2 × 2 ANOVA using an "unweighed means analysis" (Bouchard, 1972, 420).

The rating.—From the means and standard deviations for the total number of ideas produced by the two groups, it is clearly shown that the synectics procedure was significantly higher and thus, more effective than the brainstorming group on both levels of high and low-interpersonal effectiveness. All three sessions showed a higher means for the synectic performing group.

IV. Discussion

The author's findings in his experiment supported his hypothesis of the higher effectiveness rates of the synectic procedure. He executed it by comparing two different group-problem-solving techniques by having the subjects perform three different sets of problems. Bouchard admits that there is no way to determine ____ the experiment if the increased productivity of the synectics group is due to personal identification or a "generalized motivator for creating greater involvement" (1972, 421).

Evaluation

1. Bouchard's experiment is well organized in its style however, his comparisons are not too obvious which makes it hard for the reader to understand it the first time. The independent variable is more difficult to recognize than the dependent variable although both seem to correlate well with the author's hypothesis. Both were manipulated well, however, there is still some question on the way he divided the individual groups.

2. The experiment is highly credited for Bouchard's great detail in his methods. They were described adequately which facilitated reading for the general audience. His descriptive methods laid the basis for his results from which his conclusions are directly followed. He interprets his findings using descriptive and differential statistics.

3. "The author is at least 95% certain that brainstorming and synectics are truly different and that the result is not a fluke. In contrast, Bouchard states that there was no significant main effect due to group selection. He is suggesting that the high and low-interpersonal effectiveness groups are not really different, and that any apparent difference should be viewed as resulting from chance fluctuation." (Ornstein, "Brief Comments on Bouchard's (1972) Statistics", 1988)

4. Follow-up experiments should be desirable for Bouchard's experiment. Such factors which should be considered is the use of all females or a mixture of both sexes instead of using only males in the experiment. Future experiments could also divide the two groups differently. Also, what would be the outcome if the groups had *not* become acquainted with each other? Would not the results be affected if the time allotted for each problem and maybe the number of group sessions were different? Follow-up experiments should be performed to answer these questions along with others which may arise from the reading of the Bouchard experiment.

5. Advertising is a good example of when synectics and brain-

storming are used. Different companies are manufacturing new products every day. These products need names and the use of the above procedures accounts for the fact that different ones will be generated through a different tactic.

Sentence Lesson

Some students are so concerned with trying to sound like their teachers that they use words they aren't entirely familiar with, or they use words imprecisely. The result in either case is writing that is difficult to read and understand. Consider the sentences below, for example:

1. George Hillocks clearly acknowledges that research with inconclusive and conclusive evidence has something to add to the solution in developing better techniques for higher level skills in the writing process.
2. The combination of studies include the maturational process of the students paralleling writing development.
3. As we strive to better our lives, every student should immolate the great leaders of the past.
4. People who are guilty of prejudism should be reeducated so they will no longer be ingots and will be better human beings.

In the first two sentences, the meaning is so obscure that we can't really rewrite them effectively. Possible alternatives might be:

1a. George Hillocks acknowledges that research that produces conclusive and inconclusive results may help develop better techniques for teaching writing.
2a. The studies address student maturation and writing development.

Although the ideologies inherent in the second two sentences may be suspect, we can nevertheless make them more readable with some relatively simple word changes:

3a. As we strive to better our lives, every student should emulate the great leaders of the past.
4a. People who are guilty of prejudice should be reeducated so they will no longer be bigots and will be better human beings.

Before you use a word that you aren't really familiar with, you should go to your dictionary to find its meaning. Your dictionary will help you use such words precisely, which will improve your writing.

STUDY QUESTIONS

1. Read Bouchard's abstract of his report. Are all of the sections of the report—Introduction, Method, Results, and Discussion—represented in it? From your reading of this example, what would you say is the purpose of an abstract?

2. Read again the Results section of all three student papers. Which paper most exactly reports the results of Bouchard's study? What important piece of information is left out in the other two papers? How does this omission mislead readers about the actual results of the study?

3. What changes in Bouchard's method would the writers of these papers make? Which student, in your opinion, provides the most practical suggestions?

4. Point out the information in Mary's paper that you feel is unnecessary. In what way does this information make reading the paper difficult and confusing?

5. David, in Paper 5, asks a valid question: Why weren't any females used in Bouchard's study? Why might Bouchard have included only males in his research? How does this choice affect the significance of his results?

6. Point out the unanswered questions in David's evaluation. What kind of burden do these questions place on readers? How should David treat these concerns?

7. What's missing from the response Sonya gives to question 5 in her evaluation? Why is this paragraph an insufficient response to the question?

Writing Assignments

1. Write a paper that introduces and explains Bouchard's report, one that will encourage a variety of readers, beyond psychologists, to take note of his findings. In the paper, explore the implications of Bouchard's research. Explain how general readers might apply his theories concerning successful brainstorming techniques.
2. Choose another experimental research report published in the *Journal of Abnormal Psychology*. Using the formal structure employed in Psychology Assignment 2, summarize and evaluate the report.
3. Go through copies of the *Journal of Developmental Psychology* until you find a research report on language. Then go through copies of *Psychology Today* until you find another article on language. Summarize and evaluate the two articles in a way that compares and contrasts them. Identify the audience each article is designed for.

PSYCHOLOGY ASSIGNMENT 3

[Editor's Note: The following is a summary of an assignment given in an undergraduate psychology course for sophomores, juniors, and seniors. The instructor asked students to draw up an assessment report of a psychological case study using a computer simulation of an interview with a HELPLINE client. The assigned case study is part of the computer software package written and devised by the instructor, and the assignment below is extracted from the manual that accompanies the software.]

Imagine yourself as a volunteer counselor at a HELPLINE in your community. You went through some initial training in personality, psychopathology and crisis intervention before being permitted to receive crisis calls over the telephone or to conduct face-to-face interviews. In this volunteer role, you have the opportunity to meet many distressed people who share personal information with you. Though you are not a trained mental health professional capable of diagnosing and treating persons experiencing psychological difficulties, you are able to administer emotional first aid and to make an initial assessment of their personalities and problems before referring them to appropriate professionals.

You are also a psychology student. Through class meetings and readings, you have been learning about the array of biological, psychological, and social forces that act during childhood and adulthood to shape normal personality and lead, at times, to a wide range of psychological difficulties. You are also likely to have learned about the psychodynamic and behavioral perspectives on personality and psychopathology, some of the major variations within each of these theoretical systems, and the ways each paradigm seeks to understand the human experience. Through computer simulation you will see an interview of a HELPLINE client and write a comprehensive evaluation in which you apply what you are learning in class and your own insights to the individual you encounter in the interview.

Most interviewers use headings in their case formulations and assessment reports to emphasize the organization and make them easier to read. In constructing your report, use the following, commonly used outline:

- *I. Description: demographic information.*
- *II. Presenting Complaint: circumstances of the patient's interview and reasons the patient gave for coming.*
- *III. Background: the patient's social and family background.*
- *IV. Symptoms and Mental Status: summary of symptoms and observations about the patient's thinking and feelings,*
- *V. Diagnostic Impression: initial diagnosis, given how much has been learned to date.*
- *VI. Summary and Integration of Findings: comprehensive integration of all that is known.*
- *VII. Disposition: how the case was resolved.*
- *VIII. Theoretical Perspectives: comparison of major theoretical perspectives applied to the subject's life.*

Analysis of Psychology Assignment 3

This assignment is similar to Assignment 2 in that it asks students to summarize and evaluate. But what they will summarize and evaluate here is not an article in a scholarly journal but a client's psychological case. The evaluation is termed a "diagnosis," and students' ultimate goal is to arrive at the most accurate and appropriate diagnosis possible, given what's known from the case summary.

This assignment is also similar to Assignment 2 in that it requires students to use a formalized structure provided by the instructor. They will present the facts of the case in Sections I–III, make observations and pinpoint symptoms in Section IV, provide a Diagnosis in Section V, integrate all of the above and resolve the case in Sections VI and VII. Section VIII allows students to apply theoretical knowledge from the course to this particular case. Note that the report from Sections II–VII is a narration of an event, moving from the initial presentation of the case to its resolution.

Part of the assignment's challenge is to tell the events of "the story" in their proper order. Students may be tempted, for example, to present some of their diagnostic impressions when discussing the patient's background, or they may be tempted to present theoretical perspectives within the diagnosis. Neither approach is allowed in the assignment. Success will require students to consider fully each of the categories included in the structure and to "plug in" the appropriate development.

Guide for Reading

Don's paper is a complete, informative discussion and explanation of this case. He writes clearly, which means that readers don't have to struggle to determine what Don is trying to convey. His paragraphs are fully and logically developed; that is, they have ample detail, and the sentences are closely related. His sentences are varied and well constructed. The result of his skill and effort is an outstanding paper that is an excellent model for this assignment.

SAMPLE PSYCHOLOGY PAPER 7

Victor: An Assessment Report

Don S. (a junior)

I. DESCRIPTION

Victor Taylor is a twenty-three year old, "home sales manager" for a Christian publishing corporation (New Life Publications). He considers himself to be a religious Christian. He lives in a rented room in the home of the Galinsky family; he is rarely there because he spends much of his time on the road selling New Life products.

Victor called the HELPLINE yesterday evening and made an appointment with a counselor for today (Thursday) to talk about "a personal problem." I saw him during several two and three hour sessions. He is very pleasant and cooperative, though he is frustratingly adept at dodging questions that he finds uncomfortable.

II. PRESENTING COMPLAINT

Mr. Taylor's appointment was for ten o'clock Thursday morning, he arrived twenty minutes early at 9:40. He was initially very reluctant to tell me why he had arranged for an appointment.

Mr. Taylor had come seeking counseling on the advice of a District Attorney. He has been arrested for inflicting an exhibition of his genitalia upon an unwilling person, a certain person whose husband was unfortunately (for Mr. Taylor) at home and tackled Mr. Taylor before calling the police. Mr. Taylor suffered no injuries at the hands of the irate husband. Mr. Taylor has opted to go to his trial without legal counsel, wishing to represent himself. Upon the DA's advice, he wants from me a letter to the effect that he is undergoing treatment for his problem, in the hope that the judge's sentence will be more lenient.

He reports that he has been very cooperative with the authorities and he will plead "guilty" at his trial eleven days from the day of our first interview; he is out of jail on an unsecured bond. Mr. Taylor expresses desire to get over his problem quickly.

III. BACKGROUND

Mr. Taylor grew up in Topeka, Kansas. His mother, Joyce, is a devout Baptist and housewife; Mike, his father, is less religious and operates his own business selling stocks and bonds. He has one brother, Charlie, who is three and a half years Mr. Taylor's senior.

Mr. Taylor describes his mother as warm and caring, and he often mentions her comforting him and his brother with good food and back rubs. He remembers very well how she protected her sons from their overbearing, violent father. From Mr. Taylor's description of his father, I can speculate that he has alcohol-related problems. Mr. Taylor recalls his father as being strict and prone to spanking his sons when he disapproved of their behavior or was angry. It is interesting to note that Mr. Taylor was often spanked with his pants pulled down. By Mr. Taylor's account, Joy and Mike Taylor do not have a happy marriage. His father behaved abusively to the entire family and his mother mostly resisted her husband's actions passively, when she resisted. Victor Taylor reports that his father engaged in several extramarital affairs, and he frequently causes turmoil in the home by complaining of his job's stress. His mother rarely openly fought back at her husband, except when he drank alcohol and/or brought liquor into their home. She did conspire with her sons to protect them from their father. On different occasions, Mike left his family for several months at a time, always to eventually return. Once he left for six months after Joy's mother reported Mike to the authorities for repeatedly physically abusing her grandsons. Mike Taylor was never punished due to the lack of evidence in the case.

Mr. Taylor said of his brother, Charlie, that he is the "smart one" of his family. Charlie did well in school and college and has always been very popular with friends. Currently Charlie is in prison for child molestation; Mr. Taylor was very hesitant to tell me this and feels that his brother has been imprisoned unjustly.

Mr. Taylor has not seen his other relatives for quite some time. He does not visit his brother often, though he sees his parents once or twice each month. Mr. Taylor reports only one close friendship during his childhood, and that with a boy whose name he cannot remember. The man Mr. Taylor presently claims as his best friend, he sees only a few times a year and that relationship, judging from his description of it, is rather shallow. Mr. Taylor cites a lack of time to make and maintain close relationships, but he is reluctant to admit that he does not feel he has enough friends.

He has undergone psychological treatment only once before, for a period of about a month during the spring of his twelfth grade. He sought psychological treatment then, as now, under legal advice—this time from his probation officer. He saw Dr. Geri Little once each week during one-hour sessions. Mr. Taylor claims his urges to expose himself decreased during the period he met with Dr. Little. Mr. Taylor discontinued treatment, by simply missing his appointments, when he decided he no longer needed them.

Now Mr. Taylor claims he is enthusiastic about entering into psychological treatment about his exhibitionism.

IV. SYMPTOMS AND MENTAL STATUS

Victor Taylor reports neither hallucinations nor thoughts of suicide nor thoughts of violence against others. He does mention recurring urges to expose himself, an urge he tries very hard not to give into. He says he has a very good apetite and it actually seems to me that he over-eats. He complains of having trouble getting to sleep until very late at night and consequently has trouble waking up in the mornings. I would say this problem is caused and/or compounded by the fact that he drinks five to ten cups of coffee per day and relies on the caffeine to wake him up in the morning. He does not think he drinks too much coffee, nor does he make a connection between his caffeine-intake and his sleeping problems.

He reports headaches of varying duration (one to seven days) that occur every three to four weeks. He complains that they are "real bad." He has never received medical attention concerning these headaches, but he takes quite a bit of aspirin. His headaches appear exclusively while Mr. Taylor is traveling and seem to be related to stress, though there are possibly biological factors such as unhealthy eating, sleeping and exercise habits which may also play a role. Mr. Taylor's problems appear neither psychotic nor physically threatening to himself or to others. He is coherent and rational. However, he is strikingly immature for a man of his age. Mr. Taylor continues to store most of his belongings in his old bedroom at his parents' home; he is irresponsible financially and is insensitive to the feelings of others, particularly women. He is unwilling to admit faults or weaknesses in his own character and behavior, even those that are obvious and self-incriminating from his own descriptions. Mr. Taylor's aspirations for success are self-defeating and unrealistically high, considering his occupation, job-performance and education. He prefers to attribute responsibility for his moral decisions to outside sources, particularly his religion. Also, Mr. Taylor does not accept responsibility for his actions very well.

At age twelve, Mr. Taylor made his debut as an exhibitionist to young women in his neighborhood. His exhibitionism fits the pattern mentioned in <u>Abnormal Psychology</u> (p. 382); it is "compulsive, insistent and ritualistic." Victor resists urges to expose himself and finally cannot resist any longer; he has "flashed" women on repeated occasions, several times per year, and his urges to do so continue; his method of "flashing" is the same every time: he sees an attractive woman, he hides somewhere near her intended path, jumps out at her with his pants down while masturbating, and often experiences orgasm when she sees him. It is interesting to note that he is convinced that many of his victims enjoy this experience, and he says that he is most stimulated when the woman likes being "flashed."

Victor's major concern is that he wishes to stay out of jail. He has implied that he has given the responsibility for his remaining outside of prison into God's—and my—hands; an example of his <u>preparation</u> to shift the blame onto parties other than himself should he have to serve a jail sentence.

V. DIAGNOSTIC IMPRESSION

Mr. Taylor has several long-term, relatively mild, but aggravating personality problems. His inability to become involved in or to maintain long-term intense personal relationships has been present throughout his entire life. He appears to have attained a degree of social skill necessary to begin close relationships, but Mr. Taylor seems afraid to or does not know how to continue past the very casual.

Given that Mr. Taylor's parents had no real close friends, it is possible that brought up in such an environment, he may simply lack the social skills associated with keeping close friendships outside of his immediate family.

Victor Taylor is essentially very insecure and terrified of seeing himself in an unpositive light. For instance, he does not think of himself as a criminal or a dangerous person, though he has been arrested on criminal charges and his exhibitionism clearly causes emotional damage to his victims. He often assigns responsibility for his actions onto others, and his fundamentalist religious beliefs make a convenient bandage for his easily wounded self-esteem; he puts his "faith in the Lord" or he rationalizes to render himself blameless in difficult situations, instead of taking initiative or responsibility in his own life.

Taylor's emotional immaturity is further exemplified by his reluctance to live independently. He rents a room in a house from an older married couple, where they indulgently allow him to get behind in rent payments and do not require him to pay for minor things such as his long-distance phone charges. This relationship appears very much like that between parents and their dependent child.

He effectively suppresses unpleasant or undesirable thoughts, emotions and memories to the point where he has trouble recalling them and examining them in any detail or depth.

The fact that he began his exhibitionism at such a young age (twelve, and he was first arrested at about age fourteen for exhibitionism) and has continued in this behavior for approximately ten years suggests that his problem, plus his other related ones, are long-standing, not transient.

VI. SUMMARY AND INTEGRATION OF FINDINGS

Victor Taylor's problem is consistent with other "typical" exhibitionist: Victor feels sexually powerful when he can force someone to notice his sexuality without opportunity for them to reject him, nor for him to have to perform sexually and be faced with humiliation or failure.

Mr. Taylor's own heavily guilt-repressed sexuality, insecurities and need for recognition combined with his inability to positively express anger (or any of his other emotions) and his disregard for women probably contributes to his aggression towards females via his exhibitionism.

He says he has no prior sexual experience and took an interest in sexual relationships with women later than is typical for heterosexual adolescent males. Financially his situation is not stable because his salary is based on commission in an easily fluctuable industry. Victor's interest in hobbies or other activities are superficial, except for his preoccupation with violent, macho sports, like football.

VII. DISPOSITION

Given that Victor Taylor has previously sought out psychological treatment only when he is in legal trouble; that he stopped going to his only counselor when his symptoms were somewhat alleviated; his financial situation, and his ability to rationalize any decision, no matter how illogical, I would predict that he will not voluntarily continue treatment much past his trial date, assuming he does not go to prison.

I would advise to the judge that his condition would not be lessened or helped by prison conditions. I feel that continued, consistent psychological counseling/treatment would best facilitate improvement; I would recommend that it be enforced by a court order that Mr. Victor Taylor undergo treatment on an outpatient basis, assuming this is legally feasible.

VIII. THEORETICAL PERSPECTIVES

According to the behavioral/cognitive perspective, Mr. Taylor's condition can be explained in Pavlovian terms. The unconditioned stimulus of genital stimulation plus the conditioned stimulus of seeing a shocked or frightened woman produce the unconditioned response of sexual pleasure. The sight of a frightened woman as erotically stimulating became a conditioned stimulus because Mr. Taylor was receiving a reward (sexual pleasure while he masturbated) when he shocked a woman.

Psychology

To the psychodynamic perspective, Taylor formed a positive cathexis for shocking women early in his first few playful acts of exhibition. He began exhibiting himself to women as an act of rebellion against his father, recalling the incidents when Taylor was spanked with his pants pulled down. This venting of misplaced aggression at an object less threatening than his father became associated with erotic pleasure as Taylor matured [if this word can ever be used to describe Victor] physically. Thus he developed a fetish for exhibitionism, loving, and deriving sexual pleasure from shocking women.

The two explanations are very similar. The psychodynamic explanation is more complex and offers more of a why Mr. Taylor would opt to shock women in the first place. But the cognitive/behavioral model is more empirically provable and logical. Both interpretations allow for Mr. Taylor's peculiar emotional state and thought patterns concerning his inability to channel anger well and his disregard of women. Though both views bring about a greater understanding of Mr. Taylor and his paraphilia, neither one offers conclusive explanations about why or how Mr. Taylor developed a paraphilia for exhibitionism while others in similar conditions do not.

I do agree with the psychodynamic model that Victor was expressing aggression against his father when he began exhibiting his genitals. The similarities between the cognitive/behavioral and the psychodynamic approaches about how Mr. Taylor became sexually stimulated by the act of frightening unwitting women are virtually undifferentiated and I find them both agreeable. However, I also lack solid explanations as to why this came about. My theory is that somewhere in Victor's unique illogical cognitive/emotional processes, exhibitionism must have made sense.

> **STUDY QUESTIONS**
>
> 1. Do you feel that you know Victor Taylor well after reading Don's paper? Do you need any more information in sections I–IV to understand sections V–VIII? If so, what facts would you like to know?
>
> 2. The assignment states that you are to "apply what you are learning in class and your own insights to the individual you encounter in the interview." Mark these two types of information in Don's paper. Are they adequate? In other words, does he seem to know enough from class and is he sufficiently involved in Mr. Taylor's history to explain his case convincingly?

Guide for Reading

Jacci's paper is also complete and well written, and it is certainly well above average. You will notice, however, that she didn't become as involved in the case and in explaining it as Don did. Her paper is one that we can't fault, simply because there are no major problems in it. Yet it doesn't address the complexities of the case as well as Don's paper, and it lacks some of the verbal felicity that his writing exhibits. As a result, it isn't quite as good. When you read this paper, try to identify those places where Jacci fails to address complexities sufficiently.

SAMPLE PSYCHOLOGY PAPER 8

Assessment Report: Victor Taylor

Jacci Q. (a junior)

I. Description

Victor Taylor is a twenty year old, unmarried man residing in Tulsa, Oklahoma. He is a home sales manager for "New Life Publications." Mr. Taylor oversees a sales force of parttime college students in a three state area. Mr. Taylor was instructed to come into our Helpline offices when he called one evening. Upon meeting him, I found he was very outgoing and friendly.

II. Presenting Complaint

Mr. Taylor called the Helpline at 9:30 a.m. on Thursday, May 26. He asked to speak to someone about a "personal problem." Mr. Taylor made an appointment for 10:00 a.m. on Friday. He arrived twenty minutes early for his interview. His primary reason for coming to Helpline is a charge brought against him for exposing himself to a woman. This interview reveals that Mr. Taylor has been told that the DA probably wouldn't be very hard on him if he had a letter from a professional stating that he was receiving help for his problem and that he was not a danger to anyone. It is also revealed that Mr. Taylor suffers from recurring headaches.

III. Background

Victor Taylor is the younger of two boys. His father was also a salesman and his mother was a homemaker. His parents reside in Topeka, Kansas. He completed one year of college but did not return in the fall reportedly because of the money he was making during the summer. Mr. Taylor reports having been a salesman for about eight to ten years and has worked for his present company for about two and a half years. He has never married and has no children. He rents a room in a house near campus but he also has his room at his parents' home just as it was in high school. He travels a lot and therefore he spends many of his nights in motel rooms. His relationship with his mother has been close; however, his relationship with his father has been very strained. His parents seem to have had a similar relationship with his brother, Charlie. Both of his parents are living.

IV. Symptoms and Mental Status

Mr. Taylor reports that he gets these "urges" to expose himself to women several times a day to every few weeks. The urges are harder to suppress when he is tired or "feeling down." He also reports recurring headaches which last up to a week, and ___ occur every three or four weeks. Mr. Taylor sometimes has trouble getting to sleep but sleeps soundly. He appears very elated and perhaps overly optimistic about his future plans. He has no loss of appetite and has not had any hallucinations. Although he reports that he once considered suicide as a teen, he does not have any such thoughts at the present time. His main problem now is the need to receive treatment for his exhibitionism and to let the DA know of his treatment.

V. Diagnostic Treatment

Mr. Taylor appears to have a longstanding psychosomatic disorder. He reports that he has been exposing himself since age twelve and has been having the recurring headaches since early in high school. He admits he has a problem and genuinely seems to want help. The need for help has recently become more urgent because of the police charges that have been brought against him. His headaches seem to be brought on by spending time traveling in the course of his work. Given that his grandfather and father were both salesmen and given the fact that his father was very work motivated, as well as money motivated, suggests that Mr. Taylor's problems may be partly genetic as well as environmental, or learned. Given the length of time he has had problems, they seem to be enduring rather than transient.

VI. Summary and Integration of Findings

Victor Taylor appears to have a psychomatic disorder. His headaches seem to be directly related to his job and personality type. He is a very active man at times and seems to push himself very hard to work and succeed. Hard work and success were his father's main lessons to his sons. Victor shows his father's characteristics in the important role of money and hard work with little or no time for close friends. Like his father, Victor is very friendly and talkative. He likes his job and plans to stay with it.

Mr. Taylor has yet to separate from his parents as seen in the fact that he still maintains his room in their house just as he left it. He appears to be a "loner" even though he doesn't admit it. He has a very few friends he spends leisure time with. Victor's paraphilia, his psychosexual disorder of exhibitionism, is apparently his only sexual "contact" with women. He is still virgin but he does try to meet "nice" women at his church. He does have deep religious views on subjects such as alcohol and drugs. Victor has been in psychological treatment before, for a short time in high school where he stopped because he felt he was better. He does seem motivated to begin therapy.

VII. Disposition

Mr. Taylor has continued to see me on a regular basis as was his wish. He is progressing well. Part of our focus is on how to continue in his present job while structuring it around more responsible eating habits and living arrangements. Biofeedback sessions have also been useful in managing stress and tension associated with his headaches.

VIII. Theoretical Perspectives

Mr. Taylor's problems likely stem from his father's views on work. He may have unresolved feelings toward his father. Victor's mania seems to be related to his father. Victor seems to feel he has to live up to his father's image by being as good at his job as his father was. He seems to have very unrealistic goals such as returning to school and sales getting better. It seems he has never made enough money to do much more than get by, but he feels he is very good at what he does and he will make alot of money from it soon.

Since Victor's brother Charlie also appears to have a psychosexual disorder (pedophilia), it is very probable that his paraphilia is genetically based. This along with his father's attitude towards sex.

Psychodynamic theory suggests that Victor's problems may stem from conflicts between his father's loose sexual morals and his mother's strict Baptist values. This conflict in turn generates unconscious anxiety which may cause his "urges" to jump in front of women and masturbate.

> **STUDY QUESTIONS**
>
> 1. Compare the Theoretical Perspectives of Don's paper and Jacci's. Which organizes its discussion more successfully? What organizational strategy does the more successful writer use in this section?
>
> 2. Look at the Disposition section of Jacci's paper. What important aspect of Victor Taylor's case does she ignore in this section?

Guide for Reading

Sheri's paper is an average response because it does only what the assignment asks for. Her paper is not as easy or as pleasurable to read as the other two for several reasons. For example, she is not involved enough in the subject to present Victor Taylor's case to readers as completely as it should be. (As you read, you should try to identify other factors that signal a lack of involvement.) In places, Sherri presents information in a haphazard manner, and you should try to determine what effect this has on paragraph development.

SAMPLE PSYCHOLOGY PAPER 9

Assessment Report: Victor Taylor

Sheri C. (a junior)

I. Description

Victor Taylor is a twenty-two and a half year old home sales manager representing "New Life Publications". He was seen in five, one-hour long sessions conducted at the HELPLINE offices. He was very cooperative.

II. Presenting Complaint

Mr. Taylor called the HELPLINE on the evening of April 27 expressing concern for a personal problem. He was given an appointment for 10:00 a.m. the following morning. He arrived for his first interview at 9:40, 20 minutes early. His primary concerns were that he has chronic headaches and that he exposes himself to women. The latter is what brought him to the HELPLINE after he was arrested for exposing himself to a woman whose husband pressed charges.

III. Background

Victor Taylor is the younger of two children born to Joyce and Mike Taylor. He graduated from high school with mostly B's and C's and attended his freshman year of college after which he began his present job working for "New Life Publications" as a sales manager. He has never married and has no children. For the past seven months he has rented a room where he lives alone. Mr. Taylor reports being very close to his mother, enjoying her good food and her frequent backrubs. However, he reports being afraid of his father who whipped Victor and his brother when younger, frequently left for extended periods of time, and drinks accessively. Victor's brother, Charlie, is 26 years old and is currently in prison at the Canyon City Prison in Colorado after being arrested for child molesting.

IV. Symptoms and Mental Status

Mr. Taylor reports chronic headaches and "urges" to expose himself. Also, he suffers from loose bowels and insomnia. He reports no experiences of hallucinations and is not considering suicide, although, at age 16 or 17 he did feel suicidal for reasons he cannot remember. He is, however, anxious about going to trial. Victor appears competent, though not as responsible as he should be. Furthermore, Victor seems sincere in wanting to rid of his urges to expose himself.

V. Diagnostic Impression

Victor Taylor appears to have long-standing psychosexual problems. The major diagnostic issues are the extent of his chronic headaches and exhibitionism and the probable cause of both the headaches and his urges to expose himself. It is likely that his headaches are stress related being that he tries to ignore things that bother him and ___ he is concerned with his business. His loose bowels and insomnia are probably the result of his drinking 5 to 10 cups of coffee a day. It is difficult to know the extent and underlying cause of his exhibitionism. It's possible that this may be a result of his father beating Victor while he lay naked on the bed.

VI. Summary and Integration of Findings

Victor Taylor has experienced urges to expose himself since age 12 and has experienced the headaches since high school. Victor claims he is not a loner, however, he lives by himself, travels alone, doesn't "hang out" with people, doesn't date, and sees his closest friend only a couple times a year. His financial situation is unknown. He has had his present job for two and a half years. He has no bill except rent. He doesn't like to go to the doctor because he says they're crooks, they're too expensive. He says dates are too expensive so he doesn't take girls out. He bounces checks but always "makes them good". Victor is a Christian, saved at age 17. He prays every day to help him, he claims it makes him feel better. Victor attends church regularly, every Sunday and Sunday evening and Wednesday evenings if he doesn't have to work. Victor loves football, he likes to hear the helmets hit. He reported having let his anger out when he played football. He likes to watch wrestling on television. One of his favorite movies is *Friday the 13th* in which he really likes the main character, Jason. Though he enjoys all of this violence, he doesn't fish or hunt because he reportedly doesn't want to kill anything. He claims he doesn't believe in killing unless the person is evil. Victor does not date regularly. He likes cute, decent girls and does not like cheap, trashy women. He liked his former therapist but she didn't turn Victor on because she was nice and understanding and not trashy. He was once engaged while in school until she broke it off. He reports that it excites him to think about exposing himself. Victor is a virgin. Victor wants to begin therapy in order to get help for his problems in addition to getting a note for the judge for his previous arrest.

VII. Disposition

Mr. Taylor appears to be a good candidate for psychotherapy. He was referred to the North Carolina Mental Health Center for a comprehensive evaluation and treatment.

VIII. Theoretical Perspectives

Victor Taylor's current and most pressing problem of exposing himself to women shows a psychosexual disorder of the paraphilia exhibitionism (Axis I 302.40). This seems to be Victor's only form of sexual release. This psychosexual disorder may stem from a fear of sexual relationships and ___ his failure at the one romantic relationship he had. It may also be cause to believe he is emotionally immature. The only evidence of a biological basis is the connection of his brother being in prison for child molesting. The only basis for a childhood trauma would be his father whipping him while he lay naked on the bed. This in itself could cause Victor to relate a bed and/or nudeness to being punished and therefore make him fearful or inadequate in sexual relationships. A possible Axis II diagnosis for Victor would be narcissistic personality (301.81)

> ## STUDY QUESTIONS
>
> 1. Review the Summary and Integration of Findings section in Sheri's paper. How could she have better organized her material? Does she include any observations or interpretations that help readers integrate these findings? Rewrite this section so the information will seem part of a single topic instead of scattered ideas.
>
> 2. Each paper gives information not contained in the other two. What information do you feel is important enough to be included, and what is not relevant to the case?
>
> 3. Each writer gives Victor a different age. How would you explain this inconsistency?

Writing Assignments

1. Interview one of your classmates about his or her writing. Using the formal structure employed in Assignment 3, summarize your classmate's writing background, strengths and weaknesses as a writer, and writing habits. Then integrate your findings and recommend a course of action that, from your knowledge of good writing, would help your classmate improve as a writer.
2. Rewrite one of the assessment reports on Victor Taylor. Instead of using a formal structure and writing for an instructor, write an informal letter to Victor explaining the conclusions you have reached concerning his case.
3. For this assignment, the class must divide itself into teams composed of "patients" and "therapists" that are further divided into pairs. Go to the library and research psychosexual disorders. Working in pairs, the patients should write a "patient history" that outlines relevant personal characteristics and that describes the symptomatic behavior. They should then submit the history to a pair of therapists, who use it to produce an assessment report similar to the ones above.

6 Political Science

INTRODUCTION TO WRITING IN POLITICAL SCIENCE

Writing assignments in political science courses demand two special skills: summary and analysis. Many of the assignments for entry-level courses ask students to read politically oriented articles and essays and then to analyze them using information presented in class discussions or the textbook.

How well one summarizes depends in large part on how well one reads. That is, you must be able to recognize and understand the important points in an article before you can write an accurate summary of it. Because writing assignments require you to translate the gist of any reading into your own words, not copy down passages verbatim, you usually have to understand the underlying political science principles at work to do well. (In fact, this generalization applies to just about every kind of assignment you will encounter in college.) A good preparation for any assignment involving summary is to look at some of the examples of summary and paraphrase available in most writing handbooks.

Whenever you are asked to "explain the connection," "critique," or "analyze," you must do more than simply repeat information. In political science assignments that ask you to do one of the above, you are expected to show a knowledge of the principles and trends that cause or influence a specific political situation. Your ability to display this knowledge will commonly constitute the major criterion for success. Simply being able to state the facts of a situation through summary is deemed a low-level skill. Training you to apply what you are learning in class to that situation is usually the teacher's goal, and you should keep this point in mind whenever you approach any assignment.

The first two sample assignments in this chapter are from entry-level (freshman/sophomore) courses that introduce students to the basic concepts of the discipline; to a large extent, they deal with current political situations. The papers assigned in these courses are usually short, and, as mentioned above, they require summary and analysis. (Analysis plays a major part in all of the assignments in this section.) The aim of this type of assignment is to make you aware of current political events and to ask you to study and interpret them in the same manner as the historical examples in textbooks. In other words, summaries ask you to relate what a text says, and analysis asks you to tell what it means. The tasks are very similar to those we've already practiced in earlier sections.

The third sample assignment comes from an upper level (junior/senior) course in criminal justice. Although some colleges recognize criminal justice as a separate department, many others include it as part of the political science curriculum. The course this assignment came from involved class work and an internship with a law enforcement agency. The purpose of internships is to give students a chance to experience the field they have been studying, without the pressure of regular employment. The writing assignment is both a report and an analysis of the experience, a combination of what students learned in class and in the field.

POLITICAL SCIENCE ASSIGNMENT 1

Course: **Introduction to Political Science**

In order to increase their awareness about what is going on around them, students are required to read a daily newspaper or a weekly magazine of their choice which covers political and economic news and carries political and economic opinion. (Some may claim that they do not subscribe to any paper or magazine of such a kind. The library does have subscriptions to several.) Depending on the chapters of the text that have been covered at a specific time period, students are to choose an article which is relevant to the subject matter at hand. Students are then to write an integration paper using the said article.

An integration paper is a one-to-two-page paper which contains a brief summary or highlight of the main points of the chosen article and which then tries to relate these issues to the main points which have been learned from class and from the text.

In writing the paper students are to use any of the popular word processing software packages available in the computer lab in order to facilitate their work. Please indicate what software was used in generating the output.

Students should also practice all the proper rules of grammar and spelling. To get proper credit the paper should be neat and free from grammatical and typographical errors. After all, students are using word processors which have allowed for a much easier typing and editing job. Any papers with more than five red marks of any kind made by the instructor will be returned for revision before a grade for the paper will be issued.

Analysis of Political Science Assignment

This is a straightforward assignment that states clearly the topic and form of the integration paper. The paper itself is relatively simple, containing a brief summary followed by an explanation relating the article to an issue from the textbook or class discussion. In addition to format, the instructor seems very concerned that students use a word processor and produce a paper free of surface errors.

Such an assignment may falsely lull many students into thinking that it will be easy to make a good grade. A successful summary, however, involves careful reading and writing, which are not particularly simple tasks, as the following papers illustrate.

Ideally, a good integration paper will contain at the beginning a brief summary that focuses only on the main issues in the article. Students must understand the article well enough to recognize the main points; then they must express those points in their own words. Readers should have no trouble determining that the information comes from a published article, not from the student writer. After the summary, students should identify the issue from the textbook or class discussion in enough detail to substantiate its relationship to the article.

Moreover, readers should have no trouble separating the information contained in the article from the explanation of the relationship. A good summary will therefore contain specific cues to help in this regard, expressions such as "According to the article," "The author states," and "The main point of the article is." It is not necessary to quote unless a short excerpt can succinctly express the author's position and tone. Too many quotations distract readers and suggest that students responding to the assignment may be unwilling or unable to engage in independent thought.

Although many teachers, like the one who produced the above assignment, often talk about grammatical errors, few students really produce ungrammatical language. The problem is one of usage, not grammar. That is, students will use the word *effect* when the context calls for *affect*, or they will use the word *lay* when the context calls for *lie*, and so on. You should know that a huge number of people, not only teachers, view such usage errors as a sure sign of a writer's carelessness. We know, of course, that the issue is more complex than that, but you will be doing yourself a great service if you manage to avoid usage errors. One way to do this is to study the usage section in any writing handbook; it will explain the most common errors and how to avoid them.

An integration paper should contain the title and author of the article you've read. This information, plus the date, page, and title of the publication in which it is found, should be included on a reference page at the end of the paper. A commonly used documentation guide in political science is the *Chicago Style Manual*, and another is the APA. An abbreviated version of both is included in the overview to writing in the social sciences.

You may be surprised at how difficult it is to duplicate the proper format. Most students deem documentation to be a low-level skill, so they don't pay much attention to what they are doing. As a result, they rarely get it right. And because teachers *also* deem it to be a low-level skill, they see a student's inability to supply the proper documentation format as another sign of carelessness.

As a final point, we would comment on the style appropriate to this assignment, even though the assignment itself says nothing in this regard, probably because the teacher assumes (perhaps incorrectly) that students will be aware of what constitutes proper style. Your style should not be distracting. You should not strive to imitate the style of the article or to entertain readers with any kind of flourish. Don't, for example, use dramatic language, such as: "The writers of this article thrill readers with their description of the economic factors related to the recent tide of unrest in China." The purpose of political science papers is to inform readers, not to entertain them, so the writing should be objective and plain.

Class Article 1

Why Can't We Get Good People to Serve in Government?

"The flow of talent from the private sector into public service effectively has been dammed, and the results could be disastrous."

by Harry L. Freeman

Whatever happened to the tradition of eminent figures from the private sector offering public service to the nation? This custom produced statesmen who left their mark on the Washington of yesteryear as well as on history, such as Dean Acheson, Henry Stimson, and Averell Harriman. Today, the available pool of highly able recruits to public service from the private sector is growing smaller and drier—largely for lack of interest.

My concern, and the focus of this article, is directed toward political appointments—*i.e.*, that layer of people above the civil service and below Cabinet appointments. These include assistant secretaries, deputy assistant secretaries, etc.

I am concerned that we are not getting the quality of people we should be getting to fill these critical political appointments. Why is this so? Some minor disincentives put aside, plain and simple, I lay the major responsibility at the feet of the people who have run for president in recent years.

In my view, these presidential aspirants have run "against Washington" and, by doing so, have discouraged a lot of creative and talented people from coming to Washington to serve their country in the public

---

"Why Can't We Get Good People to Serve in Government?" by Harry L. Freeman, *USA Today Magazine*, January 1988. Copyright © 1988 by the Society for the Advancement of Education. Reprinted by permission.

service. The flow of talent from the private sector into public service effectively has been dammed, and the results could be disastrous.

Traditionally and classically, the dual-career, dual-perspective person came into government after achieving distinction in the private sector—in business, the law, or academic life. It helped—in fact it was essential—to have independent means, either through inheritance or business success or through what was once called a "fortunate marriage." For such people, public service was a kind of crowning touch to an already charmed life.

In addition, there was another group that joined the ranks of public servants, but for a very different reason—namely, as an alternative to unemployment. This was especially true during the Great Depression, when the only jobs available were in government.

Not so long ago, talented people from the private sector could be recruited rather readily into service not only in the Cabinet, but in the array of posts below that level. They considered public service a high calling, and looked forward to a sojourn in Washington as an exciting prospect. One need only recall the likes of John J. McCloy (High Commissioner in post-war Germany), investment banker Douglas Dillon (Treasury Secretary under Pres. Kennedy), and the Ford Motor Company executive Robert S. McNamara (Defense Secretary under Presidents Kennedy and Johnson).

Today, such able recruits from private life can still be found, but they are fewer, especially below the Cabinet level. Moreover, some of those who do serve these days seem excessively eager to cash in on their experience and contacts.

Since roughly the Administration of Richard Nixon, both Republican and Democratic presidents have been appointing young people to high government posts—more campaign aides, and representatives of the not-for-profit sector, but fewer experienced and eminent people from the nation's corporations and other elements of the private sector. There are several reasons for this, some relatively minor, one major.

The minor reasons include pay and sheer inconvenience. As compensation in the private sector has risen and the cost of living has gone up, the financial sacrifice by people who quit to enter government service has become greater. Similarly, elaborate post-Watergate reform laws, instead of simply making penalties stiffer for the few wrongdoers in public service, have created a complicated web of disclosures and divestiture requirements that at worst imply that high officials are suspect until proven innocent, and at best make entering public service complicated and bothersome.

Another nettlesome problem is the tortuous length of the confirmation process. The time between agreeing to serve and being sworn in has stretched, over the years, from a few weeks to months—months in which a highly motivated executive may be forced to put his or her life on hold or, worse, seek to return to a corporate job just given up. Given such inconveniences, why bother?

The major problem, however, is that, in recent years, our political culture has devalued the profession of public service. For example, our last two presidents (one Democrat, one Republican) have come into office by running against Washington—deriding government as part of the problem, rather than part of the solution. John F. Kennedy, as far as I can tell, is the last American president who made it a point to speak of politics and public service as a noble profession, conveying a truth that many of us who have served in both worlds have learned: there are highs and lows in both public and private life, but there is no high like that of effectiveness in public service.

By running against Washington, subsequent presidents may have won short-term political advantage, but they have also tarnished public service as a calling and made it harder to recruit talented people.

Paul O'Neill, a longtime official of the Office of Management and Budget who is now president of International Paper Inc., put the problem this way: "Leaders generally don't say that their troops are lousy, bad or ne'er-do-wells who couldn't work anyplace else. In my experience, people who work in government have been damaged, hampered and demotivated by a leadership that has said its workers are bad."

Most conspicuously talented executives I meet are conspicuously uninterested in entering public service; those who are interested think only in terms of Cabinet jobs, of which there are precious few. The gulf between the business world of New York and the political world of Washington is growing wider and deeper.

As someone who has worked on both sides of the fence, I can say without hesitation that I'm a great believer in dual careers and the dual perspectives they provide. I can say with conviction that the corporate world, in its own self-interest, needs excellence in government. It needs able, professional, imaginative public servants who have some insight into the issues that are of critical interest to the business community. While I believe many corporate leaders would readily agree, I venture that only a few will do anything to help. Why is this so?

We often imagine the interests of the public sector and the private sector to be opposed. Very often, the media is quick to highlight the points of difference and dispute, the popular stereotype being that private interest and the public interest are generally in conflict. However, that stereotype, as generally is the case with stereotypes, is misleading and inaccurate.

Today, the interests of the two sectors converge at least as often as they stand in conflict. A prosperous, productive private sector produces the tax revenues that Congress and the Administration need to finance defense programs, debt service, and Social Security. Conversely, it serves the private sector well to have skilled and professional public servants conduct trade negotiations, issue patents, write regulations, and shape tax legislation—the infrastructure and environment in which business flourishes or suffers.

To most people in professional Washington, it is simply accepted that the nation, including the private sector, needs and wants excellence in government and in public service. We think that point should be obvious. Unfortunately, what is not obvious to many people is how to bring about this excellence. How can we ensure that the right people are being considered for the right job? More importantly, how can we encourage the right people to accept the challenges of public service, especially in light of some of the disincentives that currently make that choice less than easy to make?

THE ATTACK ON EXCELLENCE

There is a great deal of complacency in our nation that excellence in government is an obvious good, and I want to attack that complacency. It is apparent to me, from my vantage point in the corporate world, that most people today, including most senior corporate officials, put rather low priority on excellence in government, or at least do not fully understand the important role they can play in achieving this excellence. In recent years, some have even questioned the very concept of excellence in government and in the public service.

In May, 1986, *The Wall Street Journal* carried a remarkable op-ed article by Terry W. Culler, an executive recruiter who, until recently, was the associate director in charge of workforce effectiveness for the U.S. Office of Personnel Management. "The government," he wrote, "should be content to hire competent people, not the best and most talented people. A good case can be made that those individuals are needed in the private sector, where wealth is produced rather than consumed.

"The government," Culler continued, "does not need top graduates . . . , administrative offices staffed with MBA's best and brightest whatevers. Government's goal should be not employee excellence, but 'employee sufficiency.'"

Later in 1986, journalist Don Feder weighed in with an even stronger version of this thesis in his nationally syndicated column, "For the Record": "I am adamantly opposed to the concept of excellence in government. The very idea is terrifying. . . . Imagine what life would be like with a highly motivated IRS, an aggressive OSHA, and a Department of Health and Human Services driven to succeed. . . . I want a government that is disorganized, lethargic, and low-performing. It's our best hope for the preservation of liberty."

To most of us with experience in Washington, such views are easily refuted heresy. Finding cures for cancer, negotiating arms-control treaties, and making trade and tax policy are matters of great consequence—even matters of life and death. For these and a thousand other undertakings, mere sufficiency will never be enough; excellence is essential.

That is our view, but is it a consensus view beyond Washington? I doubt it. Nearly two decades of government-bashing, I'm afraid, have taken their toll. The whole ethos of excellence in public service—the very notion that public service is a high calling, deserving of the best talents—is now a minority notion. The consensus supporting public service, let alone excellence in public service, has been deflated.

This breakdown in consensus is the reason that most proposals for civil-service reform and recruitment for public service seem to me to miss the point. To use a couple of highly accurate cliches—and to mix a metaphor in the bargain—they put the cart before the horse and they miss the forest for the trees.

I have no quarrel with proposals to improve the incentives for public service, including pay. I have no quarrel with reviewing the laws and regulations governing ethics and disclosure with an eye toward removing barriers to public service. I encourage these efforts; indeed, I have called repeatedly for steps to make it less burdensome and more attractive for talented leaders to make the move from the private sector into public service.

My point is this: such nuts-and-bolts reforms will not go far, perhaps nowhere, until we can rebuild a strong national consensus in support of public service as a calling. It is time to call a "time-out" to the representation of public service as a frustrating, unrewarding, no-win situation that should be avoided by all individuals of substance. Changing public attitudes about public service is not simply one of the reforms we need to achieve—it is *the reform* we need to achieve. Rebuilding the ethos of public service is not simply one change that is needed, along with pay reform—it is the fundamental change that will make all others possible.

I have no pre-wrapped, pre-tested, fool-proof program that will achieve that ambitious end. However, I *can* suggest a couple of ways in which we might begin to do it.

We need to look at the disincentives that make the move from the private sector into the public so unattractive. The long and uncertain appointment and confirmation process needs to be streamlined so that senior executives will not be left twisting in the wind for many months after making a major career choice. The disparity between private and public compensation needs to be rectified, with a careful look at the mandatory participation in the retirement programs that the "dual careerist" may never use. One of my colleagues argues that every citizen should be provided with, say, two years of exemption from taxation while in public service. This kind of creative thinking is necessary if public service is to compete with the lucrative benefits of a job in the private sector.

In addition, we need to begin our educational efforts designed to change public attitudes, with special attention made toward reshaping the attitudes of senior leaders in the American business community. I suggest this for more than one reason. These leaders have great power to influence public opinion. Yet, they are often victims themselves of ignorance and false notions about government and about public servants. Moreover, these leaders, with their wealth of talent and experience, could serve their country well, but may be reluctant to enter public service because of the "bad press" it has received. As Drew Lewis recently said, "There are highs in public and private sectors. But there is no high like a real high in the public sector."

Perhaps most importantly, we can marshal support among the presidential candidates in 1988 for a moratorium on government-bashing. The idea that government can do nothing right is one of those false and pernicious claims that, left unchallenged, will become a self-fulfilling prophecy. Unfortunately, for some time, presidential candidates of both parties have been among the most successful spreaders of that falsehood. Opinion leaders can perform a major public service by persuading the candidates in 1988 to have no part in careless, indiscriminate attacks on government and the public service, and, affirmatively, to get the candidates on a pro-excellence in government theme. An "excellence in government" theme is consistent with either a "smaller" or "bigger" government plank. A reasoned debate about the role of government, yes; mindless government-bashing, no. If necessary, we need to revive the equivalent of the old Democratic and Republican "truth squads" that followed candidates around to try and set the record straight.

Adlai Stevenson once made a tart observation about the quality of government in America. "In the end," he said, "we get the public servants we deserve." He was right. All of us, especially leaders in the corporate sector, need to remember that, if we denigrate the calling of public service, we will not get the caliber of people that make for greatness—and we'll deserve what we get.

Guide for Reading

Glenda has produced an excellent integration paper; it is informative, well organized, and written in a style that is pleasing to read. Her summary is complete without being tedious, and her own comments follow the same order as the information in the summary. Why would this organization be an advantage?

Untitled

Glenda M. (a freshman)

In this article, "Why Can't We Get Good People to Serve in Government?," Harry L. Freeman editorializes about the lack of excellence in public service. This article focuses on political appointments; those above civil service workers but below Cabinet appointments. Freeman states that traditionally public service was an honor bestowed upon one who had achieved distinction in the private sector. Since the Nixon Administration, however, presidents have appointed young, relatively inexperienced persons to government positions. According to Freeman, presidents have been forced to choose such appointees because older, more experienced persons are not willing to make the financial sacrifice required when entering government service from the private sector, nor are they willing to put their lives on hold during the confirmation process. The major reason Freeman gives for lack of excellence in public service is that "our political culture has devalued the profession of public service" (13). Our last two presidents have come into office deriding government and government workers. This attitude has tarnished public service and has made it much more difficult to recruit talented people. Freeman urges educational efforts to be undertaken to change public opinion about government service.

Much criticism is directed toward government and its bureaucrats. With most of the private sector believing that government workers work less, waste more time and money, and are greatly overpaid in comparison with private employees, it is little wonder that the experts in private industry are not interested in public service. With today's attitudes concerning bureaucrats, a move from a private to a government career would hardly be a move of which one would be proud.

Certainly, there are problems in the bureaucracy. Some of them include almost permanent tenure, self-interest, and waste. Yet it is doubtful that constant criticism will encourage better performance. Certainly the bureaucracy could be made more efficient. But what better way to do so than by recruiting excellence? Such recruitments can take place, however, only if government service is once again considered a calling of honor.

Works Cited

Freeman, Harry L. "Why Can't We Get Good People to Serve in Government?" *USA Today* January 1988: 12–14.

Analysis of Sample Political Science Paper 1

This paper does exactly what the assignment asks for. The first paragraph provides a brief summary, naming both the article and its author. Glenda notes the author's main points: the decline in experienced people appointed to political positions at the level between civil service workers and Cabinet personnel. She states the trend, presents some reasons for the trend, and then gives the author's proposed solution.

Only one quotation appears in the paper, and it is appropriate because it states succinctly the main point of the article. It supplies important information that Glenda could not have said better in her own words. Glenda also skillfully connects this statement to her own writing, so there is no distracting break between her words and the quotation.

When referring specifically to the article, Glenda effectively uses the cues mentioned in our assignment analysis: "This article focuses," "Freeman states," and "According to Freeman" are some examples. Readers know who is responsible for what information. The parenthetical reference to the page of the quotation follows proper format, allowing readers to find it if they choose.

In the second paragraph, Glenda refers to the principle presented either in her class or her textbook, describing it in enough detail to inform readers and agreeing that the trend discussed in the article is accurate. In the third paragraph, she comments on the situation and briefly evaluates the possibility for its improvement. Her paper follows

Political Science

the same order as the summary: a description of the problem followed by a suggestion of what may help the situation.

Glenda demonstrates her ability to control language in several of the sentences she constructs. You should notice how she varies sentence structure. Particularly effective are the short sentences that begin the second and third paragraphs and the second from last sentence, in the form of a question, in the third paragraph. These short sentences and the question focus attention on themselves because one idea is stated succinctly and by itself, in contrast to the more involved sentences existing throughout the paper. Changing sentence patterns is an effective way to emphasize an idea.

The Works Cited page is an appropriate part of this type of paper, although a quick glance at the APA and *Chicago* formats illustrated in the overview to writing in the social sciences will show you that Glenda seems confused about which format she should use. She appears to have combined the two in her paper. Also note that the citation indicates that Glenda's article comes from the newspaper *USA Today*. Actually, it comes from *USA Today Magazine*. This problem is significant. For example, finding a copy of the article for this textbook required many hours of effort.

Class Article 2

"After INF, the Next New Arms Race"

It was, nearly everyone took pains to say, a truly historic agreement: For the first time ever, thanks to the treaty banning intermediate-range nuclear missiles, some of the superpowers' nuclear arms would actually be *destroyed*. And though the destruction carries more symbolic than strategic importance, both Ronald Reagan and Mikhail Gorbachev insist that the INF accord, whose verification provisions are still subject to some dispute, is just the beginning. But even now, as START talks are under way to reduce longer-range strategic weapons by up to 50 percent, a quiet new arms race has begun, and weapons experts on both sides once again are hard at work in their laboratories. Their task: To improve the destructive power of strategic missiles, the heavyweights remaining in the nuclear arsenals, and to devise new non-nuclear weapons that might take the place of both some long-range arms and the midrange nukes now bound for the scrapheap.

The options under consideration range from the sublime to the fairly

---

"After INF, The Next New Arms Race" by Robert Kaylor, *U.S. News & World Report*, May 9, 1988. Copyright © 1988 U.S. News & World Report. Reprinted by permission.

obvious, though there is an element of Buck Rogers in almost all of them. Scientists are working on new strategic nuclear warheads that maneuver as they fall through the atmosphere, and penetrate deep inside the earth before exploding near buried targets. The Pentagon is now experimenting with high-power microwaves that could immobilize enemy missiles by frying their electronic innards in the same way a household microwave cooks a chicken. And researchers are looking at laser radars and other guidance improvements that could triple the accuracy of cruise missiles armed with conventional explosives, making them able to do some of the same jobs as their more-powerful nuclear-tipped cousins. "You could have the same deterrent effect with a conventional weapon," says one well-placed Pentagon official, "as you now have with a nuclear weapon."

New arms debate. Is that the way to go? Joseph Braddock, a high-level Pentagon consultant and member of its Defense Science Board, sees an emerging debate now as the U.S. and its allies begin to rethink military strategies under intermediate and strategic-arms-control agreements. Should money be spent on these technological "silver bullet" solutions? Or should it go into beefing up conventional forces? Unsurprisingly, there is no clear consensus yet. But because the new weapons systems under consideration could be used with greater efficiency against some of the same targets as the banished nukes, they are appealing to many strategists.

Possibly the most promising conventional weapon is the cruise missile, the same small, unmanned aircraft the Pentagon tipped with nuclear warheads and based in Europe. In its ground-launched version, the cruise missile is banned by the INF treaty. It is still allowed, however, on aircraft, submarines and ships. Thus the Navy is looking at ways to more than double the conventional cruise missile's range and improve its accuracy.

There are engineering problems to be worked out, but the technology looks promising. Increased range could be accomplished with prop-fan engines, which add a propeller to jet turbines. Reducing the missile's weight by replacing metal with composite materials also would help. And exotic fuels, which combine solids with liquids, could boost range still further. Longer range means nothing, however, if the missile can't be targeted accurately over the longer distances. One proposal now on the boards promises to deliver a missile to within 3 feet of its target from a distance of 1,500 miles. How? The standard inertial-guidance systems, on which cruise missiles now rely, would be augmented by radar, laser or infrared sensors to provide images the missile could compare with a detailed "picture" of the target already programed into its onboard computer. That way, experts say, a missile could be designed to be so accurate that it could strike a pretargeted pillar of a strategically located bridge. Using new technology that lets warheads crunch through more than 10 yards of reinforced concrete before exploding, and special fuses still in the development stage, the missiles could accomplish tasks that, up until now, have required the greater destructive power of nuclear weapons.

Risks and rewards. High-power microwave, or HPM in the scientists' shorthand, involves more dazzle and drama than the cruise missiles, but it would be no less a threat, experts say. Pentagon officials won't discuss their programs, but John Pike, a military analyst for the Federation of American Scientists, says HPM could be used with great effect against elusive Soviet mobile-based missiles. If it were exploded in space, a 10-megaton nuclear weapon specially constructed to generate microwave emissions could frazzle any unprotected electronics within a 2,000-mile radius, Pike and others estimate. Thus, even if the U.S. didn't know *exactly* where Soviet mobile missiles were, a microwave blast could still disable them.

There are risks in the use of HPM weapons, however. Some arms-control advocates oppose them, believing they could tempt an enemy to try a nuclear first strike before his missiles are zapped by HPM. And Carnegie Mellon University researcher H. Keith Florig, writing in the March issue of the Institute of Electrical and Electronics Engineers' *Spectrum*, notes that laboratory rats whose brain temperatures were affected by microwaves suffered convulsions, unconsciousness and amnesia. "HPM weapons that blind, burn or bake people to death," writes Florig, "may be viewed as an abhorrent addition to the arsenal." But, he adds, it may be possible to design weapons with pulses "too low to harm people but with enough peak power to burn out hardware." The Pentagon says the Soviets might be able to field a tactical HPM weapon in the 1990s, and the U.S. Navy is believed to be working on a non-nuclear-explosive device that would serve as an HPM generator, possibly to defend ships from missile attack.

Toward bigger blasts. Where HPM weapons seem more insidious, non-nuclear "enhanced blast" technology is brutally blunt. Researchers are now improving an already existing fuel-air explosive that sprays a fine liquid mist into the air, then ignites it milliseconds later in a thunderclap blast killing anything in its path. Another technique being explored for use at sea recalls the high-school-science experiment in which potassium metal is dropped into water, creating a violent reaction. In its military application, an explosion would release a large mass of molten metal into the sea, causing a huge gas bubble that would, in turn, create a shock wave that could crush a submarine or break a ship in half. "Today's enhanced-blast technology," says Pentagon munitions expert George Kopcsak, "has four to seven times the force of TNT. And we have the potential of getting a factor of 10."

Impressive as they sound, it's still far from clear that such weapons will be built and deployed. With the budget constraints the next President will inherit, there will be stiff competition for scarce dollars for new weapons systems. And should the arms talks with the Soviets hit a snag sometime in the future, some conventional weapons likely would be far less attractive. Still, weapons experts say, the U.S. has to examine all technologies, from the newest cutting-edge long-distance weapons to nuts-and-bolts improvements in weapons for the front-line battlefield. "You have to be sure the other side does not have options that it did not have before," says Braddock. "Some new technologies might turn out to be silver bullets, but it costs money to find out."

Guide for Reading

Scott's paper is average; it informs readers, covers what the assignment asks for, and is free of surface errors. The main problem with the paper that keeps it from being better is that Scott's audience is his teacher, evidenced by his vague reference to the article and to the textbook. Notice how Glenda's paper can stand alone and inform all readers, but Scott's is clearly a response to an assignment. Why would audience be a factor in responding to the assignment? If you are surprised that Scott's teacher should want students to attend to audience, even though the assignment says nothing in this regard, go back and look again at "To the Student" at the beginning of this text.

SAMPLE POLITICAL SCIENCE PAPER 2

"AFTER INF, THE NEXT NEW ARMS RACE," by Robert Kaylor from U.S. News and World Report May 9, 1988, pp. 26–31

Scott J. (a freshman)

With the signing of the INF treaty by Ronald Reagan and Mikhail Gorbachev, which placed a ban on intermediate-range nuclear missiles; and START talks underway to limit longer-range strategic weapons, it would seem that the arms race is quieting. This is far from the case, as scientists on the American side and the Soviet side are working on new technology to make strategic missiles more destructive and accurate. The sci-

Political Science 283

entists are also working on making nuclear missiles that are not included in the INF accord more destructive. Both of the super powers also hope to come up with new non-nuclear weapons.

One of the conventional weapons that is being improved by the United States is the cruise missile. These cruise missiles, which were banned from being ground-launched by the INF treaty, are allowed on aircraft, submarines, and ships. The Navy is involved in research on improving the weapon's range as well as its accuracy. One proposal being worked on is a plan to make the cruise missile capable of hitting within three feet of its target, at a range of fifteen hundred miles.

The Americans and the Soviets are also working on high-power microwave, or HPM. A nuclear weapon is exploded in space, generating microwave emissions. These emissions would destroy unprotected electronics within a two thousand mile radius. This could disable many weapons, and it would be especially useful in incapacitating missiles whose exact location is unknown.

This article ties in with our discussions about Chapter 20 in our textbook, which is the chapter relating to defense policy. We discussed defense spending, and whether or not it should be cut. We also discussed nuclear freeze and disarmament.

What I found interesting about the article was the fact that although the INF treaty has reduced intermediate-range nuclear missiles, it will not necessarily save money, as both superpowers will plow any money that is saved on intermediate-range missiles into other weapons. While advocates of nuclear freeze are probably somewhat happy about the INF treaty, it will probably leave our current level of military spending unaffected. The superpowers will still continue to spend vast amounts of money on defense, with the hope of attaining the elusive goal of gaining the upper hand on the other.

Analysis of Sample Political Science Paper 2

This paper is an adequate response to the assignment. The information in the first three paragraphs, which summarize the article from *U.S. News and World Report*, is clearly expressed and well organized. Scott has focused on the important point in the article: In spite of the INF treaty, both the U.S. and the Soviet Union are actively developing more destructive and more accurate weapons. The first paragraph states this, and the second and third paragraphs add support with examples of new weapons. The paragraphs themselves are logically developed; each has a topic sentence supported by explanation.

The main problem with this summary is that it sounds more like information Scott put together rather than a summary of someone else's article. The phrase "this article" in the fourth paragraph, although indicating some type of transition, doesn't clear up the confusion. It will force many readers back to the title page to see which article is being referred to. Scott should have made a clear reference to the article at the beginning of his summary; then he could have used cues throughout the first three paragraphs to signify that the information comes from the article. Readers would then more clearly and more quickly recognize that the first three paragraphs contain a summary of the article mentioned on the title page.

The fourth paragraph identifies the connection between the article and a specific chapter in the textbook covering defense policy, defense spending, nuclear freeze, and disarmament. The fifth paragraph contains Scott's reaction to the article and text. Thus, in terms of form, Scott provides what the assignment asked for.

But more is at issue than simply form. When discussing the relationship between the textbook material and the article, Scott supplies very little concrete information. He *refers* to the textbook material, he does not *present* it. As a result, anyone who has not read the textbook will be at a loss in determining just what relationship obtains. The problem is one of audience. Scott is clearly writing solely for the instructor, as we see explicitly when he refers to "our discussion about Chapter 20 in our textbook" (paragraph 4). We would suggest that assuming his teacher is the only reader of the paper is a significant flaw. It led to Scott's spending too much effort showing he had done his assignment and too little effort informing readers about the topic. Had he imagined his paper would be read by a wider audience, Scott might have written a better response.

Political Science

Class Article 3

"Reagans are looking for good signs"

By Johanna Neuman, Taurus
(*USA Today*, May 4, 1988, pp. 14–24)

Washington—When President Reagan (an Aquarius) and Soviet leader Mikhail Gorbachev (a Pisces) met to sign a historic arms treaty at 1:30 p.m. last Dec. 8, White House planners were puzzled.

Their original plan was for a prime-time signing ceremony before a vast TV audience. But the East Wing was insistent: First Lady Nancy Reagan (Cancer) wanted the ceremony in early afternoon. The reason: Her astrologer told her the stars were right.

"A perfect time to launch a new era," said USA TODAY astrologist Catherine Usha.

The White House reeled—mostly with jokes—at the leaked revelation Tuesday that former chief of staff Donald Regan (Sagittarius) will reveal in his kiss-and-tell book May 16 that stargazers have invaded the White House.

"I knew they were out to lunch," said Rep. Bill Gray, D-Pa. (Leo), "but I didn't know they were out to space."

Regan, banished from the White House last year at Mrs. Reagan's urging, is enjoying an old Washington custom: Don't get mad, get even.

White House spokesman Marlin Fitzwater (Sagittarius) confirmed the story: "It's true that Mrs. Reagan has an interest in astrology. She has for some time, particularly following the assassination attempt on March 30, 1981. She was very concerned for her husband's welfare, and astrology has been a part of her concern in terms of his activities."

Translation: After the assassination attempt, the first lady turned to an astrologer-friend to avoid near-tragedies in future travel plans.

In fact, ABC's *Nightline* reported Tuesday night that an astrologer warned Mrs. Reagan of an "incident" that would occur on March 30.

Reagan would only say that "no policy or decision in my mind has ever been influenced by astrology."

The White House was without defenses. Fitzwater reported Regan's horoscope on the day he was forced out: "You'll complete assignment. A burden will be lifted from your shoulders. You will grasp spiritual meanings. Events occur which place you on more solid, emotional, financial ground. Be confident."

Regan's revenge loosed a galaxy of guffaws from folks who liken astrologers to faith healers. Also from Democrats who just couldn't resist.

"It's all right with me," said Speaker Jim Wright, D-Texas (Capricorn). "I'm glad he consults somebody."

House Majority Whip Tony Coelho, D-Calif., (Gemini) quipped: "We should check whether astrologer Jeane Dixon recommended a veto of the trade bill."

All of which led CNN's Frank Sesno (Pisces) to ask Fitzwater if the Reagans worried they looked ridiculous. "It's unfortunate," he replied.

The news also brought claims of fame—and contests of will.

■ Los Angeles astrologer Joyce Jillson (Capricorn) claimed she "spent a lot of time at the White House after the assassination attempt"; picked Vice President George Bush as Reagan's running mate; and told Reagan to hold news conferences during full moons.

The White House says neither of the Reagans know Jillson.

■ Lou Cannon (Gemini) of *The Washington Post*, who has covered Reagan since his California days, reported Reagan was sworn in as governor at 12:01 a.m. because the stars smiled on a midnight ceremony.

But the White House said Tuesday Reagan took the oath early to stem last-minute judicial appointments by the outgoing Democratic governor.

Finally, the revelation of a presidential stargazer provoked a debate of sorts on astrology.

"We are pleased to hear about anyone who is interested in this science," said Sarah Cooper of the American Federation of Astrologers in Tempe, Ariz., estimating about 50 million to 70 million in the USA believe in astrology to some extent.

But Dr. Lawrence Cranberg, a physicist who co-founded the Austin Society to Oppose Pseudo-Science, said astrology isn't a science.

San Francisco State University astronomer Andrew Fraknoi said he's performed studies on astrology, finding it's wrong 90 percent of the time: "That's not the type of guidance we need from the federal government."

But Sydney Omarr (Leo), who appears daily in 300 newspapers, was angry Reagan is being knocked.

Noting that FDR and Winston Churchill were avid buffs (not to mention Adolf Hitler's interest), Omarr said: "You can make fun of Reagan for many reasons, but don't make fun of him for something that has intrigued man for 5,000 years."

Rep. Jack Davis, R-Ill., (Virgo) agreed. "It just goes to show that Mr. and Mrs. Reagan are human," he said. "I bet you 95 percent of the people read horoscopes."

Evidence of Reagan's superstition:

Political Science   **287**

- He pockets lucky charms and counts 33 as his lucky number. "It was my number on my jersey when I played football, I was the 33rd governor, and even when we were buying a ranch and I was on pins and needles as to whether we were going to get it," the deal closed at 3:33 p.m.
- Reagan often has said that Rex, the family cocker spaniel, barks when entering Lincoln's bedroom because he senses Lincoln's ghost.
- More recently, friends who bought a home for the Reagans at 666 St. Cloud in Bel Air had to change the address to 668 St. Cloud when they learned 666, among devotees of superstition, is a mark of Satan.

Reagan, called "incurably superstitious" by aide Michael Deaver, is not the only starry-eyed president.

Teddy Roosevelt (Scorpio) mounted his natal horoscope on a chessboard to study it daily; Charles De Gaulle (Sagittarius) quoted a prewar horoscope predicting he would rule France.

Actor Sylvester Stallone (Cancer), born of an astrologer, planned his son's birth so he would be a Taurus with Libra moon and Leo rising.

And Sally Quinn (Cancer), novelist, journalist and wife of *Washington Post* editor Ben Bradlee, is said to be such a devotee of astrology that editors didn't even try to lobby for a disclaimer on the daily horoscope.

"One editor told me not to expect anything, that Mrs. Bradlee is a true believer," said Cranberg about efforts to get the *Post* to run a disclaimer. Quinn, whose novel *Regrets Only* depicts a first lady who consults an astrologer, was unavailable.

Reagan, born "with Jupiter rising," has traits of being "warm and witty, yet ambitious and proud," says *American Astrology* magazine.

Astrological input or not, the stars say Reagan's trip to Chicago today for a summit speech "should be a wonderful day of travel for the president," said Usha. "It is a day to express his vision."

Contributing: Karen Peterson and Richard Latture, both Aries; Libra Peter Johnson; Aquarius Bob Minzesheimer

Guide for Reading

Carl's paper may at first impress you, but careful reading will show you that he isn't in control of his subject. What does this mean? Look for a lack of organization and for poor development. Also, consider Carl's tone. Is it consistent throughout? Is it appropriate to the task? As you read, ask yourself what Carl's primary goal seems to be. Does he strive primarily to be funny or to do what the assignment calls for?

SAMPLE POLITICAL SCIENCE PAPER 3

REAGAN POLICY—IS IT IN THE STARS? as taken from USA TODAY, May 4, 1988

Carl S. (a freshman)

Policy, domestic or foreign, can be politically described as a set of actions and intentions promulgated by our elected officials to fulfill certain goals and resolve conflicts. All of these actions have an impact on us as citizens. Truly a descriptive definition of a basic term of politics. But who sets policy, for argument's sake, foreign policy? Traditionally, as taught in certain classes such as American National Government, we learn that the President, the Secretary of State, and several other people and government agencies help and advise to determine what the goals are for our nation state in the international arena. Traditionally . . . yet these axioms of governmental truths (if there are any) were put into question this week. Claims of astrological influence have rocked the wings of the White House as journalists seek the truth and citizens seek a safe place to hide. In the May 4 article of USA TODAY, allegations of the first couple's use of astrology in making decisions are brought forth. Such claims that are filling the political air include White House planners' puzzlement over the signing of the arms treaty by President Reagan and Mikhail Gorbachev last December at 1:30 P.M. It was originally planned for a prime-time signing in order for a large TV audience, but rumor has it that Nancy Reagan insisted it be held in early afternoon, after her astrologer told her the stars would be right at that time.

In the traditional political practice of get even not mad, Donald Regan has threatened to reveal such information and more in the May 16 release of his book about his time in the White House gang. To play down such accusations, White House spokesman Marlin Fitzwater said Mrs. Reagan does have an interest in astrology, "particularly following the assassination attempt in March of 1981." USA TODAY interpreted such information to "translate" as: Nancy Reagan turned to an astrologer-friend "to avoid near tragedies" in future traveling ever since the attempted as-

Political Science

sassination. Also, astrologist Joyce Jillson has come out with claims of spending time with the Reagans after the assassination attempt. Among her claims to astrological fame: She picked George Bush to be Reagan's V.P. running mate and she has advised Reagan to hold news conferences during full moons. Both President and Mrs. Reagan deny knowing Ms. Jillson (a typical procedure in Washington politics). Reagan's only real comment (unless Marlin Fitzwater made this up) was to say that "no policy or decision in my mind has ever been influenced by astrology." Well, this must make the American people feel much better. This latest "attack" on Reagan's credibility brought many comments from many students as well as from the opposition party: House Speaker Jim Wright (D-Texas) said "It's all right with me. I'm glad he consults somebody." Rep. Bill <u>Grey</u> (D-PA.) was more disturbed in his opinion when he said "I knew they were out to lunch, but I didn't know they were out to space."

Reagan is known for his superstitious beliefs, according to close friends like Michael Deaver (and what a close friend he is), but is this really a situation to panic over? Reagan's policy is admittedly screwy in many areas, and such a thing as astrology would be a perfect scapegoat to blame his mistakes on. Yet, at the same time, this is not a laughing matter, but one that has a darker side to it. The mere thought that the President of the United States consults not his expert advisors, but astrologers, is a scary thought. All things considered, Reagan made some bad policy decisions, but it is far-fetched to make such a claim <u>as our current President</u> accepting policy advice from a bunch of star gazers. It is safe to say that it is the "traditional" view that holds true. Foreign policy, the American people can rest assured, is more than likely still handled by experts (?) in the field.

Analysis of Sample Political Science Paper 3

This paper is obviously the work of someone who enjoys the topic and the process of writing about it. At first glance, a paper like this may impress readers because the writer seems involved with the subject rather than just reporting it. The end result, however, is not a clear explanation of the article and how it is related to an issue from the text and/or class.

In this case, the result is a confusing paper that touches on the topic and on several ideas related to it but that develops none of them sufficiently.

Notice that Carl provides no summary as such—we know what is covered in the article only in the most general terms. Carl limits any mention of the article's contents to a single statement in the first paragraph: "allegations of the first couple's use of astrology in making decisions are brought froth." He fails to say anything about what the author of the article does with these "allegations." As a result, readers can judge neither the author's credibility nor Carl's perceptions, because there is no clear summary. At the worst, Carl is guilty of plagiarism because he fails to give credit to the author for his ideas.

Moreover, the paragraphs are not developed logically. We understand that the first sentence in the paper is an attempt to define foreign and domestic policy, but it is both too abstract and too subjective to be of much value. The paragraph then jumps to a vague description of who should "traditionally" set foreign policy, to allegations of astrological influence, to the signing of the arms treaty, and finally to Nancy Reagan's scheduling of the signing. All of these ideas may be connected, but readers have no real way of knowing because Carl doesn't make clear any connections; he doesn't develop the ideas or explain what the relationships are.

The next two paragraphs follow much the same pattern as the first. In the second paragraph, the first sentence is only loosely connected to what follows, the connection is not developed, and it does not appear to be relevant to the issue of astrological influence. The third paragraph is confusing because Carl's attitude toward the issue is ambiguous. Is the situation one "to panic over," does it have a "darker side to it," or is policy still being "handled by experts (?) in the field"? If he felt unable to take a definite stand, he should have explained why the issue is not clear enough to warrant an accusation or a reaffirmation of President Reagan's process of making policy decisions.

The tone of the paper is at the heart of the problem. The assignment demands a straightforward response that informs readers. Carl has made the mistake, however, of trying to be entertaining. His smugness comes through in a wide range of snide remarks and sarcasm: "if there are any," "a typical procedure in Washington politics," "and what a close friend he is," "Well, this must make the American people feel much better." Such commentary requires far more skill than Carl demonstrates. Moreover, it is inappropriate in this assignment. One suspects that Carl detected in his teacher some anti-Reagan sentiment and hoped to capitalize on it through these weak attempts at humor. He digs a deeper hole for himself by adding a touch of pomposity with statements like "to determine what the goals are for our nation state in the international arena."

In addition to these shortcomings, we note the lack of documentation throughout the paper, which is a serious omission. Readers have no idea where the quotations came from and thus have no notion of their accuracy or context. Proper documentation is important not only to avoid the charge of plagiarism but to give readers an idea of a quotation's validity and relevance.

Carl appears to have put a significant amount of energy into making this paper different from those of his classmates. But different does not mean better. Good papers stand above mediocre ones because they supply more information in a more readable way, not because they are cute. It seems clear in this case that Carl failed to understand the teacher's purpose in giving the assignment, so for him it was not a learning experience.

Writing Assignments

The following assignments are modeled on the integration papers above. The assignments increase in difficulty, based on the source for your article and on the type of analysis required. A good paper will be informative and interesting to a person who is aware of current political news. It will include a concise summary and a thoughtful analysis and/or explanation, and it will be free of surface errors.

1. In 1–2 pages, summarize a politically oriented article from a current issue of your hometown or college town newspaper. Explain how this issue reflects, on a local level, the same concerns of a current national issue.
2. In 2–3 pages, summarize an article on the same political issue from both *Time* and *Newsweek*. Based on the manner of reporting and writing, analyze the political leaning of each magazine.
3. In 3–4 pages, summarize a politically oriented article from a recent issue of *Atlantic Monthly* and explain what this article suggests about the present character of American national politics.

POLITICAL SCIENCE ASSIGNMENT 2

Course: **Introduction to Political Science**

There will be four critiques comprising the writing assignment for this course. Each critique should be 2–3 pages in length, typed and double-spaced and should include: 1) the major idea of the author, 2) what evidence he cites for his assertion, and 3) your evaluation of the author's point of view. The articles should be taken from each segment of the required readings. . . . The papers must be handed in on the days indicated. If this schedule is not followed or if the student fails to hand in a paper, 10% is subtracted from his/her grade.

Analysis of Political Science Assignment 2

This assignment is designed to be as foolproof as possible. The three points the teacher gives provide the most logical order for the critique. Because the format and source of the critiques are so clearly stated, it may seem difficult to produce one that will stand out as being better than most. It is safe to assume, however, that most students do not know exactly what a critique is. Many may believe it is merely a kind of report, similar perhaps to the integration papers in the previous assignment.

But a critique is actually a critical review or commentary, not simply a report. In this case, "critical" means characterized by careful evaluation. The better critiques, then, in addition to following the form prescribed by the assignment, will contain careful, perceptive evaluation of the author's main points.

Material covered in the course will provide a solid basis for judgment, but you should not feel limited by what has been talked about in class. Using events related to what has been discussed in class will show that you have learned principles and can apply them in appropriate situations.

The length the teacher specifies is a suggestion. Unless there is a strong emphasis on staying within a certain number of pages, you should be as complete as possible in responding to the assignment. In the case of this assignment, each of the three points certainly deserves equal at-that there is absolutely no virtue in stretching out a paper with irrelevant information and wordy constructions.

Class Article 4

"We Must Learn to Live with Revolutions"
by Frank Church[3]

America's inability to come to terms with revolutionary change in the Third World has been a leitmotif of U.S. diplomacy for nearly 40 years. This failure has created our biggest international problems in the post-war era.

But the root of our problem is not, as many Americans persist in believing, the relentless spread of communism. Rather, it is our own difficulty in understanding that Third World revolutions are primarily nationalist, not communist. Nationalism, not capitalism or communism, is the dominant political force in the modern world.

You might think that revolutionary nationalism and the desire for self-determination would be relatively easy for Americans—the first successful revolutionaries to win their independence—to understand. But instead we have been dumbfounded when other peoples have tried to pursue the goals of our own revolution two centuries ago.

Yes, the United States generally has supported political independence movements, as in India or later in Africa, against the traditional colonial powers of Europe. Those situations were easy for us—we've never been nationalists. But where a nationalist uprising was combined with a Marxist element of some kind or with violent revolutionary behavior, Americans have come unhinged.

This happened most dramatically in the biggest tragedy of American diplomacy since World War II, Vietnam. But it has happened repeatedly in other countries as well, most recently in Nicaragua and El Salvador.

Given the size and the seriousness of our failures to deal successfully with nationalistic revolutions, you might think we'd be busy trying to figure out why we've done so badly, and how we could do better in the future. But on the contrary, we simply stick to discredited patterns of behavior, repeating the old errors as though they had never happened before.

The latest example is the report of the Kissinger Commission on Latin America which painted events in Central America in ominously stark colors. The commission said that in principle America can accept revolutionary situations, but in Nicaragua and El Salvador we cannot. Why? Because of Soviet and Cuban involvement.

From Frank Church, "We Must Learn to Live with Revolutions," *Washington Post* (March 11, 1984): C-1 and C-4.

But the sad fact is that the Soviets will always try to take advantage of revolutionary situations, as will the Cubans, particularly in this hemisphere. To solve our problem we have to learn to adapt to revolutions even when communists are involved in them, or we will continue to repeat the errors of the last four decades.

Revolutionary regimes are not easy to live with—particularly for a country as conservative as the United States has become. As Hannah Arendt—no Marxist herself—noted in her classic work, "On Revolution," the United States has made a series of desperate attempts to block revolutions in other countries, "with the result that American power and prestige were used and misused to support obsolete and corrupt political regimes that long since had become objects of hatred and contempt among their own citizens."

Why does America, the first nation born of revolution in the modern age, find it so difficult to come to terms with revolutionary change in the late 20th century?

One answer involves the nature of our own revolution. It was essentially a revolt against political stupidity and insensitivity. With sparsely populated, easily accessible and abundant lands, the restless and dissatisfied in early America had an outlet for their discontent. The young United States never had to deal with the limitless misery of an impoverished majority.

In the first half of this century, when the country faced sharpened class conflict as a result of the excesses of an unbridled capitalism, we were blessed with patrician leaders, Theodore and Franklin Roosevelt, who had the foresight to introduce needed reforms. An intelligent, conservative property-owning class had the sense to accept them.

But our experience is alien to other countries which do not share our natural wealth. In poor countries a desperate majority often lives on the margin of subsistence. A selfish property-owning minority and, often, an indifferent middle class intransigently protect their privileges. Dissidence is considered subversive. It isn't surprising that those who seek change resort to insurrection.

They take their lead not from the American, but from the French revolutionary tradition where, in Arendt's phrase, the "passion of compassion" led the Robespierres of the time to terrible excesses in the name of justice for the impoverished masses.

The spectacle of violent, sometimes anarchic revolutionary activity combined with an obsessive fear that revolutions will inevitably fall prey to communism has led us to oppose radical change all over the Third World, even where it is abundantly clear that the existing order offers no real hope of improving the lives of the great majority. As a result, those who ought to be our allies—those who are ready to fight for justice for the impoverished majority—find themselves, as revolutionaries, opposed not only to the ruling forces in their own societies, but the United States.

I am not arguing that revolutions are romantic or pleasant. History is full of examples, from France to Iran, of revolutions born in brutality and often accompanied by extended bloodbaths of vengeance and reprisal, and which ultimately produce just another form of authoritarianism to replace the old. But the fact that we may not like the revolutionary process or its results is, alas, not going to prevent revolutions. On the other hand, the fact that revolutions are going to happen need not mean disaster for the United States. Our past failures do suggest a way we can adapt to revolutions without fighting them or sacrificing vital national interests.

Consider the case of Vietnam. Our overriding concern with "monolithic" communism led us grossly to misread the revolution in that country. Ignoring centuries of enmity between the Vietnamese and the Chinese, our leaders interpreted a possible victory for Ho Chi Minh's forces as a victory for international communism. The war against the French and then the war among the Vietnamese in our eyes became a proxy war by China and the Soviet Union even after those two powers had split, destroying the myth of "monolithic" communism. Indochina, in the new American demonology, was seen as the first in a series of falling dominoes.

Vietnam did fall to the communists, but only two dominoes followed—Laos and Cambodia, both of which we had roped into the war. Thailand, Malaysia and Indonesia continue to exist on their own terms. The People's Republic of China, for whom Hanoi was supposed to be a proxy, is now engaged in armed skirmishes against Vietnam.

Meanwhile, the United States, having been compelled to abandon the delusion of containing the giant of Asia behind a flimsy network of pygmy governments stretched thinly around her vast frontiers, has at last shown the good sense to make friends with China. American influence, far from collapsing, has drawn strength from this sensible new policy, and has been rising ever since. As for communism taking over, it is already a waning force. The thriving economies are capitalist: Japan, South Korea, Taiwan, Hong Kong, Singapore. You don't hear Asians describing communism as the wave of the future.

If any lessons were learned from our ordeal in Southeast Asia, they have yet to show up in the Western Hemisphere, where our objective is not simply to contain, but to eradicate communism, regardless of the circumstances in each case. In pursuit of this goal, we took heed of one restraint. The legacy of resentment against us still harbored by our Latin neighbors, stemming from the days of "gunboat diplomacy," made it advisable, wherever feasible, to substitute "cloak and dagger" methods—covert instead of overt means.

Hence the American-sponsored coup to oust a democratically elected government in Guatemala in 1954. The ousted president, Jacobo Arbenz, was by American standards, a New Deal liberal. But our cold warriors of that era decided he was a red threat. As U.S. Ambassador John Peurifoy, arriving in Guatemala on his special mission, put it: "If Arbenz is not a communist, he'll do until the real thing comes along."

In Cuba, the United States spared no effort to get rid of Fidel Castro. We financed and armed an exile expeditionary force in an attempted repeat of the Guatemalan coup, only to see it routed at the Bay of Pigs. Then the CIA tried repeatedly to assassinate Castro, even enlisting the Mafia in the endeavor; and the United States imposed against Cuba the most severe trade embargo inflicted on any country since the end of World War II.

Even where the left gained power in fair and open elections, the United States has been unwilling to accept the results. Hence the Nixon administration's secret intervention in Chile aimed first at preventing the election of and then at ousting President Salvador Allende.

Despite these and other efforts by the United States, another Marxist regime did arise in the hemisphere: Nicaragua. And, true to form, the United States has again financed, armed and promoted an exile army whose objective is its overthrow.

After spending billions of dollars, and emptying the CIA's bag of dirty tricks, what do we have to show for our efforts? Obviously, the hemisphere has not been swept clean of communism. Cuba and Nicaragua have avowedly Marxist regimes; in El Salvador, an insurrection gains momentum against an American-trained and -equipped army, despite an American-sponsored agrarian reform program and our hopes for the election of a reformist president and legislature. The result defies our grand design: the army fights indifferently; the agrarian reform is stymied, and the Salvadoran middle class and traditional landed interests remain determined to elect extreme rightists to the important legislative and executive positions.

By our unrelenting hostility to Castro, we have invested him with heroic dimensions far greater than would be warranted by Cuba's intrinsic importance in the world. We are in the process of performing a similar service for the commandantes of Nicaragua and, at the same time, discrediting the legitimate domestic opponents of their political excesses. We have left Cuba no alternative to increased reliance upon Russia, and we now seem determined to duplicate the same blunder with Nicaragua.

So by any standard, American policy has failed to achieve its objective: to inoculate the hemisphere against Marxist regimes. But are we fated to cling to the disproven policy of opposing each new revolution because of Marxist involvement, even though the insurgents fight to overthrow an intolerable social and economic order?

By making the outcome of this internal struggle a national security issue for the United States, as the Kissinger Commission does, we virtually guarantee an American military intervention wherever the tide turns in favor of the insurgents. If this happened in El Salvador, it would be difficult to imagine that the present administration would stop before it had gone "to the source," Nicaragua or even Cuba. In the process, of course, we would fulfill Che Guevara's prophecy of two, three, many Vietnams in Latin America.

We should stop exaggerating the threat of Marxist revolution in Third World countries. We know now that there are many variants of Marxist governments and that we can live comfortably with some of them. The domino theory is no more valid in Central America than it was in Southeast Asia. And it is an insult to our neighbor, Mexico, for it assumes that Mexico is too weak and unsophisticated to look out for its own interests.

We repeatedly ignore the explicit signals from Marxists in Central America that they will respect our concerns. For example, we worry that the commandantes in Nicaragua will invite the Soviets or the Cubans to establish bases in their countries. Yet, the Sandinista government in Nicaragua has explicitly committed itself not to offer such bases to the Russians or Cubans. Instead, they have offered to enter into a treaty with the United States and other regional countries not to do so. And the political arm of the insurgents in El Salvador has also committed itself to no foreign bases on its soil.

Why not take them up on these commitments? The United States, with the help of other regional powers who share our interests, including Venezuela, Mexico, Colombia and Panama, has the means to ensure that the revolutionaries keep their word. If Nicaragua violated its treaty obligation to those states, the United States would have legal grounds and regional sanction for taking action.

If the threat of communist bases is real, then a negotiated agreement precluding them would surely be perceived as a "victory" for the United States and a "defeat" for the Russians. And with a Nicaraguan treaty agreement with the United States and the countries of the region, the Salvadoran insurgents, should they prevail, would surely follow suit.

Although the Nicaraguan revolution has followed classic lines, in comparative terms it has been relatively moderate. There has been no widespread terror, and the regime has shown itself sensitive to international pressure. If we cannot come to terms with the Nicaraguan revolution, then we probably are fated to oppose all revolutions in the hemisphere.

The problem is illustrated in human terms by a vignette of the Kissinger Commission in Nicaragua. According to press accounts, the members of the commission were angered by the confrontational tone of the meetings with the Nicaraguans and their obvious reliance on Soviet and Cuban intelligence.

Imagine the setting: The commission arrives in Nicaragua one week after the *contras*, supported by the United States, blow up a major oil facility. On the one side, a largely conservative commission led by Henry Kissinger, Robert Strauss, William Clements and Lane Kirkland, men in their late 50s or 60s, expecting to be acclaimed for their willingness to listen to the upstart revolutionaries. On the other side, peacock-proud Nicaraguan *commandantes* in their 30s or early 40s, men and women, who had spent years fighting in the mountains, who had seen their friends and comrades die at their side in opposition to the U.S.-supported Somoza dictatorship, and naturally resentful of U.S. support of the counterrevolution. To them, a commission led by Kissinger, architect of the campaign to destabilize Allende, had to be seen as a facade for the American plan to bring them down. Is it a wonder there was no meeting of minds?

Whoever gains power in Central America must govern. And governing means solving mundane problems: the balance between imports and exports, mobilization of capital, access to technology and know-how. The United States, the Western European countries and the nearby regional powers, Colombia, Mexico and Venezuela, are the primary markets and sources of petroleum, capital and technology. The social democratic movements in Western Europe are important sources of political sustenance for revolutionary movements in Central America.

If we had the wit to work with our friends and allies rather than against them, the potential abuses and exuberance of revolution in Central America can be contained within boundaries acceptable to this country. There is no reason to transform a revolution in any of the countries of Central America, regardless from where it draws its initial external support, into a security crisis for us.

The objective of U.S. policy should be to create the conditions in which the logic of geographic proximity, access to American capital and technology and cultural opportunity can begin to exert their inexorable long-term pull. Russia is distant, despotic and economically primitive. It cannot compete with the West in terms of the tools of modernization and the concept of freedom.

But if we insist on painting the Cubans and Nicaraguans of this world—and there will be others—into a corner, we save the Russians from their own disabilities. If, on the other hand, we were to abandon our failed policy and adopt the alternative I suggest, pessimism might soon give way to optimism. After a while, democracy may begin to take root again. The wicked little oligarchies, no longer assured American protection against the grievances of their own people, may even be forced to make the essential concessions. The United States and Cuba might be trading again, joined in several regional pacts to advance the interests of both. And Marxist governments, far from overtaking the hemisphere, will be lagging behind as successful free enterprise countries set the standard.

We will marvel at the progress in our own neighborhood, measured from the day we stopped trying to repress the irrepressible and exchanged our unreasonable fear of communism for a rekindled faith in freedom.

Guide for Reading

The following three papers are adequate responses to the assignment, although none is outstanding. Jane's paper contains an average summary and critique. Daryl's paper has a more complete summary and the most thoughtful critique, but he asks too many questions and supplies too few answers. In addition, his tone is inconsistent. Kevin's summary is also complete, but his critique is much too brief and superficial. Because the writers know and understand the Church article, each paper could be improved with careful revising; the study questions focus on this process.

SAMPLE POLITICAL SCIENCE PAPER 4

WE MUST LEARN TO LIVE WITH REVOLUTIONS, by Frank Church

Jane E. (a freshman)

"Third World revolutions are primarily nationalist, not communist. Nationalism, not capitalism or communism, is the dominant political force in the modern world." This statement from Church's paper states the focal point the United States must come to grips with while dealing with revolutionary countries. Although the U.S. had its beginnings as a revolutionary force, revolutions in other countries are met with great fear. Vietnam represents a case of American intervention for all the wrong reasons. The result of the Vietnam war for the U.S. was a huge loss of resources and manpower and no significant accomplishment. The Main concern for the U.S. was Central Asia falling into the hands of communist governments. Despite our failure, the entire area did not become completely communist.

Church compares the situation in Central America to the Vietnam struggle. Will we again waste resources and men in a fight we do not belong in? Church points out that there are different degrees of Marxist element that we have learned to live with. How can we be allies with China and also be so afraid of a similar government that may result in Central America.

Historically, our relationship with revolutionary regimes has been bad. Future relations between our two countries are permanently scarred when the new revolution proves unsuccessful. Instead of having things go our way the new regime aligns with the Soviet Union for assistance.

We can never tell ahead of time if the revolutionary regimes will be better than the governments they replace. There are certainly no guarantees, but the people of any country should be allowed to establish what ever kind of government the desire without the interference of everyone else. Although the U.S. is quick to jump into everyone else's problems, imagine how we would react if someone tried to tell us what kind of government we should have. I believe our time would be better spent trying to create peaceful relations with whatever regime preveils. Several countries in South America have offered to enter into treaties with the U.S. to protect our mutual interests. Instead of driving these groups to other countries looking for allies, we should let them decide what government is best for them and then proceeded with peaceful negotiations.

Political Science

> **STUDY QUESTIONS**
>
> 1. In a paper containing a summary of someone else's writing, the writer should be very careful to separate the summarized information from his or her own information and thoughts. One way to do this is to use such phrases as "According to Church," "He continues by stating," and "He says that." Assuming that the first three paragraphs in Jane's paper summarize Church's article, add the necessary cues to make this point clear to readers.
>
> 2. Jane has too many sentences that mention a topic but don't develop it (for example, the fourth sentence in paragraph 1). Mark all of these and briefly describe the type of information she needs to add. As a guide, look again at suggestion 2 in the assignment.
>
> 3. Rephrase Jane's question (second paragraph) and the third sentence in paragraph 4 to make these into strong, convincing statements.

SAMPLE POLITICAL SCIENCE PAPER 5

WE MUST LEARN TO LIVE WITH REVOLUTIONS by Frank Church

Daryl T. (a freshman)

        Does the establishment of Marxist revolutionary regimes in Central America pose a threat to American security interests? Frank Church explains that we are exaggerating the spread of communism. He points out that the root of our problem is not the relentless spread of communism, but our own difficulty in understanding that Third World revolutions are primarily nationalist, not communist.

  The United States generally has supported political independence movements, but when they are combined with a Marxist element or violent revolutionary behavior, we have come unhinged. He uses the example of Vietnam. Are we to repeat the Vietnam catastrophe in Nicaragua and El Salvador? Why do we stick to these discredited patterns of behavior? The answer is because of Soviet and Cuban involvement. Because of the obsessive fear that these revolutions will fall prey to communism, we have been led to oppose radical change all over the Third World. As a result, the revolutionaries, who ought to be our allies, find themselves not only opposed to the ruling forces in their own societies, but also to the United States. The author points out numerous examples such as Vietnam, Laos, Cambodia, Cuba, and the present cases in Nicaragua and Sandinistas in which we are also failing to achieve our objectives of inoculating the hemisphere against Marxist regimes. Church claims we should stop exaggerating the threat of Marxist revolution. The domino theory is no more valid in Central America than it was in Southeast Asia.

We know that there are many variants of Marxist governments and that we can live comfortably with some of them. We worry that Nicaragua will invite the Soviets or Cubans to establish bases in their countries. Yet the Sandinista government in Nicaragua has explicitly committed itself to enter into a treaty with the U.S. and other regional countries not to do so. El Salvador has also committed itself. Why not take them up on their commitments? The United States with the help of other regional powers who share our interests have the means to ensure that the revolutionaries keep their word. If the threat of Communists basis is real, then a negotiated agreement would be a "victory" for the United States.

The author concludes by pointing out that the objective of U.S. policy should be to create the conditions in which the logic of geographic proximity, access to American capital and technology and cultural opportunity can begin with inexorable long-term pull. We must stop painting countries like Cuba and Nicaragua into a corner.

In my opinion it seems that on one side you have the Soviet Union trying to spread communism and on the other, the United States trying to spread democracy. Does anyone have the right to influence a country one way or another? Using a little common sense one would say no. If <u>you</u> have opposing forces trying to form one nation, naturally they will turn to use any means available. What if it may threaten our Nation's security? The question is, does it? So far we cannot answer this question. China was influenced by the Soviet Union but broke away, which should teach us a lesson. People must decide for themselves what is best for them and given time, they will do so either way. Communist regimes don't have to be just like the Soviet Union, and democracies don't have to be just like the United States. If you look at it from this point of view, the strain on our economy that funds all these revolutionary movements ends up a waste. I think the Soviet Union is also beginning to realize this after their <u>latest</u> failure in Afghanistan. We also have to realize that our people aren't willing to fight or sacrifice loved ones in war for the domino theory as was proven in Vietnam. If it comes down to defense there is no question that our people will die for our country, but I think we are overreaching our goals here. As long as communist countries agree to be friendly with the U.S. and commit to a treaty that it will not let the Soviet Union or Cuba establish bases on its territory, don't they have the right to choose their government?

> **STUDY QUESTIONS**
>
> 1. Rewrite Daryl's questions, making them into strong, convincing statements.
>
> 2. Point out words that seem inappropriate to the tone in most of the paper. What words would be appropriate in these places?
>
> 3. Even though Daryl's critique is thoughtful, it is disorganized. List the different topics covered in the last paragraph and write a comment directing him how to improve this part of his paper.

SAMPLE POLITICAL SCIENCE PAPER 6

WE MUST LEARN TO LIVE WITH REVOLUTIONS by Frank Church

Kevin D. (a freshman)

In this reading the author, Frank Church, tells how Americans' inability to come to terms with revolutionary change in the Third World has created our biggest international problems in the post-war era. Since we were the first successful revolutionaries to win our independence, you would think that it would be easy for us to understand the desire for self-determination and revolutionary nationalism. But because many Americans feel that communism and revolution go together, we will not support them. We have a difficulty in understanding that Third World revolutions are primarily nationalist, not communist. We have been dumbfounded when other people have tried to pursue the goals of our own revolution two centuries ago.

The United States has supported political independence movements, as in India or Africa, but where a nationalist uprising was combined with a Marxist element of some kind or with violent revolutionary behavior, Americans have become very upset. A good example of this was American diplomacy in Vietnam. This has happened repeatedly in other countries as well, most recently in Nicaragua and El Salvador.

In ____ report from the Kissinger Commission on Latin America it was said that in principle America can accept revolutionary situation, but in Nicaragua and El Salvador we cannot. The reason for this is because of Soviet and Cuban involvement. To solve our problems we have to learn to adapt to revolutions even when communists are involved in them, or we will continue to repeat the errors of the last four decades. The Soviets and the Cubans will always try to take advantage of revolutionary situations, particularly in this hemisphere.

The question is often asked as to why does America, the first nation born of revolution in the modern age, find it so difficult to come to terms with revolutionary change in the late twentieth century. It was a revolt against stupidity and insensitivity. Because of such an abundance of land, the restless and dissatisfied in early America had an outlet for their discontent. The United States never had to deal with the limitless misery of an impoverished majority. In poor countries a desperate majority often lives on the margin of subsistence, while a selfish property-owning minority protect their own privileges. We, as Americans, have never had to experience this. Many of these revolts occur in hope of improving the lives of the great majority, but this becomes very hard for them when they are opposed not only by the ruling forces in their own societies, but also the United States.

Despite many efforts by the United States to control revolutions, Marxist regimes have still been formed. We should stop exaggerating the threat of Marxist revolutions in Third World countries. There are many Marxist governments and we have seen that we can live comfortably with some of them.

We got involved in the revolution in Nicaragua because we were worried that they would invite the Soviets or the Cubans to establish bases in their country. The government of Nicaragua has explicitly committed itself not to offer such bases to the Russians or the Cubans. Instead, they have offered to enter into a treaty with the United States and other regional countries not to do so. We should just take them up on these commitments. If we cannot come to terms with the Nicaraguan revolution, then we probably are fated to oppose all revolutions in this hemisphere. We should work with our friends and allies rather than against them, if we continue to go against these countries we will only be hurting ourselves.

In conclusion, I would like to say that I agree with the authors' point of view. If we continue to get involved in other countries' problems when we are not wanted we are only going to make more enemies. We should concentrate more on making alliances, such as the one offered by Nicaragua. If they go against their agreement, then we should get involved. I think that we should start to show a little more trust toward other countries and let them start looking out for their interests, and only get involved when our help is wanted and asked for.

> **STUDY QUESTIONS**
>
> 1. Kevin's summary lacks the necessary cues to make it clear what information comes from Church's article. Add these cues, rewriting sentences if necessary.
>
> 2. Kevin's critique is much too brief, in part because he doesn't give any specific information to support his statements. Ask him questions that would force him to add the necessary specifics.

Writing Assignments

The following assignments are similar to the critique assignment above. They increase in difficulty as the readings increase in sophistication. A good paper will include an informative, concise summary and a thoughtful analysis and evaluation, and will be free of surface errors.

1. Read a political editorial from a local newspaper. In 2–3 pages, summarize the editorial, giving the author's major idea and the evidence he or she cites for the point of view expressed; then evaluate how convincing the editorial is, based on the evidence included.
2. Read a politically oriented editorial of national interest in a newspaper with national circulation (*The New York Times* or *The Washington Post*, for example). In 3–4 pages, summarize the editorial, give the evidence the author cites for his or her point of view, and agree or disagree with this point of view, giving reasons for your position.
3. Read a political essay in a current issue of one of the popular news magazines (*Newsweek, Time, U.S. News and World Report*, etc.). Explain the major idea of the author, give the evidence the author cites for his or her point of view, and evaluate that point of view, based on what you know of current political situations.

POLITICAL SCIENCE ASSIGNMENT 3

Course: **Internship in Criminal Justice**

READING AND RESEARCH COMPONENT
GENERAL DESCRIPTION

    Each student will be required to write a major paper on a topic of his/her own selection relating to his/her field placement experiences. The student may choose to write a paper based on some field research growing out of his/her placement experiences. Or he/she may choose to do extensive reading on an issue which has already been well researched and discuss its salient features in the light of his/her field experiences. In either case, the paper should identify a particular problem in criminal justice, and propose, justify, or update policies, programs, or techniques designed to solve the problem.

OBJECTIVES

    1. To enhance the student's capacity for intellectual inquiry and expository skills.

    2. To increase the student's understanding of the problem area selected by him.

    3. To develop the student's understanding and/or ability to devise realistic strategies for improving an agency's delivery of services.

COMPONENTS AND PROGRESS EXPECTATIONS

    1. The student will attempt a preliminary and informal survey of agency service activities which should assist him/her in selecting a topic of study. This phase should be completed by the second week of placement.

    2. Utilizing the above, the student will then formulate his/her area of interest into a statement of intent (with some attention to the method of inquiry planned). The student will then obtain approval from the agency administrator and campus faculty. This phase should be completed by the fifth week of placement.

    3. After obtaining approval for his/her proposal, the student will proceed with his/her field project or library research.

4. The written results will be typed and follow accepted form for term papers or research projects. Normally, the paper will be prepared in triplicate (copies for the agency, the University, and the student). The project should be completed by the date announced by the internship supervisor.

5. Whether new research is undertaken or whether a paper is created from existing research, the focus should be directed toward proposing and justifying new policies or programs, or updating old policies/programs, which could be expected to fill some identified gap in provision of services.

GUIDE FOR ANALYZING AGENCY OF PLACEMENT

The following guide is suggested as a basis for study and analysis of the agency in which you are placed. Each student should make any necessary modifications to increase the relevance of this guide to his specific situation. The guide is merely a skeleton: the student should expand it on the basis of those details which are relevant in current methods of criminal justice analysis.

I. PROBLEM(S) OF CENTRAL CONCERN TO THIS AGENCY:

This agency has arisen as a response to what social problems and conditions? With what problems is the agency presently concerned?

II. THE SOCIAL TASK OF THE AGENCY, as currently defined or "unassigned" to the agency:

1. Historically, what have been the changing shifts in conception of task? What movements and forces have helped to shape the focus of present concern? What have been the major contributions of political and reform leaders and criminal justice professionals?

2. Currently, with what parts or aspects of what social problems is the agency concerned?

3. Distinguish between what is said to be the task of the agency and the task in which it is actually, actively concerned.

4. In which of the remaining important areas of unmet need would it be appropriate for the criminal justice agency to become concerned? (This is one basis for identifying gaps.)

5. Note those variations in the definition of the task by other agencies in the community.

6. Give your own summary of the agency's task.

III. THE SERVICE SYSTEM. Organization and present functioning of programs of your agency. (What is now being done?) Selected comparisons with other agencies.
1. The network of agencies and programs:
    - Typical agency structures and functions
    - Related and fringe agency structures and functions
    - New and non-typical structures and functions
    - Extent of cooperative and coordinative efforts
2. What groups are typically served? What groups are given low priority or omitted? (For example, middle and upper classes and poor urban and rural.)
3. Geographic coverage of your agency's services.
4. How much emphasis on crime preventive services is there? Specifically, what evidences are there that preventive work is being undertaken?
5. How do public attitudes affect the extent and quality of services rendered by your agency?
6. Knowledge and skills developed in this agency.
7. Financing: extent, sources, adequacy.
8. Personnel: (examine for manpower gaps.)
    - Non-criminal justice personal in agency: numbers, classifications, qualifications, deployment, in-service training and staff development, possibilities for more effective utilization of existing staff, extent of manpower gaps.
    - Criminal justice personnel in agency (AS, BS, MA): numbers, classifications, qualifications, deployment, in-service training and staff development, possibilities for more effective utilization of existing staff, extent of manpower gaps.
9. How effective is the services system in meeting the agency's social task?
10. What are current trends in the agency's service system?

IV. SUMMARY OF MAJOR GAPS
This summary is to be derived from the above study and from the student's own experiences and observations.
1. What have been the recommendations of experts, taskforces, and study commissions?

2. Insofar as possible, it must be specified whether a "gap" is measured against a realistic *operations concept of the social task*, or against an ideal *concept of the task*.
3. To place gaps into a working perspective, there should be summary of the positive aspects of the current functioning of this network of services.

V. RESPONSIBILITIES OF THE CRIMINAL JUSTICE PROFESSION - toward closing the gaps, in varying degrees of collaboration with non-criminal justice personnel in the field and with community groups and "power structures."
1. Areas of social change effort for which criminal justice must assume primary responsibility.
2. Collaboration with others.
3. Action priorities.

Analysis of Political Science Assignment 3

This assignment comes from a 12-hour course entitled "Internship in Criminal Justice." To duplicate this assignment, you would need to participate in an internship with a criminal justice organization. You can, however, *approximate* the assignment without having to duplicate the experience.

As the assignment states, the paper is an analysis and not just a report. Hence, as well as describing the agency, you would need to explain its purpose and the reasons behind its organization; you would also need to evaluate how well the agency performs the duties it is designed for. The better papers, then, will not only present a thorough, clear description but will demonstrate a deeper understanding of the functions and goals of the agency. They will demonstrate that the writer is familiar with a wide range of details related to the agency.

In our view, the paragraph preceding the "Guide for Analyzing Agency of Placement" is important to any student who wants to complete the assignment successfully. The word *suggested* should be taken very seriously, because the professor has probably spent considerable time constructing the guide and probably wants students to follow it closely. At the same time, students should understand that they do have the freedom to modify and expand their responses to fit specific experiences.

The assignment is very elaborate, which can be intimidating. Com-

Political Science　311

pleting it successfully demands much effort to internalize the requirements. We see the length of the assignment as both a strength and a weakness because it does necessitate close study. Nevertheless, students who recognize that the teacher's goal is to help ensure that every important aspect of the agency comes under analysis will see the assignment as a guide rather than a constraint.

[Editors' note: We have numbered the paragraphs in these papers to facilitate references in the study questions.]

Guide for Reading

This analysis is a good example of a paper that follows the assignment but has, as the grading professor stated, "no real depth." Even though the author, Gary, appears to have enjoyed his internship and learned from this experience, the resulting paper is uninspiring, redundant, and tedious. If Gary had used what follows as a draft, rather than a finished paper, and reworked it to eliminate unnecessary repetition, the same information could have been conveyed in a paper one-half to two-thirds as long. At the same time, he needed to include specific details that would make this analysis apply more to the Scotland County Sheriff's Department and less to criminal justice systems in general. The result would be a more interesting and concise account of a particular law enforcement agency.

SAMPLE POLITICAL SCIENCE PAPER 7

Analysis of the Scotland County Sheriff's Department

Gary H. (a senior)

[1] The Scotland County Sheriff's Department was established to meet the need of the community for protection against criminal acts. The Sheriff's Department serves the community by answering complaints brought to them by the community. When a complaint is filed the agency will investigate and try to correct the situation. This may involve arresting the person that the complaint is against or it might mean talking with both parties to try to come to an agreement on the situation.

[2] The Scotland Sheriff's Department also serves to protect our highways. They do this by fining speeders and reckless drivers. They also enforce other highway laws, such as arresting violators of DWI laws.

[3] The Scotland Sheriff's Department is comprised of nineteen deputy sheriffs which are in four different squads. The deputies work in twelve hour shifts for four days and then they get four days off. The calls and complaints are received by the dispatchers. There are four dispatchers in the department and they work the same shifts as the deputies. Once a crime is committed and a complaint is made a deputy will respond to the crime scene. In cases of burglary or rape the deputy will need the assistance of one of the detectives to find out who, what, where, how, and why the crime was committed. Scotland County has four such detectives. There are two criminal detectives, one narcotics detective, and one juvenile detective. The detectives' main duties are to gather as much information about the crime as possible. The information gathering process is done by interviewing the victims and witnesses of the crime. During the interview the detective finds out exactly what has taken place, how the act was committed, when it was committed, where it took place, who might have committed the crime and why it was committed. It is very important to get the information in as much detail as possible. After the interview has taken place the detective will go over what the interviewee has stated to make sure everything is in the right order and correct. If the person interviewed is satisfied with the testimony given, the detective will get them to sign the statement.

[4] The detectives, the deputies, and the rest of the Sheriff's Department personnel work together under the guidance of the sheriff. The sheriff was elected into office by the community in 1986. The office of sheriff is a four year term. His main duties are to supervise the deputies and   make any necessary changes in personnel. He also handles the public relations end of the department.

[5] The Scotland County Sheriff's Department has had to undergo some change due to the fact that the criminal element is changing. With the rising attention being drawn toward drugs and

Political Science

its effect on crime, the department has had to adapt its procedures in order to deal with this.

[6] Drugs are illegal and Scotland County is fighting the existence of drugs by using an undercover drug agent. He works closely with the State Bureau of Investigations in seeking out drug dealers in Scotland. Most of his information on who is dealing drugs comes from what are called snitches. These are people who either don't like drugs and tell on people involved with them, or they are dealers who get arrested and tell who they got the drugs from. In most cases the snitches come from the latter category. In the case of drugs, the higher up on the ladder you get the better off you are. The reason for this is, if a major drug dealer is arrested then the people who buy from him are automatically out of business until they find someone else to buy drugs from. The snitch comes into play because it is difficult to arrest big dealers directly. Most initial arrests involve lower level dealers. When a dealer is arrested, he is told that the judge might go easier on him if he tells where he got the drugs from. The officers make no promises to him, they just explain to him that he would be better off if he cooperated, since he would already be in custody for having drugs. If the person agrees to cooperate, he is wired with a bug and sent to his dealer to make another purchase. Once the officers are sure a deal is going down they raid the place and are able to arrest a dealer on the next level. This procedure can go on for as long as the arrested drug dealers are willing to cooperate.

[7] Drugs effect in other ways besides being a crime directly. Drug use causes a number of armed robberies, break-ins, and larcenies. Drug users often have habits that exceed their financial capacities, so they rob stores and break in houses to gain money to support their habits. The detectives who work on these break-ins and robberies have to know what to look for in drug related crimes. The drug abusers who commit these crimes are often more dangerous than other offenders because they are desperate and they don't act in a rational capacity. Special caution must be taken when dealing with drug related crimes for that very reason.

[8] Another area of change which has taken place in Scotland

County deals with child abuse and child sexual abuse. The reason for this change is the growing concern by our nation for the welfare of its children. As a result of this growing concern more and more child abuse and molestation is being reported. Scotland County has had to adapt itself to meet these concerns. It has done this by installing the position of a juvenile detective. The juvenile detective investigates all reported child abuse and molestation cases. If the child abuse is of a domestic nature, it is required that the Department of Social Services is called in. The juvenile detective works side by side with the Department of Social Services in the investigation of these offenses. The Department of Social Services is only called in if the abuse is within the family. If it involves someone outside the family then only the Sheriff's Department is involved. The first step in investigating an abuse case is to interview the victim to see exactly what happened. Then, if there are any witnesses, they are interviewed to see what they know about the situation. If there appears to be sufficient probable cause the abuse exists, the perpetrator of the alleged abuse is questioned. If it is found, through investigation, that abuse is present, the perpetrator is charged and taken into custody. The Department of Social Services main concern is with the welfare of the child and if it appears that the child is in danger of further abuse, action is taken to remove the child from the home.

[9] Currently, the main social problems that are the concerns of this agency are abuse, teen pregnancy, and the homeless. The Scotland County Sheriff's Department deals with these concerns in reactive and proactive manner. In the reactive form they investigate all crimes that are reported. If the crime being investigated is serious enough to warrant an arrest then the suspect is taken into custody so that he cannot cause any more damage. In the proactive form, the idea is to prevent crime from happening. This prevention is done by patrolling the areas within the agency's jurisdiction. During a patrol, if the officer notices something suspicious or out of the ordinary he investigates the situation. If during this investigation illegal activities are about to take place, an arrest is made. Another method of crime prevention is school based programs. Speeches are given in surrounding schools

about how kids should deal with peer pressure, substance abuse, and public safety.

[10] An area that would be appropriate for this agency to become more involved in is domestic violence. Domestic violence and abuse cannot be reacted upon until a complaint has been made. In most cases where a complaint is made the victim of the abuse does not want the perpetrator arrested because he ___ a family member. The main reason a complaint is made is to temporarily stop the aggression. By not being able to do anything about domestic violence until after the fact, a gap in the system is created. The only time an officer can do anything about a domestic problem, other than temporarily stopping the fight, is if there is probable cause to believe the victim will be seriously injured after he leaves. In this case the officer may make an arrest in order to temporarily separate the people involved in the fight.

[11] Through my observations of the Scotland County Sheriff's Department, that task seems to be to enforce the laws of the state. In most cases this enforcement is in the proactive from. By using patrol methods a small number of crimes are stopped either while in process or are stopped prior to their commission. With the number of deputies compared to the number of citizens in the county it is not unlikely for crimes to be committed in the absence of law enforcement. When these crimes are not stopped by patrol officers then complaints are usually made by the victim to the department. After a complaint is made, the deputies will respond and if needed, the detectives will be called in. The detectives then investigate the crime to discover who committed it. After probable cause has been established as to who committed the crime an arrest is made. Another method used by the sheriff's department in reducing criminal activity is with public education programs. The "D.A.R.E." program is one such program, which teaches school children about the damages of drugs. It teaches what drugs can do to you, and it teaches them how to say no when confronted with drugs. The sheriff's department is also involved in a community task force program. This program is designed to address community problems and discuss these problems to try to find solutions.

[12] An agency which works in relationship to the sheriff's department is the probation and parole agency. This agency takes the criminals who are given probation as part of their sentence, after they have passed through the court system. The main goal of the probation officer is to assess the needs and help the convicted offender to get back on the right track. When a probation officer receives a client, the first thing that he does is get as much information from the client as he can. He gathers personal information, studies family background, and gets a criminal history on the client. The next step in the assessment of the offender is to gather information on the events of the crime. This information is gathered from talking to the client and the arresting officer. After the assessment has been completed, the probation officer will set up appointments with the mental health, drug counseling, or any other such services that the offender may need. This assessment also determines what type of probation the offender needs. There are four different types of probation that the offender can be placed on. The first type of probation is called high risk. This is the most strict type of probation. Contact must be made by the offender once every two weeks and curfews are normally set for the offender. The second type of probation is called medium risk. In this type, contact must be made once a month. Next is the intermediate type. In this type contact must be made every three months. The fourth type of probation is called selective probation. This type of probation is for people with drug problems or family and job problems. In selective probation the offender is referred to some sort of counseling program as part of their probation requirements.

[13] There are also two special types of probation which an offender can be placed in. One type is for DWI offenders. In a DWI case the probation officer will set up a community service and mental health counseling for the offender. DWI offenders are also required to take a drivers education course which is set up by the probation officer. The other type of special probation is called intensive probation. This type of probation is only for felons. Since most of our prisons are overcrowded, felons with lesser serious crimes are placed on intensive probation. Community service and strict curfews are set on these offenders.

There is also a special probation officer, who only handles intensive probation, assigned to the case.

[14] Another job of the probation and parole agency is to collect all fines owed to the court. This includes court fees, attorney fees, and community service fees.

[15] In the criminal justice system, cooperation between the different agencies is essential. Without cooperation, criminals could not be given due process of law. Each department in the judicial system has a specific duty to do and a certain time in which to do this duty. When a criminal is arrested and brought before the court for arraignment, the court must cooperate by indicting the offender; if not then he goes free. While the case is awaiting trial there must be cooperation between the lawyers and the law enforcement officers, or a case against the offender cannot be made. The clerk of the court's office and the dispatchers then cooperate by gathering the offender's criminal history information. After the trial there must be cooperation by the agency who gets the offender. If it is the probation and parole department, they must process the offender accordingly. If the offender is sent to prison, the correction department must cooperate by making room for him in their prison system. So you see, the criminal justice system can be seen as a large team. Each separate department is like a position on a football team. Every department has its duty and must cooperate with the rest of the system to properly process the criminal offenders. If one department doesn't cooperate it's like a player not playing in position which causes mistakes and ultimately will cause the system to fail.

[16] The people that are typically served in Scotland County by the sheriff's department are the people who need help. The social class which is most often served by the sheriff's department is the lower class. The reason for this is that crime is more prevalent in the lower class. Complaints which are received by the sheriff's office from these people usually involve more serious offenses. It is from this social class that most of the rapes, homicides, drugs, shooting, assaults, and domestic violence occur. The reason behind the amount and seriousness of crimes in the lower class is due to many factors. The environment is probably

the main factor. These people live in projects and trailer parks which are in close proximity to each other. They don't have any money and there are not many jobs available to them. The frustration level in these areas is often very high and alcohol and drug abuse are their frustration releasers. In an environment where one has very little and one's outlook on the future doesn't hold anything, the value of life and one's property is worth very little.

[17] The second largest group which make complaints to the sheriff's office are people from the middle and upper classes. Most of the crimes in this category are breaking and enterings, larcenies, drug related crimes and domestic violence. The environment is an important factor in these types of crimes also. Most of the crimes reported by this group are property crimes and not violent crimes. The only exception is with domestic violence which seems to be present in all social classes.

[18] In the case of which group has high priority and which group has low priority, I haven't found that any group is given such priority. The sheriff's department in Scotland County does not serve and protect according to social class. There is a priority system, but it is based on the seriousness of the crime. For example, rapes and murders are given priority over property crimes.

[19] The geographic area which is served by the sheriff's department is any and all areas within Scotland County, this being 319.33 square miles. Laurinburg is the major town within the county, and it is served by the Laurinburg Police Department. The police department patrols the city limits of Laurinburg and has jurisdiction for a one mile radius outside the city limits. The sheriff's department has jurisdiction within the city as well as in the county.

[20] Within the community served by the Scotland County Sheriff's Department there has been a major emphasis on crime prevention. The most direct approach taken to prevent crime is by patrolling the areas within the departments jurisdiction. By patrolling the area and by being seen the deputies can deter some would be criminals. They can deter these would be criminals by convincing them that there is a good chance of them being caught if they commit a crime. Community watch is also a

method of preventing crime. This is a program where the people of each neighborhood will call the sheriff's department if they see someone breaking into a neighbor's home, or if they see something suspicious going on. This program helps to supplement the patrol efforts of the deputies. By posting community watch signs in each neighborhood it may deter a criminal from breaking into a house in that neighborhood. Another preventive method which is used to deter crime is called the "D.A.R.E." program which was mentioned in detail earlier. This program prevents drug-related crime before they start by educating students about drugs.

[21] In my observations of the Scotland County Sheriff's Department I have found that public attitudes have a direct affect on the extent and quality of services rendered to them. When a deputy responds to a complaint and is confronted with a good attitude towards him, he will be more responsive to the person's needs. A good attitude lets the deputy know that the person truly needs his help and is willing to help him in return. Showing a good attitude means cooperating with the officer in answering his question to the best of their knowledge and acting in a polite manner towards the officer. This cooperation lets the officer know that the complainant wants the situation corrected and is willing to do his or her part to help the officer and the court system to correct the situation.

[22] Just as a good attitude will help the complainant get action, a bad attitude will hinder him. When a deputy responds to a complaint and is greeted with a bad attitude it will have an affect on the approach he takes in the case. A bad attitude will make the deputy feel that the people don't really want his help. It will also make him feel like he is not respected and his interference is the situation is not welcome. A bad attitude consists mainly of a hostile reaction towards the deputy while he is performing his duty. It also consists of not cooperating with the deputy by not answering his questions. If the complainant doesn't cooperate with the deputy it becomes difficult for him to know and understand what the situation consists of. It also makes it hard, if not impossible, for the deputy to correct the situation. If the attitude displayed by the complaining party becomes too hostile, the deputy might be forced to take him into custody. At any rate,

the extent and quality of services rendered to the public displaying a bad attitude will be little to none.

[23] In order for the personnel of this agency to develop the knowledge and skills required to perform their duties as law enforcement officers, they must attend a basic training school. The school lasts for thirteen weeks and teaches the officers such things as criminal law, investigative procedures, arrest tactics, firearms, patrol tactics, etc. After the thirteen weeks of training the officers take an examination on what they have learned. If they pass they are then certified and sworn in as law enforcement officers. This training is required for all first time law enforcement officers and any officer that has been out of law enforcement for more than a year.

[24] Basic training school is only the beginning of the learning process for law enforcement officers. Most of an officers development of skills and knowledge come from on the job experience. In each situation that and officer deals with he learns something. A good officer will look back on a situation, after he has handled it, and ask himself what he could have done differently to better perform his duty. This self-evaluation process will help him when he is confronted with a similar situation.

[25] Specifically an officer must learn how to effectively patrol his assigned area. He must pay attention to everything that is going on around him while on patrol. He has to check out anything that seems suspicious or out of the ordinary. If he notices that a door or window has been tampered with he must be ready and able to asses the situation and act accordingly. Caution must be taken in this type of situation because he will not know whether someone is robbing the premises. An officer also has to develop skills in dealing with a wide variety of people. Some people will be very cooperative with him, while others will act violently towards him. Probably the hardest skill to develop in law enforcement is the ability to remain calm in any situation. An officer must remain calm and rational no matter how bad the situation might get. If he loses control of himself while performing his duty he is placed in a vulnerable position. This loss of control may cause him to get seriously injured or killed. It might also cause him to necessarily injure or kill someone else.

Political Science

[26] The Scotland County Sheriff's Department is financed by the county commissioner. The fiscal year in Scotland County begins in June. At this time requests can be made for funds. It is up to the commissioner how much money is then used to pay the employees of the department, and the fund the programs and equipment used by the department. The starting salary for deputies in this county is a little over $16,000 a year. The detectives start out at $20,000 per year. In talking to different employees of the department on the adequacy of the funds that they receive, I found that they are adequate. By adequate, I mean that the department has the necessary funds their duties as a law enforcement agency. These funds are not adequate enough for the department to install programs that would better serve the community in a social capacity. If the necessary funds were available the department could install programs that would educate the community on issues like domestic violence, teen pregnancies, drug abuse, and crime prevention. These programs would demand full time personnel and specialized training in order to be effective. The programs that are presently in use are only periodic programs that are taught by existing personnel. The equipment used by this agency could also be improved with more adequate funding. While on patrol the deputies are armed with a pistol and a shotgun, which is kept under the front seat. It has become common knowledge that the criminal forces in our society have the upper hand when it comes to firearms. During a drug raid the officers place their lives in a great deal of danger. They are busting in on heavily armed drug dealers with a minimum of firepower. For the job that law enforcement officers are expected to perform, I feel that more funding is needed. The present funding is adequate only for them to do an adequate job.

[27] The Scotland County Sheriff's Department has a social task in which it must meet. This social task is to enforce the laws of the state and to arrest those who violate these laws. Through my observations of this agency I have found that the task is effectively met. Since I have been here, there have only been three unsolved cases. In one of them the perpetrators of the crime have been apprehended but the gun that was involved is still missing. The detective assigned to this case is still trying to

recover the missing gun. He is doing this by following up on information given to him by informants. The list of suspects tied in with having the gun has been narrowed down to two people. I am sure that it is only a matter of time before it is located. In another open case there was a truck driver who was shot while driving towards Greensboro. In this case there were no witnesses and no probable cause for the shooting. The State Bureau of Investigations has been brought in to help with the case. In the third case, a man was murdered in his mobile home on the week of March 13. Again, there were no witnesses. There are, however, several suspects who might have had a motive to kill this person. With the help of the S.B.I. and by investigating every possible lead, I feel that the case will be solved.

[28] Other than these three cases the department has been able to solve each case that has come up since I have been here. I feel that the detectives in this department are meeting their task in a very efficient manner. I have also found that with the degree of patrol and manpower that is available, the deputies of this department are meeting their task very efficiently.

[29] As with every sheriff's department, this department has its share of problems. The first and most important problem is the lack of manpower in this department. I mentioned earlier that this department operates with nineteen deputies. Out of these nineteen deputies there are only twelve that actually patrol the county. The other seven work in the sheriff's office. Two of them are ranking officers which do mainly paper work and the other five are jailers. The twelve patrol deputies work in squads of three. This means that there are only three deputies patrolling the entire county at one time. This lack of manpower seriously hinders the effectiveness of this agency in meeting its social task of enforcing the laws of the state.

[30] Another problem that I have found is lack of storage space in which the officers keep evidence. Each officer is assigned a locker to keep evidence in, but they are small and can only hold small items. The bulk of the evidence that is brought in must be kept in the detectives' office. This cuts down on space and clutters the office. The shortage of offices available is a problem also. The offices used by the detectives have to be shared which can

Political Science

create problems when one detective is trying to do paperwork and the other is talking to someone on the telephone. Most of the interrogations are done in the detectives' office because of the lack of space in the interrogation room. This also creates a problem for the other detective, because most interrogations are private matters. This lack of space can cause arguments between the detectives which is counterproductive.

[31] Another problem faced by the sheriff's department has to do with the juvenile division. Juveniles are arrested for the same types of crimes as adults are, but there is no place to detain juvenile offenders. When a secure custody order is placed on a juvenile he must be taken to the detention center in Fayetteville, which is forty miles away. The detention center in Fayetteville only holds twenty residents and is used by all of the counties in our district. Unless the juvenile is a serious threat to himself or others he is released into the custody of his parents. In many cases it is the juveniles home environment that caused him to get into trouble in the first place. While at home he has the opportunity to run around with the same group of friends that got him into trouble.

[32] The lack of money within the system seems to be the main cause of these problems. If more money was given to the sheriff's department the problem of the number of deputies could be solved. With more money new positions could be opened that would make it possible to better serve Scotland County. The lack of space within the department could be corrected by implementing a building fund. This would make it possible to build more office and storage space. A building fund would also make it possible to build a juvenile detention center in Scotland County. It is going to take the cooperation of the people of Scotland County and the County Commission in order for any of these problems to be solved. Nothing is going to change until they realize that this agency has problems and needs their help to solve the problems.

[33] In the time that I have been with this agency I have learned a great deal about how the criminal justice system works. Through this internship I have been able to witness, first hand, what I learned in the classroom. I have been able to get involved with the investigation of different crimes and see how the detectives han-

dle these investigations. In working with the detectives I have been exposed to things that I have never seen before. I was able to see just how delicate a rape interview is. I learned that when investigating a sex crime you have to take extreme caution in how you handle the situation. It is very easy to make the victim feel that she is being raped again with the questions she is being asked. Probably the most interesting thing that I have seen this semester was a dead body after an autopsy had been performed. I was actually able to see what the inside of a human being looked like. This internship has been an experience that I will never forget. I find this type of work very interesting and very rewarding.

BIBLIOGRAPHY

Breeden, Alvin. Probation/Parole Intake Officer. Probation classifications and procedures.

Collier, B. W. Special agent for State Bureau of Investigation-Narcotics Division. Drug investigation procedures and the use of informants.

Green, Doug. Special agent for State Bureau of Investigation-Criminal Division. Criminal investigation procedures.

Lemmond, Paul. Criminal Detective for Scotland County Sheriff's Department. Criminal investigation procedures.

Merritt, Mary. Probation/Parole Officer. Probation classifications and procedures.

Schmidt, Mike. Assistant District Attorney for Hoke and Scotland Counties. Interview techniques.

Scotland County Memorial Library. Area covered by Scotland County Sheriff's Department.

Smith, Steve. Juvenile Detective for Scotland County Sheriff's Department. Juvenile investigations and child sexual abuse investigations. D.A.R.E. program. Juvenile detention.

Wray, Robert. Deputy for Scotland County Sheriff's Department. Patrol techniques.

Political Science

> **STUDY QUESTIONS**
>
> 1. Almost any paragraph can be rewritten more concisely. Paragraph 4 could be revised to read: "The detectives, deputies, and the rest of the Sheriff's Department personnel work together under the guidance of the sheriff, elected by the community in 1986 to a four-year term. His main duties are to supervise the deputies, make necessary changes in personnel, and handle public relations." In addition to reducing the number of words by roughly one-third, this revision puts the less important ideas into phrases. With this approach in mind, rewrite paragraph 8, eliminating unnecessary repetition and combining related ideas in sentences containing subordinate clauses, phrases, and adjectives.
>
> 2. Paragraph 12 contains distracting repetition and also contains more than one topic. Rewrite this paragraph, eliminating the repetition and separating topics into their own paragraphs.
>
> 3. Another major problem with this paper is that Gary too often states the obvious. Paragraph 24 contains an idea that needs to be stated, but here it is stated in such a way that readers almost feel that their intelligence is being insulted. Mark the sentences and phrases in this paragraph that simply repeat in a different form what has just been stated. Rewrite paragraph 32, eliminating those statements that either are repetitious or are too obvious to need stating.
>
> 4. Throughout this paper, Gary says things that could be said about almost any sheriff's department. Paragraph 15 could have been lifted straight from a section on cooperation in a criminal justice textbook. By inventing specific names and details, make this

paragraph applicable only to cooperation within the Scotland County criminal justice system.

5. Paragraph 27 is an example of a problem just the opposite of the one discussed above. Here Gary has included too many irrelevant details on the three unsolved cases. Rewrite this paragraph, eliminating the irrelevancies but at the same time showing that the three unsolved cases do not detract from the performance of the Scotland County Sheriff's Department.

6. This paper contains a number of recurring grammatical errors, the most common of which is disagreement between a pronoun and its antecedent. After studying the sentence lesson below, correct this error in the first two paragraphs.

7. Gary calls the list of people he spoke with to write this report a "Bibliography." What problem does this label present?

Sentence Lesson

Pronouns are used in place of nouns in large part to reduce repeating nouns. Consider the sentences below:

1. **The criminals** were processed quickly, but the criminals could not get a court date for over a year.
1a. **The criminals** were processed quickly, but *they* could not get a court date for over a year.
2. **Our course on Third World revolutions** didn't cover any events after 1980, and our course on Third World revolutions didn't address the role of religious fanaticism in political upheavals.
2a. **Our course on Third World revolutions** didn't cover any events after 1980, and *it* didn't address the role of religious fanaticism on political upheavals.

Notice that the italicized pronouns refer to the noun phrases in bold print. If the noun in the noun phrase is plural, as in sentence (1), the pronoun must also be plural. If this match doesn't occur, the pronoun is said to disagree with its antecedent. In most circumstances, students don't have a problem in this regard, but certain words can be confusing. For example, "everyone" refers to a large group of people and would therefore seem to be plural, but it is actually singular, which leads to the problem illustrated below:

3. **Everyone** asked for *their* money at the same time.

In everyday speech, this sentence doesn't present any difficulty. In formal writing, however, it does, because the pronoun "their" doesn't agree with its antecedent, "everyone." The correct form is:

3a. **Everyone** asked for *his or her* money at the same time.

A related problem occurs when writers lose track of the noun they are referring to and make a pronoun agree with the wrong noun, as in:

4. The officer was assigned **a locker** for valuables, but *they* were so small that they couldn't hold more than a pair of shoes.
4a. The officer was assigned **a locker** for valuables, but *it* was so small that it couldn't hold more than a pair of shoes.

Guide for Reading

Although this paper certainly is not flawless, Andrew has written an interesting report and analysis of the human side of a particular police department. He has used a number of outside sources to broaden his report and has smoothly combined these with his own writing. In addition, he has given examples to let readers see for themselves the situation he is analyzing. By comparing Andrew's work with the preceding paper, you will find that you now have a good picture of the officers and their approach to law enforcement in Winston-Salem, North Carolina, as well as how they fit into the general category of law enforcement officers.

SAMPLE POLITICAL SCIENCE PAPER 8

The Person Behind the Badge

Andrew H. (a senior)

[1] You see them every day. They are out on the job twenty-four hours a day seven days a week all year long and yet the average citizen knows almost nothing about them. The public sees them as faceless uniformed automatons who either fight a never ending battle with crime or who deprive innocent citizens of their freedom of action. Television has done its part to increase the separation between the public and the police by creating the image of the supercop who drives fast, talks tough, shoots straight, and who can solve the deepest mystery in one hour. The true face of law enforcement is often shrouded by the distance that society puts between itself and the business that the police do. Even as a criminal justice major, the real identity of police officers remained largely unknown, masked by the academic detachment and philosophical theses, until as an intern with the Winston Salem Police Department, this writer had a chance to see what most outsiders never see: The person behind the badge. The genuine identity of these real people consists of internal elements, those of demographics and the police working personality, and the external forces that influence the working personality.

[2] In the area of demographics the first attribute of a police officer that anyone notices is one of gender and race. Law enforcement is still predominantly staffed by white males even in the Affirmative Action era. Statewide, white males hold 75% of all law enforcement positions, non-white males hold 11.2%, white females hold 10.8%, and non-white females hold 3%. Increasing numbers of female officers have been hired since the 1970s in all areas of police work, not just in areas considered by some people to be feminine jobs, such as traffic control, working with youth offenders, and administration. One surprising bit of information from the averages is the lack of females in upper level administration positions.[1] Since there are qualified and capable

Political Science

female officers in this field, it would seem that they are either somehow being denied a chance at promotion or simply unwilling to take on the extra responsibility.

[3] The second attribute that seems to be in the news most frequently is one of race. Because the police department is an arm of the government, it is especially subject to Federal Affirmative Action programs. In the past, many departments have drawn sharp criticism from the black community because it was felt that an insufficient number of blacks were being hired. However, the majority of blacks who fit the employment requirements get hired. The latest push in law enforcement has been promoting the hiring of non-black minority groups because of the steady influx of hispanic and far eastern immigrants into this area.

[4] The third attribute along this line is one of age. Statewide, 32.8% of all sworn law enforcement personnel are between 30 and 40 years of age. The next largest group is the 25 to 30 year olds, who comprise 23.8% of this group.[2] Law enforcement, by nature, is an intense and demanding career field. By the time most officers reach their forties, they have gotten into administration and have left the field enforcement to younger men.

[5] Winston-Salem, as a whole, seems right in line with the state averages. In the Patrol Division, there were an average of three female officers for each of the five 30-officer platoons and in the Criminal Investigation Division, there are five female detectives. One point that seemed to stick out in Winston-Salem and it was duplicated on the state averages, there are no females above the rank of Sergeant. In the past, the Winston-Salem Police Department has drawn sharp criticism from the aldermen and the NAACP because it was felt that an insufficient number of blacks were being hired. But from a personnel opinion, the ratio of black to white officers was not excessively small. As far as other minority groups are concerned, there only appeared to be only one hispanic officer and no orientals at all. This fact will probably cause some concern in the future as these minority groups increase in the Triad area. The average of the officers on the street in Winston-Salem is approximately twenty-seven years. This figure is below the state average and it makes for a

younger and relatively less experienced department. This has been brought about because of retention problems internal and because a larger city's police force is often used as a primary training ground for people who want to progress to other areas of law enforcement, especially the Federal level agencies.[3] The officers that do stay are often those who have strong ties to the community. It is this group that often progresses into the administration positions.

[6] The final major attribute of a police officer is one of background. North Carolina requires that an individual be 21 years old before becoming a sworn officer, so all members of the force have some sort of prior experience they can bring with them, whether it is military service, college credits, or prior employment.

[7] National statistics show that in 1985, 75% of all law enforcement officers have at least one year or more of college. This is an increase from 46% of all law enforcement officers ten years before.[4] This can be attributed to the increase of two and four colleges offering criminal justice degrees, a new emphasis on education, and the career development programs within the law enforcement community. Today's police officer works in a different environment than his counterpart twenty years ago. Changes in previous court rulings, new decisions by Federal and state courts on jurisdiction, extents of police power, and new techniques for arrests and surveillance, make continuing education for a police officer a must. Winston-Salem is no exception to this rule. The city's public safety attorney gives bimonthly classes to officers. The class instruction covers recent North Carolina Supreme Court decisions that affect subjects such as civil liability in pursuits and evidence admissibility. The department offers DWI investigation classes and radar certification classes "in house." The state offers courses at local Community Colleges and at the Criminal Justice Academy in Salemburg, N.C. in more specialized areas such as advanced homicide investigation and intelligence gathering. Winston-Salem also offers tuition incentives for officers working towards a degree. Many officers in Winston-Salem feel that this push in education is merited, because it contributes to the professionalism of the department. This extra education gives the officer improved skills in public relations, oral

Political Science

and written communication, and observation. The officers that have Bachelor's degrees in Winston-Salem have them in the following fields: Criminal Justice, Business Administration, Sociology and Psychology.

[8] Many police officers are military veterans. Military experience is looked upon favorably because it demonstrates an ability to work with others in a supervised environment, being able to take charge of a situation if need be, experience working under stress, and personal discipline. There are several prior service officers in Winston-Salem. The majority of them served in the US Army as Military Policemen.

[9] Many officers did not initially go into law enforcement but entered police work after pursuing a career in another field. Within the Winston-Salem department there is a former bank teller, a dockworker, and a former elementary school teacher.

[10] In addition to the physical, tangible attributes of a police officer, there is an non-tangible aspect that plays just as great a part in the day-to-day business of police work. This aspect is the police working personality. This working personality is unique to the law enforcement profession, just as a Doctor's personality is unique to the medical profession. Both personalities develop as a reaction to the work environment and the people that both professions encounter. The first factor that contributes to the working personality of police officers are the people that the police are charged to serve. When most people are asked about police work, the same images are often described as references: Chases in fast cars with lights flashing and sirens blaring; a detective in a fedora and a trench coat examing a crime scene: a patrol officer in a gun fight with an armed suspect.[5]

[11] The truth is that police work is very different from these images. After all the training in pistol marksmanship and hand to hand combat, even though the most obvious tools of the police's trade are weapons, actual crimefighting is only 10% of the police workload. Many times the officer is confronted with a situation on the street that might confound a psychologist in a clinical setting.[6] The majority of police calls are more than likely some sort of public service that usually has nothing to do with law enforcement. For example, during a routine evening shift, this writer

assisted an officer escort an intoxicated street person to one of Winston-Salem's homeless shelters. Even with all the patrol car's windows open, both he and I were overcome by the smell of our passenger. The officer turned to me and said, "It isn't like Adam-12, is it?"[7]

[12] The people with whom the average officer comes in contact on a day to day basis are often the reason many officers begin to mistrust the public at large. The longer that an officer serves on the street, the more he or she becomes suspicious of anyone with whom they have had prior contact with, either directly or indirectly. These experience often make the officer suspicious of anyone who fits into a generic criminal description: A teen with a brown bag becomes a drug courier, a woman out after dark in provocative clothing is a hooker, or the old man who sits at the same corner every day is a look-out for the drug dealer down the street. This mistrust of people stems from repeated encounters with inherent dishonesty on the public's part. Case in point: A call came in from the University Parkway Pizza Hut in Winston-Salem that a woman had pulled a gun on the manager. Upon arriving at the seen, the officer was given a description of the woman and the car she was in. During the questioning of the manager, the suspect's car passed by the front of the restaurant and the police immediately pursued. When the woman's car was stopped and searched, she admitted going by Pizza Hut that morning and gave up the pistol from her purse. However, the manager did not tell the officer the following: The woman being sought was his ex-live-in girlfriend, he gave her the pistol she was carrying, she was also carrying his unborn child and awaiting a verdict in a civil court case against him. When the manager was requestioned, he denied his earlier statement to the same investigating officer, and stated that he wished to withdraw his complaint. The officer chastised him for making a false call and left. This is one first hand example of what contributes to cynicism in the working personality of the average officer.

[13] The public's attitude about getting involved contributes to the frustration of the street officer. No one ever sees anything or wants to get involved. For these reasons so many times cases go to an inactive status because of the lack of pertinent facts that are

known by the people at the crime scene. This apathy coincides with the "felt" distance between the police and public, another factor that formulates the working personality of officers.

[14] As this working personality continues to develop in officers, they feel separated from a society who looks on them as lesser persons for the "dirty work" they do every day. The public sees the officers as a faceless "Rorschach-in-blue" with persons responding either favorably or unfavorably according to predisposition or situation. Yet, the police officer's response is set by orderly rules, learned both in school and on the street from other officers.[8] This area was particularly obvious every time this writer went out with a patrol officer. The majority of people seemed to think that they were doing something wrong because they avoided passing by or even coming near the officer or the patrol car. Amusingly enough, my presence as a plain clothed individual with uniformed officers made some even more uneasy, as that fact usually meant the intervention of some higher level law enforcement agency.

[15] Another element of a typical officer's working personality is suspicion. Officers are taught from the very beginning to observe and the pay particular attention to every person they see because anyone on the street could become a threat. Many times this suspicion is brought into sharp focus when the officer serves in a high crime area such as a housing project or low rent district.

[16] If an officer works in the "projects', he or she begins to learn the following: Checks come on the third of the month, Christmas holidays means TV and VCR stealing season, and robberies are often drug related-whether it means stealing to support the habit or the dealer stealing from the junkie to pay off the junkie's outstanding debt. Case in point: One evening there were two reported break-ins in the same general area that were almost identical: kicked in door and nothing missing from the apartment but the TV and the VCR. The officer asked the same questions from the victims: Was the TV or VCR rented? If so, how long have you been renting it? Do you owe anyone any money? Does anyone live here with you? The seasons also contribute to the officer's suspicions because the season affects what goes on in the community. Spring and summer have warmer

weather which means more people are outside and on the move. Fall and winter means more are inside and therefore there are fewer fights and cuttings but more burglaries. Almost to a different pole is the element in the typical police working personality known as an attitude of "CYA" or "cover your ass."

[17] This perspective is deeply ingrained in patrolwork and stems from the fact that one mistake on a report could potentially jeopardize the evaluation and career of the officer who write it along with that of his squad and sergeant. The sergeant plays a pivotal role here since they are the person that reviews the reports and either approves it or rejects it.[9] An example of this element at work in Winston-Salem occured one evening in October: During a routine patrol this writer observed an old man have an accident on a moped. After informing the officer present, we moved in to assist the man. The officer filled out a standard police service form and a North Carolina motor vehicle accident report. The officer's reasoning for filing a motor vehicle accident report was to assure that no matter what, if any action taken by the party involved in the accident that she would be covered procedurally. The sergeant reviewed the report and told the officer that the report was done correctly and that there were "no holes."

[18] There were other cases where officers who responded to the same call made their reports corroborate each other's reports. Therefore, both of the officers would be absolved, as much as possible, in case of any legal repercussions. The "CYA" concept means that as patrol officers spend more time on the street, they do only what they are directly told to do or become involved in through no actions of their own so that questionable situations are avoided. By being cautious, officers are also making another personal trait known.

[19] The last element to be discussed in the typical police working personality is an attitude of "don't work to hard." This comes about from the fact that working hard and enforcing the law increases the number of contact that the officer has with the public. The more contacts the officer makes with the public thereby increases the chances of making mistakes and increases the amount of paperwork that the officer has to do.[10] This ele-

ment manifests itself by the officer taking as much time as the informal norm allows to clear a call and taking more retroactive patrol measures rather than going out to actively look for violations of the laws.

[20] Public contacts are avoided because of the indifferent or antagonistic manner that many people take when in the presence of a uniformed police officer.[11] Therefore, the officer works the shift, with little meaningful contact aside from the waitress at the restaurants where they eat and the other officers in their assigned patrol. All contacts with the civilian populace are packed with anxiety and tension, even if it involves no wrong-doing on the part of the civilian. The worst encounters for both parties are traffic stops. Being stopped on a public street by a uniformed officer is a highly visible symbol of governmental authority in a freedom loving society. This almost always creates a feeling of being unfairly singled out for punishment.[12] Oftentimes, it is this attitude taken by the citizen during these encounters that result in a citation or arrest.

[21] Police officers know that encounters with the law can be stressful for the public, but they also dislike people who do not respect police authority. The individual officer has a great deal of discretion in regards to what constitutes a violation of the law serious enough for a citation or arrest, and it is the subjects attitude that determines whether or not they "hold pink" or "make the trip to the Church Street Hilton."[13] One example of a public contact came from Winston-Salem. It occured on I-40 in the eastbound lane. After clocking a car going 60 mph in a 45 mph zone and stopping the car, the officer asked the male driver if he knew how fast he was going. The driver replied that he didn't have time to talk to a police officer because he was late for a business meeting. The officer then wrote him a ticket, to which the driver replied, "You can't give me a ticket." He received one just the same. Conversely, another man was clocked on I-40 doing 85 mph in a 55 mph zone. When the man was stopped, he told the officer that his mother had been admitted to Baptist Hospital because of a heart condition and he was going to see her. The officer gave him a severe verbal warning, followed him to the hospital, and let him go. These two incidents reflect not only

the use of discretion, but the way policing styles can influence the same violation of the law to be handled differently. There are three distinct policing styles according to James Q. Wilson, author of Varieties of Police Behavior. The watchman style, the legalistic style and the service style shape the behaviors of the police officers within a department depending on the particular style the administration of that department adhers to.[14]

[22] The watchman style can be paralleled with the stereotype of the small town policeforce. The emphasis of the department is on keeping order rather law enforcement, being the seriousness of an offense by the person who committed it and if it makes the police look bad. "Private" matters such as personal arguments, gambling, and assaults among friends are ignored or treated informally unless they pose a threat to the community or to the police's authority. Juveniles are treated in a familial manner, ignoring most infractions as childish mischief and acting "in local parentis" with the more serious ones by administering punishment. The officers in such a department are often locally recruited, less trained and less well paid than their counterparts in other agencies.[15]

[23] The legalistic style is based on the view that all matters can be solved from a law enforcement perspective. This type of department issues traffic tickets at a high rate and makes arrests even when the peace has not been broken. Everyone in the community is held to the same standards of behavior and face the same punishment if those standards are breached. Juvenile offenders are all treated formally and dealt with through the system. Formal authority is repeatedly stressed in this style, with college educated better paid officers being the norm.[16]

[24] The final style is the service style, characterized by frequent interaction without as much formal action by the police. This style results from a high need for public order but no administrative demand for the strong enforcement orientation of the legalistic style. This type department maintains a high level of community relations because it has a strong orientation to maintaining the police image. Officers who fail to live up to this image are fired quickly, since they pose a threat to the police-community relationship. Violations are not overlooked, but are only dealt with formally

if the situation merits. This type of department issues just as many warning tickets as it does real ones, thereby enforcing the law without involving the legal system.[17]

[25] In assessing the Winston-Salem Police Department in light of these three styles, it would appear that this department is a service style one. Winston-Salem has taken a very interactive stand with the public by stressing Community Watch programs and foot patrols in urban areas. The department stresses intervention which often results in informal actions on the part of the officer. There appears to be a move to increase the amount of public service calls accepted beyond the current high levels. The department currently operates on a six day on, four day off schedule. This would be changed to a four day on, two day off schedule so that more manpower would be available per day. The public image of the department is an important factor to the administration. A complaint from a citizen, even if it is contrived and false, often holds more weight than the officer's own account of the situation. Although the policing style of the department and the police working personality affects the way in which an officer carries out his or her duties. There is one final factor that has to be acknowledged; that of the family.

[26] Because of the nature of policework today, officers need the dedicated support and understanding of his or her family. Law enforcement has always been a family occupation because like ministers or teachers, police families are often expected to live up to certain standards. Sadly enough, the divorce rate for police officers outdistances all other professions. The marriages that do work display a high degree of interspouse cooperation and understanding.

[27] The importance of family support ranks near the top of an officer's list of needs. The goals that he or she may have set may have worked while single, but marriage changes all that. What does their spouse want out of marriage? One female officer related the story of her first marriage. Her husband expected her to carry out the traditional roles of a housewife and could not understand why police work would not allow this. She said that this turned into resentment of her career as a police officer and resulted in their divorce.[18]

[28] Dorothy Fagerstrom, research editor for Law and Order writes: "Police officers want an ordered society where it is safe for their wives and children; they want to help those who need assistance and are too weak to help or protect themselves; they want the satisfaction of serving mankind but without any possible stigma of being a sissy. They expect their wives and families to understand that this is something they must do and to approve."[19] Early in marriage most spouses think they can cope with the stresses of a police career and it is misunderstanding of the job that is at the root of most problems.

[29] As the officer-mate team struggle with their problems to define the questions of ambitions, goals, and personal ways of coping, a new question usually presents itself—children. Do we want them? If so, how many? The wife knows that she took vows to love her husband. However, she also knows that her officer husband has a committment to work and woven through all of this is the need by both parties to have the moral and physical support of the person they love. One reocurring problem in the lives of police officers is that these questions and conflicts cause stress.

[30] Stress can affect all members of an officers family. At home, the mate often faces a lot of uncertainty about the time the family will be together. Police officers are never completely off-duty because a call could come at any time, day or night if the officer is needed. If something has been planned, how is the mate to react? Do they simply attribute this to being a part of the job and let it pass? Difficulties often arise in marriages if this is repeated too often and sadly enough they could be avoided by a more thorough description of what goes on "downtown." The daily pressure of the job carries over into the family and this puts pressure on the spirit of the family relationship. When the officer is the husband, this carry-over affects his relationship with his wife. As she reacts to this stress, her approach to the husband's demands affects his emotional stability, attitudes, and in general, his overall job effectiveness. This problem never seemed to be very widespread in Winston-Salem, but as an outsider in a closed society, some parts of an officer's life are still guarded secrets.

[31] These secrets often manifest themselves in changes that

occur in officers' lives. The rates of suicide, divorce, heart attacks, alcoholism, and ulcers among police officers are some of the highest of any career in the United States. One officer told me that he never smoked or drank until he joined the force.

[32] There are many young officers who approach their work with a spirit of upright bravado, who with the passage of time become hard, silent and insensitive to their wives and especially the tame life of home.[20] After watching these officers in this stressful occupation, the idea comes across that the constant pressure to perform in an acceptable manner is not frequently found in an equal measure in any other field. In short, in these days of technological change, few jobs offer the interpersonal challenge of police work.

[33] If the pressure to perform daily can be tolerated by the officer's body, the pressure on the soul is always there. One reason police officers develop this hardness of heart is due to what they see every day on the street. Most of the people they come in contact with are the homeless, the poor, the victims, and especially the victimizers. These people don't always have complementary opinions of those on the force.

[34] Public opinion is reflected in the subtle attitudes of people and is not always easily understood. Some citizens, it is true, have had bad experiences with police and whether justified or not, the ill feelings are very real to them. Some have merely heard or read of the bad experiences others have had.[21] This impacts the officers' families and the officer himself/herself. Often police officers feel that what is expected of them is a tough stance; to stand tall and be strong no matter how they feel inside. One officer said that being tough is a part of police training. He also said that it was like trying to live up to the screen image of John Wayne—the tough, courageous lawman who is never afraid and never backs down. It is this sort of pressure that makes for additional stress in the officers life and it carries over into their off-duty lives.

[35] Anxiety comes on stage each time the officer goes into work. All the members of the police family know in the back of their minds that every time the officer hits the street there is the chance that this shift could be the last one. There is always the

chance that something could happen because the potential for danger is ever present "out there." It is little wonder that fear sometimes clutches at the heart of these families. Wives, sons, daughters, mothers and fathers. No one is exempt. Accidents occur without warning. If they allow themselves to dwell on the disastrous events reported daily by the local and national media from around the world that involve the police, the family would go out of their minds with fear.

[36] Being an intern, you see all of these things happening in the lives of the officers you are with daily. If you look carefully you see the demographics and working personality along with the external influences played out center stage because it is no longer case studies in a textbook. It was and is live first person drama. As you watch, listen, and learn, experience imparts a greater appreciation of the job police do.

[37] Many of the younger officers enter with an idea of changing the world and cleaning up the town, but with the passage of time, the officer sees the world as it is: cold, hard, unforgiving, and ever critical of any decision made, whether right or wrong. If this hardens the soul of the officer, what are his or her reasons for serving the public? The majority of officers give the answer that most people expect to hear but is proved to be the one that was the most surprising after all these revelations. No matter how long an officer had been on the street, no matter how soured or cynical the officer had become, they ALL said they had entered law enforcement to help people.

ENDNOTES

[1] NC Department of Crime Control and Public Safety, Governor's Crime Commission, Criminal Justice Analysis Center, NC Law Enforcement Data Manual, (Raleigh, NC: State Printing Office, 1979–80) p. 50

[2] NC Law Enforcement Data Manual, p. 151

[3] Dan Chapman, "Inability to Fill Vacancies Leaves Police with Manpower Shortage," Winston Salem Journal, 8 June 1988, p. 17

[4] US Department of Labor, Employment and Training Administration, Criminal Justice Careers Guidebook, (Washington, DC: Government Printing Office, 1982) p. 5

[5] Kirkham, George L. and Wollan, Laurin A. Jr, Introduction to Law Enforcement (New York: Harper and Row Publishers, 1980) p. 332

[6] Introduction to Law Enforcement. p. 45

[7] Craig J. A., Interview conducted during and after shift at Winston-Salem Public Safety Center, 6 September 1988

[8] Omitted

[9] Manning, Peter K., and Van Maanen, John. editors Policing: A View From the Street, (Santa Monica, CA: Goodyear Publishing Company, INC. 1978) p. 126

[10] Manning and Van Maanen, p. 125

[11] Manning and Van Maanen, p. 118

[12] Manning and Van Maanen, p. 73

[13] "Hold pink" is the popular term for an issued traffic citation, "The Church Street Hilton" is one name for the Forsyth County Jail.

[14] Wilson, James Q., Varieties of Police Behavior (Cambridge: Harvard University Press, 1968) p. 141–250

[15] Wilson, p. 141–153

[16] Wilson, p. 172–188

[17] Wilson, p. 200–210

[18] Harter, A. A., interview conducted during and after shift at Winston-Salem Public Safety Center, 3 November 1988

[19] "An Open Letter to Police Wives," Law and Order, (May 1971) quoted in Pat James and Martha Nelson, Police Wife (Illinois: Bannerstone House, 1975) p. 7

[20] James, Pat and Nelson, Martha Police Wife (Illinois: Bannerstone House, 1975), p. x–xv

[21] James and Nelson, p. 85

BIBLIOGRAPHY

"An Open Letter to Police Wives," Law and Order, (May 1971) quoted in James, Pat and Nelson, Martha, Police Wife, p. 7 Illinois: Bannerstone House, 1975

Chapman, Dan. "Inability to fill vacancies leaves Police with manpower shortage," Winston-Salem Journal, 8 June 1988, p. 17

Craig, J. A., Winston-Salem Police Department, Winston-Salem, NC. Interview 6 September 1988

Harter, A. A., Winston-Salem Police Department, Winston-Salem, NC. Interview 3 November 1988

Kirkham, George L., and Wollan, Laurin A. Jr., Introduction to Law Enforcement New York: Harper and Row Publishers, 1980

Manning, Peter K., and Van Maanen, John, editors. Policing: A View from the Street, Santa Monica: Goodyear Publishing Company, INC. 1978

NC Department of Crime Control and Public Safety, Governor's Crime Commission, Criminal Justice Analysis Center, NC Law Enforcement Data Manual, Raleigh, NC: State Printing Office, 1980

Stinchcomb, James D., Opportunities in Law Enforcement and Criminal Justice, Illinois: VGM Career Horizons, 1985

US Department of Justice, National Institute of Justice. Crime and Policing, by Mark H. Moore, Robert C. Trojanowicz, and George L. Kelling. Report No. 2 Washington, DC: Government Printing Office, 1982

US Department of Labor and Training Administration, Criminal Justices Careers Guidebook. Washington, DC: Government Printing Office, 1982.

Wilson, James Q., Varieties of Police Behavior, Cambridge: Harvard University Press, 1968

Political Science

STUDY QUESTIONS

1. After carefully reading the paper, evaluate it on the basis of how well it responds to the suggested approach given in the professor's guide for analysis.

2. One weakness of the paper is the inconsistency and number of errors contained in the footnotes and bibliography. These errors have no direct effect on Andrew's analysis or presentation of information, but how do they affect the way you view Andrew as a writer?

3. Notice the dates of the outside sources. Are these sources appropriate, based on the information contained in paragraph 7?

4. Paragraph 8 contains several examples of the type of imprecision found throughout the paper. Rewrite this paragraph so that it says what you think Andrew meant to say.

5. A recurring problem in many student papers centers on pronoun/antecedent agreement. Andrew has the same problem in this paper, both with gender and number. One way to solve this problem is to use the plural whenever possible. Use the plural in the first three sentences of paragraph 12. Will this method work in other instances throughout this paper to eliminate the pronoun/antecedent problem?

6. In general, the paragraphs are put together well, focusing on a specific topic that is clear to readers. A problem occurs, however, at the end of paragraph 16/beginning of 17 and again at the end of 25/beginning of 26. Identify this problem and correct it.

7. Take one of the popular television police shows and explain, based on Andrew's paper, what parts of that show are probably not an accurate portrayal of police work.

Writing Assignments

These writing assignments duplicate, on a small scale, the internship reports and analyses above. They also ask for a report and analysis/evaluation. Instead of writing for a professor guiding you through an internship, you should write for an intelligent person who is curious but not especially knowledgeable about the subject. A good paper will include the relevant facts, an explanation of how the components work together, and a thoughtful analysis and evaluation of the organization. It should be properly documented and free of surface errors.

1. In a 4- to 5-page paper, explain how your state handles the problem of people who drink and drive. Include the standards for measuring intoxication, the penalties for first and multiple offenses, a profile of the most common offender, and the success (or lack of success) of the program in reducing traffic accidents and fatalities caused by intoxicated drivers.
2. In a 6- to 8-page paper, explain how your college or university student judicial system works. Include the following:
    a. the structure of the system
    b. the method of filling the various positions
    c. the procedure for bringing a case to court
    d. the procedure for hearing and ruling on a case
    e. an evaluation of the system and suggestions for improvement
3. In a 6- to 8-page paper, explain how your college or university security system works. Include the following:
    a. the structure of the system
    b. the duties of the officers
    c. the main problems the officers have to deal with and how they deal with them
    d. the relationship between the officers and the students
    e. an evaluation of the system and suggestions for improvement

7 Anthropology

INTRODUCTION TO WRITING IN ANTHROPOLOGY

Anthropology is the study of human physical and cultural origins and development. As a field of inquiry, it ranks with psychology, astronomy, and mathematics as one of the oldest intellectual disciplines, perhaps because humans seem to have always had an intrinsic interest in understanding their roots.

Currently, anthropology has two main branches—physical anthropology, which focuses on the study of human artifacts and remains, and cultural anthropology, which focuses on the study of human culture and societies. At some colleges and universities, these two branches are housed in a single department, whereas at others they are separated into archaeology and anthropology.

The writing in anthropology is generally characterized by the aims of its branches and the materials or facts that writers work with. For example, physical anthropology has many affinities with natural sciences such as biology, geology, and paleontology. The physical anthropologist generally collects data at a dig site, keeping a notebook to record details of procedures and finds. Once that particular trip is over, he or she then returns to a lab to study the data using a range of methods, many of which involve the high technology of scanning electron microscopes, carbon dating, and so forth. Subsequent reports draw on the records of the notebook and the lab analyses.

Because data are always missing from even the richest site, writing in physical anthropology involves a great degree of interpretation from relatively little information, based on both inductive and deductive reasoning. In fact, some physical anthropologists lightheartedly refer to themselves as "detectives" out to unravel the mysteries of the human past. This flamboyant image is captured most notoriously in the film character Indiana Jones. Writing in physical anthropology also requires clear and concise descriptive abilities, because, in spite of what the old saying tells us, a picture is not always worth a thousand words.

Unless students are fortunate enough to go on a dig and are asked to write up their notebooks, they won't have to master any special format for writing in physical anthropology. Their work often consists of descriptive essays, designed to help them practice attending to details, and research papers that ask them to learn more about a topic by examining published materials and then integrating that information with principles studied in class. The tone is relatively formal, and students are expected to approach their topics in an interesting way, which means that organization and style commonly play an important role in successful writing.

For its part, cultural anthropology, with its attention to the development of art and religion and symbols, is closely linked to the humanities. Some of its techniques, as a consequence, resemble those we find in history and English, where there is much attention to documents as reflections of human accomplishment. At the same time, however, some of its techniques, particularly close observation of human behavior, are based firmly in psychology.

Although the writing in cultural anthropology strongly resembles that in its sister branch, at least in regard to form, its methods are distinctly different. The cultural anthropologist doesn't always deal with tangible artifacts but often with the abstractions of human behavior, which tend to impose interpretation with every gesture and utterance. Still, cultural anthropology has its own field techniques, including notebooks, which help researchers reduce the level of inherent subjectivity in their work. Given that the goal is to observe in order to understand, personal biases have little place in anthropological writing.

Because the potential for misinterpretation of facts is so great in this discipline, anthropologists take great pains to ensure the accuracy of their work. This principle carries over to their writing, and students enrolled in anthropology courses will be expected to produce writing that is clear, accurate, and error-free.

The writing you do in an introductory anthropology course will most likely take the form of a research paper, similar perhaps to the first two sample assignments we present in this chapter. Both come from an introductory archaeology course and require students to do extensive research and to document their sources. Although the assignments are quite different—one is a biography of a working archaeologist, the other a prehistory of a geographical area—they are similar in that they require students to organize their material in a narrative.

The third assignment comes from the final exam in an introductory anthropology course. Our analysis recognizes that some of the most significant writing you do in a social sciences course is in a test-taking situation.

ANTHROPOLOGY ASSIGNMENT 1

Course: **Introduction to Archaeology**

> Write a short biography of a present archaeologist, focusing on his/her concern, area of interest, accomplishments, and impact on the field. Write the person first, then check Citation Index for book reviews. The paper should be at least three pages and properly documented.

Analysis of Anthropology Assignment 1

This assignment introduces students to the work archaeologists do by asking them to write a paper that focuses on the career and accomplishments of one notable scholar in the field. Students are instructed to collect information on their subject in two ways: contacting the subject of their research and locating reviews of their subject's work.

Students may be alarmed by their teacher's request that they contact the subject of their research. But handled correctly, personal interviews can be a rewarding and enlightening means of gathering material. The students in this course have been instructed to write their subject first, and this letter should be composed carefully. In the letter, students should introduce themselves, state their purpose for writing, and request specific information in a clear and courteous manner. In the letter, students may want to suggest the option of writing back with the information or contacting them by phone. If the subject chooses to talk personally, students should be prepared to take careful notes of the conversation and to run the interview in an efficient manner, which means writing all questions out in advance. Whatever information students gather, either through a letter or phone conversation, should be documented with the same care given to published material. All documentation formats have specific instructions for documenting personal interviews; check the published guides.

Students are also instructed to collect book reviews of their subject's work. These book reviews will be the best means by which students can determine where their subject is situated in his or her field of study, how their subject's work has evolved, and how this work has been accepted by other scholars. The teacher does not require students to read each of the books reviewed, but it might be worthwhile to check one or two of these works out of the library for a more careful read. Students will get a feel for the subject's style, and the author's preface to the work could provide valuable information about his or her aims and methods.

After the research process is completed, students may find themselves with a dilemma: They have an abundance of information for a paper described as "at least three pages." How do they choose what information about their subject to include? It will be helpful to remember the primary goal in this project—to present the life and work of an *archaeologist*. Information about the person unrelated to his or her work need not be included.

A successful response to this assignment will reflect careful research and a thoughtful choice of material. Students will have chosen information about the subject's life and work as an archaeologist that is both representative and interesting.

As you read through the following papers, consider the organizational strategies each writer has chosen. All three papers are, predictably, organized in chronological fashion. Many students take a plodding approach to this form of writing, beginning their paragraphs with transitional phrases such as, "Professor Smith was born in 1930"; "In 1960 Professor Smith wrote," "The next year he published." Narration, as all of us who have read a good story know, need not be humdrum, but it requires that the writer find interesting ways to yoke the parts of the paper together. The following papers have dealt with this problem with varying degrees of success.

Guide for Reading

David makes good use of his source material in this paper and produces an outstanding response to the assignment. Note the manner in which he integrates quotes, paraphrases, and summary to create well-developed paragraphs. Another strength is his well-structured and varied sentences. David's organization is functional, but better use of transitional phrases and other connecting devices could make his paper flow more smoothly. As you read, try to determine what kinds of transitions would help integrate the paper.

SAMPLE ANTHROPOLOGY PAPER 1

A Biography of Peter S. Wells

by David K. (a freshman)

Peter S. Wells' main interest lies in the European origins of Western civilization and culture. Admittedly, his focus seems to be on the rise of iron production and trade in central Europe. Most of his work, along with his four books, concerns this subject.

Wells was born in Boston, Massachusetts on October 9, 1948. He attended Harvard University, majoring in Anthropology. His summers were spent in Italy, Ireland, France, Lebanon, and Labrador, Canada on various digs and projects trying to gain as much experience as possible in a variety of areas. Wells spent all but one year of his graduate schooling at Harvard University also. This other year was spent at the University of Tubingen in Germany. His graduate work was concerned with cultural contacts between Europe north of the Alps and the Mediterranean world. His graduate dissertation led to his first book.

Culture Contact and Culture Change, was published in 1980. Although this subject has been dealt with many times, Wells wanted to do a "modern study of the impact of Greek and Etruscan cultures on the European cultures" (Wells, Peter S.).

Peter Wells' next book, *The Emergence of an Iron Age Economy*, was published in 1981. This book was partly a catalogue of the items in the Mecklenberg Collection, a collection of iron-age artifacts and remains from various burials excavated in central Europe. The remainder of the publication discusses the behavioral pattern changes and the changes in the structure of society when iron mining and production became an important aspect of European culture.

In *Rural Economy in the Early Iron Age*, published in 1983, Wells examines the question of why the societies of Europe followed a course of cultural development different from that of other regions. This book summarized and revealed the findings of the excavations at Hascherkeller, Germany which took place between 1978 and 1981. "The aim of the excavation project at Hascherkeller has been to study, through a real exposure of the surface of a settlement, the economic organization of a typical community of the beginning of the final Millenium B.C. in central Europe" (Wells, Peter S., *Rural Economy in the Early Iron Age*).

Wells' latest book is a chronological overview of the history and cultural development of Europe in the 1000 years before Christ. In *Farms, Villages, and Cities*, he discusses the lack of development of true cities and towns in central Europe until contact with Mediterranean cultures. Previously, the rise of towns and cities had been atributed to the introduction of Mediterranean luxury items, but in this book Wells proposes that "it was not the arrival of Mediterranean luxury goods and their distribution in Europe that led to the formation of the commercial centers; it was rather the organizational efforts to produce goods to exchange for those desired luxuries" (Wells, Peter S., *Farms, Villages, and Cities*). He suggests that the European cultures with their consistent and temperate environment had it too good and were able to prosper without cities. Therefore agricultural irrigation and administrative and ceremonial centers were unnecessary.

J. D. Muhly calls this book a "short, but attractive survey of prehistoric Europe during the first millenium B.C." (Muhly, D., *Review of Farms, Villages, and Cities*), but calls Wells' historical interpretations rather simplistic, even to the point of being naive. Klaus Randsborg says the weakest part of the work was the fact that it devoted only twenty pages to the first 1000 years A.D. and that more extensive research of this period may have led Wells to consider several factors other than trade in the formation of urban centers in Europe. Still, it is considered and "excellent summary" (Ibid_) of various excavations and contains "valuable discussions" (Ibid_) of the development of salt and iron production.

Presently, Dr. Wells is in charge of the administration of the center for Ancient Studies at the University of Minnesota.

END NOTES

[1] Peter S. Wells.

[2] Peter S. Wells, *Rural Economy in the Early Iron Age* (Boston: Harvard University Press, 1963).

[3] Peter S. Wells, *Farms, Villages, and Cities* (Itaca: Cornell University Press, 1984).

[4] D. Muhly, *Review of Farms, Villages and Cities*, by Peter Wells, in *American Historical Review* 91 (December, 1986): 1970

[5] Ibid.

WORKS CITED

J. D. Muhly. *Review of Farms, Villages, and Cities*, by Peter S. Wells. In American Historical Review v. 91 (December, 1986): p. 1170.

Klaus Randsborg. Review of *Farms, Villages, and Cities*, by Peter S. Wells. In Science v.228 (May 10, 1985): p. 713.

Wells, Peter S. *Emergence of an Iron Age Economy*. Boston: Harvard University Press, 1983.

Wells, Peter S. *Farms, Villages, and Cities*. Ithaca, NY: Cornell University Press, 1984.

Wells, Peter S. *Rural Economy in the Early Iron Age.*

Analysis of Sample Anthropology Paper 1

David has written a readable, well-integrated research paper on the work of Peter S. Wells. He handles the various tasks involved in this assignment in an organized, knowledgeable fashion.

David's skillful use of sources is the most notable feature of his paper. Though one doubts that he had the time to read all of Wells' works, he is sufficiently familiar with each to allow him to summarize and discuss them in an intelligent fashion. He uses quotations and paraphrases from these works in conjunction with his own summary, which gives a nice texture and development to his paragraphs. (The third paragraph, where he discusses *Culture Contact and Culture Change*, is the only one not developed in this way.) David also uses material from book reviews wisely. He probably read reviews for all of Wells' books, but he chooses to focus on the reception of the latest. This paragraph is commendable for its expert handling and ordering of a variety of judgments. Using brief quotations and paraphrases, David does an excellent and exact job of summing up the praise and complaints of the book's reviewers.

David's organization is based on a chronological examination of Wells' work. He sets this structure up adequately, but, unfortunately, the movement from paragraph to paragraph is often choppy. Rather than rely solely on chronology for dictating the progression of his paragraphs, he needs to provide substantive, explicit links between the books he discusses. He could have accomplished this by stating, for example, that "The themes developed in *Culture Contact and Culture Change* are explored from a different perspective in Wells' latest book."

Transitional sentences like the one above would also have enabled David to discuss in more detail how the books are related—a significant lack in the paper as it stands. Some information is clear from their titles, of course, but David nevertheless missed an opportunity here to make his paper even better. Instead, he makes only passing reference to this important point, in the introduction, where he notes that the focus of Wells' career has been "the rise of iron production and trade in central Europe" and where he states that "most of his work, along with his four books, concerns this subject."

On a negative note, David's endnotes and references have some problems that mar his paper.

Guide for Reading

Mary's paper is written in a lively style, beginning with her introduction, and that liveliness may prompt many readers to judge her writing to be better than David's. She is by no means slavish in her reliance on chronology to organize her paper; in fact, Mary's biography would be clearer if she gave more consideration to the order in which the events in this biography took place. A factor that affects the quality of this response, and that ultimately makes it slightly less well written than David's, is the fact that she provides no indication that she used the Citation Index to collect her book reviews. How might she have solved this problem?

SAMPLE ANTHROPOLOGY PAPER 2

Wilburn Allen Cockrell: Underwater Archaeologist

Mary T. (a freshman)

When one hears the word, "archaeology," the thought that comes to mind is that of an archaeologist who digs and directs his or her group of workers to dig at a specific spot of land, marking off the land in square blocks, sifting through the soil smoothly and evenly in search of features, fossils, pottery, etc. Wilburn Allen Cockrell is one such archaeologist but his work is not conducted on land. His work takes place under water.

At the present Wilburn Cockrell is the director of Warm Mineral Springs Archaeological Research Project in Warm Mineral Springs, Florida. He is a member of the Advisory Council for the Conference on Underwater Archaeology and is also on the Technical Advisory Council; Monitor Marine Sanctuary, NOAA. He is living in Tallahassee with his wife and has two daughters and two sons.

Wilburn Cockrell was born on April 24, 1941 in Sikeston, Missouri. He attended Murphy High School in Mobile, Alabama then the University of Alabama where he received his Bachelor of Arts degree in Anthropology in 1963. In 1970 he received his Masters of Arts degree in Anthropology from Florida State University and did his thesis on the Archeology of Marco Island. In 1972 he completed work at Arizona State University for his Ph.D. in Anthropology. His dissertation topic was, "Concern With Distribution of Paleo-Indians in Florida."

Cockrell has had a vast amount of experience in the field of Archaeology and is a prize-winning published photographer and poet. He was also the first archaeologist to use video under water in recording a site and has even appeared on network and syndicated television. He has had a great number of other publications as well, as is apparent in his vita. He has also given over one hundred lectures to scientific and historical organizations as well as to civic, school, college, and university groups.

Cockrell feels very strongly toward the preservation of shipwreck remains and expressed his views in his article, "The Trouble With Treasure—A Preservationist View of the Controversy," (*American Antiquity*, Vol. 45, No. 2.) He feels that there should be laws which keep amateurs from taking treasure from sites, therefore allowing professionals to study the whole picture instead of only parts of the remains.

Cockrell has done quite a lot of shipwreck archaeology but he is most interested in the study of early man. This is where Warm Mineral Springs in southwest Florida in Sarasota County comes into the picture. In his article, "The Warm Mineral Springs Archaeological Research Project: Current Research and Technological Applications," (*The Proceedings of the Sixth Annual Scientific Diving Symposium*, Charles T. Mitchell, Editor.) he explains the Spring and his work there. Native American peoples lived there as early as 12,000 years ago. The remains have been very well preserved in the mineral spring due to the lack of dissolved oxygen in the water. There are three areas of archaeological interest; 1) the uplands site; 2) the 13 meters below the surface ledge which was once dry land and contains human, animal, and plant remains dating back 12,000 years, and lastly, 3) the massive volume of deposits on the bottom. In 1973 Cockrell found the nearly complete skeleton of an adult Paleo-Indian male. The peat which surrounded it was dated at around 11,000 years old. Bones of Ice Age mammals were found as well; a saber-tooth cat and giant ground sloth believed to be 12,000 years old. Cockrell considers this spring to be a museum of Florida's past and continues with his research layer by layer to learn more and more about Early man.

"Dawn cold, the man slowly awakens, painfully probing the new day."

—*Man the Hunter*, by Wilburn Cockrell

Analysis of Sample Anthropology Paper 2

Mary's essay gets off to a superb start with an exemplary introduction. The movement is from general to specific. She opens her introduction with a detailed and vivid description of the work that archaeologists do, creating a picture of someone who works closely with the land. When she does refer to the particular subject of her paper at the end of her introduction, it is with an element of surprise: "Wilburn Allen Cockrell is one such archaeologist but his work is not conducted on land. His work takes place under water."

This introduction makes the reader want to read more about this unusual archaeologist. Mary goes on to give additional interesting facts about her subject: He was the first archaeologist to use video under water in recording a site, he holds strong views on shipwreck preservation, and he has found the nearly complete skeleton of an adult Paleo-Indian male. She does a good job of representing the diverse interests of her subject.

As we mentioned in the analysis to this assignment, a common weakness in student narration is a dogged reliance on chronology for structure. Surprisingly, Mary's difficulties are of the opposite nature: She does not provide enough chronology. She organizes her paper around Cockrell's accomplishments and interests. This organization would be successful if she consistently allowed readers to locate in Cockrell's career when these accomplishments took place, when these interests evolved. At what point in his career did Cockrell first use video in recording a site? In what year did he publish "The Trouble With Treasure—A Preservationist View of the Controversy"? Because the assignment is defined as a biography, Mary needs to spend more time *clarifying* the chronology of her subject. Dates are implicitly important.

Like David in Sample Paper 1, Mary demonstrates knowledge of her subject's published work and provides excellent summary of two of these publications. But if she has read book reviews of Cockrell's work, she provides no evidence of it, which necessarily weakens her response to the assignment. Mary has otherwise written a detailed biography in an engaging style.

Guide for Reading

This essay has much potential both in terms of the interesting choice of subject matter and the amount of research material the student has collected. The lack of sentence variety, however, produces what can best be described as a wooden style: The sentences force readers to plod through similar patterns in paragraph after paragraph. Look closely, for example, at the first paragraph; then look at paragraphs 3 through 6. Moreover, Caleb's failure to provide interpretation and connection keeps any potential from being fully realized. As you read, try to identify where Caleb missed opportunities for interpretation.

SAMPLE ANTHROPOLOGY PAPER 3

Biography of Dr. Alice Kehoe

by Caleb S. (a freshman)

Dr. Alice Kehoe was born in New York, New York, on September 18, 1934. Her first job was at the American Museum of Natural History's Department of Anthropology at Barnard College in New York and she graduated in 1956. She then moved to Montana and worked on the Blackfeet Reservation at the Museum of the Plains Indian. After marrying the director of the Museum, Thomas Kehoe, in 1957, they enrolled at Harvard. At Harvard, Dr. Kehoe was forced to change the focus of her graduate study to ethnology because she was not allowed to work in the same field as her husband. Her dissertation was on the Ghost Dance religion of the Dakota Indians. She has taught anthropology at Marquette University since 1968. She has published a textbook, *North American Indians: A Comprehensive Account*, and several articles examining social science and why theories become popular.

The textbook, *North American Indians: A Comprehensive Account*, is widely used. It covers the different regions of North America from prehistory to modern times. A major focus of this work is to see American Indians as people engaged in the struggle for life. Malcolm McFee of the University of Oregon says, "Kehoe's Indians are neither all sages nor pawns of destiny, but rational people—including the good, the bad, the successful, and the failures—humans trying to maintain or achieve a meaningful life through the millennia" (1). Charles D'Aniello of the State University of New York at Buffalo says: "As a consequence of its social science focus it offers insights from a non-white perspective" (2) Dr. Kehoe's textbook is full of information about all of the tribes of the North American Indians. McFee says: "Kehoe has given us a superb and scholarly synthesis of the work done by archaeologists, ethnologists, and ethnohistorians in the past few years. The style is lively, and an amazing amount of detail is present as she carries her own perspective, strongly but without polemic, through the thicket of differing interpretations of data and perceptions of events."

In *The Ghost Dance Religion* (4), Kehoe describes her 1964 dissertation in length. The religion, taught by the Paiute prophet Jack Wilson, had been accepted by a Dakota community outside of Prince Albert, Saskatchewan, Canada. The findings contradicted Bernard Barbers' 1941 claim that the Ghost Dance had died in 1890, at the Wounded Knee massacre.

In *Women's Preponderance in Possession Cults: The Calcium-Deficiency Hypothesis Extended* (5), Kehoe and Dody H. Gilleti discuss the connection between vitamin deficiency and women in possession cults. In Old World traditional societies, women were either not allowed or unable to eat as much as men were, and the deficiencies affected the central nervous system. The involuntary symptoms of deficiency were interpreted as manifestations of spirit possession.

In *Points and Lines*, Dr. Kehoe criticizes the evolution of archaeology. She states: "Nineteenth-Century prehistoric archaeology focused on producing evidence for human antiquity; Twentieth-Century prehistoric archaeology focused on 'Tatting endless taxonomic rosettes out of the same old ball'; New Archaeology tried to substitute pigeonholes created by statistical methods for those developed more intuitively . . ." (6).

In *Evolution, Cultural Evolutionism, and Human Societies*, Kehoe critically reviews the ideas of Spencer and Morgan about cultural evolution. She rejects the modern "Nineteenth-Century notions of human progress" (7) model of cultural evolution and suggests using the adaptation concept of modern evolutionary biology to explain culture.

Dr. Kehoe has been a board member of the American Anthropological Association (1979–1982), she will be the president of the Central States Anthropological Society in 1989, and she is the chair of the Public Relations Committee of the Society for American Archaeology. Alice is just back from Bolivia and is on her way to the Society for Ethnohistory meeting to gather information for the revision of *North American Indians: A Comprehensive Account.*

Works Cited

(1) McFee, Malcolm. Review of *North American Indians: A Comprehensive Account.* "American Anthropologists," Volume 84. June, 1982: p. 469.

(2) D'Aniello, Charles. Review of *North American Indians: A Comprehensive Account.* "Library Journal," Volume 86. July, 1981: p. 1418.

(3) Kehoe, Alice Beck. *The Ghost Dance Religion*, "Case Studies in Cultural Anthropology." Holt, Rinehart, and Winston, 1988.

(4) Giletti, Dody H. and Alice Kehoe. *Women's Preponderance in Possession Cults: The Calcium-Deficiency Hoypothesis Extended*, "American Anthropologist," Volume 83(3): pp. 549–561.

(5) Kehoe, Alice B. *Points and Lines*, speech read to the American Anthropological Association, 1987.

(6) Kehoe, Alice B. *Evolution, Cultural Evolutionism, and Human Societies*, "Canadian Journal of Anthropology." Volume 3(1). Fall, 1982.

Analysis of Sample Anthropology Paper 3

Caleb's paper and Mary's paper serve as interesting contrasts, especially in terms of style. Both have chosen fascinating biographical subjects: a female specialist in North American Indian cult and religious behavior and an underwater archaeologist. But whereas Mary seems fully engaged in presenting the exciting career of her subject, Caleb does not.

The first hint readers get of Caleb's lack of engagement with his subject is the introduction. His opening statement is routine: "Dr. Alice

Kehoe was born in New York, New York, on September 18, 1934." He then goes on to list his subject's different degrees and academic positions. He concludes his introduction by stating that Kehoe has "published a textbook . . . and several articles examining social science and why theories become popular." A quick glance at the titles of Kehoe's works on Caleb's own Works Cited list shows just how inexact this statement is. It's clear that Caleb needs to consider more carefully how he presents and characterizes his subject.

Two other features also suggest Caleb isn't engaged in his subject. He tends to overuse quotations throughout the paper. In the second paragraph, for example, he strings together three quotations from reviews of Kehoe's textbook, without providing any comment. The fifth paragraph is, except for an opening sentence, one long quotation. To Caleb's credit, all of these quotations are well attributed and are introduced clearly. He has done extensive reading, clearly, both of Kehoe's work and reviews of it, and he offers solid summary of two of Kehoe's books. But his overuse of quotations and the lack of interpretation suggest that Caleb doesn't really understand what he is supposed to do with the knowledge he has gained. His approach is simply to present information without comment, which is antithetical to the assignment.

Given how much Caleb relies on sources, the errors in his documentation are especially troublesome. He skips citing note 3, which throws off his numbering. He fails to use italics properly with titles.

The way Caleb begins his paragraphs is also problematic. Notice that four out of seven of his paragraphs begin with exactly the same sentence structure: "In (name of book), Kehoe." He offers no transitions to bridge the gap between paragraphs. These structural difficulties demonstrate that no matter how much material a student collects in research, style is something that can't be neglected.

Writing Assignments

1. Personal interviews are an important research tool in the social sciences. They may be used, as in the above assignment, to more accurately narrate the story of one individual, or they may be used to collect data and make generalizations about the behavior of a group. Imagine that you are contributing to a series in your college newspaper highlighting the interests and accomplishments of a variety of professors on campus. Choose a professor and request an interview. When preparing for your interview, keep in mind that the focus of your paper will be the professor's career as a scholar and academic:

how it has developed, where he or she sees it moving. Write a biographical sketch of the professor's life as a scholar.
2. Choose one of the following three eminent anthropologists and research his or her career: Clifford Geertz, Margaret Mead, Horace Miner. Using the Citation Index, collect book reviews of his or her most recent book. Write a biography that charts the development of his or her career, interests, and impact on the field.

ANTHROPOLOGY ASSIGNMENT 2

Course: **Introduction to Archaeology**

In a minimum of five pages, write the prehistory of an era. The prehistory should begin with the earliest appearance of man and woman in the area and end with the first recorded history. The focus of your research should be on the human history of the area.

Analysis of Anthropology Assignment 2

On the surface, this assignment appears very straightforward. Students are to select a particular geographic area and describe human activity there, stopping with the beginning of recorded history. The task involves library research and perhaps use of class notes, because in an introductory course in archaeology students usually don't have opportunities to participate in digs.

It also appears that the goal of the assignment is to involve students in the subject matter more deeply than the class lectures allow, and in this sense it is an example of writing to learn. Students would be expected, therefore, not only to present detailed information about the geographic area they select but also to relate that information to principles and topics covered in class. Any interpretation students do would be associated with linking facts obtained from published sources to general principles of physical anthropology. The inherent danger in this task is that the writing easily takes on the characteristics of a test, where students are merely demonstrating that they have read the material, not displaying a real interest and enthusiasm for the subject.

Anthropology

A more critical analysis of this assignment reveals that the teacher is looking for something slightly different from the straightforward approach. The first clue lies in the way the gist of the assignment appears three times: (1) write a prehistory of the area; (2) begin with first appearance of men and women and end with first recorded history; (3) write a human history of the area. Each of these statements conveys almost the same information, so astute students, knowing that people often repeat themselves when they want to make a particular point and aren't sure if they have, will be alerted.

We begin to see the real focus of the assignment when we consider two points. First, the teacher has written that the paper should cover the appearance of men and women in the area. There is nothing extraordinary about this requirement or the way it is expressed. Over the last 15 years or so, social conventions have shifted in such a way that writers need to be sensitive to gender issues. The most visible result of this shift is the consensus in publishing to ban as sexist the pronoun *he* and the noun *man* as generic terms that traditionally were used to refer to every member of the human race, males and females alike. When we get to the underlined word *human*, however, it seems clear that the teacher is interested in more than conventions related to gender. What this assignment is asking for is a paper that balances the prehistoric activities of men and *women* in the selected geographic area. Grouping everyone together as prehistoric "people" is not part of the expectations for this paper.

An immediate and reasonable question at this point might be why the teacher didn't simply *direct* students to devote a significant part of their papers to the activities of prehistoric females in the area. Students then wouldn't have to spend as much energy figuring out what to do, and they wouldn't have to try to "psych out" the teacher. We agree that such an approach would have been easier, and we wish we had an acceptable answer regarding why so many teachers build implicit criteria for success into their assignments. We sense that such criteria are very often linked to initiation into a discipline: Students with the motivation required to master the ways of knowing in a particular field will seek help from their teachers and will receive information that those with less motivation won't obtain.

One outcome of the dependence on implicit criteria is that teachers find it hard to grade down those papers that meet all the explicit criteria while failing to meet the implicit ones. The next paper below is an excellent example of this problem.

Guide for Reading

Susan's paper is an intelligent, well-researched response to the assignment. She provides a relatively detailed discussion of the Nile River Valley's prehistory, and she presents the facts she has collected in an organized manner. We can say, therefore, that Susan's paper is a very good one, although not outstanding.

From our perspective, the weaknesses in Susan's writing are fairly immediate. For example, she has a bibliography, but there are no citations in the text, suggesting that she doesn't quite understand the relationship between reference sources and her own writing. The writing is also flat as a result of Susan's failure to focus on one feature of prehistory life in the area, providing elaboration that would give the paper presence. Instead, she treats every fact in the same way, with equal emphasis, which is always a mistake. Without a single descriptive detail explored in depth, the writing has the quality of a monotone, full of facts but without any one being sufficiently interesting to make us remember what she has just said when we reach the end of the paper.

Although Susan's teacher gave the paper an A−, the comments suggest the teacher hated every word. As you read, see if you can figure out why.

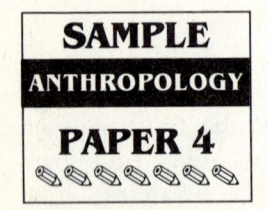

SAMPLE ANTHROPOLOGY PAPER 4

The Prehistory of Egypt

by Susan R. (a freshman)

Egypt is the birthplace of one of the world's oldest civilizations. The Nile River which extends two to three miles in width and six hundred miles in length is credited with the coming of the Egyptian civilization. The Nile kept men confined to the valley where villages formed. The resources of limestone, sandstone, granite, gold, copper, turquoise, and black silt that the Nile deposited annually contributed to the beginning of civilization. The river demanded control, thus cooperation, organization, and centralization were necessities. The prehistory of Egypt, the time before the pharaohs developed hieroglyphics and Lower and Upper Egypt united as one (1300 BC), is when the ideas of civilization originated.

Anthropology

Paleolithic man, the nomadic hunter and gatherer, first arrived in Egypt many thousands of years ago when he followed wild herds across the grassy plains of northeastern Africa. In the gravel, crude stone implements of early hunters were found. These implements were the same as the ones found in western Europe and imply that the same cultural groups were on either side of the Mediterranean. It is thought that Paleolithic man made his way between the two continents by way of the narrow strait, Gibraltar. In the plateau above the cliffs of western Thebes, many flint implements were found. These are deep brown in color which signify centuries of exposure to elements. The flint implements contain natural nodules which were chipped to shape by blows from a hammerstone. The coupe de poing or hand axe is the chief characteristic of the Paleolithic period. The coupe de poing is a triangular tool tapered at one end to a point and rounded at the other to fit in the palm of the hand. The coupe de poing was used to cleave, chop, scrape, saw, skin, and stab. The flakes sheared off when making a large tool such as a hand axe were made into small scrapers, knives, and punches.

During the Late Paleolithic period, the climate began to become dry and arid and it proved to be more profitable for man to stop his nomadic way of life and settle in the area near the river. This is proven by earthen hearths and piles of kitchen refuse found on the beaches of the Nile and the shores of prehistoric lakes and swamps. Among the findings were the shells of edible mollusks, fish and animal bones, ivory and stone. Numerous small flint and sandstone implements were found including saw toothed blades. The earliest stone mills and grind stones were also found and give evidence that cereal grains, whether wild or sown, were part of the Late Paleolithic man's diet. The knowledge of bow and arrow and harpoons was developed during this time for arrow tips made of flint, ivory, and bone were found.

The Neolithic period was when man adopted the settled mode of life and his livelihood depended on agriculture, the domestication of animals, and the Nile River. Man built houses for his family and tribes sharing the river merged to form the first villages of Egypt. These villages have to be credited to the farmer because it was he who saw the need for land reclamation and irrigation. Swamps had to be drained and the land had to be protected from floods by the building of dikes. The land also had to be irrigated by the construction of basins, ditches, and wells. To produce an abundant harvest the river had to be controlled. This could not be achieved by one individual, and therefore villages had to work together. Cooperation meant groups had to be highly organized. So, by the demands of the river the first villages were formed. During the Neolithic period pottery vessels were made to prepare, serve, and store food. These pottery vessels were made of the brown Nile clay shaped by hand and unevenly fired. Archaeologists found a bowl with a spout and piece of pottery with rows of vertical lines, the first attempt to decorate pottery. At a site in Merimden Beni Salamen, in the west Delta, polished celts or axes, pear shaped maceheads, and chipped winged arrowheads were found. Querns and grindstone, flint sickle blades, and wheat grains were also found and gave evidence that early Neolithic man farmed and ate bread. Bone awls and spatulas were found leading archaeologists to believe industries existed demanding specialized tools. Clay spindle whorls show that thread was being spun and man was weaving linen cloth. Implements were beginning to be retouched, ground and polished. In the northern edge of the Fayyum, worked arrow tips and scraper saws were discovered. Also for the first time a long lance head and a large curved knife were found. These findings illustrate the skill of Neolithic man.

In Deir Tasa, late Neolithic man's burial and funeral remains were found. The Tasians buried the dead in cemeteries along the edge of the desert away from their settlements. They dug an oval hole only a few feet deep and placed the body covered with skins and cloth on his side. Sometimes a leather pillow was placed under the head. In the hole the corpse's worldly possessions were also placed. Found in such a grave at Deir Tasa were pottery bowls for food and drink, ivory bracelets, beads, shells, bones fishhooks, ivory cosmetic spoons, palettes for eye and face paint, polished stone axes, and mills. This technique shows the Tasians' belief in life after death. They regarded that life just

Anthropology

as the one on earth. The possessions were placed in the grave so that the dead could enjoy and use them in his afterlife. The form of burial and ideas stayed the same throughout the prehistory of Egypt.

The Chalcolithic period or Copper and Stone Age was the last era before the beginning of written history of Egypt. Stone was still the chief sorce for the making of tools and weapons, but copper tools were beginning to be produced. During the Chalcolithic period two main cultures developed, one in the south which was of African origin and one in the north which originated in the Mediterranean and Asia regions.

The Badarians were the earliest of the southern group of Chalcolithic cultures. In el Badari which lies in Middle Egypt, many artifacts were found that give evidence to their way of life. The Badarians were agricultural and unwarlike. They did not hunt for in the graves and settlements no hunting weapons were found. Amulets in the form of animal heads were found and give insight to their religion. However, it is believed if man wanted to attain courage, strength, or swiftness he would wear the animal that represente that characteristic around his neck. The ox, dog, sheep, and goat were considered sacred and ___ buried like the man. The pottery of the Badarians was solid black, turned by carbonization and topped with brown. Polished red pottery fired all over was found at el Badari and thus it was concluded a potter's kiln was invented. Tusks of hippopotamus and African elephant were found carved into decorated spoons and combs, vases, and statues of women. Cosmetic palettes in the simple rectangular form were found with malachite and galena remains. The Egyptians used malachite and galena as eye paints. Smelting and the working of metal also arose during the Badarian civilization. Bone and ivory were used primarily for objects such as needles and awls but copper pins and beads were found in a Badarian cemetery. The jewelry advanced notably in el Badari. Shells were strung, stones were drilled, and imitations of beads cut from semi precious stones were being made by applying a glaze to the stone. Badarian grave contents reveal that the Badarians had contact with other cultures and were trading with them. Elephant ivory from the south, copper from the north, turquoise from Sinai, and shells from the Red Sea coast were found.

The Predynastic culture of Upper Egypt developed from the Badarian civilization and the most significant contribution of this culture is to Egyptian art. The objects found in the Predynastic cemeteries are the same as the Badarian in all ways except during the Predynastic era man began to carve, model, draw, paint, and decorate objects being produced. In Upper Egypt, pottery vessels were found. They were all brown river clay with dark red slip burnished by rubbing with a smooth pebble. The outcome varied with black vessels topped with red, solid black ones, polished red vessels, and red with white line decoration. Oval flasks, double vases, u-shaped jars, bowls shaped in the form of animals and birds were found. The objects were decorated with linear designs but also with pictures of things around them: palm branches, hippopotamus, crocodiles, and hunting expeditions. Eye makeup palettes were also found in new forms; the cosmetic plates were elongated diamonds, fishes, birds, and other animals. Figure sculpture first began to appear. Men, women, and animal figurines were found. From these sculptures, archaeologists gather what Predynastic man looked like: slim, small-boned, long narrow heads, pointed beards, dressed in tubular sheaths.

Compared to the Predynastic culture of Upper Egypt, the Predynastic culture of Lower Egypt was more advanced. Graves were oval and rectangular and the walls were lined with matting, wood, and mud brick. The cemeteries became more elaborate. Compartments were added to receive offerings. The position of the body was different than that of Upper Egypt. In Lower Egypt, the face was turned toward the direction the sun rose. This indicates the people of lower Egypt had some form of solar religion. The pottery also differed. "Wavy-handled" vases were produced to form a better grip for the fingers. Pottery was gray or pale pink decorated with elaborate red line drawings of oared ships, antelopes, flamingos, and other Nile scenes. Materials such as granite, diorite, basalt, serpentine, breccia, marble, and schist were being used to make stone vases. The glaze founded in Badarian times was used on vessels and beads; it was known as "Egyptian faience." Metal working advanced. Not only were necklaces and bracelets being hammered but harpoons, daggers, and small trays beaten from copper were found. As in Upper Egypt, statues were found. However, in lower Egypt the figurines depicted deities: Horus of Bidhet, the falcon god and Hat-Hor.

In 1898, at Hierakonopolis, the slate commemorative palette of Horus Namer was found. The pictures on this cosmetic show the king wearing his crown of Upper Egypt on one side and on the other he is wearing the crown of lower Egypt. This palette shows the union of Upper and Lower Egypt (3100 BC) under one pharaoh. The palette also contains written characters of the Egyptian language. Thus prehistory ends with the written ___ and the first dynasty, along with history begins.

Bibliography

Aldred, Cyril. *The Egyptians*, Great Britain: Thames and Hudson Ltd., 1984.

Casson, Lionel. *Ancient Egypt*, Time Incorporated, 1965, pp. 11–17, 29–34.

Fagan, Brian M. *The Rape of the Nile: Tomb Robbers, Tourists, and Archaeologists in Egypt.* New York: Charles Scribners and Sons, 1975.

Hayes, William C. *The Scepter of Egypt: A Background for the Study of the Egyptian Antiquities in the Metropolitan Museum of Art*, Harvard Press, 1953, pp. 8–27.

Sherratt, Andrew. *The Cambridge Encyclopedia of Archaeology*, Crown Publishers, Inc. 1980.

Wendorf, Fred. "Use of Barley in the Egyptian Late Paleolithic," *Science*, September, 1979, vol. 205, number 4413, pp. 1341–7.

STUDY QUESTIONS

1. Suppose Susan had asked you to read a draft of this paper and give her some feedback she could use to make it better. You know that if she will focus more on a single feature of the prehistory she can improve the quality of the paper, and you tell her so. Which feature would you ask her to elaborate? How should she go about rewriting that portion of the paper? What should she add?

2. Without any citations, we have no way of clearly separating Susan's thoughts from those of her sources, nor do we have any way of getting more specific information about individual topics, unless we are willing to go to the bibliography and read through all her sources. Look carefully at any three consecutive paragraphs and indicate those places where you think Susan could have supplied references to help you read her paper.

3. The teacher's comments on Susan's paper were scathing. For example, in paragraph 3 Susan writes that cereal grains "were part of late Paleolithic man's diet." The comment in the margin reads, "Since women aren't doing anything I guess they don't need to eat either." What effect, if any, did Susan's failure to use current conventions regarding gender have on you as you read her paper? Why do you think she might want to be more sensitive to those conventions in the future, aside from the obvious desire to please her teachers?

4. A weakness in Susan's writing is her overuse of the passive voice. Study the Sentence Lesson below and rewrite one of her paragraphs, changing passive sentences into active ones.

Sentence Lesson

Passive construction: Fred was kicked by Rita.
Active construction: Rita kicked Fred.
Passive construction: The car was driven away.
Active construction: Someone drove the car away.

The social sciences, like the life and applied sciences, allow (and sometimes expect) writes to use passive constructions. They do not, however, allow passives in every situation. The guideline is that a writer should use passives only in those instances where the agent of an action is unknown or where it is desirable to provide a higher degree of distance and objectivity, as in the case of the procedures one followed in collecting data. In all other instances, writers should use active constructions, which have identifiable agents.

The sentences below, taken from Susan's paper, illustrate both acceptable and unacceptable uses of the passive. An asterisk marks the unacceptable sentences:

1. *In the northern edge of the Fayyum, worked arrow tips and scraper saws were discovered.
2. *Oval flasks, double vases, u-shaped jars, bowls shaped in the form of animals and birds were found.
3. The objects were decorated with linear designs but also with pictures of things around them: palm branches, hippopotamus, crocodiles, and hunting expeditions.
4. *Eye makeup palettes were also found in new forms; the cosmetic plates were elongated diamonds, fishes, birds, and other animals.
5. "Wavy-handled" vases were produced to form a better grip for the fingers.

Although Susan may not have known the names of the researchers who found the arrow tips and scraper saws, she could have produced an active sentence by writing: "Archaeologists discovered arrow tips and scraper saws along the northern edge of the Fayyum.

Guide for Reading

Mary's paper never quite comes together. She begins by describing the geology of the islands, which isn't really relevant to the topic. In her discussion of the prehistory of the islands, she supplies detail, but not very much, which makes the paper seem too general to be very interesting. In fact, the level of generality and vagueness suggests strongly that Mary isn't particularly interested in the topic and is just putting words down on paper to fulfill the assignment. This perception is aided by lack of any organization. Notice how her third paragraph begins by talking about vegetation that existed on the islands when the first people arrived and ends by talking about the kind of canoe people used to colonize the islands. Overall, her response is slightly below average.

SAMPLE ANTHROPOLOGY PAPER 5

The Prehistory of the Hawaiian Archipeligo

Mary M. (a freshman)

Hawaii's diverse array of exotic plants, animals, and inhabitants, some of which are still indigenous only to the archipeligo, make the islands one of the most recondite and unique areas to visit in the world. Hawaii's mother to over 1,400 different species of plants, 10,000 species of insects and over 100 various species of birds (Kanahele, p. 2). This seemingly unexplainable phenomenon has made the Hawaiian islands prey to much archaeological investigation.

The islands themselves are the very tops of immense mountains that have been built up from the ocean floor. Scientifically, these mountains started forming about twenty-five billion years ago. They have been created by molten rock eruptions that were forced up through the earth's crust, the ocean floor, from the Earth's trembling mantle. Within the Earth's mantle, molten, fluid rocks, called magma, rose to produce a series of volcanoes. The magma that overflows from a volcano onto the Earth's surface is called lava. Billions of years ago, when the magma started seeping through the cracks, it flowed onto the ocean floor. Gradually, more and more magma seeped out creating a lava and this buildup eventually rose high enough to surface above sea level. These lava mountains, after thousands of years, started to form soil from the ashes and weathering of the lava rocks. Still, the island was deplete of life form .

Now, it is believed that when the first humans reached the island a few ferns and roots existed, as well as a few transitory birds. These life forms were transported to the distant islands by strong gusts of wind, ocean currents, and migratory birds. The only raw materials the islands could offer were refuge from the sea and fresh drinking water. Generally, archaeologists have concluded that the first inhabitants were indeed sea voyagers from Central Polynesia in the Marquesas Islands, most likely. These peoples arrived approximately 1200 years BC and brought a variety of agricultural, bestial, and cultural contributions to the islands. Archaeologists like this theory because there is no other explanation for the existence of these species. The pioneers brought with them taro, breadfruit, yams, bananas, coconuts, etc., and domestic dogs, chickens, and pigs. They also inherently brought their language, customs, rituals, social sanctions, arts, and handicrafts (National Park Service). The only mammals to proceed the humans were the seals and bats (Kanahele, p. 3). The Hawaiian archipilego was the last to be colonized because of the vast expanse of ocean isolating it from all other colonies. It is believed that about fifty men, women, and children sailed in a huge double canoe for 2,400 miles until they reached land (National Park Service).

Archaeologists started their investigations in 1950. Emory, on the island of O'ahu, conducted the first stratigraphic excavation within the archipelego. Since then, all of the islands have been studied with the exception of Ni'ihau which is privately owned. Pinning down of the actual human arrival date has been an arduous task for archaeologists for a number of reasons: the short time span of the Hawaiian prehistory, the locating of the earliest sites within the vast archipilego, and the uncertainty of C_{14} dating (Kirch, p. 244). Archaeologists do have valid evidence that the chain was settled by approximately AD 300–500. This evidence stems from the early steam beach site on O'ahu, traces of human activity on the slopes surrounding Kawainui Marsh circa AD 500, Halawa and Moloka'i, two early sites where agricultural burning was discovered in several valleys, and the Pu'u Ali'i sand dune site on Hawai'i (Kirch, p. 224).

Two early settlement sites, Bellows and Halawa, have been

identified by the unearthment of remnants of dwelling structures, cooking facilities, burial grounds, and domestic tools. Stone alignments and postmoulds studied at the Halawa site indicated a pattern of small, round-ended huts. Evidence of food substance at both sites was the finding of remnants of fishing tools, shellfish, and the exploitation of wild birds, animal husbandry, and agriculture (Kirch, p. 245). Domestic pig and dog remains were found there also. Social differentiation was made evident in an elaborate burial of a young female who was adorned with a pigtusk anklet (Kirch, p. 245). The Polynesians seemed to have adapted well and rather quickly to the land; for example, they developed an effective two hook fish hook to better suit their needs.

Archaeologists believe that by AD 900–1100, about four to seven centuries after the initial colonization, the population increased and permanent settlements were established. Examples of these settlements are Kuli'ou'ou and Makaha valleys on O'ahu and at Anaeho'omalu on Hawaii island (Kirch, p. 245). These being based on the larger number settlements found in the area. By AD 1400–1500, most of the lowlands were thought to be under some form of occupation, civilization, and/or exploitation (Kirch,p. 245).

The Halawa Valley archaeological evidence is typical of that found in valleys throughout the islands. Halawa is a plush valley located on the East Moloka'i mountains. It is broad, deep, and encircles the river in which two waterfalls cascade. The terrain was excellent for the Polynesians to propogate non-irrigated crops. It is thought to have been the home for approximately five hundred persons. The archaeological investigation was conducted in 1969 through 1970. The major areas excavated included: an early steam-beach maiden site, an intensive settlement pattern, inland residential sites, and irrigation fields and ditches (Kirch, p. 246). This project was divided into three phases: the Kaawili phase (AD 650–1350), the Kaio phase (AD 1350–1650) and the Mana phase (AD 1650–1800). Taking a closer look at the Kaawili phase as an example, one can more clearly understand the findings from the site. The settlement pattern consisted of a "coastal village at an ecological focal point" (Kirch, p. 248). The archaeologists found ovoid houses of pole

Anthropology

and thatch construction with internal hearths, and separate cookhouses. Evidence of food was fish, dogs and pigs, and irrigation technology. They found several "portable artifacts" as well. For example, early type fish hooks, dog-tooth ornaments, etc. There was no data found pertaining to burials, ceremonial architecture, or the number of inhabitants. An approximate population size was fifty around AD 650 and one hundred and fifty around AD 1350 (Kirch, p. 248). The religious and ceremonial traces were a little less evident during this phase.

This excavation, along with many others, helped archaeologists solve the Hawaiian prehistory enigma. Without the extended investigations of archaeologists over the years, the origins of thousands of plants, animals, and people would be unknown; leaving the intricate history of Hawaiian Archipilego a mystery.

Bibliography

Hawaii Volcanoes National Park. National Park Service, Department of the Interior.

Kanahele, George. *Ku KANAKA Stand Tall.* University of Hawaii Press, 1986.

Kanahele, George. *MALAMA AINA (Caring for the Land).* University of Hawaii Press, 1988.

Kirch, Patrick. *The Evolution of the Polynesian Chiefdom.* New York: University of Cambridge, 1984.

STUDY QUESTIONS

1. Titles often tell readers a great deal about a piece of writing, and they sometimes tell readers something about the writer. Look carefully at Mary's title. What does it tell you about her and her work?

2. Mary's writing is handicapped by the surface errors throughout the paper. Identify where in the paper you found these errors most troublesome. What corrections or changes would you make to improve the readability of that section?

3. The final comment Mary's teacher put on the paper was "a little too brief." If you were asked to help Mary revise this paper, what additional information would you ask her to supply?

Guide for Reading

Kim's paper is an unacceptable response to the assignment for several reasons. One of the more immediate is that she devotes the first two pages to discussing the geology and history of Peru, failing to identify her area quickly and failing to focus on its prehistory. In addition, Kim's writing doesn't meet minimal expectations in a college class. The errors range from faulty sentence structure to no capitalization at the beginning of sentences. The surface problems are so severe that we have no way of knowing whether Kim is a bad typist and an equally bad proofreader or whether she doesn't understand the conventions of formal writing. In any event, Kim's teacher refused to assign a grade to this paper, telling her that it needed to be rewritten completely.

Anthropology

> **SAMPLE ANTHROPOLOGY PAPER 6**

Peru: A Study of the Chillon Valley

by Kim B. (A freshman)

Peru is a country located in the northwest portion of South America. The countries which border Peru are Ecuador, Colombia, Brazil, Bolivia, and Chile. The Pacific Ocean also borders the west side of Peru. The Andes mountain range begins in Peru and in its valleys is where some of the earliest remains of a civilization can be found.

Archaeologists and explorers have been interested in the history of Peru and its people for centuries. The first person that is known to explore Peru in an archaeological sense, is Pedro Cieza de Leon. Leon was a Spanish soldier who first began to explore Peru in 1553. His observations were the first to be documented and his notes of ancient ruins and artifacts sparked an interest to other people and explorers (Lanning, 19).

Even though Leon first documented his observations in the sixteenth century, it was not until the nineteenth century that scholars began studying ancient sites. The idea of excavating an area and studying the buildings and artifacts could be an effective method by which one could reconstruct the history of a culture (Lanning, 19).

From 1899–1900, a German archaeologist, Max Uhle, excavated extensively in cemeteries along the coast of Peru. Uhle is given credit for first identifying many of the cultures that are today famous in the prehistory of South America. Uhle is also given credit for evolving any type of organization of time or cultures. The periods in which Uhle developed for Peru are: pre-Tiahuanaco and Inca. Even today these periods are used in trying to place cultures and peoples properly into time sequence (Lanning, 20).

During the 1920's and 1930's is when the science of archaeology began to fluish. some of the more prominent archaeologists of this time were Wendell C. Bennett and Julio C. Tello. These men, along with others, excavated many parts of Peru and discovered new information on the cultures that were found by Uhle (Lanning, 20).

As interest in the history of Peru grew, so did the information that was being discovered. archaeologist John H. Rowe proposed that the informations and time references be organized by time periods more so than stages. Rowe suggested the periods of the Ceramic stage and the Preceramic stage periods were derived from Thomas C. Patterson. The stage, period and dates are as follows:

Stage	Period	Dates
Ceramic	Late Horizon	1476–1534 A.D.
	Late Intermediate	1000–1476 A.D.
	Middle Horizon	600–1000 A.D.
	Early Intermediate	B.C. 200–600 A.D.
	Early Horizon	B.C. 900–200
	Initial Period	B.C. 1800–900–1500
Preceramic	Period VI	B.C. 2500–1500–1800
	Period V	B.C. 4200–2500
	Period IV	B.C. 6000–4200
	Period III	B.C. 8000–6000
	Period II	B.C. 9500–8000
	Period I	B.C. ?–9500

This chart was compiled to help organize the material in a universal manner (Lanning, 24 & 25).

Peru is mainly composed of valleys. The valleys are grouped into regions. The seven regions of Peru are the far north, north, north central, central, south central, south and the far south. The region in which will be discussed in this paper is in the central region. The central region includes the Chancay, Chillon, Rimac,

Anthropology

Lurin and Chilca Valleys. The area which will be concentrated on will be the Chillon Valley area.

The Chillon Valley is located in the valley of the central portion of the Andes mountains. the earliest sites found in the Central Andes are located in the lower part of the Chillon Valley. These sites and artifacts are some of the earliest that have been found throughout Peru. The findings consist of chipped stone tools and weapons that were found in the valley bottom near the pacific ocean (Lanning, 39).

In the Chillon Valley, archaeologists have also found remains of food and other artifacts. These findings seem to suggest that seeds and root plants were the main food source of the early natives. this is due to the fact that the Chillon Valley is a lomas. A lomas is an area in which the vegetation is supported by moisture due to the fog more so than rainfall (Lanning, 48).

the people of early Peru were different in many ways. They varied in their economy as well as their cultures. In the Chillon Valley, evidence seems to lead us to conclude that the people were blade and burin makers. This is partially due to the find of stone chips and shavings that were mentioned earlier. In other areas we find hunters in the highlands, food gatherers in the central coast, and elephant hunters on the north coast region (Lanning, 56).

the information that archaeologists seem to find, leads us to believe that the Chillon Valley is where the formation of the Peruvian architecture took place (Keatinge, 72). This has been shown in many of the excavation findings. During Period VI (see chart) on the central coast and in the valleys, this is where ceremonialism reached its peak. The first of the great pyramids and temples were built at this time. One of the temples, which is considered of preceramic Peruvian architecture, is located in the lower portion of the Chillon Valley at Chuquitanta. The buildings are enormous in size covering an area of 90 by 650 yards. The temples are in the same location, landward of the hills, where the Chivateros and Oquendo people occupied during Periods I and II (Lanning, 69 & 70).

During the Early Intermediate period, portions of the central coast have little evidence of life. The valleys of the Chillon, the Rimac, and the Lurin rivers have a complex history during the

Early Intermediate Period. In some sites, pottery in the Miramar style have been found. In other sites, small, village-scale pyramids have been found. This suggests that they are remembrance of an earlier large construction (Keatinge, 154).

The largest preceramic site known is El Paraiso (or Chuquitanta) in the Chillon Valley. It lies about two kilometers from the mouth of the Chillon River. The site is made up of 13 or 14 mounds, 3 and 6 meters high, over an area of about 60 hectares. The order in which the mounds are arranged is of mainly free space of a regular outline that's open at one end. It is not sure what the purpose of such a site would have served to the ancient people. Most of the evidence leans toward the open ground between the mounds being used for agricultural activities (Keatinge, 72).

There are nine buildings at the site in Chuquitanta. The buildings are made of stone blocks that are laid flat. The blocks are set in a clay mortar then plastered with a fine clay (Lanning, 70). the buildings are arranged in a manner which was found in later northern Peruvian areas: a central temple with two wings going outward and a large patio which is open at the opposite ____ of the temple. The wings are the largest buildings of ancient Peru (Lanning, 71).

The temple at Chiquitanta is built on an artificial mound. At first, it was not sure whether the wings of the temple were for residential purposes or not. The wings could have housed at least 1,000 persons. At this time, the Chillon Valley did not have that large of a population. This is why it seems more reasonable for the temple to have served as a center for ceremonial rituals of Peru (Lanning, 71).

It is thought that Chuquitanta once may have had a large population. Most of the remains have been disrupted by years of plowing. For this reason, finding means of primary economic activity has been difficult.

Peoples in the valleys depended on the water for food. Through excavating the mounds of El Paraiso, it is found that even though the cultivation of crops increased, seafood still played an important part of the natives diet. This is seen through the discovery of the large amount of marine products in the debris of the mounds (Keatinge, 82). Archaeological surveys show that in the Chillon Valley, cultivation terraces were built on the western side of the Andes. The natives grew mainly coca and maize (Keatinge, 262).

The Chillon Valley is one of the two most studied valleys during the Early Intermediate period. At this time, the population grew. Two settlements, which had several thousand people, were Plaza Grande and Cerro Culebura. Temples seem to be the center of each of these settlements (Lanning, 118).

The architecture of the Central Coast shows organized communal and cultural activity during the Preceramic Period and Early Horizon (Keatinge, 92). Through the evidence in this paper, one can see that the people of the central coast of Peru contributed greatly to the architecture and general evolution of the natives of Peru.

Bibliography

Richard W. Keatinge, ed. *Peruvian Prehistory.* Cambridge University Press; Great Britain, 1988.

Lanning, Edward P.; *Peru Before the Incas.* Prentice-Hall, Inc., 1967.

Luis G. Lumbreras, *The Peoples & Cultures of Ancient Peru.* Smithsonian Institute Press; Washington, D.C., 1974.

A Long Line of Brilliant Societies. (Andean cultures of Peru) by Garth L. Baulden v42, *Archaeology*, May–June, 1989 p. 54.

The High Life in Prehistoric Peru, v134, *Science News*, October 8, 1988 p. 237.

The Lost Story of Peru (ancient city) by William F. Allman v6, *Science*, 1985, May 1985, p16.

A "Lost City" Revisited; Unraveling a Pre-Inca Mystery, by Natalie Angier v125, *Time*, February 11, 1985.

STUDY QUESTIONS

1. Lack of organization is one of the problems Kim has in this paper. Reread it carefully and make an organizational outline of the information she presents. Then revise that outline into a more coherent one, asking yourself why certain sections should go together.

2. Kim's paper has numerous surface errors. It's unlikely that she could be expected to correct all of them on the rewrite that her teacher has asked her to do, but she may be able to correct two patterns of errors, capitalization, commas, subject/verb agreement, and so forth. Pretend she has asked for your help on the rewrite. What two patterns of error do you think she should concentrate on? Why? How would you help her eliminate these patterns from this and future papers?

3. Many of Kim's paragraphs seem undeveloped. Point out those paragraphs that need further development, then describe what additional information Kim should have supplied.

4. Kim's bibliography has many errors. Revise it using the documentation guide in the overview to writing in the social sciences.

Writing Assignments

1. Using library materials as your primary source of information, write a prehistory of your hometown. Rather than trying to be comprehensive, provide background details and then focus on one event or characteristic that makes the prehistory of your hometown special. The paper should be 5–7 pages and should be well documented.
2. Make a visit to a local antique shop or a junk store and find an old object (the older the better) that strikes you as being unusual or interesting. In a 5- to 7-page paper, invent a "history" for the object from its manufacture to its trip to the antique shop or junk store, but focus on one event or episode that makes its history special.

ANTHROPOLOGY ASSIGNMENT 3

Course: **Cultural Anthropology**

Final Exam

Essay
Plan on spending 30–40 minutes on the following question. Your answer should be a complete discussion of the question with appropriate references to the text and to your personal experience. Content is of foremost importance, but you are expected to write an organized essay with few grammatical errors.
QUESTION:
Choong Soon Kim's book tells us something about the American South from the viewpoint of a nonwesterner. To what extent is the South different from the rest of the country from the author's and your own point of view?

Analysis of Anthropology Assignment 3

This question is one part of the final exam for cultural anthropology, a course designed to develop in students an understanding of differences among cultures. This course is required for anthropology majors but is open to interested students at the freshman and sophomore levels. The exam was given in class; no one had access to texts or notes. Because the rest of the exam was objective, the essay question gave students a chance to show what they knew about a book that was part of the assigned reading for the semester.

   The queston limits answers to a very specific topic: students must explain how the South is different from the rest of the country, both from the author's and their own point of view. The better answers will show that students read and understood the book by Kim and that they are also able to make some intelligent cultural judgments about the South and the United States. The teacher does not want just a report on what Kim says about the South, but does want students to include appropriate references to the book. In addition, the teacher wants students to discuss the cultural features of the South from their own experience, either as native Southerners or as students from another part of the country attending a university in North Carolina.

As in all essay exam questions, conciseness is essential. Answers to such questions are not designed to enlighten a diverse audience of readers; instead, they are designed to show teachers that a certain body of material has been read, understood, and applied. Students should not include formal introductions and conclusions, and they should certainly avoid any information irrelevant to the question, even if the information shows that they know more than what the question calls for. At the same time, however, students must not assume that their teacher will fill in the gaps in their knowledge.

The directions state that good writing is important. Even if this were not stated in the directions, students should spend a few minutes planning their answer around several specific points, and then they should use these points as topics for well-developed paragraphs. It is also smart to save a few minutes to proofread the answer to eliminate errors in punctuation and spelling. The "grammatical errors" mentioned in the directions are usually surface mistakes that indicate carelessness on the part of writers. No teacher expects perfection in writing on an exam, but surface errors indicate that the writer was careless or, worse, ignorant of the formal conventions of language.

Guide For Reading

Joe's answer focuses directly on the question: the differences in the South from the rest of the U.S. He gives specifics from Kim's book, which shows that he has read it carefully and remembers the important points. In the last paragraph, he gives his own point of view, comparing Charlotte, North Carolina, with Columbus, Ohio. This essay answer is concise, complete, and readable.

SAMPLE ANTHROPOLOGY PAPER 7

Joe M. (a freshman)

Choong Soon Kim's book *An Asian Anthropologist in the South* gives a good view of what the South appears to be through the eyes of a nonwestern.

Kim has several main views about the South being different from the rest of the U.S. Kim believes southerners are much more formal in their speech than other Americans. Kim observed

Anthropology

that people almost always addressed each other in the manner of: yes sir, no sir (etc.). He also felt that the Southerners were much nicer to foreigners than other Americans. He realizes this from his own experiences and the story of a Nigerian student. The student stated: "When I was in the North I was just black, but in the South I am a Nigerian exchange student and deserve special treatment." Kim also contended that racism was not as bad in the South as believed by the rest of the U.S. There was still widespread segregation in the work and social areas, but it was always magnified by the press. For example, the riots over school desegregation in Boston, Mass. were not painted as a racial confrontation, but in the South they would have been attributed to bigotry. Kim saw the South as very neocolonialistic. It seemed that the South was still providing the raw materials for the North's heavy industry, and thus staying undeveloped. Yet, at the end of his research he saw a different growing South. This misconception still haunts the South, from the point of view of Kim. When Kim first landed in California, he was constantly told not to study in the backward South, with its backward people (rednecks). Kim realized these were wrong stereotypes. Kim concluded that the South is multifaceted and pluralistic.

I believe the South is great. I moved here from Columbus, Ohio with the same misconceptions Kim experienced. After going to school with my first black classmate, I realized how far the South has come in equality. The southern schools are desegregated (a rarity in the north) and racial tensions are low (from my experience in Charlotte). Racism occurs everywhere but what separates the South from the rest of the U.S. are unfair prejudices dating back to the Civil War. It has been over 120 years since slavery and the South is growing up. I believe the rest of the country should too.

STUDY QUESTIONS

1. Rewrite Joe's introduction so it will provide a better indication of the content of his answer. Remember that a good introductory statement incorporates part of the question from the exam.

2. Point out the general statements from Kim's book that Joe includes. Do the specific examples that follow convince you that Joe understands the cultural implications of what Kim discovered? Does this information focus specifically on the question? Are the examples relevant?

3. Joe's own point of view is expressed rather briefly. Do you feel that this part of his answer is adequate? If not, what other information do you think that he, as a college freshman, would be qualified to include?

Guide For Reading

Ruth chose to blend information from Kim's book with what she knows from personal experience. In a sense, she is judging the accuracy of Kim's research from her own point of view. This is a good way to organize the answer because it makes Ruth seem closely involved with the topic. One problem, however, is that she isn't specific enough in her references to Kim's book; she's hoping that her teacher will assume that she knows more than she is expressing. This slight flaw keeps her answer from being as good as Joe's.

SAMPLE ANTHROPOLOGY PAPER 8

Ruth C. (a freshman)

The author believes in this book (and by his research) that the South is discriminated against as a whole. For example, if a racist act is performed in the North, the town and specific place is mentioned. However, if the same incident occurred in the South, the South would be blamed for the incident (as a whole).

The author also found the South to be kinder and more considerate (in manners) than Yankees. I feel that this is true. Since I was born and raised in the South I saw many of the values he attributed to Southerners in myself. As a child, I was taught to say yes ma'am, no ma'am, yes sir and no sir. If I didn't I was spanked. To this day I still show this "respect" to people.

In this book, he highlighted the friendliness and hospitality of the Southerner. I believe that that is definitely found in the South. He also highlighted the curiosity and gossip. This is a definite quality of the South. My grandmother is the supreme example of the southern gossip. She makes sure she knows who did what, when, and who was there.

Choong Soon Kim studied small communities in the South. I believe ___ in the larger cities much less of the "Old South" exists. For example, Charlotte is trying to become a "banking capital." The small communities that he studied are typical of many in the South. They depend on one or two industries (mills, etc.) for their well being.

What Choong Soon Kim encountered with racism in the towns is correct. Even in large cities racism is present. For example, at my high school in Charlotte, the whites ate the first part of lunch and the blacks ate after we did. It seems ironic to me that the system that basically introduced bussing and desegregation would be this way in 1988. And if at my school you said something about another race and a Yankee was present they would usually accuse you of racial prejudice.

I have traveled North and West and have never found people as nice as those in the South. I agree with Kim's statement that graduates from southern schools are not looked upon as being quite as intelligent. The rest of the U.S. tends to believe that the South is repressed, ___ the people are all rednecks, ___ that they are lazy and have no self worth.

I could even understand Kim's misunderstanding of relationships between Blacks/Whites and Indians. It is hard to let go of prejudices that are so old and such an element of the culture.

> **STUDY QUESTIONS**
>
> 1. Point out the places in Ruth's answer where she needs to include more information from Kim's book. How will these additions help enrich her answer?
>
> 2. The strength of Ruth's answer is that she is able, as a Southerner, to describe some of the cultural characteristics of the South. Point out the information that shows that she sees the South as a unique part of the U.S. Is this information relevant to the question?
>
> 3. Can you determine from her answer that Ruth has actually read Kim's book?

Guide For Reading

Mike's answer doesn't address the question. It focuses on a few characteristics of the South, but it doesn't compare the South with the rest of the U.S. It seems that Mike read Kim's book (or parts of it), but he didn't become involved with it enough to apply the information. He also put very little effort into expressing his own point of view, which indicated to his teacher that he never became culturally aware and that he therefore failed to achieve an important goal of the course.

SAMPLE ANTHROPOLOGY PAPER 9

Mike M. (a freshman)

The South does differ from the rest of the U.S. If you'll remember the author talked about when he went to the factories and wanted to pass out questionaires but the head people wouldn't let him. One went as far to say we moved down here because cost was low and workers didn't complain (no unions). Kim says that the management of the factories were imported from the North. They were always very formal.

   He felt the South was very hospitable to him if he was playing the role of a foreigner. However when he was an "American" he was treated like another minority.

Kim could see major racial boundaries between whites and blacks in the South, as well as upper and lower classes. Whites rarely affiliated with blacks and vise versa.

I believe that there are major differences. I myself can say this from experience. I moved down here from a town in Wisconsin, mostly from the standpoint of an economic status. But in a social situation not much difference. Ex. hospitality, clothes. I also believe that racism is more prevalent down here. Ex. when any black is killed in the South many times it is perceived as racially motivated.

I enjoyed the class. Thanks.

STUDY QUESTIONS

1. Point out the places in Mike's answer where he deals with the question—the differences between the South and the rest of the United States. Do you think these are sufficient to rate his response as adequate?

2. Mike's own point of view is vaguely expressed. It seems that he may be saying that the South differs from Wisconsin economically and racially, but not socially. Rewrite this last paragraph to express these points clearly.

3. How do you think the teacher would react to Mike's compliment and thanks?

Writing Assignment

The following question should be answered under exam conditions—that is, with a time limit and no extensive revising.
QUESTION:
Pair up with a classmate who has a background different from yours. The background can include such differences as economic status, family size, gender, home site (urban or rural), race, religion, geographic location, and so on. After you have decided which difference to focus on, each of you should spend no more than 10 minutes describing to the

other what it was like growing up under these conditions. In the next 30 minutes, write an essay explaining to a third person what you have discovered. This essay should include specifics, but it should also focus on what these differences mean as far as your growth and development are concerned.

Part Three : HUMANITIES

WRITING IN THE HUMANITIES

Overview

Intellectual disciplines may be defined as different ways of looking at and trying to reach an understanding of the human experience. Each brings a set of goals, assumptions, critical tools, standards of proof, and methodologies to the enterprise. In related fields, certain commonalities exist, and such is the case for history, fine and applied arts, English, and philosophy—the disciplines in this text that together are classified under the humanities.

Humanists, like their counterparts in the social sciences and the life and applied sciences, interpret facts as they examine the human experience, but certain fundamental differences exist. For example, their "facts" tend to consist of or reside in documents (such as poems, plays, novels, and historical records) and works of art (such as paintings, sculptures, and films). Humanists aren't likely to engage in direct observation of experience for the material they analyze and interpret. As a consequence, we can call their method of inquiry *nonempirical*.

The sciences are much concerned about the generalizability of conclusions, but the humanities are not. Humanists often view their facts as inherently characteristic of the human experience, such that they are universally representative—and therefore intrinsically generalizable. They assume, in other words, that the subjects of discussion convey some meaningful statement and that the role of the writer is to interpret that statement for others. On this account, we can say that the facts considered appropriate for interpretation differ not only in kind from those in the sciences (empirical versus nonempirical) but also in nature. In the humanities, the assumption that a literary work or a piece of art reflects the human experience is a given seldom open to interpretation. Assessing what that experience is or what it means on an individual level, however, is very much open to interpretation; indeed, we may say that it is central to what the humanities are about.

Stated another way, scientists commonly work in a very focused manner with relatively small data sets, and their analyses and interpretations attempt to build over time a larger picture that approximates a model of reality. Humanists, on the other hand, tend to begin with the larger picture as represented in a work of art or a document, and they interpret it in terms of individual human experiences. They strive to explain what these works can tell us about ourselves. In this respect, they share a goal: Necessarily, the interpretations deal with emotional and personal and social values, dimensions rarely encountered in scientific writing.

The assumptions that underlie writing in the humanities influence both the act and form of composition. Whereas writing in the sciences generally requires discussion of the particular theoretical framework that will be used to help explain and interpret observed facts, in the humanities writers are expected to set forth their claim very early and then to move on to the analysis. In most cases, shared assumptions and shared goals make the presentation of a theoretical framework unnecessary. It already exists in the background knowledge that readers in the humanities bring to a composition. These readers value writing that explains some feature of a work by exploring a new way of interpreting its meaning and that argues the validity of that interpretation successfully. To the extent that members of a discipline define what it is, we can say that the writing you produce for courses in the humanities will be constrained by the assumptions and goals, and therefore the expectations, of the people in them.

For example, emphasis on "the individual" colors all dimensions of writing in the humanities. It means that different people will bring their unique experiences to a document or a work of art and will interpret through the filter of those experiences. The range of possible interpretations is almost unlimited. As evidence, consider the many different interpretations of Shakespeare's plays that have emerged during more than 300 years of scholarship. The massive nature of this work doesn't inhibit new interpretations, which are ongoing and are likely to remain so, because each new generation must reevaluate Shakespeare in light of its own needs, perceptions, and aspirations.

Interpretations are seldom going to be judged "right" or "wrong," but they will be judged, in the larger arena, by how reasonably they meet a generation's needs and, in the smaller arena, how reasonably they meet readers' needs. In other words do the interpretations help clarify a given society's particular view of the world itself, and its members? Do they help readers understand themselves and their fellow men and women better? The issue here is complex, suggesting as it does that people writing in the humanities must think deeply about values and the repetitive pattern of human existence if they are going to make meaningful interpretations. They must understand not only the work under discussion but also their society, because their interpretation will be accepted or rejected on the basis of whether it is reasonable or *valid* in a given context, for a given community of readers.

Determining what makes an interpretation valid requires learning quite a bit about a particular discipline, which normally takes much more than a single term. Nevertheless, we can make some generalizations related to standards of proof. Valid interpretations in the humanities show a thorough familiarity with the work under discussion, and they frequently demonstrate knowledge of other, related works. They are fundamentally argumentative, and they draw support for their claims primarily from the work itself. Suppose, for example, that you read *Romeo and Juliet* and view the play to be something other than a simple love story with a tragic end. You believe it has a message, which is that people who don't exercise some control over their emotions are bound to have serious problems.

You could readily turn to the character Friar Lawrence to find support for your interpretation. In act 2, at the end of scene 3, the Friar tells Romeo, "Wisely and slow, they stumble that run fast." In scene 6, he tells Romeo that "violent delights have violent ends." In the context of the play, such statements foreshadow the tragedy that occurs. They stand out as good advice that Romeo ignores in the heat of his passion, and they can be viewed as urging restraint and control of the raging emotions that lead Romeo and Juliet to kill themselves. Just as the two people fell wildly and, as it turns out, hastily in love without a single thought to their circumstances, so the two commit suicide just as hastily, just as thoughtlessly. Using the lines from Friar Lawrence to help support your claim is therefore quite reasonable and prompts readers to judge your interpretation as a valid one. (Keep in mind, of course, that there are other, equally valid interpretations.)

Another way to make your interpretation valid is to find support outside the work, in the writing of experts on the subject. If you are able to locate books and articles whose authors agree with your interpretation of *Romeo and Juliet*, it suggests that reputable people in the field have also looked at the play in this light. Your perception is shared by others, which makes it seem more reasonable. The problem, of course, is that if other readers have already made this particular interpretation, you aren't bringing anything new to the analysis of the play. Perhaps this reading is so obvious that everyone sees it—in which case they don't need your paper to help them better understand what the play is about.

We see, then, another assumption of writing in the humanities: That an interpretation should have some degree of originality that enhances people's understanding of a work. For students like you, this assumption can be one of the more problematic parts of an assignment, because you haven't spent years studying the discipline or the topic, so you don't know what has been said before. Your teachers do know, which makes it pretty easy to embarrass yourself by saying something obvious. The solution is to use your teachers' greater knowledge as a *resource*. Talk to them about writing assignments and your interpretations; seek their advice. They will be able to tell you if a specific idea is worth pursuing or if you should try another approach.

Each discipline in the humanities has a slightly different focus as it addresses the human experience. Writing in literature and the visual arts, for example, tends to engage questions of meaning. What message is the author conveying? Writing in history commonly engages questions of cause and effect. Nevertheless, the writing conventions in each discipline are essentially the same. Characteristically, papers are organized into three parts: (1) a brief section identifying the topic or subject, (2) a section describing and analyzing the topic or subject, and (3) a section that presents the writer's interpretation. We encourage you to use this organization as a strategy for dealing with writing assignments. Thinking of papers as consisting of three interrelated parts can be very useful in deciding what to include to support your interpretation.

Documentation

If you use someone else's words or *ideas* to support your writing, you are obligated to provide accurate references for them, giving credit to the originators. Failure to do so constitutes plagiarism.

There are two widely used documentation formats in the humanities: the Modern Language Association (MLA) style and the Chicago style, which was covered in the section on documentation in the Social Sciences. Both are published in book form as style guides and are available in most book stores.

In addition to specifying how to present references in the text of a paper and in a bibliography, both guides discuss a range of stylistic information, such as how to format quotations, when to write out a number and when to use the Arabic numeral, what to include on the title page, what size margins to use, and so forth. Note that this information is not the same in the two guides, so make certain you know which style your humanities teacher expects to see in your papers.

Generally, your teachers in English, drama, music, film and art will want you to use the MLA style. Your teachers in history and philosophy may want you to use the Chicago style, although we sense that some are beginning to move away from it because of its complexity.

Although we drew on these published guides to offer a brief summary of the two forms of documentation, the summary is far from being comprehensive. We therefore recommend that you buy the guides and keep them as references.

MLA

In this style, if you provide a direct quotation, you refer to the source parenthetically in the text of your paper. You can do this two ways. As Example 1 shows, you can incorporate the quotation into your text and then give the reference, which will consist of the author's last name and the pages where the quotation appears in the author's work. Or as Example 2 shows, you can give the author's name in your text, in which case you will put the *pages only* in parentheses.

Example 1

> The biggest problem with the third Indiana Jones film is the shoddy editing. In one scene, for example, a German tank plunges over a cliff. When it hits an outcrop, the turret blows off. Then another camera picks up the descent from a different angle, showing the tank roll and bounce down the cliff before hitting level ground, where it explodes in a ball of fire. Somehow, between the first camera and the second, the turret managed to re-attach itself to the tank, prompting one critic to remark that "the tank was truly a miracle of German engineering" (Henderson-Smyth 13–14).

Example 2

> Other, equally amateurish, examples of bad editing occur throughout the film. What are we to make of the fact that, at the beginning of the airplane chase sequence, Indiana and his father have the rear rudder of their airplane machine-gunned off, only to have it appear *intact* in the next series of camera shots? Henderson-Smyth suggests that the success of the earlier films produced "an arrogant complacency on the part of the director and a pathetic contempt for the ticket-buying public" (15). Certainly, not much else serves to explain such gross ineptness.

If you are not quoting a passage but are referring to a writer's entire work, you don't have to provide any parenthetical information. You simply need to give the writer's name, as shown in Example 3:

Example 3

> Henderson-Smyth suggests throughout his article that the problems in *Indiana Jones: The Last Crusade* are characteristic of sequels and that they argue strongly against Hollywood's tendency to milk successful films, and their audiences, for every last nickel.

Finally, you may occasionally want to provide a quotation longer than two or three lines. When you do, separate it from the body of your text by indenting both sides, producing what is called a "block quotation." Don't single-space this quotation—keep it double spaced like the rest of your paper. The author's name should appear in your text, and the reference, which should consist simply of the page number(s), will be at the end of the quotation, outside the period.

Example 4

> Although the third Indiana Jones is bad, the problems are primarily technical and represent mere sloppiness, reprehensible as that is. More problematic are films like *E.T., The Extraterrestrial*, which project themes that reinforce some of our worst inclinations. In this regard, Henderson-Smyth notes that:
>> At no time during the history of Western Civilization has so much money been made off of so much sentimental nonsense. Far worse, the nonsense has an insidious side, for Spielberg portrays adults in general and scientists in particular as hideous, heartless criminals willing to slay the ugly alien for the sake of "knowledge." In

a world with few real villains but much complaisance, a little scientist bashing may seem harmless enough, but it nevertheless reveals the sort of anti-intellectual, anti-technological message that young people don't need. It is characteristic of the sort of touchy-feely, superstitious mysticism one associates with astrology and palm reading, out-of-the-body experiences and reincarnation. If left unchallenged it will lead us all into a dark age where a life-time subscription to *National Enquirer* is an intellectual status symbol. (122)

The list of materials your used for your paper should be presented as a separate section at the very end of your work. Double-space all entries, and indent second and succeeding lines five spaces. Generally, you should include only those references you have actually cited, and the section should be titled "Works Cited." Sometimes a teacher may ask you to include not only the works you cited but also those you consulted during your writing. In that case, the section should be titled "Works Consulted."

BOOKS

A Book by One Author

Smith, James A. *The Thrill of It All: An Analysis of J. T. Boone's Banjo-Picking Style*. New York: Scribners, 1989.

Two or More Books by the Same Author

Robinson, Fred. *The New Art in an Artless Society: The Making of Meaning*. Los Angeles: U of California P, 1990.
———.*Performance Art: From Product to Process*. New York: Random, 1989.

A Book by Two or Three Authors

Winters, Mary, and Fritz Guggenheim. *Poetry for Daily Living*. New York: HarperCollins, 1991.
Clevenger, Betty, Merle Roundtree, and Sandra Mitchel. *Modern Drama*. Seattle: U of Washington P, 1988.

A Book by More than Three Authors

Rose, Bambi C. et al. *Film and the Forging of the American Experience*. New York: Appleton, 1987.

A Book with an Editor

    Zador, Leslie T., ed. *The Complete History of Film Music*. Los Angeles: Sage, 1990.

A Work in an Edited Volume

    Frankel, Debra. "The Downfall of Dictators." Ed. Nick Ceausescu. *The Christmas of 1989*. New York: New Liberty, 1990.

A Multivolume Work

    McEachren, Ashley. *How to Destroy a Relationship: Three Detailed Lessons*. 3 vols. San Francisco: Kwan-Sun, 1985.

A Translation

    Gunterstrasse, Karl. *A Postmodern Interpretation of Thomas Mann's Work*. Trans. Freda Bunderstadt and Robert Heissenberg. New York: Avon, 1988.

ARTICLES

Journals

    Harty, Barbara. "Cinematography and Costume Design: An Unhappy Union." *Cinematography* 33 (1988): 212–223.

Periodicals

    Richardson, Storm. "Synthetic Drums and the Death of Rock 'n' Roll." *Rolling Stone* 30 Sep. 1990: 7–15.

FILMS AND TELEVISION PROGRAMS

    Escape from Moscow. Dir. Douglas Weiskopf. With Feather Tippetts, Nikki Koloshnokoff, and Victoria Kessler. Crown. 1966.

    "Starlight." *The Universe*. Created by Robert Oppenheimenn. Dir. Judy Smith. PBS. KCET, Los Angeles. 31 May 1989.

CHICAGO

The Chicago style is different from the MLA style in some significant ways. For example, it requires two entries for each reference. The first appears as a reference footnote, and the second appears as a bibliographic entry at the end of the paper. In each case, the information conveyed is very similar; what varies is the format. In Example 1 below, you can see how the reference footnote appears at the bottom of a page of text. In Example 2, you will find the corresponding bibliographic entry:

Example 1

The move to establish a national high school curriculum has been hampered by the fact that, historically, states and in many cases local districts have been responsible for deciding what students learn in school.[1] As a consequence, the quality of education differs radically from one state to the next, even from one district to the next. It is a situation that Chester Finn, President of the National Association of Educational Progress, describes as being "a hodgepodge of texts, content, and standards that must be viewed as a complete disaster."[2]

---

[1] Rita Moreno Smith. *Educating America* (Los Angeles: Westwood Books, 1989), pp. 18–20.

[2] Chester Finn. "Creating a National Standard for Education," *Harvard Educational Review 30* (May 1989): 159.

Example 2

Finn, Chester. "Creating a National Standard for Education." *Harvard Educational Review* 30 (May 1989): 159–174.

Smith, Rita Moreno. *Educating America.* Los Angeles: Westwood Books, 1989.

The Chicago style differs from the MLA style in several other respects. Block quotations, for instance, are single, not double, spaced. Bibliographic entries are on a separate page, but they are titled "List of References" rather than "References."

One of the more difficult features of this format is the common use of Latin abbreviations to direct readers to sources cited more than once. These are

ibid. = *ibidem,* in the same place
loc. cit. = *loco citato,* in the place cited
op. cit. = *opere citato,* in the work cited

You should notice that the abbreviations are not be underlined. In addition to the above, this format uses the Latin term "idem," meaning "the same person," when referring to multiple works by the same author, as we will show below.

The rationale for using these abbreviations can be confusing, and the entire process can be most taxing and frustrating. The system is based on the *order of repeated references*. Suppose, for example, that the writer of the paper above has another reference to Chester Finn's article that immediately follows the one indicated in note 2. In this case, the second reference would be indicated by the abbreviation "ibid." If the citation is from a page different from the one first indicated, "ibid." is followed by the appropriate page number. If the writer follows that reference with one from another source, which is in turn followed by another reference to Finn's work, he or she would provide the author's last name, Finn, followed by either "loc. cit." or "op. cit." If the reference is to the same page used previously, "loc. cit." is correct. If the reference is to a different page, "op. cit." is correct and should be followed by the appropriate page number. This procedure is illustrated in the example below:

Example 3

There is no question that reaching agreement on what a national curriculum should consist of will be a major challenge. Special interest groups abound that will try to block or influence any proposals. One of the largest of these is the National Education Association (NEA), a group that Finn says is "interested only in the next cost of living increase for its members, who don't give a fig for improving education."[3] NEA Under-Secretary Jane Gabor has recently labeled Finn's assertion "ridiculous and beneath contempt,"[4] but Finn has not wavered in his condemnation of special interest groups like the NEA, calling them a "clear and present danger to American education."[5]

---

[3] Ibid.

[4] Jane Gabor, "The Problem with a National Curriculum," *The American Educator* 10 (October 1989): 15.

[5] Op. cit., Finn, p. 164.

The examples below illustrate how to document various sources using the Chicago style. In each instance, we give the reference footnote first, as indicated by reference number, and the bibliographic entry second.

BOOKS

A Book by One Author

[1] Rita Moreno Smith, *Educating America* (Los Angeles: Westwood Books, 1989), pp 18–20.
Smith, Rita Moreno, *Educating America*. Los Angeles: Westwood Books, 1989.

Two or More Books by the Same Author

[2] Martin Martinez, *The American Presidency, 1900–1960* (Cambridge, MA: Harvard University Press, 1990), p. 211.
Martinez, Martin. *The American Presidency*. Cambridge, MA: Harvard University Press, 1990.
[3] Idem, *America in Transition, 1960–1975* (Cambridge, MA: Harvard University Press, 1991), p. 57.
Martinez, Martin. *America in Transition, 1960–1975*. Cambridge, MA: Harvard University Press, 1991.

A Book by Two or Three Authors

[4] Jesus Winegate and Mary McIntry, *Change in Society* (Boston: Houghton Mifflin Co., 1989), pp. 45–47.
Winegate, Jesus, and McIntry, Mary. *Change in Society*. Boston: Houghton Mifflin Co., 1989.
[5] Fred MacMurry, Edward H. Horse, and Freda Roberts, *Studies in Communication* (New York: Lawrence Erlbaum, 1990), p. 123.
MacMurry, Fred; Horse, Edward H.; and Roberts, Freda. *Studies in Communication*. New York; Lawrence Erlbaum, 1990.

A Book by More than Three Authors

[6] Mary A. Popins et. al., *Umbrellas in Nineteenth Century England* (Chicago: Waterhouse Press, 1987), pp. 22–23.
Popins, Mary A.; Mental, Jonathan; Wilson, Ted C.; Glenn, Cheryl. *Umbrellas in Nineteenth Century England*. Chicago: Waterhouse Press, 1987.

A Book with an Editor

[7] Roberto Duran, ed., *Boxing as Social Commentary* (Panama City, Panama: Republica, 1988), p. 323.

Duran, Roberto, ed. *Boxing as Social Commentary*. Panama City, Panama: Republica, 1988.

A Work in an Edited Volume

[8] Raisa Gorbachev, "Affairs of State: Affairs of Fashion," in *Significant Statements of the Twentieth Century*, ed. Edward M. Koch (New York: Scandalous Press, 1992), pp. 169–170.

Gorbachev, Raisa. "Affairs of State: Affairs of Fashion." In *Significant Statements of the Twentieth Century*, edited by Edward M. Koch. New York: Scandalous Press, 1992.

A Multivolume Work

[9] Willard Scott, *How to Make a Fortune by Being a Clown*, 10 vols. (New York: CBS Books, 1988–1989), vol. 2: *From Bozo to Ronald McDonald: The Lean Years*, p. 643.

Scott, Willard. *How to Make a Fortune by Being a Clown*, 10 vols. (New York: CBS Books, 1988–1989), vol. 2: *From Bozo to Ronald McDonald: The Lean Years*, p. 643.

A Translation

[10] Boris Spassky, *Chess and Politics*, trans. Bobbi Fisher (New York: Bantum Books, 1978), p. 36.

Spassky, Boris. *Chess and Politics*. Translated by Bobbi Fisher. New York: Bantum Books, 1978.

ARTICLES

Journals

[11] Edward J. H. K. Simpson, "Latin America: Revolving Dictators," *South* 58 (May 1990): 178–180.

Simpson, Edward J. H. K. "Latin America: Revolving Dictators." *South* 58 (May 1990): 178–180.

Periodicals

[12] Linda Reed-Johnson-Greely-Hope, "The Good Earth: Death of a Rain Forest," *National Review*, June 1991, pp 75–91.

Reed-Johnson-Greely-Hope, Linda. "The Good Earth: Death of a Rain Forest." *National Review*, June 1991.

FILMS AND TELEVISION PROGRAMS

[13] *Escape from Moscow*, dir. Douglas Weiskopf. Crown International Pictures, 1966.
Escape from Moscow. Directed by Douglas Weiskopf. Crown International Pictures, 1966.
[14] PBS, "The Universe," 31 May 1989, "Starlight," Austin Williams, narrator.
PBS, "The Universe," 31 May 1989, "Starlight," Austin Williams, narrator.

8 English

INTRODUCTION TO WRITING IN ENGLISH

Almost all writing in English is based on texts. In elementary and high school, such papers often take the form of book reports, in which students summarize the plot of a story or play and describe the main characters. At the college level, however, a different sort of writing is required.

In the field of college English, the fundamental question concerning literary texts is "What do they mean?" The answer to this question may not be as straightforward as one might think. For example, the obvious response, "Whatever the authors intended them to mean," is difficult to accept because we know that people often intend to communicate one thing only to end up communicating something quite different. In addition, many authors refuse to state what they intended to communicate, or they are unable to do so. Unless we discover some hitherto hidden statements of Shakespeare, we'll never know what he intended *The Merchant of Venice* to tell us. Likewise, the response, "The text means whatever the words on the pages say," is problematic both because language has multiple layers of meaning and because different readers respond to different layers. We know that texts have both literal and figurative meanings as well as direct and indirect meanings. For example, if you ask someone at the dinner table, "Can you pass the salt?" you don't expect a yes or no answer. You are making a request instead of inquiring into the person's ability to pass salt. A literal interpretation to the above question might startle all who heard the exchange.

Over the last several years, scholars have come to believe that comprehending texts is a constructive process. In this view, meaning doesn't reside on the pages of a book; it is something readers construct on the basis of what they know about how the world operates, using the words on the page as cues to trigger that stored knowledge. In the salt example above, familiarity with human behavior during meals enables us to understand the question as a request for a specific action. In the same way, we respond to a text out of our understanding of our world. Determining what a literary text means, therefore, consists of passing the author's language through the filter of our own understanding and experience to reconstruct it as meaning on a personal level.

As a result, writing in English deals almost entirely with *interpretation*. Anyone who talks about stories, plays, or poems on the surface level of what they *say* is ignoring the deeper, more important level of what they *mean*. On this account, summaries of plot and descriptions of characters must always be of secondary importance when writing in English. They should appear only to support writers' interpretations of meaning.

The focus of interpretation itself is very broad. It concerns what we may vaguely call "life" or "the human condition." Literary texts are instructional in that they generally strive to help readers gain a better understanding of what life is all about, encouraging a moment of reflection that can enhance daily living. Acts of interpretation, therefore, should address this underlying educational message. For example, *Romeo and Juliet* isn't simply about the joys of youthful love; it is, more subtly, about the tragedies that occur when people have no control over their emotions. *Huckleberry Finn* isn't simply denouncing slavery and its evils but is, more memorably, about the power of friendship to overcome social barriers and about the strength of human dignity to withstand oppression. Both the literal and deeper meanings are necessary aspects of literature, but interpretive writing should always go beyond the literal. The author William Faulkner once called such messages "the eternal verities," meaning that literature always deals with fundamental human truths.

The interpretive nature of writing in English doesn't mean that anything goes. One can't decide, say, that *Don Quixote* is about a poor man possessed by devils. The meaning of a text is always constrained by the society in which it is read and by the genre it follows. Moreover, some interpretations will be more valid than others, on the basis of the knowledge and experience a set of given readers bring to the text. Those who have lived more, read more, and thought more about life and literature will be able to produce more valid interpretations of literary works. This fact doesn't discount alternative readings, of course, but it reinforces the point that the more worthwhile interpretations come from the more informed and thoughtful readers. In addition, it should indicate that writing in English can function powerfully as a way of learning.

Because each reader must construct his or her individual interpretation of meaning, the primary goal of writing in English is to convince readers that this particular interpretation is a valid one. Thus, the form of writing in English is argument. The claim, or thesis, usually appears in the opening paragraph, clearly and directly. The thesis acts as an assertion about the writer's interpretation that must be supported. The remainder of the paper consists of the support, which must come largely from the text under discussion. Going outside the text is risky because students have to make certain that whatever information they draw on is relevant to the argument. Secondary sources—that is, books or essays written about the work being discussed—can provide valuable support, but students have to be careful to document these sources appropriately and to avoid padding the paper with long quotations.

The conclusion of the paper shouldn't be a paraphrase of the introduction, as many students mistakenly believe. It should be forward-looking. It should state the meaning of the text to readers in a somewhat personal way, shifting the focus from the work to the readers' understanding and experiences. Alternately, it should direct readers to apply the insights gained in the paper to other, similar works.

English has its own conventions for documentation, so you need access to the *Modern Language Association* (MLA) *Style Guide*. Please refer to the overview that marks the beginning of writing in the humanities; there you will find a brief summary of MLA documentation.

ENGLISH ASSIGNMENT 1

Course: **Freshman Honor Seminar in Literary Criticism**

Analysis of Theme in a Play
Your task for this assignment is to identify what you perceive as the dominant theme in Sam Shepard's Buried Child, and to illustrate in your essay the ways in which the play reveals, ex-

pands, illuminates, exemplifies, describes, even subverts that theme. Imagine as your audience a group of readers who have either seen or read <u>Buried Child,</u> and who are therefore somewhat familiar with the play.

As is true of nearly all literary analyses, this essay should be a formal exposition of a carefully and clearly stated idea. The essay should be logically organized, well supported with specific examples from the play, and mechanically and grammatically correct. The introduction should identify the play and its author and explain the purpose of your essay; the conclusion should summarize your findings or briefly identify other approaches to the play.

The following suggestions might help you as you read the play, think about it, and then draft your essay:

1. Read all the stage directions carefully several times. Shepard's sets are highly symbolic, as are the characters' appearance and clothes. Indulge in mental theater; imagine what the stage looks like; picture what the characters are wearing and how they move.

2. Be aware of act and scene changes. What is happening at the beginning of a scene or act? At the end? What is said first? Last? How much time elapses between the divisions of the play? How do scenes and acts build on each other?

3. Read closely and carefully. Who says what? In what tone? What gestures or body language accompany the dialogue? Can you identify any of the characters by their speech patterns or by characteristic expressions? Shepard's plays display his fascination with language, especially in the long monologues in which some of the characters indulge. Study those monologues for clues to what the play is about.

4. Ask yourself what the play is about beyond the obvious surface action. Does the action parallel anything in "real life," or does it comment through contrast?

5. Readers and audiences have identified as major themes in Shepard's plays the following: the betrayal of the American Dream; the decay of our national myths; the growing mechanization of our lives; the search for roots and identity; the disintegration of the American family. You may use one of these as the

focus for your paper, or you may discover a theme that has not yet been identified.

6. Don't panic if you discover that your focus is different from those of your classmates. People bring different experiences and ideas to their reading and viewing of plays, and these different experiences and ideas inevitably lead to differing interpretations. What you should be concerned with is proving and illustrating your thesis.

7. Remember that the most important part of your essay is the body, in which you show that your interpretation of <u>Buried Child</u> is a valid one. You need specific examples—direct quotes, descriptions of actions or incidents, paraphrases—from the play. Don't generalize or assume that your reader will know what you mean.

Analysis of English Assignment 1

This assignment is from a freshman honors seminar, a course designed primarily as an introduction to literary criticism. The works studied are by contemporary authors, most of whom have yet to be considered major writers. The poems, short stories, plays, and novels are especially challenging because quite often they are experiments in form and content.

Making sense of Sam Shepard's *Buried Child* and expressing what you have discovered in a coherent essay is a difficult task, one that demands careful reading and careful analysis. The assignment is designed and written in a way to provide valuable help, both in understanding the play and in writing the essay. The first two paragraphs explain the subject and the form of the analysis, identify the audience, and even give suggestions for an introduction and conclusion.

The analysis should contain a strong, clearly identified thesis ("a carefully and clearly stated idea") that is supported with specific references to the play. For example, the introduction should inform readers about the point the author is making, and the body of the paper should contain support and explanations to convince readers that the writer's interpretation is valid. Too often when students write analyses, they think that an example automatically supports the point they are making. It's necessary, however, to explain *how* the example supports the point, guiding readers toward the writer's conclusion.

The seven suggestions are not questions to be answered as such. They should be used as guides for reading and writing that will help you discover a thesis. These suggestions are especially valuable because they are for *Buried Child* specifically. Number 5 even suggests particular themes, any one of which would be a legitimate focus for your essay.

Typically, readers of this sort of analysis will be familiar with the work analyzed, so avoid retelling any parts of the story unless they specifically support a point you are making. You do, however, need to explain carefully how these examples support your points; don't depend on readers to figure out relationships for themselves. Avoid writing, "Throughout the play Tilden brings in vegetables from the garden." Readers already know this from reading the play. At the same time, you shouldn't just write, "The vegetables symbolize hope." This alone may not be convincing; you need to explain how you reached this conclusion, and you must make specific reference to the text of the play where we can find support for this interpretation. The balance between summarizing too much of the play and providing too few examples and explanations may be difficult to determine. As a guide, remember that in your analysis you don't have to explain what happened; you task is to explain *what it all means*.

From *Buried Child*,
by Sam Shepard

Act Two

SCENE: *Same set as act 1. Night. Sounds of rain.* DODGE *still asleep on sofa. His hair is cut extremely short and in places the scalp is cut and bleeding. His cap is still center stage. All the corn and husks, pail and milking stool have been cleared away. The lights come up to the sound of a young girl laughing off stage left.* DODGE *remains asleep.* SHELLY *and* VINCE *appear up left outside the screen porch door sharing the shelter of* VINCE'S *overcoat above their heads.* SHELLY *is about nineteen, black hair, very beautiful. She wears tight jeans, high heels, purple T-shirt and a short rabbit fur coat. Her makeup is exaggerated and her hair has been curled.* VINCE *is* TILDEN'S *son, about twenty-two, wears a plaid shirt, jeans, dark glasses, cowboy boots and carries a black saxophone case. They shake the rain off themselves as they enter the porch through the screen door.*

"Buried Child," from *Seven Plays* by Sam Shepard. Copyright © 1979 by Sam Shepard. Used by permission of Bantam Books, a Division of Bantam Doubleday, Dell Publishing-Group, Inc.

SHELLY: (*laughing, gesturing to house*) This is it? I don't believe this is it!
VINCE: This is it.
SHELLY: This is the house?
VINCE: This is the house.
SHELLY: I don't believe it!
VINCE: How come?
SHELLY: It's like a Norman Rockwell cover or something.
VINCE: What's a' matter with that? It's American.
SHELLY: Where's the milkman and the little dog? What's the little dog's name? Spot. Spot and Jane. Dick and Jane and Spot.
VINCE: Knock it off.
SHELLY: Dick and Jane and Spot and Mom and Dad and Junior and Sissy!
(*She laughs. Slaps her knee.*)
VINCE: Come on! It's my heritage. What dya' expect?
(*She laughs more hysterically, out of control.*)
SHELLY: "And Tuffy and Toto and Dooda and Bonzo all went down one day to the corner grocery store to buy a big bag of licorice for Mr. Marshall's pussy cat!"
(*She laughs so hard she falls to her knees holding her stomach.* VINCE *stands there looking at her.*)
VINCE: Shelly will you get up!
(*She keeps laughing. Staggers to her feet. Turning in circles holding her stomach.*)
SHELLY: (*continuing her story in kid's voice*) "Mr. Marshall was on vacation. He had no idea that the four little boys had taken such a liking to his little kitty cat."
VINCE: Have some respect would ya'!
SHELLY: (*trying to control herself*) I'm sorry.
VINCE: Pull yourself together.
SHELLY: (*salutes him*) Yes sir.
(*She giggles.*)
VINCE: Jesus Christ, Shelly.
SHELLY: (*pause, smiling*) And Mr. Marshall—
VINCE: Cut it out.
(*She stops. Stands there staring at him. Stifles a giggle.*)
VINCE: (*after pause*) Are you finished?
SHELLY: Oh brother!
VINCE: I don't wanna go in there with you acting like an idiot.
SHELLY: Thanks.
VINCE: Well, I don't.
SHELLY: I won't embarrass you. Don't worry.
VINCE: I'm not worried.
SHELLY: You are too.

VINCE: Shelly look, I just don't wanna go in there with you giggling your head off. They might think something's wrong with you.
SHELLY: There is.
VINCE: There is not!
SHELLY: Something's definitely wrong with me.
VINCE: There is not!
SHELLY: There's something wrong with you too.
VINCE: There's nothing wrong with me either!
SHELLY: You wanna know what's wrong with you?
VINCE: What?
  (SHELLY *laughs.*)
VINCE: (*crosses back left toward screen door*) I'm leaving!
SHELLY: (*stops laughing*) Wait! Stop! Stop! (VINCE *stops*) What's wrong with you is that you take the situation too seriously.
VINCE: I just don't want to have them think that I've suddenly arrived out of the middle of nowhere completely deranged.
SHELLY: What do you want them to think then?
VINCE: (*pause*) Nothing. Let's go in.
  (*He crosses porch toward stage right interior door.* SHELLY *follows him. The stage right door opens slowly.* VINCE *sticks his head in, doesn't notice* DODGE *sleeping. Calls out toward staircase.*)
VINCE: Grandma!
  (SHELLY *breaks into laughter, unseen behind* VINCE. VINCE *pulls his head back outside and pulls door shut. We hear their voices again without seeing them.*)
SHELLY'S VOICE: (*stops laughing*) I'm sorry. I'm sorry Vince. I really am. I really am sorry. I won't do it again. I couldn't help it.
VINCE'S VOICE: It's not all that funny.
SHELLY'S VOICE: I know it's not. I'm sorry.
VINCE'S VOICE: I mean this is a tense situation for me! I haven't seen them for over six years. I don't know what to expect.
SHELLY'S VOICE: I know. I won't do it again.
VINCE'S VOICE: Can't you bite your tongue or something?
SHELLY'S VOICE: Just don't say "Grandma," okay? (*she giggles, stops*) I mean if you say "Grandma" I don't know if I can stop myself.
VINCE'S VOICE: Well try!
SHELLY'S VOICE: Okay. Sorry.
  (*Door opens again.* VINCE *sticks his head in then enters.* SHELLY *follows behind him.* VINCE *crosses to staircase, sets down saxophone case and overcoat, looks up staircase.* SHELLY *notices* DODGE'*s baseball cap. Crosses to it. Picks it up and puts it on her head.* VINCE *goes up the stairs and disappears at the top.* SHELLY *watches him then turns and sees* DODGE *on the sofa. She takes off the baseball cap.*)
VINCE'S VOICE: (*from above stairs*) Grandma!

(SHELLY *crosses over to* DODGE *slowly and stands next to him. She stands at his head, reaches out slowly and touches one of the cuts. The second she touches his head* DODGE *jerks up to a sitting position on the sofa, eyes open.* SHELLY *gasps.* DODGE *looks at her, sees his cap in her hands, quickly puts his hand to his bare head. He glares at* SHELLY *then whips the cap out of her hands and puts it on.* SHELLY *backs away from him.* DODGE *stares at her.*)

SHELLY: I'm uh—with Vince.

(DODGE *just glares at her.*)

SHELLY: He's upstairs.

(DODGE *looks at the staircase then back to* SHELLY.)

SHELLY: (*calling upstairs*) Vince!

VINCE'S VOICE: Just a second!

SHELLY: You better get down here!

VINCE'S VOICE: Just a minute! I'm looking at the pictures.

(DODGE *keeps staring at her.*)

SHELLY: (*to* DODGE) We just got here. Pouring rain on the freeway so we thought we'd stop by. I mean Vince was planning on stopping anyway. He wanted to see you. He said he hadn't seen you in a long time.

(*Pause.* DODGE *just keeps staring at her.*)

SHELLY: We were going all the way through to New Mexico. To see his father. I guess his father lives out there. We thought we'd stop by and see you on the way. Kill two birds with one stone, you know? (*she laughs,* DODGE *stares, she stops laughing*) I mean Vince has this thing about his family now. I guess it's a new thing with him. I kind of find it hard to relate to. But he feels it's important. You know. I mean he feels he wants to get to know you all again. After all this time.

(*Pause.* DODGE *just stares at her. She moves nervously to staircase and yells up to* VINCE.)

SHELLY: Vince will you come down here please!

(VINCE *comes half way down the stairs.*)

VINCE: I guess they went out for a while.

(SHELLY *points to sofa and* DODGE. VINCE *turns and sees* DODGE. *He comes all the way down staircase and crosses to* DODGE. SHELLY *stays behind near staircase, keeping her distance.*)

VINCE: Grandpa?

(DODGE *looks up at him, not recognizing him.*)

DODGE: Did you bring the whiskey?

(VINCE *looks back at* SHELLY *then back to* DODGE.)

VINCE: Grandpa, it's Vince. I'm Vince. Tilden's son. You remember?

(DODGE *stares at him.*)

DODGE: You didn't do what you told me. You didn't stay here with me.

VINCE: Grandpa, I haven't been here until just now. I just got here.
DODGE: You left. You went outside like we told you not to do. You went out there in back. In the rain.
(VINCE *looks back at* SHELLY. *She moves slowly toward sofa.*)
SHELLY: Is he okay?
VINCE: I don't know. (*takes off his shades*) Look, Grandpa, don't you remember me? Vince. Your Grandson.
(DODGE *stares at him then takes off his baseball cap.*)
DODGE: (*points to his head*) See what happens when you leave me alone? See that? That's what happens.
(VINCE *looks at his head.* VINCE *reaches out to touch his head.*
DODGE *slaps his hand away with the cap and puts it back on his head.*)
VINCE: What's going on Grandpa? Where's Halie?
DODGE: Don't worry about her. She won't be back for days. She says she'll be back but she won't be. (*he starts laughing*) There's life in the old girl yet! (*stops laughing*)
VINCE: How did you do that to your head?
DODGE: I didn't do it! Don't be ridiculous!
VINCE: Well who did then?
(*Pause.* DODGE *stares at* VINCE.)
DODGE; Who do you think did it? Who do you think?
(SHELLY *moves toward* VINCE.)
SHELLY: Vince, maybe we oughta' go. I don't like this. I mean this isn't my idea of a good time.
VINCE: (*to* SHELLY) Just a second. (*to* DODGE) Grandpa, look, I just got here. I just now got here. I haven't been here for six years. I don't know anything that's happened.
(*Pause,* DODGE *stares at him.*)
DODGE: You don't know anything?
VINCE: No.
DODGE: Well that's good. That's good. It's much better not to know anything. Much, much better.
VINCE: Isn't there anybody here with you?
(DODGE *turns slowly and looks off to stage left.*)
DODGE: Tilden's here.
VINCE: No, Grandpa, Tilden's in New Mexico. That's where I was going. I'm going out there to see him.
(DODGE *turns slowly back to* VINCE.)
DODGE: Tilden's here.
(VINCE *backs away and joins* SHELLY. DODGE *stares at them.*)
SHELLY: Vince, why don't we spend the night in a motel and come back in the morning? We could have breakfast. Maybe everything would be different.
VINCE: Don't be scared. There's nothing to be scared of. He's just old.

SHELLY: I'm not scared!
DODGE: You two are not my idea of the perfect couple!
SHELLY: (*after pause*) Oh really? Why's that?
VINCE: Shh! Don't aggravate him.
DODGE: There's something wrong between the two of you. Something not compatible.
VINCE: Grandpa, where did Halie go? Maybe we should call her.
DODGE: What are you talking about? Do you know what you're talking about? Are you just talking for the sake of talking? Lubricating the gums?
VINCE: I'm trying to figure out what's going on here!
DODGE: Is that it?
VINCE: Yes. I mean I expected everything to be different.
DODGE: Who are you to expect anything? Who are you supposed to be?
VINCE: I'm Vince! Your Grandson!
DODGE: Vince. My Grandson.
VINCE: Tilden's son.
DODGE: Tilden's son, Vince.
VINCE: You haven't seen me for a long time.
DODGE: When was the last time?
VINCE: I don't remember.
DODGE: You don't remember?
VINCE: No.
DODGE: You don't remember. How am I supposed to remember if you don't remember?
SHELLY: Vince, come on. This isn't going to work out.
VINCE: (*to* SHELLY) Just take it easy.
SHELLY: I'm taking it easy! He doesn't even know who you are!
VINCE: (*crossing toward* DODGE) Grandpa, look—
DODGE: Stay where you are! Keep your distance!
(VINCE *stops. Looks back at* SHELLY *then to* DODGE.)
SHELLY: Vince, this is really making me nervous. I mean he doesn't even want us here. He doesn't even like us.
DODGE: She's a beautiful girl.
VINCE: Thanks.
DODGE: Very Beautiful Girl.
SHELLY: Oh my God.
DODGE: (*to* SHELLY) What's your name?
SHELLY: Shelly.
DODGE: Shelly. That's a man's name isn't it?
SHELLY: Not in this case.
DODGE: (*to* VINCE) She's a smart-ass too.
SHELLY: Vince! Can we go?
DODGE: She wants to go. She just got here and she wants to go.

VINCE: This is kind of strange for her.
DODGE: She'll get used to it. (*to* SHELLY) What part of the country do you come from?
SHELLY: Originally?
DODGE: That's right. Originally. At the very start.
SHELLY: L.A.
DODGE: L.A. Stupid country.
SHELLY: I can't stand this Vince! This is really unbelievable!
DODGE: It's stupid! L.A. is stupid! So is Florida! All those Sunshine States. They're all stupid. Do you know why they're stupid?
SHELLY: Illuminate me.
DODGE: I'll tell you why. Because they're full of smart-asses! That's why.
(SHELLY *turns her back to* DODGE, *crosses to staircase and sits on bottom step.*)
DODGE: (*to* VINCE) Now she's insulted.
VINCE: Well you weren't very polite.
DODGE: She's insulted! Look at her! In my house she's insulted! She's over there sulking because I insulted her!
SHELLY: (*to* VINCE) This is really terrific. This is wonderful. And you were worried about me making the right first impression!
DODGE: (*to* VINCE) She's a fireball isn't she? Regular fireball. I had some a' them in my day. Temporary stuff. Never lasted more than a week.
VINCE: Grandpa—
DODGE: Stop calling me Grandpa will ya'! It's sickening. "Grandpa." I'm nobody's Grandpa!
(DODGE *starts feeling around under the cushion for the bottle of whiskey.* SHELLY *gets up from the staircase.*)
SHELLY: (*to* VINCE) Maybe you've got the wrong house. Did you ever think of that? Maybe this is the wrong address!
VINCE: It's not the wrong address! I recognize the yard.
SHELLY: Yeah but do you recognize the people? He says he's not your Grandfather.
DODGE: (*digging for bottle*) Where's that bottle!
VINCE: He's just sick or something. I don't know what's happened to him.
DODGE: Where's my goddamn bottle!
(DODGE *gets up from sofa and starts tearing the cushions off it and throwing them downstage, looking for the whiskey.*)
SHELLY: Can't we just drive on to New Mexico? This is terrible, Vince! I don't want to stay here. In this house. I thought it was going to be turkey dinners and apple pie and all that kinda stuff.
VINCE: Well I hate to disappoint you!
SHELLY: I'm not disappointed! I'm fuckin' terrified! I wanna' go!
(DODGE *yells toward stage left.*)
DODGE: Tilden! Tilden!

(DODGE *keeps ripping away at the sofa looking for his bottle, he knocks over the night stand with the bottles.* VINCE *and* SHELLY *watch as he starts ripping the stuffing out of the sofa.*)

VINCE: (*to* SHELLY) He's lost his mind or something. I've got to try to help him.

SHELLY: You help him! I'm leaving!

(SHELLY *starts to leave.* VINCE *grabs her. They struggle as* DODGE *keeps ripping away at the sofa and yelling.*)

DODGE: Tilden! Tilden get your ass in here! Tilden!

SHELLY: Let go of me!

VINCE: You're not going anywhere! You're going to stay right here!

SHELLY: Let go of me you sonuvabitch! I'm not your property!

(*Suddenly* TILDEN *walks on from stage left just as he did before. This time his arms are full of carrots.* DODGE, VINCE *and* SHELLY *stop suddenly when they see him. They all stare at* TILDEN *as he crosses slowly center stage with the carrots and stops.* DODGE *sits on sofa, exhausted.*)

DODGE: (*panting, to* TILDEN) Where in the hell have you been?

TILDEN: Out back.

DODGE: Where's my bottle?

TILDEN: Gone.

(TILDEN *and* VINCE *stare at each other.* SHELLY *backs away.*)

Guide for Reading

Diane's paper is a very good analysis of *Buried Child*. As you read it, notice how she follows most of the points covered in the Introduction to Writing in English as well those in the Analysis of this assignment. You should also sense that she is writing to communicate her discoveries to readers so they will gain a better understanding of the play from her analysis.

SAMPLE ENGLISH PAPER 1

A Critical Analysis of <u>Buried Child</u>

Diane K. (a freshman)

The Pulitzer is an extremely prestigious <u>prize</u> honor bestowed on the authors of only the finest and most influential works of modern literature. In 1979, Sam Shepard wrote an exceptional play meeting these qualifications. *Buried Child* appears to be a sequence of unrelated, inexplicable events. Reading between the lines, though, reveals an ingenious structure explaining a family's inability to cope with the breakdown of their Cleaver-esque life. More abstractly, the play can be seen as a metaphor for the failure of America to live up to the dreams of the founding fathers.

The generally accepted definition of the "American Dream" is a middle class family living in a house in the country or the suburbs with two or three children who grow up to be intelligent, successful, and healthy-for example, the families portrayed in "Leave It To Beaver," "My Three Sons," and "Father Knows Best." In the early years, Dodge's and Halie's family was the model of the "American Dream," with fertile farmland of their own and three promising young sons-Tilden, Bradley, and Ansel. As Dodge said, "We were a well-established family once. . . . All the boys were grown. The farm was producing enough milk to fill Lake Michigan twice over. . . . All we had to do was ride it out." Old pictures on Halie's wall showed a thriving farm, the boys waving straw hats in a field of corn, and a young, red-haired Halie holding a baby that, as Shelly says, looks "like it didn't even belong to her."

As the years progressed, each son eventually failed to fulfill the expectations of Dodge and Halie, as well as their expectations of themselves. Tilden, who wore letters on his chest and medals around his neck in high school, became burned out on drugs, spent time in a Mexico jail, and finally followed his trail of brain cells back to Dodge and Halie's house, where he now lives. After cutting his leg off with a chain saw, Bradley became an invalid in his own mind and, as Halie put it, "can hardle look after himself." Finally the honorable soldier and supposedly the most intelligent of the three sons, Ansel, was killed in a motel room by his Roman Catholic wife.

All the while, Dodge and Halie are watching their own "American Dream" unravel in their face. None of their sons have managed to reach their potential, or even come close, the farm has stopped producing as it once did, and it is alleged that Halie is fooling around. The inability to cope with this breakdown leads to the conception of the fourth son of Halie and Dodge. He is created as a psychological defense mechanism enabling the family to deal with all of their disappointments, and is at all times a symbol, not a reality (although any given person can interpret the child's importance in a different way.) The drowning and burial of the child by Dodge is a metaphor for the repression and "burial" of all the lost hopes and dreams of this "typical" midwest family. In essence, the buried child represents the transplanting the blame of their failure to a vehicle they can understand and deal with somehow. At the end of the play, Tilden unearths the child and carries the decayed body back into the house. This is symbolic of the family finally coming to grips with it's past, instead of merely explaining and rationalizing, as a result of Shelly's honest, outsider's point of view questions and Vince's dramatic, violent metamorphosis.

Tilden's discovery of corn and carrots in the backyard is also an extremely important metaphor in *Buried Child*. They represent hope. Hope that just as corn could grow in such a fertile environment as the backyard; things could change for the better in such a fertile environment as that house. Also, in the same way that corn and carrots must be peeled to get to the good parts, the belief in the buried child and all it meant must be shed in order to realize the saving graces of the family.

One of the more ironic instances in the play is the remarks that Shelly makes before her and Vince enter the house. She makes a reference to the house as being "like a Norman Rockwell cover or something," and then goes on to make jokes about how Vince's family is the mega-average, Dick and Jane-style storybook family. Of course this is ironic because the family is more like "Dallas's" Ewing with psychological problems. Perhaps Shepard is illustrating the point that no family is perfect like Norman Rockwell or the Cleavers would have you believe.

Finally, the higher purpose of *Buried Child,* above all of the smaller, lesser metaphors, is to display how America failed to achieve what the founding fathers had attempted to create. When writing the Constitution, they had a nearly perfect society in mind in which everyone was equal, free, and able to make a living. The early years of Dodge's and Halie's family represent this ideal. As the nation matured, though, war, drugs, and inequality among

English

people, whether it be because of race, handicap, age, or sex, began to rip the nation apart and render the founding fathers' ideal almost imbecilic. This is represented in the play by the sons and Dodge's senility and denial of the past, respectively. Father Denis represents the inability of religion to act as an adequate cohesive force and hold the nation together. The use of the buried child to dispel the family's frustrations about its failures is a metaphor for the attempts of post-depression movies and television to ignore the problems of America and exude an image of a euphoric, middle class nation. At last, there is Shelly and Vince. They symbolize the young people of the United States during the social revolution of the late sixties. Vince's dramatic change at the end of the play can be likened to the "hippie" generation that would no longer accept the bull that mainstream American society was trying to make them believe. Shelly's inquisitive nature represents the question of that generation that woke America up to the injustices found in our country, just as Shelly's questions forced Dodge and Halie's family to bring their secret out in open and, eventually, exhume the buried child and all it stood for.

Analysis of English Sample Paper 1

Diane has written a very good analytical paper on *Buried Child*. It is thoughtful, her examples are well chosen, and her explanations are likely to convince readers that her interpretation is valid.

The introduction does exactly what the assignment calls for; it identifies the author, the play, and the claim (thesis) of the paper. Readers know that Diane recognizes that the play depicts the breakdown of an American family, which in this case is a minimal requirement to a meaningful interpretation. The point she wants to make goes beyond this recognition to something other than the obvious, and we see her propose that the play expresses the failure of America to realize the ideals of the Founding Fathers. After stating this proposal, the next task is to provide good reasons for the interpretation, with examples and convincing explanation.

In paragraphs 2 through 6, Diane does not tell what happens in the play. Instead, she explains what has happened to the family in the past, basing her analysis on the action and dialogue in the play. She has synthesized her impressions into a coherent account of the family, and then she uses these impressions as evidence for her viewpoint. Notice how she uses bits of dialogue and incidents from the text to support her analysis and then explains how these led her to specific conclusions. Understanding the past of Dodge and Halie's family is essential to understanding its present condition, which in turn enables readers to accept Diane's interpretation. All of the examples directly support a point she is making; none is there simply to refresh the reader's mind about what happens.

Diane wants readers to see that the play is a metaphor—a text with a meaning other than its literal one. She builds up to this point by carefully explaining the concrete details necessary to grasp the metaphor. In paragraph 4 she focuses on the burial of the child and provides explanations of what other incidents represent or symbolize. These explanations work because Diane has already prepared readers for her interpretation. She isn't simply reaching out and grabbing for anything that might represent something else; her metaphors and her analysis of them support *her specific reading* of the play.

The last paragraph functions to elaborate her interpretation of the play as a metaphor for America's failure to live up to the ideals of the Founding Fathers. With the previous paragraphs acting as foundation, these final remarks work effectively to bring the paper to a close. Diane supports her position with information from the play and with her general knowledge about trends in America. Sometimes it is dangerous to "leave the play" to explain it, but in this case she has stayed within the bounds of reasonable interpretation. She shows that her conclusion is logical, both by building up to it with careful analysis and complete explanation and by including specifics from America's past showing that her connections make sense.

After reading her paper, we understand that Diane wants to help readers understand *Buried Child* better. She makes it clear that her interpretation is not the only one (her parenthetical comment in paragraph 4), but at the same time she clearly believes that hers is a valid one. Traditionally, a critic's purpose is to enlighten readers, and Diane does this nicely in her paper.

On a negative note, we would mention that Diane's paragraphs sometimes are too long. The last paragraph, for example, could easily be divided into two, which would make it easier to read. In addition, Diane may well be idealizing America's founding fathers and ignoring their own failures to live up to their dreams and expectations. Had she viewed them more realistically, her interpretation might have been more complex.

Guide for Reading

The following paper is an average one that fulfills the basic requirements of the assignment. As you read it, you may feel that Sam is telling you what you already know and isn't giving you any information to enhance your understanding of the play. He has limited himself to reminding readers of incidents that to him reflect the disintegration of the family, without attempting to explain why these incidents happen.

SAMPLE ENGLISH PAPER 2

The Disintegration of the Family

Sam L. (a freshman)

In "Buried Child" by Sam Shepard the reader is aware of the strangeness of the family just by viewing the stage. The set is considerably bare with only an old staircase with frayed carpet, a couch with the stuffing coming out, and a television giving off a flickering blue light. This sets the mood by giving the audience the feeling something is wrong with the family that lives here—and there is. Although there are many themes in this book the most important is the disintegration of the family. Evidence of this is seen in the family's sense of being lost, the deep secret that is not to be discussed, and the obligation of Vince to save the family.

It is evident near the beginning of the play that there is a sense of being lost when Vince, Dodge and Halie's grandson, returns home to see his family after six years of absence. No one, including Vince's father, Tilden, recognizes him. Vince expects everything to be "normal" and quite different than the strange situation he walks into. Dodge says, "Who are you supposed to be?" "Who are you to expect anything?" It is safe to say that when someone doesn't or chooses not to recognize a member of the family destruction is close. Another sign of the family's bewilderment is the lack of trust and compassion between them. Throughout the play Tilden constantly protests his innocence. He sounds guilty and scared when he claims, "I didn't do anything," and later, "I didn't do anything wrong." This testimony shows the lack of understanding and trust between Tilden and his family. It also foreshadows his involvement in the family's unspeakable secret. The tension between Tilden and his father is seen when Tilden covers Dodge's body with corn husks. It is as if he would like to bury his father. "He gathers more husks and repeats the procedure until the floor is clean of corn husks and Dodge is completely covered except for his head." Halie expresses her sense of being lost to Dodge when she says, "Nobody's going to look after us." "I had no idea in the world Tilden would be so much trouble." This family constantly blames their troubles on one another without each accepting part of the responsibility.

There are many leaks and hints by the family about their secret through what they say and their actions. Halie wears black the first time she is seen. She seems to still be mourning a loss of a loved one. She talks about her dead son, Ansel, but this son, according to her, was a man when he died. More of the secret slips out when Tilden says to Vince, "I had a son once but we buried him." Dodge quickly looks at Tilden and most likely with scorn. Tilden finally tells Shelly, Vince's girlfriend. He says that Dodge killed a baby by drowning it. "He's the only one who knows where it is buried. The only one. Like a secret buried treasure." Dodge again gets angry at this outburst. His guilt and resentment of his son is evident once again when Dodge says, "You think just because people propagate they have to love their offspring?" "You never seen a bitch eat her puppies?" This shows that because of this secret the family not only resents each other, they also have definite feelings of hatred toward one another. The entire secret is revealed by Dodge near the end of the play. He says, "I wanted to pretend that I was its father. She wanted me to believe in it. Even when everyone around us knew. Everyone. All our boys knew. Tilden knew." Dodge uncovers, not literally, the root of the family's disintegration by claiming, "Everything was cancelled out by this one mistake." "This one weakness." Shepard seems to be saying that the family destroys itself. The family causes its own disintegration by an immoral flaw and is, in this family's case, unable to pull back together.

The saddest evidence of the family's disintegration is Vince's obligation to his desperate family. It seems that Vince is inevitably following in his father's footsteps. Tilden came home because he "didn't know where else to go." Now Vince comes home to visit and one of the first things his father says is "I thought I saw a face inside his face." This symbolizes the link between Vince and his strange family. Halie expresses her hope for the family by saying, "Vincent was an angel. A guardian angel. He'd watch over us. He'd watch over all of us." When Vince returns he is strange like the rest of his family. He claims, "I am a murderer." This statement hints that Vince already realizes his inevitable link with his family. He again expresses this when he asks Shelly is the family has her prisoner in the house. Dodge tells Vince to take over the house and Vince "buries" himself when he tells Shelly, "I've gotta carry on the line." The line of disintegration? Evidently not to the rest of the family because in the end Halie sees the imaginary corn and vegetables growing in her back yard. This symbolizes hope just as the return of Vince does to Halie. However Vince seems to be just like the rest of the family now and will probably only be able to help with further destruction of his family.

In "Buried Child" Shepard exemplifies the hopelessness and weaknesses of the family. The family destroys its self. Vince feels obligated to help his family and in the end only destroys his own chances of becoming a sane and rational person. Because of this choice he also becomes a "buried child." Indeed, in some ways, there is a "buried child" in all people.

Analysis of Sample English Paper 2

After reading Sam's essay, you may feel that you haven't learned much that you didn't already know about the play. Part of the problem is that Sam argues that the play is simply about "the disintegration of the family," an obvious point that few readers of *Buried Child* would fail to recognize. Sam doesn't seem aware of the fact that Shepard uses the status of the family as a means of getting at broader and therefore more generalizable statements about life. As a result, the paper fulfills the basic requirements of the assignment (it does analyze the play and use supporting examples), but it doesn't enlighten readers or challenge them to reconsider the play. In other words, it lacks a crucial component of all outstanding papers: the student's willingness to go beyond basic requirements.

Most of what Sam uses as support is merely a recounting of incidents or dialogue. Although he uses them in the proper places in his paper, they don't provide any new information; they don't suggest that Sam has thought deeply about the work. He needs to explain what the incidents mean, supporting his interpretation with other information from the play. For example, he tells readers, "It is safe to say that when someone doesn't or chooses not to recognize a member of the family destruction is close." He then uses common knowledge to support this proposition.

Although writers need to assume that they share with readers a certain amount of knowledge, they shouldn't use this knowledge to support a claim about a text. Such common knowledge is just too general. It could apply to almost any text, which means that it isn't very revealing about individual texts such as *Buried Child*. The support must come from the play itself. It is also true that literary texts of any depth often force us to question and discard this type of common knowledge. Sam should explain why Dodge and Tilden refuse to recognize Vince, using what he has learned about the family from the play. It is clear that the family is close to destroying itself; Sam doesn't need to point out this fact to readers. But as the analyst, he needs to explain *why*.

Sam, however, seems intent on avoiding explanations, content to limit his writing to a series of truisms. Notice how often he says that one thing "means," "represents," or "symbolizes" something else without explaining why. For example, readers don't know why "this testimony shows the lack of understanding and trust between Tilden and his family" (paragraph 2), or why the "face inside his face . . . symbolizes the link between Vince and his strange family" (paragraph 4). These may be valid interpretations, but Sam needs to explain what led him to them if he wants readers to follow the same path and reach the same conclusions. Without an explanation, such statements make it seem as though he is trying to force readers into accepting his interpretations at face value. But few readers will be inclined to do so. They need Sam to connect the symbols he perceives into a coherent reading that will deepen their appreciation of the play.

Sam's paper is problematic on other grounds, perhaps the most annoying being the way he uses words inaccurately and imprecisely. For example, in paragraph 1, sentence 2, he tells us that the stage is "considerably bare." To what degree of emptiness is he referring? In the fourth sentence, he refers to the play as "this book," which is simply inaccurate. Then, in paragraph 2, sentence 9, he calls Tilden's claims of innocence "testimony," which reflects a misunderstanding of what this word means.

In general, Sam's paper has the form of an analysis, but it falls short of being a good one. What he identifies as the theme is so obvious that it doesn't lend itself to analysis and argument, so the paper lacks any convincing explanation of what the play means. This difficulty, combined with the imprecision in his writing, makes Sam's an average paper.

Guide for Reading

The following paper is very weak for several reasons. Robert's claim cannot really by called a thesis because it doesn't make a definitive statement about any aspect of the play and therefore isn't an arguable point. In an effort to develop this idea, he has focused on summarizing parts of the action and adding a small amount of interpretation or explanation. Although he does say something about the action in the play, Robert doesn't go beyond the surface, producing a paper that repeatedly states the obvious. Notice how most paragraphs begin with a reference to a particular part of the text, followed by a comment or two on what this part might mean. This pattern is a good indication that the writer is looking for something to say instead of being guided by a central theme. Finally, Robert's sentences are similar enough in length to give his paper a monotonous rhythm. The combination of these problems makes this paper an inadequate response to the assignment.

SAMPLE ENGLISH PAPER 3

Sam Shepard's *Buried Child*

Robert A (a freshman)

Sam Shepard's play Buried Child is a study of what results from the failure to live up to the expectations of one's self and of others. The story encompasses two major themes: that of failure and that of cyclical change that results from the aging process, from dependence to independence, and back again.

Dodge starts out obsessed with the idea of becoming the typical, midwestern American. He has a wife, sons, and a productive farm. At this point in his life his dreams have been fulfilled and his future is set before him. His sons will take over the family property and the family name. He has every reason to believe that his sons Tilden and Bradley will turn out to be competent and responsible men.

At this point the conflict arises. Dodge's wife has an unexpected child, and he is sure that it is not his own. This awkward turn of events is a threat to his dreams of having the ideal American family; it is a disgrace to the family name and a disruption of the orderly succession of generations.

The reader is led to believe that Tilden is the father of the child. Dodge tells us that he and his wife have not slept together for six years prior to the child's birth. Also, Dodge tells the reader that Tilden was the only one who paid any attention to it.

The Characters spend the rest of their lives trying to cover up this problem. In his attempts, Dodge goes as far as killing the child. Halie, the mother of the child, creates an imaginary biography for the child. She makes him out to be an all-American hero. Dodge spends the rest of his life sitting on the couch, drinking cheap whiskey and watching television. Bradley, Dodge's other son, has lost his leg (allegedly to a power saw) and becomes a cripple, in his case a physical cripple.

The story begins with the reader observing Dodge, now a decaying elderly man who is sitting in front of the television. Once an independent, self-sufficient farmer, he is now at the mercy of others. He is like a child, reverting back to a state of total dependence on his family.

The reader is given the picture of a family whose members are seemingly detached from one another. Halie speaks to Dodge as a nagging Mother speaks to her young, helpless child. He pays as much attention to her as she pays to him. At one point in the story, she goes as far as having his hair cut when she is expecting company. She still wishes hers to appear like a normal family.

The next character to come on stage is Tilden, who is carrying a basket of vegetables from the back yard, a yard which supposedly has not been sowed for at least thirty years. This suggests to the reader that there is new life continuing the cycle. The reader knows that something of life is out there. Tilden brings in corn from the yard, and covers Dodge up with the husks, suggesting a burial of sorts. This would explain one of the many interpretations of the metaphor in the title. Dodge is now a buried child in the sense that he is someone with a child-like dependence who is now actually covered. At the same time, the infant he has murdered is buried in the yard outside.

The next series of action occurs when Tilden's son, Vince, after being away for six years, comes to visit. Accompanying him is his girlfriend, Shelly, who is a total outsider to the situation. She is expecting to see what Vince has prepared her for, a typical Mid-western farm family, like the ones depicted in the portraits of Norman Rockwell. Her illusion is shattered as soon as she enters. She finds herself alone with Dodge, and is shocked because he is not what she expected to find. Soon after, Tilden enters, and seems not to know who Vince is at all. Shelly demands to know why everyone is acting so strangely. She is shocked when Vince leaves again to get his grandfather a bottle of whiskey. While he is gone, Halie returns with a tipsy preacher. Dodge begins explaining to Shelly how all of this has come about. He explains to her that his wife gave birth to an unexpected child whom he murdered. He tells her that all along, they have been trying to cover up. With his death, there is no longer any reason to cover up.

Dodge, as he is dying, formally leaves his farm to Vince. The reader sees the drunken Vince, waxing poetically about how he will live his days, as a typical mid-western farmer. The reader knows he will be just as disillusioned as Dodge was. While this is happening, Tilden returns with the buried child. At this point the secret is uncovered, and the cycle has come back full swing.

Analysis of Sample English Paper 3

Robert's essay is a plot summary with a small portion of analysis thrown in haphazardly. It is not an adequate response to the assignment and needs to be completely reworked before it can be considered an analytical essay.

In the first paragraph, Robert tries to establish a thesis by stating that *Buried Child* is a story of failure and cyclical change. As a thesis statement or point to be argued, this one has some potential, but it is never realized. If in this first paragraph Robert had mentioned some of the reasons for the failure and the change (the burial of the child, sublimation of the tragedy, and so on), he would have given himself and readers a guide for his analysis. Instead, he loses sight of the real goal of the paper and focuses on summarizing the plot.

Parts of the essay do contain some interpretation. In paragraphs 2 through 4, Robert provides background information on the family that is necessary for understanding their present condition. The problem is that he doesn't explain why any of this happened or what the results of these incidents were. Readers need to know how the unexpected child is a threat to Dodge's dream, what chain of events resulted from this unfortunate occurrence, why it's important that Tilden might be the father, and how these events caused the family to fail. Instead of trying to explain or answer these questions, Robert tells more of the story. What he tells shows the family's failure, but the play does the same thing.

A play such as *Buried Child* is full of clues that need to be examined carefully if it is to be understood at all. Among these are the stage directions and the dress and appearance of the characters (suggestion number 1). It seems that Robert relied only on the action of the play and ignored other aspects that are equally important.

Moreover, we can't help but notice the style of Robert's writing. As mentioned earlier, too many of the sentences are about the same length, which gives the paper a monotonous rhythm that makes reading difficult. Thus, even if he had managed to do more than merely summarize the play, his paper wouldn't be outstanding because it's awkwardly written at the sentence level. Although combining some of these short sentences into longer ones would help the paper a great deal, this sort of stylistic fix is no substitute for having something meaningful to say.

Sentence Lesson

Learning how to vary sentence patterns requires some discipline, although the task itself is relatively easy. The discipline involves forcing yourself to reread your sentences and to evaluate how long they are and what pattern they follow. For example, if you rarely subordinate parts of your sentences with constructions beginning with such words as "because," "as," and "although," chances are that you won't achieve much variety. The easiest way to increase variety is by combining short sentences into longer ones.

Consider the sentences below, which come from Robert's paper:

English

1. The reader is led to believe that Tilden is the father of the child. Dodge tells us that he and his wife have not slept together for six years prior to the child's birth. Also, Dodge tells the reader that Tilden was the only one who paid any attention to it.

Although these sentences have other problems that combining won't solve, we can join the first two easily, producing the following:

2. The reader is led to believe that Tilden is the father of the child when Dodge tells us that he and his wife have not slept together for six years prior to the child's birth. Also, Dodge tells the reader that Tilden was the only one who paid any attention to it.

A more thorough revision, of course, would also fix the problem inherent in shifting from using "the reader" and "us" in the same paragraph (Robert doesn't seem to know who his audience is):

3. Dodge makes two statements that suggest that Tilden is the child's father: First, he says that he and his wife haven't slept together for six years; and second, he says that Tilden is the only person who paid any attention to the child.

Writing Assignments

The following assignments increase in difficulty, and the subsequent assignments demand that you understand more about drama and literary analysis. The first is essentially a character analysis, the second is a comparison/contrast of theme, and the third is an analysis of genre. The plays themselves also become more difficult to work with, moving from the accepted and often-performed *Death of a Salesman* to Sam Shepard's experimental works, relegated to Off-Broadway theater.

1. Pretend that you have been cast as Willy Loman in *Death of a Salesman* or Josie in *Moon for the Misbegotten*. Describe the character you have chosen by analyzing his or her speech and actions and by paying close attention to the playwright's comments in the stage directions. Following this characterization, explain how you would play the character.
2. TYPE OF PAPER: Theme Analysis
SPECIFIC FOCUS: To determine a similar theme in the two plays *Death of a Salesman* and *A Long Day's Journey into Night*.
FORMAT: Comparison/Contrast. You are to explain that, in spite

of some substantial differences, these two plays share a theme.

A POSSIBLE WORKING OUTLINE:

a. Introduction—a brief discussion of the important differences in the two plays; a statement concerning the importance of recognizing the similarities; your thesis.

b. A full discussion of the shared theme as it is expressed in both plays.

c. A point-by-point discussion of how each play presents this theme. You will need to treat each point from each play in a separate paragraph. In other words, if the past of each family is a factor in their present condition, you will first discuss this as presented in *Death of a Salesman,* and follow it with a paragraph on the same topic for *A Long Day's Journey into Night.* This method works well if you have definite parallel points to discuss.

d. An alternative to the suggestion above is to discuss all the points for *Death of a Salesman* first and then do the same for *A Long Day's Journey into Night.* This method works well if there are no clear parallel points to compare directly.

e. Conclusion—a brief discussion of what these similarities mean. Remember that all of your points must be supported with specific references to both plays and with a complete explanation of how these examples support your thesis.

3. TYPE OF PAPER: Genre Analysis

SPECIFIC FOCUS: To determine whether Shepard's *Buried Child* or *Curse of the Starving Class* is tragedy or comedy, and whether that tragedy or comedy is in the realistic or the naturalistic mode.

FORMAT: Argument/Persuasion. (In other words, you are—with this essay—attempting to prove to your reader that your determination of genre is correct.)

A POSSIBLE WORKING OUTLINE:

a. Introduction—a brief discussion of the controversy about genre and the play you have chosen; a statement about the importance of resolving that conflict; your thesis.

b. A summary of the arguments in favor of the genre you have NOT chosen.

c. A comprehensive definition of the genre and mode you intend to discuss; specific examples from other works of literature to support your definition.

d. Several paragraphs in which you state your proof (that the play is tragedy or comedy, realistic or naturalistic), explain that proof, and support your ideas with specific references to the play.

Each reason you give in support of your claim must be discussed in a separate paragraph. You should have four to six good reasons.
e. Conclusion.

ENGLISH ASSIGNMENT 2

Course: **Contemporary Literature for Freshmen and Sophomores**

Write a 7–9 page essay comparing and contrasting two of the novels and/or plays we've discussed so far:
  Atwood, The Handmaid's Tale
  Pomerance, The Elephant Man
  Fugard, "Master Harold" . . . and the boys
  Thomas, The White Hotel

Come up with your own thesis. Build this essay around your own impressions of the texts (remember: using outside texts is not necessary). Use parenthetical citations to show the source of each passage you quote. Your audience is someone who has read both the texts you're discussing—and therefore does not need a cumbersome plot summary.

You might use the discussion question from our midterm as a model . . .

> Offred describes a conversation with Moira about the latter's being lesbian. Moira told her that "the balance of power was equal between women" (222). Both this novel and the play about J. Merrick show us a great deal about power and about relationships between men and women. Come up with a thesis about what a contemporary reader can learn from these two texts about power and about relationships between women and men. Write a thoughtful, clearly organized essay that uses specific references to both texts to support your point.

In this essay, as in that discussion question, I'll expect you to use specific references to support your point.

Remember that this assignment counts 20 per cent of your final grade. In grading your essay, I'll look for the same strengths I looked for in your midterm discussion question: clarity, directness, effective organization, and effective, correct use of sources. Your paper is to be typed (double-spaced, please) and should be free of serious grammatical errors.

Analysis of English Assignment 2

All of the works covered in this class were written during the last fifteen years, and some of the authors are experimenting with both form and content. The assignment calls for a substantial paper, indicated both by the number of careful instructions and by the percentage it counts in the final grade. It is in some way a culmination of the semester, asking that you use the reading and analytical skills you've learned to discover something in common between two works of literature.

The form of the essay is comparison/contrast, one that you should be familiar with. For this assignment, a good essay will have a claim, or thesis, that focuses on a similarity that is not readily obvious to someone reading the two works. You would want to discover a similarity in what at first appear to be two different themes. For example, one author focuses on race and another on gender; you discover that both present a struggle between the races or genders in which one side has social power and the other has moral power. This discovery, which comes only after careful reading and analysis, means that the two authors are dealing with the same concern, but in different ways.

When writing a comparison/contrast paper, you must discuss similarities and differences in some depth. Generally, the best way to proceed is to identify two or three larger issues, such as theme and character, as your major points of focus. The individual details that fill the works under analysis can then be discussed in terms of how they develop similar or different larger issues. Many students make the mistake of turning their comparison/contrast papers into mere lists: "These characters were different, but these other characters were the same"; "The plots were different, but the locales were the same," and so on. Such lists aren't particularly informative, and they certainly don't reveal much about your understanding of the work you've studied.

As in all essays that analyze works of literature, you must support your points with both examples and explanation. Even when this isn't stated, it is always good practice to cite the page (or act and scene) of any direct quotations you use. This assignment specifically requires that you do this in MLA style with parenthetical documentation, which is illustrated in the summary provided in the overview to writing in the humanities.

The last paragraph in the assignment is also very important. It describes the basis for evaluating your paper: "clarity, directness, effective organization, and effective, correct use of your sources." This means that you must write to inform your readers, not to impress them with your use of the language; that you must organize your essay so readers can follow your argument; and that your references must be well chosen and correctly documented. Clearly, then, this paper is not one that you can write in a hurry at the last minute. A good essay will result from careful reading, thoughtful analysis, and several revisions of your efforts to explain your discoveries.

From *The Handmaid's Tale,* by Margaret Atwood

21

It's hot in here, and too noisy. The women's voices rise around me, a soft chant that is too loud for me, after the days and days of silence. In the corner of the room there's a bloodstained sheet, bundled and tossed there, from when the waters broke. I hadn't noticed it before.

The room smells too, the air is close, they should open a window. The smell is of our own flesh, an organic smell, sweat and a tinge of iron, from the blood on the sheet, and another smell, more animal, that's coming, it must be, from Janine: a smell of dens, of inhabited caves, the smell of the plaid blanket on the bed where the cat gave birth on it, once, before she was spayed. Smell of matrix.

"Breathe, breathe," we chant, as we have been taught. "Hold, hold. Expel, expel, expel." We chant to the count of five. Five in, hold for five, out for five. Janine, her eyes closed, tries to slow her breathing. Aunt Elizabeth feels for the contractions.

Now Janine is restless, she wants to walk. The two women help her off the bed, support her on either side while she paces. A contraction hits her, she doubles over. One of the women kneels and rubs her back. We are all good at this, we've had lessons. I recognize Ofglen, my shopping partner, sitting two away from me. The soft chanting envelops us like a membrane.

A Martha arrives, with a tray: a jug of fruit juice, the kind you make from powder, grape it looks like, and a stack of paper cups. She sets it on the rug in front of the chanting women. Ofglen, not missing a beat, pours, and the paper cups pass down the line.

I receive a cup, lean to the side to pass it, and the woman next to me says, low in my ear, "Are you looking for anyone?"

"Moira," I say, just as low. "Dark hair, freckles."

"No," the woman says. I don't know this woman, she wasn't at the Center with me, though I've seen her, shopping. "But I'll watch for you."

"Are you?" I say.

"Alma," she says. "What's your real name?"

I want to tell her there was an Alma with me at the Center. I want to tell her my name, but Aunt Elizabeth raises her head, staring around the room, she must have heard a break in the chant, so there's no more time. Sometimes you can find things out, on Birth Days. But there would be no point in asking about Luke. He wouldn't be where any of these women would be likely to see him.

The chanting goes on, it begins to catch me. It's hard work, you're supposed to concentrate. Identify with your body, said Aunt Elizabeth. Already I can feel slight pains, in my belly, and my breasts are heavy. Janine screams, a weak scream, partway between a scream and a groan.

"She's going into transition," says Aunt Elizabeth.

One of the helpers wipes Janine's forehead with a damp cloth. Janine is sweating now, her hair is escaping in wisps from the elastic band, bits of it stick to her forehead and neck. Her flesh is damp, saturated, lustrous.

"Pant! pant! pant!" we chant.

"I want to go outside," says Janine. "I want to go for a walk. I feel fine. I have to go to the can."

We all know that she's in transition, she doesn't know what she's doing. Which of these statements is true? Probably the last one. Aunt Elizabeth signals, two women stand beside the portable toilet, Janine is lowered gently onto it. There's another smell, added to the others in the room. Janine groans again, her head bent over so all we can see is her hair. Crouching like that, she's like a doll, an old one that's been pillaged and discarded, in some corner, akimbo.

Janine is up again and walking. "I want to sit down," she says. How long have we been here? Minutes or hours. I'm sweating now, my dress under my arms is drenched, I taste salt on my upper lip, the false pains clench at me, the others feel it too, I can tell by the way they sway. Janine is sucking on an ice cube. Then, after that, inches away or miles, "No," she screams. "Oh no, oh no oh no." It's her second baby, she had another child, once, I know that from the Center, when she used to cry about it at night, like the rest of us only more noisily. So she ought to be able to remember this, what it's like, what's coming. But who can remember pain, once it's over? All that remains of it is a shadow, not in the mind even, in the flesh. Pain marks you, but too deep to see. Out of sight, out of mind.

Someone has spiked the grape juice. Someone has pinched a bottle, from downstairs. It won't be the first time at such a gathering; but they'll turn a blind eye. We too need our orgies.

"Dim the lights," says Aunt Elizabeth. "Tell her it's time."

Someone stands, moves to the wall, the light in the room fades to twilight, our voices dwindle to a chorus of creaks, of husky whispers, like grasshoppers in a field at night. Two leave the room, two others lead Janine to the Birthing Stool, where she sits on the lower of the two seats. She's calmer now, air sucks evenly into her lungs, we lean forward, tensed, the muscles in our backs and bellies hurt from the strain. It's coming, it's coming, like a bugle, a call to arms, like a wall falling, we can feel it like a heavy stone moving down, pulled down inside us, we think we will burst. We grip each other's hands, we are no longer single.

The Commander's Wife hurries in, in her ridiculous white cotton nightgown, her spindly legs sticking out beneath it. Two of the Wives in their blue dresses and veils hold her by the arms, as if she needs it; she has a tight little smile on her face, like a hostess at a party she'd rather not be giving. She must know what we think of her. She scrambles onto the Birthing Stool, sits on the seat behind and above Janine, so that Janine is framed by her: her skinny legs come down on either side, like the arms of an eccentric chair. Oddly enough, she's wearing white cotton socks, and bedroom slippers, blue ones made of fuzzy material, like toilet-seat covers. But we pay no attention to the Wife, we hardly even see her, our eyes are on Janine. In the dim light, in her white gown, she glows like a moon in cloud.

She's grunting now, with the effort. "Push, push, push," we whisper. "Relax. Pant. Push, push, push." We're with her, we're the same as her, we're drunk. Aunt Elizabeth kneels, with an outspread towel to catch the baby, here's the crowning, the glory, the head, purple and smeared with yoghurt, another push and it slithers out, slick with fluid and blood, into our waiting. Oh praise.

We hold our breath as Aunt Elizabeth inspects it: a girl, poor thing, but so far so good, at least there's nothing wrong with it, that can be seen, hands, feet, eyes, we silently count, everything is in place. Aunt Elizabeth, holding the baby looks up at us and smiles. We smile too, we are one smile, tears run down our cheeks, we are so happy.

Our happiness is part memory. What I remember is Luke, with me in the hospital, standing beside my head, holding my hand, in the green gown and white mask they gave him. Oh, he said, oh Jesus, breath coming out in wonder. That night he couldn't go to sleep at all, he said, he was so high.

Aunt Elizabeth is gently washing the baby off, it isn't crying much, it stops. As quietly as possible, so as not to startle it, we rise, crowd around Janine, squeezing her, patting her. She's crying too. The two Wives in blue help the third Wife, the Wife of the household, down from the Birthing Stool and over to the bed, where they lay her down and tuck her in. The baby, washed now and quiet, is placed ceremoniously in her arms. The Wives from downstairs are crowding in now, pushing among us, pushing us aside. They talk too loud, some of them are still carrying their plates, their coffee cups, their wine glasses, some of them are still chewing, they cluster around the bed, the mother and child, cooing and congratulating. Envy radiates from them, I can smell it, faint wisps of acid, mingled with their perfume. The Commander's Wife looks down at the baby as if it's a bouquet of flowers: something she's won, a tribute.

The Wives are here to bear witness to the naming. It's the Wives who do the naming, around here.

"Angela," says the Commander's Wife.

"Angela, Angela," the Wives repeat, twittering. "What a sweet name! Oh, she's perfect! Oh, she's wonderful!"

We stand between Janine and the bed, so she won't have to see this. Someone gives her a drink of grape juice, I hope there's wine in it, she's still having the pains, for the afterbirth, she's crying helplessly, burnt-out miserable tears. Nevertheless we are jubilant, it's a victory, for all of us. We've done it.

She'll be allowed to nurse the baby, for a few months, they believe in mother's milk. After that she'll be transferred, to see if she can do it again, with someone else who needs a turn. But she'll never be sent to the Colonies, she'll never be declared Unwoman. That is her reward.

The Birthmobile is waiting outside, to deliver us back to our own households. The doctors are still in their van; their faces appear at the window, white blobs, like the faces of sick children confined to the house. One of them opens the door and comes toward us.

"Was it all right?" he asks, anxious.

"Yes," I say. By now I'm wrung out, exhausted. My breasts are painful, they're leaking a little. Fake milk, it happens this way with some of us. We sit on our benches, facing one another, as we are transported; we're without emotion now, almost without feeling, we might be bundles of red cloth. We ache. Each of us holds in her lap a phantom, a ghost baby. What confronts us, now the excitement's over, is our own failure. Mother, I think. Wherever you may be. Can you hear me? You wanted a women's culture. Well, now there is one. It isn't what you meant, but it exists. Be thankful for small mercies.

From "Master Harold"... and the boys
by Athol Fugard

SAM All right, Hally, all right. What you got for homework?

HALLY Bullshit, as usual. (*Opens an exercise book and reads*) "Write five hundred words describing an annual event of cultural or historical significance."

SAM That should be easy enough for you.

HALLY And also plain bloody boring. You know what he wants, don't you? One of their useless old ceremonies. The commemoration of the landing of the 1820 Settlers, or if it's going to be culture, Carols by Candlelight every Christmas.

SAM It's an impressive sight. Make a good description, Hally. All those candles glowing in the dark and the people singing hymns.

HALLY And it's called religious hysteria. (*Intense irritation*) Please, Sam! Just leave me alone and let me get on with it. I'm not in the mood for games this afternoon. And remember my Mom's orders . . . you're to help Willie with the windows. Come on now, I don't want any more nonsense in here.

SAM Okay, Hally, okay.

(HALLY *settles down to his homework; determined preparations . . . pen, ruler, exercise book, dictionary, another cake . . . all of which will lead to nothing*)

(SAM *waltzes over to* WILLIE *and starts to replace tables and chairs. He practices a ballroom step while doing so.* WILLIE *watches. When* SAM *is finished,* WILLIE *tries*) Good! But just a little bit quicker on the turn and only move in to her after she's crossed over. What about this one? (*Another step. When* SAM *is finished,* WILLIE *again has to go*)

Much better. See what happens when you just relax and enjoy yourself? Remember that in two weeks' time and you'll be all right.

WILLIE But I haven't got partner, Boet Sam.

SAM Maybe Hilda will turn up tonight.

WILLIE No, Boet Sam. (*Reluctantly*) I gave her a good hiding.

SAM You mean a bad one.

WILLIE Good bad one.

SAM Then you mustn't complain either. Now you pay the price for losing your temper.

WILLIE I also pay two pounds ten shilling entrance fee.

SAM They'll refund you if you withdraw now.

WILLIE (*Appalled*) You mean, don't dance?

From *"Master Harold"... and the boys* by Athol Fugard. Copyright © 1982 by Athol Fugard. Reprinted by permission of Alfred A. Knopf, Inc.

SAM Yes.
WILLIE No! I wait too long and I practice too hard. If I find me new partner, you think I can be ready in two weeks? I ask Madam for my leave now and we practice every day.
SAM Quickstep non-stop for two weeks. World record, Willie, but you'll be mad at the end.
WILLIE No jokes, Boet Sam.
SAM I'm not joking.
WILLIE So then what?
SAM Find Hilda. Say you're sorry and promise you won't beat her again.
WILLIE No.
SAM Then withdraw. Try again next year.
WILLIE No.
SAM Then I give up.
WILLIE Haaikona, Boet Sam, you can't.
SAM What do you mean, I can't? I'm telling you: I give up.
WILLIE (*Adamant*) No! (*Accusingly*) It was you who start me ballroom dancing.
SAM So?
WILLIE Before that I use to be happy. And is you and Miriam who bring me to Hilda and say here's partner for you.
SAM What are you saying, Willie?
WILLIE You!
SAM But me what? To blame?
WILLIE Yes.
SAM Willie . . . ? (*Bursts into laughter*)
WILLIE And now all you do is make jokes at me. You wait. When Miriam leaves you is my turn to laugh. Ha! Ha! Ha!
SAM (*He can't take* WILLIE *seriously any longer*) She can leave me tonight! I know what to do. (*Bowing before an imaginary partner*) May I have the pleasure? (*He dances and sings*)
"Just a fellow with his pillow . . .
Dancin' like a willow . . .
In an autumn breeze . . ."
WILLIE There you go again!
(SAM *goes on dancing and singing*)
Boet Sam!
SAM There's the answer to your problem! Judges' announcement in two weeks' time: "Ladies and gentlemen, the winner in the open section . . . Mr. Willie Malopo and his pillow!"
(*This is too much for a now really angry* WILLIE. *He goes for* SAM, *but the latter is too quick for him and puts* HALLY's *table between the two of them*)
HALLY (*Exploding*) For Christ's sake, you two!

WILLIE (*Still trying to get at* SAM) I donner you, Sam! Struesgod!

SAM (*Still laughing*) Sorry, Willie . . . Sorry . . .

HALLY Sam! Willie! (*Grabs his ruler and gives* WILLIE *a vicious whack on the bum*) How the hell am I supposed to concentrate with the two of you behaving like bloody children!

WILLIE Hit him too!

HALLY Shut up, Willie.

WILLIE He started jokes again.

HALLY Get back to your work. You too, Sam. (*His ruler*) Do you want another one, Willie?

(SAM *and* WILLIE *return to their work.* HALLY *uses the opportunity to escape from his unsuccessful attempt at homework. He struts around like a little despot, ruler in hand, giving vent to his anger and frustration*) Suppose a customer had walked in then? Or the Park Superintendent. And seen the two of you behaving like a pair of hooligans. That would have been the end of my mother's license, you know. And your jobs! Well, this is the end of it. From now on there will be no more of your ballroom nonsense in here. This is a business establishment, not a bloody New Brighton dancing school. I've been far too lenient with the two of you. (*Behind the counter for a green cool drink and a dollop of ice cream. He keeps up his tirade as he prepares it*) But what really makes me bitter is that I allow you chaps a little freedom in here when business is bad and what do you do with it? The foxtrot! Specially you, Sam. There's more to life than trotting around a dance floor and I thought at least you knew it.

SAM It's a harmless pleasure, Hally. It doesn't hurt anybody.

HALLY It's also a rather simple one, you know.

SAM You reckon so! Have you ever tried?

HALLY Of course not.

SAM Why don't you? Now.

HALLY What do you mean? Me dance?

SAM Yes. I'll show you a simple step—the waltz—then you try it.

HALLY What will that prove?

SAM That it might not be as easy as you think.

HALLY I didn't say it was easy. I said it was simple—like in simple-minded, meaning mentally retarded. You can't exactly say it challenges the intellect.

SAM It does other things.

HALLY Such as?

SAM Make people happy.

HALLY (*The glass in his hand*) So do American cream sodas with ice cream. For God's sake, Sam, you're not asking me to take ballroom dancing serious, are you?

SAM Yes.

HALLY (*Sigh of defeat*) Oh, well, so much for trying to give you a decent education. I've obviously achieved nothing.
SAM You still haven't told me what's wrong with admiring something that's beautiful and then trying to do it yourself.
HALLY Nothing. But we happen to be talking about a foxtrot, not a thing of beauty.
SAM But that is just what I'm saying. If you were to see two champions doing, two masters of the art . . . !
HALLY Oh, God, I give up. So now it's also art!
SAM Ja.
HALLY There's a limit, Sam. Don't confuse art and entertainment.
SAM So then what is art?
HALLY You want a definition?
SAM Ja.
HALLY (*He realizes he has got to be careful. He gives the matter a lot of thought before answering*) Philosophers have been trying to do that for centuries. What is Art? What is Life? But basically I suppose it's . . . the giving of meaning to matter.
SAM Nothing to do with beautiful?
HALLY It goes beyond that. It's the giving of form to the formless.
SAM Ja, well, maybe it's not art, then. But I still say it's beautiful.
HALLY I'm sure the word you mean to use is entertaining.
SAM (*Adamant*) No. Beautiful. And if you want proof, come along to the Centenary Hall in New Brighton in two weeks' time.
(*The mention of the Centenary Hall draws* WILLIE *over to them*)
HALLY What for? I've seen the two of you prancing around in here often enough.
SAM (*He laughs*) This isn't the real thing, Hally. We're just playing around in here.
HALLY So? I can use my imagination.
SAM And what do you get?
HALLY A lot of people dancing around and having a so-called good time.
SAM That all?
HALLY Well, basically it is that, surely.
SAM No, it isn't. Your imagination hasn't helped you at all. There's a lot more to it than that. We're getting ready for the championships, Hally, not just another dance. There's going to be a lot of people, all right, and they're going to have a good time, but they'll only be spectators, sitting around and watching. It's just the competitors out there on the dance floor. Party decorations and fancy lights all around the walls! The ladies in beautiful evening dresses!
HALLY My mother's got one of those, Sam, and, quite frankly, it's an embarrassment every time she wears it.
SAM (*Undeterred*) Your imagination left out the excitement.

(HALLY *scoffs*)
Oh, yes. The finalists are not going to be out there just to have a good time. One of those couples will be the 1950 Eastern Province Champions. And your imagination left out the music.

WILLIE Mr. Elijah Gladman Guzana and his Orchestral Jazzonions.

SAM The sound of the big band, Hally. Trombone, trumpet, tenor and alto sax. And then, finally, your imagination also left out the climax of the evening when the dancing is finished, the judges have stopped whispering among themselves and the Master of Ceremonies collects their scorecards and goes up onto the stage to announce the winners.

HALLY All right. So you make it sound like a bit of a do. It's an occasion. Satisfied?

SAM (*Victory*) So you admit that!

HALLY Emotionally yes, intellectually no.

SAM Well, I don't know what you mean by that, all I'm telling you is that it is going to be *the* event of the year in New Brighton. It's been sold out for two weeks already. There's only standing room left. We've got competitors coming from Kingwilliamstown, East London, Port Alfred.

HALLY (*starts pacing thoughtfully*)

HALLY Tell me a bit more.

SAM I thought you weren't interested . . . intellectually.

HALLY (*Mysteriously*) I've got my reasons.

SAM What do you want to know?

HALLY It takes place every year?

SAM Yes. But only every third year in New Brighton. It's East London's turn to have the championships next year.

HALLY Which, I suppose, makes it an even more significant event.

SAM Ah ha! We're getting somewhere. Our "occasion" is now a "significant event."

HALLY I wonder.

SAM What?

HALLY I wonder if I would get away with it.

SAM But what?

HALLY (*To the table and his exercise book*) "Write five hundred words describing an annual event of cultural or historical significance." Would I be stretching poetic license a little too far if I called your ballroom championships a cultural event?

SAM You mean . . . ?

HALLY You think we could get five hundred words out of it, Sam?

SAM Victor Sylvester has written a whole book on ballroom dancing.

WILLIE You going to write about it, Master Hally?

HALLY Yes, gentlemen, that is precisely what I am considering doing. Old Doc Bromely—he's my English teacher—is going to argue with me, of course. He doesn't like natives. But I'll point out to him that in strict anthropological terms the culture of a primitive black society includes its dancing and singing. To put my thesis in a nutshell: The war-dance has been replaced by the waltz. But it still amounts to the same thing: the release of primitive emotions through movement. Shall we give it a go?

SAM I'm ready.

WILLIE Me also.

HALLY Ha! This will teach the old bugger a lesson. (*Decision taken*) Right. Let's get ourselves organized. (*This means another cake on the table. He sits*) I think you've given me enough general atmosphere, Sam, but to build the tension and suspense I need facts. (*Pencil poised*)

WILLIE Give him facts, Boet Sam.

HALLY What you call the climax . . . how many finalists?

SAM Six couples.

HALLY (*Making notes*) Go on. Give me the picture.

SAM Spectators seated right around the hall. (WILLIE *becomes a spectator*)

HALLY . . . and it's a full house.

SAM At one end, on the stage, Gladman and his Orchestral Jazzonions. At the other end is a long table with the three judges. The six finalists go onto the dance floor and take up their positions. When they are ready and the spectators have settled down, the Master of Ceremonies goes to the microphone. To start with, he makes some jokes to get the people laughing . . .

HALLY Good touch! (*As he writes*) ". . . creating a relaxed atmosphere which will change to one of tension and drama as the climax is approached."

SAM (*Onto a chair to act out the M.C.*) "Ladies and gentlemen, we come now to the great moment you have all been waiting for this evening . . . . The finals of the 1950 Eastern Province Open Ballroom Dancing Championships. But first let me introduce the finalists! Mr. and Mrs. Welcome Tchabalala from Kingwilliamstown . . ."

WILLIE (*He applauds after every name*) Is when the people clap their hands and whistle and make a lot of noise, Master Hally.

SAM "Mr. Mulligan Njikelane and Miss Nomhle Nkonyeni of Grahamstown; Mr. and Mrs. Norman Nchinga from Port Alfred; Mr. Fats Bokolane and Miss Dina Plaatjies from East London; Mr. Sipho Dugu and Mrs. Mable Magada from Peddie; and from New Brighton our very own Mr. Willie Malopo and Miss Hilda Samuels."

(WILLIE *can't believe his ears. He abandons his role as spectator and scrambles into position as a finalist*)

WILLIE Relaxed and ready to romance!

SAM The applause dies down. When everybody is silent, Gladman lifts up his sax, nods at the Orchestral Jazzonions . . .
WILLIE Play the jukebox please, Boet Sam!
SAM I also only got bus fare, Willie.
HALLY Hold it, everybody. (*Heads for the cash register behind the counter*) How much is in the till, Sam?
SAM Three shillings. Hally . . . your Mom counted it before she left.
(HALLY *hesitates*)
HALLY Sorry, Willie. You know how she carried on the last time I did it. We'll just have to pool our combined imaginations and hope for the best. (*Returns to the table*) Back to work. How are the points scored, Sam?
SAM Maximum of ten points each for individual style, deportment, rhythm and general appearance.
WILLIE Must I start?
HALLY Hold it for a second, Willie. And penalties?
SAM For what?
HALLY For doing something wrong. Say you stumble or bump into somebody . . . do they take off any points?
SAM (*Aghast*) Hally . . . !
HALLY When you're dancing. If you and your partner collide into another couple.
(HALLY *can get no further.* SAM *has collapsed with laughter. He explains to* WILLIE)
SAM If me and Miriam bump into you and Hilda . . .
(WILLIE *joins him in another good laugh*)
Hally, Hally . . . !
HALLY (*Perplexed*) Why? What did I say?
SAM There's no collisions out there, Hally. Nobody trips or stumbles or bumps into anybody else. That's what that moment is all about. To be one of those finalists on that dance floor is like . . . like being in a dream about a world in which accidents don't happen.
HALLY (*Genuinely moved by* SAM's *image*) Jesus, Sam! That's beautiful!
WILLIE (*Can endure waiting no longer*) I'm starting! (WILLIE *dances while* SAM *talks*)
SAM Of course it is. That's what I've been trying to say to you all afternoon. And it's beautiful because that is what we want life to be like. But instead, like you said, Hally, we're bumping into each other all the time. Look at the three of us this afternoon: I've bumped into Willie, the two of us have bumped into you, you've bumped into your mother, she bumping into your Dad. . . . . None of us knows the steps and there's no music playing. And it doesn't stop with us. The whole world is doing it all the time. Open a newspaper and what do you read? America has bumped into Russia, England is bumping into

India, rich man bumps into poor man. Those are big collisions, Hally. They make for a lot of bruises. People get hurt in all that bumping, and we're sick and tired of it now. It's been going on for too long. Are we never going to get it right? . . . Learn to dance life like champions instead of always being just a bunch of beginners at it?

HALLY (*Deep and sincere admiration of the man*) You've got a vision, Sam!

SAM Not just me. What I'm saying to you is that everybody's got it. That's why there's only standing room left for the Centenary Hall in two weeks' time. For as long as the music lasts, we are going to see six couples get it right, the way we want life to be.

HALLY But is that the best we can do, Sam . . . watch six finalists dreaming about the way it should be?

SAM I don't know. But it starts with that. Without the dream we won't know what we're going for. And anyway I reckon there are a few people who have got past just dreaming about it and are trying for something real. Remember that thing we read once in the paper about the Mahatma Gandhi? Going without food to stop those riots in India?

HALLY You're right. He certainly was trying to teach people to get the steps right.

SAM And the Pope.

HALLY Yes, he's another one. Our old General Smuts as well, you know. He's also out there dancing. You know, Sam, when you come to think of it, that's what the United Nations boils down to . . . a dancing school for politicians!

SAM And let's hope they learn.

HALLY (*A little surge of hope*) You're right. We mustn't despair. Maybe there's some hope for mankind after all. Keep it up, Willie. (*Back to his table with determination*) This is a lot bigger than I thought. So what have we got? Yes, our title: "A World Without Collisions."

SAM That sounds good! "A World Without Collisions."

HALLY Subtitle: "Global Politics on the Dance Floor." No. A bit too heavy, hey? What about "Ballroom Dancing as a Political Vision"?

(*The telephone rings.* SAM *answers it*)

SAM St. George's Park Tea Room . . . Yes, Madam . . . Hally, it's your Mom.

HALLY (*Back to reality*) Oh, God, yes! I'd forgotten all about that. Shit! Remember my words, Sam? Just when you're enjoying yourself, someone or something will come along and wreck everything.

SAM You haven't heard what she's got to say yet.

HALLY Public telephone?

SAM No.

HALLY Does she sound happy or unhappy?

SAM I couldn't tell. (*Pause*) She's waiting, Hally.
HALLY (*To the telephone*) Hello, Mom . . . No, everything is okay here. Just doing my homework. . . . What's your news? . . . You've what? . . . (*Pause. He takes the receiver away from his ear for a few seconds. In the course of* HALLY'S *telephone conversation,* SAM *and* WILLIE *discretely position the stacked tables and chairs.* HALLY *places the receiver back to his ear*) Yes, I'm still here. Oh, well, I give up now. Why did you do it, Mom? . . . Well, I just hope you know what you've let us in for. . . . (*Loudly*) I said I hope you know what you've let us in for! It's the end of the peace and quiet we've been having. (*Softly*) Where is he? (*Normal voice*) He can't hear us from in there. But for God's sake, Mom, what happened? I told you to be firm with him. . . . Then you and the nurses should have held him down, taken his crutches away. . . . I know only too well he's my father! . . . I'm not being disrespectful, but I'm sick and tired of emptying stinking chamberpots full of phlegm and piss. . . . Yes, I do! When you're not there, he asks *me* to do it. . . . If you really want to know the truth, that's why I've got no appetite for my food. . . . Yes! There's a lot of things you don't know about. For your information, I still haven't got that science textbook I need. And you know why? He borrowed the money you gave me for it. . . . Because I didn't want to start another fight between you two. . . . He says that every time. . . . All right, Mom! (*Viciously*) Then just remember to start hiding your bag away again, because he'll be at your purse before long for money for booze. And when he's well enough to come down here, you better keep an eye on the till as well, because that is also going to develop a leak. . . . Then don't complain to me when he starts his old tricks. . . . Yes, you do. I get it from you on one side and from him on the other, and it makes life hell for me. I'm not going to be the peacemaker anymore. I'm warning you now: when the two of you start fighting again, I'm leaving home. . . . Mom, if you start crying, I'm going to put down the receiver. . . . Okay . . . (*Lowering his voice to a vicious whisper*) Okay, Mom. I heard you. (*Desperate*) No. . . . Because I don't want to. I'll see him when I get home! Mom! . . . (*Pause. When he speaks again, his tone changes completely. It is not simply pretense. We sense a genuine emotional conflict*) Welcome home, chum! . . . What's that? . . . Don't be silly, Dad. You being home is just about the best news in the world. . . . I bet you are. Bloody depressing there with everybody going on about their ailments, hey! . . . How you feeling? . . . Good . . . Here as well, pal. Coming down cats and dogs. . . . That's right. Just the day for a kip and a toss in your old Uncle Ned. . . . Everything's just hunky-dory on my side, Dad. . . . Well, to start with, there's a nice pile of comics for you on the counter. . . . Yes, old Kemple brought them in. *Batman and Robin,*

Submariner ... just your cup of tea ... I will. ... Yes, we'll spin a few yarns tonight. ... Okay, chum, see you in a little while. ... No, I promise. I'll come straight home. ... (*Pause—his mother comes back on the phone*) Mom? Okay. I'll lock up now. ... What? ... Oh, the brandy ... Yes, I'll remember! ... I'll put it in my suitcase now, for God's sake. I know well enough what will happen if he doesn't get it. ... (*Places a bottle of brandy on the counter*) I *was* kind to him, Mom. I didn't say anything nasty! ... All right. Bye. (*End of telephone conversation. A desolate* HALLY *doesn't move. A strained silence*)

SAM (*Quietly*) That sounded like a bad bump, Hally.

HALLY (*Having a hard time controlling his emotions. He speaks carefully*) Mind your own business, Sam.

SAM Sorry. I wasn't trying to interfere. Shall we carry on? Hally? (*He indicates the exercise book. No response from* HALLY)

WILLIE (*Also trying*) Tell him about when they give out the cups, Boet Sam.

SAM Ja! That's another big moment. The presentation of the cups after the winners have been announced. You've got to put that in.
(*Still no response from* HALLY)

WILLIE A big silver one, Master Hally, called floating trophy for the champions.

SAM We always invite some big shot personality to hand them over. Guest of honor this year is going to be His Holiness Bishop Jabulani of the All African Free Zionist Church.
(HALLY *gets up abruptly, goes to his table and tears up the page he was writing on*)

HALLY So much for a bloody world without collisions.

SAM Too bad. It was on its way to being a good composition.

HALLY Let's stop bullshitting ourselves, Sam.

SAM Have we been doing that?

HALLY Yes! That's what all our talk about a decent world has been ... just so much bullshit.

SAM We did say it was only a dream.

HALLY And a bloody useless one at that. Life's a fuck-up and it's never going to change.

SAM Ja, maybe that's true.

HALLY There's no maybe about it. It's a blunt and brutal fact. All we've done this afternoon is waste our time.

SAM Not if we'd got your homework done.

HALLY I don't give a shit about my homework, so, for Christ's sake, just shut up about it. (*Slamming books viciously into his school case*) Hurry up now and finish your work. I want to lock up and get out of here. (*Pause*) And then go where? Home-sweet-fucking-home. Jesus, I hate that word.

English 445

(HALLY *goes to the counter to put the brandy bottle and comics in his school case. After a moment's hesitation, he smashes the bottle of brandy. He abandons all further attempts to hide his feelings.* SAM *and* WILLIE *work away as unobtrusively as possible*)

Guide for Reading

The following paper is an excellent response to the assignment. Notice how in paragraphs 3 and 4 Lisa states her thesis directly. Notice also how she deals with each work separately when she explains the theme of power and then brings the two works together when she explains the similarities. This method gives readers a good sense of how each work handles the theme of power as well as a thorough explanation of how they are similar.

SAMPLE ENGLISH PAPER 4

Social and Moral Power in *The Handmaid's Tale* and "Master Harold" . . . and the Boys

Lisa D. (a sophomore)

Power. The word conjures up great and mighty images: strength, success, leadership, military prowess, the ruling party, the ultimate winner. The powerful end up on top. Powerful is what you should strive to be.

But what about those who are secretly powerful? What is there to be said about the "power" behind the real powers? One saying suggests that behind powerful men are equally powerful (yet unseen) women. The Bible says that those who do not appear to be powerful-the meek and mild-will someday be the most powerful. Today, powerful people surround themselves with networks of other powerful people to assist them. This often leads us to question where the power really does lie.

It is this division of powerful forces that I will address in this paper. I believe that a distinction needs to be made between those who possess *social power*-those who are in positions of leadership within the establishment, and between those who possess *moral power*-those who may or may not belong to the established leadership ranks but who, more importantly, contribute a show of force stemming from their moral and ethical convictions.

I propose that in Margaret Atwood's *The Handmaid's Tale* and Athol Fugard's *"Master Harold" . . . and the boys,* the two protagonists, Offred and Sam respectively, do not possess the social power awarded to those who belong to the establishment. Both of these characters possess the moral power so often lacking in other characters, namely those who are establishment-based. Since Offred and Sam do possess this moral power, the reader has hope that they will ultimately prevail over the socially powerful because they represent justice and equality.

I would like to begin by looking at Offred, the woman who tells us her story in *The Handmaid's Tale*. Because she is a fertile woman in (generally speaking) infertile times, she has been relegated to the ranks of surrogate mother-a handmaid. Though the ability to reproduce is in theory esteemed, the handmaid suffers discrimination and hostility from all sides of the society they live in: they are spat upon by women of the "less powerful" rank than they (the Econowives); it is implicitly shown that the "more powerful" women (the wives) resent their presence in the households; they are constantly being watched by the "all-powerful" components of the society (the Eyes). Everyone in the Society of Gilead has some way to exert power over the handmaids. Yet, there are some ways in which the handmaids can wield the little power they have.

One such way is through sexual power. Offred learns that although the society is set up so there is no "extramarital sex" (no sex between a handmaid and a man other than her commander and his wife), there are times when this rule is broken. She learns of Doctors sleeping with handmaids, the Guards having affairs with the handmaids, and later in the story, she finds a place where some women, ex-handmaids included, have found a place to exert sexual power in an "open" and unabashed way-at Jezebels.

Though Offred learns of the power of her sexuality she does

not choose to use that power for her own gain. She certainly has the opportunity when she begins her meetings with the Commander and comes to realize that he is a lonely man seeking companionship and, probably, a sexual release. He is surprised when she asks for very little in return for the meetings.

But just because Offred does not take advantage of her sexual power is this proof of her moral power? In and of itself no. But I do believe it is one proof of it. But more importantly, the evidence of Offred's moral power lies in her refusal to forget life as it was, mistakes and all, and her refusal to "buy into" the Gileadian idealogy. She keeps her own hopes alive, stronger at certain times than at others. She strives to understand her new world, to understand how it could have happened, and to look for solutions and answers to the problems that have been created. Offred does not necessarily do anything heroic, but more importantly, she does not act like a coward.

An example of this throughout the novel is Offred's frequent flashbacks to her life before the Gilead regime. These are not picture-perfect reminiscences. She remembers resenting her mother (p. 234), laughing and feeling exasperated with her friend Moira (pp. 73–74), and the feelings of fear and panic while trying to escape (pp. 96–97). Most of the memories are quite painful for her. But she needs them to keep her perspective, to remember. And some of the most important memories for her are those of her daughter. These memories transcend time and become more like the actual presence of her daughter with her at certain times. It is these memories especially that offer her hope and reason to live on.

The story of Sam in *"Master Harold" . . . and the boys* closely resembles that of Offred. This is in part due to the fact that both Sam and Offred suffer from discrimination because they are part of the socially powerless minorities. Sam is a black man in a white-ruled world. Offred is a woman in a male-ruled world. Sam has no social power whatsoever and has no immediate hopes of having any. But this does not leave Sam without hope. Instead, Sam works within the confines of the world that other "powers" have created for him to try and create the hope for a less discriminating world in the future.

Sam does this through Master Harold whom he knows better as Hally. This young white boy has unofficially become Sam's charge—and especially so in Sam's eyes. Sam hopes to change Hally through the experiences he has growing up. The immediate result he hopes to achieve is to make Hally's life easier and happier. A more long-term goal is to change the thinking of one who will be socially powerful over Sam some day. In fact, Hally has some controlling social power over Sam even as a young child. He is able to give the "boys" household orders and by the age of 17 is able to directly tell them what to do and not to do.

Like Offred, Sam refuses to "buy into" the system that the socially powerful whites have created. One prime example of this is the name that Sam calls Master Harold. He has familiarized the boy's name to Hally and makes him appear to be on a more equal footing with Sam and Willie rather than as their "master." At the end of the play when Hally insists that Sam call him by his real (socially powerful) name (p. 54), one very important link between the socially and morally powerful has been broken.

Sam also shows his moral power through his desire to learn. Education is the key to overthrowing the socially powerful who do not also possess the qualities of moral power. Therefore, education is denied to the ones who do not have social power. But Sam realizes that education is important and pursues learning. He is also fulfilling his role as "guardian" to Hally by helping him to study and do well in school. By challenging Hally to do his best, to learn as much as he can, he again may be helping to change the thinking of a white boy who will some day possess a great amount of social power.

Sam's ultimate example of his moral power comes at the end of the play. Hally cannot deal with the news that his father will be returning from the hospital. He does not know how to discuss what he is feeling with either Sam or Willie. But since they are there in the room with him, he takes his anger and frustration and hurt out on the "boys" verbally and eventually, physically. He ends up spitting on Sam. Sam becomes enraged that this "boy" has spit on him—a boy he has helped raise and whose life he helped form. But rather than take retaliation in the form of physical violence (though he threatens to), Sam walks away instead.

This may be the most important moral lesson Hally will ever witness. And this brave, moral act gives the reader and the audience hope that the Sam's and Hally's of the world can work things out eventually.

I believe that Sam and Offred's determination not to succumb in spirit to the socially powerful is the most important example of their moral power. It has been argued that because they did not risk being heroes/heroines in the traditional sense of doing extraordinary deeds to prove to the populous that they were indeed moral beings, they cannot be identified as truelly moral. I disagree.

Had either of these characters sought to prove their points in a radical or outspoken way, their aims could not have been achieved. Both Offred's and Sam's purpose was to show us, the reader, that there is hope for social/moral change within our worlds as well. They each worked within the system they live in. They sought to change what they could given the circumstances they found themselves in. Both character's "worlds" might appear very foreign and far-fetched to many readers, though perhaps a closer look may reveal more similarities than can be comfortably acknowledged.

Granted, both Sam's and Offred's changes are small. There is certainly some question as to what changes they were each able to produce. But the fact remains that they each *tried* to change things. They made conscious efforts to make their worlds work better for the socially moral and less prejudiced toward the socially powerful.

STUDY QUESTIONS

1. Even though Lisa doesn't state her claim, or thesis, in one sentence, she conveys it very clearly to readers. Underline the sentences (in paragraphs 3 and 4) that together form her thesis. In your own words, write a one-sentence statement that could be used as a thesis for this paper. What does Lisa gain by not including such a sentence in her introductory paragraphs?

2. Mark all sentences that contain a specific reference to the texts. Which of these simply remind readers what happens and which are used to support a point Lisa is making?

3. Has Lisa employed a point-by-point or a subject-by-subject comparison? Is her choice the proper one for this paper? Why or why not?

4. Evaluate this paper on the points stated in the last paragraph of the assignment: "clarity, directness, effective organization, and effective, correct use of sources." Give specific examples from the paper to support your evaluation.

Guide for Reading

The following paper is an inadequate response to the assignment. Angie never clearly states a claim, or thesis, and the rambling nature of her paper indicates that she has no clear idea of what she wants to say. Toward the end, she is simply pointing out different types of discrimination in the three works. Because she is saying something about the texts and not just summarizing, she may have given herself the illusion that she is analyzing, but this information is not guided by a single purpose.

English

SAMPLE ENGLISH PAPER 5

Discrimination in Society: Three Views by Contemporary Authors

Angie M. (a sophomore)

Margaret Atwood, Athol Fugard, and Bernard Pomerance, three prominent contemporary authors have opened a Pandora's box full of controversial issues dealing with discrimination. These three writers, respectively, in the novel *The Handmaid's Tale,* the play *"Master Harold" . . . and the boys* and the play *The Elephant Man* reveal to American society the inadequacies in our own system of thoughts concerning sexism, racism and physical discrimination. Atwood's *The Handmaid's Tale* deals primarily with the assertion of superiority of men over women. Fugard's *"Master Harold" . . . and the boys* is a look at the white minorities rise over the black majority in South Africa. Furthermore, Pomerance's *The Elephant Man,* adapted from the life of John Merrick, a hideously deformed human being, centers its theme around the trials and tribulations of physical discrimination. Each of these pieces relates to the other, yet shows a different view of the discriminatory patterns prevalent in society.

Margaret Atwood reveals to her audience a futuristic look at societies views on politics and sex. She thoughtfully explores what it means to be a woman and a man. The discriminatory patterns she melodramatically emphasizes puts the reader in a position to look further into the patterns of his own environment.

The society that we live in today places males at the top of the hierarchic ladder. The male race is considered leader; the strongest and the most knowledgable. Their duties require protecting the female race. Females on the other hand are to serve their male counterparts and function as a link in the reproductive chain. This sexism or exploitation and domination of one sex by the other is the key to Atwood's plot. She takes these ideas, exaggerates them and shows us that sexism should not be part of society.

Atwood's handmaid society is a personification of the most

extreme form of discrimination against women. For example, to be a woman means to be controlled. Women are not allowed to read, write, or go out alone. They are also divided among each other-the Commanders wives being the highest and the econo-wives being the lowest-so as to keep their race weak and unable to unite as one against males. This ranking is based upon each ones ability to bear children and their marital status before the hostile takeover of this all male regime. The handmaids such as Offred, represent this child producing form of sexual discrimination. Sexuality means of or involving sex, the sexes or sex organs. It is ironic and very clever of Atwood to use such a pun in the representation of the handmaid's and society. Atwood exploits sexuality the most with the handmaids whose sole job is to reproduce, that is, with sex or sex organs. According to the commander women should merely "fulfill their biological destinies" (284).

The all powerful male regime is the basis of what it means to be a man. They are the controllers of all the money, power and knowledge. They have sex drives and needs where as the women should not have any desires except to have babies and please men. As the slogan goes at the Red Center "From each according to her ability; to each according to his needs" (151). Sayings such as this are the basis for the sexuality in Atwood's novel.

These two extremes, male power and female servitude, that for too long have gone together, are what makes Atwood's tale so illuminating. Society today is trying to rid itself of these stereotypes and Atwood reveals to us that we should. One of the scenes between Offred and the Commander best exemplifies the problems of a sexist society. The Commander proceeds to tell Offred why her society has changed from the one she knew before. At first the Commander's argument seems valid. Women were always unhappy . . . "singles bars," "blind dates," "the meat market." Now women are "protected." "What did we overlook?" the Commander asks Offred. her reply, "Love" (284). There was a lack of companionship between men and women in Atwood's society. Atwood heartfully reveals the human condition in her novel, a loss of integrity and individuality. Her message? Society should not lose this individuality in a mass of discrimination because without it there would not be interaction, except what was necessary for life, between the sexes.

These same themes of discrimination, sexism and individuality are seen in *The Elephant Man* by Bernard Pomerance. Though, in the play, Pomerance addresses these issues somewhat differently then Atwood. For example, in scene XV Ross asks Merrick if he has "had a woman" because to Ross this is what makes a man (53). Due to the fact that Merrick has not been with a woman sexually, he is not a man in Ross's mind. To be a man means to be sexual, yet to be a woman means to be pure. This contradiction, moreover, relates to scene XIV in which Mrs. Kendal shows her naked body to Merrick. Treves walks in and asks if Mrs. Kendal has any sense of decency. Such acts by women are "forbidden" (50). Pomerance's presentation of sexuality and sexism, therefore, is somewhat different than Atwood's. Individuality concerning women should not be permitted, yet to be a man means individuality and sexuality. Therefore, sexism and discrimination.

Sexism is not the only type of discrimination society today has to deal with. Racism or racial discrimination has been more prevalent than sexism in times past. Athol Fugard's play "Master Harold" . . . and the boys deals with this topic as it relates to the South African apartheid (a policy of segregation and political and economic discrimination against non-Europeans in the Republic of South Africa) of the 1950's and present. In the past, as not so much as today, society has been plagued with racial tensions, especially between blacks and whites. Fugard reveals to us this pattern and the power that whites have over blacks.

"Master Harold" . . . and the boys is a story about a young white boy, Hally, of age seventeen and his "friends," Sam and Willie, who are in their mid forties. This friendship has evolved since Hally was a small boy of about five. The irony of the play is that Hally is essentially Sam and Willie's "master." Hally has the power to tell Sam and Willie what to do. For example, at one point Willie throws a slop rag at Sam and it accidently misses him and hits Hally. To this Hally responds, "Act your bloody age! Cut out the nonsense now and get on with your work" (13). In a society such as ours today it would be very disrespectful for a boy of such an age to say this to a grown man, black or white.

Fugard tests the limits of racism. He challenges us to look at this kind of discrimination and to see its injustice. At the end of the play, Fugard dives into deep water by actually reproducing a dispute with black against white. Hally has the power to win the arguement with Sam, but the audience is never quite sure if he really does. Fugard also makes several racial remarks against blacks. During the disagreement Hally tells Sam that he is "only a servant in here (the tea room) and don't forget it" (53). Hally also tells Sam that taking orders from a white man is "good enough for you" (53). Fugard even goes so far as to tell, through Hally, a joke about black skin color. These types of statements relate to the reader the inadequacy of racial imbalance. It forces white society today to make a judgement about its own actions toward blacks because the scales of black power are still more than slightly tipped in favor of whites.

Fugard shows us the white-black pattern, yet, in the end seems to show us that wisdom may be deeper than skin color. The audience almost feels that Sam is superior to Hally. Hally has had all the possible advantages of education and lifestyles a young man could be offered, though he is very confused due to his dealing with a crippled father with a drinking problem. Sam has not had the opportunity to receive a formal education or a nice environment because of his color. His wisdom has stemmed from his association with Hally and his life experiences. Even though background and skin color has made Hally the master, he proves only to be inferior to Sam in many ways. Sam has nurtured Hally and given him almost as much knowledge as Hally has given him. This same scenario could be reproduced with two whites and two blacks. Though, Fugard forces us to take a look at racism. The social power one young white boy has over a black man twice his age and the power this same man has over the boy.

Racism also show up in The Handmaid's Tale by Atwood. The society that Offred lives in is all white. The blacks and other minorities have been shipped to other parts of the United States, primarily as we know South Dakota. Atwood calls this the "Resettlement of the Children of Ham" to "National Homeland One" (107). Although here there is only a small trace of racism and

"Master Harold" ... and the boys addresses the whole issue, they are the same. Both Fugard and Atwood show the discriminatory process and make a statement that it is wrong.

A third type of discrimination is physical discrimination or exploiting others on the basis of their physical features. This is most seen in Bernard Pomerance's The Elephant Man. John Merrick, the elephant man, was socially outcast and made fun of because of his appearances. He was exploited by Ross for the sake of money until Treves took him in. Pomerance shows his readers that one does not have to be shunned from society. Merrick, under the care of Treves, eventually becomes friends with some of the most prominent people in London. They find him very much like themselves despite his crude exterior. For example, in scene XII Mrs. Kendal, Bishop How, Carr Gomm, Merrick's other visitors and even Treves each say how much Merrick resembles themselves. All make statements such as "He seems practical, like me" (Gomm, "For I know he is discrete. Like me." (the Duchess) and "I think him curious, compassionate, concerned about the world, rather like myself, Freddie Treves" (39–40). Each one treats Merrick as a human, unlike Ross who treats him like an animal. Pomerance makes a very bold statement, based on this true story, that humanity and the human condition are deeper than the physical exterior of a person.

Physical discrimination is also briefly dealt with in The Handmaid's Tale by Margaret Atwood. In Offred's society all the babies born that are in some way not healthy or physically deformed are sent away. We as readers do not really know what happens to them but due to the harshness of this society it would not be improbable to assume they were killed. This type of action taken against a human being simply based upon their physical features is most inhumane. Compared to The Elephant Man, Atwood takes a completely different approach to physical discrimination. She does not exploit the babies to the humiliation of growing up but takes more extreme measures and rids others of the tolerance of such deformities. One cannot say which situation, Atwood's or Pomerance's is more humane.

All three authors, Atwood, Fugard and Pomerance, convey to society the injustice and immoral acts of discrimination. In a culture such as ours today we can not rid ourselves of these inadequacies. These writers though, have attempted, in several different ways, to make each one of us look at discriminatory situations and make a choice as to how we will act. In the words of John Merrick "It is done" (66).

STUDY QUESTIONS

1. Point out information that, although it may be correct, seems irrelevant to Angie's discussion.

2. Mark sentences that contain specific references to the text. Which of these clearly support points Angie is making, and which simply remind the readers what happens?

3. Angie includes references both to the real world as she knows it and to the worlds created by the authors. Using "our" world, or common knowledge, as a means of explaining a literary text can be risky and confusing unless it is done skillfully. Are Angie's references enlightening, confusing, and/or irrelevant? Would she have more success in enlightening readers if she focused more on the text? Why or why not?

ENGLISH ASSIGNMENT 3

Course: **Survey of British Literature**

Essay Exam

Instructions:
  1 Answer the question in essay form (that means sentences and paragraphs in some sort of organized fashion). Don't worry about introductions and conclusions—go straight to the core of the question and deal with it.

2 Answer the entire question. Some have more than one part—be sure that you cover all parts.

3 Support and illustrate your ideas and statements with specific details from the works covered in this course. Titles and authors alone are not enough—you must explain why a chosen example illustrates your point. Please note that generalizing won't get you very far on this test.

4 You will be graded primarily on content (how well and how thoroughly you answer the questions you have selected). This test is designed to see if you can make connections between forms and concepts, and literary works.

5 Grammar? Obtrusively bad grammar and poor spelling (you will be expected to spell correctly author's names, characters' names, titles) will not be ignored, and will produce minor point deductions. This is, after all, an English class.

Question:
Pride and Prejudice *is a satire on the upper middle class in a provincial English town. Jane Austen satirizes social customs and conventions, priorities, values, lifestyles, and even certain professions. Explain.*

Analysis of English Assignment 3

This assignment is one of three questions from the final exam for a survey of British literature, a course open for sophomores, juniors, and seniors. The exam was closed-book and was written in class.

Instruction 1 stresses the fact that time is limited by suggesting students eliminate the traditional introduction and conclusion. This advice is valuable for several reasons. An exam is designed to let you show what you know on a specific topic within a certain time frame. Any information that doesn't address the topic specifically is irrelevant. Including irrelevant points makes it appear that you don't understand the questions or are trying to cover up the fact that you don't know enough to deal only with the topic. Your instructor will have many exams to read and grade and will not appreciate having to wade through "padding." The best type of essay exam answer contains the thesis early (usually the first sentence), lists the main points to be discussed, and then treats each point individually. Quite often the question or statement for you to explain can be reworded into a thesis statement. Using this statement as the opening sentence of your essay guides both you and your teacher straight to the point you are making, and at the same time it will prevent you from inserting irrelevant information.

Many students may find the teacher's abrupt "Explain" a bit cryptic, and with good reason. It presumes a high level of "test awareness" on the part of students. In the context of an essay exam, "Explain" means that students should analyze the work in order to provide textual support for the thesis, which the teacher has provided. They must offer examples and explanation, as instruction 3 illustrates, and in each case the support should come directly from the text, not from outside sources or common knowledge.

The ideal essay for the above assignment would cover Jane Austen's satire of upper-middle-class social customs and conventions, priorities, values, lifestyles, and professions. For each of these categories, writers would need to explain how Austen satirizes it, and then they would need to give at least one appropriate example. (It is, of course, crucial that you understand satire so you can explain how this literary device is used.) In other words, students will have to know the novel very well to respond successfully.

In instruction 5, the teacher emphasizes the importance of grammatically correct writing. What the teacher really means is that he or she expects students to spell and punctuate accurately and to apply standard usage with some degree of consistency. Grammar as such isn't at issue because few native speakers of English produce ungrammatical language. Yet the pressure of timed writing often causes "slips of the pen" that, if left uncorrected, can be interpreted as carelessness or, even worse, outright ignorance. For this reason, we recommend that students reserve some time for proofreading the exam after they have written it. Taking a few minutes to read your response and to make a few corrections can often raise a grade by half a letter.

From *Pride and Prejudice*
by Jane Austen

CHAPTER 1

It is a truth universally acknowledged, that a single man in possession of a good fortune, must be in want of a wife.

Excerpt from *Pride and Prejudice* by Jane Austen. Reprinted by permission of Oxford University Press.

However little known the feelings or views of such a man may be on his first entering a neighbourhood, this truth is so well fixed in the minds of the surrounding families, that he is considered as the rightful property of some one or other of their daughters.

"My dear Mr. Bennet," said his lady to him one day, "Have you heard that Netherfield Park is let at last?"

Mr. Bennet replied that he had not.

"But it is," returned she; "for Mrs. Long has just been here, and she told me all about it."

Mr. Bennet made no answer.

"Do not you want to know who has taken it?" cried his wife impatiently.

"*You* want to tell me, and I have no objections to hearing it."

This was invitation enough.

"Why, my dear, you must know, Mrs. Long says that Netherfield is taken by a young man of large fortune from the north of England; that he came down on Monday in a chaise and four to see the place, and was so much delighted with it that he agreed with Mr. Morris immediately; that he is to take possession before Michaelmas, and some of his servants are to be in the house by the end of the week."

"What is his name?"

"Bingley."

"Is he married or single?"

"Oh! single, my dear, to be sure! A single man of large fortune; four or five thousand a year. What a fine thing for our girls!"

"How so? how can it affect them?"

"My dear Mr. Bennet," replied his wife, "how can you be so tiresome! You must know that I am thinking of his marrying one of them."

"Is that his design in settling here?"

"Design! nonsense, how can you talk so! But it is very likely that he *may* fall in love with one of them, and therefore you must visit him as soon as he comes."

"I see no occasion for that. You and the girls may go, or you may send them by themselves, which perhaps will be still better, for as you are as handsome as any of them, Mr. Bingley might like you the best of the party."

"My dear, you flatter me. I certainly *have* had my share of beauty, but I do not pretend to be any thing extraordinary now. When a woman has five grown up daughters, she ought to give over thinking of her own beauty."

"In such cases, a woman has not often much beauty to think of."

"But, my dear, you must indeed go and see Mr. Bingley when he comes into the neighbourhood."

"It is more than I engage for, I assure you."

"But consider your daughters. Only think what an establishment it would be for one of them. Sir William and Lady Lucas are determined to go, merely on that account, for in general you know they visit no new comers. Indeed you must go, for it will be impossible for *us* to visit him, if you do not."

"You are over scrupulous surely. I dare say Mr. Bingley will be very glad to see you; and I will send a few lines by you to assure him of my hearty consent to his marrying which ever he chuses of the girls; though I must throw in a good word for my little Lizzy."

"I desire you will do no such thing. Lizzy is not a bit better than the others; and I am sure she is not half so handsome as Jane, nor half so good humoured as Lydia. But you are always giving *her* the preference."

"They have none of them much to recommend them," replied he; "they are all silly and ignorant like other girls; but Lizzy has something more of quickness than her sisters."

"Mr. Bennet, how can you abuse your own children in such a way? You take delight in vexing me. You have no compassion on my poor nerves."

"You mistake me, my dear. I have a high respect for your nerves. They are my old friends. I have heard you mention them with consideration these twenty years at least."

"Ah! you do not know what I suffer.'

"But I hope you will get over it, and live to see many young men of four thousand a year come into the neighbourhood."

"It will be no use to us, if twenty such should come since you will not visit them."

"Depend upon it, my dear, that when there are twenty, I will visit them all."

Mr. Bennet was so odd a mixture of quick parts, sarcastic humour, reserve, and caprice, that the experience of three and twenty years had been insufficient to make his wife understand his character. *Her* mind was less difficult to develop. She was a woman of mean understanding, little information, and uncertain temper. When she was discontented she fancied herself nervous. The business of her life was to get her daughters married; its solace was visiting and news.

Guide for Reading

None of the sample papers is an outstanding response to the assignment. The following one is average because Nathan shows an understanding of the question and the novel. He supports his thesis with relatively good examples from the text, and he summarizes them in a way that shows he grasps their significance in relation to the novel. But Nathan recollects the plot inaccurately, and he weakens his credibility by consistently misspelling Austen's name. Moreover, he asks readers to figure out for themselves *how* his examples work as satire. As you read, identify some places where Nathan could have explained the text better.

SAMPLE ENGLISH PAPER 6

Nathan F. (a junior)

Pride and Prejudice by Jane Austin is a form of Horatian satire that ridicules the customs, values, and lifestyles of the upper-middle class in England. The novel ridicules the customs of marriage to a great degree. The main interest of the book seems to be concerned with getting married to the right person. With this in mind, it is quite obvious that Mrs. Bennet is trying to arrange all of the marriages for all five of her daughters. Mrs. Bennet seems to contend that marriage is an institution designed to strengthen the family structure. However, as Austin points out, money is the primary impetus for marriage.

The reasons for getting married are wide ranged. Charlotte and Mr. Collins get married for convenience. Charlotte feels as if the picking is as good as it will ever get. Lydia and Mr. Wickham also get married for all the wrong reasons. Their motive for marriage is infatuation. This type of spontaneous love leads to their eloping. The only marriage that is exemplary and has any worth to it is that of Elizabeth and Mr. Darcy. These two get married because they are truly in love with one another. When Elizabeth refuses Darcy's proposal at first and then tells him to ask again in five years, one gets the impression of how strong their bond truly is. Elizabeth and Darcy are genuine friends at the end of the story.

Another problem that Austin points out with regard to English society is the amount of gossip that takes place. Everyone in the novel, except for Jane Bennet, thoroughly enjoy gossiping about who's seeing who, who gave the last party, and what each person wore to dinner.

The intent of social gatherings was to introduce prospective males and females to each other. The Bennet's, not true to form, expose and display all of their daughters in the same hall at the same time. It seems as if it would be more proper to just allow the eldest daughters out socially until they are properly married. This practice of keeping the younger ones "confined" longer would eliminate any jealousy that may develop between siblings.

Pride and Prejudice does not attack government or politics in any way. The only real "stab" it takes toward religion involves Mr. Collins who is a corrupt country clergyman. This novel ridicules the leisure class because it does not have work to do. Therefore, there is no reason why the class should exist. The only people that seem to work is the servant class.

STUDY QUESTIONS

1. Do you feel that Nathan has a clear understanding of Jane Austen's satire, or of the concept of satire itself? If so, point out in his essay the information that discusses satire.

2. In the last paragraph of his essay, Nathan states that *Pride and Prejudice* attacks both religion and the leisure class. Reread the question and then summarize what he has not included in this part of his response.

Guide for Reading

In her essay, Susan shows that she understands what Jane Austen focused on in *Pride and Prejudice*. This understanding, along with the fact that she covers the topic in a readable manner, makes her response adequate but no better than average. Notice, however, that in paragraph 5 she leaves the topic of satire and discusses how the title of the novel is reflected in the characters. Even though what she says may be correct, she is padding her essay with information irrelevant to the test question. When you reach this section, you may want to look again at the question to see how far she deviates.

English

SAMPLE ENGLISH PAPER 7

Susan K. (a sophomore)

Pride and Prejudice satirized the social customs of marriage and of social classes. The upper class lifestyles were also satirized, along with some professions, and the attitudes, priorities, and values concerning these things.

Marriage was satirized by Mrs. Bennet. Her main goal was to get her daughters married off. She spent each day gossiping and planning and watching for eligible men. Jane Austin is satirizing the 18th century view of marriage and how people often married for the wrong reasons. Marriage to Mrs. Bennet was a way of assuring her that her daughters would be kept up after they (Mr. and Mrs. Bennet) died. She didn't really care if the girls loved the men, as seen when she tried to make Elizabeth marry Mr. Collins. She was constantly looking for balls or excuses to have her girls seen, like when she sent Jane to Mr. Bingley's in the rain on horseback so that she'd have to stay there overnight. She was a nosey woman who bragged about her home, girls, and such to everyone, especially the Lucas' and an eligible bachelor.

Lady Catherine and Miss Bingley satirized the snobbery of the upper class. They were rude and didn't care to watch other people's feelings. They were full of pride and prejudice in a disheartening way. They showed how, just because they were rich, they thought they could tell others what to do. As Lady Catherine constantly tells Mr. and Mrs. Collins what to do: and when she tried to tell Elizabeth what to do about not marrying Mr. Darcy.

Mr. Collins' profession is satirized. He is in the clergy, but not by desire. He is a cynic and hypocrite who is only concerned with looking nice and good to others. As seen when he was explaining to Elizabeth the reasons for his wanting to get married, not of which were love. And after her refusal, he ran out to Charlotte and asked her to marry him. He was a proud and vain man. The militia was also satirized through Mr. Wickham as he ran off with Lydia and eloped to get money from Mr. Darcy.

The exemplars in *Pride and Prejudice* were Jane and Mr. Bingley and the Gardners. They were the only ones who weren't blinded by pride or prejudice and who liked people for what they truly were, instead of what they thought they should be.

Mr. Darcy was blinded by his pride and upbringing. He couldn't see, for a while, that he had any reason to communicate with those lower than himself. He finally realized that although he was rich he wasn't necessarily happy. His happiness grew from falling in love with Elizabeth. He had to forget the false pretensions of Elizabeth not being good enough for himself to love her. He had to get the pride and prejudice out of his life.

Jane and Elizabeth both valued marriage. Jane had no pride or prejudice. But Elizabeth had pride once she heard Mr. Darcy refuse her at the ball. She still valued love and wanted to marry only out of love, as seen when she refused Mr. Collins. She had to be shown that Mr. Darcy was innocent from the accusations of Mr. Wickham before she could love him. She and her father discussed the value of love to a marriage when she talked with him after Mr. Darcy's proposal. Unlike Charlotte and most of the 18th century belief, they married for the right reasons. (The 18th century belief was changing however and allowing the children to pick their partners—at the opportunity of being vetoed by the parents). Marriage was more than a social custom and rule. Jane Austin shows this through the silliness of obsession of Mrs. Bennet with marriage, and by the waiting of Jane and Elizabeth for the real and right reasons for marriage.

English

> ## STUDY QUESTIONS
>
> 1. Susan begins her first four paragraphs with the following:
>
>   "*Pride and Prejudice* satirized the social customs of marriage and of social classes."
>
>   "Marriage was satirized by Mrs. Bennet."
>
>   "Lady Catherine and Miss Bingley satirized the snobbery of the upper class."
>
>   "Mr. Collins' profession is satirized."
>
>   What is inconsistent and incorrect about these four statements?
>
> 2. Mark the paragraphs that have nothing to do with satire. Read the exam question again. Are those paragraphs completely irrelevant to the question? Could these paragraphs be rewritten so they are relevant? In other words, has Susan chosen appropriate examples from the text but simply not explained them in correct terms?
>
> 3. Count how many times Susan uses the terms "Pride" and "Prejudice" in the paper. What effect does this repetition have on readers?

Guide for Reading

Although it is obvious that Amy has read the novel and has some understanding of what Jane Austen is saying, she appears to have ignored most of the question in planning her essay. She focuses on two points in the question (social customs and conventions) and then explains the methods Mrs. Bennet employs to get her daughters married. Amy's essay is an inadequate response, not because it contains incorrect information (the information is correct), but because it doesn't address the question.

SAMPLE ENGLISH PAPER 8

Amy H. (a junior)

Pride and Prejudice is about an upper middle class family, the Bennetts. They have five daughters. The mother, Mrs. Bennett, is only concerned with getting her daughters married off to a rich man. Mr. Bennett, the father, is sort of henpecked. His wife gets on his nerves most of the time so he spends a lot of time in his study. No one in this family works. They just run around, gossip, and try to get married. They treat their servants as though they weren't real people, and call all of them Betty or Charles. Mrs. Bennett's nerves are her ailment and when she is feeling bad or upset she blames it on her nerves. No one is concerned with politics, religion, or any thing of much importance. They sort of live in a fantasy world. No one works. Money is a key factor in finding a husband - *the richer the better.*

The custom is to get the oldest daughters married first and then let the youngest get married. The older daughters were supposed to be the only ones going out but Mrs. Bennett sent all her daughters out together. She really didn't care who got married first as long as they all get married - preferably to someone rich. Other families only sent their oldest daughters out. The Bennett girls, especially the 2 youngest, Kitty and Lydia, ran wild. They were always looking for soldiers because they were so cute in their uniforms.

Their top priority was to get married - preferably to a rich man. They didn't seem to care about work or important issues, such as religion or politics. They tended to judge people on first impressions. If they were wealthy they usually liked them. Except for Mr. Darcy. They thought he was a snob and didn't like him even though he was very rich. Later, when Elizabeth fell in love with him and he proposed to her the family was shocked. But they quickly learn to adjust. Mrs. Bennett had a hard time dealing with it at first but she eventually got over it and was happy for her "Dear Lizzy."

Girls weren't supposed to read or be very excited about learning anything of that sort. Mary the middle daughter didn't seem to let this bother her. She read a lot, sang, etc. Needless to say, she was one of the last two daughters left at home.

Marriage, once again, was important. It really didn't matter who got in your way. For example, Elizabeth liked Mr. Wickham but he went away to England. Then Elizabeth's younger sister ran away with Mr. Wickham and got married. Also, Mr. Collins, the cousin of the Bennett family, was in love Elizabeth but she refused his proposal. So he married her next door neighbor, Charlotte Lucas. It was though people were only concerned with getting married and they didn't care who they hurt or who it was they married - as long as they got married.

STUDY QUESTIONS

1. In what ways is Amy's opening paragraph not appropriate according to the instructions?

2. Based on the references to the text in Amy's essay, what specific social customs and conventions, priorities, lifestyles, and professions do you think Jane Austen is satirizing in *Pride and Prejudice?*

3. Pick one of the above categories and write a paragraph explaining how Jane Austen satirizes this particular aspect of the upper-middle class. Use your knowledge of satire and the references to the text in Amy's essay. Treat this one paragraph as the answer to an essay question, following the guidelines on the assignment and the analysis. You will see that Amy knows what Jane Austen is doing in *Pride and Prejudice,* but in her essay she hasn't expressed much knowledge.

4. Like Susan in the previous paper, Amy repeats certain phrases too frequently. Identify the most repeated phrase and describe how Amy's redundancy affects readers.

Writing Assignments

The following questions are characteristic of the sort students are likely to encounter on an essay exam for a survey of British literature. The works in the questions are those typically covered in such a course. Go to your college library and find copies of *The Canterbury Tales* and *King Lear* (make certain that the copy of *The Canterbury Tales* you select is written in modern English). Read the Prologue to *The Canterbury Tales* and all of *King Lear*, then answer the questions below. Try to simulate an exam situation. Give yourself 30 minutes for each, and write without stopping. Use the instructions from Assignment 3.

1. The Prologue to *The Canterbury Tales* is a valuable social document because it describes and comments on almost the entire range of social classes—as well as a wide variety of professions, occupations, and physical types—in fourteenth-century England. Explain.
2. *King Lear* is dominated by the motifs of sight and blindness, clothing, childhood, and madness. Discuss each of these, and explain how each motif contributes to the overall intent and effect of the play.

9 History

INTRODUCTION TO WRITING IN HISTORY

The popular view of what history is about is fairly limited. It holds that history consists of recording and reporting "facts," such as the date of the American Revolution, the events that led to World War I, and so forth. Only those people initiated into the nature of the discipline understand that recording and reporting "facts" is merely the basis for the real task of the discipline, which is interpreting events to understand them better. Historians do this by presenting facts in a context that gives them meaning.

Writing in history is therefore largely argumentative. Writers are involved in making a claim about the meaning, or in some cases the consequences, of an event, and they use historical evidence to support their thesis. For example, everyone knows that the Civil War took place. It is a historical fact. But historians have been intrigued for generations by what caused the war. For years it was widely believed that the central cause was the dispute between the North and the South over the morality of slavery, but more recently that argument has been challenged by writers who argue that economic tensions caused the war. Other writers have proposed that the war started because of different ideological views on the power of the state versus the power of the federal government, an argument that expressed itself through the issue of slavery. Thus a single historical fact—here, the Civil War—can be interpreted many different ways from many points of view as researchers attempt to explain its causes.

An important goal of most writing assignments in history, therefore, is to help students grasp the interpretive aspect of the discipline. Assignments typically ask writers to use historical information to support their personal interpretations of events. Admittedly, this task is challenging because few undergraduates have the background necessary to discuss the complex forces that bear on significant historical events. But most teachers recognize the limitations of their students and perceive writing in history at this level as training in the intellectual processes of the discipline. That is, they are more concerned about students' ability to develop reasonable theses or arguments and to use historical evidence in support of a thesis than they are about students' ability to make an important contribution to historical research.

The form of writing in history is similar to that found in other disciplines in the humanities. Papers begin with an introduction that both presents some background information to set the scene for the argument and offers the thesis. The paragraphs that follow should support the thesis through the careful analysis of historical information. Because nearly all of this information will come from secondary sources—books and journals available in the campus library—students must be certain to document accurately. Historians use either the *MLA Style Guide* or the *Chicago Style Guide*.

At this point, it may be worth mentioning that history is peculiar in that at some schools it is classified as one of the humanities, whereas at other schools it is classified as one of the social sciences. In our experience, the consequences can be significant. We found when compiling this text that when history was deemed a social science, the faculty tended to be more involved in measuring, analyzing, and interpreting contemporary events. Their work resembles what one might find in a sociology department. When history was deemed part of the humanities, on the other hand, the faculty tended to be more involved in interpreting noncontemporary historical documents. These different emphases necessarily result in different writing conventions. As you read the assignments and responses that follow, you may find it interesting to speculate on the nature of the history departments that generated them.

HISTORY ASSIGNMENT 1

Course: **American History for Sophomores and History Majors**

History Book Review
   Format:
   1. On the title page you should include the title of your review essay, your name, and the complete citation for the book. (Author, Title, City of Publication, Publisher, Date of Publication, No. of pages.)
   2. A book review is an essay that should be formally written. There must be a logical format to your discussion, proper grammar, correct spelling, a conclusion, etc.

Helpful Hints:
   1. Every book has a thesis or point of view. Usually you can find the author's thesis in the introduction. It is the underlying message of the book—the statement the author is trying to make. The thesis is not necessarily the same as the purpose of the book, which may simply be to fill a void in a particular research area.
   2. While you must describe the contents of the book, you cannot cover everything in the allotted space. As the reviewer, you must be selective with the information you include. Give an overview and then stress what you feel are the most important points or incidents.
   3. Remember to write as if readers are unfamiliar with the book but [have] a general knowledge of American history. You are informing [them] of the book's contents and value. Do not write directly to me (the instructor) or assume that I know what you are writing about. Your grade will reflect both your level of knowledge about the book and your ability to explain the thesis of the book to someone else.
   4. Analyze and evaluate the book. Consider the following gen-

eral questions in addition to others which might relate more specifically to the book:
   A. Does the author prove his thesis?
   B. Is his information correct? Is it consistent with the text, the discussion in this course, and other historical evidence you may personally be aware of? Does the author leave out or neglect important information or evidence?
   C. Is the book well written? Does the argument flow well? Is the discussion clear?
   D. How does this book help our understanding of the person/event and our understanding of this period of history?
   E. Was this book enjoyable to read? What value does it hold for others not yet familiar with it? Would you recommend it?
5. If your selection is a historical novel, comment on its relevance to American history. Is the fictional environment consistent with information covered in class? How helpful was the novel in constructing a believable environment?
6. With any book, be aware of the publication date. Does the period in which your book was published give any key as to the author's overall interpretation? Was the book a product of some cultural bias?

Analysis of History Assignment 1

We begin this chapter with a book review to reinforce the notion that intellectual disciplines frequently work with the same materials but apply different perspectives to them. In this case, the topic of analysis is the book *Huckleberry Finn,* a novel you might assume would be more appropriately studied in an American literature course. From the historian's point of view, however, this book offers revealing insights into some of the personal and social values of the early mid-1800s. It isn't a historical novel, and technically it isn't a historical document, but it nevertheless can tell us much about the past.

   An assignment as detailed as this one has been well planned by the instructor, which means that he or she expects the students' reviews to be carefully written. Before students select a book, therefore, they should read the assignment closely to determine what they will need to include in the review. They can then make notes and write down ideas on what to cover while they read the book.

A good book review must contain a complete summary of the work, but as the assignment states, the review cannot contain everything the book contains. A good summary focuses on the most important points, giving readers an overview of the structure and/or events and letting them know what the book is about. If you have written a good summary, your readers can place within the context of the whole work the details or scenes you discuss as part of your evaluation.

When you follow an assignment as detailed as the one above, you must resist the temptation to do nothing but answer the questions. Keep in mind that they are guides. Although you will supply answers, your review should not read as a list. Instead of writing, "The author proves his thesis," you could write, "The author's argument is convincing because his points are fully supported and documented with appropriate sources." This makes your review sound as if you are explaining what is important about the book.

It is also important to recognize that the choice of a book will make some of the hints in the assignment inappropriate and others especially important. The author of a work of fiction is not required to develop and argue a thesis in as formal and obvious a manner as the author of a nonfiction book. At the same time, a novel is expected to be more entertaining than informative, which puts a greater burden on a novelist's creativity than on his or her need to be historically accurate. In other words, the analysis should consider the aims of the book, not reader expectations of what it should be. If students are uncertain about its aim, they should talk to their instructor.

Note that the questions in this assignment ask you to take a historical rather than a literary perspective. You should avoid any extensive discussions of literary devices such as symbols, allusions, use of language, style, and so on. Focus instead on the book's value as a source of historical information.

Although your opinion will be the basis for much of your evaluation, you must support it with information from the book. If the author has been careless with facts, your readers need examples to be convinced of this. Keep in mind, though, that your examples need to be appropriate and only long enough to support your points.

Class Article 1

From *Adventures of Huckleberry Finn*
by Mark Twain

CHAPTER 17

About half a minute somebody spoke out of a window, without putting his head out, and says:

"Be done, boys! Who's there?"

I says:

"It's me."

"Who's me?"

"George Jackson, sir."

"What do you want?"

"I don't want nothing, sir. I only want to go along by, but the dogs won't let me."

"What are you prowling around here this time of night, for—hey?"

"I warn't prowling around, sir; I fell overboard off of the steamboat."

"Oh, you did, did you? Strike a light then, somebody. What did you say your name was?"

"George Jackson, sir. I'm only a boy."

"Look here; if you're telling the truth, you needn't be afraid—nobody'll hurt you. But don't try to budge; stand right where you are. Rouse out Bob and Tom, some of you, and fetch the guns. George Jackson, is there anybody with you?"

"No, sir, nobody."

I heard the people stirring around in the house, now, and see a light. The man sang out:

"Snatch that light away, Betsy, you old fool—ain't you got any sense? Put it on the floor behind the front door. Bob, if you and Tom are ready, take your places."

"All ready."

"Now, George Jackson, do you know the Shepherdsons?"

"No, sir—I never heard of them."

"Well, that may be so, and it mayn't. Now, all ready. Step forward, George Jackson. And mind, don't you hurry—come mighty slow. If there's anybody with you, let him keep back—if he shows himself he'll be shot. Come along, now. Come slow; push the door open, yourself—just enough to squeeze in, d' you hear?"

Samuel Langhorne Clemens, *Adventures of Huckleberry Finn*. W. W. Norton and Company, 1961, 1962, pp. 79–86.

I didn't hurry, I couldn't if I'd a wanted to. I took one slow step at a time, and there warn't a sound, only I thought I could hear my heart. The dogs were as still as the humans, but they followed a little behind me. When I got to the three log door-steps, I heard them unlocking and unbarring and unbolting. I put my hand on the door and pushed it a little and a little more, till somebody said, "There, that's enough—put your head in." I done it, but I judged they would take it off.

The candle was on the floor, and there they all was, looking at me, and me at them, for about a quarter of a minute. Three big men with guns pointed at me, which made me wince, I tell you; the oldest, gray and about sixty, the other two thirty or more—all of them fine and handsome—and the sweetest old gray-headed lady, and back of her two young women which I could see right well. The old gentleman says:

"There—I reckon it's all right. Come in."

As soon as I was in, the old gentleman he locked the door and barred it and bolted it, and told the young men to come up with their guns, and they all went in a big parlor that had a new rag carpet on the floor, and got together in a corner that was out of range of the front windows—there warn't none on the side. They held the candle, and took a good look at me, and all said, "Why *he* ain't a Shepherdson—no, there ain't any Shepherdson about him." Then the old man said he hoped I wouldn't mind being searched for arms, because he didn't mean no harm by it—it was only to make sure. So he didn't pry into my pockets, but only felt outside with his hands, and said it was all right. He told me to make myself easy and at home, and tell all about myself; but the old lady says:

"Why bless you, Saul, the poor thing's as wet as he can be; and don't you reckon it may be he's hungry?"

"True for you, Rachel—I forgot."

So the old lady says:

"Betsy" (this was a nigger woman), "you fly around and get him something to eat, as quick as you can, poor thing; and one of you girls go and wake up Buck and tell him—Oh, here he is himself. Buck, take this little stranger and get the wet clothes off from him and dress him up in some of yours that's dry."

Buck looked about as old as me—thirteen or fourteen or along there, though he was a little bigger than me. He hadn't on anything but a shirt, and he was very frowsy-headed. He come in gaping and digging one fist into his eyes, and he was dragging a gun along with the other one. He says:

"Ain't they no Shepherdsons around?"

They said no, 'twas a false alarm.

"Well," he says, "if they'd a ben some, I reckon I'd a got one."

They all laughed, and Bob says:

"Why, Buck, they might have scalped us all, you've been so slow in coming."

"Well, nobody come after me, and it ain't right. I'm always kep' down; I don't get no show."

"Never mind, Buck, my boy," says the old man, "you'll have show enough, all in good time, don't you fret about that. Go 'long with you now, and do as your mother told you."

When we got up stairs to his room, he got me a coarse shirt and a roundabout and pants of his, and I put them on. While I was at it he asked me what my name was, but before I could tell him, he started to telling me about a blue jay and a young rabbit he had catched in the woods day before yesterday, and he asked me where Moses was when the candle went out. I said I didn't know; I hadn't heard about it before, no way.

"Well, guess," he says.

"How'm I going to guess," says I, "when I never heard tell about it before?"

"But you can guess, can't you? It's just as easy."

"*Which* candle?" I says.

"Why, any candle," he says.

"I don't know where he was," says I; "where was he?"

"Why he was in the *dark*! That's where he was!"

"Well, if you knowed where he was, what did you ask me for?"

"Why, blame it, it's a riddle, don't you see? Say, how long are you going to stay here? You got to stay always. We can just have booming times—they don't have no school now. Do you own a dog? I've got a dog—and he'll go in the river and bring out chips that you throw in. Do you like to comb up, Sundays, and all that kind of foolishness? You bet I don't, but ma she makes me. Confound these ole britches, I reckon I'd better put 'em on, but I'd ruther not, it's so warm. Are you all ready? All right—come along, old hoss."

Cold corn-pone, cold corn-beef, butter and butter-milk—that is what they had for me down there, and there ain't nothing better that ever I've come across yet. Buck and his ma and all of them smoked cob pipes, except the nigger woman, which was gone, and the two young women. They all smoked and talked, and I eat and talked. The young women had quilts around them, and their hair down their backs. They all asked me questions, and I told them how pap and me and all the family was living on a little farm down at the bottom of Arkansaw, and my sister Mary Ann run off and got married and never was heard of no more, and Bill went to hunt them and he warn't heard of no more, and Tom and Mort died, and then there warn't nobody but just me and pap left, and he was just trimmed down to nothing, on account of his troubles; so when he died I took what there was left, because the farm didn't belong to us, and started up the river, deck passage, and fell overboard; and that was how I come to be here. So they said I could have a home there as long as I wanted it. Then it was most daylight, and everybody went to bed, and I went to bed with Buck, and when I waked up in the morning, drat it all, I had forgot what my name was. So I laid there about an hour trying to think, and when Buck waked up, I says:

"Can you spell, Buck?"

"Yes," he says.

"I bet you can't spell my name," says I.

"I bet you what you dare I can," says he.

"All right," says I, "go ahead."

"G-o-r-g-e J-a-x-o-n—there now," he says.

"Well," says I, "you done it, but I didn't think you could. It ain't no slouch of a name to spell—right off without studying."

I set it down, private, because somebody might want *me* to spell it, next, and so I wanted to be handy with it and rattle it off like I was used to it.

It was a mighty nice family, and a mighty nice home, too. I hadn't seen no house out in the country before that was so nice and had so much style. It didn't have an iron latch on the front door, nor a wooden one with a buckskin string, but a brass knob to turn, the same as houses in a town. There warn't no bed in the parlor, not a sign of a bed; but heaps of parlors in towns has beds in them. There was a big fireplace that was bricked on the bottom, and the bricks was kept clean and red by pouring water on them and scrubbing them with another brick; sometimes they washed them over with red waterpaint that they call Spanish-brown, same as they do in town. They had big brass dog-irons that could hold up a saw-log. There was a clock on the middle of the mantel-piece, with a picture of a town painted on the bottom half of the glass front, and a round place in the middle of it for the sun, and you could see the pendulum swing behind it. It was beautiful to hear that clock tick; and sometimes when one of these peddlars had been along and scoured her up and got her in good shape, she would start in and strike a hundred and fifty before she got tuckered out. They wouldn't took any money for her.

Well, there was a big outlandish parrot on each side of the clock, made out of something like chalk, and painted up gaudy. By one of the parrots was a cat made of crockery, and a crockery dog by the other; and when you pressed down on them they squeaked, but didn't open their mouths nor look different nor interested. They squeaked through underneath. There was a couple of big wild-turkey-wing fans spread out behind those things. On a table in the middle of the room was a kind of lovely crockery basket that had apples and oranges and peaches and grapes piled up in it which was much redder and yellower and prettier than real ones is, but they warn't real because you could see where pieces had got chipped off and showed the white chalk or whatever it was, underneath.

This table had a cover made out of beautiful oil-cloth, with a red and blue spread-eagle painted on it, and a painted border all around. It come all the way from Philadelphia, they said. There was some books too, piled up perfectly exact, on each corner of the table. One was a big family Bible, full of pictures. One was "Pilgrim's Progress," about a man that left his family it didn't say why. I read considerable in it now and then. The statements was interesting, but tough. Another was "Friendship's Offering," full of beautiful stuff and poetry; but I didn't read the poetry. Another was Henry Clay's Speeches, and another was Dr. Gunn's Family Medicine, which told you all about what to do if a body was sick or dead. There was a Hymn Book, and a lot of other books. And there was nice split-bottom chairs, and perfectly sound, too—not bagged down in the middle and busted, like an old basket.

They had pictures hung on the walls—mainly Washingtons and Lafayettes, and battles, and Highland Marys, and one called "Signing the Declaration." There was some that they called crayons, which one of the daughters which was dead made her own self when she was only fifteen years old. They was different from any pictures I ever see before; blacker, mostly, than is common. One was a woman in a slim black dress, belted small under the armpits, with bulges like a cabbage in the middle of the sleeves, and a large black scoop-shovel bonnet with a black veil, and white slim ankles crossed about with black tape, and very wee black slippers, like a chisel, and she was leaning pensive on a tombstone on her right elbow, under a weeping willow, and her other hand hanging down her side holding a white handkerchief and a reticule, and underneath the picture it said "Shall I Never See Thee More Alas." Another one was a young lady with her hair all combed up straight to the top of her head, and knotted there in front of a comb like a chair-back, and she was crying into a handkerchief and had a dead bird laying on its back in her other hand with its heels up, and underneath the picture it said "I Shall Never Hear Thy Sweet Chirrup More Alas." There was one where a young lady was at a window looking up at the moon, and tears running down her cheeks; and she had an open letter in one hand with black sealing-wax showing on one edge of it, and she was mashing a locket with a chain to it against her mouth, and underneath the picture it said "And Art Thou Gone Yes Thou Art Gone Alas." These was all nice pictures, I reckon, but I didn't somehow seem to take to them, because if ever I was down a little, they always give me the fan-tods. Everybody was sorry she died, because she had laid out a lot more of these pictures to do, and a body could see by what she had done what they had lost. But I reckoned, that with her disposition, she was having a better time in the graveyard. She was at work on what they said was her greatest picture when she took sick, and every day and every night it was her prayer to be allowed to live till she got it done, but she never got the chance. It was a picture of a young woman in a long white gown, standing on the rail of a bridge all ready to jump off, with her hair all down her back, and looking up to the moon, with the tears running down her face, and she had two arms folded across her breast, and two arms stretched out in front, and two more reaching up towards the moon—and the idea was, to see which pair would look best and then scratch out all the other arms; but, as I was saying, she died before she got her mind made up, and now they kept this picture over the head of the bed in her room, and every time her birthday come they hung flowers on it. Other times it was hid with a little curtain. The young woman in the picture had a kind of a nice sweet face, but there was so many arms it made her look too spidery, seemed to me.

    This young girl kept a scrap-book when she was alive, and used to paste obituaries and accidents and cases of patient suffering in it out of the *Presbyterian Observer,* and write poetry after them out of her own head. It was very good poetry. This is what she wrote about a boy by the name of Stephen Dowling Bots that fell down a well and was drownded:

>ODE TO STEPHEN DOWLING BOTS, DEC'D.
>And did young Stephen sicken,
>   And did young Stephen die?
>And did the sad hearts thicken,
>   And did the mourners cry?
>
>No; such was not the fate of
>   Young Stephen Dowling Bots;
>Though sad hearts round him thickened,
>   'Twas not from sickness' shots.
>
>No whooping-cough did rack his frame,
>   Nor measles drear, with spots;
>Not these impaired the sacred name
>   Of Stephen Dowling Bots.
>
>Despised love struck not with woe
>   That head of curly knots,
>Nor stomach troubles laid him low,
>   Young Stephen Dowling Bots.
>
>O no. Then list with tearful eye,
>   Whilst I his fate do tell.
>His soul did from this cold world fly,
>   By falling down a well.

> They got him out and emptied him;
> Alas it was too late;
> His spirit was gone for to sport aloft
> In the realms of the good and great.

If Emmeline Grangerford could make poetry like that before she was fourteen, there ain't no telling what she could a done by-and-by. Buck said she could rattle off poetry like nothing. She didn't ever have to stop to think. He said she would slap down a line, and if she couldn't find anything to rhyme with it she would just scratch it out and slap down another one, and go ahead. She wasn't particular, she could write about anything you choose to give her to write about, just so it was sadful. Every time a man died, or a woman died, or a child died, she would be on hand with her "tribute" before he was cold. She called them tributes. The neighbors said it was the doctor first, then Emmeline, then the undertaker—the undertaker never got in ahead of Emmeline but once, and then she hung fire on a rhyme for the dead person's name, which was Whistler. She warn't ever the same, after that; she never complained, but she kind of pined away and did not live long. Poor thing, many's the time I made myself go up to the little room that used to be hers and get out her poor old scrapbook and read in it when her pictures had been aggravating me and I had soured on her a little. I liked all that family, dead ones and all, and wasn't going to let anything come between us. Poor Emmeline made poetry about all the dead people when she was alive, and it didn't seem right that there wasn't nobody to make some about her, now she was gone; so I tried to sweat out a verse or two myself, but I couldn't seem to make it go, somehow. They kept Emmeline's room trim and nice and all the things fixed in it just the way she liked to have them when she was alive, and nobody ever slept there. The old lady took care of the room herself, though there was plenty of niggers, and she sewed there a good deal and read her Bible there, mostly.

Well, as I was saying about the parlor, there was beautiful curtains on the windows: white, with pictures painted on them, of castles with vines all down the walls, and cattle coming down to drink. There was a little old piano, too, that had tin pans in it, I reckon, and nothing was ever so lovely as to hear the young ladies sing, "The Last Link is Broken" and play "The Battle of Prague" on it. The walls of all the rooms was plastered, and most had carpets on the floors, and the whole house was whitewashed on the outside.

It was a double house, and the big open place betwixt them was roofed and floored, and sometimes the table was set there in the middle of the day, and it was a cool, comfortable place. Nothing couldn't be better. And warn't the cooking good, and just bushels of it too!

Guide for Reading

James' review is very good. He has a clear thesis, which he develops and supports convincingly in his paper. Notice how James' summary gives a good overview of the novel and at the same time focuses on those events relevant to his thesis. He does a particularly effective job of using specific parts of the novel to support his claims.

SAMPLE HISTORY PAPER 1

Huckleberry Finn: An Experiment in Equality

by James R. (a freshman)

Twain, Mark. *Adventures of Huckleberry Finn.* New York: NAL Penguin, Inc., 1959 (1884), 288 pages.

In the historical novel, *Adventures of Huckleberry Finn,* author Mark Twain presents a look at life on the Mississippi River during the nineteenth century, as seen through the eyes of a homeless boy. The boy, Huckleberry Finn, shares a series of adventures with a runaway slave named Jim, who teaches the boy the real meaning of friendship and moral obligation. The boy comes to realize that black people are not property, but human beings; and that they share the same emotions that white people do. In this masterpiece, the author does three important things. He shows the inner workings of the slave trade; and how this colored the white man's perception of blacks. He describes the significance of the Mississippi River. And most importantly, he suggests an equality between blacks and whites that was uncommon during that era.

Adventures of Huckleberry Finn begins by introducing the main character, Huck Finn, his friend Tom Sawyer, and their gang of friends. They were young boys living along the banks of the mighty Mississippi, in the state of Missouri. The time was pre-Civil War, perhaps the 1850s. Huck's friend Tom is a respectable boy who lives in comfort with his Aunt Polly. Huck has no mother, his father is a drunk and a bum, and Huck is forever getting into trouble. Huck and Tom both have six thousand dollars that they found in a cave. Even with the money, Huck is an outcast and practically an orphan.

Huck had been living with the Widow Douglas and her sister, Miss Watson. Mrs. Douglas was trying to "civilize" Huck, and had some small success. Overall, the experiment failed. Huck was too coarse to be tamed. His father, a mean and vile drunkard, kidnapped him and took him to live in the wilderness. Huck escaped by feigning his own murder. He then "borrowed" a canoe and began his journey down the Mississippi. While in flight, he came across Miss Watson's slave, Jim, who had escaped bondage. The two decided to run away together, making their down river on a raft.

One of their first adventures was the discovery of a floating house that was carrying a dead body. This fact is important later in the story. The pair floated at night and hid during the day. There were adventures at every turn. Once they boarded a wrecked steamship that was harboring criminals. Later they became separated in the fog, and each thought the other was dead.

The fog incident was important because it hinted at an equality between the two. While Huck was scouting in the canoe, Jim stayed on the raft. They were separated by an island for some time. Huck found Jim asleep on the raft. He pretended that the separation was a dream. When Jim found out the truth, he was very hurt. Huck realized he had hurt his friend and he apologized, making the two equal at that point.

After Huck observed a southern "family feud" first hand, Huck and Jim acquired two passengers: the "Duke" and the "King." This "royal" duo was a pair of swindlers who only brought trouble to Huck and Jim. Their greatest swindle was pretending to be the brothers of the late Peter Wilks. The con men almost cheated the Wilks family out of a large sum of money, but Huck secretly prevented this from happening.

In a town called Pikesville, the fiends committed their meanest act. They sold Jim to the Phelps family. Fortunately, this is the last Huck sees of the two men, but the damage has already been done. Huck goes to the Phelps' farm posing as Tom Sawyer, the Phelps' cousin who is expected that day on a visit. Tom arrives the same day and "became" cousin Sid, after Huck found him and told him what was happening. Huck tells Tom about Jim, and how he had been sold to the Phelps. At this stage, all Huck wants is to free his friend Jim. It would be easy to steal Jim because he was being held in a tiny shack without guards. Huck wants to get Jim out as soon as possible, but Tom has other plans.

Tom is an avid reader with a fierce imagination. He knows how "real" prisoners escape, and he hatches an elaborate plan that confounds Huck, but it is used anyway. After many days, the plan is carried out and the boys free Jim. In the process, Tom is shot in the calf, Jim is recaptured, and the truth is exposed.

Jim had been free for some time and Tom knew this. He only went through the plan "for the fun of it." It is also revealed that the dead man in the floating house was Huck's father. As the book ends, Huck decided to run off again because Aunt Sally Phelps wants to adopt him and "civilize" him. Huck Finn was an orphan now, but more than that, he was free.

Mark Twain did a remarkable job in describing the attitude shared by whites towards blacks in that era. Black people were not seen as human beings but as property: "someone's nigger." Even Huck, who begins to see the humanity of Jim cannot escape this attitude completely. A letter he writes, but does not send, to Miss Watson, refers to Jim as "your runaway nigger." This shows that while Huck sees Jim as a friend, he cannot escape the "spirit of the times" completely.

The great Mississippi is paid homage to by Twain, who does not hide his love of that river in any of his works. The entire story is centered around this grand waterway. The Mississippi was the economic and social hub of the American west during the mid-1800's. Major cities like St. Louis and New Orleans supported much trade on the Mississippi. The old steam riverboats are highlighted in the novel. The docks were busy with passengers, slaves, sailors, and cargo, all awaiting passage on the vessels. In those days, mail was delivered via riverboat to those who lived in river towns. Huck and Jim encountered many such craft, and they were once thrown from their raft after being struck by such a vessel. It could be said that the mighty Mississippi was blood, and steamboats were the life-giving oxygen, that served the "body" of the American West during the mid-nineteenth century.

As stated earlier, Twain captured the "spirit of the times" in this book. He shows how blacks are viewed as property and referred to as "niggers." However, it seems that Twain is trying to transcend the old attitudes in *Adventures of Huckleberry Finn*. He portrays Jim as a man, capable of feelings, and at times, equal to Huck Finn. Huck is often caught between the prevailing attitude about blacks and his deep friendship with Jim. He even sees this dilemma as a moral problem since southern theology supported the slave system. Huck and Jim's friendship was an experiment in equality. It would be many painful years before the United States would see the black man on Mark Twain's terms.

There is no better way to understand the south in those pre-Civil War days, than to meet the characters in Twain's novel. The Grangerfords represent the elite planter class. The middle class farmer is represented by the Phelps family. Huck's father was the epitome of the poor white class. Jim was representative of both the runaway slave, and later, the free black. The Phelps' slaves were the slaves still within the system. These characters help Twain paint a portrait of the south before the war.

The book flows well and is hard to put down. One aspect of the book does slow the reading pace a bit. It is hard to read the dialogue of Jim and the other blacks. Of course it was written like this to present the way blacks talked, so this small problem is understood.

The novel serves the history student well as it presents the attitudes and feelings of those who would later go to war to protect their interests. It is shown that the southerner felt he had to fight as he was protecting his very way of life. By examining the everyday lives of the people, their fears, hopes, and ideas, greater understanding of how the Civil War came about can be gleaned.

The most important thing Twain did was to put readers on the raft with Huck and Jim. Readers must ask themselves the same question that Huck asked. The questions asked almost mirror Thoreau in *Civil Disobedience*. How far should one follow the government, when the government is committing acts that seem morally and ethically wrong. Painful choices have to be made at times, and these choices often lead to the persecution, and even death of the voices of opposition. But these questions must be asked so that previous mistakes will not be repeated.

In writing *Adventures of Huckleberry Finn,* Mark Twain wrote, perhaps, the greatest American novel ever. He put his reputation on the line in writing about the friendship of a white boy and a runaway slave. Many readers did not or could not see Twain's true intentions. Others saw the subtle suggestions, but ignored them. And perhaps some people read between the lines and saw Twain's intentions. And maybe some were persuaded to take up the causes of reform and equality after reading this book. The battle for equality has been an uphill struggle since the book was published in 1884. Blacks have achieved many rights since those days after the Civil War, but there is still room for more equality.

Analysis of Sample History Paper 1

James has written a very good review of the novel. He provides a complete plot summary without becoming tedious, and he accurately focuses on the social and historical significance of *The Adventures of Huckleberry Finn*. His introduction clearly states what he plans to do, and he fulfills this plan in the review. The result is an organized and thoughtful discussion of the novel that informs people who have not read the book before and enlightens those who have.

Recognizing the impossibility of retelling the story in such a short paper, James develops a clear and narrow thesis and uses it as a guide for what to focus on. His statement that "the author does three important things" leads him to choose those events in the novel that deal with the slave trade and the white man's perception of blacks, the river itself, and the suggestion of equality between blacks and whites. This clear focus not only gave James a guide, but it also enables readers to follow and understand the review more easily.

Without seeming to be answering questions directly, James has responded to the questions in hints number 4, 5, and 6 in the assignment. Beginning with the twelfth paragraph, he responds to those points that are appropriate for a book review assignment for a history class. Although James may have been aware of the important literary issues surrounding *The Adventures of Huckleberry Finn*, he was right in avoiding those in his review.

The one problem James had in writing this review was an uncertainty with verb tense. The accepted convention calls for discussing literature in the present tense, because the events happen as they are read. A novel is fiction, so the events never really happened; in this sense they are timeless and happen every time the novel is read. The same convention also applies to nonfiction; the author or book *states* or *says*, even though the book was written in the past. In the sciences and social sciences, the convention is the opposite; writers use the past tense when making references.

Guide for Reading

Karen's review is below average, mainly because she has no clear thesis and because she is unclear about what historical period the novel belongs to. While reading Karen's review, you may get the sense that she is simply looking for enough to say to fill the required number of pages. Certainly, this was her teacher's impression, and this effort was marked accordingly. As you read, identify those places where the writing lacks focus.

SAMPLE HISTORY PAPER 2

A Review of *The Adventures of Huckleberry Finn*

by Karen C. (a freshman)

Twain, Mark. *The Adventures of Huckleberry Finn.* New York: Bantam Books, 1988, 292 pages.

The Adventures of Huckleberry Finn is a fun and innerjetic book to read. The author, Mark Twain, does a superior job in writing this adventure story. In the "notice" of the book the author states that "persons attempting to find a motive in this narrative will be persecuted, and persons attempting to find a plot will be shot" (p. 2). Mark Twain may not have had a motive, or a plot in mind, but the adventures of Huckleberry Finn give readers a good look at society during the late 1800's.

The book is written for pleasure and to be exciting. Huck Finn's life is adventerous and exciting with an added lonliness and depression. Each adventure could be published as it's own short story and would be just as exciting. The adventure starts off when

Huck Finn is living with a woman from the community. His father is supposedly dead and Huck is put into the care of the Widow Douglas, who is trying to civilize him. At first Huck felt cramped but with time he began to get used to the widow and her kind of civilization.

Huck did not seem to care about his father's death. His father was known to be a drunk. When he was under the influence he would beat Huck. As time passed and Huck got used to the widow and school his father stepped back into his life. Huck was not pleased to see his father and his father was not pleased that Huck was attending school and living with the Widow Douglas. Eventually Huck's father kidnapped him and locked him into a cabin in the woods. At first, according to Huck, "I was kind of lazy and jolly, laying off comfortable all day, smoking and fishing, and no books nor study" (p. 24). This life was right up Huck's alley until his father began to beat him more. "But by and by pap got too handy with his hick'ry, and I couldn't stand it. I was all over welts" (p. 24). With time Huck schemed a way to escape, which he was able to pull off. During Huck's escape he met up with Jim, a slave, and they started a long trail of adventures.

Along with the ongoing adventures that Huck finds himself in, the book takes on another character. The people that Huck and Jim come in contact with give readers a sense of the beliefs and personality of the time period in which they lived. Slaves were very common during Huck's day. A runaway slave was breaking the law which was an unforgiving crime, even to Huckleberry Finn. Huck begins to have a problem with his conscience when thinking of Jim's freedom. "Well, I can tell you it made me all over trembly and feverish, too, to hear him, because I began to get it through my head that he was most free—and who was to blame for it? Why, me" (p. 85). Huck felt that by helping Jim he was betraying Jim's owner. "What did that poor old woman do that you could treat her so mean?" (p. 85). In the long run, Huck decides it would be too much trouble to do the right thing so he does not turn Jim in.

Huck and Jim become good friends living on the raft together. The only obstacle is that Jim is a nigger. Huck often refers to Jim as a nigger, even though he respects him. "Well, he was right; he was most always right; he had an uncommon level head for a nigger" (p. 74). Society said that niggers were of lower intelligence and the only place they had in society was to be slaves. Huck was not as civilized as some, but even he knew where blacks stood in society.

Another characteristic of this book is the religious beliefs during this time period. Religion was very contradictory during Huck's day. On one occasion the widow told Huck that he would get everything he prayed for. Huck did not believe this was true. "Once I got a fishline, but no hooks. I tried for hooks three or four times, but somehow I could not make it work" (p. 12). Huck felt like religion was some sort of magic and he was unable to get the hang of it.

Religion was also something a person could use when he wanted something from another person. The author points this out on occasions. The first being when Huck's father wants whiskey. Pap, as Huck calls his father, gave the judge a sob story saying he was going to turn over a new leaf. "There's a hand that was the hand of a hog; but it ain't no more; it's the hand of a man tha's started in on a new life, and'll die before he'll go back" (p. 23). After the judge's family had gone to sleep, Pap snuck out and traded his new coat for a jug of whiskey. He has played on the religious beliefs and kindness of the judge. The author again illustrates this idea when Huck and Jim encounter the King and the Duke. The supposed king makes money by deceiving people at camp meetings. He told the people at the meeting that he found religion because of them and even though he had no money he would spend his life, "trying to turn the perator unto the true path" (p. 128). The people at the camp meeting decided to pass around a hat for him, to show their trust and faith. In turn the King used the money to get drunk.

A third example of societies religious beliefs is uncovered when Huck meets the Grangerford's. The Grangerfords and the Shepherdsons are involved in a feud, which takes precedence over all matters. Both families attended church on Sunday where the sermon was on Brotherly love. The whole Grangerford commented on what a good sermon it was, but the next day a battle broke out that killed Buck Grangerford.

Mark Twain attempts to write an adventure story to entertain young boys. What the author may not have expected was that this book would be used as a historical novel. The book can be enjoyed by everyone. Huckleberry Finn's life was exciting and sometimes scary. The book gives a fascinating view of the people whom Huck encountered. The book gives insight to the beliefs and personalities of society during the late 1800's.

Analysis of Sample History Paper 2

Although it is obvious that Karen enjoyed reading *The Adventures of Huckleberry Finn*, her review has no clear focus. The summary covers only a few episodes and completely fails to give an overview of the novel. It appears that she assumed her readers had read and remembered the book, and as a result she discusses points without providing a context. The summary actually covers only the early part of the novel, to the point when Huck escapes from his father. Although later incidents are mentioned, they make sense only to someone who already knows the complete story. She has failed to "describe the contents of the book," as point 2 of the assignment requires.

The two issues that Karen touches on are race and religion. These are valid points to discuss, but there is no sense that Karen set out to make them the focus of her review. According to the first two paragraphs and the conclusion, *The Adventures of Huckleberry Finn* is basically an adventure story that inadvertently contains some historical truths about society. This evaluation seems to reflect a fundamental reading error: Karen took seriously the author's ironic "notice" in the beginning of the book, where he states that the story contains no motive or plot. We can see that a problem in reading causes equal problems in writing. Had Karen been more perceptive and caught Twain's irony, she would have realized that the novel was intended to do much more than simply entertain.

There are times when quotations are necessary to support points the reviewer is making. They should be used only for support, and they should never be used to make the reviewer's point. In the case of fiction, quotations are appropriate as examples when the author's style and use of language are being discussed. Long book reviews may contain quotations as examples of the author's humor, style, vocabulary, and so forth. Karen has used too many in her review, and none is really essential. She could have summarized or paraphrased the information, and the review would seem more like her own writing instead of an assembly of quotations.

Another problem that may cause readers to question Karen's authority as a reviewer is her historical inaccuracy. Twice she mentions that the novel reflects society in the late 1800s, when in fact the setting is pre-Civil War, or early to mid-1800s. She hasn't made the connection between Huckleberry Finn's society and its historical setting. This error undermines Karen's evaluation of the novel as a historical document.

Finally, you should note that Karen's writing doesn't meet academic expectations because it doesn't follow accepted standards of correctness. In the very first sentence, for example, she spells "energetic" *innerjetic*. Immediately, our image of her as a person who cares about her work falls several notches. If this paper had been written in class without the benefit of a handy dictionary, we might be more inclined to view this invented spelling as a slip of the pen—but the paper was written outside of class, and Karen had ample time to proofread her work.

In a similar vein, look at the second sentence of the second paragraph: "Huck Finn's life is <u>adventerous</u> and exciting with an added <u>lonliness</u> and depression." Again, the invented spelling is distracting, but notice how the sentence itself just doesn't sound right. In fact, it sounds as though Karen is saying that loneliness and depression, when added to Huck's life, made it adventurous and exciting. But that can't be what she means. The problem lies in the fact that the sentence, as structured, doesn't properly focus on Huck; instead it focuses on "adventurous and exciting." More time spent revising the paper through several drafts, using feedback from classmates and perhaps from her teacher, would have helped significantly. Maybe then Karen would have found a better way of expressing her thought, such as, "Huck leads an exciting and adventurous life, but he is nevertheless lonely and depressed much of the time."

Writing Assignment

Review a novel using the guidelines in History Assignment 1. You may not be in a history class, so it may be necessary for you to replace the second sentence in hint number 5 with: "Is the fictional environment consistent with what you know of the period covered by the book?" Part of your review concerns the accuracy of the author's portrayal of the setting, so it is also necessary for you to choose a book whose setting is a time and place you are familiar with. Remember that you don't need to cover every aspect of the novel. After you have read the book, make a specific claim that deals in some way with its historical significance. Your audience consists of those in the general public who enjoy reading and who check reviews as a guide for selecting books. Write a review that would be appropriate for the Arts and Entertainment page of the Sunday edition of a large newspaper.

HISTORY ASSIGNMENT 2

Course: **U.S. History for Freshmen and Sophomores**

Write a well-organized, interpretative essay of 1000–1500 words on the following topic. You are expected to use factual data from the course material (class notes, textbook, paperbacks, and supplementary articles) along with your considered opinion formed upon reflection. Be creative and solid.

TOPIC: Assume that you have invented a time machine that allows you to offer customers the ultimate vacation: a one-month trip anywhere back in time. Your tourists will pick an initial destination and a day of their choice and then travel successively from year to year every 24 hours. They will be allowed to participate fully in the events they come into contact with though they will not be allowed to "interfere" in history; you have designated a brain program which allows them to understand the relevance of their situation but prevents them from speaking of or making any movement which would in the slightest way alter history. For the moment you have only one important reservation. There are still some minor bugs to be worked out and your vacation package is only "safe" as far back as 100 years. You decide to offer three basic packages for which you must heavily advertise: 1896 to 1925, 1926 to 1955, and 1956 to 1985. You choose your favorite time period and write an advertising campaign for it while employees work on the other two. As a part of your campaign, discuss what advantages a time traveler might have in making a trip to that time period. What historically significant events might he/she witness? What precautions would be in order for your "tourists"? In general, you are to write an in-depth historical portrait of the period, telling your customers all they "need" to know before embarking on their tour. Be sure to cover all the major bases (i.e., political climate of the period, economic advantages or disadvantages, social movements to take advantage of or beware of, military conflicts to take note of, and cultural trends to enjoy).

Analysis of History Assignment 2

This assignment calls for a blend of knowledge and creativity, as stated in the first paragraph: "Be creative and solid." A good paper, then, will be a clearly expressed, well-explained chronology of the 30-year segment expressed in the language and format of a travel brochure.

Its nature as a history assignment mandates that the "solid" part be attended to first. If you were responding to this assignment, you would want a complete list of the events that took place within the time segment so you could choose those that are important and at the same time interesting and exciting to witness. In addition, you would need to understand the importance and the effects of each event, because you will have to explain why you have chosen it. The assignment asks for more than just those well-known events or scenes most of us are familiar with; the teacher wants students to understand that quite often a peripheral or connected event is more interesting and actually more significant than those covered in history tests. For example, the personal financial losses suffered by Winston Churchill in the American stock market crash pinpoint both the worldwide effects of the crash and Churchill's own precarious financial situation throughout the thirties.

The creative part of this assignment is not as easy as it sounds. Although nothing in the assignment explicitly directs students to additional study, you should know that successfully imitating the format and language of a travel brochure requires some reading of this type of advertising. Ambitious students would therefore give careful study to several of these brochures (available at any travel agency). The language of advertising is simple and direct, and it is designed to make readers feel as if they are being talked to personally.

Guide for Reading

Marie's paper is a good response to the assignment, better than average, but not outstanding. The paper is strong in its coverage of historical events and trends; the events give readers a good sense of what happened between 1926 and 1955. As a travel brochure, however, the paper is weak. Imagine you are a potential customer for such an experience, and ask yourself where Marie's paper seems to ignore that part of the assignment. Would you want to take this trip?

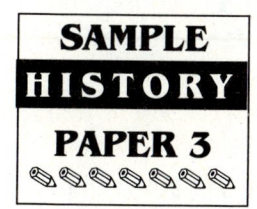

> **SAMPLE HISTORY PAPER 3**

A Winter Wonderland

Marie M. (a sophomore)

[1] Having a rough time thinking of a gift to give that special person on your Christmas list? Well, Time Voyagers, Inc. has the perfect gift. Give that special person on your list a trip back to a "winter wonderland." This December only Time Voyagers is offering a one month trip back to the years of 1926 through 1955. Yes, it's time travel. Due to a recent discovery, we here at Time Voyagers are able to offer our customers the ultimate vacation. On this particular trip, you or that special person will be able to experience the second Industrial Revolution and see the political and economic effects of the Great Depression. You will see America develop its international relations with the Good Neighbor policy only to retreat to a policy of neutrality with the fear of war. During the last few weeks of your trip you will gain insight into World War II and the Cold War. Finally, the last twenty-four hours of your vacation will be spent enjoying the post-war era by celebrating Christmas with your family of 1955. Hence, Time Voyagers has prepared this information packet to inform our customers of the events that took place during these years. We will describe the places where you will be traveling and will discuss the historical significance of each event.

[2] With the second Industrial Revolution, American industrial output nearly doubled and the national product rose about forty percent. Most of this tremendous growth took place in consumer ____ producing industries. These industries produced such items as automobiles, appliances, furniture, and clothing. American workers became the highest paid in history and were able to buy the new goods that were turning out on the assembly lines.

[3] The first stop on your trip will be Detroit, Michigan. Here you will experience the second Industrial Revolution by touring one of Henry Ford's automobile manufacturing plants. The automobile industry became the nation's largest in the 1920's. By the end of the decade, twenty-six million cars were on the road. This industry also had an effect on the rest of the economy. The mass production of the assembly line, which was pioneered by Henry Ford, required large quantities of steel to produce a car. Rubber factories boomed with the demand for tires. Paint and glass suppliers experienced a noticeable increase of business. Thus, the whole economy was strengthened with the automobile industry.

[4] Your second stop will be New York City. Here you will experience the new urban culture and the Roaring Twenties. During the decade of the twenties, metropolitan areas grew rapidly as people came seeking jobs in the new consumer industries. The skyscraper became the most prominent feature of the city. You will see the construction of the 102-story Empire State Building, which was not completed until 1930.

[5] The Roaring Twenties was a time for heroes, excitement, and frivolity. Remember to bring your autograph book because you will be meeting many heroes of the late twenties. One such hero will be Charles Lindbergh. Lindbergh is famous for his solo flight across the Atlantic in 1927. Oh, we here at Time Voyagers must warn you that alcoholic beverages are not allowed on the trip because of Prohibition. We do not allow bootleggers on our tours. However women are permitted to smoke. You will be attending several dances so brush up on the Charleston and listen to that jazz music.

[6] Before leaving New York you will visit the New York Stock Exchange and see the prosperity of the twenties come to an abrupt halt. On October 14, 1929 the stock market crashed. Prices dropped eighty percent below their 1929 highs. This was the beginning of the Great Depression. The Great Depression lasted for ten years. Finally it loosened its grip on the nation with the outbreak of World War II.

[7] The Depression led to a profound shift in political loyalties. The Republicans, dominant since the 1890s, gave way to a new

Democratic majority. The result was the election of Franklin D. Roosevelt in 1933 as Herbert Hoover's successor. President Roosevelt developed a broad program of relief, recovery, and reform that increased the role of government on American life. This program was called the New Deal.

[8] Your next stop will be Chicago, Illinois. Here you will see the economic effects of the Great Depression. We must warn you that the repercussions of the stock market crash are harsh. For example, men and women who were victims of the stock market crash lived in lean-tos made of scrap wood and metal. Families went without meat and fresh vegetables for months. Their diet consisted of soup and beans. There were massive lines where the unemployed stood waiting for their relief checks. Veterans sold apples and pencils on the street corners.

[9] Roosevelt's New Deal attempted to solve America's economic problems. The New Deal lasted for five years and its impact on American life was enduring. Franklin D. Roosevelt managed to preserve the traditional capitalistic system with a thin overlay on federal control. However, he did little to alter the distribution of wealth throughout America. Most of the changes brought about by the New Deal were reflected in the society. The government acknowledged its responsibility to provide for the welfare of those unable to care for themselves with the adoption of the Social Security. The Wagner Act stimulated the growth of labor unions, called for a balance of corporate power, and provided a minimum wage law.

[10] Roosevelt was a brilliant politician. He was successful in appealing to the people. He filled people with the sense of purpose and provided the "psychological lift" they needed to endure and survive the Great Depression.

[11] After seeing the dreadful effects of the Great Depression, you will be transported back to the year 1936. You will tour Latin America for three days. It is here that you will see America develop its international relations. As a result of the Depression, American trade with Latin America had drastically declined. Roosevelt moved quickly to solidify the improved relations and gain economic benefits. He proclaimed the Good Neighbor policy and renounced the imperialism of the past. You will see

Roosevelt actually sign this new policy in Buenos Aires. The President believed that cooperation and friendship were more effective tactics than threats and armed intervention.

[12] Aside from the Good Neighbor approach in the Western Hemisphere, America was unsure of where it stood concerning foreign policy. The Americans wanted peace and noninvolvement. Thus, came the neutrality legislation of the Nye Committee.

[13] After touring Latin America, your next stop will be New Jersey. While staying in New Jersey, you will visit Princeton University. Here you will see student demonstrations against the war. Pacificism swept across college campuses due to the growing fear of war. Students carried signs reading "Abolish the R.O.T.C." and "Build Schools-Not Battleships."

[14] For two years the United States tried to remain at peace while war raged in Europe and Asia. On May 10, 1940 the Germans unleashed the blitzkreig or lightning war on the Western front. Using tanks and dive bombers, the Germans cut deep into the Allied lines dividing the French and British forces. Thus, France fell to the victorious Hitler.

[15] Your next stop will be Charlottesville, Virginia. Here you will hear Roosevelt invoke a policy of all-out aid to the Allies. The President made a commitment to involve America in the Second World War. He denounced Germany and Italy as "the gods of force and hate" in his speech at Charlottesville.

[16] America became involved in the fighting when Japan attacked Pearl Harbor on December 7, 1941. With this attack Mr. Roosevelt asked Congress for a declaration of war. The whole country united behind Roosevelt to seek revenge for Pearl Harbor.

[17] After World War II many decisions had to be made concerning Europe. So Truman, who was made President after Roosevelt's death, met with Stalin and Churchill to make some decisions. You will be transported to Potsdam in East Germany to see this conference of the big three. Reparations of Europe was the crucial issue. It was agreed that each side would take reparations primarily from its own occupation zone. This signaled the future division of Germany.

History

[18] Even though a compromise was reached in Potsdam, the conflict over world power still existed between America and the Soviet Union. The nations tried to adjust their differences of postwar economic aid and the atomic bomb though discussion and negotiations. However, the Americans still remained suspicious of the Russians. Thus, out of this suspicion came the Truman Doctrine. The Truman Doctrine marked an informal declaration of Cold War.

[19] The Truman Doctrine was put to the test with the outbreak of the Korean War. The Soviet Union supported the industrial, Northern part of Korea and America supported the agrarian South. On June 25, 1950, the North Korean army crossed the thirty-eighth parallel attacking South Korea. It is presumed that Stalin built up the North Korean forces and ordered an attack in order to expand the Soviet sphere. Assuming that this was a sign of Soviet aggression, Truman sent American troops over to Korea to engage in war against the Communists.

[20] From East Germany, you will be traveling to Washington to see the inauguration of President Eisenhower. America's foreign policy changed under the leadership of Eisenhower. He made the Cold War the primary issue in his presidential campaign. Eisenhower wanted to end the Cold War and issue a detente. He emphasized nuclear warfare and reduced military spending. Someday he hoped to end the arms race between America and the Soviet Union. The grand finale of your trip will be spending Christmas with your family of 1955. You will notice that family togetherness is emphasized. Also, you will quickly notice all the packages under the tree. The second World War brought about the revival of the consumer industries. The Korean War helped overcome a brief recession and ensured continued prosperity. Families of the fifties marveled at the television and kitchen appliances. Remember to bring your Christmas gifts along?

[21] We here at Time Voyagers hope that you or that special person in your life will join us on this Christmas excursion to a "winter wonderland." Make this a Christmas to remember. For reservations and more information 725-459-7412. Ask for Santa Claus.

STUDY QUESTIONS

1. A good introductory paragraph provides readers with a guide for what follows. Make a list of the points covered in Marie's first paragraph and then compare this list with the information that follows. Does this introduction do a good job preparing you for the paper? What changes (if any) in the introduction would you recommend?

2. Does Marie properly prepare her potential travelers for any hazards or problems that may occur in the course of their journey? If so, what are they? If not, what do you think travelers would need to know in this regard?

3. The main problem with Marie's paper is that it is more solid than creative. Throughout the paper she focuses more on summarizing history than on providing a tour. This focus could easily be altered by changing the wording and by choosing events that are visually interesting. Rewrite paragraphs 6, 10, and 16 so readers will feel as though they will be taken somewhere to see something important happen instead of simply being told about the event.

4. One final feature of this paper that needs attention is style. Marie tends to use short sentences that should be connected. A series of these short sentences makes Marie sound as if she is writing ideas down as they come to her. For example, paragraph 13 would read better if revised to something similar to the following: "After touring Latin America, you will visit Princeton University, where you will see student demonstrations against the war. As pacifism swept across the country because of the growing fear of the war, students carried signs reading 'Abolish the R.O.T.C.' and 'Build Schools, Not Battleships.'" Rewrite paragraphs 15 and 20 using clauses, phrases, and adjectives to eliminate the

> strings of short, simple sentences. Keep the important points in the main clauses and use subordinate parts of the sentence for the less important ideas.

Sentence Lesson

One of the more subtle features of good writing is related to what is called "parallel structure." The convention inherent in this term is that when two or more ideas in a sentence are similar in function, they should be phrased in the same grammatical form. Noun and verb construction cause writers the most difficulty, as you can see in the sentences below, taken from sample history papers 2 and 3:

1. Society said that niggers were of lower intelligence and the only place they had in society was to be slaves.
2. Huck felt like religion was some sort of magic and he was unable to get the hang of it.
3. On this particular trip, you or that special person will be able to experience the second Industrial Revolution and see the political and economic effects of the Great Depression.
4. Before leaving New York you will visit the New York Stock Exchange and see the prosperity of the twenties come to an abrupt halt.
5. Roosevelt moved quickly to solidify the improved relations and gain economic benefits.

Look carefully at how we have rewritten the sentences to make their structure parallel. Pay particular attention to what we have underlined:

1a. Society said _that_ niggers were of lower intelligence _and that_ the only place they had in society was to be slaves.
2a. Huck felt _that_ religion was some sort of magic _and that_ he was unable to get the hang of it.
3a. On this particular trip, you or that special person _will experience_ the second Industrial Revolution _and will_ see the political and economic effects of the Great Depression.
4a. Before leaving New York you _will visit_ the New York Stock Exchange _and will see_ the prosperity of the twenties come to an abrupt halt.
5a. Roosevelt moved quickly _to solidify_ the improved relations _and to gain_ economic benefits.

Guide for Reading

In many ways, Kimberly's paper captures the pace and bounce of the language of advertising: short paragraphs, the use of appropriate jargon, and the careful avoidance of anything tedious. As a response to this particular assignment, however, it is below average because the historical information is not solid. Notice how Kimberly mentions events and trends without explaining them in any depth. The result is a paper that is *too much* like an advertisement: a series of images designed to trigger an emotional, but not a thoughtful, response.

SAMPLE HISTORY PAPER 4

The Ultimate Time Journey

Kimberly S. (a sophomore)

[1] Journey back to the thrilling and exciting years of 1956 through 1985. Experience 30 fun filled days that you will remember for a lifetime. See and participate in the decades, 50's, 60's, 70's, and 80's, that helped mold our culture and life today. This marvelous journey allows you to spend 24 hours per day through the gamut from 1956 to 1985. Experience the politics, economy, social conflicts and cultural trends of the era. Witness the period first hand; tell your friends, "I was there!"

[2] In the era you are about to witness, you will travel through some rough times in politics yet you get to experience the economic prosperity and the cultural highs. From Eisenhower to Reagan, from rhinestone-speckled shoes to jeans ripped from the thighs, and from Elvis to the discos, this era is certainly one to remember and experience.

[3] Our journey starts you off in the late 1950's, during Eisenhower's administration. During this time racial riots are at their highs. You are welcome to join in on these riots, just watch out for the National Guard, for they are famous for being called to break up anti-black rioting. You may be better of standing behind Martin Luther King, Jr., for he is one of the main segregational leaders of this time. See first hand the origins and means of the Civil Rights ____.

History

[4] The Americans at this time had a feeling of atomic-anxiety. In J. Robert Oppenheimer's words, "The U.S. and the USSR are like two scorpions in a bottle, each capable of killing the other but only at the risk of his own life. . . . The atomic clock ticks faster and faster."

[5] Most Americans looked to the time-honored virtues of home, church, and community. It was a time to find group acceptance. The economic times booming brought about the men in their suits going to work and the wives staying at home making a family.

[6] This was a time of stern undergarmets such as boned girdles and stiff, pointed or padded bras.

[7] You'll see that these times were based on the motto, "The family that prays together stays together." Songs like "love and Marriage" were blockbusters like the movie "The Ten Commandments." The family was well illustrated with the TV hit shows "Father Knows Best" and "Leave it to Beaver." Part of the fads you'll see as a result of this are crew cuts, white bucks, and hula hoops.

[8] Soon the fads change and you'll have a chance to rock and roll, the teenage "fad." Buy yourself a felt skirt with sequined appliques and some rhinestone-speckled plastic shoes. Pull up a chair and enjoy a TV dinner.

[9] Share in America's grief as the Russians launched their "Sputnik" into space. American technology was a "bit" set back with the creation of the Edsel. Now is your time to test drive that all time manufacturing flop.

[10] Experience the excitement of seeing the premieres of "As the World Turns," and "The Price is Right." Just as well, the movies "Invasion of the Body Snatchers," "War and Peace," and "The King and I."

[11] Dance to "Hound Dog," "Love Me Tender," and "Que Sera, Sera."

[12] The decades of the 60's begins with John Kennedy's administration. These times as you'll see were times of technological advancements, economic prosperity, and unfortunately tragic assasinations.. Now is your chance to experience the Cuban missile crisis and ____ see how we faltered at the Bay of Pigs.

[13] Witness the tragic and senseless death of an ideal American, Kennedy. Get involved in the still alive racial riots such as the boycotting of segregated busses. Hear "The King" say, "I have a dream."

[14] You'll see the dress and grooming codes change during this era. Hair, even for men grew longer, skirts rose higher and bras were discarded. This was known as the time of the hippies where life was doing your own thing. A time of "making love not war" and a time of intense drug use shaped the country. Visit this time and you can enjoy the Beatles and join in the acid rock.

[15] College campuses became the place for demonstrations. Join in the marches for peace and love. Join in on the marches against war, the Vietnam War! A time the people did not know the reason or the how of Vietnam. This war was a tragic time and a cheap excuse for the loss of so many young American people.

[16] Presidential elections were close yet the vote went to Nixon. Now is your chance to experience Nixon's reign, and failure. Find out for yourself what really happened and see if you would still have him resign.

[17] This is a good time to buy yourself some Superbowl tickets and witness the stars like Joe Namath and Cassius Clay in action. Or if football is not your game then be one of the 500,000 who gathered at Woodstock for a free concert.

[18] Still, America made its advances in space. Neil Armstrong made his successful leap onto the moon, be there to see it!

[19] Next on our voyage, we arrive in the 70's. Gerald Ford was appointed President. By this time, there had been a tally of over fifty thousand soldiers were dead as a result of the war.

[20] Soon Carter is to enter into our travels. You'll see for yourself how he was a Christian from the deep South. You'll also experience the growing double digit inflation during this time.

[21] The blacks were, in film, role models and ordinary people, rather than stereotyped and victims. Witness the blockbuster best-seller "Roots" of Alex Haley.

[22] This era was also a monumental era for the women and their rights. Now's your chance to play your part in the ERA movement. This movement brought about movies such as "Kramer vs Kramer."

History

[23] Women wore whatever they pleased. The skirts were of all lengths.

[24] Movies of divorced men such as "The Odd Couple" were products of the new ERA Movement.

[25] With a new decade to come, comes a new leader to help out. Ronald Reagan becomes our president and helps free the hostages that Iran took during Carter's administration.

[26] With Reagan we will witness the meetings with Gorbachav. We'll see first hand what Reagan is doing as a defence on Star Wars. We will see views on the peace talks about armament at Geneva.

[27] People during this era are concerned with South Africa and Apartheid. Hard Rock and Heavy metal mold our society into a damned group.

[28] Men walk around with long hair and mohawks and earrings. The society is aware of diseases and is concerned about their children.

[29] This ultimate journey is one you cannot miss. No part of what is today. Join in the fun, learn and understand, grieve and laugh. The best and the worst of the past, whatever you wish to see and experience can be yours today.

STUDY QUESTIONS

1. This is a creative paper with some weaknesses that keep it from being as solid as it should be. Kimberly has caught the essence of the language of advertising, and as a result this paper reads like a travel brochure. Identify what makes the paragraphs, sentences, and focus resemble the language of advertising.

2. a. Make a list by number of those paragraphs that do not adequately explain the significance of the event that is focused on.
b. Make a list of those paragraphs that need examples so you will know exactly what Kimberly is talking about.

c. Make a list of those paragraphs that tell you something about history but do not seem appropriate for a journey.
Rewrite one paragraph from each of these three categories to make it appropriate for the assignment.
Make a list of those paragraphs that do not adequately explain the significance of the event Kimberly describes.

3. Throughout the paper, Kimberly produces some unclear sentences and incomplete explanations of historical events.
a. Rewrite paragraphs 5 and 15 so the sentences will say clearly what you think Kimberly meant to say.
b. Rewrite paragraph 9, expressing more accurately the reaction to Sputnik and the flop of the Edsel. You may want to express the state of America's technology in more than one paragraph.
c. Try to make some sense out of paragraph 27 and express what you think Kimberly meant to say. Here again you may want to write more than one paragraph.

4. At various places in her paper, Kimberly makes historically inaccurate or incorrect statements. She writes in paragraph 3, for example, that the National Guard was "famous" for being called to break up "anti-black rioting." In paragraph 17, she suggests that Cassius Clay was a football player. Use your library to determine the role the National Guard played during race riots in the 1950s and to determine the sport Cassius Clay participated in. Then reread Kimberly's paper to see if you can find other historical inaccuracies. What effect do these problems have on the paper?

Writing Assignments

For the following assignments, assume that you are able to offer the same type of time travel described in the above assignment for U.S. History. Although the length of the assigned papers remains the same, assignments 2 and 3 demand a greater knowledge of history than number 1. For all three, however, you will need a good sense of the time and place of choice. A good paper will accomplish two things: It will make your readers want to take the trip to discover the time for themselves, as a good advertisement would, and it will demonstrate your knowledge of the period covered. As always, logical organization, clear explanations, and correct grammar are necessary elements of good writing.

1. Using a week's sequence of your local or hometown newspaper, design a day-long tour covering those events that are both visually interesting and important in understanding the character of the town. Your readers are contemplating moving to this town. In a 4- to 6-page paper, describe your tour in a way that will persuade them to do so.
2. Using an issue of *Life* magazine, design a week-long tour covering those events that are visually interesting. In a 4- to 6-page paper, describe your chosen events so your readers will want to witness them and at the same time will understand what the world was like during that particular period.
3. Using a week's sequence of a major newspaper (*The New York Times, The Washington Post*, etc.) from at least five years ago, design a week-long tour of the United States covering those events that are both interesting in themselves and significant to what is happening today. In a 4- to 6-page paper, describe your chosen events so readers will want to see them happen and will also understand the significance of each event.
4. Pretend you are a time traveler who has decided to go back in time to interfere with some major historical event that has influenced who and what we are today. In a 6- to 8-page paper, describe your chosen event, explain its significance, and tell why you chose to alter it. Then describe what you would do and explain what the consequences would be for our own time.

HISTORY ASSIGNMENT 3

Course: **Religious Fundamentalism and American Culture, a Seminar for Junior History Majors**

> You will write a research paper (15 to 20 pages) on a major figure, movement, or event directly connected with the fundamentalist movement in America. Your paper should focus on the character of the person (or people) involved and the chronology of the person's life, event, or movement, and also explain the historical significance of your subject. Assume that your reader knows nothing of your subject but has a general knowledge of American history. Your goal is to enlighten this reader on one aspect of American fundamentalism.
>
> Your paper must be fully researched and carefully and appropriately documented with end notes and bibliography. While content is of paramount importance, your paper should be grammatically correct, well organized, and clearly written. The result should be an interesting, informative paper that is a pleasure to read.

Analysis of History Assignment 3

This assignment is for a seminar for junior history majors, the major assignment for the semester in place of a final examination. It constitutes almost all the writing students do for the term, so it understandably asks for extensive research and careful writing.

The paper is actually a history of one specific aspect of American fundamentalism focusing on a single person as emblematic of that aspect. Writing a good history means more than simply presenting a chronology of random facts. There must be a clear purpose (or thesis) to the history, which means that the facts chosen must be relevant to this purpose. In preparing such a paper, writers need to conduct a complete overview to know what their purpose is and what is essential to this purpose. Before handing in their final copies, writers should be able to state, in one good sentence (a thesis statement), what the paper says in 15 to 20 pages. This statement should make a significant connection between an aspect of American fundamentalism and the life of a particular person.

The three words in the assignment that should guide the preparation and writing of the paper are *character*, *chronology*, and *significance*. After reading the paper, readers should know the person or people involved as real people, the significance and order of the relevant events, and the importance of the subject as an aspect of American fundamentalism.

It is clear from the assignment that the instructor assumes students are familiar with the requirements of scholarly research and the characteristics of good writing. When attempting such an assignment, students can benefit from referring to an English handbook for clarifying the mechanical details of documentation. It is necessary for you to understand how to summarize, paraphrase, quote and document sources correctly.

Sometimes the phrase "a pleasure to read" can be taken amiss. You should not labor to produce elaborate sentences and "cute" remarks to make the reading pleasurable. Style is much less important than content and organization. Writers who are involved in their topics and who want to present their knowledge and enthusiasm to their readers invariably produce the more pleasurable papers. Students responding to this assignment should choose a topic of interest, become completely involved in it to learn as much as the resources and time allow, and then write as naturally as possible to enlighten and interest readers.

Guide for Reading

Robert's paper is not flawless, but it presents an excellent picture of Dwight L. Moody and explains his place within the fundamentalist evangelical movement. As you read it, notice how all of Robert's information on Moody explains the type of person he was, how he became an evangelist, and how he was able to make such a mark in the world. What is the value of providing the amount of detail Robert provides?

SAMPLE HISTORY PAPER 5

Dwight L. Moody: A Man Who Met a Challenge

by Robert W. (a junior)

[1] When the popular evangelist from Northfield, Dwight L. Moody died in December of 1899, the magazines and newspapers in the United States and Europe wrote exten-

sive articles and obituaries. Most sources agree that D. L. Moody had spoken to more people than any other person in the history of the world. Although figures that could provide exact numbers of people spoken to and the numbers of converts are incomplete, enough evidence remains to ensure him as a likely candidate for the title of "most listened to man in the world" before mass media devices.[1]

[2] D. L. Moody's influence as a religious leader was phenomenal. He saw himself as an ordinary man with minimal education, but totally available as a businessman, Sunday School teacher, organizer of schools and institutions, conference leader, pastor, evangelist, and in many other capacities. Moody was not blessed with a great speaking voice or wide vocabulary, but was best known for being a speaker who could capture listeners attention and present the message of Christ with conviction. Moody joined with Ira Sankey, a talented musician, to organize campaigns that inspired a boom in religion following the Civil War. Evangelism was nothing new, but the crowds Moody attracted were overwhelming. Religion seemed to be in keeping with the times, as Americans were adjusting to the machine age.[2] Moody and Sankey are recognized then and today as pioneers of big-time evangelism.

[3] As the Lord Jesus was born in the lowly town of Bethlehem, D. L. Moody also seemed to come out of nowhere. He was born in the poverty-stricken area of Northfield, Massachusetts, in 1837, one of a large family. His parents, Edwin and Betsy were dirt poor, living in a mortgaged clapboard homestead. Moody's father died at age forty-one completely bankrupt. The widow Moody was left to raise seven children and would soon after give birth to twins.[3] Although some of her neighbors urged her to split her struggling family among homes outside of friends, Betsy Moody kept the family intact with help from her brother and her local church.[4]

[4] Moody's early life was typical of most rural families, consisting of hard work on the farm for six days and old-time religion on the seventh.[5] By age seventeen, Moody was far too restless to be hooked to a plow for life. He announced to his family his intentions to leave for "the big city" of Boston in 1854, where an

uncle owned a shoe store. It was here that D. L. Moody, a man with a meager education, would accept Christ and begin his great mission.

[5] Finding work in Boston as an unskilled, uneducated young man was not immediate for Moody. He eventually turned to his uncle, who agreed to hire ___ on the following conditions: "that he would board where he was told to, keep off the streets at night, avoid questionable places of amusement, and regularly attend the Mount Vernon Church."[6] Moody agreed to the terms and soon became a good shoe clerk. His Sunday School teacher, Mr. Edward Kimball, described Moody as "embarrassingly ignorant" of Biblical terms. Yet, Kimball took a keen interest in the young man and invited him to trust Christ in the shoe store. At the age of eighteen, Moody accepted Jesus Christ as his personal savior. From this moment on his life was drastically changed.[7] Mr. Kimball later said, "I've seen few persons whose minds were spiritually darker than his when he came into my Sabbath School class, or who seemed unlikely ever to become Christians of clear, decided views of gospel truth, still less to fill any sphere of extended public usefulness."[8]

[6] The Mount Vernon Church deferred Moody's request for membership due to his initial examination before the committee. However, the church saw his desire to know more of God and appointed three members to instruct him. Moody later said that the church had acted wisely in giving him further instruction because a convert should always be ready to give a reason for the hope that was in him.[9]

[7] The following year Moody decided to leave the shoe store and with his carpet bag and a five dollar ticket, he set out for Chicago and the challenge of the growing West. Moody in later life admitted to always having been a man of impulse. By having moved West in search of his fortune, he displayed this characteristic.[10]

[8] His initial work was again in retail shoe sales. Moody was making good money and invested it wisely in land. His employers, Charles and Augustus Wiswall, predicted that one day Moody would be a millionaire. His business blossomed despite an economic crash in 1857.[11] By the time Moody was twenty-

four, he had an annual income of $5,000 and over $7,000 in savings and investments.[12]

[9] The business world demands a tough, firm, competive nature from those who seek to be successful. Moody was a gritty competitor but maintained an integrity backed by Christian principles. Moody saw obedience to the scriptures teachings as an asset. in writing a letter to his mother in 1858, D. L. Moody mentioned financial success, yet he spent more time asking her to pray that he would live a consistent Christian life before the many young men he hoped to see accept Christ.[13]

[10] Moody and Chicago seemed to be made for each other. Chicago was one of the fastest growing cities in America, and the agressive and wise people were enjoying success. Yet Moody was being drawn toward the challenge of soulwinning. He joined the Plymouth Congregational Church, yet he was unhappy because he was often asked to refrain from speaking with his poor grammar.[14] This hardly shook his faith and he proceeded to ask a mission Sunday School's superintendent on North Wells Street if he could teach a class. Moody was told he could teach everyone he would get to attend the mission. The following Sunday he showed up with eighteen street kids, all dirty, undernourished, barefooted, and in need of Christ. He had more than doubled the school's enrollment of sixteen members. "That was the happiest Sunday I have ever known," wrote Moody. "I had found what my mission was."[15]

[11] Moody's first class met on a piece of driftwood next to Lake Michigan, but soon he was able to rent an old saloon building on Illinois Street. Some of his early students included twelve to fourteen year old boys from local gangs including Darby the Cobbler, Billy Bucktooth, and Madden the Butcher. Most of the kids were living in "The Sands," one of the roughest areas in Chicago. The classes were still meeting without seats when Moody invited a wealthy merchant friend, John Farwell, to attend one Sunday. The following week Mr. Farwell purchased seats for the class. When he returned for a look during next Sunday's meeting, he was elected superintendent by acclamation.[16]

[12] "Crazy Moody" as business associates referred to him, continued to work in this unique training ground for his future

ministry. From daylight to past dark, he worked tirelessly seeking recruits. Moody was gaining experience that he would use for many years as he continued in "rescue work," moving among the affluent who could be led to give to worthwhile mission endeavors and distributing these gifts to the needy. Moody later referred to this early experience as a seminary, noting that, "If a whaling ship was Herman Melville's Yale and his Harvard, then "The Sands" was my divinity school."[17]

[13] D. L. Moody was a big man weighing well over 200 pounds. This served him well; few took issue toward his working in the rough areas. Moody believed that Christians should always avoid fighting. He often ran from angry or drunken men only to later return as he sought recruits for his Bible School. Many parents came to respect Moody for his determination and obvious concern for people. Moody bought a pony to help him recruit and carry boys to school and was referred to as the "urban circuit rider." By 1859, his school was averaging six hundred and was divided into eight classes, one of which was being led by Emma Revell, his future wife. Moody's students loved him and he referred to them as his "bodyguards." During a Thanksgiving service Moody asked the children, "What are you thankful for?" The young Christians exclaimed, "There's nothin' we're so thankful for as you, Mr. Moody."[18]

[14] As Moody's school continued to prosper, he steadily lost interest in continuing in business. A major concern for the school was space with over a thousand children attending by 1859. To finance the construction of a building, Moody issued 40,000 "shares" at a quarter each and convinced businessmen to contribute both money and time as teachers.[19] By 1860, the school was a Chicago institution and many influential people, including President-elect Abe Lincoln, visited the school. The future President challenged the boys to listen by telling them how he came from being a poor country boy to standing at the threshold of the Presidency of the United States.

[15] While visiting and leading people to attend the school, Moody always allowed elders and others to talk with the students about their souls. One week he substituted for an ill teacher in a rowdy class of young girls. Later in the week the teacher asked

Moody to join him in visiting the girls. Moody later realized the teacher's concern for the girls spiritual condition was compelled by his declining health. Moody went and prayed with him as God saved each of the girls. Shortly thereafter the teacher died, and Moody led the class in a prayer meeting. This experience greatly influenced Moody to devote his life to full-time religious work.[20]

[16] D. L. Moody had moved to Chicago with an ambition to become a successful merchant but that ambition was now gone. In 1861 he decided to give up his career as a businessman to give more than his already full-time attention to religious work. He referred to this as "the hardest struggle I ever had in my life." Others noted it to be a lucky day for his competitors and a dark one for Satan.[21] During this time Moody was married to Emma Revell, who faithfully assisted him throughout his religious work. Without assurance of financial support from any organization, he was determined to live on savings and any donations that God would supply. D. L. Moody never regretted his choice because God opened doors immediately; wherever he went revival broke out. In a letter to his concerned mother, he wrote: "I have been to prayer meeting every night but two for eight months."[22]

[17] Within four years of quitting his retail job, Moody had built the Illinois Street Church, which held fifteen hundred people and was used constantly seven days a week. In addition Moody was still working with the Sunday School, which now was known as the North Market Sabbath School. When asked the secret of his success, he quoted Henry Varley's challenge, "The world has yet to see what God can do with and for and through and in a man who is fully and wholly consecrated to Him."[23] Moody knew he couldn't be a great man, or a learned man, or clever man or eloquent man. But he could be totally consecrated so that is what he set out to be.

[18] Moody first noticed the Young Men's Christian Association (YMCA) shortly after arriving in Boston and later volunteered while he was still working as a businessman in Chicago. These were tough times for the recently established association, and Dwight L. Moody's energetic leadership was noticed and channeled by the association to build a solid base in Chicago. He was devoting much of his time to the YMCA when the Civil War be-

gan. Many of the young men and associates of Moody in Chicago were being recruited and stationed at Camp Douglas, located south of the city.

[19] Moody felt compelled to serve but his feelings about combat were similar to the Quakers, for he could not willingly take a gun and shoot down a human being. Moody and others in the YMCA formed a committee to offer assistance to soldiers. With assistance from J. V. Farwell, B. F. Jacobs, and others, Moody established a chapel for the soldiers where regular meeting were conducted. An army hymn book with a flag donning its cover was issued without cost to the soldiers in both Union and Confederate armies. Moody also conducted meetings for prisoners on many occasions at Camp Douglas; at times the camp held more than nine thousand captives. During these meetings many men trusted Christ. In addition, a branch of the YMCA was established at the camp with officers, soldiers, and prisoners enrolled as members.[24] Moody was well aware of the necessity to share Christ at every opportunity, as men were always faced with the possibility of death. He urged others to share Christ "now," arguing that many would surely die without Christ if they delayed.

[20] In working with wounded men on the front lines in battle, Moody moved quickly and was said to have left "dying saved men" to search for others who needed to be kept alive while there was yet a chance for their conversion.[25] After witnessing to a dying young man, Moody asked him if he had any message for his mother. The soldier replied, "Oh yes, tell my mother that I died trusting in Jesus!"[26] Moody later recalled that this had to have been one of the sweetest messages ever told. The ministry of mercy performed by Moody and others during the Civil War demanded a tremendous amount of stamina and zeal; D. L. Moody was also recognized by many as an intense worker with a heavenly purpose.

[21] In 1865 the Civil War ended and D. L. Moody was again engaged in Sunday School work. His work in Chicago continued to expand rapidly, and workers in religious education traveled many miles to visit the famous school and find out its methods. Whether Moody actually started the mission school movement is not certain, but he certainly popularized it and helped provide the

strength and momentum necessary to keep it moving. Moody did this through personal recruiting and always had candy, oranges, or maplesugar in his pockets to attract the children. He also followed-up on his members, visiting them when they were either sick or absent. The "scholars" as Moody referred to them became devotedly attached to him. When Moody needed a teacher he would recruit one for he seldom waited for anything.

[22] Moody's continued involvement with the YMCA provided him with numerous opportunities to speak at conventions. In most cases these meetings and conventions were turned into revivals since Moody always went to these affairs with the idea of making them into something other than a showcase for aspiring preachers.[27] He had soon built a reputation as a "demon fund raiser" for missions, schools, and churches. One contemporary called him "the lightning Christian of the lightning city."[28] His success as a fundraiser was clear in his work to built the YMCA buildings in Chicago. Fire completely destroyed the first building only four months after its dedication. It was stated that Moody had a new building of greater value paid for by the time the fire was out![29] Moody had a hand in building three YMCA buildings; the second building was also destroyed by the same fate in the Great Chicago Fire of 1871.

[23] During the later part of the 1860s and into 1870s, D. L. Moody seemed to have established enough work in Chicago alone to last even a person with his spunk a lifetime. His work during this time included being: YMCA President, Pastor at Illinois Street Church (although he was never ordained), President of the Sunday School, and a popular speaker in conventions and meetings.[30]

[24] While attending a YMCA convention in Indianapolis in 1870, his life would take another major turn. It was here that Moody made his acquaintance with Ira Sankey, whose professionalism in leading congregational music caught the preacher's attention. After Sankey sang "There is A Fountain Filled With Blood" at a prayer meeting, Moody felt that he was the man God wanted to join him in evangelistic campaigns. Moody quickly questioned Sankey about his work and his marital status. Before Sankey could reply, Moody said, "I've been looking for you for

eight years, you will have to give that up."[31] Sankey was astonished that Moody would think he would leave a good position to work without assurance of a salary. The following day Moody left word for Sankey to meet him on a certain street corner at six o'clock. He then proceeded to make a stage out of wooden boxes and instructed Sankey to lead a hymn. In a few minutes, a substantial sidewalk meeting was taking place. Seeing Moody in action convinced Sankey to give up his position with the government and join the evangelist's mission efforts. Little did either of them know that the names Moody and Sankey were going to become household words both in the U.S. and in Europe during the next two decades.[32]

[25] Moody gave credit for the success of his work to consistent prayer from three women in Illinois Street Church. These ladies always sat prayerfully on the front pew and said, "We have been praying for you." Moody once asked why they prayed for him instead of the people. "Because," they answered, "you are the one who needs the power of the spirit."[33] Until then Moody felt he had power since he was pastoring the largest church in Chicago and seeing many conversions, in addition to his other activities in Sunday School and YMCA. Shortly thereafter, he was speaking in New York when he was approached by an elderly man who pointed at him and said, "Young man, when you speak again, honor the Holy Ghost."[34] This statement left Moody with a great hunger for the Holy Spirit to fill him, and he remembered that this probably influenced him more than any single experience in his life. Later he was again in New York when he experienced a stunning renewal:

> God revealed himself to me, and I had such an experience of his love that I had to ask him to stay his hand . . . I was all the time tugging and carrying water. But now I have a river that carries me.[35]

This was the beginning of his work in revivalism. The sermons he preached were not different, but the servant was. His messages had been well received previously, reaching a few people consistently; hundreds were responding to his messages.[36]

[26] D. L. Moody's preaching was simple and to the point.

Many preachers were known for either boring or "scaring the hell" out of their congregations; Moody focused on preaching God's love for all men. He had a unique ability to bring the gospel message into a current setting. He often used situations of praying mothers and wayward sons to illustrate God's concern for those who were lost in sin. Many said Moody did not preach to his audience but rather talked to them as if he were speaking to people on an individual basis. One person said, "As he spoke it seemed to me that he held me by the coat collar with one hand while he said, 'Young man, I have a message for you, and I want you to hear it.' "[37] Moody's sermon outlines generally features the three R's - Ruin by sin, Redemption by Christ, and Regeneration by the Holy Ghost. Salvation of lost souls was Moody's primary goal. His most quoted statement to defend this concern was, "I look on this world as a wrecked vessel. God has given me a lifeboat and said to me, 'Moody, save all you can.' "[38]

[27] Moody was always keenly aware of his lack of education. He was often able to keep newspapermen from being overly critical when quoting him verbatim by using as much direct quotation from the Bible as possible.[39] Moody was also a master at avoiding problems in services. His organizational methods were precise and his work prior to meetings covered issues such as temperature control, ushers' responsibilities, publicity, overflow accommodations, and many more. Critics, skeptics, agnostics, and drunkards who occasionally attended a Moody campaign in hope of ridiculing the famous evangelist were quickly silenced by this husky preacher who took charge of meetings in the fashion of a successful businessman. He tended to waste no time with introductory remarks, but plunged at once into his subject. Every item of a Moody and Sankey campaign was carefully planned to stay within a certain frame. When assistants or preachers tended to get lengthy or dull with remarks or in prayers, Moody would often cut them short. His favorite method was to stride up to the speaker, firmly grasp his shoulder and say, "Now, sir, that is perfect; if you add one single word you will spoil it. Let us sing hymn number 173."[40] When asked if the interruption was not offensive, Moody always said it was better to offend people than to lose a soul through boredom.

[28] In the spring of 1873, the Moody and Sankey families sailed to England to begin what would become a three-year campaign. Initially, they received a cold, suspicious welcome as they worked their way toward Scotland. While in the city of Edinburg, the tide turned in their favor. In November of 1873 they were speaking to audiences of 2,000 each night. By February, 1874, they were speaking to crowds of 5,000 listeners in Kibble Palace, while an overflow crowd of 2,000 outside was addressed by local ministers. Later that year in Dublin, with only 40,000 Protestants in the city, Moody spoke to 12,000 one afternoon. Moody and Sankey's reputation began to spread throughout England; estimated numbers attending the Birmingham campaign totaled 156,000 people in eight days. By the time they reached London, Moody and Sankey were national celebrities. Their London campaign was held in five separate auditoriums over a four month period. Though figures include repeating attenders, the results were nonetheless amazing. The Moody-Sankey team pulled over three million people through the doors.[41] Moody's meeting reached people from all walks of life. In addition to challenging poor mothers to come and bring their babies, he encouraged the most wealthy to attend as well. The London Journal reported that notable people such as the Prince of Wales, the Duke of Marlborough, the Earl of Shaftesbury, and many others came to listen.

[29] Moody experience opposition to his work. Some British papers referred to him as a "ranter of the worst kind." A New York Times writer stated that Moody's visit to england was being financed by P. T. Barnum Circus. Other critics referred to the Americans as "a fresh supply of opium for the common people, purchased by the British ruling classes."[42]

[30] Despite the limited criticism, Moody and Sankey came home as conquerors returning from battle. The peak years of their evangelistic work continued until 1881. Cities in the United States where Moody's campaigns were especially successful were Brooklyn, Philadelphia, New York, Chicago, Boston, Baltimore, St. Louis, and San Francisco. Moody continued to preach God's love, but was also certain to make clear to his listeners that those who rejected Christ would experience God's wrath. He said:

If you don't accept his love, if you reject his salvation, do not think that God will receive harlots, and drunkards, and sinners, unredeemed, into his Kingdom. If you die in your sins there is not one ray of hope to show that there will be opportunity to repent hereafter.[43]

Though numbers do not tell the complete story of revival work, one figure reports that between the years 1870–1880 a growth of 3,400,000 members were added to evangelical churches. Many agree that Moody's influence in revivalism is shown in these figures.[44]

[31] D. L. Moody must have been a man who loved God; how else could a man spend over 10,000 days and nights in meetings? This total represents over twenty-five years continuous revival.[45] In 1881, Moody sensed that his efforts should again shift toward religious organization and training others to win souls. He still worked as tirelessly as before leading conferences and founding the Moody Bible Institute, the Northfield Seminary for Girls, and the Mt. Herman School for boys. His faith that God would continue to provide even when the money was not there was always sure. In 1888, Moody knelt on a lot near LaSalle Street and Chicago Avenue and asked the Lord to give the land to him so he could build a men's dorm. Within a year, students moved into the new facility.[46]

[32] in 1899, Moody led his final meeting. Though rapidly weakening from illness, he completed his final campaign in Kansas City. By the time he arrived at his home in Northfield, he was unable to walk. Friends carried him to his room where he died several days later. The Chicago Tribune obituaries portrayed how the public felt about the death of Dwight L. Moody.

[33] It is now forty-three years since Brother Moody dedicated himself to his life work. During all that time he never wavered in his advocacy of "the plain, practical gospel," and thousands of men and women have been made better by it. His was an honest, earnest, sincere, well-founded life. A good man has passed on to his reward.[47]

[34] Fittingly, his monument read:

History

> Some day you will read in the papers that D. L. Moody, of East Northfield, is dead. Don't you believe a word of it! At that moment I shall be more alive than I am now, I shall have gone up higher, that is all; die. That which is born of the Spirit will live forever.[48]

[35] The influence of this man who lived each day as a servant, fully consecrated to his Lord, greatly influenced revivalism and left many lasting effects for Christians today. D. L. Moody was a man who met a challenge.

End notes

[1] Rollin W. Quimby, "How D. L. Moody Held Attention," Quarterly Journal of Speech, 43 (October, 1957).

[2] Barnard A. Weisberger, "Evangelists to the Machine Age," American Heritage Journal v. 6, n. 5 (August, 1955).

[3] Gordon L. Hall, The Sawdust Trail: The Story of American Evangelism (Philadelphia, Macrea Smith Company, 1900), p. 80.

[4] William R. Moody, The Life of D. L. Moody, by His Son. (Murfreesboro, TN.: Sword of the Lord Publishers, 1900), p. 21.

[5] Weisberger, p. 21.

[6] Elgin S. Moyer, Great Leaders of the Christian Church. (Chicago, Moody Press, 1951) p. 459.

[7] W. R. Moody, p. 41.

[8] Moyer, p. 459.

[9] W. R. Moody, p. 44.

[10] W. R. Moody, p. 46.

[11] Hall, p. 89.

[12] Weisberger, p. 21.

[13] W. R. Moody, p. 53.

[14] Hall, p. 89.

[15] Hall, p. 90.

[16] Richard E. Day, Bush Aglow: The Life Story of D. L. Moody, Commoner of Northfield, (Philadelphia, The Judson Press, 1936).

[17] Bernard A. Weisberger, They Gathered at The River: The Story of the Great Revivalists and Their Impact Upon Religion in America, (New York Times Book Company, 1958), p. 183.

[18] Day, p. 76.

[19] Weisberger, "Evangelists to the Machine Age" p. 22.

[20] W. R. Moody, pp. 64–65.

[21] Weisberger, "Evangelists to the Machine Age" p. 22.

[22] W. J. Smart, Six Mighty Men, (New York, The McMillan Company, 1957), p. 37.

[23] Moyer, p. 462.

[24] W. R. Moody, p. 84.

[25] Weisberger, They Gathered at the River, p. 189.

[26] W. R. Moody, p. 86.

[27] W. R. Moody, pp. 98–99.

[28] Weisberger, "Evangelists to the Machine Age," p. 22.

[29] W. R. Moody, p. 116.

[30] Weisberger, "Evangelists to the Machine Age," p. 22.

[31] Hall, p. 100.

[32] Weisberger, "Evangelists to the Machine Age," p. 22.

[33] Smart, p. 38.

[34] Raymond V. Edman, They Found the Secret. (Grand Rapids, Zondervan Publishing House, 1960), pp. 82–83.

[35] Hall, p. 102.

[36] Edman, p. 83.

[37] Quimby, p. 282.

[38] Mark A. Noll, Erdman's Handbook to Christianity in America. (Grand Rapids, William R. Erdman's Publishing Company, 1983) p. 294.

[39] Paul D. Moody, My Father: An Intimate Portrait of Dwight Moody. (Boston, Little, Brown, and Company, 1938) p. 111.

[40] Quimby, pp. 281–282.

[41] Weisberger, "Evangelists to the Machine Age," p. 23.

[42] Weisberger, "Evangelists to the Machine Age," p. 23.

[43] Shelton, Smith, Robert T. Handy, and Lefferts A. Loetscher, American Christianity: An Historical Interpretation with Representative Documents v. 2. 1820–1960. (New York, Charles Scribner's Sons, 963) p. 321.

[44] Moyer, p. 463.

[45] Day, p. 274.

[46] Vergilium Ferm, Pictorial History of Protestantism. (New York, Philosophical Library, 1957) p. 38.

[47] The Chicago Tribune. December 23, 1899. p. 12.

[48] W. R. Moody. p. 1.

Bibliography

Obituaries, "Death of Brother Moody," The Chicago Tribune. December 23, 1899.

Day, Richard Ellsworth. Bush Aglow: The Life Story of D. L. Moody, Commoner of Northfield. Philadelphia, The Judson Press, 1936.

Edman, Raymond V. They Found the Secret. Grand Rapids: Zondervan Publishing House, 1960.

Ferm, Vergilius, Pictorial History of Protestantism. New York, Philosophical Library, 1957.

Hall, Gordon L. The Sawdust Trail: The Story of American Evangelism. Philadelphia: Macrae Smith Company, 1964.

Moody, Paul D. My Father: An Intimate Portrait of Dwight Moody. Boston, Little, Brown, and Company, 1938.

Moody, William R. The Life of D. L. Moody, By His Son Murfreesboro, TN, Sword of the Lord Publishers, 1900.

Moyer, Elgin S. Great Leaders of the Christian Church. Chicago, Moody Press, 1951.

Noll, Mark A. Erdman's Handbook to Christianity In America. Grand Rapids, William B. Erdman's Publishing Co., 1983.

Quimby, R.W. "How D. L. Moody Held Attention, Quarterly Journal of Speech 43 October 1957.

Smart, W. J. Six Mighty Men. New York, The McMillon Company, 1957.

Smith, Shelton H., Robert T. Handy, Lefferts A. Loetscher. American Christianity: An Historical Interpretation With Representative Documents v. II.

Weisberger, Bernard A. "Evangelism to the Machine Age" American Heritage Journal. v. 6, n. 5, August 1955.

Weisberger, Bernard A. They Gathered at the River: The Story of the Great Revivalists and Their Impact Upon Religion in America. Boston, Little Brown, and Co., 1958 3rd edition, Quadrangle/The New York Times Book Co.

STUDY QUESTIONS

1. In addition to explaining Moody's place among evangelists, Robert lets us see Moody as a person. Mark the information in this paper that tells us about his personality. In what ways does this information help you understand what type of evangelist Moody was?

2. What is Robert's method of organization? Is it appropriate for the subject? Is another method possible, appropriate, or more appropriate?

3. Compare paragraphs 26 and 27. Paragraph 26 is clearly focused on a single topic, Moody's method of preaching, which is stated in the first sentence. Although paragraph 27 could be considered a single topic, it seems to touch on several related topics.

History

> Rewrite this paragraph in such a way that all the information in it is clearly a part of the same general topic. (Hint: Quite often the key lies in an introductory sentence that encompasses the subject of the paragraph.)
>
> 4. How do you suppose Robert feels about Dwight L. Moody? Point out some specifics in the paper that indicate Robert's personal opinion. Do you think Robert's paper is helped or hurt by the inclusion of personal opinion?
>
> 5. Notice the documentation and the bibliography. Do you feel that Robert's research has been extensive enough and that throughout the paper he gives proper credit to his sources? Do you, as the reader, feel that you have been given an accurate and unbiased picture of D. L. Moody?

Guide for Reading

Although informative, William's paper is an average but not an outstanding response to the assignment. With some revising, however, his history of the Scopes Trial could be "a pleasure to read" and could be informative as well. As you read, consider what revisions would be required to improve the paper; you may want to pay special attention to the amount of unnecessary information. Did William become so involved in the details of the trial that he overlooked the significance of the event in the context of American fundamentalism?

SAMPLE HISTORY PAPER 6

Scopes, Bryan, Darrow, and the Monkey

William S. (a junior)

[1] Early in the year 1925, two great forces collided in the state of Tennessee. On one side there was religion, particularly fundamentalist Christianity, while on the other

side, there was science and the theory of evolution. The fundamentalist Christians were constantly on the lookout for a windmill to attack. As a matter of fact, this segment of Christianity has always been embroiled in some type of conflict. Following World War I, this group had helped to push through Prohibition; now they were turning to science. The theory of evolution was an obvious enemy to attack. Fundamentalists believed that the Bible should be interpreted literally and evolution seemed to go against the idea of a divine creation. In the early 1920's, fundamentalists tried to pass anti-evolution laws in several states. In Kentucky, the group tries to get a law passed but professors at the University of Kentucky, along with other intellectuals, pressured the legislature to vote against it. Nevertheless, in 1925, an anti-evolution law was passed in Tennessee that would change American education and ideas of religion to the present.

[2] In 1921, a preacher came through a small town in Macon County, Tennessee telling a story about a girl who went off to college and came back believing in evolution instead of the Bible. One of the people in the audience was William Butler, a member of the Tennessee State Legislature. Butler was a good and sincere man, but he had very little education. It was said that Butler believed that the King James Bible was handed down from God to Moses in English.[1] Being a devout man, he felt it was his duty to keep such damaging ideas from students, so, in January of 1925, he introduced an anti-evolution law to the legislature. The law stated:

> Be it enacted by the General Assembly of the State of Tennessee that it shall be unlawful for any teacher in any of the universities, normals, and all other public schools of the State, which are in whole or in part supported by the public school funds of the State, to teach any theory that denies the story of the divine creation of man as taught in the Bible and to teach instead that man has descended from a lower grade of animals.

On January 28, 1925, the law passes the Lower House by a vote of 71 to 5; it then passed the Upper House by a vote of 24 to 6.

[3] There were two main reasons why the law passed so eas-

ily in Tennessee. In the first place, there was no organized resistance against the law like there had been in Kentucky. This may have had to do with the fear that politicians had of the fundamentalists. Fundamentalists comprised a large part of the constituencies of these politicians. The university community feared the fundamentalists for a different reason. At the same time the law was being proposed, the Baptist Convention was about to make a substantial contribution to the University of Tennessee. The school was afraid that it might lose the money. The second reason has to do with the rivalry between Baptists and Methodists. At the same time Nashville was the capital of Methodism and the Methodists were the primary rival to the Baptists. Methodism set less stock in words than in deeds and in grace than in works; generally they were inactive in fundamentalist debates. Since Methodists would not take a stand on such an important issue, Baptists took a firm stand for the law. Zealous Baptists viewed this as a chance to use this emotional issue to bring new members into the Baptist Church and beat their chief competitors.[2]

[4] Tennessee's very popular and progressive governor at the time was Austin Peay. During his administration, he improved the highways and worked hard to improve education on all levels. It was also his job to sign the evolution bill into law. Privately he opposed the law and saw it as a step backwards; yet in order to get his other ideas to pass he needed the votes of rural farmers and their representatives, like Butler. Peay was also a Baptist and was getting pressure from the churches. Thus, on March 21, 1925, he signed the bill into law and it took effect immediately. In explaining his actions to the legislature, he stated that the state constitution mentioned the people's belief in God and immorality. If a man is to be judged after his death, Peay argued, he must be judged by some law, and God's law is the Bible. In addition, Peay moved that the Butler Act did not require public school to teach any one interpretation of the Biblical creation account; thus the law did leave some room for individual ideas. Finally, the governor felt that the law would never be applied.

[5] Southern culture made it possible for such a law to be passed. The south was very unique in that the growth of industry,

cities, and education stimulated the growth of the church, while in other parts of the country, church membership decreased as industrialization grew.[3] Between 1906 and 1926, church membership grew fifty percent. An example of this growth would be in Memphis where the population in this period grew twenty-three percent while church membership increased by sixty-two percent. Two reasons for this growth are that the largest denominations, the Southern Baptists and the Methodists, were revivalistic and that these churches controlled much of the higher education. The major denominations felt that they should provide schools for both men and women. The typical college curriculum at one of these religious schools consisted of religion courses and the classics.

[6] Another thing that made such a law possible was the Southern mentality. Walter Hines Page claimed that the chief element distinguishing Southerners from people in the North was their utter lack of intellectual curiosity.[4] Many Southerners believed that the only thing a person needed to know was the Bible. Georgia legislator Hal Kimberly stated,

> "Read the Bible. It teaches you how to act. Read the hymn book. It contains the finest poetry ever written. Read the almanac. It shows you how to figure out what the weather will be. There isn't another book that is necessary for anyone to read, and therefore I am opposed to libraries."[5]

Senator Huey Long of Louisiana claimed in the United States Senate, "It is true that I am an ignorant man. . . . I know the hearts of my people because I have not colored my own. I know what is right in my own conscience." Some of the leaders of Southern politics had no desire or inclination to know more. They saw no need for new intellect. In the 1920s a writer wrote in Christian Fundamentalism that the only believers in evolution were almost always the university crowd or the social reds.[6] Not only did preachers and politicians support the law, but so did many prominent Southern lawyers and businessmen.

[7] Soon as the law was passed, the American Civil Liberties Union began to seek a test case to see if the law was constitutional. They first tried to find someone willing to go on trial in

Chattanooga, but no one was willing to come forward. The Chattanooga Times then ran an article explaining the law and publicizing that the ACLU was willing to pay the expenses of anyone willing to be put on trial to test the law.

[8] Dayton was a small town located forty miles northeast of Chattanooga in Rhea County, Tennessee. The population of the town was only 1800 and there was only one high school. The business district of the town consisted of a hardware store, mercantile and furniture stores, Robinson's and Brady's drugstores, the Aqua Hotel, a movie theater, and J. R. Darwin's "Everything to Wear." The Southern Railway also went through Dayton, but rarely stopped. Going to church made up the majority of the social life in the town and most of the people were church members.

[9] In 1924 the Rhea County Board of Education hired a young college graduate to coach football and teach at the high school. His name was John Thomas Scopes. Scopes was born on August 3, 1900 in Paducah, Kentucky. His father was from the slums of London while his mother was a Kentucky Belle of Scotch-Irish descent. Scopes' father had an unorthodox view of the Christian religion; he accepted the teachings of Jesus without the myths and miracles of Christian dogma.[7] He did not believe in heaven or hell. At one time Scopes' father had been an elder in the Presbyterian Church, but left because of what he felt was intolerance to other views. John Scopes entered college in the fall of 1919 at the University of Illinois at Urbana. At the end of his first year he developed a severe case of bronchitis and had to leave school. His grades were good enough that he still passed his freshman year. In 1921 he enrolled as a sophomore at the University of Kentucky where in 1924 he graduated. In the same year he filed records with the teacher placement bureau at the university and, when offered the job at Dayton, he took it for $150 a month.

[10] As a football coach Scopes led Dayton to a successful season even though he lacked experience in the sport. He knew of the Butler Act when it came out in March 1925, but he did not worry about it because he was not the biology teacher. He did not agree with the law and felt that Darwin's theory was right. Scopes

said, "As I saw it, the fundamental teachings of Christ had little in common with the preachings of fundamentalism, which polluted the words of Jesus."[8] On May 1 the first term ended, and Scopes' contract was extended for another year. He had planned to leave Dayton for the summer as soon as school ended so that he could visit his family, but two events kept him from going, and at the same time made him available to be the defendant in the most famous trial in United States history. In the first place two of his students were hospitalized following an automobile accident. The second event that kept him was his introduction to a girl who invited him to a church social. On May 5 he was playing tennis with two of his students when he was summoned to Robinson's Drugstore. At the drugstore there was a discussion about the new anti-evolution law. When Scopes arrived he found four men involved in the discussion, "Doc" Robinson, the owner of the store, was the chairman of the school board as well as the school book supplier. Sue Hicks and Wallace Haggard were both local lawyers. George Rappelyea was in charge of several coal mines in the area. The men had figured out a way to put Dayton on the map. All of the men except Rappelyea had lived in the town for many years. Scopes could understand why they wanted to make Dayton famous, but he could not figure out why Rappelyea was involved. Scopes said of him, "Possibly he hoped to open the Tennessee coal business or win some industry as a result. I didn't see how he could gain from the trial; at the same time I knew him well enough to realize he wouldn't have done the things he did if he didn't have a good angle." They asked Scopes if he would like to be involved in a trial to test the Butler Act. They told Scopes that if he would volunteer to test the case, The ACLU would pay the expenses of anyone willing to go on trial. They knew that on April 24, 1925 Scopes had substituted for the principal who served as the regular biology teacher. During the class Scopes had taught evolution. At the time he was not even aware that he had broken the law. He taught straight out of the book. Scopes figured that if anyone had broken the law, and should stand trial, it would be the principle. The men in the drugstore had already asked the principal to stand trial, but he declined because he had a family. Scopes then consented to be put on trial because he thought that the law was a bad one. On May 7 Scopes was arrested and an indictment was soon brought against him.

[11] As soon as the newspapers reported the arrest of Scopes, John Randolph Neal showed up to represent him. Neal insisted that, "The great question is whether the Tennessee legislature has the power to prevent young minds of Tennessee from knowing what has been taught and said by the world's greatest scientists, and thus prevent them from forming their own judgement in regard to questions of life and science."[9]

[12] The case was assigned to the Eighteenth Judicial Circuit Grand Jury which was to meet the first Monday in August. Bond for Scopes was set at one hundred dollars. There was still a chance that some other town might take the case before Dayton. While Dayton business men saw the trial as a way to revitalize the town, Judge Raulston saw it as a way to get more votes in the upcoming elections. The judge was not only a Republican politician, but also a lay preacher at the local Methodist Episcopal Church. He did not hesitate to move the trial date since duty to God, duty to country, and duty to self could be fulfilled at the same time.

[13] The judge called a special session of the grand jury that met on May 25. Walter White, the country school superintendent, became the plaintiff in the case, and thirteen men were sworn in on the jury. The judge then proceeded to read a copy of the Butler Act followed by a reading of the first chapter of Genesis. Seven students that were in the class the day that Scopes taught, testified that he taught evolution. The grand jury took an hour to return an indictment, and Judge Raulston set the trial date for July 10, 1925.

[14] On May 13, William Jennings Bryan, a two-time nominee for president and Secretary of State under President Wilson, agreed to represent the World's Christian Fundamentals Association as a special prosecutor for the case. Bryan was an ardent fundamentalist, and during his day he was the leading spokesman for the fundamentalists. When accepting the position of special prosecutor, Bryan stated,

> "We cannot afford to have a system of education that destroys the religious faith of our children. There are five thousand scientists, and probably half atheists, in the United States. Are we going to allow them to control our schools? We are not."[10]

Bryan felt that he was on a crusade for religion against atheism. He rested all religion on the Bible's exact wording, and believed that the Bible should be taken literally. Following World War I, he had begun speaking tours to disprove evolution and put down the evolutionist threat. He stated

> "When a Christian nation understands the demoralizing influence of its godless doctrine, they will refuse it to be taught at public expense. Christianity is not afraid of the truth, because truth comes from God, no matter how it is discovered or proclaimed, but there is no reason why Christians should tax themselves to pay teachers to exploit guesses and hypothesis as if they were true. The only thing that Christians need to do is bring the enemies of the Bible into the open and compel them to meet the issue as it is."[11]

[15] The main lawyer for the defense was Clarence Darrow. He spent his whole life arguing that man was the sum of his heredity and environment. He was a brilliant lawyer who often got his clients off death row through appeal. John Scopes, in his autobiography, stated that, "Next to my father Darrow has influenced me more than anyone else." Darrow probably never would have taken the case had it not been for Bryan entering the case and turning it into a religious issue.[12]

[16] The stage was now set for what H. L. Mencken, a famous Baltimore journalist, called "The Monkey Trial." This trial would become one of the most famous trials of all time, and the publicity that the trial received was world wide. European press ran stories about it and, the British press expressed amazement at the insistence by the state of Tennessee to prevent the teachings of a known fact of evolution. As the things heated up, and the trial date grew closer, the ACLU leaders wanted very much to avoid a fiasco, and the only way to avoid this would be to have the trial

moved from Dayton. Ideally the leaders wanted the trial moved to Federal Court where the constitutionality of the law would be tested. Darrow promised that he would do this, but Bryans presence caused a problem with having the trial moved. Bryan was so popular in the state, and so many fundamentalists wanted to see him defend the Bible, that it would have been political suicide had a judge had the trial moved.

[17] As July approached, Dayton took on a carnival atmosphere. People from all over the surrounding area flocked into the town so that they could get a seat. Store windows had cotton monkeys, and monkey signs in them. Street vendors were all over the streets selling their goods. As the day grew closer almost one hundred reporters flooded into town.

[18] On July 7, William Jennings Bryan came into town. Upon his arrival, store owners took down the monkeys and replaced them with religious signs. Bryan brought a truck with him that had a large loud speaker on the top of it. It drove around town advertising land that Bryan was trying to sell in Florida. In a sermon that Bryan gave, he spoke of the joys of retiring to Florida. Bryan saw nothing wrong with selling his land even though he was in Dayton to handle a trial.

[19] Darrow arrived the next day to less fanfare. The town hurridly threw together a party in order to make him feel welcome. At the party the celebrated lawyer was given the honrary title of "Colonel." He spent the rest of the time before the trial getting to know the townspeople and preparing for the trial.

[20] The trial began on July 10, 1925. The day began with prayer as was the custom of the court. Judge Raulston then proceeded to call a new grand jury. It had been so long since the first indictment that the judge was afraid that the case would be overturned over a technicality. The grand jury was called and sworn in. The judge then read the Butler Act and the first chapter of Genesis. The jury brought back the same indictment charging Scopes with violating the act. The rest of the morning session was taken up by introducing council for both sides. The council for the prosecution consisted of William Jennings Bryan, General Ben Mckenzie, Sue and Herbert Hicks, E. T. Stewart, Walter White, W. C. Haggard, and William Jennings Bryan Jr. The coun-

cil for the defense consisted of Clarence Darrow, John R. Neal, and Dudley Field Malone.

[21] From the beginning of the trial Darrow wanted to know if scientific evidence would be admitted. The judge said that he could not rule on the motion until both sides had outlined their theories of the case. That could not be done until the jury had been chosen.

[22] Also during the first session the major issues were defined. Could the defense prove that evolution was valid and did not conflict with the Bible? Would the issue be limited to the factual question of whether Scopes violated the Butler Act? When the court reconvened after lunch, it began to choose the jury. It took only two and a half hours to pick all twelve members of the jury. The jury consisted of nine farmers, a school teacher, and a shipping clerk. The first dispute of the trial came when the prosecution requested that the jury not be sworn in until Monday morning. Darrow was against this because he was afraid that the jury might get prejudiced before the trial started. The judge ruled that if the jurors were sworn in on Friday the court would not be dismissed until way after 4:30. The court adjourned until 9:30 Monday morning.

[23] After the weekend recess, Neal made a motion that the indictment be quashed. He stated that the Tennessee state constitution was violated on six grounds. Article 2 section 12 required the state to cherish science and literature. Article 2 section 17 said that no bill in the legislature could embrace more than one subject and it must be dealt with clearly. In article 1 section 3, the constitution stated that no preference could be given by law to any religious establishment or mode of worship. The Butler Act also violated Article 1 sections 8 and 9 which dealt with due process and freedom of speech. Finally it violated article 2 section 8 which stated that all laws must be of general application. Neal then went on to explain that the law violated the Fourteenth Amendment to the Federal Constitution which forbade infringement of life, liberty, or property.

[24] After the defense presented the motion to quash the indictment the prosecution requested that the judge have the jury removed. The judge asked the jury to retire for the afternoon. In

having the jury retire, Judge Raulston violated the constitution. The constitution of Tennessee said that the jury is judge of the law as well as the facts. Darrow protested the removal of the jury, but to know avail.

[25] In the afternoon session the state proceeded to make an arguement for the law. Stewart stated that the public owned the schools and paid the teachers. The public thus had the right to direct the teachers in what was said in class.

[26] Stewart then proceed to answer the defenses motion to quash the indictment. He stated that the case did not involve religious questions at all and that freedom of religion applies only to churches. He claimed that the Butler Act was an effort by the legislature to control the expenditure of state funds. Darrow argued back that the act gives preference to the Bible over any other religious work. The two sides argued over this point for the rest of the day.

[27] The next day the trial began to heat up. The judge tried to open the day up with a prayer and Darrow objected on the grounds that it would prejudice the jury. The judge over ruled the objection stating that there was no way to prejudice a jury by opening with a prayer. That afternoon a question was brought to the court by a group of Unitarian congregationalists, and Jewish ministers. They wanted to be allowed the opportunity to open the court sessions in prayer. The judge left it up to the ministers association.

[28] The entire trial lasted only eight days, but only half a day was for witnesses. As its first witness the state called Walter White, the school superintendent. White testified that on April 24, 1925, Scopes taught evolution out of Hunter's Civic Biology. Under cross examination Darrow discovered that the book that Scopes taught out of was the state approved text book. Had Scopes not taught evolution, he would have been guilty of a crime; while at the same time, by teaching evolution he was guilty of another crime. The state then called two students to testify against as was F. E. Robinson. When Stewart tried to have the Bible admitted as evidence, Darrow protested. The Butler Act referred to the Bible, but never stated which one. Darrow went on to explain that there were several different versions of the prot-

estant Bible, there was the Catholic Bible, and the Greek and Hebrew Bibles. Darrow said that if the law did not specifically say which version, then none were admissable as evidence. The judge over ruled this objection.

[29] Darrow, as his first witness called on Dr. Metcalf to come and explain evolution to the court. Darrow felt that in order for the jury to understand that the Bible and evolution were not in conflict, they must first understand what evolution is. Dr. Metcalf stayed on the stand the rest of the day. The very next day Darrow wanted to put the doctor back on the stand, but the state objected claiming that the scientific testimony had no bearing on the case since Scopes had already pleaded guilty. The state then made a motion that all scientific evidence be stricken from the record. The jury was again dismissed while the lawyers argued over the relevance of the testimony. The judge adjourned the court until he could rule on the scientific evidence.

[30] On the sixth day Judge Raulston ruled that the scientific testimony was unimportant to the case. He then told the scientists that they could write a fourteen thousand word brief explaining the theory of evolution and the evidence to support it. This brief would then be added to the court records. This made Darrow angry, and he made a slur at the judge. The judge replied, "I hope you don't think that the court is being unfair," to which Darrow replied, "Your honor has the right to hope." The court was then adjourned for the weekend.

[31] First thing Monday morning Darrow was cited for contempt of court. Darrow apologized for the comments that he had made and the judge forgave him.

[32] The highlight of the trial came when Darrow called Bryan to the stand as a Biblical expert. Bryan was eager to get on the stand and to end the evolution nonsense. Darrow asked Bryan questions that he could not answer. Bryan was unable to tell where Cain's wife came from, where the great fish came from that swallowed Jonah, or what would happen if the earth stopped its rotation. When Bryan admitted that the days of creation might have been longer than the normal day, Darrow had him because this left reasonable doubt as to whether evolution could have taken place in a Biblical context.

[33] Though he hoped to get Bryan on the stand the next day, Bryan never got his chance. Judge Raulston felt that the case was getting out of hand so, he sent the jury out to deliberate. The jury returned with a guilty verdict and fined Scopes one hundred dollars.

[34] The appeal to the case was heard on June 26, 1926. The lawyers for Scopes stressed how indefinite the law was. The court upheld the law but reversed the decision against Scopes on a technicality in the way the fine was administered.

[35] What was the significance of the Scopes trial on the nation and to the fundamentalists? The trial caused the fundamentalists to lose credibility which they were not able to regain until the 1980s. For a few years after the trial the group continued to lobby for anti-evolution bills, but they were not successful. Their efforts continued until 1928, then with the depression, and the repealing of prohibition the fundamentalists went underground, and have just in the past decade begun to resurface. As for the rest of America creation is not taught in the schools while evolution is. The Scopes Trial seriously discredited the fundamentalists and gave them an image that still lingers today. Most people view this group as being uneducated, narrowminded, and intolerant. Even though the fundamentalists won the trial they lost in the long run.

Footnotes

[1] Gail Kennedy, Evolution and Religion (Boston: Heath, 1957), p37

[2] Ray Ginger, Six Days or Forever? (London: Oxford University Press, 1958), p4

[3] Ibid, p15

[4] Ibid, p15

[5] Ibid, p21

[6] Ibid, p15

[7] John Scopes, Center of the Storm (New York: Holt, Reinhart, and Winston, 1967), p22

[8] Ibid, p39
[10] Ginger, p21
[11] Scopes, p51
[12] Kennedy, p39

Bibliography

Ginger, Ray. Six Days or Forever?, London: Oxford University Press, c 1958.

Kennedy, Gail. Evolution and Religion:The Conflict Between Science and Theology in Modern America, Boston: Heath c 1957.

Levy, Leonard W. The Worlds Most Famous Court Trial, New York: De Capo Press, c1971

Scopes, John Thomas. Center of the Storm, New York: Holt, Reinhart, and Winston. c1967

STUDY QUESTIONS

1. The main problem with William's paper is that he has included too much information. Put parentheses around the information in paragraphs 8, 9, and 10 that is not necessary or relevant to the significance of the trial. Rewrite these paragraphs so they will still be informative but less tedious.

2. When writers include names, readers assume that these names are important. Which names in paragraph 10, if any, are important? What would you do to make this paragraph more focused and more relevant?

3. Beginning with paragraph 12, William recounts the steps in Scopes' trial. Based on the assignment, what personalities and events should he have fo-

cused on in this section of his paper? What information would you like to see included that William left out?

4. The use of direct quotations is an important consideration in any research paper. In this type of paper, quotations are most effective in defining character and in providing support for the author. What would be lost if William had paraphrased Hal Kimberly (paragraph 6) and William Jennings Bryan (paragraph 14)? Are there any quotations that you believe should be left out?

5. What other quotations would you like to see included that would give you a better idea of the personalities involved in this trial?

6. Do you think that William has accurately documented his information? If not, where does he need to indicate a specific source for his information? What effect does careless documentation have on you as the reader?

7. Both the notes and the bibliography are inconsistent. Use the summary of the *Chicago* style guide provided in the overview to the humanities to make necessary corrections.

10 Philosophy

INTRODUCTION TO WRITING IN PHILOSOPHY

The word *philosophy* means the love of wisdom, and philosophers pursue wisdom through constant inquiry into the human condition. Their work focuses on four broad areas. The first is *values*, which includes ethics, aesthetics, and social and political philosophy. The second is *epistemology*, which is the study of knowledge and the limits of human knowledge. The third is *metaphysics*, which is the study of being and reality. And the last is *logic*, which includes language as well as the study of critical thinking and the rules of reason.

Because clear, reasoned argumentation is a fundamental priority in philosophy, students learn to argue for or against difficult theoretical concepts in an ordered, unambiguous fashion. They learn to state a proposition and spell out the assumption upon which the proposition rests. They learn to define their terms with precision and to use language with care.

Although students commonly complain of the abstract, other-worldly nature of philosophical writing, the field nevertheless places high value on specificity and the grounding of theoretical arguments in down-to-earth examples. Philosophers seek vivid, understandable images and metaphors to make difficult concepts accessible.

For example, the classical Greek philosopher Plato wanted to provide a provocative description of how, in his view, most people lead unen-

Philosophy

lightened lives. He used a cave as his metaphor. To someone residing inside the cave who had never been outside and who couldn't even look outside, the outer world would be knowable only as shadows projected onto the walls. Not having experienced the solid objects that cast the shadows into the cave, these dwellers would perceive their shadowy world as being real. Even if brought forth out of the cave, they might persist in maintaining the superior truth of the shadows, because their minds had been conditioned by their experience. In Plato's view, we are in fact all like cave dwellers in that we believe the world of our everyday senses is the real world and in that our experiences with this world and our insistence on its reality prevent us from attaining the greater truth that lies outside the world of the senses. He uses the cave, in other words, as a vivid metaphor for unenlightened human existence.

Students writing philosophy papers have the opportunity to use their imaginations and to exercise their evidence-generating skills. The focus of their papers will be on argumentative discourse that attempts to substantiate a claim. It is therefore understandable why many philosophy majors go on to study law. As shown in the sample papers that follow, successful writers will be those who provide interesting and thoughtful proofs to support their arguments.

PHILOSOPHY ASSIGNMENT 1

Course: **Introduction to Modern Philosophy**

Use available library materials to determine Marx's theory of the alienation of labor. Paraphrase it as clearly as possible. Does his theory apply today (if it ever did)? If you disagree with Marx's theory, what are your objections to it? If you agree with Marx's theory, why do you find it convincing? You may use examples from history, the contemporary world, or your own experience to support your stance. Length: 3–5 typed pages.

Analysis of Philosophy Assignment 1

The format of this assignment is one students will see frequently: a list of questions followed by rather cursory instructions. Many students find such assignments forbidding. They believe they should respond to every question but fear that the teacher is simply restating some, not posing clearly distinct questions. They worry over which question they should answer first. They want to write a coherent, unified paper, but they don't know if they can sort out all the assignment's questions and still do so.

These concerns are understandable but can be diminished through practice in interpreting such assignments. One point students should remember is that no teacher wants to read a repetitive, disorganized, incoherent paper. Therefore, most teachers will make each question clear and distinct, will present the questions in the order in which they should be answered, and will expect some kind of unifying theme or point to emerge from the final product. Often, however, teachers may not explicitly state that they expect a thesis.

Unfortunately, even the best teachers can occasionally produce less-than-adequate tasks, so students should study every assignment carefully for repeated questions and for illogical ordering of questions. Asking your teacher to clarify vague points can often help you write a better paper and can help your teacher recognize where the assignments may be unclear.

The assignment above does present clear and distinct questions in a logical order. It gives the student two objectives: to define Marx's theory and to argue for or against its present application. These two objectives are interrelated. You should be able to recognize the relationship between them and to construct an argument for or against Marx's theory that proceeds smoothly from the definition. Those papers that argue against Marx's theory will give a definition of it different in tone and orientation from papers arguing for it.

In its cursory instructions, the assignment emphasizes the need for argumentative support. The richest responses will use all three types of support suggested: examples from history, from the contemporary world, and from the student's own experience. Though many students justifiably feel uncomfortable using their own experience in a paper, this teacher clearly considers such support appropriate for the assignment. Indeed, personal experience, when used selectively and concisely, can often enhance the distinctiveness and credibility of your argument. It's important to remember, however, that personal experience is best used *in conjunction* with other types of support.

Guide for Reading

Vicki's paper is very good, almost but not quite outstanding. Her method of organization is so clear and straightforward that you may think her response is overly simple. She has taken a rather elaborate philosophical theory and presented it to readers with clear explanation and familiar examples. But comparing this paper with the two that follow will convince you that Vicki understands both Marx's theory of alienation and what readers need to know to understand it as she does. In other words, she has accomplished what good writers are expected to accomplish: She has analyzed a body of information and explained what it means in a way that readers can understand and accept.

SAMPLE PHILOSOPHY PAPER 1

Analysis of Marx's Theory of Alienation

Vicki K. (a sophomore)

Marx's theory regarding the alienation of labor puts forth two major tenets. The first of these is the idea that workers are alienated from the enjoyment of their work and from the pride in the final product because of the nature of modern assembly-line production. The second tenet is that the worker is controlled by the machinery that he himself has built. In other words, when a worker builds a machine that is meant to help in the production process, he is in essence caging himself in with the effects of his own labor.

This second part of the theory is generally used for economics applications and the first part is more often the subject of philosophical debate. This paper will therefore concentrate on the first of these ideas, on how Marx supports his assertions, how they have held true or been proven false throughout time, and how they apply today.

There are several components to the concept of alienation of labor. Perhaps the most significant of these is the idea that because the worker is involved with a final product in a limited way, he has little opportunity to identify with the product that he has created and therefore he is unable to feel much satisfaction with his job. This was viewed by Marx as a direct contrast to the situation of the medieval artisans, who took pride in the products that they created because of the personal relationship that they had with the product during the production phase.

Another aspect of the alienation theory is that the worker feels frustrated because he is unable to properly develop his body and his mind as a result of his virtual imprisonment in the role of an unskilled labor. The worker has little or no opportunity to use his imagination or to create, rather he is forced to perform a menial chore in a repetitive fashion that provides no personal gain whatsoever. This lack of potential for growth combined with the worker's resentment of his alienation from the final product creates a general feeling of unhappiness that pervades every aspect of the worker's life. The ultimate low is achieved when the worker makes the realization that he does not even receive the benefits of the product that he has created. The laborer perceives that his efforts do not even belong to himself, rather they belong to to the capitalist who exploits him.

To a large extent, there is much validity in Marx's theory of the alienation of labor. Particularly in the time of the industrial revolution that Marx was witnessing there was much merit in criticizing the manner that the capitalists exploited the labor of their workers. Historical evidence such as workers' revolts leads us to believe that the majority of the workers were very unsatisfied with their working conditions and that the sense of alienation from their work augmented their frustration.

While much has changed in terms of working conditions since the industrial revolution, the sense of alienation from the final product continues. For example, it is very difficult for a person working on an automobile assembly-line, performing some very small part of the overall production process, to feel much satisfaction in his work. This is aggravated by the fact that there is very little deviation in the task. Unless the worker buys a car made by his company, he will have no direct experience with the fruits of his labors.

Even assuming that the worker does drive a car manufactured by his company, it may be difficult for the worker to identify with the particular item in the car that he himself worked on. So much of the automobile is the result of the labor of others that it is difficult for a single person to conceive of the importance of his own labors in the production process. Although there may be a few individuals who are capable of looking past the psychological barriers so as to take satisfaction in their work, there is strong evidence that the vast majority of assembly-line workers feel alienated from their work.

There are a few things that deserve to be said in terms of the changes that have taken place over the years. Most importantly, the workers are not as confined to their jobs as they were during the time that Marx presented this theory. The contemporary worker has greater control over his economic status depending on his degree of initiative. In general, upward mobility is not out of the question even though it may require a great deal of hustle and some intelligence as well.

The other subject of note in recent times is the amount of publicity that has been given to the methods that the Japanese have been using to motivate their employees in large companies. Close contact with management, a sense of comraderie among workers, and an instilled sense of pride in the final product have contributed in creating an environment and attitude that seems to challenge the logic of Marx. Although this system may not remain intact over time, it has definitely provided food for thought for the present.

On a final note, I would like to stress the importance of perspective. It appears that the assembly-line worker will always feel some degree of resentment as long as he is in a position where he cannot use creativity to tailor a product to his individual tastes and to meet his individual desires. However, this view is not necessarily held by all of the people involved in the production process. The manager or owner of a company will clearly have a different perception of the workers' relationship with their work. In order for the workers' plight to be remedied, it will be necessary to have a sufficient number of non-laborers in support of policies to help the laborers. Until this happens, western society, by its own choice, will continue to live in a world where the laborer feels alienated from his product.

Analysis of Sample Philosophy Paper 1

This paper is a good example of a clearly constructed response to the assignment. Notice how Vicki uses the first sentence of each paragraph to signal its content and to move her argument along logically: "There are several components to the concept of alienation of labor"; "To a large extent, there is much validity in Marx's theory of the alienation of labor"; "There are a few things that deserve to be said in terms of the changes that have taken place over the years"; "On a final note, I would like to stress the importance of perspective." Vicki chooses to follow exactly the organization suggested by the assignment, and the result is an easy-to-follow, coherent paper.

But the paper is not, by any means, simplistic. Vicki answers the question "Does Marx's theory apply today?" in a careful, considered manner. She does not give a simple yes or no answer. Instead she states that Marx's theory does have some application today—many workers are still involved in alienating labor—but the system is no longer closed; new management methods have improved the worker's lot. Such an answer reflects Vicki's willingness to consider her subject fully and objectively.

Vicki's argument is moderate but not wishy-washy. In fact, in her conclusion, she strongly urges specific action—the intervention of outside forces in behalf of the interest of the worker. Her moderate stance is convincing because she supports it with specifics. She refers to the assembly-line worker in an automobile factory to discuss the potentials for alienating labor in modern industry. She refers to the American ideal of upward mobility and to new Japanese management methods to illustrate the difference between worker's conditions today and working conditions in Marx's time. She chooses to use two out of three of the types of support the assignment encourages: examples from history and examples from the contemporary world.

Although this paper is quite good, it could be better. Note that the definition section is not as concrete as it could be. Here Vicki needed to refer directly to some of Marx's works. Also, the Japanese management methods confirm the problem of worker alienation. They don't challenge Marx's logic but, instead, diminish the problem he defined. And an upwardly mobile worker may still feel alienated in his or her work—a problem not limited to the unskilled. Nevertheless, her definition of the theory and her evaluation of its current application are clear, systematic, and well integrated. Finally, like many students, Vicki seems unable to use commas correctly. The number of surface errors in the paper are distracting for most readers.

Sentence Lesson

Many students use commas haphazardly, having studied the guidelines for usage but never having learned them. Although you should refer to a handbook to understand the full range of guidelines governing comma usage, we can provide a quick lesson here by using Vicki's paper.

Vicki's comma problems fall into two major categories. The first is related to "clauses," those structures that have a subject and a predicate. Consider the sentence below:

1. This second part of the theory is generally used for economics applications and the first part is more often the subject of philosophical debate.

This sentence has two clauses. The first begins with "This" and ends with "applications"; the second begins with "and" and ends with "debate." The word *and* serves to join the two clauses, but by convention *and* must be preceded by a comma. Failure to provide the comma doesn't make the sentence ungrammatical, but it violates the convention and signals to readers that Vicki either doesn't understand the conventions of formal writing (ignorance) or that she doesn't care enough about her work and her readers to apply the convention (apathy). Neither signal is desirable because it leads to a negative evaluation of the writing. Fixing this comma problem would result in the sentence below:

1a. This second part of the theory is generally used for economics application, and the first part is more often the subject of philosophical debate.

Vicki's second problem is related to phrases that introduce sentences. A phrase, unlike a clause, doesn't consist of a subject and a predicate; it functions to provide modification, or additional information, to the sentence. Introductory phrases should almost always be set off with a comma. Look at the sentence below from Vicki's paper:

2. Particularly in the time of the industrial revolution that Marx was witnessing there was much merit in criticizing the manner <u>that</u> the capitalists exploited the labor of their workers.

Although this sentence has more wrong with it than punctuation—"the manner that" should be "the manner in which"—it nevertheless serves to illustrate the point that introductory phrases need to be punctuated. In this case, the sentence should be:

2a. Particularly in the time of the industrial revolution that Marx was witnessing, there was much merit in criticizing the manner <u>that</u> the capitalists exploited the labor of their workers.

You may have had a writing teacher tell you at some point that commas correspond to the pauses you make when you read a sentence. Consequently, you may rely on this advice rather than on any understanding of the formal conventions. If so, your writing will reflect comma problems the opposite of Vicki's: rather than leaving them out, you will put them in—almost always in the wrong places. The advice that commas correspond to pauses is inaccurate and is pretty useless.

Here are the three primary uses for commas that you should study in your handbook:

1. Use a comma along with a conjunction (*and, but, for, or, nor, yet*) to join two clauses.
   Example: The wind blew through the trees, and the rain beat down.
   Note that when you join noun and verb constructions (rather than clauses) with a conjunction, you shouldn't use the comma.
   Example: The jury deliberated for days without reaching a verdict and finally told the judge that they were hung.
   Putting a comma after *verdict* would be incorrect because it would split the verb construction.
2. Use a comma to set off phrases that serve as initial and/or nonessential modifiers.
   Example: Democratic pluralism, the principle that argues for the value of disparate points of view, has recently adopted a tyrannical stance that brooks no criticism.
   Example: When the world's population crosses a heretofore undefined threshold, we will see famine on a scale unimagined in our worst nightmares.
3. Use a comma to set off items in a series.
   Example: Language is recursive, associational, and innate.

Philosophy

Guide for Reading

Alice's paper is well organized, and it focuses on a single topic, private property, that is dealt with in the definition and argument sections. You may find it more difficult to read than the preceding paper, mainly because Alice isn't as concrete in her explanations and examples as Vicki is. Compared to Vicki, she refers more to Marx's text, which helps anchor the paper to a specific source. As you read, you may want to note the places where a concrete example would help make clear a reference to Marx's theory.

SAMPLE PHILOSOPHY PAPER 2

Karl Marx: A Man Whose Theories Time Has Passed

Alice L. (a sophomore)

Karl Marx, one of the foremost political and economic philosophers of the last 200 years, addresses the problem of what he terms "estranged labor" in his Economic and Political Manuscripts of 1844. Behind the rhetoric appears a genuine concern for the plight of the exploited labor class present in his day. He considers the causes of, and results from, participation in a political economy which leads to the separation of the "property owners and the propertyless workers."

In the portion of his writings entitled "Estranged Labor", Marx attacks the foundation of a political economy. He develops his argument showing how the laborer sinks to the level of commodity as he is forced to participate in the system. In so much as the worker becomes a commodity, he becomes estranged from himself and the system. The act of estranging human labor proceeds from two points as Marx explains it. First is the relation of the worker to the product of his labor. In this capacity, "the more objects the worker produces, the less he can possess and the more he falls under the sway of his product, capital." Second is the relation of the laborer to the act of production within the labor process. Marx believes that labor is external to the laborer because it is not essential to his being; therefore the labor is forced and unwanted.

Through the estrangement process there develops the loss of man's ability to make free and conscious choices. He is forced to participate in a system which yields no personal benefit, essentially having no control over what he does or the results of his labor.

Looking at man's inability to own or control the product of his labor or himself, who then does control it? Marx says it is other men, the owners and controllers of the means of production who dictate to the workers.

The culmination of the estrangement of the labor force is the creation of private property. Political economy, as Marx explains it, starts from labor as the real soul of production, then the resulting products translate into money for the company and private property for society; therefore, the wages earned are the direct consequence of the relation between labor and private property. Marx attempts to make it clear that though private property appears to be the source, the cause of alienated labor, it is rather the consequence. Private property, therefore, is the product of alienated labor and it also is the means by which labor alienates itself.

Marx concludes that "since wages are a direct consequence of estranged labor, and estranged labor is the direct cause of private property, then the downfall of one must involve the downfall of the other." If this is true then the elimination of private property would translate into the emancipation of the worker. This is the principle force driving his economic theory, and its implications on society.

Consider the following images: dimly lit, hazardous factories; men, women, and children alike working under abhorrent conditions; dirty overpopulated urban slums. History texts are inundated with images which illustrate the great poverty and hardships many people endured during the great step forward in industrialization during the 1800's. It is upon these images which Marx wants us to dwell as we consider his economic and political theories.

One must understand that the image Marx paints allows only

the connection of what he describes to be the alienation of labor to what occurred at THAT time in history. This is what the crucial point of consideration should be. Admittedly in the 1800's a grossly unfair system did exist and people were taken advantage of with little concern for their individual well-being. This was done as a necessity for effective growth of industry. Unfair as it was, without such measures, the industrial prosperity known today would not be realized. But, aside from the environment of industry, 100 – 150 years ago, presently such a situation does not exist in great enough proportion to make any of Marx's theories applicable, especially among the established industrialized nations of the world.

Even if it were warranted in today's society, the application of Marxism would be a highly impractical means to deal with the problem. In fact those countries which have latched on to Marxist ideals have not provided a cure to the worker's plight, but have merely altered the circumstances under which they work. For example, in the Soviet Union, rather than allowing the individual to control the means of production, it is the state who carries out that function. The very nature of the system refuses to allow any labor control. In fact, they appear to have even less control and far less freedom than the workers in most capital-based industries. For those Marxist-Communist societies, the failure of such a system is fast becoming evident. The Soviet Union, for example, which adamantly supports the basic ideas of Marxism has found them economically unwise to strictly continue, especially if they are to be competitive on world markets. In an attempt to strengthen their economy and stimulate growth and innovation, they have begun to allow limited experiments in free enterprise . . . which are working.

I find the greatest forum of debate, however, to be in his assertion that the elimination of private property would emancipate the worker. Wages and the pursuit of private property are a necessary by-product of a successful economic system. Wages, as Marx explains, are equal to the product of one's labor and is the necessary consequences thereof. Wages are subsequently altered into private property, and subsequently, the elimination of either would take away the need for a useful monetary system. I urge that this would not improve the life of the worker but rather would worsen it. In a capital based, competition-oriented society, wages are more than just means to enable the worker to subsist, they work as incentive mechanisms. Man inherently wants to do more than merely survive, and that is why private property exists in the first place, as a measure of his life's work. The scaled compensation for the quality and quantity of work is the key to the economic machine. Without the incentives to work, there exists a highly inefficient and stagnant economy. The drive and motivation for an individual to strive for advancement are also absent, thus leaving him even more tied to his present station as a mere laborer. Consequently, it does not follow that elimination of private property would improve the workers situation at all, much less free him from the bondage of his labor.

In the time and context in which they arose, the theories of Marx had great relevance to the plight of the common laborer. Now, however, in an age where industrialization is allowing more people than ever to enjoy its benefits, the theories have become outmoded and antiquated. It is not to say that Marx's writings and theories may not bring to light some injustices which have become entrenched in the system, they do. As was briefly shown, it's merely that they are not effective ways, in the modern era, to handle them.

Analysis of Sample Philosophy Paper 2

As Vicki did in Paper 1, Alice organizes a neat, well-ordered definition of Marx's theory of alienated labor. The definition paragraphs flow smoothly, moving from the origins of alienated labor to its consequences. Alice focuses on the role of private property and returns to it in the argument section of the paper, thereby unifying its two sections. Although she fails to introduce all her questions, Alice is more successful than Vicki at incorporating direct references to the assigned text.

Given these pluses, why is this paper slightly weaker than the first? The answer lies primarily in the argument section, which has some development problems as well as some doubtful assumptions. Although Alice argues that present working conditions are more humane that those in Marx's time, she fails to refer to specific changes that have taken place; she simply states that our situation is now "different." She might have considered researching the subject of present labor policies as part of her prewriting work—the assignment does not prohibit outside research and does encourage students to use support from the contemporary world. Most teachers write assignments that leave students room to exercise their own initiative. Alice fails to exercise this initiative fully. For example, she needs to be aware, but isn't, that her supporting material is insufficient to demonstrate her thesis. She believes that the modern worker has significant advantages over the worker in Marx's day, but she seems unsure about how she arrived at this belief, because she fails to pinpoint what led her to this conclusion.

Alice could have offered specifics from a number of sources. Perhaps she has read about labor reforms in a class on American history. Perhaps a family member has experience in labor relations and can serve as a resource. Researching the subject or interviewing someone who knows the history of labor would be perfectly acceptable prewriting activities that would generate much-needed support for the thesis.

Guide for Reading

Micky's paper contains the same problems that Alice's has, but to a much greater degree and without the redeeming factor of a clear focus on the topic. His language is much too theoretical and awkward. (Consider, for example, the first three sentences, where Micky uses the word *through* four times.) His use of commas doesn't follow modern standards of usage, which forces readers to reread many sentences, mentally removing commas before they can understand exactly what each sentence means. When Micky tries to be concrete, he uses a cliché or an inappropriate example, which adds confusion to what is already a confusing topic to most readers. Although the paper shows promise, it doesn't deliver enough substantial information to be an adequate response to the assignment.

SAMPLE PHILOSOPHY PAPER 3

The Human Race

Micky R. (a sophomore)

The body of this paper will be divided into two main parts: a discussion of Marx's theory of estranged labor, and evidence of human evolutionary progress through competition. The text will attempt to delineate a causal chain through which we can follow the evolution of estranged labor through competition. It seems that through a necessary progression for human survival, estranged labor evolved in conjunction with competition, on route to the production of a dominant species, "man". In short, making each individual in society a happy equal, is not necessarily a good foundation on which to build the road to progress. I think that there is little doubt that labor is estranged, but what Marx is overlooking is the beauty of competition, and the positive aspects of greed. Man has always been wrapped up in the drama of "building a better mousetrap."

I have divided Marx's theory of estranged labor into three main points: estrangement of labor, estrangement of life production activities, and the estrangement of species. To understand the estrangement of labor, we must recognize that labor has become a material object. Marx calls this occurence "objectification". Labor, which is the act of working for a given period of time, has become an object that can be bought or sold. The problem here is that the value of the object produced by labor, is lost from the laborer as its value is not owned by the laborer, but by the boss/owner. Marx calls this phenomenon "loss of realization". The loss for the laborer occurs due to the inequality of the value of his/her labor, with respect to the compensation of his/her labor. This produces a devaluation of the world of objects for the laborer, through the estrangement of his/her labor.

"The laws of political economy express the estrangement of the worker in his object thus: the more the worker produces, the less he has to consume; the more values he creates, the more valueless, the more unworthy he becomes; the better formed his product, the more deformed becomes the worker; the more civilized his object, the more barbarous becomes the worker; the more powerful labor becomes, the more powerless becomes the worker; the more ingenius labor becomes, the less ingenius the worker becomes, and the more he becomes nature's bondsman."(109)

There is also the life production activities estrangement, which is similar to the estrangement of labor itself. The life production activities become external to the essential being of the laborer. If labor was not compensated for, and thus not a means to survival, the laborer would not work for someone else's benefit. Thus the need to survive compells the laborer to labor, just as the nomadic hunter and gatherer, hunts and gathers. The underlying reason for laboring, is that the laborer considers it an easier way to fulfill life sustaining needs. Again the loss for the laborer occurs due to the inequality of the value of his/her labor, with respect to the compensation for his/her labor. The basic business laws of profit and loss can account for this inequality. The fact that the laborer considers labor an easier or possibly the only mode of producing lifes necessities, is the basis for the estrangement of his/her life production activities. The worker could benefit from realizing that he is producing far more than his actual survival needs in work hours: subsitence profit. An example of this overproduction can be drawn from our primate relatives. Animals generally only produce for themselves, and produce no surplus. Thus the distinction between animal labor, and estranged human life production activities.

Finally, Marx discusses the estrangement of the species. Estranged labor produces a change in production and progress, from the life of the species (the good of all), to the life of the individual, Marx claims that this division has undercut the cooperating power of man, and forced us into the archaic system of "every man for himself". This is most notable through the estrangement of man from man via the boss/worker relationship. The formation of complex social stratigraphies such as upper, middle, and lower class "working dogs", is a direct result of the boss/worker relationship. This is where I think the cooperating power of man is. Marx views this stratification as the root of man's eventual decline, and____ that estranged labor is evidence of our regression.

To accept estranged labor as a regression, would be like accepting labor as the only means to survival. Are we really regressing, or is estranged labor not unlike the modern day result and continuance of the survival of the fittest strategy? It would seem possibly honorable to sympathize with the plight, bondage, and degradation of the laborer, but would it not be more logical to admit that the laborer has made his own bed, and____ hope that he is comfortable in it? Throughout history, and even pre-history, competitive subsistence strategies, complex social stratifications, and economic stratifications have been the hallmarks of human progression. The drive of greed, competition, and the desire for progress are the main reasons we don't live in trees anymore! The progression of human evolution has always been from less complex to more complex in every aspect of life. Marx seems to have a rather tainted view of competition and greed as witnessed by this quote: "The only wheels which political economy sets in motion are greed and the war amongst the greedy—competition." Greed and competition are the driving gears of progress. The relation between greed and competition can be formulated into an equation: "lesser work + greater gains = what we call progress." From this equation we can empathize with the bosses who have thousands of employees. Those thousands of employees work millions of hours, and those millions of hours turn into millions of dollars, and those millions of dollars belong to the boss, who works very few hours. That's progress. It is the progress of people who have devised methods of less work and more gain that have propelled us to the very standards of living that we now call normal. Our "normal" standard of living may vary greatly from person to person, but it is living proof of our progress, even in the case of the laborer. I would think it safe to assume that most humans would rather truck on down to McDonalds 5 times a week for 3.35 dollars an hour, live in an apartment, and eat when they are hungry than brave the cold of winter in a cave, and face the reality that when hunger strikes, its time to go throw rocks at bison.

    In conclusion, competition and greed have combined together as a team, and helped us to strive for progress if not perfection. The opportunities and choices we have as modern humans, are what allow us to become multi-millionaires, or estranged laborers. It's a tough race, and some of us are still driving Pontiacs, but it's the distinction between Pontiacs and Ferraris that drives us. To cut off competition and greed, would be like cutting off the gas-line to the engine of human progression. Granted there might be some cars lost in the race, but we must remember, it is "THE HUMAN RACE".

Analysis of Sample Philosophy Paper 3

This paper is problematic for several reasons, but perhaps the most glaring are the following: first, the simplistic, smug tone is quite inappropriate to the task; second, the definition of important terms are far too narrow for an intelligent audience; and third, Micky's surface errors keep forcing readers to back up and start sentences over.

Micky's difficulties begin almost immediately in the introductory paragraph when he states: "I think that there is little doubt that labor is estranged, but what Marx is overlooking is the beauty of competition, and the positive aspects of greed." Micky goes on to state that "The drive of greed, competition, and the desire for progress are the main reasons we don't live in trees anymore!" Later he points out that "most humans would rather truck on down to McDonalds 5 times a week for 3.35 dollars an hour, live in an apartment, and eat when they are hungry than brave the cold of winter in a cave, and face the reality that when hunger strikes, its time to go throw rocks at a bison."

The first statement can be faulted for its questionable assertion of causality (can the writer be sure it was greed rather than some other motivation that civilized man?) and the second for its setup of an either/or fallacy (most humans assume options for themselves other than working at McDonald's or throwing rocks at bison). Micky's careless logic contributes to the tone that prevails here: Either he isn't seriously engaged in the issues Marx presents, or he is trying too hard to bring levity or a "modern" touch to a serious discussion. Rather than treat the subject thoughtfully, he uses fallacious reasoning and a glib tone in an attempt to make Marx's theories appear out of touch with reality. Whether one agrees or disagrees with Marx's theories, the fact that they are among the world's more influential merits some measure of respect, even in light of the recent collapse of Marxist governments.

Micky's word choices and phrasing contribute to his difficulties. Note the tired metaphor in the following: "It would seem possibly honorable to sympathize with the plight, bondage, and degradation of the laborer, but would it not be more logical to admit that the laborer has made his own bed, and ___ hope that he is comfortable in it?" To make matters worse, the metaphor is confounded by faulty logic and lack of convincing support—why would it be "more logical" to believe that laborers caused their own conditions? If Micky wants to challenge Marx (and he certainly should if he finds grounds to do so), he must base this challenge on concrete weaknesses. But he doesn't, and his faulty logic traps him in positions from which there is no escape and certainly no appeal. Consider his contention, for example, that those who labor least should enjoy the rewards of their successful exploitation of others. Does this mean that Micky condones slavery?

Although this paper is very weak, it isn't beyond redemption. In fact, it could be an enlightening and delightful paper because Micky wants to take issue with Marx. To improve it, Micky would need to drop the cavalier attitude and approach the topic with the same seriousness and thoughtfulness that Marx demonstrates. And in this recommendation lies an important principle of mastering writing in a given discipline: One is expected to approach topics with the same tone and consideration they are accorded in the field. The goal is to master the tenor of the insider, even while one is formulating his or her individual voice.

Micky would also need to reevaluate his understanding of fundamental concepts. For example, he defines human progress in strictly financial terms. A broader definition of progress, one that also includes cultural and social factors, would certainly allow him more leeway for some insights into his subject. In the same manner, a broader definition of competition—one less aligned with greed and more open to forms of cooperation—would present the term in a much more positive light. Micky could certainly argue that competition furthers a society not only economically but culturally and politically. He could even use the metaphor of the race—one of the more appealing aspects of the paper—to make this point. Might competition help us as individuals to acquire faster cars and as a society to build safer, better-quality cars?

Micky also needs to realize that his readers will not automatically believe or even *accept* what he says. Careful explanation and relevant examples are essential before he can show readers he has a valid claim. If Micky were to evaluate his subject in all its complexity and implications, rather than slight it through an offhand tone and narrow approach, his work would show dramatic improvements. As it stands, however, this paper is an inadequate response to the assignment because it fails to recognize the complexities of its subject.

Sentence Lesson

As noted above, punctuation is one of Micky's problems in this paper. As with Vicki's paper, the errors fall into two major categories, but they are different categories. The first involves quotation marks. In American English, the convention dictates that commas and periods go inside quotation marks. Look at the examples below from Micky's paper:

1. ... and forced us into the archaic system of "every man for himself".
2. ... but we must remember, it is "THE HUMAN RACE".

Micky has reversed the convention. The proper punctuation is

1a. ... and forced us into the archaic system of "every man for himself."
2a. ... but we must remember, it is "THE HUMAN RACE."

Like most people who don't understand this convention, Micky is inconsistent in how he punctuates quotation marks: sometimes he does it correctly, sometimes incorrectly.

The second category of error is related to commas. When a subject is followed immediately by its predicate, there should be no intervening comma. In other words, a sentence like the one below is punctuated incorrectly:

3. The woman, bought the dress.

Micky, however, regularly punctuates his sentences in this way. Look at these sentences:

4. To accept estranged labor as a regression, would be like accepting labor as the only means to survival.
5. The opportunities and choices we have as modern humans, are what allow us to become multi-millionaires, or estranged laborers.
6. The underlying reason for laboring, is that the laborer considers it an easier way to fulfill life sustaining needs.

Correcting these sentences would involve removing the comma in each instance.

Writing Assignments

1. Using your dictionary, personal experience, interviews with others, and any other sources available, define one of the following terms used in the above papers: *democracy, success, alienation, progress*. In a 3- to 5-page paper, argue that this term, as you have defined it, either is or is not descriptive of some aspect of American society. For example, you may discover that we cannot really call the American government a democracy. A successful paper will include a definition of democracy that is broad enough for most readers to accept

followed by an argument that is carefully explained and supported with relevant examples.
2. Using sources available in your library, write a 5-page paper that summarizes one of Marx's ideas. Following the summary, explain why people in America in the last decade of the twentieth century should be aware of this idea. You may want to think of answering one or more of the following questions: (1) What does this idea have to do with me? (2) How does this idea affect my daily life? (3) Should we as a society try to change the conditions that this idea represents?
3. Interview two faculty members in your college's English department and two in the political science department to determine their views of Marx's influence on contemporary society. In a 5- to 7-page paper, report the results of your interviews and provide a conclusion that summarizes what you've learned.
4. Rewrite Micky's paper to show how competition might further human progress without alienating labor.

PHILOSOPHY ASSIGNMENT 2

Course: **Introduction to Ethics**

In the world we find a variety of differing ethical and moral systems. Two stances that one can take toward this diversity are ethical relativism and ethical absolution. Explain the terms ethical relativism and ethical absolutism. What problems do the adherents of each of these ethical positions face when attempting to act in the world? Which of these theories do you think is the correct position for humans to adopt? Why? Length: 3–5 typed pages.

Analysis of Philosophy Assignment 2

This assignment, like Assignment 1, offers a clear procedure students can use to structure their response. The assignment encourages students to use a comparison/contrast approach to organize and develop their argument.

Whenever students are provided with two related subjects to compare and evaluate—in this case, ethical relativism and ethical absolutism—

they must decide whether they will take a point-by-point approach or a subject-by-subject approach to organizing their argument. All the responses to the assignment presented here represent the subject-by-subject approach. That is, the writers discussed one of the ethical systems entirely and then moved on to the second ethical system, rather than discussing one after another the point-by-point similarities and differences between the two systems.

The approach the students below chose is suitable for a 3- to 5-page assignment. Ordinarily, a point-by-point structure is too cumbersome and confusing for a relatively short comparison/contrast assignment. It is also inappropriate if the two subjects don't have many points that correspond directly. When you choose the subject-by-subject approach to organizing an argument, you must keep three important factors in mind. First, you must strive to make your presentation of both subjects parallel and closely related. In other words, corresponding points should be discussed in the same order for each subject. Second, you must choose wisely which subject to discuss first and which subject to discuss last. When using comparison and contrast as a method of evaluation, as in this assignment, it is usually best to discuss the subject you favor last. And third, you must be careful to ensure that both parts of your paper are related, but at the same time, you should avoid slipping into a point-by-point evaluation in the second half.

Class Article 1

"Anthropology and the Abnormal,"*

by Ruth Benedict

Modern social anthropology has become more and more a study of the varieties and common elements of cultural environment and the consequences of these in human behavior. For such a study of diverse social orders primitive peoples fortunately provide a laboratory not yet entirely vitiated by the spread of a standardized worldwide civilization. Dyaks and Hopis, Fijians and Yakuts are significant for psychological and sociological study because only among these simpler peoples has there been sufficient isolation to give opportunity for the development of localized social forms. In the higher cultures the standardization of

---

* "Anthropology and the Abnormal" by Ruth Benedict, *Journal of General Psychology*, 10 (1934): 59–80. Reprinted with permission of the Helen Dwight Reid Educational Foundation. Published by Heldref Publications, 4000 Albemarle St., N.W., Washington, DC 20016. Copyright 1934.

custom and belief over a couple of continents has given a false sense of the inevitability of the particular forms that have gained currency, and we need to turn to a wider survey in order to check the conclusions we hastily base upon this near universality of familiar customs. Most of the simpler cultures did not gain the wide currency of the one which, out of our experience, we identify with human nature, but this was for various historical reasons, and certainly not for any that gives us as its carriers a monopoly of social good or of social sanity. Modern civilization, from this point of view, becomes not a necessary pinnacle of human achievement but one entry in a long series of possible adjustments.

These adjustments, whether they are in mannerisms like the ways of showing anger, or joy, or grief in any society, or in major human drives like those of sex, prove to be far more variable than experience in any one culture would suggest. In certain fields, such as that of religion or of formal marriage arrangements, these wide limits of variability are well known and can be fairly described. In others it is not yet possible to give a generalized account, but that does not absolve us of the task of indicating the significance of the work that has been done and of the problems that have arisen.

One of these problems relates to the customary modern normal–abnormal categories and our conclusions regarding them. In how far are such categories culturally determined, or in how far can we with assurance regard them as absolute? In how far can we regard inability to function socially as diagnostic of abnormality, or in how far is it necessary to regard this as a function of the culture? . . .

The most spectacular illustrations of the extent to which normality may be culturally defined are those cultures where an abnormality of our culture is the cornerstone of their social structure. It is not possible to do justice to these possibilities in a short discussion. A recent study of an island of northwest Melanesia by Fortune describes a society built upon traits which we regard as beyond the border of paranoia. In this tribe the exogamic groups look upon each other as prime manipulators of black magic, so that one marries always into an enemy group which remains for life one's deadly and unappeasable foes. They look upon a good garden crop as a confession of theft, for everyone is engaged in making magic to induce into his garden the productiveness of his neighbors'; therefore no secrecy in the island is so rigidly insisted upon as the secrecy of a man's harvesting of his yams. Their polite phrase at the acceptance of a gift is, "And if you now poison me, how shall I repay you this present?" Their preoccupation with poisoning is constant: no woman ever leaves her cooking pot for a moment untended. Even the great affinal economic exchanges that are characteristic of this Melanesian culture area are quite altered in Dobu since they are incompatible with this fear and distrust that pervades the culture. . . . They go farther and people the whole world outside their own quarters with such malignant spirits that all-night feasts and ceremonials simply do not occur here. They have even rigorous religiously enforced customs that forbid the sharing of seed even in one family group. Anyone else's food is deadly poison to you, so that communality of stores is out of the question. For some months before harvest the whole society is on the verge of starvation, but if one falls to the temptation and eats up one's seed yams, one is an outcast and a beachcomber for life. There is no coming back. It involves, as a matter of course, divorce and the breaking of all social ties.

Now in this society where no one may work with another and no one may share with another, Fortune describes the individual who was regarded by all his fellows as crazy. He was not one of those who periodically ran amok and, beside himself and frothing at the mouth, fell with a knife upon anyone he could reach. Such behavior they did not regard as putting anyone outside the pale. They did not even put the individuals who were known to be liable to these attacks under any kind of control. They merely fled when they saw the attack coming on and kept out of the way. "He would be all right tomorrow." But there was one man of sunny, kindly disposition who liked work and liked to be helpful. The compulsion was too strong for him to repress it in favor of the opposite tendencies of his culture. Men and women never spoke of him without laughing; he was silly and simple and definitely crazy. Nevertheless, to the ethnologist used to a culture that has, in Christianity, made his type the model of all virtue, he seemed a pleasant fellow.

An even more extreme example, because it is of a culture that has built itself upon a more complex abnormality, is that of the North Pacific Coast of North America. The civilization of the Kwakiutl, at the time when it was first recorded in the last decades of the nineteenth century, was one of the most vigorous in North America. It was built up on an ample economic supply of goods, the fish which furnished their food staple being practically inexhaustible and obtainable with comparatively small labor, and the wood which furnished the material for their houses, their furnishings, and their arts being, with however much labor, always procurable. They lived in coastal villages that compared favorably in size with those of any other American Indians and they kept up constant communication by means of sea-going dug-out canoes.

It was one of the most vigorous and zestful of the aboriginal cultures of North America, with complex crafts and ceremonials, and elaborate and striking arts. It certainly had none of the earmarks of a sick civilization. The tribes of the Northwest Coast had wealth, and exactly in our terms. That is, they had not only a surplus of economic goods, but they made a game of the manipulation of wealth. It was by no means a mere direct transcription of economic needs and the filling of those needs. It involved the idea of capital, of interest, and of conspicuous waste. It was a game with all the binding rules of a game, and a person entered it as a child. His father distributed wealth for him, according to his ability, at a small feast or potlatch, and each gift the receiver was obliged to accept and to return after a short interval with interest that ran to about 100 per cent a year. By the time the child was grown, therefore, he was well launched, a larger potlatch had been given for him on various occasions of exploit or initiation, and he had wealth either out of usury or in his own possession. Nothing in the civilization could be enjoyed without validating it by the distribution of this wealth. Everything that was valued, names and songs as well as material objects were passed down in family lines, but they were always publicly assumed with accompanying sufficient distributions of property. It was the game of validating and exercising all the privileges one could accumulate from one's various forebears, or by gift, or by marriage, that made the chief interest of the culture. Everyone in his degree took part in it, but many, of course, mainly as spectators. In its highest form it was played out between rival chiefs representing not only themselves and their family lines but their communities, and the object of the contest was to glorify oneself and to humiliate one's opponent. On this level of greatness the property involved was no longer represented by blankets, so many thousand of them to a potlatch, but by higher units of value. These higher units were like our bank notes. They were incised copper tablets, each of them named, and having a value that depended upon their illustrious history. This was as high as ten thousand blankets, and to possess one of them, still more to enhance its value at a great potlatch, was one of the greatest glories within the compass of the chiefs of the Northwest Coast. . . .

Every contingency of life was dealt with in . . . two traditional ways. To them the two were equivalent. Whether one fought with weapons or "fought with property," as they say, the same idea was at the bottom of both. In the olden times, they say, they fought with spears, but now they fight with property. One overcomes one's opponents in equivalent fashion in both, matching forces and seeing that one comes out ahead, and one can thumb one's nose at the vanquished rather more satisfactorily at a potlatch than on a battle field. Every occasion in life was noticed, not in its own terms, as a stage in the sex life of the individual or as a climax of joy or of grief, but as furthering this drama of consolidating one's own prestige and bringing shame to one's guests. Whether it was the occasion of the birth of a child, or a daughter's adolescence, or of the marriage of one's son, they were all equivalent raw material for the culture to use for this one traditionally selected end. They were all to raise one's own personal status and to entrench oneself by the humiliation of one's fellows. A girl's adolescence among the Nootka was an event for which her father gathered property from the time she was first able to run about. When she was adolescent he would demonstrate his greatness by an unheard of distribution of these goods, and put down all his rivals. It was not as a fact of the girl's sex life that it figured in their culture, but as the occasion for a major move in the great game of vindicating one's own greatness and humiliating one's associates.

In their behavior at great bereavements this set of the culture comes out most strongly. Among the Kwakiutl it did not matter whether a relative had died in bed of disease, or by the hand of an enemy; in either case death was an affront to be wiped out by the death of another person. The fact that one had been caused to mourn was proof that one had been put upon. A chief's sister and her daughter had gone up to Victoria, and either because they drank bad whiskey or because their boat capsized they never came back. The chief called together his warriors. "Now, I ask you, tribes, who shall wail? Shall I do it or shall another?" The spokesman answered, of course, "Not you, Chief. Let some other of the tribes." Immediately they set up the war pole to announce their intention of wiping out the injury, and gathered a war party. They set out, and found seven men and two children asleep and killed them. "Then they felt good when they arrived at Sebaa in the evening."

The point which is of interest to us is that in our society those who on that occasion would feel good when they arrived at Sebaa that evening would be the definitely abnormal. There would be some, even in our society, but it is not a recognized and approved mood under the circumstances. On the Northwest Coast those are favored and fortunate to whom that mood under those circumstances is congenial, and those to whom it is repugnant are unlucky. This latter minority can register in their own culture only by doing violence to their congenial responses and acquiring others that are difficult for them. The person, for instance, who, like a Plains Indian whose wife has been taken from him, is too proud to fight, can deal with the Northwest Coast civilization only by ignoring its strongest bents. If he cannot achieve it, he is the deviant in that culture, their instance of abnormality.

The head-hunting that takes place on the Northwest Coast after a death is no matter of blood revenge or of organized vengeance. There is no effort to tie up the subsequent killing with any responsibility on the part of the victim for the death of the person who is being mourned. A chief whose son has died goes visiting wherever his fancy dictates, and he says to his host, "My prince has died today, and you go with him." Then he kills him. In this, according to their interpretation, he acts nobly because he has not been downed. He has thrust back in return. The whole procedure is meaningless without the fundamental paranoid reading of bereavement. Death, like all the other untoward accidents of existence, confounds man's pride and can only be handled in the category of insults. . . .

These illustrations, which it has been possible to indicate only in the briefest manner, force upon us the fact that normality is culturally defined. An adult shaped to the drives and standards of either of these cultures, if he were transported into our civilization, would fall into our categories of abnormality. He would be faced with the psychic dilemmas of the socially unavailable. In his own culture, however, he is the pillar of society, the end result of socially inculcated mores, and the problem of personal instability in his case simply does not arise.

No one civilization can possibly utilize in its mores the whole potential range of human behavior. Just as there are great numbers of possible phonetic articulations, and the possibility of language depends on a selection and standardization of a few of these in order that speech communication may be possible at all, so the possibility of organized behavior of every sort, from the fashions of local dress and houses to the dicta of a people's ethics and religion, depends upon a similar selection among the possible behavior traits. In the field of recognized economic obligations or sex tabus this selection is as non-rational and subconscious a process as it is in the field of phonetics. It is a process which goes on in the group for long periods of time and is historically conditioned by innumerable accidents of isolation or of contact of peoples. In any comprehensive study of psychology, the selection that different cultures have made in the course of history within the great circumference of potential behavior is of great significance.

Every society, beginning with some slight inclination in one direction or another, carries its preference farther and farther, integrating itself more and more completely upon its chosen basis, and discarding those types of behavior that are uncongenial. Most of those organizations of personality that seem to us most incontrovertibly abnormal have been used by different civilizations in the very foundations of their institutional life. Conversely the most valued traits of our normal individuals have been looked on in differently organized cultures as aberrant. Normality, in short, within a very wide range, is culturally defined. It is primarily a term for the socially elaborated segment of human behavior in any culture; and abnormality, a term for the segment that that particular civilization does not use. The very eyes with which we see the problem are conditioned by the long traditional habits of our own society.

It is a point that has been made more often in relation to ethics than in relation to psychiatry. We do not any longer make the mistake of deriving the morality of our own locality and decade directly from the inevitable constitution of human nature. We do not elevate it to the dignity of a first principle. We recognize that morality differs in every society, and is a convenient term for socially approved habits. Mankind has always preferred to say, "It is morally good," rather than "It is habitual," and the fact of this preference is matter enough for a critical science of ethics. But historically the two phrases are synonymous.

The concept of the normal is properly a variant of the concept of the good. It is that which society has approved. A normal action is one which falls well within the limits of expected behavior for a particular society. Its variability among different peoples is essentially a function of the variability of the behavior patterns that different societies have created for themselves, and can never be wholly divorced from a consideration of culturally institutionalized types of behavior.

Each culture is a more or less elaborate working-out of the potentialities of the segment it has chosen. In so far as a civilization is well integrated and consistent within itself, it will tend to carry farther and farther, according to its nature, its initial impulse toward a particular type of action, and from the point of view of any other culture those elaborations will include more and more extreme and aberrant traits.

Each of these traits, in proportion as it reinforces the chosen behavior patterns of that culture, is for that culture normal. Those individuals to whom it is congenial either congenitally, or as the result of childhood sets, are accorded prestige in that culture, and are not visited with the social contempt or disapproval which their traits would call down upon them in a society that was differently organized. On the other hand, those individuals whose characteristics are not congenial to the selected type of human behavior in that community are the deviants, no matter how valued their personality traits may be in a contrasted civilization. . . .

The problem of understanding abnormal human behavior in any absolute sense independent of cultural factors is still far in the future. The categories of borderline behavior which we derive from the study of the neuroses and psychoses of our civilization are categories of prevailing local types of instability. They give much information about the stresses and strains of Western civilization, but no final picture of inevitable human behavior. Any conclusions about such behavior must await the collection by trained observers of psychiatric data from other cultures. Since no adequate work of the kind has been done at the present time, it is impossible to say what core of definition of abnormality may be found valid from the comparative material. It is as it is in ethics; all our local conventions of moral behavior and of immoral are without absolute validity, and yet it is quite possible that a modicum of what is considered right and what wrong could be disentangled that is shared by the whole human race. When data are available in psychiatry, this minimum definition of abnormal human tendencies will be probably quite unlike our culturally conditioned, highly elaborated psychoses such as those that are described, for instance, under the terms of schizophrenia and manic-depressive.

Class Article 2

"Ethical Relativism"
by Walter T. Stace
(from *The Concept of Morals,* 1937)

Any ethical position which denies that there is a single moral standard which is equally applicable to all men at all times may fairly be called a species of ethical relativity. There is not, the relativist asserts, merely one moral law, one code, one standard. There are many moral laws, codes, standards. What morality ordains in one place or age may be quite different from what morality ordains in another place or age. The moral code of Chinamen is quite different from that of Europeans, that of African savages quite different from both. Any morality, therefore, is relative to the age, the place, and the circumstances in which it is found. It is in no sense absolute.

This does not mean merely—as one might at first sight be inclined to suppose—that the very same kind of action which is *thought* right in one country and period may be *thought* wrong in another. This would be a mere platitude, the truth of which everyone would have to admit. Even the absolutist would admit this—would even wish to emphasize it—since he is well aware that different people have different sets of moral ideas, and his whole point is that some of these sets of ideas are false. What the relativist means to assert is, not this platitude, but that the very same kind of action which *is* right in one country and period may *be* wrong in another. And this, far from being a platitude, is a very startling assertion.

It is very important to grasp thoroughly the difference between the two ideas. For there is reason to think that many minds tend to find ethical relativity attractive because they fail to keep them clearly apart. It is so very obvious that moral ideas differ from country to country and from age to age. And it is so very easy, if you are mentally lazy, to suppose that to say this means the same as to say that no universal moral standard exists,—or in other words that it implies ethical relativity. We fail to see that the word "standard" is used in two different senses. It is perfectly true that, in one sense, there are many variable moral

---

Reprinted with permission of Macmillan Publishing Company from *The Concept of Morals* by W. T. Stace. Copyright 1937 by Macmillan Publishing Company, copyright renewed © 1965 by Walter Stace.

standards. We speak of judging a man by the standard of his time. And this implies that different times have different standards. And this, of course, is quite true. But when the word "standard" is used in this sense it means simply the set of moral ideas current during the period in question. It means what people *think* right, whether as a matter of fact it *is* right or not. On the other hand when the absolutist asserts that there exists a single universal moral "standard," he is not using the word in this sense at all. He means by "standard" what *is* right as distinct from what people merely think right. His point is that although what people think right varies in different countries and periods, yet what actually is right is everywhere and always the same. And it follows that when the ethical relativist disputes the position of the absolutist and denies that any universal moral standard exists he too means by "standard" what actually is right. But it is exceedingly easy, if we are not careful, to slip loosely from using the word in the first sense to using it in the second sense; and to suppose that the variability of moral beliefs is the same thing as the variability of what really is moral. And unless we keep the two senses of the word "standard" distinct, we are likely to think the creed of ethical relativity much more plausible than it actually is.

The genuine relativist, then, does not merely mean that Chinamen may think right what Frenchmen think wrong. He means that what *is* wrong for the Frenchman may *be* right for the Chinaman. And if one enquires how, in those circumstances, one is to know what actually is right in China or in France, the answer comes quite glibly. What is right in China is the same as what people think right in China; and what is right in France is the same as what people think right in France. So that, if you want to know what is moral in any particular country or age all you have to do is to ascertain what are the moral ideas current in that age or country. Those ideas are, *for that age or country,* right. Thus what is morally right is identified with what is thought to be morally right, and the distinction which we made above between these two is simply denied. To put the same thing in another way, it is denied that there can be or ought to be any distinction between the two senses of the word "standard." There is only one kind of standard of right and wrong, namely, the moral ideas current in any particular age or country.

Moral right *means* what people think morally right. It has no other meaning. What Frenchmen think right is, therefore, right *for Frenchmen.* And evidently one must conclude—though I am not aware that relativists are anxious to draw one's attention to such unsavory but yet absolutely necessary conclusions from their creed—that cannibalism is right for people who believe in it, that human sacrifice is right for those races which practice it, and that burning widows alive was right for Hindus until the British stepped in and compelled the Hindus to behave morally by allowing their widows to remain alive.

When it is said that, according to the ethical relativist, what is thought right in any social group is right for that group, one must be careful not to misinterpret this. The relativist does not, of course, mean that there actually is an objective moral standard in France and a different objective standard in England, and that French and British opinions respectively give us correct information about these different standards. His point is rather that there are no objectively true moral standards at all. There is no single universal objective standard. Nor are there a variety of local objective standards. All standards are subjective. People's subjective feelings about morality are the only standards which exist.

To sum up. The ethical relativist consistently denies, it would seem, whatever the ethical absolutist asserts. For the absolutist there is a single universal moral standard. For the relativist there is no such standard. There are only local, ephemeral, and variable standards. For the absolutist there are two senses of the word "standard." Standards in the sense of sets of current moral ideas are relative and changeable. But the standard in the sense of what is actually morally right is absolute and unchanging. For the relativist no such distinction can be made. There is only one meaning of the word "standard," namely, that which refers to local and variable sets of moral ideas. Or if it is insisted that the word must be allowed two meanings, then the relativist will say that there is at any rate no actual example of a standard in the absolute sense, and that the word as thus used is an empty name to which nothing in reality corresponds; so that the distinction between the two meanings becomes empty and useless. Finally—though this is merely saying the same thing in another way—the absolutist makes a distinction between what actually is right and what is thought right. The relativist rejects this distinction and identifies what is moral with what is thought by certain human beings or groups of human beings. . . .

I shall now proceed to consider, first, the main arguments which can be urged in favor of ethical relativity; and secondly, the arguments which can be urged against it. . . . The first is that which relies upon the actual varieties of moral "standards" found in the world. It is easy enough to believe in a single absolute morality in older times when there was no anthropology, when all humanity was divided clearly into two groups, Christian peoples and the "heathen." Christian peoples knew and possessed the one true morality. The rest were savages whose moral ideas could be ignored. But all this changed. Greater knowledge has brought greater tolerance. We can no longer exalt our own morality as alone true, while dismissing all other moralities as false or inferior. The investigations of anthropologists have shown that there exists side by side in the world a bewildering variety of moral codes. On this topic endless volumes have been written, masses of evidence piled up. Anthropologists have ransacked the Melanesian Islands, the jungles of New Guinea, the steppes of Siberia, the deserts of Australia, the forests of central Africa, and have brought back with them countless examples of weird, extravagant, and fantastic "moral" customs with which to confound us. We learn that all kinds of horrible practices are, in this, that, or the other place, regarded as essential to virtue. We find that there is nothing, or next to nothing, which has always and everywhere been regarded as morally good by all men. Where then is our universal morality? Can we, in face of all this evidence, deny that it is nothing but an empty dream?

This argument, taken by itself, is a very weak one. It relies upon a single set of facts—the variable moral customs of the world. But this variability of moral ideas is admitted by both parties to the dispute, and is capable of ready explanation upon the hypothesis of either party. The relativist says that the facts are to be explained by the non-existence of any absolute moral standard. The absolutist says that they are to be explained by human ignorance of what the absolute moral standard is. And he can truly point out that men have differed widely in their opinions about all manner of topics including the subject-matters of the physical sciences—just as much as they differ about morals. And if the various different opinions which men have held about the shape of the earth do not prove that it has no one real shape, neither do the various opinions which they have held about morality prove that there is no one true morality.

Thus the facts can be explained equally plausibly on either hypothesis. There is nothing in the facts themselves which compels us to prefer the relativistic hypothesis to that of the absolutist. And therefore the argument fails to prove the relativist conclusion. If that conclusion is to be established, it must be by means of other considerations.

This is the essential point. But I will add some supplementary remarks. The work of the anthropologists, upon which ethical relativists seem to rely so heavily, has as a matter of fact added absolutely nothing *in principle* to what has always been known about the variability of moral ideas. Educated people have known all along that the Greeks tolerated sodomy, which in modern times has been regarded in some countries as an abominable crime; that the Hindus thought it a sacred duty to burn their widows; that trickery, now thought despicable, was once believed to be a virtue; that terrible torture was thought by our own ancestors only a few centuries ago to be a justifiable weapon of justice; that it was only yesterday that western peoples came to believe that slavery is immoral. Even the ancients knew very well that moral customs and ideas vary—witness the writings of Herodotus. Thus the principle of the variability of moral ideas was well understood long before modern anthropology was ever heard of. Anthropology has added nothing to the knowledge of this principle except a mass of new and extreme examples of it drawn from very remote sources. But to multiply examples of a principle already well known and universally admitted adds nothing to the argument which is built upon that principle. The discoveries of the anthropologists have no doubt been of the highest importance in their own sphere. But in my considered opinion they have thrown no new light upon the special problems of the moral philosopher.

Although the multiplication of examples has no logical bearing on the argument, it does have an immense *psychological* effect upon people's minds. These masses of anthropological learning are impressive. They are propounded in the sacred name of "science." If they are quoted in support of ethical relativity—as they often are—people *think* that they must prove something important. They bewilder and over-awe the simple-minded, batter down their resistance, make them ready to receive humbly the doctrine of ethical relativity from those who have acquired a reputation by their immense learning and their claims to be "scientific." Perhaps this is why so much ado is made by ethical relativists regarding the anthropological evidence. But we must refuse to be impressed. We must discount all this mass of evidence about the extraordinary moral customs of remote peoples. Once we have admitted—as everyone who is instructed must have admitted these last two thousand years without any anthropology at all—the principle that moral ideas vary, all this new evidence adds nothing to the argument. And the argument itself proves nothing for the reasons already given. . . .

The second argument in favor of ethical relativity is also a very strong one. And it does not suffer from the disadvantage that it is dependent upon the acceptance of any particular philosophy such as radical empiricism. It makes its appeal to considerations of a quite general character. It consists in alleging that no one has ever been able to discover upon what foundation an absolute morality could rest, or from what source a universally binding moral code could derive its authority.

If, for example, it is an absolute and unalterable moral rule that all men ought to be unselfish, from whence does this *command* issue? For a command it certainly is, phrase it how you please. There is no difference in meaning between the sentence "You ought to be unselfish" and the sentence "Be unselfish." Now a command implies a commander. An obligation implies some authority which obliges. Who is this commander, what this authority? Thus the vastly different question is raised of *the basis of moral obligation.* Now the argument of the relativist would be that it is impossible to find any basis for a universally binding moral law; but that it is quite easy to discover a basis for morality if moral codes are admitted to be variable, ephemeral, and relative to time, place, and circumstance.

In this book I am assuming that it is no longer possible to solve this difficulty by saying naïvely that the universal moral law is based upon the uniform commands of God to all men. There will be many, no doubt, who will dispute this. But I am not writing for them. I am writing for those who feel the necessity of finding for morality a basis independent of particular religious dogmas. And I shall therefore make no attempt to argue the matter.

The problem which the absolutist has to face, then, is this. The religious basis of the one absolute morality having disappeared, can there be found for it any other, any secular, basis? If not, then it would seem that we cannot any longer believe in absolutism. We shall have to fall back upon belief in a variety of perhaps mutually inconsistent moral codes operating over restricted areas and limited periods. No one of these will be better, or more true, than any other. Each will be good and true for those living in those areas and periods. We shall have to fall back, in a word, on ethical relativity.

For there is no great difficulty in discovering the foundation of morality, or rather of moralities, if we adopt the relativistic hypothesis. Even if we cannot be quite certain *precisely* what these foundations are—and relativists themselves are not entirely agreed about them—we can at least see in a general way the *sort* of foundations they must have. We can see that the question on this basis is not in principle impossible to answer—although the details may be obscure; while, if we adopt the absolutist hypothesis—so the argument runs—no kind of answer is conceivable at all. . . .

This argument is undoubtedly very strong. It *is* absolutely essential to solve the problem of the basis of moral obligation if we are to believe in any kind of moral standards other than those provided by mere custom or by irrational emotions. It is idle to talk about a universal morality unless we can point to the source of its authority—or at least to do so is to indulge in a faith which is without rational ground. To cherish a blind faith in morality may be, for the average man whose business is primarily to live aright and not to theorize, sufficient. Perhaps it is his wisest course. But it will not do for the philosopher. His function, or at least one of his functions, is precisely to discover the rational grounds of our everyday beliefs—if they have any. Philosophically and intellectually, then, we cannot accept belief in a universally binding morality unless we can discover upon what foundation its obligatory character rests.

But in spite of the strength of the argument thus posed in favor of ethical relativity, it is not impregnable. For it leaves open one loop-hole. It is always possible that some theory, not yet examined, may provide a basis for a universal moral obligation. The argument rests upon the negative proposition that *there is no theory which can provide a basis for a universal morality.* But it is notoriously difficult to prove a negative. How can you prove that there are no green swans? All you can show is that none have been found so far. And then it is always possible that one will be found tomorrow. . . .

It is time that we turned our attention from the case in favor of ethical relativity to the case against it. Now the case against it consists, to a very large extent, in urging that, if taken seriously and pressed to its logical conclusion, ethical relativity can only end in destroying the conception of morality altogether, in undermining its practical efficacy, in rendering meaningless many almost universally accepted truths about human affairs, in robbing human beings of any incentive to strive for a better world, in taking the lifeblood out of every ideal and every aspiration which has ever ennobled the life of man. . . .

First of all, then, ethical relativity, in asserting that the moral standards of particular social groups are the only standards which exist, renders meaningless all propositions which attempt to compare those standards with one another in respect to their moral worth. And this is a very serious matter indeed. We are accustomed to think that the moral ideas of one nation or social group may be "higher" or "lower" than those of another. We believe, for example, that Christian ethical ideals are nobler than those of the savage races of central Africa. Probably most of us would think that the Chinese moral standards are higher than those of the inhabitants of New Guinea. In short we habitually compare one civilization with another and judge the sets of ethical ideas to be found in them to be some better, some worse. The fact that such judgments are very difficult to make with any justice, and that they are frequently made on very superficial and prejudiced grounds, has no bearing on the question now at issue. The question is whether such judgments have any *meaning.* We habitually assume that they have.

But on the basis of ethical relativity they can have none whatever. For the relativist must hold that there is no *common* standard which can be applied to the various civilizations judged. Any such comparison of moral standards implies the existence of some superior standard which is applicable to both. And the existence of any such standard is precisely what the relativist denies. According to him the Christian standard is applicable only to Christians, the Chinese standard only to Chinese, the New Guinea standard only to the inhabitants of New Guinea.

What is true of comparisons between the moral standards of different races will also be true of comparisons between those of different ages. It is not unusual to ask such questions as whether the standard of our own day is superior to that which existed among our ancestors five hundred years ago. And when we remember that our ancestors employed slaves, practiced barbaric physical tortures, and burnt people alive, we may be inclined to think that it is. At any rate we assume that the question is one which has meaning and is capable of rational discussion. But if the ethical relativist is right, whatever we assert on this subject must be totally meaningless. For here again there is no common standard which could form the basis of any such judgments.

This in its turn implies that the whole notion of moral *progress* is a sheer delusion. Progress means an advance from lower to higher, from worse to better. But on the basis of ethical relativity it has no meaning to say that the standards of this age are better (or worse) than those of a previous age. For there is no common standard by which both can be measured. Thus it is nonsense to say that the morality of the New Testament is higher than that of the Old. And Jesus Christ, if he imagined that he was introducing into the world a higher ethical standard than existed before his time, was merely deluded. . . .

I come now to a second point. Up to the present I have allowed it to be taken tacitly for granted that, though judgments comparing different races and ages in respect of the worth of their moral codes are impossible for the ethical relativist, yet judgments of comparison between individuals living within the same social group would be quite possible. For individuals living within the same social group would be subject to the same moral code, that of their group, and this would therefore constitute, as between these individuals, a common standard by which they could both be measured. We have not here, as we had in the other case, the difficulty of the absence of any common standard of comparison. It should therefore be possible for the ethical relativist to say quite meaningfully that President Lincoln was a better man than some criminal or moral imbecile of his own time and country, or that Jesus was a better man than Judas Iscariot.

But is even this minimum of moral judgment really possible on relativist grounds? It seems to me that it is not. For when once the whole of humanity is abandoned as the area covered by a single moral standard, what smaller areas are to be adopted as the *loci* of different standards? Where are we to draw the lines of demarcation? We can split up humanity, perhaps,—though the procedure will be very arbitrary—into races, races into nations, nations into tribes, tribes into families, families into individuals. Where are we going to draw the *moral* boundaries? Does the *locus* of a particular moral standard reside in a race, a nation, a tribe, a family, or an individual? Perhaps the blessed phrase "social group" will be dragged in to save the situation. Each such group, we shall be told, has its own moral code which is, for it, right. But what *is* a "group"? Can anyone define it or give its boundaries? This is the seat of that ambiguity in the theory of ethical relativity to which reference was made on an earlier page.

The difficulty is not, as might be thought, merely an academic difficulty of logical definition. If that were all, I should not press the point. But the ambiguity has practical consequences which are disastrous for morality. No one is likely to say that moral codes are confined within the arbitrary limits of the geographical divisions of countries. Nor are the notions of race, nation, or political state likely to help us. To bring out the essentially practical character of the difficulty let us put it in the form of concrete questions. Does the American nation constitute a "group" having a single moral standard? Or does the standard of what I ought to do change continuously as I cross the continent in a railway train? Do different States of the Union have different moral codes? Perhaps every town and village has its own peculiar standard. This may at first sight seem reasonable enough. "In Rome do as Rome does" may seem as good a rule in morals as it is in etiquette. But can we stop there? Within the village are numerous cliques each having its own set of ideas. Why should not each of these claim to be bound only by its own special and peculiar moral standards? And if it comes to that, why should not the gangsters of Chicago claim to constitute a group having its own morality, so that its murders and debaucheries must be viewed as "right" by the only standard which can legitimately be applied to it? And if it be answered that the nation will not tolerate this, that may be so. But this is to put the foundation of right simply in the superior force of the majority. In that case whoever is stronger will be right, however monstrous his ideas and actions. And if we cannot deny to any set of people the right to have its own morality, is it not clear that, in the end, we cannot even deny this right to the individual? Every individual man and woman can put up, on this view, an irrefutable claim to be judged by no standard except his or her own.

If these arguments are valid, the ethical relativist cannot really maintain that there is anywhere to be found a moral standard binding upon anybody against his will. And he cannot maintain that, even within the social group, there is a common standard as between individuals. And if that is so, then even judgments to the effect that one man is morally better than another becomes meaningless. All moral valuation thus vanishes. There is nothing to prevent each man from being a rule unto himself. The result will be moral chaos and the collapse of all effective standards. . . .

But even if we assume that the difficulty about defining moral groups has been surmounted, a further difficulty presents itself. Suppose that we have now definitely decided what are the exact boundaries of the social group within which a moral standard is to be operative. And we will assume—as is invariably done by relativists themselves—that this group is to be some actually existing social community such as a tribe or nation. How are we to know, even then, what actually *is* the moral standard within that group? How is anyone to know? How is even a member of the group to know? For there are certain to be within the group—at least this will be true among advanced peoples—wide differences of opinion as to what is right, what wrong. Whose opinion, then, is to be taken as representing *the* moral standard of the group? Either we must take the opinion of the majority within the group, or the opinion of some minority. If we rely upon the ideas of the majority, the results will be disastrous. Wherever there is found among a people a small band of select spirits, or perhaps one man, working for the establishment of higher and nobler ideas than those commonly accepted by the group, we shall be compelled to hold that, for that people at that time, the majority are right, and that the reformers are wrong and are preaching what is immoral. We shall have to maintain, for example, that Jesus was preaching immoral doctrines to the Jews. Moral goodness will have to be equated always with the mediocre and sometimes with the definitely base and ignoble. If on the other hand we said that the moral standard of the group is to be identified with the moral opinions of some minority, then what minority is this to be? We cannot answer that it is to be the minority composed of the best and most enlightened individuals of the group. This would involve us in a palpably vicious circle. For by what standard are these individuals to be judged the best and the most enlightened? There is no principle by which we could select the right minority. And therefore we should have to consider every minority as good as every other. And this means that we should have no logical right whatever to resist the claim of the gangsters of Chicago—if such a claim were made—that their practices represent the highest standards of American morality. It means in the end that every individual is to be bound by no standard save his own.

The ethical relativists are great empiricists. *What* is the actually moral standard of any group can only be discovered, they tell us, by an examination on the ground of the moral opinions and customs of that group. But will they tell us how they propose to decide, when they get to the ground, which of the many moral opinions they are sure to find there is *the* right one of that group? To some extent they will be able to do this for the Melanesian Islanders—from whom apparently all lessons in the nature of morality are in future to be taken. But it is certain that they cannot do it for advanced peoples whose members have learned to think for themselves and to entertain among themselves a wide variety of opinions. They cannot do it unless they accept the calamitous view that the ethical opinion of the majority is always right. We are left therefore once more with the conclusion that, even within a particular social group, anybody's moral opinion is as good as anybody else's, and that every man is entitled to be judged by his own standards.

Finally, not only is ethical relativity disastrous in its consequences for moral theory. It cannot be doubted that it must tend to be equally disastrous in its impact upon practical conduct. If men come really to believe that one moral standard is as good as another, they will conclude that their own moral standard has nothing special to recommend it. They might as well then slip down to some lower and easier standard. It is true that, for a time, it may be possible to hold one view in theory and to act practically upon another. But ideas, even philosophical ideas, are not so ineffectual that they can remain forever idle in the upper chambers of the intellect. In the end they seep down to the level of practice. They get themselves acted on.

Guide for Reading

The following three papers are adequate responses to the assignment. None is outstanding, but each presents both types of moral systems relatively completely. All three exhibit the same problem: They lack a strong sense of argument. Instead, they seem to be discussing the strengths and weaknesses of each system before claiming that a particular one is the correct one for humans to adopt.

It is possible for writers to argue effectively by not stating their claim till the argument is complete. This works, however, only if readers are guided through the writer's decision-making process in such a way that the conclusion seems valid, perhaps even inescapable. Without such a guide, readers are likely to wonder what point the information is leading to, a problem that the following papers share.

Guide for Reading

Ricardo's paper gives the clearest information on the strengths and flaws of each ethical system. Most of his sentences are very well constructed and lucid, making his argument a pleasure to read. As mentioned above, however, Ricardo's paper has no strong sense of argument; moreover, he leaves too many unanswered questions, which forces readers to do the work Ricardo was supposed to do.

SAMPLE PHILOSOPHY PAPER 4

Ethical Systems

Ricardo G. (a junior)

[1] Ethical relativism and ethical absolutism are two ethical positions which refer to the subject of ethics in general rather than to specific moral systems. Ethical relativism is that position which maintains that there is not

one moral standard which can be applied to all of humanity. Rather groups of people each have their own moral standard which they not only think is right but is in fact right for them. Ethical absolutism is the exact opposite of this. It states that there is just one moral standard for everyone. What people may think is right may vary from group to group but what is actually right is the same for all. The basic question therefore is which position is true. Are there many moral standards each of which is ethically right or is there just one absolute standard?

[2] At first glance there appears to be many standards. This is supported by the diversity of ethical systems which exist in the world today. A few of them which Joel Feinberg refers to in his book *Reason and Responsibility* are ethical egoism, utilitarianism, and Rawl's contractarian theory. Each of these systems has a different basis. For example, in utilitarianism an action is defined as morally right by the amount of happiness it promotes in the greatest amount of people including oneself, whereas in ethical egoism a morally right act is one in which a person seeks his or her own well-being without considering the welfare of any other people. With such opposing moral systems how can a single absolute moral standard exist among them all?

[3] Another piece of evidence against ethical absolutism and in support of ethical relativism is seen in cultural anthropology. Cultural anthropology has shown how different societies can have very different moral systems. For example, Ruth Benedict in her paper "Anthropology and the Abnormal" discusses an island of northwest Melanesia. The people of this island "look upon each other as prime manipulators of black magic." As a result, the people are very distrustful of each other and consider everyone to be their enemy. They take their distrust to such an extreme that even when they are starving they will not accept food from another person for fear it will be poison. Acceptance of the food is considered to be a morally wrong action for which a person can be alienated from the society. To a society which does not believe in black magic such a morality would be considered abnormal and downright silly. This difference indicates how societies base their moral systems on their cultures. "Normality, in short, within a wide range is culturally defined." Con-

sequently, given the variations among the numerous cultures throughout the world and throughout time, moral systems must vary. Therefore, how can there be one absolute moral standard?

[4] What the ethical absolutist would argue is that even though these various moral standards exist both in the past and the present, they are not all valid. Only those systems which are based on the absolute moral standard correctly define what is morally right and what is morally wrong. The other moral systems only define what people think is right and wrong. This reasoning may be true; however, it can only be proven as such through the absolute moral standard. So what is this standard? This question is the basic problem of ethical absolutism. The entire theory is based upon an absolute moral standard which as of yet has not been found. Therefore, how can ethical absolutism be true? The absolutist would defend his position by stating that just because this standard has not been found does not mean that it does not exist. In support of this argument Walter Stace in his paper "Ethical Relativism" uses the example of green swans. As he says, "How can you prove that there are no green swans? All you can show is that none have been found so far. And then it is always possible that one will be found tomorrow. . . ."

[5] This may be true; however, this example is not applicable to absolutism for if a green swan is ever found there will be no question of its color. Everyone will agree that the swan is green. There can be no argument over it because the swan is either green or is not green. But absolutism is not as easy to distinguish as color. To be absolute a standard must define what is ultimately morally right and what is ultimately morally wrong. But how are people supposed to know when a standard has such a definition? How is the world supposed to recognize when a moral standard is absolute?

[6] For the ethical relativist such a recognition is impossible because an absolute moral standard does not exist. Instead individual groups have their own concept of what is right and of what is wrong with no concept being better or worse than another. In view of the evidence against ethical absolutism this may seem to be true. However, this theory of relativism is not without its problems, especially those that it poses for today's world. The

first problem is that of moral progress. As Stace points out, it is natural for groups of people to compare themselves with other groups from both the present and the past. He refers to it as a habit. this is seen in religion continually. Every Sunday TV evangelists preach to millions of viewers about how their religion is better than all others that have ever existed. It is the best. By following its principles people will "see the light" and be truly good and moral.

[7] The ethical relativist would never accept this for it implies there is an absolute moral standard against which all religions can be compared. But the exact opposite is the basis of this theory. Consequently, in the world of ethical relativism there can never be any moral progression. No group religious or secular can ever rise up and be morally better than another. This is contradictory to what people want to believe, but it may be the truth. For example, a "civilized" country like the United States naturally believes that it is morally superior to the "savage" tribes of past civilizations. True, these tribes probably had weird rituals in which people were tortured and sacrificed needlessly according to today's standards, but such tribes never chained an entire race to a life of slavery; they never intentionally dropped two atomic bombs on cities full of innocent people; nor did they create enough nuclear arms to destroy the entire world.

[8] The next point which Stace brings up against ethical relativism is that even though various groups may not be able to be compared to each other since there is no absolute moral standard, individuals within a group can be since they all have the same standard, that being the one of the group. Therefore, according to Stace, it is possible "for the ethical relativist to say quite meaningfully that President Lincoln was a better man than some criminal or moral imbecile of his own time and country." The relativist, however, cannot say this. Even though an imbecile, a criminal, and President Lincoln may have been from the same country and the same time the three had to have led very different lives and consequently had to have developed very different moral systems. As a result, they cannot be compared as to who is morally better since they belong to different groups with different moral standards. The question which Stace then raises

is if people from the same country and the same time do not define a group with the same moral standard, what does? Does a state, a country, a town, a family? It appears as if only an individual can define such a "group" because if morality is culturally defined as cultural anthropology shows, the likelihood of even two people having the same standards is small since different people experience a culture in different ways.

[9] This has a serious effect on ethical relativism. If every individual has his or her own moral standard and no one moral standard is better than another, a person would only be bound to him or herself. Every man, woman, and child could do whatever he or she thought was morally right to do. This system would work out well if everyone lived isolated from one another. But in a society where everyone must live and work together such a system would lead to, as Stace says, "moral chaos and the collapse of all effective standards."

[10] So what is humanity to do? If people adopt the position of the ethical absolutist there will be an absolute standard on which to base morality for everyone. But discovering such a standard is nearly impossible. If people adopt the position of the ethical relativist there will be no need to discover an absolute standard. Everyone will be able to have his or her own morality. But such a system would lead to complete chaos. Therefore, a compromise must be met between ethical absolutism and ethical relativism. People must be able to have their own morality. This is only natural as proven by the diversity of ethical systems which exist. But somehow a single standard must be found to link together these individual moralities so that people may live together as a society. An example of this is seen in the United States. Not everyone in this country has the same morality, but everyone believes in democracy. It is the concept which the entire country holds as morally right. In short it is the standard which binds this country together. This is what must be done for all of humanity. A standard must be decided upon that will allow individuals to have their own morality, but at the same time let the human race live together as a whole.

STUDY QUESTIONS

1. Questions can serve as useful prompts to get readers to agree to a particular point of view. They can also inspire readers to disagree with the writer's argument. Which of Ricardo's questions make you want to agree with him, and which make you inclined either to disagree or resent the fact that he hasn't provided an answer?

2. When you use sources, it is important to respond to the material you present, to engage in a dialogue with it. How does Ricardo do this in paragraphs 5 and 6?

3. Ricardo's paper is organized around showing the problems involved in ethical relativism and ethical absolutism. Which subject does he reserve for final discussion? Outline this paper in terms of its subject-by-subject approach.

4. In paragraph 7, Ricardo creates a false comparison. What is it?

5. In the conclusion, what stance does Ricardo ultimately take? Does he support ethical absolutism, ethical relativism, or both? Do you find his conclusion satisfactory?

Guide for Reading

Chris's paper provides good information, but it is difficult for most readers to put all of this information together. For example, the paragraphs don't flow very well from one to the next, mainly because Chris hasn't tried to connect the information so it will build into a convincing argument. The use of connecting phrases would help, as would a clear indication in the introduction of where the paper is going. As you read, consider the other changes that would help integrate the paper.

SAMPLE PHILOSOPHY PAPER 5

Ethical Relativism and Ethical Absolutism

Chris, L. (a sophomore)

Ethical absolutism and ethical relativism are two different philosophies of morality. Ethical relativists believe that there is no single moral standard. They claim that morality depends on the age, place, and circumstance, and no society can be justly labeled as more moral than another. Ethical absolutists believe that there is only one absolute moral standard. People of all ages and customs are subject to this one standard. Since there is only one standard, we can meaningfully compare ethical systems and learn from past systems.

Benedict backs up the ethical relativist theory. She focuses on the extreme differences in the moral standards of different societies. Since there are so many different cultures, she claims it would be impossible to judge every system by one moral standard. For example, she discusses the Melanesian culture in which family members are paranoid of each other. In such an ethical system, deceit and disloyalty are not considered wrong. Ethical relativists claim that we are unable to judge the Melanesians by our standards since the Melanesians are from a completely different ethical system. What the Melanesians think is right is actually right for them.

Stace brings up another problem with ethical absolutism. No one has actually discovered the source of the absolute morality. If we don't know the foundation for absolute morality, how can we be sure that it exists? Just because we don't know the reasoning behind something does not mean that it does not exist. This argument should not rule out ethical absolutism. For example, humans did not discover gravity until Newton's time, but it always existed. We were effected by it before we understood it.

Ethical absolutism has several strong points where relativism fails. Ethical relativists claim that the majority (or ruling class) is always moral. This may not always be true. We can safely assume that the ruling class was immoral in Hitler's era when the

Nazis unjustly condemned the Jews. The relativist would have to claim that Hitler was moral. In this case, ethical absolutism seems more valid. It allows us to label the majority as immoral.

In addition, Stace argues that ethical relativism undermines the concept of moral progress. To the relativist, moral progress would be virtually meaningless. Moral progress deals with a comparison of past ethical systems to those of the present. But in ethical relativism we are unable to make such comparisons. We would be considered no more moral than ancient cave men who could kill another human being without feeling any remorse. The word "moral" takes on different meanings for each culture so that the general term "moral" becomes meaningless. If someone were to ask, "Is it moral to kill a stranger because he stole your bread?" there would be no single answer. "Moral" in this question would have no meaning to the ethical relativist.

Under ethical relativism, the same act can be both moral and immoral depending on the culture. This may be quite disturbing. For example, let us assume that the Chinese do not consider rape immoral. If a Chinese man came to the United States and raped a woman, we could not justly condemn him because according to his standards he was acting morally. However, from the point of view of the ethical absolutist, we could say that our laws are more moral than the laws of the Chinese. Therefore we could say that the Chinese man acted immorally, and we could punish him.

Stace also points out that it is difficult to define who should be placed in a special ethical group. For example, should North Carolinians be judged as an ethical unit, or should we include the whole United States? Indeed this distinction is difficult, if not impossible, to make. It is difficult to say if hermits should be judged by their own personal moral standard or by an established moral system. Even if the boundaries of an ethical unit are determined, who is to lay down the actual ethical guidelines? The majority could provide the standard, but the majority is not necessarily right. These ambiguities seem to weaken the ethical relativists' argument.

Stace presents the problem that under ethical relativism, it would be impossible to judge other societies. Since there is no basis for comparing ethical systems, we are wrong to interfere in other groups that may need help. This would provide a problem for the United States in dealing with backward foreign countries. The relativist position seems to advocate an isolationist foreign policy. The United States would have no right to interfere with apartheid in Africa because the ethical relativist would say that Apartheid is moral for the Africans.

I disagree with Benedict's statement that "the concept of the normal is properly a variant of the concept of the good." It is not always true that what is normal is good. In fact, we may consider the normal to be immoral. For example, a recent study has shown that at least fifty percent of Durham's high school students have pre-marital sex. It seems that sex at a young age is the norm, but society in general still feels that it is immoral.

Ethical absolutism seems to be the more favorable theory. Like ethical relativism, it allows for ethical systems to be different. But it blames the differences on human error, thus allowing for the majority and the norm to be wrong; whereas ethical relativism says the norm is always right. It seems that ethical relativism leaves many loopholes. For example, it is unclear exactly who should be included in a given ethical system. Also it is difficult to say who should have the authority to judge what is moral and what is immoral. Ethical absolutism seems to be strong where ethical relativism is questionable.

STUDY QUESTIONS

1. Chris wisely refers to two authorities in the field of ethics, Walter Stace and Ruth Benedict. But how successful are these references? What does Chris tell us about his sources? What details should be included when one first refers to an outside source? (You may want to refer to the section on documentation in the overview to writing in the humanities.)

2. When using outside sources, it is important to mark clearly where reference to a source material ends and where your response to the source material begins. Chris fails to do so in paragraph 3. Revise the paragraph so that it flows smoothly from outside source material to the writer's own argument.

3. Writers of philosophical arguments often use hypothetical examples to test a theory's validity. In paragraph 6, Chris unwittingly uses a hypothetical example that many would find insensitive to the Chinese. Propose a different hypothetical example that would test the validity of ethical relativism without offending any potential audience.

4. Characterize Chris's style in this paper. Does he use effective transitions? Does he use a variety of sentence structures?

Guide for Reading

Anthony's paper presents the *clearest* argument of the three because he states his claim in the fourth paragraph and supports it in the following paragraphs. His paper is still the *weakest* of the three, however; the information isn't complete, his support isn't always relevant, and his simplistic view of what caused World War II effectively undermines his authority as a logical thinker.

A Theory of Ethics

Anthony P. (a junior)

SAMPLE PHILOSOPHY PAPER 6

It is a known fact that there are many different ethical and moral systems in the world. Different cultures have different beliefs in what is right and what is wrong, what is normal and what is abnormal. An action or belief that is right in one society may be wrong in another society. This diversity in ethics and morals has posed a problem for philosophers (Feinberg 474). "When individuals disagree in their moral judgments about other persons, or about their actions or policies, how can they determine by rational means whose judgment is correct?" (Feinberg 462). How can an individual, or a society for that matter, truly know what is right, and what are they to base their decision on? Over the years, two distinct arguments have emerged that can be taken toward this diversity. One is ethical relativism, and the other is ethical absolutism.

The ethical relativist believes that morality is culturally defined, and that "morality is relative to the age, the place, and the circumstances in which it is found." (Feinberg 474). He argues that "there is not merely one moral law, one code, one standard." (Feinberg 474). Rather, there are several different systems of ethics and morals and a society's system is defined by that society and may be quite different from the ethics and morals of another society. Normal actions are actions that a particular society has approved and that fall "within the limits of expected behavior for [that] particular society." (Feinberg 472). The relativist believes that an "absolute" set of morals and ethics that everyone follows is non-existant. On the other hand, the ethical absolutist, like the relativist, is "aware that different people have different sets of moral ideas" (Feinberg 474), but he argues that some of these sets of beliefs are false. The absolutist believes that there is one "absolute" and universal moral code. "His point is that although what people think right varies in different countries and periods, yet what actually is right is everywhere and always the same." (Feinberg 475).

No matter which stance a person takes in choosing his/her set of morals and ethics, that person will be faced with problems. If he/she takes the stance of the relativist, the individual will be confronted with conflicting ideas in the world about what is right and what is wrong, and the person will have to choose which set of ideas is correct. But this decision will be a very difficult one since there are no rational grounds on which to base his/her choice and the person is usually forced to adopt the morals and ethics of the society in which he lives. If, however, the individual takes the stance of the absolutist, he/she claims that his/her set of morals is right and that all others are wrong. Again, there are no rational grounds on which to base this argument that his/her morals are right and not somebody else's. There also exists the problem that if a universal morality exists, who or what is the authority that established this moral code (Feinberg 476–477)?

Of the two arguments, the relativistic point of view appears to be the stronger one. Although the absolutist argument accounts for the varied moral systems, it does not say which one is "right" and which of the others are wrong. The absolutist claims that there exists one moral code which governs all societies, but fails to define the values of this code and does not identify the source of its authority, at least in a rational way. Christians would claim that God is the authority figure that defined this universal system of morals. But not all people are Christians, and consequently this system of morals is not universal, and therefore not "absolute".

The relativist, instead of discounting some systems of morals as false and defining one moral code, explains the reasons for the variability of morals and ethics between societies, and proves that morals are culturally defined. "Every society, beginning with some slight inclination in one direction or another, carries its preference farther and farther, integrating itself more and more completely upon its chosen basis, and discarding those types of behavior that are uncongenial." (Feinberg 472). Therefore each society develops a set of morals that reflect the needs and interests of the people in that society. Since each society has different needs and interests, each society develops a different system of morals and ethics. Another explanation is that "no one civilization can possibly utilize in its mores the whole potential range of human behavior." (Feinberg 472). There is a large number of possible behaviors that humans can perform, and for any single civilization to define every single behavior as good or bad, right or wrong, according to that society's moral code is absurd if not impossible. Therefore, the existence of several different moral systems is essential if not necessary.

Although the absolutist's position seems to be the easier stance to take, humans should adopt the relativist's position. The simplicity of ethical absolutism is very deceiving, in that if there exists one moral code, then why are there so many variations in ethical systems and why doesn't the one society that follows the "absolute" moral system, if it exists, stand up and say that it is right and all others are wrong? The answer to this question is simple and can be answered with an actual example. The Germans, under Hitler, thought themselves to be the supreme race and that their society was superior to everyone else's, and their only objective was to destroy any and all societies that did not follow their "moral code". As a result, World War II broke out and caused a devastating effect on the world killing many people. Granted that this is an extreme example, but if every society were to stand up and claim that their system of morals is "absolute", then the world would become a chaotic and disorganized place to live. Therefore in order to maintain social sanity, humans should accept the fact that there are many different moral systems and that each system is "right" for the particular society that it governs, even if it conflicts with our morals and ethics.

References

Feinberg, Joel, ed. Reason and Responsibility: Readings in Some Basic Problems of Philosophy. 6th ed. Belmont, California: Wadsworth Pub. Co., 1985. 462–479.

STUDY QUESTIONS

1. Throughout this paper, Anthony fails to introduce quotations used from his source. Why is it necessary to provide parenthetical documentation as well as introductions to quotations? What are some examples of appropriate introductory phrases?

2. Compare Anthony's documentation format with the *MLA* format in the overview to writing in the humanities. What would you do to Anthony's documentation to make it conform to *MLA* style?

3. How would you describe the organization of Anthony's paper? Is it entirely a subject-by-subject approach? Are both subjects, ethical absolutism and ethical relativism, discussed in detail?

4. In his final paragraph, Anthony refers to the rise of Hitler in Germany as an argument against ethical absolutism. He is wrong in this regard. Fascism was based on moral relativism, on there not being any external absolute value or truth. Can you suggest a better example to use in arguing against ethical absolutism? What effect is this mistake likely to have on readers? That is, how will it influence their perception of Anthony?

5. Does Anthony take into account counterarguments against relativism? What arguments against relativism—some of which we have seen in previous papers—could the writer address?

Writing Assignments

1. Construct a dialogue between two scholars on the subject of ethical relativism and ethical absolutism, using the articles included in this section. Give the scholars names and have them argue (in their own words) the merits of the system they are proposing. Although neither scholar needs to concede to the other, readers should feel that one system is more appropriate than the other. A good paper will be

creative and solid—the two scholars will become real people, and each will argue convincingly for his or her chosen position.
2. In a 4- to 6-page paper, explain your own moral system and how you apply it in a fairly specific situation (in a particular community, in your college or university environment, in a specific work place, and so forth). Your purpose is twofold: to convince readers that your system is appropriate for the situation and to explain the basis for your system (religion, common sense, experience, and so on). Good papers will provide clear explanations and interesting, relevant examples.

PHILOSOPHY ASSIGNMENT 3

Course: **Introduction to Aesthetics**

What is art or an aesthetic experience? Many people think art is found in museums and concert halls. Some think this is where art belongs. Do you agree? Support your position with reference to the work of Dewey, Schiller, or Benjamin (or a combination thereof). Be sure to clearly indicate where your chosen thinker comes down on this question. Tell me if you agree and why. Personal experience as well as theoretical arguments may be appropriate support for your position.

Analysis of Philosophy Assignment 3

This assignment gives students practice in a form of writing necessary to all disciplines and especially important to philosophy: definition. Philosophical writing often grapples with difficult questions that hinge on the definitions of abstract concepts. Students are often asked to define *truth, justice, freedom, evil,* and so forth.

The assignment above asks for a definition of art, an important task in the branch of philosophy we call aesthetics. It also requires students to relate their definition of art to the thinking of noted aestheticians they have studied—Dewey, Schiller, and Benjamin. We would point out that the teacher, already having a fairly good understanding of what art is, is *not* interested in a dictionary definition. In this respect, the assignment has a hidden agenda—it requires students to ponder the concept of art and to arrive at an understanding or an insight that reflects their minds at work.

The paper falls under the category of what we call an "extended definition," and students have a variety of approaches that they can apply to the task. For example, they can define art by referring to representative examples, or they can address the function it plays on social and/or personal levels. They can also define art by pinpointing what is not art, by giving a negative definition of the term.

The last two sentences in the assignment—"Tell me if you agree and why. Personal experience as well as theoretical arguments may be appropriate support for your position"—mean that the teacher wants students to go beyond summarizing some authority's view on the subject. Students should have their own thoughts on art and aesthetic experience, and they should use these along with support from an authority to present a convincing definition. The better papers will be based primarily on personal experience supported with relevant examples and theoretical argument.

The papers that follow address the assignment in different ways, with a range of success. Even the best paper, however, is problematic in some respects. Each writer focuses on a single assigned text, although Paper 7 does bring in some outside source material; in each case, the writer supports wholeheartedly the attitude toward art espoused therein. Moreover, each paper fails to consider seriously any definitions of art other than the one offered in the text the student is using. As a group, all three students neglect to address fully any counterarguments to their definitions, and they do not appropriately critique the texts they use, which is the real challenge in this assignment.

Guide for Reading

In her paper, Natalie provides a thoughtful discussion on the problem of defining art. She does more than just work with Benjamin's ideas; she shows that she has thought about the problem as well. Her references to movements and specific artists help make connections between what Benjamin states and what these movements and artists advocate.

The main problem with Natalie's paper is that she doesn't take a strong stand herself. As a result, her paper is more a discussion of the problems of defining art than it is an argument for a particular definition. What's lacking, in other words, is the element of personal interpretation.

> **SAMPLE PHILOSOPHY PAPER 7**

Changing Art

Natalie J. (a sophomore)

The twentieth century has been filled with people (who may be called artists) who have challenged traditional perceptions of art. As early as the Impressionists, who broke away from the academic style of painting, art began to take on many new shapes and forms. Mechanical reproduction, film, and photography have greatly changed the art world and how the public perceives art, Walter Benjamin points out. What makes art and what role it should play are personal definitions, but whatever that definition, art does not exist for an elite group. The age of mechanical reproduction has brought art out of the museums and concert halls and made it more accessible to the average person. The artist can now reach more people with his message, if he has one. Film, photography, and other forms of mechanical reproduction are very suitable art forms for our age. As society changes so must art, for new inventions and new ideas cause the traditional definition to be inadequate. New ones must be made.

The definitions of art vary. What one person considers art another may not. In Dadaism, for example, the artist would create a collage or poem by putting the pieces together totally at random. Someone who feels that art must have planning and intention behind it, would feel that Dadaism was not art. Art forms also differ in the roles they perform. German Expressionists, for example, used their art for social and political commentary. Matisse, on the other hand, wanted his art to soothe. "What I dream of is an art of balance, of purity and serenity devoid of troubling or depressing subject matter" (133). To some a work of art must evoke a feeling in the viewer. To someone like this, what would then be a masterpiece of art? Would it be the work which evokes the strongest feeling in the audience or the one which evokes a feeling that is closest to the artist's intention? Yet, in the latter case it is difficult to determine the artist's intention because few artists tell the public exactly what they mean. Secondly, the result of a work may be totally unplanned and far from what the artist expected. Is it still art?

This brings up another question. Does art have to be well made? For example, there are two paintings before me. One was done by a three-year-old, the other by Rembrandt. The Rembrandt is obviously more skillfully rendered (provided the three-year-old is not a miraculous prodigy). I call the Rembrandt art and the other not art. At least the Rembrandt is of a higher degree of art for it is better crafted. However, I have disregarded the feelings evoked by the works. If I were the child's mother, the feelings evoked from the child's picture would probably be stronger than those from the Rembrandt. Nevertheless, I cannot help but admire something which is extremely well done.

As times change definitions of art change as new mediums are brought into use. As Picasso said, "Art does not evolve by itself. The ideas of people change and with them their mode of expression" (264). Walter Benjamin said something similar in "The Work of Art in the Age of Mechanical Reproduction." Benjamin recounts the initial controversy upon the development of film and photography as to whether or not these inventions could produce art. Benjamin feels, however, that the important question is not if they can be classified as art but how they have changed the art world and people's perceptions of art. Film and photography as well as other forms of mechanical reproduction such as audio recording and print making have greatly increased the audience of the art world. As Benjamin says, "The quality of its [the art work's] presence is always depreciated." The reproduction does not carry the "aura" of the original. However these reproductions are beneficial to society. They diminish the elitist quality of art and allow many others to experience it. In other words, reproductions take art out of the museums and enable "the original to meet the beholder halfway" (Benjamin 851). Posters, for example, take the great works out of museums and put them in rooms across the country. This increases their appreciation. It may also help the artist, if he or she is still living, for the artist may be able to get more income from the reproduction and sale of his or her works. It may also make the artist more widely known. This increased interest may cause more demand for original and reproduced works.

Benjamin does not qualify the change in art as good or bad. He sees it simply as a readjustment to a new way of living. This is why he feels the question of whether or not these new forms are art is irrelevant. They are new forms of art for a new society. The old definitions of art do not apply.

What kind of a world is it into which film and photography fit so neatly as art forms? According to Benjamin, people, in general, are in a state of distraction, and film is a very effective way of communicating to a distracted audience. He says that "reception in a state of distraction" is increasing today, and "the film with its shock effect meets this mode of reception halfway." (Benjamin 868) Indeed, it seems few people stop to contemplate anything. Our lives move too fast. Art forms have had to change to reach an audience whose method of noticing things has changed.

New innovations in art—the Impressionists, Abstract Expressionism, and Dadaism among others—have always met with criticism. Yet years later they are accepted as art forms. Initially, these art forms are judged by past traditions of art and their artistic value is questioned. Eventually, however, they pave their own way. They change the art world and modify definitions of art and its role like film and photography have done. The influence between society and art is circular. As society and its technology, beliefs, and perceptions change, so does its modes of expression—its approach to art. In return, the changing world of art affects the perceptions of society.

References

Benjamin, Walter. "The Work of Art in the Age of Mechanical Reproduction." *Film Theory and Criticism.* Ed. Mast and Cohen. NY: Oxford University Press, 1979. 848–871.

Matisse, Henri. "Notes of a Painter." *Theories of Modern Art.* Ed. Herschel B. Chipp. Los Angeles: University of California Press, 1968. 130–137.

Picasso, Pablo. "Statement." *Theories of Modern Art.* Ed. Herschel B. Chipp. Los Angeles: University of California Press, 1968. 263–266.

> **STUDY QUESTIONS**
>
> 1. Natalie begins paragraph 2 with the statement, "The definitions of art vary." How does she develop this topic sentence throughout the paragraph? How does she link the examples she gives?
>
> 2. In paragraph 3, Natalie brings up the question of the role of craft in defining art and suggests that, in her opinion, all art is well crafted. But she fails to return to this issue again. How might she incorporate this point into her paper more fully and thus strengthen the unity of her writing?
>
> 3. In paragraph 4, Natalie neatly integrates two of her references. What are they and how does she connect them?
>
> 4. In the conclusion, Natalie states that no one definition of art can be made, for art is continually changing and expanding. What objections to this relativist stance might one propose? Has Natalie anticipated these objections in her conclusion?

Class Article 3

Chapter 1: "The Live Creature"
by John Dewey

(from *Art as Experience*)

By one of the ironic perversities that often attend the course of affairs, the existence of the works of art upon which formation of an esthetic theory depends has become an obstruction to theory about them. For

---

"The Live Creature" from *Art as Experience* by John Dewey, pp. 3–19. Reprinted by permission of the Putnam Publishing Group, Inc. Copyright © 1934 by John Dewey.

one reason, these works are products that exist externally and physically. In common conception, the work of art is often identified with the building, book, painting, or statue in its existence apart from human experience. Since the actual work of art is what the product does with and in experience, the result is not favorable to understanding. In addition, the very perfection of some of these products, the prestige they possess because of a long history of unquestioned admiration, creates conventions that get in the way of fresh insight. When an art product once attains classic status, it somehow becomes isolated from the human conditions under which it was brought into being and from the human consequences it engenders in actual life-experience.

When artistic objects are separated from both conditions of origin and operation in experience, a wall is built around them that renders almost opaque their general significance, with which esthetic theory deals. Art is remitted to a separate realm, where it is cut off from that association with the materials and aims of every other form of human effort, undergoing, and achievement. A primary task is thus imposed upon one who undertakes to write upon the philosophy of the fine arts. This task is to restore continuity between the refined and intensified forms of experience that are works of art and the everyday events, doings, and sufferings that are universally recognized to constitute experience. Mountain peaks do not float unsupported; they do not even just rest upon the earth. They *are* the earth in one of its manifest operations. It is the business of those who are concerned with the theory of the earth, geographers and geologists, to make this fact evident in its various implications. The theorist who would deal philosophically with fine art has a like task to accomplish.

If one is willing to grant this position, even if only by way of temporary experiment, he will see that there follows a conclusion at first sight surprising. In order to understand the meaning of artistic products, we have to forget them for a time, to turn aside from them and have recourse to the ordinary forces and conditions of experience that we do not usually regard as esthetic. We must arrive at the theory of art by means of a detour. For theory is concerned with understanding, insight, not without exclamations of admiration, and stimulation of that emotional outburst often called appreciation. It is quite possible to enjoy flowers in their colored form and delicate fragrance without knowing anything about plants theoretically. But if one sets out to *understand* the flowering of plants, he is committed to finding out something about the interactions of soil, air, water and sunlight that condition the growth of plants.

By common consent, the Parthenon is a great work of art. Yet it has esthetic standing only as the work becomes an experience for a human being. And, if one is to go beyond personal enjoyment into the formation of a theory about that large republic of art of which the building is one member, one has to be willing at some point in his reflections to turn from it to the bustling, arguing, acutely sensitive Athenian citizens, with civic sense identified with a civic religion, of whose experience the temple was an expression, and who built it not as a work of art but as a civic commemoration. The turning to them is as human beings who had needs that were a demand for the building and that were carried to fulfillment in it; it is not an examination such as might be carried on by a sociologist in search for material relevant to his purpose. The one who sets out to theorize about the esthetic experience embodied in the Parthenon must realize in thought what the people into whose lives it entered had in common, as creators and as those who were satisfied with it, with people in our own homes and on our own streets.

In order to *understand* the esthetic in its ultimate and approved forms, one must begin with it in the raw; in the events and scenes that hold the attentive eye and ear of man, arousing his interest and affording him enjoyment as he looks and listens: the sights that hold the crowd—the fire-engine rushing by; the machines excavating enormous holes in the earth; the human-fly climbing the steeple-side; the men perched high in air on girders, throwing and catching red-hot bolts. The sources of art in human experience will be learned by him who sees how the tense grace of the ball-player infects the onlooking crowd; who notes the delight of the housewife in tending her plants, and the intent interest of her goodman in tending the patch of green in front of the house; the zest of the spectacular in poking the wood burning on the hearth and in watching the darting flames and crumbling coals. These people, if questioned as to the reason for their actions, would doubtless return reasonable answers. The man who poked the sticks of burning wood would say he did it to make the fire burn better; but he is none the less fascinated by the colorful drama of change enacted before his eyes and imaginatively partakes in it. He does not remain a cold spectator. What Coleridge said of the reader of poetry is true in its way of all who are happily absorbed in their activities of mind and body: "The reader should be carried forward, not merely or chiefly by the mechanical impulse of curiosity, not by a restless desire to arrive at the final solution, but by the pleasurable activity of the journey itself."

The intelligent mechanic engaged in his job, interested in doing well and finding satisfaction in his handiwork, caring for his materials and tools with genuine affection, is artistically engaged. The difference between such a worker and the inept and careless bungler is as great in the shop as it is in the studio. Oftentimes the product may not appeal to the esthetic sense of those who use the product. The fault, however, is oftentimes not so much with the worker as with the conditions of the market for which his product is designed. Were conditions and opportunities different, things as significant to the eye as those produced by earlier craftsmen would be made.

So extensive and subtly pervasive are the ideas that set Art upon a remote pedestal, that many a person would be repelled rather than pleased if told that he enjoyed his casual recreations, in part at least, because of their esthetic quality. The arts which today have most vitality for the average person are things he does not take to be arts: for instance, the movie, jazzed music, the comic strip, and, too frequently, newspaper accounts of love-nests, murders, and exploits of bandits. For, when what he knows as art is relegated to the museum and gallery, the unconquerable impulse towards experiences enjoyable in themselves finds such outlet as the daily environment provides. Many a person who protests against the museum conception of art, still shares the fallacy from which that conception springs. For the popular notion comes from a separation of art from the objects and scenes of ordinary experience that many theorists and critics pride themselves upon holding and even elaborating. The times when select and distinguished objects are closely connected with the products of usual vocations are the times when appreciation of the former is most rife and most keen. When, because of their remoteness, the objects acknowledged by the cultivated to be works of fine art seem anemic to the mass of people, esthetic hunger is likely to seek the cheap and the vulgar.

The factors that have glorified fine art by setting it upon a far-off pedestal did not arise within the realm of art nor is their influence confined to the arts. For many persons an aura of mingled awe and unreality encompasses the "spiritual" and the "ideal" while "matter" has become by contrast a term of depreciation, something to be explained away or apologized for. The forces at work are those that have removed religion as well as fine art from the scope of the common or community life. The forces have historically produced so many of the dislocations and divisions of modern life and thought that art could not escape their influence. We do not have to travel to the ends of the earth nor return many millennia in time to find peoples for whom everything that intensifies the sense of immediate living is an object of intense admiration. Bodily scarification, waving feathers, gaudy robes, shining ornaments of gold and silver, of emerald and jade, formed the contents of esthetic arts, and, presumably, without the vulgarity of class exhibitionism that attends their analogues today. Domestic utensils, furnishings of tent and house, rugs, mats, jars, pots, bows, spears, were wrought with such delighted care that today we hunt them out and give them places of honor in our art museums. Yet in their own time and place, such things were enhancements of the processes of everyday life. Instead of being elevated to a niche apart, they belonged to display of prowess, the manifestation of group and clan membership, worship of gods, feasting and fasting, fighting, hunting, and all the rhythmic crises that punctuate the stream of living.

Dancing and pantomime, the sources of the art of the theater, flourished as part of religious rites and celebrations. Musical art abounded in the fingering of the stretched string, the beating of the taut skin, the blowing with reeds. Even in the caves, human habitations were adorned with colored pictures that kept alive to the senses experiences with the animals that were so closely bound with the lives of humans. Structures that housed their gods and the instrumentalities that facilitated commerce with the higher powers were wrought with especial fineness. But the arts of the drama, music, painting, and architecture thus exemplified had no peculiar connection with theaters, galleries, museums. They were part of the significant life of an organized community.

The collective life that was manifested in war, worship, the forum, knew no division between what was characteristic of these places and operations, and the arts that brought color, grace, and dignity, into them. Painting and sculpture were organically one with architecture, as that was one with the social purpose that buildings served. Music and song were intimate parts of the rites and ceremonies in which the meaning of group life was consummated. Drama was a vital reënactment of the legends and history of group life. Not even in Athens can such arts be torn loose from this setting in direct experience and yet retain their significant character. Athletic sports, as well as drama, celebrated and enforced traditions of race and group, instructing the people, commemorating glories, and strengthening their civic pride.

Under such conditions, it is not surprising that the Athenian Greeks, when they came to reflect upon art, formed the idea that it is an act of reproduction, or imitation. There are many objections to this conception. But the vogue of the theory is testimony to the close connection of the fine arts with daily life; the idea would not have occurred to any one had art been remote from the interests of life. For the doctrine did not signify that art was a literal copying of objects, but that it reflected the emotions and ideas that are associated with the chief institutions of social life. Plato felt this connection so strongly that it led him to his idea of the necessity of censorship of poets, dramatists, and musicians. Perhaps he exaggerated when he said that a change from the Doric to the Lydian mode in music would be the sure precursor of civic degeneration. But no contemporary would have doubted that music was an integral part of the ethos and the institutions of the community. The idea of "art for art's sake" would not have been even understood.

There must then be historic reasons for the rise of the compartmental conception of fine art. Our present museums and galleries to which works of fine art are removed and stored illustrate some of the causes that have operated to segregate art instead of finding it an attendant of temple, forum, and other forms of associated life. An instructive history of modern art could be written in terms of the formation of the distinctively modern institutions of museum and exhibition gallery. I may point to a few outstanding facts. Most European museums are, among other things, memorials of the rise of nationalism and imperialism. Every capital must have its own museum of painting, sculpture, etc., devoted in part to exhibiting the greatness of its artistic past, and, in other part, to exhibiting the loot gathered by its monarchs in conquest of other nations; for instance, the accumulations of the spoils of Napoleon that are in the Louvre. They testify to the connection between the modern segregation of art and nationalism and militarism. Doubtless this connection has served at times a useful purpose, as in the case of Japan, who, when she was in the process of westernization, saved much of her art treasures by nationalizing the temples that contained them.

The growth of capitalism has been a powerful influence in the development of the museum as the proper home for works of art, and in the promotion of the idea that they are apart from the common life. The *nouveaux riches,* who are an important byproduct of the capitalist system, have felt especially bound to surround themselves with works of fine art which, being rare, are also costly. Generally speaking, the typical collector is the typical capitalist. For evidence of good standing in the realm of higher culture, he amasses paintings, statuary, and artistic *bijoux,* as his stocks and bonds certify to his standing in the economic world.

Not merely individuals, but communities and nations, put their cultural good taste in evidence by building opera houses, galleries, and museums. These show that a community is not wholly absorbed in material wealth, because it is willing to spend its gains in patronage of art. It erects these buildings and collects their contents as it now builds a cathedral. These things reflect and establish superior cultural status, while their segregation from the common life reflects the fact that they are not part of a native and spontaneous culture. They are a kind of counterpart of a holier-than-thou attitude, exhibited not toward persons as such but toward the interests and occupations that absorb most of the community's time and energy.

Modern industry and commerce have an international scope. The contents of galleries and museums testify to the growth of economic cosmopolitanism. The mobility of trade and of populations, due to the economic system, has weakened or destroyed the connection between works of art and the *genius loci* of which they were once the natural expression. As works of art have lost their indigenous status, they have acquired a new one—that of being specimens of fine art and nothing else. Moreover, works of art are now produced, like other articles, for sale in the market. Economic patronage by wealthy and powerful individuals has at many times played a part in the encouragement of artistic production. Probably many a savage tribe had its Maecenas. But now even that much of intimate social connection is lost in the impersonality of a world market. Objects that were in the past valid and significant because of their place in the life of a community now function in isolation from the conditions of their origin. By that fact they are also set apart from common experience, and serve as insignia of taste and certificates of special culture.

Because of changes in industrial conditions the artist has been pushed to one side from the main streams of active interest. Industry has been mechanized and an artist cannot work mechanically for mass production. He is less integrated than formerly in the normal flow of social services. A peculiar esthetic "individualism" results. Artists find it incumbent upon them to betake themselves to their work as an isolated means of "self-expression." In order not to cater to the trend of economic forces, they often feel obliged to exaggerate their separateness to the point of eccentricity. Consequently artistic products take on to a still greater degree the air of something independent and esoteric.

Put the action of all such forces together, and the conditions that create the gulf which exists generally between producer and consumer in modern society operate to create also a chasm between ordinary and esthetic experience. Finally we have, as the record of this chasm, accepted as if it were normal, the philosophies of art that locate it in a region inhabited by no other creature, and that emphasize beyond all reason the merely contemplative character of the esthetic. Confusion of values enters in to accentuate the separation. Adventitious matters, like the pleasure of collecting, of exhibiting, of ownership and display, simulate esthetic values. Criticism is affected. There is much applause for the wonders of appreciation and the glories of the transcendent beauty of art indulged in without much regard to capacity for esthetic perception in the concrete.

My purpose, however, is not to engage in an economic interpretation of the history of the arts, much less to argue that economic conditions are either invariably or directly relevant to perception and enjoyment, or even to interpretation of individual works of art. It is to indicate that *theories* which isolate art and its appreciation by placing them in a realm of their own, disconnected from other modes of experiencing, are not inherent in the subject-matter but arise because of specifiable extraneous conditions. Embedded as they are in institutions and in habits of life, these conditions operate effectively because they work so unconsciously. Then the theorist assumes they are embedded in the nature of things. Nevertheless, the influence of these conditions is not confined to theory. As I have already indicated, it deeply affects the practice of living, driving away esthetic perceptions that are necessary ingredients of happiness, or reducing them to the level of compensating transient pleasurable excitations.

Even to readers who are adversely inclined to what has been said, the implications of the statements that have been made may be useful in defining the nature of the problem: that of recovering the continuity of esthetic experience with normal processes of living. The understanding of art and of its rôle in civilization is not furthered by setting out with eulogies of it nor by occupying ourselves exclusively at the outset with great works of art recognized as such. The comprehension which theory essays will be arrived at by a detour; by going back to experience of the common or mill run of things to discover the esthetic quality such experience possesses. Theory can start with and from acknowledged works of art only when the esthetic is already compartmentalized, or only when works of art are set in a niche apart instead of being celebrations, recognized as such, of the things of ordinary experience. Even a crude experience, if authentically an experience, is more fit to give a clue to the intrinsic nature of esthetic experience than is an object already set apart from any other mode of experience. Following this clue we can discover how the work of art develops and accentuates what is characteristically valuable in things of everyday enjoyment. The art product will then be seen to issue from the latter, when the full meaning of ordinary experience is expressed, as dyes come out of coal tar products when they receive special treatment.

Many theories about art already exist. If there is justification for proposing yet another philosophy of the esthetic, it must be found in a new mode of approach. Combinations and permutations among existing theories can easily be brought forth by those so inclined. But, to my mind, the trouble with existing theories is that they start from a ready-made compartmentalization, or from a conception of art that "spiritualizes" it out of connection with the objects of concrete experience. The alternative, however, to such spiritualization is not a degrading and Philistinish materialization of works of fine art, but a conception that discloses the way in which these works idealize qualities found in common experience. Were works of art placed in a directly human context in popular esteem, they would have a much wider appeal than they can have when pigeon-hole theories of art win general acceptance.

A conception of fine art that sets out from its connection with discovered qualities of ordinary experience will be able to indicate the factors and forces that favor the normal development of common human activities into matters of artistic value. It will also be able to point out those conditions that arrest its normal growth. Writers on esthetic theory often raise the question of whether esthetic philosophy can aid in cultivation of esthetic appreciation. The question is a branch of the general theory of criticism, which, it seems to me, fails to accomplish its full office if it does not indicate what to look for and what to find in concrete esthetic objects. But, in any case, it is safe to say that a philosophy of art is sterilized unless it makes us aware of the function of art in relation to other modes of experience, and unless it indicates why this function is so inadequately realized, and unless it suggests the conditions under which the office would be successfully performed.

The comparison of the emergence of works of art out of ordinary experiences to the refining of raw materials into valuable products may seem to some unworthy, if not an actual attempt to reduce works of art to the status of articles manufactured for commercial purposes. The point, however, is that no amount of ecstatic eulogy of finished works can of itself assist the understanding or the generalization of such works. Flowers can be enjoyed without knowing about the interactions of soil, air, moisture, and seeds of which they are the result. But they cannot be *understood* without taking just these interactions into account—and theory is a matter of understanding. Theory is concerned with discovering the nature of the production of works of art and of their enjoyment in perception. How is it that the everyday making of things grows into that form of making which is genuinely artistic? How is it that our everyday enjoyment of scenes and situations develops into the peculiar satisfaction that attends the experience which is emphatically esthetic? These are the questions theory must answer. The answers cannot be found, unless we are willing to find the germs and roots in matters of experience that we do not currently regard as esthetic. Having discovered these active seeds, we may follow the course of their growth into the highest forms of finished and refined art.

It is a commonplace that we cannot direct, save accidentally, the growth and flowering of plants, however lovely and enjoyed, without understanding their causal conditions. It should be just a commonplace that esthetic understanding—as distinct from sheer personal enjoyment—must start with the soil, air, and light out of which things esthetically admirable arise. And these conditions are the conditions and factors that make an ordinary experience complete. The more we recognize this fact, the more we shall find ourselves faced with a problem rather than with a final solution. *If* artistic and esthetic quality is implicit in every normal experience, how shall we explain how and why it so generally fails to become explicit? Why is it that to multitudes art seems to be an importation into experience from a foreign country and the esthetic to be a synonym for something artificial?

We cannot answer these questions any more than we can trace the development of art out of everyday experience, unless we have a clear and coherent idea of what is meant when we say "normal experience." Fortunately, the road to arriving at such an idea is open and well marked. The nature of experience is determined by the essential conditions of life. While man is other than bird and beast, he shares basic vital functions with them and has to make the same basal adjustments if he is to continue the process of living. Having the same vital needs, man derives the means by which he breathes, moves, looks and listens, the very brain with which he coördinates his senses and his movements, from his animal forbears. The organs with which he maintains himself in being are not of himself alone, but by the grace of struggles and achievements of a long line of animal ancestry.

Fortunately a theory of the place of the esthetic in experience does not have to lose itself in minute details when it starts with experience in its elemental form. Broad outlines suffice. The first great consideration is that life goes on in an environment; not merely *in* it but because of it, through interaction with it. No creature lives merely under its skin; its subcutaneous organs are means of connection with what lies beyond its bodily frame, and to which, in order to live, it must adjust itself, by accommodation and defense but also by conquest. At every moment, the living creature is exposed to dangers from its surroundings, and at every moment, it must draw upon something in its surroundings to satisfy its needs. The career and destiny of a living being are bound up with its interchanges with its environment, not externally but in the most intimate way.

The growl of a dog crouching over his food, his howl in time of loss and loneliness, the wagging of his tail at the return of his human friend are expressions of the implication of a living in a natural medium which includes man along with the animal he has domesticated. Every need, say hunger for fresh air or food, is a lack that denotes at least a temporary absence of adequate adjustment with surroundings. But it is also a demand, a reaching out into the environment to make good the lack and to restore adjustment by building at least a temporary equilibrium. Life itself consists of phases in which the organism falls out of step with the march of surrounding things and then recovers unison with it— either through effort or by some happy chance. And, in a growing life, the recovery is never mere return to a prior state, for it is enriched by the state of disparity and resistance through which it has successfully passed. If the gap between organism and environment is too wide, the creature dies. If its activity is not enhanced by the temporary alienation, it merely subsists. Life grows when a temporary falling out is a transition to a more extensive balance of the energies of the organism with those of the conditions under which it lives.

These biological commonplaces are something more than that; they reach to the roots of the esthetic in experience. The world is full of things that are indifferent and even hostile to life; the very processes by which life is maintained tend to throw it out of gear with its surroundings. Nevertheless, if life continues and if in continuing it expands, there is an overcoming of factors of opposition and conflict; there is a transformation of them into differentiated aspects of a higher powered and more significant life. The marvel of organic, of vital, adaptation through expansion (instead of by contraction and passive accommodation) actually takes place. Here in germ are balance and harmony attained through rhythm. Equilibrium comes about not mechanically and inertly but out of, and because of, tension.

There is in nature, even below the level of life, something more than mere flux and change. Form is arrived at whenever a stable, even though moving, equilibrium is reached. Changes interlock and sustain one another. Wherever there is this coherence there is endurance. Order is not imposed from without but is made out of the relations of harmonious interactions that energies bear to one another. Because it is active (not anything static because foreign to what goes on) order itself develops. It comes to include within its balanced movement a greater variety of changes.

Order cannot but be admirable in a world constantly threatened with disorder—in a world where living creatures can go on living only by taking advantage of whatever order exists about them, incorporating it into themselves. In a world like ours, every living creature that attains sensibility welcomes order with a response of harmonious feeling whenever it finds a congruous order about it.

For only when an organism shares in the ordered relations of its environment does it secure the stability essential to living. And when the participation comes after a phase of disruption and conflict, it bears within itself the germs of a consummation akin to the esthetic.

The rhythm of loss of integration with environment and recovery of union not only persists in man but becomes conscious with him; its conditions are material out of which he forms purposes. Emotion is the conscious sign of a break, actual or impending. The discord is the occasion that induces reflection. Desire for restoration of the union converts mere emotion into interest in objects as conditions of realization of harmony. With the realization, material of reflection is incorporated into objects as their meaning. Since the artist cares in a peculiar way for the phase of experience in which union is achieved, he does not shun moments of resistance and tension. He rather cultivates them, not for their own sake but because of their potentialities, bringing to living consciousness an experience that is unified and total. In contrast with the person whose purpose is esthetic, the scientific man is interested in problems, in situations wherein tension between the matter of observation and of thought is marked. Of course he cares for their resolution.

But he does not rest in it; he passes on to another problem using an attained solution only as a stepping stone from which to set on foot further inquiries.

The difference between the esthetic and the intellectual is thus one of the places where emphasis falls in the constant rhythm that marks the interaction of the live creature with his surroundings. The ultimate matter of both emphases in experience is the same, as is also their general form. The odd notion an artist does not think and a scientific inquirer does nothing else is the result of converting a difference of tempo and emphasis into a difference in kind. The thinker has his esthetic moment when his ideas cease to be mere ideas and become the corporate meanings of objects. The artist has his problems and thinks as he works. But his thought is more immediately embodied in the object. Because of the comparative remoteness of his end, the scientific worker operates with symbols, words and mathematical signs. The artist does his thinking in the very qualitative media he works in, and the terms lie so close to the object that he is producing that they merge directly into it.

The live animal does not have to project emotions into the objects experienced. Nature is kind and hateful, bland and morose, irritating and comforting, long before she is mathematically qualified or even a congeries of "secondary" qualities like colors and their shapes. Even such words as long and short, solid and hollow, still carry to all, but those who are intellectually specialized, a moral and emotional connotation. The dictionary will inform any one who consults it that the early use of words like sweet and bitter were not to denote qualities of sense as such but to discriminate things as favorable and hostile. How could it be otherwise? Direct experience comes from nature and man interacting with each other. In this interaction, human energy gathers, is released, dammed up, frustrated and victorious. There are rhythmic beats of want and fulfillment, pulses of doing and being withheld from doing.

All interactions that effect stability and order in the whirling flux of change are rhythms. There is ebb and flow, systole and diastole: ordered change. The latter moves within bounds. To overpass the limits that are set in destruction and death, out of which, however, new rhythms are built up. The proportionate interception of changes establishes an order that is spatially, not merely temporarily patterned: like the waves of the sea, the ripples of sand where waves have flowed back and forth, the fleecy and the black-bottomed cloud. Contrast of lack and fullness, of struggle and achievement, of adjustment after consummated irregularity, form the drama in which action, feeling, and meaning are one. The outcome is balance and counterbalance. These are not static nor mechanical. They express power that is intense because measured through overcoming resistance. Environing objects avail and counteravail.

There are two sorts of possible worlds in which esthetic experience would not occur. In a world of mere flux, change would not be cumulative; it would not move toward a close. Stability and rest would have no being. Equally is it true, however, that a world that is finished, ended, would have no traits of suspense and crisis, and would offer no opportunity for resolution. Where everything is already complete, there is no fulfillment. We envisage with pleasure Nirvana and a uniform heavenly bliss because they are projected upon the background of our present world of stress and conflict. Because the actual world, that in which we live, is a combination of movement and culmination, of breaks and re-unions, the experience of a living creature is capable of esthetic quality. The live being recurrently loses and reëstablishes equilibrium with his surroundings. The moment of passage from disturbance into harmony is that of intensest life. In a finished world, sleep and waking could not be distinguished. In one wholly perturbed, conditions could not even be struggled with. In a world made after the pattern of ours, moments of fulfillment punctuate experience with rhythmically enjoyed intervals.

Inner harmony is attained only when, by some means, terms are made with the environment. When it occurs on any other than an "objective" basis, it is illusory—in extreme cases to the point of insanity. Fortunately for variety in experience, terms are made in many ways—ways ultimately decided by selective interest. Pleasures may come about through chance contact and stimulation; such pleasures are not to be despised in a world full of pain. But happiness and delight are a different sort of thing. They come to be through a fulfillment that reaches to the depths of our being—one that is an adjustment of our whole being with the conditions of existence. In the process of living, attainment of a period of equilibrium is at the same time the initiation of a new relation to the environment, one that brings with it potency of new adjustments to be made through struggle. The time of consummation is also one of beginning anew. Any attempt to perpetuate beyond its term the enjoyment attending the time of fulfillment and harmony constitutes withdrawal from the world. Hence it marks the lowering and loss of vitality. But, through the phases of perturbation and conflict, there abides the deep-seated memory of an underlying harmony, the sense of which haunts life like the sense of being founded on a rock.

Most mortals are conscious that a split often occurs between their present living and their past and future. Then the past hangs upon them as a burden; it invades the present with a sense of regret, of opportunities not used, and of consequences we wish undone. It rests upon the present as an oppression, instead of being a storehouse of resources by which to move confidently forward. But the live creature adopts its past; it can make friends with even its stupidities, using them as warnings that increase present wariness. Instead of trying to live upon whatever may have been achieved in the past, it uses past successes to inform the present. Every living experience owes its richness to what Santayana well calls "hushed reverberations."*

To the being fully alive, the future is not ominous but a promise; it surrounds the present as a halo. It consists of possibilities that are felt as a possession of what is now and here. In life that is truly life, everything overlaps and merges. But all too often we exist in apprehensions of what the future may bring, and are divided within ourselves. Even when not overanxious, we do not enjoy the present because we subordinate it to that which is absent. Because of the frequency of this abandonment of the present to the past and future, the happy periods of an experience that is now complete because it absorbs into itself memories of the past and anticipations of the future, come to constitute an esthetic ideal. Only when the past ceases to trouble and anticipations of the future are not perturbing is a being wholly united with his environment and therefore fully alive. Art celebrates with peculiar intensity the moments in which the past reënforces the present and in which the future is a quickening of what now is.

To grasp the sources of esthetic experience it is, therefore, necessary to have recourse to animal life below the human scale. The activities of the fox, the dog, and the thrush may at least stand as reminders and symbols of that unity of experience which we so fractionize when work is labor, and thought withdraws us from the world. The live animal is fully present, all there, in all of its actions: in its wary glances, its sharp sniffings, its abrupt cocking of ears. All senses are equally on the *qui vive.* As you watch, you see motion merging into sense and sense into motion—constituting that animal grace so hard for man to rival. What the live creature retains from the past and what it expects from the future operate as directions in the present. The dog is never pedantic nor academic; for these things arise only when the past is severed in consciousness from the present and is set up as a model to copy or a storehouse upon which to draw. The past absorbed into the present carries on; it presses forward.

---

* "These familiar flowers, these well-remembered bird notes, this sky with its fitful brightness, these furrowed and grassy fields, each with a sort of personality given to it by the capricious hedge, such things as these are the mother tongue of our imagination, the language that is laden with all the subtle inextricable associations the fleeting hours of our childhood left behind them. Our delight in the sunshine on the deep-bladed grass today might be no more than the faint perception of wearied souls, if it were not for the sunshine and grass of far-off years, which still live in us and transform our perception into love." George Eliot in "The Mill on the Floss."

There is much in the life of the savage that is sodden. But, when the savage is most alive, he is most observant of the world about him and most taut with energy. As he watches what stirs about him, he, too, is stirred. His observation is both action in preparation and foresight of the future. He is as active through his whole being when he looks and listens as when he stalks his quarry or stealthily retreats from a foe. His senses are sentinels of immediate thought and outposts of action, and not, as they so often are with us, mere pathways along which material is gathered to be stored away for a delayed and remote possibility.

It is mere ignorance that leads then to the supposition that connection of art and esthetic perception with experience signifies a lowering of their significance and dignity. Experience in the degree in which it *is* experience is heightened vitality. Instead of signifying being shut up within one's own private feelings and sensations, it signifies active and alert commerce with the world; at its height it signifies complete interpenetration of self and the world of objects and events. Instead of signifying surrender to caprice and disorder, it affords our sole demonstration of a stability that is not stagnation but is rhythmic and developing. Because experience is the fulfillment of an organism in its struggles and achievements in a world of things, it is art in germ. Even in its rudimentary forms, it contains the promise of that delightful perception which is esthetic experience.

Guide for Reading

Michael's paper is one that does only what the assignment states and no more. He shows that he has read Dewey's article and understands the ideas therein to a limited degree, just enough to apply one of them to personal experience. What this paper lacks is the sense that Michael has really done what he claims to have done.

As you read, ask yourself the following questions: Does Michael understand the Athenians' experience that led them to create the Parthenon? Does he understand Dewey's concept of "tension" and "separation" between "man and his environment"? Does he understand the art of a mechanic's job? Even though you may not agree with Dewey's ideas, this paper could still be successful if Michael proved, through concrete detail, that he tested these ideas and found them right for him.

Ordinary Art

Michael D. (a junior)

In the first chapter of his book *Art as Experience,* John Dewey argues against the conventional view of art. Dewey criticizes the aura placed upon art and the fact that it is isolated upon a pedestal. Works of art are confined to museums and galleries which restrict its true nature. Dewey does not dispute the fact that these works are, in fact, art but rather says the simpler meaning of art is distorted. According to Dewey, art is closely related to common experience. Each work of art expresses some facet of ordinary life. In order to understand each work, one must be familiar with their origins and how they relate to one's own life. Dewey states, "When artistic objects are separated from both conditions of origin and operation in experience, a wall is built around them that renders almost opaque their general significance, with which esthetic theory deals." Dewey is therefore critical of the sacred label bestowed upon art because it separates art from common life and therefore distorts its esthetic value.

I share Dewey's view and have some personal experiences to support his argument. A few years ago, my family and I took a trip to Athens, Greece where I saw the Parthenon. At this time, I held the conventional idea of art as confined to museums and galleries. Therefore, when I saw the Parthenon I was filled with awe and thought how fortunate I was to experience this world-acclaimed and historical monument. But I was merely experiencing the physical, external esthetic value of this work of art. If I was to share the true esthetic value of the Parthenon, I had to become aware of its origins and the meaning it held for the ancient Athenians. As Dewey says, "The one who sets out to theorize about the esthetic experience embodied in the Parthenon must realize in thought what the people into whose lives it entered had in common with people in our own homes and on our own streets." Now that I reflect on that experience, it has more meaning for me. The Athenians constructed the Parthenon as an expression of their experience, just as I had done in the past when I built something with my father's tools in the garage. The Parthenon may be more impressive in appearance, but it has the same esthetic value as my own creations.

While I have attempted to clarify the misconception placed upon art, I have not explained what is meant by "esthetic value" or "esthetic experience." Basically, an esthetic experience is one which helps an individual grow. Dewey believes that growth arises through "tensions", a break with the equilibrium established between man and his environment. When this separation occurs, man attempts to re-unify himself. Through this cycle, he grows. Dewey states, "If its [man's] activity is not enhanced by the temporary alienation, it merely subsists. Life grows when a temporary falling out is a transition to a more extensive balance of the energies of the organism with those of the conditions under which it lives." Art is an expression of these temporary separations and subsequent reunions. This is why Dewey believes something as ordinary as a mechanic fixing a car has esthetic value. The mechanic encounters a difficulty in his repairs, resolves his complication and has acquired valuable experience. He has gained more knowledge in the field of auto mechanics and perhaps learned to be more patient in his labor. In this manner, he has grown. Not everyone is gifted enough to share his esthetic experiences through painting or sculpture, therefore we must look for them in daily life as well.

Dewey expresses his belief that modern conventions have distorted art and placed it upon a pedestal, far from man's everyday experiences. By removing art in this way, we only experience it in museums and galleries and merely see its physical beauty. But Dewey brings art down to earth. Any expression of esthetic value is art, whether it be the Mona Lisa or a mechanic repairing an automobile. Esthetic experiences help one grow in life and art works are expressions of these events. One who realizes this can gain more from watching a football game than the ignorant person visiting the Louvre.

STUDY QUESTIONS

1. In his introductory paragraph, Michael uses summary, paraphrase, and quotation to present the ideas in Dewey's first chapter of *Art as Experience*. How does he introduce each reference to the source material so that ideas are clearly attributed to Dewey?

2. In the second paragraph, Michael uses personal experience to support Dewey's definition of art. Does he provide any other such support in subsequent paragraphs?

3. In his concluding paragraph, Michael claims that the Mona Lisa as well as a mechanic repairing an automobile are expressions of art. Do you agree? What objections to this claim could a writer anticipate?

4. Do you believe Michael has provided an appropriate analysis of Dewey's argument? Does he tend simply to summarize Dewey, or does he analyze and develop his point?

Guide for Reading

Maura's paper looks closely at her personal views of art as inspired by Dewey's article. Her agreement with Dewey is carefully and convincingly explained in the third paragraph. From the fourth paragraph on, however, she seems either to lose her convictions or to fail to understand Dewey's argument, and as a result the paper begins to wander toward a weak conclusion. Maura could have written a better paper (the one promised by the first three paragraphs) had she agreed in part with Dewey and then challenged those ideas she felt were inappropriate. As you read, consider what sorts of challenges Maura could have made.

Art: What Are Its Limits?

Maura F. (a sophomore)

The Louvre. The Parthenon. The ritual of visiting famous museums and monuments has long been one practiced by cultures of today as well as those of the past. The search for beauty has always preoccupied the thoughts of man. But, we must ask, "Is this beauty of art found in a few appointed locations such as museums and music halls or can it be experienced continuously in our everyday lives?" "The Live Creature" from John Dewey's *Art as Experience* helps one shed some light on the philosophy of the fine arts as well as other art with respect to aesthetic values.

Art's attributes, as we will see, are not confined to the limits of museums, music halls, or any of the institutions of the fine arts. Art can be found in a much larger realm of experience in our lives. The problem with museums is that the person who looks at a piece of art as a classic can only have limited "interactions" with the art, therefore minimizing its aesthetic value. Dewey urges the reader to forget the artistic object and concentrate on its background or its functions in order to gain an understanding of the object. It however is not necessary to understand the object to appreciate its beauty, but understanding it enhances and intensifies the object's aesthetic value. Dewey's purpose in his writing is to indicate "theories which isolate art and its appreciation by placing them in a realm of their own (museums), disconnected from other modes of experiencing, are not inherent in the subject matter but arise because of specific extraneous conditions." Once the observer loses contact with the true environment of the artpiece, he no longer is integrated with the aesthetic worth of the piece itself, rather the aesthetic air or aura of the new surrounding or museum where it is encased. One's preconceived notion of the intricate handwork behind the work can be somewhat diminished in this framework. The emotion that is spawned by means of a visit to a museum may only be a feeling towards the entire institution of museums not the specific piece that you have come to see. For art to be aesthetically valuable it must inflict some emotion in the viewer. Its rarity and monetary worth are unimportant.

For example, as I am writing this paper in my dorm room, in front of me is a poster. Not just any poster, but one with the Marshall University basketball schedule, pictures of the Thundering Herd (school mascot), and Kemper Arena (sight of the 1988 Final Four) indicating the school's aspiration for the season. This has some meaning to me. It arouses thoughts, emotions of my present, past, and future. Images of home, times with my father at games, friends and excitement of winning and the disappointment in defeat are all scenes flashing through my mind. On the other hand, roommates feel no sense of artistic worth or aesthetic value to this piece since they have never experienced Marshall basketball like I have, they tend to label it as worthless. But, of all the posters in our room, I consider this to be the best in artistic and aesthetic value. Picture if you will that I have been a Marshall basketball fan and cheered them on all my life. I can be labeled a participant or maybe even a "player." I should be more captivated than they. Just as beauty is in the eye of the beholder, aesthetic value is in the mind of the player.

I also realize that the importance of aesthetics need not reflect emotions of happiness or victory but images of pain and anguish are also responses to art. This art comes in numerous forms ranging from music, sculptures, nature, sports, and dance. It need not be a representation of stability, but may exhibit turbulence giving way to "living consciousness an experience that is unified and total."

At this stage it easy to surmise that art is not only confined to the museum and music halls as may have been previously believed. The genre of art must extend through the bounds of handwork. A carpenter or glassblower are two such people whose professions offer many useful aspects to our lives. The hands of a doctor also produce works of art by repairing the body. All these professions require great understanding of the art by the "artisan." The numerous possible actions and their consequences allow for the deep sense of utility. But the limits of art do not stop here.

As the main title suggests, man must view art as experience. The birds singing after a seemingly relentless rain, lawnmower cutting grass along with that distinct smell of freshly cut grass soon after, accident are all types of experience we are captivated and moved by, with some uncovering our emotions more vividly than others. I use these examples in the hope to point out the significance of art as experience, emotion varying from intense fear and anxiety with the car accident to a peaceful sense of security as the birds indication of a return to normality after the rain sounds.

Can we truly call this art of aesthetic value? On the broadest scale, yes, we can. It depends on your connotative meaning of "art." If you feel that art may be something originated from a source other than one dubbed an artist or artisan or even one who tries to recreate those skills, you would probably agree with the reply to the question just stated. Natural occurences would be included. After all, moods, emotions, and thoughts can be created by nature (including interactions of man and himself, man and man, nature and nature, and man and supernatural). So now we have answered what can be considered art with aesthetic value. But what of those who feel the limits of art are those denotatively defined by Webster's New Collegiate Dictionary as the "Conscious use of skill and creative imagination especially in the production of aesthetic objects." There must be some limit of this great thing called "art" for those who want to exclude nature as art, although I honestly do not have the assurance to definitely say this.

It seems that the meaning of art with aesthetics simply described is that which is made which "inflicts" upon the observer emotions of sorts. The heart of aesthetics is therefore intrinsically subjective.

STUDY QUESTIONS

1. Maura defines art as an artifact that "inflicts" emotions on the observer. After the introduction, each paragraph of the paper comments on the relationship between art and emotion, except one. Which paragraph strays from the focus? What would you suggest Maura do to remedy this break in her train of thought?

2. Maura suggests that all experience that invokes an emotional response can be considered aesthetic. She even cites the case of a car accident. How does this example hurt her argument? What was your response to this example?

3. In her concluding paragraph, Maura refers to the dictionary definition of the term *art*. How does this definition compare with the writer's own? Does she define art as being either conscious or unconscious? Does she discuss the role of skill and creative imagination in art? If not, is her definition of art complete?

4. Look up the definition of *art* in your dictionary. Then look up the definition of *nature*. Are these terms mutually exclusive? What is Maura's attitude to the relationship between art and nature?

5. A successful conclusion clarifies and solidifies the position developed throughout the paper. If this is the case, why might we consider Maura's concluding paragraphs weak?

Writing Assignments

1. In a 3- to 5-page paper, give your personal definition of art based on the type of art that appeals to you. Assume that your readers have only a general knowledge of art (they can picture the Mona Lisa and can differentiate between Picasso and the Impressionists). You will need to describe your chosen art carefully and to explain what elements make this "art" to you.

2. In an age in which people seem compelled to validate every human action, the popular view appears to hold that almost everything is art: the art of motorcycle maintenance, the art of roofing, the art of accounting, the art of successful relationships, and so on. Using Dewey's essay as a basis for discussion, defend or attack this popular view.

11 Fine and Applied Arts

INTRODUCTION TO WRITING IN THE FINE AND APPLIED ARTS

In addition to the standard characteristics of good writing (logical organization, clear explanation and description, standard grammar, and so on), assignments in the arts call for special skills in analysis and evaluation. Usually, the subjects of analysis and evaluation are not written or spoken (art and music), relying on shapes and sounds rather than on words as a means of expression. In those cases where words are used (drama and film), they constitute only one part of the means of expression. To write perceptive, informative papers in the arts, then, students' powers of observation must be broadened and sharpened so they can respond to nonverbal nuances presented by shape, color, sound, voice, tone, setting, costume, and gesture.

Fine and Applied Arts

In most of the assignments in this chapter, writers don't have the luxury of flipping pages to refresh their memory of their topics. When analyzing and evaluating a play or a musical concert, writers have no opportunity to hear or see that particular performance again. Consequently, they must observe several aspects of the performance at the same time: the work being presented, the relationships among the characters or components within the work, and the quality of the performance.

If the assignment is for an art or film paper, students may have the chance (and probably should) to return to the work of art or to view the film again. If the subject is a painting or a sculpture, the task is to verbalize what the lines, colors, and arrangements of figures and shapes suggest but do not explicitly state. When reviewing a movie, a concert, or a stage performance, students must be aware of which techniques are employed for which purposes, and they must be able to evaluate their degree of success. Writing in the arts, therefore, demands not only objective attention to verbal and nonverbal communication but also an awareness of artistic technique.

Stated another way, writing in the arts has some common goals. One of the more important is to allow writers to learn about a work by analyzing its various components. Often, such learning asks students to contextualize a work and its creator. For example, determining how the compositions, say, of Mozart differ from and are similar to those of his contemporaries can lead to a better understanding of his music. A second important goal is to look beyond what may be thought of as the structural features of a work to the message it conveys. This task is clearly interpretive, and carrying it out successfully usually involves sharing a work's meaning with readers, helping them discover aspects of a work of art that they may not have considered before. In challenging situations, students are asked to combine these goals and to analyze, interpret, and edify in a single paper. Many introductory classes, however, will limit assignments to simple analysis.

The better papers in this chapter reflect certain skills in writing, and they also reflect a high level of alertness on the part of students as they were experiencing their subjects. The papers are characterized by the writers' strong desire to explain a particular art form and to enlighten readers. You will see that, after reading the following papers and attempting one or more of the assignments, analyzing and evaluating a work of art demands much more concentration than merely enjoying that work.

ART ASSIGNMENT 1

Course: **Introduction to Art**

> As a class we will go to the Catherine Smith Art Gallery and view the exhibition that is set up. Look at all the art and pick a favorite piece. While you are looking at the piece, write a response to it, describing your reaction and the piece, using information learned in the course. Since you will hand in what you write in the gallery, I don't expect a polished essay. Nevertheless, I do expect about a page of well-organized, coherent writing focusing on the piece and your reaction to it.

Analysis of Art Assignment 1

This assignment does not appear to be highly structured, but the page limit and the conditions under which it will be completed impose certain structures. Students are asked to focus on two points in the paper: a description of the piece of art and their reaction to it. These points should be controlled by material learned in class, and students are expected to write from the perspective of someone reasonably knowledgeable about art.

A good description of a work of art is much like a summary of a piece of writing; it covers the important points that combine to shape an overall impression. On such assignments, you would not want to describe every detail. If a painting has a sense of gloom, you should focus on those details that convey its gloominess. Usually, the better responses will present descriptive information of the art in the order a viewer is likely to notice it. This order will give you a structure that resembles a narrative: "The first thing that struck me was the sinister figure emerging out of the darkness just to the right of the center...." From this point, you can describe the painting as the elements relate to one another.

A good reaction should include more than just "I like..." or "I don't like...." Expressing your tastes is appropriate as long as you give reasons for your likes and dislikes. It isn't necessary, however, to say whether you like an aspect of a piece of art. Describing the mood or

Fine and Applied Arts

impression (mysterious, frightening, gloomy, friendly) is a legitimate reaction because you are interpreting and reacting to certain aspects of the work. On the other hand, with assignments like this one, it is important to avoid becoming self-absorbed in the analysis. Keep in mind that art has a universal element and that your interpretive reaction should be one others can share, given the benefit of your insight.

This assignment doesn't give you a chance to do any extensive revision, so you should plan your paper carefully, using notes and maybe a brief outline before you actually begin composing. Brainstorming by listing adjectives that reflect the work and your reaction to it may help you focus on the essence of the piece. Outlining or brainstorming may also help organize your thoughts; you don't want a reaction and description that is simply a list of information. Strive for a well-developed paragraph (or several, if necessary).

Guide for Reading

The following paper is an above-average response to the assignment. Catherine covers the technical and expressive qualities of the painting in a way that allows readers to form an impression of the work, even without being able to see it. As you read, consider what additional details Catherine might have provided to make this impression clearer.

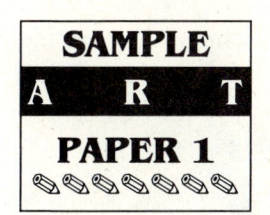

Art Review

Catherine M. (a sophomore)

"A Figure on Black Background #14" by Junko Chodos is a very interesting work. The colors are a vivid mixture of various hues that are brought together very well. The contrasting crimson and almost lime green would appear to be very startling, yet___work very well together. The black background is brought out even more by the black line running throughout the figure, which gives it its actual shape.

Line quality in the work provides the piece with a sense of motion, as if the figure were halted in mid-action. The expression on his face is one of perhaps pain and/or determination. This and the seemingly oriental line quality lead me to picture the figure as perhaps a Sumo wrestler or something akin to that.

The work has little, if any, decorative texture, yet would appear to be heavily textured by the paint if one could touch it.

The painting is balanced by one leg exiting on the bottom left corner and the upper body exiting on the upper right corner.

I really like this piece—I'd like to own it!

Analysis of Sample Art Paper 1

Catherine describes what she believes are the painting's important features. It is composed of various hues (some of them bright and startling) on a black background, with black lines giving shape to a figure engaged in some kind of action. Catherine has done a good job avoiding saying simply that these features are there. Instead, she explains how they work together and how they affect her. She is describing, reacting, and evaluating at the same time, using knowledge from the course. The second paragraph is perhaps the best, in which she gives her *interpretation* of an abstract painting. This interpretation is not used to guess what the artist was attempting but to give readers a better idea of what the painting looks like. Notice that Catherine is careful to say that the expression and lines "lead me to picture," which is an effective way of acknowledging that others may see something different.

Catherine's paper covers four aspects of the painting: colors, lines, texture, and balance. Thus she integrates her description of the painting with her awareness of technique. This method gives structure to her paper and prevents her from attempting to do too much in the time and space she was working in. Her reaction to the painting is covered by her evaluation and interpretation.

Guide for Reading

Tim's review is weak because he doesn't present a clear description of the painting: some of his expressions are vague and inaccurate, and he contradicts himself in his evaluation. His paper sounds like his very first reaction to the painting instead of the result of careful observation and reflection.

Fine and Applied Arts

SAMPLE ART PAPER 2

Kerr, "A Nude Study"

Tim O. (a junior)

The artist uses dark skin tones along with dark colors in his depiction of the nude. His color patterns include many tones of red. It seems that the colors move from brown to red.

In the proportion of the woman, her head seems much larger and out of proportion to the rest of her. She is very skinny and is sitting in a relaxed position which may lead to this depiction. She seems to be sitting in a window seat, looking at the floor. This alone may lead us to our reasoning of her large head.

The artist seems to be attempting to paint a beautiful woman, but in his layering of paint and his slightly abstract figure he does not succeed. The woman has nice qualities, but alot of them are covered up by the artist style. His use of dark colors also helps to set a suttle if not depressing mood.

The artist, Kerr, did an excellent job depicting this woman. He has shown detail in his stylized form.

Analysis of Sample Art Paper 2

Tim has given us a fairly good description of the painting, but overall his paper is confusing and inconsistent. The second paragraph gives us the most details about the work: a skinny woman with a large head, sitting on a window seat looking at the floor. This information, along with the colors mentioned in the first paragraph, indicates that Tim at least saw the painting, however briefly.

But Tim has trouble with his evaluation. If there is some logic behind his attempt to explain the nude's large head (her position on the window seat), it is not at all apparent. He seems to be attributing her lack of proportion to some hidden purpose of the artist, not to the perspective of the viewer. In the same manner, he assumes that the artist attempted to paint a beautiful woman, but did not succeed, perhaps owing to incompetence. It is always dangerous to base an analysis on what one *thinks* the artist attempted to do. For an assignment like this one, the focus should be entirely on the finished product—what the artist *has* done.

The last two sentences in the third paragraph are very confusing. The phrases "nice qualities," "artist['s] style," and "suttle if not depressing mood" are too vague to tell readers much. Readers need to know exactly what qualities Tim considers "nice" and how the artist managed to cover these up. The description of the mood is equally confusing, especially because "subtle" and "depressing" are generally not adjectives that can be used to describe the same thing.

Tim's conclusion is a disappointing way to end his analysis. He contradicts what he said in the previous paragraph about the success of the artist, which makes him sound uncertain about his reaction to the painting. He could have written a much better paper if he had continued to describe carefully in the third paragraph, giving examples of the "nice qualities" and the "artist['s] style," and if he had tried to explain how these contribute to the mood. If he had wanted to express his own taste or opinion, the concluding paragraph is a good place for it. Here he could have said something like, "To me the woman is not beautiful, although she could be made so with a few minor changes."

Guide for Reading

Even though his list of characteristics shows that Jason observed his chosen painting very carefully, his "paper" is unacceptable because the assignment calls for "a page of well-organized, coherent writing." A list simply doesn't meet the requirements of the assignment.

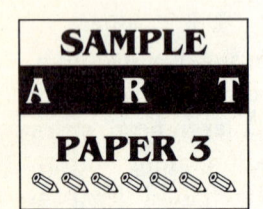

Junko Chodus "Figure on Black Background"

Jason H. (a sophomore)

Aspects of painting - elements
 1) Line uses expressive lines. Wide fast lines, suggesting strength, directness, boldness & movement.
 2) Shape: incorporates soft edge & implied shape. Appears to be the lower half of a person running.
 3) Dynamic form: appear lively & moving.
 4) Texture: visual texture by repetition; continually uses round & arc like shape.
 5) Color: uses a large variety of cool colors; seems to come off the painting. Uses black, white, pink, blue, green, & yellow.

Fine and Applied Arts

6) Balance: fairly well balanced, top seems a little heavier than bottom; sides balanced evenly.

7) Variety: transitional variety - uses same basic shape, slowly changing from small arcs to large ones. Also uses some wiggly lines leading into arcs.

8) Repetition: repeats single design element - arc; arcs differ in line (wide, thin) & color (uses a variety). All appear to be dynamic form and texture.

Analysis of Sample Art Paper 3

Although the assignment did not emphatically state that the paper should be in essay form, it should be clear that a list of features is not appropriate. The phrase "a page of well-organized, coherent writing" eliminates the suitability of a list, even one as complete as Jason's. His response is really nothing more than a set of notes, a good way to begin a writing task but not something most teachers want to see.

If Jason had organized this list into several paragraphs, he might have produced a very good description and analysis of the "Figure on Black Background." As it stands, however, he failed to meet the requirements of the assignment, even though his depth of observation shows great interest in the painting.

ART ASSIGNMENT 2

Course: **Introduction to Art**

Write a one-page paper about your favorite piece of sculpture. We have seen all of the ten pieces in this year's show, so you shouldn't have to spend too much time picking a favorite.

You will need to write in paragraph form and talk about why you like this piece. You may want to discuss the formal *(visual elements: line, shape, form, color, and texture)*; or *visual principles (rhythm, balance, unity, variety)*; technical *(welded steel, combination of materials)*, and expressive *properties in the works.*

Analysis of Art Assignment 2

This assignment is for a class (freshman through senior) in which students analyze architecture, sculpture, painting, crafts, and industrial design in relationship to their historical periods. The subjects of their papers are outdoor sculptures placed around the campus. Each year, ten new pieces are chosen to replace the current ones, so to a degree they represent trends in sculpture.

For the last class of the semester, the students view the sculpture of their choice and write the paper described in the assignment. The instructor doesn't expect the papers to be revised extensively; at most, they might be copied over for neatness and minor revisions.

A good response to this assignment will include a description of the sculpture, clear enough so readers can picture it. The description should cover the formal and technical aspects mentioned in the assignment. The expressive properties of the work may be the most difficult to verbalize coherently. Although most people automatically react to a work of art, they often have difficulty expressing this reaction in a way that allows someone else to appreciate it. Reactions are abstract, and people frequently can't find the right words to express them. The best approach is to base abstract qualities firmly on concrete qualities. For example, large sculptures commonly produce sensations of strength and grandeur, and writers could relate these sensations of strength to the size of the work.

In addition to including the three aspects called for in the assignment, adding a fourth could produce an excellent paper. The course deals with sculpture (along with other forms of art) in relation to its period, so explaining where a sculpture fits in with trends in sculpture would make a paper stand out. Writers would demonstrate that they can view the work of art as an individual creation that has been influenced by past and present trends. Although the assignment doesn't ask for this type of information, it is especially appropriate because it includes knowledge learned in the course.

As with any in-class writing, special care must be taken in planning and organizing such a paper. Making a list of points to include and writing an informal outline would help produce a better-than-average response.

Guide for Reading

George has written a good response to the assignment, integrating his descriptions of the technical and expressive qualities of the work into a

Fine and Applied Arts

pleasing analysis. His playful conclusion, however, is a weakness. It seems written merely as a comment to his teacher, and it is expressed in a way that will distract most readers.

> **SAMPLE ART PAPER 4**

After the Rape of Persephone

George S. (a junior)

    After the Rape of Persephone combines the visual and compositional elements into an evocative marble sculpture [Figure 11.3]. A mangled woman's form of realistic size is reclining on a pillar; headless and with amputated limbs. She is split down the middle of the torso and her pelvic area looks as though it were deformed even before the rape. Standing a few feet behind the figure is a vertical marble about eight feet tall.

    The most noticeable visual elements used in the piece are

texture and form. The marble used in Persephone is of a smoother grade than her bed and the vertical stone behind. The surreal arrangement of body parts suggests that more than one woman modeled for the sculpture, a technique which may imply that all women are victims in the Rape of Persephone. The ripple of the left rib cage is very realistic. The sunken right chest and sagging breast are obviously modeled from an older woman. These features reveal the artistic skill and astute conception of human anatomy.

Of the compositional elements, good balance seems to stand forth. There is something magical about having three components.

This sculpture appeals less to the intellect than to one's emotions. Certainly it is a statement of the victimization of women. I am also compelled to try to remember who the hell Persephone was. My first primary reaction comes from the gut, though. There is a woman plundered and abused. Could that vertical marble be Mr. Goodbar?

Guide for Reading

Cynthia's paper is an average response to the assignment. She has explained the expressive qualities well, although she needs to support her reaction with more concrete details. Her description of the physical qualities is the weakest part of her paper, especially for a sculpture that tells her so much. Are there qualities she could have included but didn't?

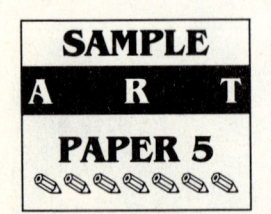

SAMPLE ART PAPER 5

After the Rape of Persephone

Cynthia H. (a sophomore)

"After the Rape of Persephone" is a light gray piece of sculpture. There are two legs and two torsos lying on a flat slab of marble that looks like a small table or bench. The marble has been smoothed into an interlocking of man and woman after a rape.

Fine and Applied Arts

This work makes a strong statement about man's dominance over woman. The man has just raped Persephone. That is the most obvious statement. Then there are more suggestions. Both figures are lying on their left sides, but the man's torso is above the woman's. He may be resting on his elbow. His leg is on top of her leg, possibly holding her down. She lies in front of him, but under him, not struggling. The rape is over but she is not trying to get away. She has surrendered completely.

The man and woman are made of the same material, gray marble, as we are in life, flesh and blood. But somehow man has risen above and taken over woman. There is a tall white marble pillar behind his sculpture which emphasizes the theme. It is a phallic symbol which states: As man has taken control of this woman in a rape, so it is in the world.

Guide for Reading

Kristin's paper is a poor response to the assignment because it is so short and vague. She doesn't seem to have become involved with either the task of viewing the sculpture or writing about it. Notice that she mentions mental and emotional depth, symbolism, and meaning without ever identifying these terms or explaining how the sculpture conveys them.

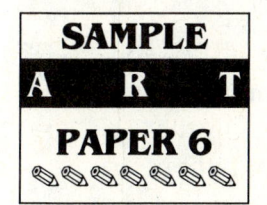

SAMPLE ART PAPER 6

Meaning in a Sculpture

Kristin A. (a sophomore)

The Rape of Persephone, a piece of modern art on campus, has great mental and emotional depth which makes it a favorite of students. It consists of two pieces of marble with varying textures. The textures have a lot to do with the symbolism in the piece. The smooth form of the body shows the delicacy of human form; where as the places that are more rough show the harshness and brutality of the rape. One piece of the sculpture is a type of monument, a possible tombstone for the death of a part of Persephone caused by the rape. In the human form, there is a piece that has been cut away, leaving the surface rough. This missing part makes the form look twisted and torn. This "tear" is right in front of the monument or tomb. The symbolism I find in this sculpture through its texture, missing pieces, and placement gives this sculpture meaning.

STUDY QUESTIONS

1. Each of the three authors describes the sculpture differently. Which of the three do you think provides the most accurate description of the sculpture's formal and technical aspects? Point out specific parts of the paper to support your choice.

2. Which of the three papers seems to convey most closely the experience of viewing the sculpture? What are some of the techniques used that help convey the sculpture's expressive qualities?

3. Because your reaction to a work of art is so personal, you need to explain why it represents a certain thing to you. Which of the three authors provides good reasons for his or her interpretation?

4. Which (if any) of the authors shows an awareness of the historical significance of either the subject or the style of the sculpture?

5. All three authors describe the "Rape of Persephone" differently. Do you have a problem with the fact that they all saw something different in the same work of art? What does this tell you about art, especially abstract art?

Writing Assignments

The following assignments take examining art one step beyond the two assignments above. The first one could be done in a gallery, although the length of the paper really demands careful planning and thoughtful revision. The second assignment demands some research before viewing and writing the evaluation.

Fine and Applied Arts 631

1. Using the photographs on pages 631–632 or your local art museum, write a 3- to 4-page paper comparing two works of art (two paintings, or one painting and one sculpture, or some combination of different media) on the following dimensions:
   Formal: What formal properties are dominant in each work of art?
   visual elements: line, shape, color, texture, form
   visual principles: balance, repetition, rhythm, unity, variety, proportion, and scale
   Technical: What art media were used, and what techniques were used to make the works?
   Expressive: What human feelings are embodied in the works of art?
2. After studying the processes by which critics (connoisseurs) examine and judge works of art, write a 3- to 4-page paper evaluating a current exhibit of art (in a local museum, a campus exhibit, etc.). Magazines such as *Time, Newsweek, Art News,* and *Connoisseur* often include critiques of individual pieces and art shows.

632   Part Three   HUMANITIES

DRAMA ASSIGNMENT 1

Course: Survey of Dramatic Literature

Notes on Papers

1. 5–7 typed pages: Use standard margins and double space. If you use a computer, use 12 pt. plain type. If you do not have access to a typewriter, you may use the one in the theater lounge afternoons or evenings.
2. Don't summarize the plot unless this is a point of comparison and then only briefly.
3. State your thesis (that is the specific idea you want to present in the paper) and use references to the plays and quotes from the plays to support your points. Limit your topic to one or two points of comparison and discuss them in depth.
4. You may also use other reference materials, but you must not use them as your only ideas. Draw your own conclusions from the plays.
5. If you use a long quote, indent it 5 spaces and single space it.
6. Use end notes, footnotes, or internal notes to give references for quotes and ideas. Notes are used whenever you use material and ideas not commonly known, not just for direct quotes. Be sure to include page or act and scene numbers.
7. Also include a bibliography of sources consulted including the plays you use. Use the correct bibliographic form.
8. Be careful to proofread for typos, spelling, incomplete sentences, etc.
9. Avoid slang, catch phrases and casual writing. Don't include yourself in the discussion; write in third person not first.
10. Suggested topics:
    a. Discuss the similarities and differences in two versions of the same story (i.e., The Menaechmi and Comedy of Errors,

Hippolytus and *Phedre*, *Medea* by Euripides and Seneca, *Dr. Faustus* and *Faust*, etc.)
b. Compare and contrast the actions, motivations, etc. of the heroes of two plays (i.e. Oedipus and Hamlet)
c. Discuss the structure of two similar plays or one which is derivative from the other (i.e. *Everyman* and *Dr. Faustus*, *The Spanish Tragedy* and *Hamlet*)
d. Discuss the use of particular devices in two or more plays (i.e. the use of the "dumb show" in *The Spanish Tragedy*, *Hamlet*, and *The Duchess of Malfi*)
e. Discuss how certain faults or "sins" are treated in different plays (i.e. adultery, gluttony, miserliness, hypocrisy)

Analysis of Drama Assignment 1

This assignment calls for a comparison/contrast paper, a mode that should be familiar to most students. Although comparison/contrast papers are fairly straightforward, they require careful analysis and a thoughtful organization.

Successful papers will avoid the obvious and will discuss similarities and differences not readily apparent to readers. Commenting on the obvious is at best simply an exercise in writing and of no real value to writers or readers. The first step, then, is to find important similarities in what appear to be quite different situations or to find important differences in what appear to be similar situations. In short, you should delve beyond the obvious and seek a more profound understanding.

But the assignment asks for more. As Note 3 above indicates, students must state their thesis clearly. But to do so, writers must first have an interpretation worth advocating. Simply arguing that certain similarities and differences exist, even if they are subtle ones, isn't enough. The thesis must be related to the human truths drama attempts to convey. For example, if you discover that adultery is treated differently in two plays from the same culture, this knowledge may suggest to you that the society that produced these plays is not sure how to view this "sin" or even whether to consider it a sin. At this point, you have something worth arguing; you have a thesis.

Note 3 above also states a point that students must take seriously: "Limit your topic to one or two points of comparison and discuss them in depth." At first it may seem impossible to write five to seven pages on

Fine and Applied Arts 635

just one or two points. The purpose of this limitation, however, is to force students to choose points that are not obvious and that need to be discussed completely.

The inherent danger is plot summary; many students will want to fill the required number of pages with such summaries. But what the teacher wants after the opening paragraph is support for the thesis. The bulk of the paper should therefore contain analysis and examples that will convince readers that this particular thesis is a valid one.

Guide for Reading

The following paper is an average response to the assignment. Lisa enlightens only those readers who are willing to work through her scattered comments and belatedly discovered thesis. Notice that she appears to be discovering a thesis in the process of writing the paper, a thesis she states clumsily and weakly in the last sentence. Why is it that the first sentence of the paper is not the thesis?

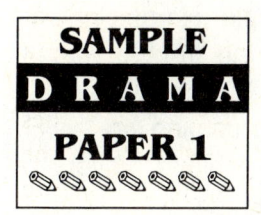

SAMPLE DRAMA PAPER 1

Oedipus and Hamlet
A Comparison in Character and Motive

Lisa M. (a sophomore)

Oedipus and Hamlet are both excellent examples of the tragic hero: a man either whose nature or motive eventually brings him to disaster. Both are forced into downfall. Oedipus is doomed by prophecy. Hamlet is doomed by the revenge sought by the ghost of his father. Both seek retribution for a dead king.

Oedipus obtained the crown by saving Thebes from the curse of the Spinx. His power which aided him was that of high intellect. Yet, it was this same, almost scientific curiosity that blinded him to the consequences of the truth. Another factor that influenced Oedipus was a prophecy that he would murder his father and marry his mother. He therefor exiled himself from Corinth in order to avoid the prophecy.

So far, there are two qualities driving Oedipus-curiosity and fear. Another baffle that he erects is his temper. It is a rage that is easily kindled and fuddles his reason. His temper is so bad that it even drives him to try to exile Creon without conclusive evidence of treason.

Finally, we have the vengence factor. But this does not seem to be an inherent characteristic to Oedipus. Instead, he is forced to find and banish, or slay, the killer of Laius as decreed by Apollo. To find the killer and pay him back for his crimes would free the city of Thebes.

Oedipus is a good king. He is noble, truthful, and cares for his people very much. But his wild temper would be evidence of a deeply seated paranoia which might possibly be rooted within the fear of the prophecy affecting him.

Hamlet was crown prince of Denmark, next in line for the throne. However, Hamlet the king died and his brother, Claudius, married the widowed Gertrude forming a somewhat incestual brother-in-law/husband, sister-in-law/wife relationship. In addition, it is revealed in the play that the corruption of the court reflects the condition of the country. For example, Horatio and Bernardo in the very opening scene discuss the trouble with Prince Fortinbras. Then they meet the ghost of old Hamlet and Horatio says, " . . . And prologue to the omen coming on, . . . Unto our climatures and countrymen." So it is possible at the very opening of the play to imagine that Hamlet could be jealous of having the throne stolen from him by his uncle. Matters are then only made worse that Claudius is a poor king as was revealed by Hamlet in Act II scene 4 . . .

> Here is your husband; like a mildewed ear,
> Blasting his wholesome brother. Have you eyes?
> Could you on this fair mountain [King Hamlet]
> Leave to feed, and batten on this moor? [Claudius]

So already Hamlet had two motivators for his actions; jealousy, and a want to see his country whole again. But then Hamlet learns of his father's murder from the ghost. The ghost of Hamlet demands vengeance upon Claudius and his son can but comply not only out of love for his father but also because honor demands it. This, beyond all other factors is the driving force behind Hamlet's desire for revenge.

Oedipus' paranoia is evident in his interview with Tiresias the

Prophet. Tiresias merely wished to hide Oedipus from himself, but in an anger prompted by Oedipus, ___ proclaimed him his own wanted man. Enraged, Oedipus immediately assumes Creon put Tiresias up to this in an attempt to usurp the throne. The accusation is apparently baseless because it seems that there had been no animosity between Creon and Oedipus before then. This could easily be caused by the paranoia resulting from the prophecy and the fact that his kingdom is falling apart under the curse. The problem that occurs is that because of his uncertainties, Oedipus is looking for those who might betray him, making him blind during the investigation of Laius' murder. Oedipus might have begun to think that if he found who killed Laius, he would also uncover the conspiracy to the throne-even though there wasn't, nor had there been, one. Instead of looking at the evidence at face value, then, he took some hidden meaning to be found. Therefore, it might be said that Oedipus walked blindly into the answer that was the last thing he wanted to hear: that his wife was his mother was also currently his wife, and that Laius was indeed his father. Thus, the prophecy that Oedipus feared so much had already come to pass.

In contrast, Hamlet knew exactly where he was headed if not to what toll the revenge would exact. He feigned insanity to possibly catch his uncle unawares or at least ___ distract him until the time was ripe. Gertrude and Claudius were puzzled over Hamlet's insanity, but Polonius was sure that it was Hamlet's unrequitted love of Ophelia and made steps to prove and correct the problem.

On the first attempt, Hamlet tries to get rid of Ophelia as if to get her away from the future events. But at the play, Hamlet made a turnaround and accepts her affection making us believe that it might be for the last time. Maybe he realizes that any relationship with Ophelia would be impossible after the coming confrontation with his mother and Claudius. Polonius' death was unforeseen but does not really seem to affect Hamlet. It is possible that he sees the death as merely something inevitable to begin with.

If Hamlet was not mad to begin with, he certainly was by the closing scene. He seems to take his duel with Laertes with nonchalence, just as long as his end goal is accomplished. And so it is, yet Gertrude unknowingly was pulled into the deaths with her draught of Hamlet's wine. This makes Hamlet's revenge twice earned: that for his father, and that for his mother.

So both were driven by vengeance, but for different reasons. And both suffered equally, but by a different end. And though the code was death before dishonor, I believe that the playwrights might have had a different opinion. That any obsession holds the capability of tragedy.

Analysis of Sample Drama Paper 1

Lisa has chosen a good topic for this paper, one that asks her to understand Oedipus and Hamlet as real people. To understand their characters and motives, she has to analyze them on the basis of what they say and do, which forces her to read carefully and then to explain to her readers what she has discovered. This type of topic has a degree of difficulty greater than average, but at the same time, it gives students more to work with, is more interesting to write, and is certainly more interesting to read.

The main weakness of Lisa's paper is that she seems unsure of her thesis. In fact, Lisa seems to have discovered a meaning to her analysis only at the end of the paper, where her last sentence (actually a fragment) hints at a reason for the similarities she has found. It is not unusual to discover something important in the process of writing. When this happens, however, the entire paper should focus on the discovery. This paper would have been much better had Lisa used, from the beginning, the idea of obsession as a major characteristic of both Oedipus and Hamlet. She then could have shown how obsession led to tragedy. This approach would have provided an excellent point to focus on, giving her paper the unity it lacks. Because she didn't have a clear thesis, Lisa fell back on a method that doesn't produce a cohesive paper. She summarized a bit of the action or dialogue from one play, commented on it, and then tried to parallel this summary with something from the other play. The result is an array of comments that confuse readers because they don't lead to any particular point.

Throughout her paper, Lisa summarizes only what is necessary to support her points. She expects her readers to have read both plays and so doesn't burden them with tedious information. Notice, in paragraph 2, that Lisa explains how Oedipus' talent for solving the riddle of the

Fine and Applied Arts

Sphinx is the same talent that brought about his tragedy. This is a good example of using action from the play to explain character. She does the same in the third paragraph to explain Oedipus' temper and again in the sixth paragraph to identify Hamlet's motives. In these sections, we see signs of analytical thinking that could enlighten readers had Lisa been working from a specific thesis.

The paper begins to wander toward the end of paragraph 8. The information here and in the next two paragraphs does not support any particular point. Although Lisa may have thought the contrary, she does not provide readers with necessary connections. She should have explained, for example, how Hamlet's feigned insanity, his problems with Ophelia, and his reaction to the death of Polonius lead to his disaster. Instead, she gives too much summary and not enough explanation. At this point, Lisa seems to be padding with summary, either to fill up the required number of pages or to make sure she says enough about the play.

In addition to the content problems, the sentences in this paper need work; they are riddled with surface errors, some so severe that we can only guess at her meaning. Moreover, short sentences can be used for emphasis, but too many make it seem as if the student is writing down thoughts as they come instead of putting similar ideas together. As an example, the last four sentences in the first paragraph should be combined because they express the same idea. One way of doing this would be to write: "Both are forced into downfall; Oedipus is doomed by prophecy; Hamlet, by the revenge sought by the ghost of his father; and both seek retribution for a dead king." Even though the words have not been changed, the semicolons indicate that the following clause is closely related to the preceding one. The first sentence in the fourth paragraph ("Finally, we have the revenge factor") is another one that needs reworking. This type of sentence doesn't say anything about the topic and as a result doesn't inform readers. Another way of introducing this paragraph would be: "Although revenge does not seem to be an inherent characteristic of Oedipus, he is forced by the decree of Apollo to find and banish, or slay, the killer of Laius." This one sentence contains the same information that is now spread out over three sentences.

Guide for Reading

Chris's paper is an inadequate response to the assignment. His claim in the last sentence of the introduction states the obvious, something that is readily apparent to readers of the plays. The paragraphs that follow ignore this claim and simply juxtapose similarities that occurred to

Chris. Another weakness is the number of distracting surface errors, indicating that he wrote hastily and didn't proofread his paper.

SAMPLE DRAMA PAPER 2

Murder, Incest, and Revenge in Hamlet and Oedipus Rex

Chris P. (a freshman)

In the story of Oedipus the King, the action takes place in pre-Christian times, and the standards of morality and conduct differ accordingly from that in Shakespeare's Hamlet. However, the two stories are significantly similar in that they both deal with murder, incest, and revenge.

There are two sides to Prince Hamlet: one, the sensitive young intellectual and idealist who expresses himself with beautiful poetry and is dedicated to the truth; the other is a barbaric Hamlet who treats Ophelia very cruelly, who slays Polonius and then calls him a fool for having been behind the curtain where he shouldn't be, and one who thinks nothing of sending Rosencrantz and Guildenstern to their deaths. Oedipus also has two sides to his personality. He has a side that is loving and loyal and a dedicated ruler, and the other side is mean and cruel. This side of Oedipus is seen when Oedipus kills Laius and threatens to do the same to Creon.

Hamlet takes vengeance into his own hands when he kills Claudius, the new ruler of Denmark, and Oedipus controls his own fate by blinding himself as punishment for his crime of killing his father and marrying his mother. Each tragic hero has a belief in a greater being or beings, but neither of them chooses to leave vengeance up to the heavens.

King Hamlet's ghost functions in the same way that the chorus does in Oedipus Rex. He appears to Hamlet to persuade him to avenge his death. Hamlet is not sure that the ghost is telling him the truth. He later discovers that he is indeed telling the truth because of Claudius' reaction to the players who are acting out the death of King Hamlet. The chorus approaches Oedipus and beg him to free them of the plague that is on the city by finding the person responsible for the death of Laius and punishing him accordingly. The chorus however, is not aware that Oedipus is the man that they are searching for.

Oedipus could have justified his actions of killing his father and marrying his mother by shifting the blame onto his parents. Had Laius and Jocasta not listened to the oracle about Oedipus, and had not left him on the mountainside to what they thought would be his death, then the prophecy could have been prevented. Laius was not a sensitive nor compassionate man. His actions were not kind and he was often brutal, yet his death still had to be avenged. Although King Hamlet's murder was not justified, he was not always a compassionate person. He took over the kingdom of Denmark from King Fortinbras. Both Laius and King Hamlet were not model citizens, yet their deaths cause the ruin of tragic heroes like Oedipus and Prince Hamlet.

Claudius is fully aware that his marriage to Gertrude is incestuous according to canon law, which is based on the dictum that man and wife become one flesh. He is also aware that even if the marriage were not incestuous, it took place much too hastily. Typically, royal periods of mourning last for a full year, but this marriage took place within two months of king hamlet's death. Claudius however obtained approval for his marriage by his court. This is revealed by his words in the first twenty-five lines of his opening speech, concluding with "So much for him" He rationalizes his act by saying that reason is set against grief and nature. Gertrude is referred to first as "sometimes sister" then as Queen, and finally as "Imperial jointress" of Denmark. Claudius is in effect trying to convince his audience that he has been motivated by a high sense of public duty.

Oedipus is not aware that his marriage to Jocasta is incestuous but it took place none the less much too quickly after Laius was killed. Oedipus was made king by answering the riddle of the Spinx and Jocasta was part of his reward since she was already Queen.

Claudius is viewed as the antagonist of Hamlet, and Oedipus maintains a heroic image in *Oedipus Rex* even though many of his actions are similar to Claudius. Claudius is a ruler who exhibits decisiveness and capability as a ruler. Although Denmark fears an invasion led by young Fortinbras, the court and the people rest assured that their king will take proper action. Claudius shows tact for all concerned when he ascertains that Polonius will not oppose his son's departure. King Claudius' public image is a favorable one because the people do not realize the role he played in the death of his own brother, King Hamlet.

The people of Thebes are loyal to oedipus because they too are unaware that their king is responsible for the former king's death. At the beginning of the play, the chorus of townspeople comes to Oedipus to seek help in freeing them from that will only vanish if Laius' murderer is found. Oedipus vows to do this even though he is unaware that it is himself he is searching for. The townspeople of Thebes feel confident that their leader will help them. Oedipus is, like Claudius, a king that exhibits great capability as a ruler.

Another common characteristic of *Hamlet* and *Oedipus Rex* is that both Claudius and Oedipus display moments of paranoia. Claudius fears that Prince Hamlet is trying to overthrow his throne. He tries to have him killed by sending a message to England with Rosencrantz and Guildenstern, but the crafty Hamlet switches the messages and Rosencrantz and Guildenstern are killed instead. Oedipus feels that Creon is trying to overthrow his throne and become king. Oedipus thinks that Creon sent the blind prophet to tell him of the oracle because Creon was desirous of his crown, but Creon was merely trying to help him discover the truth. Oedipus says in a moment of anger that he believes Creon is "about to stab me in the back." Hamlet could also be a bit paranoid also. He thinks for a short while that the ghost of King Hamlet is actually a devil in disguise, and he also thinks that Claudius is spying on him from behind a curtain in his mother's bedroom, but it is actually Polonius.

Another aspect of these two plays that make them very similar is the fact that Gertrude and Jocasta are both oblivious to the sins of their second husbands. Nothing that Queen Gertrude says or does actually confirms that she was in on the plot to kill Hamlet. She is obviously undisturbed by her status as wife/sister to Claudius, but her concern for her son seem to be that of a genuinely loving mother. If Claudius' words tend to arouse suspicion as to his true motives, this is not the case with Gertrude. Her plea, "Let not thy mother lose her prayers, Hamlet" has the ring of sincerity. gertrude is not completely innocent however, as Hamlet can not forget that she married too soon, and to his uncle.

Unlike Gertrude, Jocasta does not go to her grave not knowing the truth about her husband. Jocasta takes her place as an unsympathetic character along with Laius when she allows her child to be carried off to die. She does not take place in the death of Laius, and she is initially not aware that she wed her own son, but she suffers punishment just the same. The Queens of Oedipus Rex and Hamlet live in ignorance of the vile sins that surround them, but in the end they both suffer the consequences.

One last point to ponder on the similar themes of *Oedipus* and *Hamlet* is the overwhelming desire of the tragic heros of each play to inflict harm on themselves as a form of punishment or escape. so great is Hamlet's despair that, were it not for the religious injunction against suicide, that ultimate act of despair and thus a mortal sin, he would take his own life: "O, that this too too solid flesh would melt . . ." is the passage where Hamlet contemplates suicide.

Oedipus does not have the strong religious convictions against suicide and he feels that forcing himself to live a life groping in darkness is a more terrible fate than death. He leaves his children and dead wife to live a life of exile.

Oedipus leaves the audience with the feeling that he is indeed a hero because he chooses to suffer for his sins. Hamlet does not leave us with the feeling that he is the "king killer" but retains his sense of honor in his death. The moving words of Horatio, who knew him best, provide the best epigraph:

> "Now cracks a noble heart. Good night, sweet prince,
> And flights of Angels sing thee to thy rest."

Analysis of Sample Drama Paper 2

The main problem with Chris's paper is that he chose, according to his introduction, to discuss rather obvious differences and similarities. But obvious points don't need to be discussed; readers will already be aware of them. Consequently, Chris searches desperately for something significant to say and fails. The paper is poorly developed, without a real focus and without any interpretive insight.

An informal outline of paragraph topics may enable you to see better what this paper does and why it fails to develop any topic.

> Paragraph 2: the two sides of Hamlet and Oedipus
> Paragraph 3: the manner in which Hamlet and Oedipus handle vengeance
> Paragraph 4: the function of the ghost and the chorus
> Paragraph 5: the justification of the murders; the characters of Laius and Claudius
> Paragraph 6: the incestuous marriage of Claudius and Gertrude
> Paragraph 7: the incestuous marriage of Oedipus and Jocasta
> Paragraph 8: Claudius as a ruler
> Paragraph 9: Oedipus as a ruler
> Paragraph 10: the paranoia of Claudius and Oedipus
> Paragraph 11: the innocence of Gertrude
> Paragraph 12: the crime and ignorance of Jocasta
> Paragraph 13: Hamlet's desire to inflict harm on himself
> Paragraph 14: Oedipus' desire to punish himself
> Paragraph 15: the heroic nature of Oedipus; the nobility of Hamlet

We can see from this outline that the paper has neither focus nor purpose. It doesn't even have a thesis. It reads as if Chris made a list of things that might be discussed as similarities or differences and then used this list as the paper. Obviously, outlining can be valuable if it is used properly. Several of these paragraph topics (especially those in paragraphs 3, 4, 13, 14, and 15) could serve as good topics for the paper, provided Chris had been willing to read and think carefully. What Chris did was ignore the part of the assignment that states: "Limit your topic to one or two points of comparison and discuss them at length."

Writing Assignments

In assignments involving comparison/contrast, you need to be aware that the purpose is to say something meaningful about the similarities or differences and not just to point them out. The purpose of the paper is not just to compare. A good paper will have a clear thesis, detailed explanation, and specific examples from the sources, and will be free of surface errors.

Fine and Applied Arts

1. Take a modern play and create an additional scene of dialogue between two of the characters. You must re-create the language (speech patterns and vocabulary), the subjects, and the attitudes appropriate to these two characters. Insert this in a spot in the play where these two characters would likely be talking to each other. This scene should not change the outcome of the play; instead, it should add information readers would find interesting and enlightening. Remember that your stage directions should not interpret; they tell the actors and actresses what to do.
2. In a 5- to 7-page paper, compare a play's text with the screen version. Focus on something significant about the effects of the medium on the story, characters, plot, and so on. The following are a few of the many modern plays that have also become movies: *'night, Mother, A Soldier's Story, Amadeus, Crimes of the Heart, Biloxi Blues,* and *Brighton Beach Memoirs.*

DRAMA ASSIGNMENT 2

Course: **Introduction to Drama**

Students' Guide to Writing Papers

This is intended as a guide to writing reports on the plays you see. In all reports, give your own feelings about the subject but back them up with specific examples. Do not simply answer the questions posed below with a yes or no. Elaborate and illustrate your answer with specific instances from the production.

TOPICS

I. Acting

a) Choose the performers you liked best—with illustrations from the production. Things they did well: gestures, movements, etc.
b) How was the performer's voice, movement, interpretation of the role?
c) Separate the actor or actress from the role. You can dislike a character but admire the performance.

d) Discuss the way the performers did or did not relate to one another. Did they listen to each other and respond?

II. Directing

a) Has the director helped the actors perform convincingly?
b) Do the actors and actresses play together, as an ensemble?
c) Is it easy to see and hear what is going on?
d) Are entrances and exits smooth? Scene changes?
e) Is the stage space well used? Are some areas ignored?
f) Does the pace or rhythm seem right? Does it drag or move swiftly?

III. Environment

a) The size and shape of the theater building
b) The atmosphere
c) The stage arrangement
d) The actor-audience relationship
e) Is the environment proper for the play or not?

IV. Scenery

a) Is the scenery helpful to the play? To the performers?
b) Is it a hindrance? Too distracting? Too overbearing?
c) Does it contribute to the mood? Is it appropriate to the style?
d) Is there a symbolic element in the scenery? In the shape and/or colors?
e) Is it exciting and appealing?

V. Costumes

a) Are the costumes right for the play?
b) Are they right for individual characters? In personality, station in life, occupation, etc?
c) Is the design good? The colors?

VI. Lighting

a) Is the lighting realistic, fantastic, or non-realistic?
b) Does it create mood?
c) Are all the actors properly lit? Can we see their faces?

Fine and Applied Arts

    d) How does lighting use color and direction (where does it come from: above, below, behind, etc.)?
    e) Are light changes made slowly or quickly? Is this right for the play?

VII. Characters

    a) Are the characters clearly defined?
    b) Are they realistic or symbolic?
    c) Which characters are in conflict? How do minor characters relate to major ones? Are they: mirror images, contrasts, parallels?
    d) Which characters are badly presented? Are they: incomplete, inconsistent, unbelievable?
    e) Which characters do you most closely identify with? Why?

VIII. Content, substance and meaning of the Play

    a) What is the play about? Is it easy to understand or not?
    b) Does it present the subject clearly?
    c) Does the author take sides, or is he or she neutral?
    d) Is the theme brought out in words? In actions? In symbols?
    e) Is there more than one theme? Are they consistent with one another?

IX. Type of play; Structure

    a) Is it serious or comic? Realistic or fantastic?
    b) If serious, is it tragic or more down to earth?
    c) Does it simply present life, or does it have a message?
    d) If comic, is it plain comedy, or farcical with exaggerations?
    e) Does it mix elements? Serious with comic? Realistic with fantastic?
    f) Is the play written in the climactic form? Episodic? Some other form? Give specifics.

REMEMBER: You are to see different kinds of plays in different environments. The above questions are guides in approaching the various subjects. Look at them before going to a performance, so you will have some idea of what to look for.

—From Theater Experience by Edmund Wilson

Analysis of Drama Assignment 2

This assignment presents a real challenge—collecting into an integrated whole the dramatic fragments represented by the 44 different "topics" the teacher provides. After reading the teacher's guide, you may think it will be impossible to remember all of the points while watching the play and equally impossible to respond to all of them in a relatively short paper. You would most likely be right in this assessment, which means that you have to devise an alternative strategy.

You may think that the key lies in the fact that there are only nine major categories for analysis: "directing," "costumes," "characters," "content," and so on. Most of these categories should be familiar to you from other literary analyses, and those that aren't (such as "Type of play") are obvious analytical features and don't require any special knowledge or skill. You may therefore believe that your goal should be to memorize the nine major categories before the performance. This approach is possible, but it isn't very efficient.

We suggest that on this assignment and others like it, students will write better papers if they merely read through the list of topics a couple of times before the performance. The goal is to get a general impression of what features the teacher wants to focus on (in this particular case, everything). Thus, if you were responding to this assignment, you should focus your energy on the play, not the list of topics. You should exercise your memory on the details of the play, not the guide.

If you are successful, the next day you will be able to use the guide as a questionnaire to trigger your recall of the performance. Try to write two to four sentences in response to each of the teacher's questions. These will form the foundation of your paper, the points you will develop into analytical and argumentative paragraphs. You probably will decide that you can't use all the questions and answers, and then you will have to make some decisions about what to cut and what to keep. These decisions represent another challenge, because they will determine the shape and content of the paper and whether you produce a coherent, well-integrated analysis.

Guide for Reading

Kathy's review is a well-written, honest evaluation of *The Fourposter*. She has blended many of the topics from the assignment in a manner that prevents her review from sounding as if she answered a list of questions.

Fine and Applied Arts

One weakness is that her review is too brief; as you read it, ask yourself what additional information Kathy should have included.

SAMPLE DRAMA PAPER 3

Review of *The Fourposter*

Kathy B. (a sophomore)

I enjoyed the theater's production of Jan de Hartog's *The Fourposter.* Karen Duckett and Keith Smith, who made up the two member cast, were very convincing in their roles as Agnes and Michael. They related well to each other as performers, which was especially essential since they were playing a married couple. I almost felt as if I were spying on the private moments of a husband and wife while watching the play. The characters were clearly defined and very personable. I found them to be realistic and believable. After seeing both performers also play in *Heathen Valley,* I was impressed with their ability to feign mannerisms and accents of a different era and culture so easily. Another example of their skill as actors can be found when Agnes was about to go into labor with her first child. I sympathized with the nervousness the couple must have experienced, while realizing their were "only pretending."

The costumes used by the cast were suitable for *The Fourposter.* They were very appropriate for the period and style of the play. As the characters aged during the duration of the story, I found their costumes helped me judge the years that had elapsed since the previous act. The costumes became heavier and darker as the couple grew older. They also reflected the increasing affluence of Agnes and Michael. Touches of gray to their hair, and for instance Michael's glasses and Agnes's mane rolled up into a bun, made the aging characters more realistic.

I. G. Greer Arena Theater was a good location for the production. Because of its small size, it made it possible to view the expressions and gestures of the performers more easily. Also, since the content of the play dealt with the private lives of individuals, the size added to the intimacy. The stage arrangement was simplistic, yet it possessed all of the elements necessary. The scenery helped contribute to the performance. It was not anything spectacular, but then that would have been distracting to the action of the play.

I was glad I went to watch The Fourposter. More than anything, I think the actors made the show worthwhile.

> **STUDY QUESTIONS**
>
> 1. List the topics in the guide that Kathy included. How has she covered these points without sounding as if she is answering direct questions?
>
> 2. List the topics in the guide that Kathy omitted that you feel she should have included. How would these help you understand more about the play and the performance?
>
> 3. For her paper to be outstanding, Kathy needed to include more details from the performance. Imagine that this is a draft; write comments throughout the paper telling Kathy what to add.

Guide for Reading

In the following paper, Tony makes an effort to cover as many aspects of the performance as he can. Unfortunately, he fails to realize that breadth without some depth is a weakness. He offers merely a superficial treatment of each topic. In fact, you may get the impression as you read that Tony was more anxious to finish the paper than to enlighten readers. This superficiality makes his paper an inadequate response to the assignment.

"The Fourposter"

Tony G. (a freshman)

SAMPLE DRAMA PAPER 4

The play *The Fourposter* is a realistic and serious play with some funny moments. It tells about a couple growing old together and how they deal with their children, affairs, and other crisis that face a typical family. I thought the play simply presented life. The play was climatic because it was a realistic play, it involved unit and time, and the cast was very small. It was very easy to understand. I think the author presented the play with a neutral attitude. She presented both characters with conflicts. Their actions while in conflict help to bring out the theme of the play. Their physical struggles represented the many struggles in a marriage and that it isn't always perfect.

The characters were clearly defined and realistic. Michael represented the young groom as anxious and the retired man as stubborn. Agnes represented the young bride as scared and unsure and an old insecure woman. Both characters are faced with conflict. The characters are well represented and believable. I don't identify with any character.

I enjoyed the two performers very much but I enjoyed J. Keith Smith performance the best. His gestures were very typical and believable especially in his role as the "concerned" father. His interpretation of the role was excellent. The performers together did an excellent job and responded well with each other.

The directing must be commended. The actors worked together with their acting and gestures as an ensemble which made their performance convincing. It was easy to follow what was going partly because the pace of the place was swift. I like the way the lights were dimmed in order the ensure smooth exits and entrances. I also liked the way the props crew wore black and didn't talk while changing the scenes. They took good advantage of the stage space and used all areas of the stage.

The size and shape of the theater building played a great part in the actor-audience relationship. By the theater being small it made the audience feel apart of the play. I think the enviroment was proper for the play. If it would have been in a larger theater it wouldn't have been as effected.

The scenery was helpful to the play. The scenery used fit the times of the 1800's and 1900's. It helped to create the mood. The symbolic element used was the bed which had hearts carved in the headboard which I think represented love and romance. The play was very appealing and kept my attention.

The costumes correlated with the period and style of the play. For example, for night clothes Michael wore a gown and a sleeping cap. Agnes also wore a long lace gown. A lot of curves were used in Agnes's costumes and light colors to represent her feminine qualities. Michael wore suits and tuxedos because he was a professional man.

The lighting used was realistic. It created a mood according to the mood of the play. The light coming from above lit the actors faces well and everything was visible. The lighting was soft which was appropriate for this play.

STUDY QUESTIONS

1. Mark the places in Tony's paper where he mentions, but doesn't identify or explain, topics important to his review.

2. Write comments throughout Tony's paper that tell him what he needs to do to make it informative and enlightening to readers.

3. Take paragraph 6 in Tony's review and rewrite it, eliminating short, choppy sentences and any information off the topic, and add illustrations or details from the play (you may have to invent some).

Writing Assignment

Use the guide above to write a 3- to 4-page review of a play produced by a local theater group. Imagine that you are writing for the arts section of a local newspaper, informing readers about the quality of the produc-

Fine and Applied Arts 653

tion. Let honesty be your guide: A good performance deserves commendation; a poor one needs constructive criticism. Imagine that some readers will have seen the performance and will want to know what a "critic" thinks about it. Other readers will want to know if they would enjoy the show.

FILM ASSIGNMENT 1

Course: **Introduction to Film**

> Write a 2–4 page review of a recent film of your choice. Include in your review the date, director, and principal actors and actresses and a brief summary of what the film is about.
> Points to consider (when appropriate to your choice of film):
> a) The director's purpose or theme and whether or not the movie successfully conveyed it.
> b) The performance of the actors and actresses.
> c) Special effects.
> d) Any special camera work, music, editing, etc. that are especially effective.
> e) Your personal reactions to the film and reasons for liking or disliking it.

Analysis of Film Assignment 1

This assignment calls for a basic film review, similar to those that can be found in a weekly magazine such as *Newsweek* or *Time*. The purpose of such a review is to inform readers about certain aspects of the movie—those five listed above. People read reviews to help them decide whether they want to see the movie or to help explain something about a movie they have seen. In either case, they will want to sense that the reviewer is honestly trying to explain and evaluate the movie.

To write a good review, you must be very familiar with the movie. This often means that you'll need to watch it more than once, taking notes relating to the five points listed above. If you have previously watched movies only for entertainment, you're likely to experience some difficulty observing and remembering details necessary to your review. For your first paper, you may find it helpful to watch the movie with several friends so that afterwards you can talk about it together, an activity that will help you recall more information than you would otherwise.

Reviews do not tell the complete story or give away information that is necessary for suspense. They give just enough information for readers to know what the movie is about. Avoid describing the film's ending in any concrete way.

The first four points in the assignment are relatively simple and straightforward, requiring careful viewing and note taking. The fifth point, however, is one that you need to approach with caution. Your reaction to the movie is important, but it must be based on an objective evaluation. You must be careful not to be swayed by personal tastes that prevent you from seeing either the good or bad features of a movie. If you simply dislike serious movies and choose one to review, you shouldn't fault the movie for not being comic. If a happy ending is necessary for you to enjoy a movie, keep in mind that sometimes such an ending is not appropriate. You'll have to remember to base your evaluation on how well the movie accomplishes what it promises to do.

There are two important points about reviews that are not mentioned in the assignment. One is that you need to use examples from the movie to support your points. These examples need to be very brief but complete enough to show readers that you are basing your analysis and evaluation on specific parts of the movie. The assignment also doesn't address the importance of clear, error-free writing.

A good way to approach this assignment would be to write it as if your review would be published in a local or a school newspaper. Don't think of it merely as something to be read by your instructor. You want your readers to feel that they are being informed by someone who is an authority, on movies and on writing. Although you are not providing your readers with the same experience as watching the movie, your review should still be a pleasure to read. You may want to use the professional review that follows as a model.

Class Article 1

"Turf Wars"
by Janet Maslin

The ascension of Dennis Hopper from classic hipster to classic burnout to grand old man of the American cinema is at least as crazy as many of the things Mr. Hopper has done on the screen, but it's real. His new film, "Colors," proves this beyond doubt. "Colors," Mr. Hopper's look at violent Los Angeles street gangs and the police assigned to control them, has a superb eye for the poisonous flowering of gang culture amid ghetto life, and an ear to match; along with brilliant cinematography by Haskell Wexler, it's also got a fierce, rollicking sense of motion. Though its story has the makings of standard stuff, and is sometimes sketchily told, nothing about "Colors" is ordinary.

"Colors," which opens today at Loews Astor Plaza and other theaters, has been accused of glorifying gang warfare, but its sense of frustration is much too powerful to support that claim. Equally strong is its sense of impending doom. The film introduces two L.A.P.D. officers assigned to track the gangs, and then builds its tension around the differences in their tactics and philosophies. The painful, unavoidable implication is that nothing can stop the gang mentality from perpetuating itself.

Bob Hodges (Robert Duvall) is the seasoned veteran who's learned a lot from long experience, while the hot-tempered newcomer Danny McGavin (Sean Penn) has learned nothing and knows it all. The difference between these two men is aptly summarized by a joke that is not repeatable here, but one that works very well in Michael Schiffer's screenplay. Mr. Hopper has assembled a huge cast of actors to play various racially-mixed gang members and street types, and all of them speak in realistic-sounding, tough-guy slang (the form of address "homes," short for "homeboy," is used as often as "man" was used in Mr. Hopper's "Easy Rider," and in much the same way). This adds greatly to its feeling of authenticity, even if the actors speak all at once or make very little sense. That, as the film makes clear, is part of the gang world, too.

What "Colors" does best is to create a sense of place and a climate of fear, to capture the vivid mark that gang life has left upon the downtown Los Angeles landscape. The look of this film, with its hard-edged,

---

Review of "Turf Wars" by Janet Maslin, from *The New York Times* (April 1988). Copyright © 1988 by The New York Times Company. Reprinted by permission of The New York Times.

brightly sunlit urban settings and its constant threat of unanticipated motion, is genuinely three-dimensional and utterly enveloping. But the film has a narrative vagueness, too. Though it all comes together, most tragically, at the conclusion, "Colors" is less notable for its plot than for its chilling urgency and its sense of pure style.

Mr. Duvall, who gives a terrific performance and provides a solid, reassuring presence, is seen during the early parts of the film teaching his new partner the lay of the land. As the policemen and the camera cruise the streets warily, Hodges demonstrates that he knows better than to leap at every small provocation, and it's a lesson he imparts to everyone around him. "Hey, kid, what's your heart beatin' for?" he asks a 14-year-old boy who's caught in a possible drug bust, and he leans down and gently feels the boy's chest as he speaks. McGavin, who favors more direct tactics, doesn't see the point of this at first, nor does he have Hodges's talent for commanding respect from gang members. But by the end of the film, he's beginning to learn.

"Colors" depicts the continuing warfare between two rival gangs, who snipe at each other with shotguns from moving cars, and whose battle is taking a terrible toll. A mesmerizing early sequence finds members of the two groups in jail, separated by bars and sporting the red or blue ragtag outfits that establish their identity, while the camera swims back and forth between them and rap music is heard above the general uproar.

The violence between these two groups is such a fact of their lives that they even have customs surrounding it, like the wearing of "In Memory of" gang shirts for a member's funeral. Some of these details go by in a blur, since it's not Mr. Hopper's style to emphasize any of the particulars, but they add significantly to the overall mood. Everything from a police crowbar emblazoned "May I Come In?" to a man who wears only underwear and a shower cap and seems desperately in love with a lifesized stuffed bunny contributes to the real and threatening atmosphere.

That none of the actors in "Colors" appear to be acting very strenuously is a great credit to the director, who keeps the film remarkably free of bogus-looking behavior. Mr. Penn keeps his muscle-flexing to a minimum and gives a tightly controlled performance; the rapport between the two principals is well-established. Among the actors playing gang members, who indeed look and sound believably tough, Glenn Plummer stands out as a hapless drug dealer who has the bad luck to antagonize Mr. Penn, and Grand Bush is memorable as a strong, silent kingpin. Trinidad Silva is also good as a kind of elder statesman, who wonders along with the policemen what this new generation is coming to. "Colors" is not without its occasional flashes of wry humor.

Mr. Hopper may be a great director of hip, street-smart male char-

Fine and Applied Arts

acters, but he's miserable when it comes to women. Maria Conchita Alonso, as a restaurant worker who becomes a girlfriend of McGavin's, conducts herself in admirable spitfire fashion but has a nonsensical role. The gang members' girlfriends are shown to have a much more thankless lot than even verisimilitude would require. And several scenes involve amazingly gratuitous nudity that, despite all the violence and the luridness, sounds this film's only real note of exploitation.

Guide for Reading

Mary's paper covers all the points listed in the assignment in an organized, well-expressed manner. If you've seen the movie, Mary's references and explanations will enhance your memories and understanding of *Colors*. If you haven't seen it, this review will help you decide whether you might want to. Unfortunately, the overall quality of her response is affected by the number of mechanical errors in spelling, sentence structure, and so forth that appear throughout the paper. How would you respond to them if they appeared in a published review?

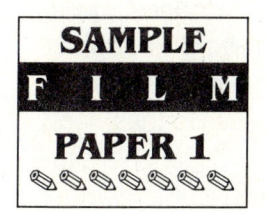

SAMPLE FILM PAPER 1

An Analysis and Discussion of *Colors*

Mary S. (a junior)

Colors, as directed by Dennis Hopper, and starring Robert Duvall and Sean Penn, is an incredibly violent film. While violence is not always necessary in a movie, *Colors* requires it in order to accurately portray its subject of Los Angeles gangs. The violence adds to the relative believability of the movie and increases its drama and its ability to move the audience. With fine acting, a good script, and a director who essentially specializes in this type of film, *Colors* turned out to be better than expected.

As discussed in class, *Colors* is basically a war film; there is an ongoing war between the two gangs, but there is also a war between the gangs and the police. Without any knowledge or experience of life in L.A., the actions seem realistic and true to life. While making an action-packed and entertaining movie, Dennis Hopper also managed to make several statements about society. First, the plight of the blacks and hispanics is illustrated and an explanation is given as to why they join gangs and why the gangs will never be wiped out. The very first scene shows a gang member getting his chest blown away. This is what will eventually happen to nearly every member of a gang: death or prison, but nothing even close to resembling a normal, productive life. The local residents accurately explain why the blacks and hispanics join the gangs and why the tragedies will never end when they become irate during a town meeting. There are no jobs available for these men and boys, they have no hope, so what else are they going to do? All the gangs have left is their territory and their pride and they will defend both to their death.

The second statement *Colors* makes is about the police and their similarity to a gang, but whether this is good or bad is a value judgement left to the audience. The police, like the gangs, have their own color, code of ethics, idea of acceptable behavior, and expectations of each other. This idea of the police as a gang is evident when Robert Duvall's character, Hodges, tells, McGavin, played by Sean Penn, that his offensive and aggressive methods make him no better than a gang member.

An interesting relationship exists between Hodges and McGavin; it is a father-son or mentor-apprentice relationship similar to that seen in *Bull Durham* between Crash and Nuke. Hodges thinks that McGavin is hotheaded and rash and feels that they do not make a good team so he tells McGavin that he has requested a new partner. While McGavin thinks Hodges and his methods are slow and useless, he is hurt that Hodges does not want him as a partner. In the end, as in any "coming-of-age" or "maturing" story, the mentor is gone, in this case Hodges is dead, and the apprentice must demonstrate how much he/she has learned. McGavin accomplishes this by telling his new partner, who is just as hotheaded and aggressive as he first was, the joke about the two bulls and the cows; it takes him a while to get it right, but it is clear that in time, this new style he has developed will become second nature. The good versus evil motif is also developed and expressed through the characters. The police are the "good guys" and the gangs are the "bad guys" or the "enemies," so where does Louisa fit in? McGavin things she is good when he takes her out and eventually sleeps with her, but then he sees her as a "home girl" sleeping with a gang member and he is physically at the sight or mere thought of it. His black and white ideals of right and wrong and good and bad have become fuzzy gray areas with which he must eventually come to terms.

The setting and special effects of Colors are typical of that of any police movie, but the cinematography and lighting are just a little bit more sensational than usual. In the scene in the jail when both gangs are being held for questioning, an interesting shade of red is used in the lighting which adds a little more to the violent and hostile atmosphere already present. Also effective are the night scenes in which the ground is lit from the helicopter above. Most memorable of these scenes is when Hodges dies. It is both lit and viewed from above, first at a close range and then moving farther away. The pain belongs to McGavin because, as the camera moves back to expose the rest of the set, the audience sees that no one else is effected by or really notices Hodges' death.

Adding to the power and drama of the scene is the sound. As the camera pulls away, McGavin releases a primal scream in anguish over his loss; however, this scene quickly turns into the pounding of the helicopter. Sound, especially in the form of music, is effectively employed in the film. More than anything else, the rap song Colors makes a strong statement about the gangs, stronger than any monologue or dialogue could possible have been.

The film's editing was done smoothly; the audience was not left in a state of confusion because of jump cuts or any such vice and while Colors is not a deep or profound movie, it is thought-provoking. The audience may not leave the theater wondering what happened, but they may leave wondering what they think and how they feel about it and that is one sign of a truly good movie.

Analysis of Sample Film Paper 1

Mary has written a very good review of Colors. She begins with the essential information of title, director, and principal actors. In addition to containing this information, her first paragraph identifies the type of movie (violent), the subject, the quality of the acting, and her own reaction. This is all done quickly, leaving her the remainder of the review to discuss specific features of the movie.

Although she never actually summarizes the story, Mary has told her readers enough for them to know what the movie is about and what genre it belongs to (war films). In the process, she suggests possible themes or purposes of the movie: the war among gangs and police, the similarity between the police force and a gang, the relationship between the veteran cop and the rookie, and the good versus evil motif that pervades the entire movie. In the first four paragraphs, Mary has covered points (a), (b), and (e), information that readers of reviews are usually most interested in.

In her last three paragraphs, Mary covers the mechanical aspects: special effects, camera work, and editing—points (c) and (d). These paragraphs deal with the artistic nature of the movie, letting readers know that the director used appropriate devices and methods to enhance the story. Discussing specific effects in this way shows that Mary is a perceptive viewer, looking for more than just the story.

Notice that Mary uses specific examples throughout her review to support her points. They convince readers that she watched the movie carefully and based her analysis on specific elements and not just on a general impression.

The conclusion is good because it sums up the movie (and the review) without repeating anything that has already been stated. Mary leaves her readers feeling one of two ways: if they like violent movies, they will enjoy *Colors*; if they don't like this type of movie, *Colors* is at least a thoughtful and carefully conceived movie of gang and police warfare.

The weakest part of Mary's review is the surface features of her writing. For example, her paragraphs are a bit too long. Paragraph 4 would be easier to read if it were divided into three paragraphs; the first break would come at the sentence that begins "While McGavin thinks," and the second would come at the sentence that begins "The good versus evil motif."

In addition, there are some typing errors that most readers will find distracting. Toward the end of paragraph 4, Mary writes, "McGavin things she is good." In that same sentence, she leaves out the word *sick* when she writes, "he is physically at the sight or mere thought of it."

Some revisions and proofreading would probably have eliminated these problems.

Fine and Applied Arts 661

Guide for Reading

Rodney's review is an average response to the assignment. It informs readers of the action in the movie, but it doesn't discuss or evaluate any other features. You may get the sense that Rodney viewed *Colors* as most moviegoers do; he watched the action carefully enough to remember the basic story and some of the more vivid scenes, but he never focused his attention sufficiently to perceive some of the more subtle features of the film. As you read, use Mary's review to identify some of the important points Rodney left out.

SAMPLE FILM PAPER 2

Colors

Rodney D. (a junior)

Colors is a movie about the LAPD's war against crack-dealing, teenage killer-zombies of east L.A. It shows how outnumbered the police force is by gangs and gang members. It examines the everyday life of a C.R.A.S.H. officer, and it shows how much violence an officer is exposed to. For example, in the beginning of the movie the Crips drive by in a van and shoot a Blood with a shotgun for no reason at all. Duvall and Penn are called to the scene where they discover the body. They also see how upset the deceaseds' mother is. *Colors* is also about the color-coded, machine gun-toting Bloods and Crips. It's about them getting high and blowing each other away. For example, in the beginning of the movie, the Crips are riding around in a van getting stoned. Shortly after that they kill a Blood in a drive-by shooting. Then when the funeral is going on for the blood, the Crips drive by and pepper the funeral with machine-gun fire. Another time is when the mexicans are having a party and the Crips start shooting threw the window and kill an innocent woman. Then in turn, the mexicans go to the Crips hideout and kill them. Afterwards the mexicans go to one of their hangouts and get stoned. The cops show up, and while they are being arrested, one member tries to be a vigilante and shoots Hodges. After he shoots Hodges he too is killed; by the police.

The relationship between Penn and Duvall is one of tension.

The two ride around in an unmarked ___ and stay at each others throat. Duvall, as hodges, is rational, ingratiating, and mistrustful of Penn (McGavin). The senior partner seems marked for death right from the start. There is something popery about his presence and his chuckle. Penn's character is concerned about his image; perfecting himself. For example, he is always looking in the mirror at himself making sure his hair isn't out of place. He is all slit eyes and swagger. He is at once hopped up and constrained.

Colors presents and inescapable racist view of the ghetto. The slums of east L.A. are a kind of zoo without walls. The movie has a hyperbolic sense of place. It isn't until the end of the movie that there is even a glimpse of a skyscraper, it is as if east L.A. is a third world country.

Analysis of Sample Film Paper 2

Although Rodney has given enough information for his readers to have an idea of what *Colors* is about, his review is not conceived or put together carefully. He ignored most of the assignment—points (b) through (e), replacing these with descriptions of specific scenes from the movie. The result is a review that contains only what most people remember of a movie they watch simply for entertainment.

Rodney never mentions the director, and he can't decide what to call the two main characters. Directors are important because a movie is basically their product and bears their stamp. Many people decide whether to see a movie on the basis of who directed it. It is also important to identify the actors, in this case Sean Penn and Robert Duvall, and then to describe the characters they play in the movie. From this point on, their movie names (McGavin and Hodges) should be used when the story is being discussed, and their real names should be used when their performances are being evaluated. This convention separates the actors from the characters they are portraying, something all actors strive to do. It isn't until the third paragraph, however, that Rodney seems to be aware that Penn and Duvall are playing the characters of McGavin and Hodges. Until that point, he seems unable to separate Penn and Duvall from the characters they play, which is a fundamental error.

Rodney's first two sentences give his readers a good idea of what the movie is about, but he includes too many examples that illustrate only this one point. He has left out an evaluation of the actors' performances

Fine and Applied Arts 663

and of any special effects that are part of the movie. We don't know how well Penn and Duvall portrayed the cops McGavin and Hodges, although we do know a little bit about their characters (paragraph 3). We learned from the first review that the cinematography, lighting, sound, and editing were carefully planned and are effective in enhancing the drama, but Rodney has completely ignored these features. This omission indicates that when he viewed the film he focused only on the story and not on any of the techniques.

Rodney didn't tell us his reaction to the movie. Although readers may not really care whether or not he liked *Colors*, it is important that he mention his reaction in his review. Deciding on an opinion and supporting it would force him to view the movie more carefully and critically than he did, and what this review desperately needs is the sense that the author did more than just watch the movie.

Guide for Reading

This review is an unacceptable response to the assignment. George did not try to review the movie *Colors;* he used the assignment as means of expressing his anger at police and movies in general. His paper illustrates what can go wrong with a paper when a writer uses an assignment as a platform for venting personal frustrations. Such an approach is deemed unprofessional and unacademic.

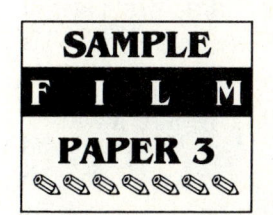

SAMPLE FILM PAPER 3

Colors

George M. (a sophomore)

Among the many important ingredients in a good film, the ability to convey as essential theme, or point, is the most important. So, one could ask about the film "Colors": Does it have an essential point, theme, or reason? If so, is it well communicated? Is the film built around any central idea?

Perhaps the theme of "Colors" was to give a realistic look into the lives of two ordinary policeman doing their best to combat the rampage of violence associated with Los Angeles gangs. Were the two central characters realistic in anyway? Were they in any way realistic enough to remotely identify with? Were they even likable? Sean Penn's character was not likable in any way. He was not even liked by anyone in the film. The only redeeming quality Pac-man has was that he was probably the most realisticly portrayed character. He reminded me of every local cop I have ever had the misfortune of meeting. His partner, with his high ideals, and general superiority complex, was completely unrealistic. Did the two main characters accomplish anything during the course of the movie? Well, one accomplished getting shot, and dying. That was about it.

Maybe the central theme of the movie was to give a realistic portrayal of L.A. gang members, and to provide an insight into their values and motivation. Were the gang members realisticly portrayed? Did most of these people look like tuff, angry, killers? Most of these so-called gangmembers do not look as if they could bully a sixth grade class. The gang members at the funeral looked the most realistic. Most of the gangmembers were poorly dressed. Most had no jewelry on. In reality Los Angeles street gangs are well financed by the crack trade. In the movie they would shoot a $400 gun, but drive a $200 car. It just simply did not seem realistic. A gang member seen talking to a cop would be shot on sight. They had hang-outs with no look-outs posted. The one redeeming character was Frog. He was likeable and more easily identified with than most of the film's characters. I still don't think that he would have told a cop, "I owe you one."

So, what the hell was the movies point? The movies point was probably, like most movies, to make money. In that regard it was probably a success.

Analysis of Sample Film Paper 3

George's review is characterized by poor writing and invective. By focusing only on his reaction—point (e) in the assignment—he has avoided providing readers any important information about the movie.

In his first paragraph, George gives himself an adequate guide for a review, even though it isn't expressed very smoothly. Had he honestly tried to find a central theme to the movie, and then discussed how it was conveyed, he could have written a relatively informative review. With his first suggested theme ("a realistic look into the lives of two ordinary policeman"), he allowed his personal problems with policemen to pre-

Fine and Applied Arts

vent him from treating the two main characters with any objectivity.

It is clear that George wants readers to think that all cops are like Pac-man, who has no likeable characteristics, and that it is impossible to conceive of a cop with high ideals. He even tells us that this completely unlikeable character resembles "every local cop I have ever had the misfortune of meeting." George is using this review more as an opportunity to display his anger at the police than as a chance to evaluate a movie.

He attacks the movie's ability to carry out his second suggested theme ("to give a realistic portrayal of L.A. gang members") with what seems to be limited knowledge. We would all agree that portraying gang members as benevolent but misguided kids would be unrealistic. At the same time, however, expensive jewelry, clothes, and guns and cheap cars are not things that all gang members have in common. Had George really wanted to persuade readers that *Colors* presented unrealistic characters as gang members, he should have supported his opinion with information from an authority on the street gangs of L.A.

The last paragraph in this review makes George seem angry, not only at the police and this movie, but at movies in general. Such anger makes us wonder if he would have liked any movie he chose to review. Plenty of movies deserve to be criticized harshly because they are hastily thrown together only to make money for someone. The main problem with George's approach is that he seemed inclined to find fault before he had watched the movie, instead of finding faults with the movie itself. This inclination caused him to ignore the assignment and to write an illogical complaint about personal dislikes.

FILM ASSIGNMENT 2

Course: Introduction to Film

Watch *E.T.* and write a two- to four-page paper about the movie. Your paper should focus on one of the following: theme(s), character(s), or techniques. Do not tell the story, but tell your readers enough so they will understand the point you are making. You are not expected to write a formal review, but you are expected to say something intelligent about the movie.

Analysis of Film Assignment 2

This was the first writing assignment of the semester in this course, and it was designed to let students exhibit whatever viewing and writing skills they had developed in the early part of the term.

Although the assignment doesn't state it explicitly, this paper must have a clear, well-developed thesis, a necessary ingredient for any paper that says "something intelligent" about a subject. The assignment is representative of many you may receive for which the teacher expects you already to know what features to include in a paper. Instead of writing about random ideas that are connected to the movie, you will need to develop and support a claim about some feature of the film, such as the themes, characters, or techniques as they relate to the entire movie. You should expect to watch the movie several times.

In many ways, this paper will resemble an analysis of a short story or novel, and you would certainly reread parts or all of the work in the process of writing such a paper. After you have chosen a thesis, you must assess all relevant information from the movie that supports your claim. The paper shouldn't sound as though you are choosing just a few of the many examples that support your point. At the same time, you don't want to have to write 10 or 15 pages, so concentrate on providing a balanced discussion.

We have provided a professional model that does an excellent job of analyzing *E.T.* We encourage you to read this analysis before examining the student papers that follow.

Class Article 2

"Well *I* Don't Love You, E.T."

by George F. Will

The hot breath of summer is on America, but few children feel it. They are indoors, in the dark, watching the movie "E.T." and being basted with three subversive ideas:
    Children are people.
    Adults are not.
    Science is sinister.
    The first idea amounts to counting chickens before they are hatched.

"Well *I* Don't Love You, E.T." by George Will from *Newsweek* (July 19, 1982). Copyright © 1982 by Newsweek, Inc. All rights reserved. Reprinted by permission of Newsweek, Inc.

The second is an exaggeration. The third subverts what the movie purports to encourage: a healthy capacity for astonishment.

The yuckiness of adults is an axiom of children's cinema. And truth be told, adults are, more often than not, yucky. That is because they are human, a defect they share with their pint-size detractors. (A wit once said that children are natural mimics who act like their parents in spite of all efforts to teach them good manners.) Surely children are unmanageable enough without gratuitously inoculating them with anti-adultism. Steven Spielberg, the perpetrator of "E.T.," should be reminded of the charge that got Socrates condemned to drink hemlock: corrupting the youth of Athens.

It is not easy to corrupt American youth additionally. Geoffrey Will, 8, like all younger brothers in the theater, swooned with pleasure while sitting next to his censorious father watching the little boy in "E.T." shout across the dinner table at the big brother: "Shut up, penis breath!" "E.T." has perfect pitch for child talk at its gamiest. Convincing depictions of a child's-eye view of the world are rare. George Eliot's "The Mill on the Floss" and Henry James's "What Maisie Knew" are two. But those delicate sensibilities could not have captured the scatological sounds of young American male siblings discussing their differences.

Ethnocentric: I feel about children expressing themselves the way Wellington felt about soldiers. He even disapproved of soldiers cheering, because cheering is too nearly an expression of opinion. The little boy in "E.T." did say something neat: "How do you explain school to a higher intelligence?" The children who popped through C. S. Lewis's wardrobe into Narnia never said anything that penetrating. Still, the proper way to converse with a young person is:

Young person: What's that bird?
Older person: It's a guillemot.
Young person: That's not my idea of a guillemot.
Older person: It's God's idea of a guillemot.

I assume every American has spent the last month either in line to see, or seeing, "E.T." In the first month it earned $100 million—$17.5 million during the Fourth of July weekend. But in case you have been spelunking beneath Kentucky since May, "E.T." is about an extraterrestrial creature left behind in a California suburb when his buddies blast off for home. He is befriended by a boy in the American manner: the boy tosses a ball to E.T. and E.T. chucks it back.

It is, I suppose, illiberal and—even more unforgivable—ethnocentric (or, in this case, speciescentric) to note that E.T. is not just another pretty face. E.T. looks like a stump with a secret sorrow. (Except to another E.T. As Voltaire said, to a toad, beauty is popeyes, a yellow belly and spotted back.) E.T. is a brilliant, doe-eyed, soulful space elf who waddles into the hearts of the boy, his big brother and little sister. But a wasting illness brings E.T. to death's door just as a horde of scary scientists crashes through the door of the boy's house.

Throughout the movie they have been hunting the little critter, electronically eavesdropping on the house and generally acting like Watergate understudies. They pounce upon E.T. with all the whirring, pulsing, blinking paraphernalia of modern medicine. He dies anyway, then is inexplicably resurrected. He is rescued from the fell clutches of the scientists by a posse of kid bicyclists and boards a spaceship for home. This variant of the boy-sundered-from-dog theme leaves few eyes dry. But what is bothersome is the animus against science, which is seen as a morbid calling for callous vivisectionists and other unfeeling technocrats.

A childish (and Rousseau-ist) view of children as noble savages often is part of a belief that nature is a sweet garden and science and technology are spoilsome intrusions. But nature is, among other things, plagues and pestilences, cholera and locusts, floods and droughts. Earlier ages thought of nature in terms of such afflictions. As Robert Nisbet says, this age can take a sentimental view of nature because science has done so much to ameliorate it.

Wonder: Disdain for science usually ends when the disdainer gets a toothache, or his child needs an operation. But hostility to science is the anti-intellectualism of the semi-intellectual. That is in part because science undercuts intellectual vanity: measured against what is unknown, the difference between what the most and least learned persons know is trivial. "E.T." is, ostensibly, an invitation to feel what we too rarely feel: wonder. One reason we rarely feel wonder is that science has made many things routine that once were exciting, even terrifying (travel, surgery). But science does more than its despisers do to nurture the wonderful human capacity for wonder.

U.S. missions have revealed that Saturn has braided rings and a ring composed of giant snowballs. The space program is the greatest conceivable adventure; yet the government scants it and Philistine utilitarians justify it because it has yielded such marvels as nonstick frying pans. We live in (let us say the worst) an age of journalism: an age of skimmed surfaces, of facile confidence that reality is whatever can be seen and taped and reported. But modern science teaches that things are not what they seem: matter is energy; light is subject to gravity; the evidence of gravity waves suggests that gravitic energy is a form of radiation; to increase the speed of an object is to decrease the passage of its time. This is science; compared with it, space elves are dull as ditchwater.

The epigram that credulity is an adult's weakness but a child's strength is true. Victoria Will (21 months) croons ecstatically at the sight of a squirrel; she sees, without thinking about it, that a squirrel is a marvelous piece of work—which, come to think about it, it is. For big people, science teaches the truth that a scientist put this way: the universe is not only queerer than we suppose, it is queerer than we can suppose.

Guide for Reading

Sara has written an excellent analysis of the movie *E.T.* Her claim is clearly stated and then supported with explanations and relevant examples from the movie. In addition to analyzing, her paper conveys her delight with the character E.T. and the movie. As you read this analysis, notice how Sarah has explained and supported her claims in a way that convinces readers she is making a valid statement about *E.T.*

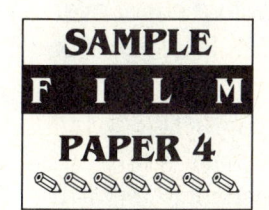

SAMPLE FILM PAPER 4

E.T. - The Extra-terrestrial

Sarah A. (a sophomore)

Steven Spielberg's "E.T. - The Extra-Terrestrial" is, in my opinion, the perfect study of the depth and beauty of pure, child-like love, shown through the relationship between a boy named Elliot and a "space" man named E.T. Spielberg's E.T. is wonderfully gentle and lovable and seems to bring out the awe and innocence of childhood not only all the film's characters, but in the audience as well. The film is a celebration of love and devotion to a true friend, no matter how different that friend may be. E.T.'s physical attributes, the special things he does, and his bond with Elliot all come together to make "E.T. - Extra-Terrestrial" a film with an incredibly powerful emotional appeal, a film that brings out the child in all of us. } Thesis

When E.T. first arrives in California, we're not sure what to make of this squatty (*short*) creature with long arms and an unusually large head. But the uncertainty doesn't last long: E.T. is obviously different, but he is obviously gentle as well. The sounds he makes are like a cat purring, he has strangely graceful hands, and he has beautiful, big (and again, gentle) blue eyes. When he learns to talk, his voice is soft and almost reassuring. In every encounter E.T. has, with Elliot or with anyone else, Spielberg does an excellent job___making sure that there is nothing frightening, nothing intimidating, about E.T.

From the beginning of the film E.T.'s actions serve only to make us understand him and love him. After being lured into Elliot's room with Reese's Pieces, he wants to see and touch (even eat) everything, just like a curious child. It is obvious that E.T. is an incredibly intelligent and peaceful creature without an ounce of malice. E.T. brings a dying flower back to life with just a look, and when he sees his friend Elliot has cut his finger and is hurting, E.T. heals it with a touch. When Elliot, his brother, and their friends are trying to help get E.T. home, E.T. unknowingly makes every kid's dream come true - he makes them fly! Seeing this little visitor waddling around on Halloween with a sheet over his head can't help but make him appealing. E.T. is capable of building a communicator to send a message into space from toys and tools around the house - again he is obviously intelligent, but he is untainted and full of love, like a child.

Perhaps the strongest emotionally powerful aspect of this film is the bond between E.T. and Elliot. From their first Elliot begins to feel what E.T. feels. A perfect example is the hilarious chaos when E.T., hidden away at home, has his first experience with beer, and Elliot, at school, feels the results. E.T.'s feelings, which are frequently Elliot's, result in quite an adventure as Elliot frees all the frogs in his science class from impending dissection and steals a kiss from the class beauty. Even though E.T. wants to go home right from the beginning, his connection with Elliot becomes stronger as the film progresses. Elliot even speaks of E.T. as "we." When finally the foreboding forces of the "adult" world catch up with E.T., the depth of his bond with Elliot is revealed. As faceless doctors and scientists run tests on both E.T. and Elliot, we discover that even their breathing and their heartbeats match. Both are very ill, but in order to save his friend, E.T. releases Elliot from this bond, giving Elliot back his life, while giving up his own. Luckily, the return of his people to earth brings E.T. back to life. We are overjoyed that E.T. is alive, and yet as he prepares to board the spaceship waiting to take him home, our hearts are breaking. E.T. and Elliot, although from two entirely different worlds, have become as close as any two could through the simple, wonderful phenomenon of the unbiased love of a child, a love that, advanced and intelligent as he is, E.T. understands. As he leaves, with his heart hurting, he touches Elliot's forehead and says, "I'll be right here," and we know it is true. The bond between E.T. and Elliot has become as real and strong as any we have known, or will know.

Steven Spielberg has given us, in "E.T. - The Extra-Terrestrial" a wonderful dream of what life in other worlds may be like. E.T. is so powerful because he represents all the good things we know, gentility, kindness, humor, and intelligence. We truly believe in E.T., just as a child would, because he brings out the best in us. The film, as well as Elliot, and of course E.T. himself, will always hold a special place in the world of film, because they have challenged us to not be afraid to believe.

STUDY QUESTIONS

1. Identify the claim, or thesis, in Sarah's paper. Next, mark all statements she makes that expand and support the thesis. Finally, mark all of the references to the movie. By doing this, you will see the structure of this review: a thesis, followed by supporting statements, which are in turn followed by supporting references.

2. Sarah hasn't retold the story of E.T., but she has given enough information for readers to understand the plot. Using Sarah's paper (not your own knowledge of the movie), write an outline of the plot.

Guide for Reading

If you find reading this paper a real struggle, don't blame yourself. Mike's writing overflows with abstractions, parenthetical expressions, and strings of modifiers that obscure the topic and the sense of his sentences. Pay special attention to paragraph 3. His paper is not a failing one: Mike has analyzed the movie, and he shows real skill with sentence structure and vocabulary. But before he can write a good paper, he needs to discipline his talents and write to inform, not to impress, readers.

SAMPLE FILM PAPER 5

The Human Element in Spielberg's *E.T.*

Mike B. (a junior)

Stephen Spielberg's *E.T., The Extraterrestrial* presents, on the surface, the tale of a lost, lovable little being from a distant, green planet who is befriended by a lonely, sensitive young boy. The film, however, actually operates on several levels; its very title, in fact, suggests a certain multiplicity of meaning. E.T. is not just the visitor from outer space, an alien presence in a human world. The adjective "extra," in the sense of "leftover" or "excess," applied to the noun "terrestrial," evokes an image of E.T., or at least some aspect of the creature, as rejected and out of place, the leftover human. The suffix "extra-" also refers to something which is "beyond" or "above," and the implication is that E.T. may represent something which surpasses the human while simultaneously sharing the same roots.

E.T.'s origins, coming from the verdant fertility of a faraway, unspoiled world, and his emergence from the misty dimness, the still, womblike enclosure of the forest, establish a vital connection between this interstellar botanist and the forgotten primeval headsprings of man's own origins. E.T.'s symbiotic interaction with his natural environment—he is, in essence, a living extension of that environment—emphasizes, through contrast, man's profound estrangement from his own and the generalized direction of his antagonistic impulses.

The fecund warmth of the natural matrix stands in stark juxtaposition to the cold sterility of the artificial California environment. Man is systematically trapping himself in a prison of his own making; with the rational cruelty of scientific calculation, he erects the steel girders of technological imperative and sets in place the bricks of homogeneity. As he reconstructs his surroundings to conform to his own gaunt image, heeding only the dictates of his supreme diety, Progress, he designs a grave, new world in which only the cold, the sterile, and the same can flourish.

E.T. cannot live in this environment; the fundamental spirit of human warmth which he embodies only wilts and dies, and into its place creeps a callous cynicism, a lingering insentience. Perhaps, upon E.T.'s "death," Elliot feels the first chilling caresses of the encroaching numbness, and he mourns not only the death of his friend, packed in ice, but the loss of the capacity to feel. For he and E.T., their reciprocity of feeling is a sustaining source of rejuvenation, and it prevents them from submerging, like many others, into the icy depths of obliviousness.

This communion between E.T. and Elliot, their love story, is the film's center of gravity, a boy embracing, all at once, the vulnerable "other" and the best in himself, the capacity to feel and be hurt, to love. *E.T.,* on its most basic level, speaks to its audience about a potentiality for the human. Although he is alienated from himself and bent on violence, modern man is not irretrievably lost. A few young souls still retain an intangible commodity, the latent capacity to respond to suffering with genuine compassion.

STUDY QUESTIONS

1. Identify the claim in Mike's paper. Is this claim appropriate to the assignment? Why or why not?

2. Mark the places in Mike's paper where you need specific references to the movie to be convinced that his claim is valid.

3. Use a dictionary to define any words you don't understand in the first two sentences of paragraph 3. Rewrite these sentences so they will inform rather than call attention to themselves.

4. How does paragraph 3 fit into the paper? What arguments could you make for deleting it?

Guide for Reading

Steve's paper is an inadequate response to the assignment. It doesn't focus on a single idea; instead, it mentions a number of topics briefly, making it read as responses to a list of questions. The final sentence in the first paragraph makes a claim that could be the thesis of the paper. Had Steve explained and supported this idea, his paper would contain a subject and focus appropriate to the assignment.

SAMPLE FILM PAPER 6

E.T.

Steve T. (a sophomore)

Steven Spielberg's film, *E.T.* fulfilled each of the three main reasons for making a movie. It was one of the most successful movies ever at the box office and it experiences huge profits again when it was released on video tape in December of 1988. It still provides exciting entertainment for the young and old. I have a four year old nephew and he has watched it at least fifteen complete times on tape. Finally it expressed several points to the public. It showed that intense family problems can be saved from an outside force. That it is good to hold on to a good portion of childhood and fantasies. The most important point to me, though, would be that the innocent can overcome and outwit harmful forces.

The casting and acting for this film was exceptional, especially for that of the character "Elliott." I can see much of my own personality in Elliott. I still have much of my childhood in me - much more than most of my peers, especially those in high school. One can be teased to the point where it hurts under these conditions. However, I think that it will make a person better in the long run and more aware of he needs of the innocent and abused.

The camera angles I enjoyed the most were the ones when the audience got to see a huge and a scary world through E.T.'s eyes. This was used when E.T. was dressed up for Halloween.

The uses of light were effective. At the beginning of the movie the jagged movements of flashlights by the scientists represented

Fine and Applied Arts

danger and the unknown. While the light in E.T.'s finger represented good and magic. The voice of E.T. was the voice of "innocence." It was perfect. The selection of music was also good. It made the audience become more involved.

The appearance of E.T. was inviting. His body movements were like those of a three year old and this made you want to help him. I think the scene where the bikes begin to fly is one of the best in movie history. It enables E.T. to meet his ship and it gives the boys a memory for a lifetime.

At the beginning of the movie when the scientists were running through the forest with flashlights you could also hear keys bouncing. Those keys might be serving as symbols. Such as E.T. would need to return to the same forest to return home. That E.T. is the "key" in Elliott's happiness and satisfaction in his desires. Also that E.T. is the "key" in the world realizing the need for goodness even if it requires deep sacrifices.

This movie will be enjoyed for generations to come and if there has ever been a perfect movie made, this would have to be it.

STUDY QUESTIONS

1. In paragraph 2, Steve uses personal experience as a means of explaining the character of Elliott. Does this personal reference enlighten or confuse you?

2. Make a list of the topics Steve mentions. Take one and explain what he needs to do to develop it into a convincing analysis.

MUSIC ASSIGNMENT 1

Course: **Music Appreciation**

In the course of this semester you will attend eight musical events (concerts or recitals) and write a review for each of them. Your reviews should include the time of the concert, the performer(s), the titles and composers of the selections, and an evaluation of the concert. The evaluation, the most important part of your review, should briefly describe each selection, reflecting, whenever possible, what we have covered in class. This evaluation must be objective; when you express your opinion, you must make it clear that it is your opinion and not an objective statement of evaluation. These reviews should be typed, at least one page long and never over two pages. Any paper that appears sloppily written and contains many spelling and grammar errors will be returned ungraded.

Analysis of Music Assignment 1

This assignment is from an entry-level music appreciation course designed to introduce students to classical music. Its goal is to enhance their understanding and appreciation. You should note, however, that appreciating and liking something are not the same things, and you should keep this point in mind as you read the papers that follow.

If you were asked to respond to an assignment like this one, there are several things you would need to consider. After you have attended a concert and have listened carefully to the music, perhaps even taking notes, you would want to look again at the assignment before you started writing. The assignment allows you to choose which concerts you attend, so you must identify the concert and the performer(s), usually in the first paragraph of your review. When you mention each selection, describe it musically, based on what you have learned in class. You should also evaluate how the musicians performed each piece, giving examples of their strengths and weaknesses. Up through this point in the review, your tastes are not important. You want to show that you understand what you have learned in class and that you can apply this knowledge intelligently to the music performed at the concert.

According to the assignment, you may express your opinion as long as you make it clear to readers that you are doing so. Nevertheless, there is no point in simply saying that you did or did not like the concert. A reader's response most likely will be, "So what?" To avoid such a totally defeating question, *explain* why you liked or disliked the concert. Provide detailed reasons related to the performance of the music.

A good way to approach one of these reviews is to write for a general audience, not your instructor. You might want to consider trying to publish the review in the arts page of your college or hometown news-

Fine and Applied Arts

paper, for example. Having a real audience in mind (rather than the artificial audience of your teacher) will help you produce a more detailed, informative, and interesting review.

You should take the length guidelines of any assignment seriously. In this case, the teacher specifies that students' reviews should be "at least one page long and never over two pages." Such guidelines usually reveal how difficult or how detailed a teacher believes a given task is.

Guide for Reading

Tamara's paper is a fairly good response to the assignment, and it has the potential to be outstanding. Notice that her first two paragraphs show that she listened carefully and applied class material to her descriptions of the Bach Concerto. The third paragraph, however, is a disappointment because it lacks the details necessary to inform and convince readers. As you read this paragraph, consider what details you would want in the paper.

SAMPLE MUSIC PAPER 1

University Chamber Orchestra

Tamara W. (a freshman)

On March 29, the University Chamber Orchestra performed at the Broyhill Music Center. This was an especially interesting concert for two reasons: <u>The first, being the diversity of the tone color of the instruments</u>. The overall effect was that of a full, well-rounded sound that held the audience's attention. The second reason I found the concert interesting, was that the pieces performed were all from the Baroque period. The pieces were distinctly different from those I had heard from the Classical and Romantic eras.

The performance began with J.S. Bach's Concerto in C minor for Two Harpsichords. This piece consisted of three movements: Allegro, Adagio, and Allegro. Featured in this piece were harpsichordists H. Max Smith and Rodney Reynerson. I would definitely classify the harpsichord melody as contrapuntal. The harpsichords' melodies were deeply interwoven and intertwined.

though each harpsichord strain was dependent <u>upon</u> its opposing strain. It definitely made for an interesting performance.

The final piece was Concerto Grosso in D major, Op. 6, No. 4, by Arcangelo Corelli. This composition also consisted of three movements: Adagio-Allegro, Adagio-Vivace, and Allegro. This piece definitely showed the skills and expertise of the orchestra. The soloists also demonstrated their virtuosity and expressive interpretations of the music. The conductor, William Wilson, did an excellent job at keeping the orchestra on cue and in tempo. I really enjoyed the concert, and am glad to have had the opportunity to attend it.

Analysis of Sample Music Paper 1

According to the instructor who received these papers, Tamara's is one of the best in a class of 75 to 100 students. We can see that it does indeed follow the points of the assignment, and Tamara has shown that she listened carefully and perceptively. She gives good reasons for finding the concert interesting in the first two paragraphs; she seems convincing, and most readers aren't likely to suspect that she is just trying to please her instructor. Identifying the pieces as Baroque and different in sound from Classical and Romantic music shows that she can make a connection between class material and the music it applies to.

The second paragraph is the strongest in the review. Describing the melodies as "contrapuntal" and "deeply interwoven and intertwined" shows that Tamara listened carefully to the first selection and recognized what was going on musically. Although by some standards her description isn't very sophisticated, it meets the expectations better-trained readers would have for a good student in a general music appreciation class.

The third paragraph, however, doesn't match the second. Tamara compliments the soloists, the orchestra, and the conductor, but she gives no descriptions of how the performers showed their skills, expertise, and virtuosity. Although we get some idea what Bach's Concerto in C minor for Two Harpsichords *sounds* like, we don't learn much about Corelli's Concerto Grosso. Tamara doesn't even tell us who the soloists were. Moreover, how did this piece show the "skills and expertise of the orchestra"? How did the soloists show their "virtuosity and expressive interpretations"? After such a good beginning, this last paragraph makes it seem as though Tamara either didn't listen carefully to the Corelli

Fine and Applied Arts

Concerto or was just anxious to finish writing her review. She could have done what was necessary and still kept within the two-page limit.

Guide for Reading

Charles' review is an unacceptable response to the assignment. Although he shows that he listened carefully and enjoyed the performance, his review doesn't focus on the music at all. He has used the assignment to confess to his teacher that he didn't want to attend the concert, but that once he was there he enjoyed the music in spite of himself. His teacher may have experienced some pleasure in learning that Charles realizes now that required concerts need not be a burden, but the teacher probably didn't appreciate the fact that Charles' paper fails to do what the assignment asked for.

SAMPLE MUSIC PAPER 2

Untitled

Charles F. (a freshman)

A concert that appeared at first to be just another ego-trip for a great performer, and just another boring college have-too turned into a real treat. Mr. Ervin Monroe was vary impressive, not only as a Flutist, but as an entertainer and teacher. Mr. Monroe with Mr. Allen Kindt teamed up and provided a lucky few with a great evening of music and entertainment.

As the concert started it seemed as though Mr. Monroe had very little respect for the accompanying Pianist. The facial expressions, and the body language seemed to indicate a vary snotty professional. However, it became clear vary quickly, that such was not the case, but just the opposite. Mr. Monroe praised the playing of Mr. Kindt at every point possible through out the concert. This , along with Mr. Monroe giving a brief overview of each selection, warmed up the audience, and provided a enjoyable evening.

A bit of history on each selection, and some joking around can really add a lot to a concert. Not that the music, was not excellent in itself. Mr. Monroe clearly demonstrated how a flute should be played. At times he seemed to be able to confuse the listener, as it actually seemed as if there were several flutes, or even other instruments playing with him. In his own selections, which he had written, he used unconventional devices in his playing, such as humming into the flute and clicking of his tongue to produce a much different tone color than one would normally hear from a flute.

    Over all Mr. Monroe turned out to be a vary personal, and humors entertainer, not to mention his wonderful ability to play the flute. The combined tone color of the flute and piano turned out to be a vary enjoyable evening of music.

Analysis of Sample Music Paper 2

Charles seems to have based his review on the fact that he didn't expect to enjoy the concert. He praises the performers for saving him from a dull evening when he should be focusing more on the music itself. He does show that he listened and was impressed with Mr. Monroe's expertise with the flute (third paragraph), but this analysis is a minor part of his review. In fact, Charles ends up making this important component of the concert seem a bit trivial. He states in paragraph 3, "not that the music, was not excellent in itself," and in paragraph 4 "not to mention his wonderful ability to play the flute." Moreover, Charles exhibits three problems that should be avoided in a review of this type. The first is sarcasm. In the opening sentence, he writes, "just another ego-trip for a great performer." This appraisal serves no purpose other than to reveal Charles' negative attitude toward solo performers.

    The second is the reference to the concert as a college requirement ("just another boring college have-too"). Again, Charles is revealing his bad attitude, dangerously so in this case, because his criticism of the requirement is unavoidably a criticism of the teacher who will grade his paper. In addition, of course, by indicating that he disapproves of the occasion for writing this review, Charles discredits himself as a reviewer to be taken seriously.

    The third problem is judging the musicians' characters in a way that is unrelated to their performance. In the second paragraph, Charles describes his misconceptions about the character of Mr. Monroe based on facial expressions and body language. Even had Mr. Monroe been the arrogant professional Charles originally thought he was, this information is inappropriate as expressed in this section of the review. It is true that a performer's character can adversely affect his or her performance and the audience's enjoyment of it. Whenever such is the case, reviewers need to explain the problem objectively just as they would explain any other problems that affected the performance.

In the final analysis, we finish this review knowing perhaps more than we would like about Charles' bad attitudes, but we know very little about the concert he attended. The image Charles creates of himself isn't enhanced any by the surface errors that riddle his paper. His consistent use of "vary" for "very" and other misspellings indicate a careless disregard for the assignment and for readers.

Writing Assignments

The difficulty of the following assignments depends mainly on your own taste and knowledge of music. To do well for each one, you will have to listen to the music much more carefully than you are probably accustomed to doing. A good author will inform readers of the significance of sounds that a normal listener is not aware of. The papers should reflect a thoughtful analysis of the music and should be free of surface errors.

1. Write a two-page review of a recently released album. Include, where appropriate:
   —a very brief comparison to other albums by the same person/group
   —a discussion of lyrics as a theme of the album
   —a description of the sound
   —the musical genre
   —an evaluation of how this album rates alongside others by the same person/group or alongside others in the same genre
   —specific examples of songs, lyrics, and sounds as support for your discussion
   Rolling Stone magazine provides good examples of album reviews in its "Recordings" section.
2. Take the same song recorded by two different artists and compare the two versions in a two-page paper. Focus on such aspects as tempo, instruments, voices, key, and overall sound. Evaluate the two versions, answering the question: In what ways (if any) is the new version an improvement over the old? Use specific examples to support your discussion.
3. Attend a concert of classical music (a chamber orchestra, a full orchestra, a recital) and write a review appropriate for the arts

section of your school newspaper. Include the date of the concert, the performer(s), the selections played, a description of the movements and featured instruments of each selection, and an evaluation of the concert. Avoid letting your personal taste show. Instead, focus on how well the music was performed and how appropriate the selections seemed for the audience.

MUSIC ASSIGNMENT 2

Course: **Analytical Techniques**

Analysis of a Piece of Music

You are to analyze a piece of music (approved by the instructor) in an eight- to twelve-page paper. This analysis should include an explanation and description of the following:

a) structure
b) melody
c) harmony
d) formal elements
e) rhythmic elements

Your paper will be graded on the accuracy of your analysis and appropriate use of terminology. In addition, your paper should exhibit the characteristics of good writing: logical organization, correct grammar, and a pleasing style.

Your reader is someone who is familiar with the piece of music and with the methods and terminology of music analysis.

Analysis of Music Assignment 2

This assignment is for the final paper in a senior music class entitled Analytical Techniques. The paper takes the place of a final exam and is designed to show what has been learned in the course.

After reading the assignment and the papers, you will recognize that no one can respond adequately to this assignment without extensive training in analyzing music. The paper is expected to be a sophisticated analysis for two reasons: first, it is for an upper-level class;

Fine and Applied Arts   **683**

second, it is the culmination of the semester's work. If you were assigned such a paper in this type of class, you would be expected to exhibit a sound knowledge of the techniques of analysis as well as the ability to explain a piece of music to an informed reader. Because your reader is knowledgeable, your analysis must be perceptive and correct and should not contain an explanation of your methods and terminology.

   Preparation for this assignment involves listening to a piece of music many times very carefully. You would want to be completely familiar with what the piece sounds like. In addition, you would need to use the score (the written form for the entire orchestra) so you could explain what the composer wrote, note by note and measure by measure when necessary. Although such analysis may seem tedious and unrelated to the ability to enjoy music, it is nevertheless an important step in the process of understanding classical compositions. For example, after reading the two sample papers for this assignment, you will realize that composers of classical music work within a recognizable structure.

Guide for Reading

Steve's paper exhibits his familiarity with Mozart's Symphony No. 40 and with appropriate analytical methods. It also demonstrates his ability to explain his analysis to readers. Even if you aren't familiar with the music or the methods of analysis, you can appreciate the careful analyzing and clarity of expression in Steve's paper, because he interprets the music for his readers.

SAMPLE
M U S I C
PAPER 3

Mozart—Symphony No. 4 in G Minor—an Analysis

Steve G. (a senior)

              Movement one—*Allegro Molto*
   The Mozart Symphony in G Minor (k. 550) is a stunning work of art. It would seem that one could study it forever and continually find new things to fascinate one about its artful conception. This work is one which is fascinating to sit an listen to and record impressions about its characteristic sound and dig deep to find

out why it sounds so. Adjectives to describe this G minor symphony might be words like intense, persistent, driving, and maybe even forboding. It seems that although the piece takes excursions into pleasant lilting passages, the intense, driving g-minor mood persistently asserts itself from beginning to end. The mood Mozart creates through this work is accomplished by an amazingly simple device—the minor second. In discussing this work, it will be impossible to do so without addressing this symphony's persistent motif—the minor second.

The work begins with a fairly straightforward sonata-allegro first movement. The opening theme occurs immediately without an introduction and the first thing heard in the melody is a minor second going from E-flat to D. This theme creates a certain amount of a feeling of unrest almost immediately. Examination shows that the melody begins on the fifth scale degree. The melody without the added tension of the E-flats is lonely sounding enough. The melody does not find its way to a tonic note until measure four and not again until measure 11 (except in passing). All of these effects combine together for the mood Mozart creates at the onset. The first musical period structure is then ended with a hammering half-cadence. This additional tension created by the extended half-cadence continues almost unmercifully for it is only resolved in a pianissimo chord in the strings which is further covered by a stretto bringing in the next phrase. Even on the big V-chords, the minor-second motive appears in the C-sharp moving to D. This happens over a rather assertive unison D played in the strings. Next, the main theme re-enters only to be cut short by the entrance of the transition theme with its abrupt *forte* entrance. It almost seems like a ray of light with its bright B-flat major feel. However measure 34 insists on bringing back the major second interval in the flutes, clarinets, bassoons, and strings with its persistent tension. As in the opening theme, this major second motive is leaning on the dominant scale degree. Measure 42 caps off this section with a half cadence and a grand pause lasting an entire measure. This dramatic pause sets up a perfect stage for the secondary tonal area coming up.

This secondary theme is more subdued and engages in a lot of statement-answer devices between strings and woodwinds.

However, the second-minor motive is not missing. It is evident in the chromatic melody of the second theme and especially measure 58 where it becomes obvious. This section is closed by a PAC in measure extended to measure 72.

Measure 73 brings the closing area with its minor-second motive in the violins and then the basses written in half notes. This sighing motive is suddenly disturbed by a big *forte* passage bringing back material from the principal theme. This is all repeated ending on a PAC in measure 88 which is extended several times building to a big extended PAC ending in measure 99. This is the end of the exposition even though there is one more chord, a dominant chord in G-minor, before the repeat sign in measure 100.

The development begins with a stretto in measures 104 and 105 bringing the principal theme back in F-sharp minor. Then it is interesting to note that the theme begins a rapid descent through several keys. It might be added that this descent is by none other than minor seconds. This is evident by observing the bass line beginning in measure 105 then picking up with the bassoons in measure 107. The line moves down through F-sharp, E-sharp, D, and then drops to C.

Mozart has to bring in his fugal section and it comes in measure 115. This fugato is built around the beginning of the principal theme so the minor seconds are still persistently creeping up with their forboding aura. The principal theme is traded between bass and treble instruments. This fugato ends in measure 134 followed by a change of color in measure 139. For the sake of conciseness, all instances of minor seconds will not be discussed. The motive is developed thoroughly in the remainder of this section. Its presence is obvious. The fact of such a thorough development of the minor second motive gives evidence of its purposeful usage as opposed to an accidental device brought on only by chromaticism.

The recapitulation begins in measure 165 with a stretto. The recap is the same as in the beginning exposition, except for a new counter melody in the bassoon (m. 168), up until measure 185 where the entrance of some A-flats take the melody off in a new direction. The new direction leads to E-flat major in measure

191. This key is across from its parallel place in the exposition which is in B-flat major. Here in measure 191, it is not only a different key, but a different texture as well, the bass instruments having a line running in counterpoint to the theme which goes back to the arpeggiated pattern from the beginning in measure 193. Measure 199, though, brings back this fugato which extends the transition a bit. Finally measure 211 looks a little more like what is supposed to be here. It is finally in G-minor and the material is more like in the beginning and the secondary theme comes in, finally, in measure 227. To understand what is happening, it is necessary to go back to measure 191, where the transition theme first enters. It is hard to understand why it is in E-flat major. The transition theme in the exposition was in B-flat, the parallel major of G-minor. The message becomes clearer when the theme comes in again in the basses in measure 198. This entrance is in F minor, but the picture is still unclear until the theme finally comes in in G minor. The listener is led to believe by the structure of the rest of the movement that maybe Mozart is going to leave this happy theme in a major key, but with this type preparation, the second theme appears in G-minor. The key of G minor ominously asserts itself now. This theme is somehow not the same in G minor as it was in B-flat major. Maybe hearing it first in a major key and then later in a minor key makes the minor key seem odd. Nevertheless, G minor asserts itself as the home key of this work.

Things finish in a fairly predictable manner with the closing theme and its characteristic motives. The question arises as to where the movement ends. Is there a coda? The best answer for this analysis is that, yes, there is a coda. The reason lies in that all the material is similar to the exposition ending except a segment from measure 281–193. This section brings back to principal theme like a coda does and is of a softer, declining character. It has no ideas that link it to the preceding phrase. Mozart must have decided to interrupt before the cadence to insert his coda and then insert the final cadence and extensions from the recap. Thus, it sounds as if there is really not a coda at first, but there is not another explanation for the purpose of this material. The coda almost seems to be there for the purpose of

Fine and Applied Arts

bringing ___ back to minor second one more time. In measure 281, the orchestra ascends chromatically building tremendous minor-second tension preparing for the last statement of material from the exposition.

Movement Two—*Andante*

This *Andante* movement stands out as the bright spot of the symphony being the only movement really in a major key, E-flat. The opening theme seems so pleasant and serene as the violas immediately establish the tonic note and reinforce it over two bars of repetition. This movement seems to be in huge contrast to the first movement but is artfully integrated with the rest of the symphony by the use of the minor second. Amid this placid theme, notice the base line in measure two. It contains minor seconds. Also measure 4 begins the violins with an A-flat to G minor second. Measures 5 and 6 become more bold in minor second usages with the appogiatura on the down beat. Is this just an accident or the product of a wonderfully organized mind? It is surely a stamp that makes this movement inherently a part of this symphony. In measure 7, the motif is again present. This instance could very well be a shadow of the first movement principal theme. Suppose the original theme were in six-eight time. It might look like this:

Compare that to:

The similarities are possible. Other minor second instances abound, but for brevity, only important instances will be noted.

This movement seems to be a *sonata-allegro* form, but certain complications make it difficult to identify all the sections of the *sonata-allegro* form. The exposition runs fairly smoothly with the PTA concluding in measure 19. The next theme seems like a secondary theme without a transition entering abruptly in the dominant key. One thing that is difficult to explain with this idea is the primary theme statement entering in measure 29 in D-flat major. The only logical explanation is that it must be a transition. Therefore, measures 20 through 36 must be transitional modulating to the dominant key. The secondary theme then enters in measure 37.

The second theme, in the key of the dominant, is another light theme like the first. It begins with the pick-up notes to measure 37. It extends to the repeat sign in measure 52 with a PAC in the dominant key.

The development goes back to the principal theme for material. Interestingly enough, what is seen right away in the strings (m. 53 with pick-up) is a minor second. The section continues with the thirty-second-note motive and other fragments of the primary theme until measure 74 where a recapitulation eases in. The primary theme is restated only partially, ending in measure 85. The transition theme comes back in measure 86, but in measure 88, seemingly out of nowhere comes something else probably derived from the bass line in measure 2 of the piece. Measure 90 continues only for this new motive to interrupt again in measures 92 and 93. Then the primary theme finishes off till the thirty-second-note theme enters again through measure 98. Mozart, here, seems to be combining fragments of all the themes for the modulation back to tonic E-flat. Finally, after this rather extensive bridge, the second theme is back in measure 108. Actually, beginning in measure 97, everything is synchronized with the exposition. This movement ends without a coda.

Movement Three—*Menuetto and Trio*

The Menuetto is in a continuous rounded binary form beginning in G minor, cadencing in the dominant key in the middle (m. 14) then moving back to G minor. This movement again manifests again that elusive minor second especially in measures 16 and 17. The violin line contains a counter to the melody. In measure 16 the melody has a D against an E-flat in the violins and bassoon. This E-flat is resolved by a minor second to D. This device again pierces through with that ever present unrest.

The trio is a pleasant diversion. Notice the minor second resolution in measure 12 in the flute. Here is another binary form moving off the dominant and back. The trio provides lovely contrast before the *Da Capo* brings it back to the *Menuetto.*

This whole movement would be an A-B-A form. With a contrasting B section and harmonically closed sections, the whole movement would then be full sectional ternary.

Movement Four—*Allegro Assai*

A rocket theme opens up the *Allegro Assai* movement. At the top of the rocket motive (m. 2) is an appoggiatura resolving down by—oh no—another minor second. The bass line in measure 3 holds minor seconds also. With the chords going I-V-I-V-I-V in measures 3 and 4, why did Mozart not just give the basses G-D-G-D-G-D, the roots of these chords? Obviously he wanted that minor second. Also, it is interesting to note that the material in measures 3 and 4 is right out of the first movement. In these measures, the rhythm is:

In the opening theme in the first movement the rhythm is:

There must be a relation here. Additionally, the violins in measures 3 and 4 carry a motive straight from movement one. It can be found in measure 98 of the first movement as well as measure 296 in the violin part. These devices work for an amazing sense of unity throughout the symphony.

The PTA ends and the transition begins with another motive from measure 276 of movement one. The primary theme is developed through the transition until a half cadence brings a halt in measure 70. The second theme, abounding in minor seconds begins in measure 71 and ends in measure 101. The closing area picks up in measure 101 with themes derived from the PTA. The exposition then ends in measure 124.

The beginning of the development is an interesting case. It is strings and woodwinds in unison. In these eight measures the notes can be paired up by those notes which form diminished seventh intervals. This shows that Mozart could have been simply outlining a series of diminished seventh chords.

One theoretician has suggested a different idea for the beginning of the development. Heinrich Jalwowetz in his article entitled "On the Spontaneity of Shoenberg's Music" (*Music Quarterly*— 1944) points out this section as being the closest thing to twelve-tone writing in classical music. He points out that beginning with the C on the third beat of measure 2 to measure 9 (disregarding the triplet in m. 4) there are ten tones of the chromatic scale. They are treated with equal value and not as traditional chromaticism. He states that because Mozart wrote it as a unison passage, that leads one to believe that he conceived it from a melodic standpoint. This is seemingly a leap into something new for Mozart. However, the very boldness of this venture gives it validity.

The development moves on abounding in minor seconds creating an air of mystery and expectancy such that enough tension is built up that a long dominant pedal is not necessary. Two measures with a pedal in the horns (ms. 202 and 203) seem to be ample in setting the stage for the recapitulation. In the meantime, several familiar ideas pop up such as the bassoon and oboe line in measures 133 and 134. This comes from movement one. The primary theme is thoroughly developed by fragmentation and other means. Again, Mozart remains faithful to creating fugal sections within the transition using the primary theme and creating points of imitation with it.

The tension builds to a grand pause and the recapitulation begins. The primary theme is abbreviated ending in measure 222. The retransition is not unlike the transition and it makes its way back to a half cadence in G minor where the second theme begins in measure 247. The remainder of the recapitulation is altered slightly from the exposition for the purpose of building up to a big ending. The cadence finally comes in measure 302 and is extended to the end.

In the final analysis, this work is thoroughly G minor and thoroughly integrated. Every movement fits with others like a puzzle to form the symphony. The key to this is the first interval of the first theme of the work. Similarly, Beethoven's entire *Symphony No. 5* revolves around the motive in the first two measures of the piece. Mozart uses the minor second with its unforgiving restlessness to unify a monumental work.

STUDY QUESTIONS

1. Point out the specific aspects of Steve's paper that show he has listened to Mozart's Symphony No. 40 attentively.

2. In what ways does Steve blend technical and emotional analysis?

3. Briefly explain how Steve ties his paper together in the same way that Mozart tied his symphony together.

4. Read each section of Steve's paper until you feel familiar with the patterns he describes. Listen to the corresponding movement of the symphony. In what ways is your enjoyment of the music enhanced by the information in Steve's analysis?

5. Look carefully at the title of Steve's paper. Mozart indeed wrote a Symphony No. 4, but he did so as a child. What effect is Steve's error likely to have on his intended audience?

Guide for Reading

George seems to have rushed through this assignment, because his analysis is confusing and tells readers very little about Sulek's Sonata. His surface errors and incomplete explanations obscure most of his analysis. What we *can* understand of George's work makes his shortcomings seem all the more unfortunate; it appears that Sulek was experimenting with standard forms and produced an intriguing variation on them. But George doesn't tell us much more than this.

> **SAMPLE**
> **MUSIC**
> **PAPER 4**

Stjepan Sulek's *Sonata for Trombone and Piano*

George L. (a senior)

Stjepan Sulek's *Sonata for Trombone and Piano* is a contemporary piece that consists of only one movement. The fact that this sonata only has one continues movement instead of three contrasting movements makes it interesting to look into its form.

The first section, a simple melody line on the trombone is accompanied by the complex sextuplets figure of the piano. This section is the introduction section of the piece. By looking forward into the next section which is a faster section and the fact that the tonal center of the section is "F" (which is the dominant of B-flat), the key of the next section further shows that this is the introduction. The introduction consists of four phrases that all end on a half cadence, which gives the section a dominant pedal feel through out (m. 3, 6, 12, 16–20). From measure 16 through 20, the dominant preparation is very obvious with this extension. All the half cadences make the form of this section a phrase group which is very often found in an introduction.

The beginning of the section after the introduction is very obvious. The tempo change, melodic changes from simple calm to rhythmic, the accompaniment change from busy sextuplets to easy eighth and articulation change from legato to staccato are all very easy to see. This section consists of a short melodic motive that is only a phrase long. The motive is repeated but with the trombone and piano changing roles (m. 28). End of measure 36 something new happens but it is not a new section; it is in fact a transition into the next section. At this point this piece seems to be very much like a sonata form with introduction and now a simple short section that merely points out the key "B-flat," is very much like the PTA of the form. If this next section (m. 37) is truly a transition, it should take the piece into a new key of the STA. In fact the piece does go into a new tonal area at measure 45. The two measure introduction to the STA (m. 47) is already in the tonal area of "C". At measure 53 something strange happens: the tonal center goes to "G-flat" and the melody is repeated in "G-flat". The problem is that the key of C and G-flat are both far away from the original B-flat. Anyway at measure 62 there is a change. First the solo trombone drops out, also the texture of the piano thickens and finally the tempo goes down again, a new section (m. 66). What is this section? If the form of this piece is indeed a sonata form, this section will have to be the closing theme. But with the transitory characteristic of this section without a conclusive cadence, it is time to doubt—is this a sonata form?

Transition comes again (m. 74) with the new tempo and the texture changes from five or more voices to four voices in octaves. The tonal center finally falls into "A-flat" at measure 107. The new section after this transition is in fact not new. The melody is based on the motive of the section right after the introduction which is the PTA theme. It is stretched out and is done in the way of the introduction style with simple melody and complex accompaniment (this time sixteenth). To get back to the form and try not to be lost, the following is the form up to this point: Intro—PTA—trans 1—STA—trans 2—CT—trans 3—PTA—. After all this the trans 1 theme comes back in the same key but develops into a larger section and ends up in the key of F. Is this a dominant preparation for the tonic? (measure 144 STA comes back in the key of F then goes into the key of C-flat just like the previous time, down a 4th). Transition 2 comes back just the same with the transitory CT following. Finally transition 3 brings the key back to the original tonic B-flat (m. 175). If this is truly a sonata form, now is the time for the recapitulation, but not in this case. An intense section that moves through keys and lands back in B-flat. Perhaps this is a codetta? But this codetta is transitory again. The last section of the piece comes with no warning and it is the "introduction."

Intro—PTA—trans 1—STA—trans 2—CTA—trans 3—PTA—

trans 1—STA—trans 2 CT (dominant key)—trans(-Ending (Intro). Looking at the form of the piece, one can only conclude that it is a free form. But can one say more about this free form? It is obvious that this is a continuous free form with all these transitions; it is hard not to be continuous. The sections of this piece so closely resemble the sections of a sonata form and the A-B-C-D-B-C-D-A structure also resembles a *rondo* structure (with a lack of refrains), plus the tempo changes resemble closely the fast-slow-fast feelings of an ordinary sonata movement, giving the piece a condensed feeling of a complete sonata. Perhaps the composer has successfully condensed the classic sonata form.

STUDY QUESTIONS

1. George's paper would have to be completely rewritten to be informative, mainly because his listening and analyzing skills are so poor. The paper itself contains problems that further confuse readers. Rewrite the following sentences so they will be correct and informative: sentence 3 in paragraph 2, sentence 6 in paragraph 4, and sentence 11 ("If this is truly") in paragraph 4.

2. Even though George's paper is not generally informative, it is not totally devoid of information. Make a list (however short) of what you have learned about Selek's *Sonata for Trombone and Piano*. Make a list of questions that you feel need to be answered for the analysis to be comprehensive.

Writing Assignment

Even though you may not have the knowledge and skills to analyze a classical composition in the manner required by the above assignment, you can analyze a piece of music you are familiar with by focusing on less technical aspects of music. In a 3- to 5-page paper, analyze a relatively short piece of music (3–6 minutes in length) that you enjoy and are familiar with. Describe and explain the following:

a. instrument used
b. performers
c. rhythmic elements
d. harmonic elements
e. interplay between vocals and instruments (if appropriate)
f. emotive qualities
g. genre

Your readers are people who listen to music but who may not be familiar with your choice. Your paper should make readers aware of how your chosen piece of music sounds and fits in with the other music of its period.

Part Four **BUSINESS**

WRITING IN BUSINESS

Overview

Most of the writing produced in this country is related to either business or government, so it isn't surprising that business schools around the country stress the importance of producing readable prose. Some of the larger schools have their own communications departments. Others ask students to take business writing classes offered through English departments.

The popularity of business as a major has increased significantly over the last decade and a half, and now it isn't unusual to find colleges where over 50 percent of the undergraduates are business majors. At the same time, many larger universities, such as UCLA and UNC Chapel Hill, have either eliminated or are planning to eliminate the undergraduate degree to focus their energy on graduate training. Competition in the remaining undergraduate programs is intense as a result.

On many campuses, freshmen and sophomores are not allowed to enroll in business courses. The first two years of college are viewed as a screening process to reduce the strain on business schools; therefore, juniors and seniors often take very demanding courses in business for which they have little preparation, particularly regarding writing. They frequently experience serious difficulties with papers because the writing they must do for their business classes is quite different from what they were asked to do in their general education courses in history, English, philosophy, and so on. Business writing tends to be much more practical than anything students encounter in freshman composition or other liberal arts courses. Such courses generally ask students to analyze and reflect, whereas, in a tangible sense, business writing is used to get things done.

The pragmatism in business writing reflects the nature of the field. Certainly, the popular image of business people, especially executives, suggests that their lives consist almost entirely of hurrying off to power meetings, closing multimillion dollar deals, and making crucial command decisions at a staccato pace. But like so many of our popular images, this one is more the product of Hollywood imaginations than of reality. Absent are the more mundane but vital aspects of conducting business, such as keeping records and writing memos, reports, and letters of all types. The professional image that successful business people have of themselves is in many ways contrary to the popular one: They value both their ability to keep accurate and accessible records and their ability to communicate far more highly than they do the speed of their decision-making. This attitude may even be reinforced by historical factors. Archaeological evidence indicates that the origin of writing is linked to the need ancient business people had to keep records and to communicate orders and invoices to distant customers.

Successfully meeting the demands for clear, timely documents can be very challenging, even for those who receive some training in business writing during college. As the size and complexity of a company increase, so do its written communications. Memos become a daily routine for managers who must keep employees apprised of goals, policies, decisions, and so forth. Although the telephone has become an indispensable tool in businesses of all sizes, those who use it understand the necessity of following up important phone conversations with a letter confirming the contents of the conversation. Putting the key points of a conversation in writing provides a permanent record of decisions and agreements, which is crucial in view of the fallibility of human memory. It also recognizes that people don't always understand one another very well and allows parties to amend or clarify points that seemed lucid over the telephone but actually were not. Such records take time, however—in some instances, up to an hour for each letter.

Usually the province of bigger companies, reports offer an efficient way of communicating information to large groups of people, whether they be employees or stockholders. Proposals, on the other hand, are often unrelated to the size of a business. In fact, startup companies owned by one person or by a partnership may succeed or fail on the basis of an effective proposal. For example, the federal government has numerous set-aside programs designed to help small businesses owned by traditionally marginalized groups, such as women and blacks. The Clean Air Act Amendments of 1990 illustrate how these programs operate: 20 percent of the total budget of $15 billion is set aside for such groups, and access to these funds hinges on a company's ability to write an effective proposal to request contracted work.

The challenge of producing readable, timely documents is heightened by the typical office environment. Offices are usually noisy and full of distractions. Recent college graduates often find that even a relatively simple task, such as writing an internal memo, can be difficult because they are used to working in the quiet of their rooms. In addition, the flow of work across one's desk doesn't halt just because an important project is due. Success depends, in part, on being able to handle several tasks simultaneously and on being able to set priorities for projects. It also depends on being able to meet deadlines. If a report wasn't needed yesterday, chances are it is needed before noon tomorrow. Because the consequences of turning a paper in late to a teacher are relatively minimal, many people new to the business world have trouble adjusting to the pressures of unalterable project deadlines. Students who are used to having time to work through several revisions of a paper for college are often dismayed to discover that in business the schedule may not allow for more than one attempt. In other words, they frequently have to get it right the first time.

Much of the writing students do in school is understood to be a reflection of their effort and mastery of course material. A good paper—as well as one that isn't so good—therefore says something about the writer who produced it. Business writing, however, is more inclusive. The people who produce the proposals, reports, and letters of daily enterprise characterize their companies as well as themselves. The public image of a company is enhanced or diminished with every circulated document. Given this reality, we can readily appreciate the value business places on high-quality writing.

Documentation

Business does not have a preferred style of documentation, and in this respect it resembles writing in the sciences. Some organizations and journals ask writers to use the APA style, which is outlined in the overview to writing in the social sciences. Other organizations and journals ask writers to use the Chicago style or the numeric style. The Chicago style is also outlined in the overview to writing in the social sciences, whereas the numeric style is outlined in the overview to writing in the life and applied sciences.

Although a variety of styles is acceptable, there is no question that business deems accurate and proper documentation to be important. The need for documentation is generally limited to reports and proposals, but it is a need informed by the principles we have discussed in other portions of this text. Accurate documentation reflects the care and diligence writers bring to their work. The effort is tedious, it's true, but writers and businesses cannot afford carelessness.

12 Business Writing

INTRODUCTION TO WRITING IN BUSINESS

The writing people produce in business falls into four major categories: memos, letters, proposals, and reports. Courses in business communication concentrate on teaching students how to generate these forms of writing. Many business classes, however, often limit writing tasks to analyses of reading, asking students to apply principles studied in the course to a situation described in an article. Other classes ask students to study case problems—scenarios reflecting real business situations—and to write responses that solve them.

If you are thinking about becoming a business major, you will probably take a business writing course in your junior or senior year. This single chapter isn't intended to substitute for such a course; it aims simply to provide a brief introduction to the kinds of writing that students in business courses are asked to complete. The first assignment, for example, involves a case study from a business administration course. The second involves analyzing a magazine article about business. The criteria for success on these assignments are very similar to those discussed in detail throughout the earlier chapters: They include going beyond the minimum response; providing a reasonable interpretation of the "facts" under analysis; avoiding errors in analysis and in writing, and so on.

For those students who are interested in learning a bit more about the kinds of writing that business people produce, we have included the following summary.

Memos

Memos are brief written documents circulated inside an organization, and they are designed to convey important information to employees quickly. In large companies, reading and writing memos are part of every day's activities. Unfortunately, the sheer volume of memos that people have to read in large organizations means that some messages are ignored or filed away in the waste basket. The key to writing successful memos lies in getting the information across clearly and quickly. For very important memos, the writer may attach a checklist of the recipients' names that will circulate back to him or her to indicate that the message has been read.

A general format has evolved to facilitate the goal of getting information across clearly and quickly, and it involves identifying the sender, the receiver or receivers, the date, and the subject of the communication. A memo about security problems, for example, might begin as follows:

TO: All Swing-Shift Employees
FROM: Patty Smith, Chief of Security
DATE: May 31, 1993
SUBJECT: Office Security

The memo would then describe the problem in two or three sentences and suggest a course of action, such as locking purses and other personal belongings in desks when the employees are away from their work areas, double-locking doors at the end of the day, and so on. The writer might want to conclude with a cordial or encouraging remark to help personalize the communication.

Although the audiences and purposes of memos differ from one situation to the next, students should keep in mind the value of both audience awareness and organization. The former is especially important when a memo conveys unpleasant information or when it aims to get the recipients to do something they aren't inclined to do. The senior editor

Business Writing

of this text, for example, once had to send a memo out to a large group of graduate instructors asking them to be more conscientious about their personal hygiene, because a number of freshmen had complained about body odors making teacher/student conferences unpleasant. The situation was delicate. Audience awareness dictated a humorous approach, which worked in all but a couple of cases.

An analysis of effective memos shows that they have four general features:

1. They state the purpose of the memo immediately.
2. They briefly outline the background that motivates the memo.
3. They present the facts succinctly.
4. They ask for some action/response and close with a cordial comment.

Letters

The volume of business correspondence keeps increasing every year. The United States Postal Service estimates that the amount of business mail it handles annually is approaching 200 *billion* pieces. Because people, companies, and circumstances vary significantly, it's reasonable to assume that the number of different kinds of letters is unlimited. There's no denying that the task of describing each kind of letter is formidable if one takes a case-by-case approach. Grouping letters into categories, however, makes the analysis a bit more manageable.

There are six general types of letters in business:

1. Sales
2. Requests
3. Replies to requests
4. Confirmation
5. Good news
6. Bad news

Each of these categories includes multiple variations. Although this introduction cannot analyze all six categories, much less the variations, it can offer some insight into their structure. The sales letter, for example, can take several different forms. It can offer a product or service to clients, it can provide an employment recommendation for a colleague, or it can even be the cover letter attached to one's resume. Request letters can ask for delivery of a product, information about a service, an increased credit line on a credit card, and so forth.

Generally, sales letters begin by setting the scene. If the aim is to get a client to purchase goods or services, the letter is likely to suggest that the client has a problem that the writer can solve. In the middle portion of the letter, the writer describes how to solve the problem through the use of the offered goods or services. The writer will generally offer evidence to support the claim of a solution by inviting the reader to sample the product or service at a reduced cost or no cost, or will cite testimonials from satisfied customers who have already benefited. In the last part of the letter, the writer shifts to a more personal tone that attempts to get the reader to identify with the problem-solution scenario. Sometimes this takes the form of a rhetorical question: "If *you* were evaluating two similar proposals, which one would you choose—the one produced in black and white or the one produced in full color on the EFG Color Laser Printer?" The letter concludes with a suggestion for action: "Call our toll-free number today to schedule a demonstration."

We can use the above analysis to identify the structure of the sales letter, which is usually unaffected by its content. The letter will have three main parts that function to accomplish the following:

1. Set the scene
2. Establish the claim
3. Encourage action

The structure of the bad-news letter is in some respects similar to the sales letter. But before discussing that structure, it's important to mention that having a heightened sense of audience awareness is crucial to writing an effective bad-news letter. Most of the time, writers should try to convey the bad news without leaving the recipient feeling angry, rejected, or threatened, which makes the task challenging. A large percentage of bad-news letters are written in response to a request that must be denied, so they must also attempt to lessen the disappointment the recipient will naturally feel over not having the request granted.

There are two ways to construct a bad news letter: the direct method and the indirect method. Both set the scene in a way that buffers the bad news to follow. In the indirect approach, however, the buffer is longer, a full paragraph or two. In the direct approach, the bad news often appears in the first sentence, but it usually follows an introductory phrase that offers some explanation or reason.

Perhaps the biggest difference, however, is the middle portion of the two letters. An indirect letter is likely to devote considerable space to the circumstances related to the bad news. If the topic is a company's price increases, for example, the writer will want to discuss inflation, the depressed economy, rising labor and materials costs, and so forth at length. The actual statement about the price increases should be included almost as an afterthought to this tale of economic woe throughout the nation. The aim is to portray the company as well as the customer as victims of larger market forces over which they have no control. In other words, writers should link the fates of the company and the customer, suggesting that both are negatively affected by the bad news.

The final part of the indirect letter should attempt to leave the reader with a positive attitude and a sense of goodwill. Of course, the specific means to this end will differ from writer to writer and from situation to situation, but we can nevertheless identify a couple of strategies. One is to remind the recipient of the good business relationship that has existed in the past. (Companies try to avoid sending bad news letters to new or prospective customers.) The aim is to build a sense of camaraderie and shared experience. The other is to suggest that the situation may change for the better in the future. In both instances, the intention is to close on a positive note.

Very often, the direct approach is used to deny claims against a company (or an individual). In such cases, writers will want to state clearly the reason or reasons for rejecting the claim, so this approach uses the middle portion of the letter to express them. A brief example will help illustrate this strategy. A businesswoman shared with us the following situation, which her company found itself in after she had ordered some office supplies from a mail-order firm. By the time the supplies arrived, she had found a local supplier who sold the same items for much less, so she returned the order. The credit department neglected to note the return and continued to bill the company for three months, adding finance charges regularly. When the return was finally credited, the finance charges remained, and the mail-order firm became very demanding regarding what it considered a delinquent account. Attempts over the telephone to get the charges removed weren't successful.

Finally, when the mail-order firm threatened legal action, our businesswoman responded in writing. The bad news letter she sent stated at the outset that her company refused to pay the amount allegedly owed. It then reviewed very quickly the history of the order and the return and repeated the rejection of the demand for payment "because finance charges cannot be levied when no purchase is made."

This simple, straightforward statement was followed by a short concluding paragraph that, like the conclusion of the indirect approach letter, strove to end the message on a positive note. The writer expressed her expectation that the mail-order company would be willing to cooperate with her on resolving the situation, thus finishing on a positive note. This expectation of cooperation was an important part of the letter, because the mail-order firm had conveyed the same message as part of its perceived role of victim asking a customer to "do the right thing." Our businesswoman reversed the respective roles, in other words, characterizing the mail-order firm as being difficult and threatening and her company as being the victim.

This positive note was tempered by our businesswoman's perception that the mail-order firm might well be disinclined to straighten out their accounting. She therefore reversed as well the firm's threat of legal action by stating that, should it refuse to cooperate, she would view continued efforts to collect the finance charges as harassment and would turn the matter over to her company's legal department. In this case, the threat was appropriate because it served to motivate a resolution.

Our analysis of both indirect and direct bad news letters indicates that they have the following structure:

1. An introduction—even if it is only a phrase—that functions to buffer the bad news.
2. A body that offers a reason or reasons for the bad news.
3. A conclusion that sets a positive tone and an expectation for an improved situation in the future.

Proposals and Reports

Proposals and reports are often, but not always, closely related. For example, in many instances an employee, a group of employees, or an entire firm will propose an endeavor, and if the proposal is accepted, it will be followed by one or more reports that describe the work performed. In other instances, such as financial statements, reports may exist independently.

Although business proposals and reports are significantly argumentative, and consequently employ many of the conventions we've already discussed in earlier chapters of this book, they also use some conventions that don't exist in fields such as history or English. They should include a cover letter that explains their purposes and goals. They may also describe any special procedures or techniques related to the endeavor.

As you might expect, formats differ greatly, depending on the nature of the business and the nature of the proposal or report, so any specific statements regarding organization would be misleading. Nevertheless, a general understanding is possible of how proposals and reports are organized. In addition to a title page, proposals and reports will usually include a table of contents. In many instances, they provide an executive summary that offers an overview of the document's key points. Recipients of proposals and reports don't always read them in their entirety, in part because of their length and complexity. Instead, such documents are often read in sections, with portions going to those who can best understand them—technical information going to programmers, engineers, or scientists; budgeting information going to accountants; and so forth. Managers, on the other hand, need an overview of the entire document so they can make sense of what their specialists recommend. The executive summary provides this overview.

Business proposals and reports, like some kinds of writing in the sciences and social sciences, frequently use subheadings to make the writing more accessible. They commonly have an introduction section that explains the reason for the document, followed by the body with its various sections, followed by a conclusion section. In the case of a proposal, the conclusion will reiterate why an endeavor should be performed by the writer or writers. In the case of a report, the conclusion will provide recommendations for action, state the significance of the information conveyed, summarize the information in a way that serves to forecast future business, and so on. You will see some of these conventions in the reports students produced in response to Assignment 1.

It seems worth noting at this point that business people tend to be more concerned about a document's surface appearance than people in other fields. Poor spelling or sloppy editing on a paper submitted to a political science teacher may simply indicate ignorance, a bad attitude, or both. In the business world, however, an unprofessional image created by poorly prepared documents can also cost firms money, and few business teachers are willing to bear the blame for sending fresh graduates out into the marketplace who are going to lose money rather than make it. Consequently, you may find that teachers in business courses are far less forgiving when it comes to matters of surface correctness. We recommend that you make significant use of a handbook.

The assignments and papers that follow reflect the two common types of writing business students have to do—reports and analyses. They are not representative of the work students do in a business writing course. Studying these assignments and papers, however, should give you a good sense of the conventions and expectations of writing in the undergraduate business curriculum.

BUSINESS ASSIGNMENT 1

Course: Introduction to Business Administration

[*Editor's note: Students in this junior-level business administration class had formed a mock company so they could engage in a range of simulated business activities. The company was a textile and wholesale clothing manufacturer, and with the exception of three students who served as chief administrators, the class was divided into the following departments: Marketing, Personnel, Finance, and Public Relations. Students responded to various problem cases that the teacher introduced and then matched their responses and predicted outcomes with what actually happened. Writing assignments generally asked students to report on simulated activities conducted in class.*

In one case, a strike had shut down the company's largest textile mill, and negotiations had ceased altogether. Without fabric, the clothing division was also threatened, so students decided to permanently close the mill and open a new one in Mexico, where labor is cheap and there are few strikes. Some of the following cases are related to this move.]

Depending on which division you belong to, respond to one of the following scenarios in a 5–7 page report. Make your report as informative as possible, keeping in mind that part of your evaluation will depend on the judgment you use to solve the problem presented by the case. The other part will depend on the clarity and quality of your writing.

Case 1

The company's market share has been static for the last two fiscal periods, and the CEO approved a proposal to enter the

Canadian market. The major obstacle is distribution, because the company's warehouse closest to Canada is in Atlanta. How should we deal with this problem?

[The students' solution was to lease warehouse space for a distribution center either close to the Canadian border or actually in Canada. This solution agreed with what actually occurred.]

Case 2

Opening the mill in Mexico will require transferring numerous executives and middle-level managers from the United States. Other companies in similar situations have reported significant adjustment problems on the part of these managers, and the problems have in turn affected productivity. What would be a way of avoiding relocation difficulties?

[The students' solution was to provide a company-sponsored orientation program to help ease the transition to the new facility. In reality, this solution was part of a broader approach that included paid "furloughs" back to the USA during the first six months of relocation and recycling employees back to the States on a permanent basis at the end of 18 months.]

Case 3

An older woman who worked selling industrial winches was wearing one of the company's suits with extra-wide shoulder pads. She leaned over to inspect a customer's operating winch and caught one of her pads in the gears, dislocating her shoulder and breaking her collar bone. Although she has recovered as well as can be expected, she alleges physical and psychological trauma that prevents her from returning to work. She is suing the company for $20 million, and the associated negative publicity has damaged sales in Southern California, the company's largest market, where the incident occurred.

[The students' solution was to take the suit through trial and to propose judgment in favor of the company. This solution was not deemed acceptable; the actual case was settled out of court, and students were told that they should have worked more aggressively to reach such a settlement in the simulation.]

Analysis of Business Assignment 1

This assignment looks fairly simple as it's presented here, but keep in mind that the class was involved in simulating a business and that the complex interaction among students and teacher cannot be captured adequately in the pages of this text. The teacher's goals in the assignment are twofold. First, students are to engage in problem solving; hence the cases present real difficulties encountered by a business similar to the one the students formed. Therefore, simply writing a report that is clear and informative won't adequately meet the requirements for success; the report must also present the *correct* information. Second, the reports must be well written. In a business context, this means no surface errors, no hard-to-read sentences, no clichés, and paragraphs that get quickly to the point.

It should be obvious from looking at the case problems and the actual solutions that no special business training is needed here. In each instance, the solution is attainable through reflecting on the nature of the problem and through applying a certain amount of common sense. Students who struggle with their notes, a textbook, or library materials in an effort to do well on the assignment are therefore misdirecting their energies. The teacher wants to give students an opportunity to develop their decision-making abilities, not their research skills.

Guide for Reading

Karima has responded well to the assignment in that she has successfully analyzed the problem presented in the case and has made an accurate decision about how to solve it. Also, the detail she provides concerning how to implement the solution is noteworthy. On the negative side, however, Karima's writing is characterized by numerous mechanical errors. In a business setting, where image is a crucial component of success, these errors mean disaster. Her teacher commended Karima's analytical and decision-making skill but was forced to give her a low grade because of the surface errors.

SAMPLE BUSINESS PAPER 1

Was the Orientation Process a Success?

Karima D. (a junior)

Executive Summary

The purpose of this report is to indicate weather the orientation process used for personnel relocated to Oxaca, Mexico was a success. The program was evaluated by two methods. The first method was a survey completed by relocated personnel. The results of the survey indicate that personnel experienced minimal culture shock and have very positive attitudes towards the move to Oxaca. The second instrument was an evaluation of relocated individuals productivity to determine weather they were performing at targeted levels. The results showed that relocated employees were performing above predicted levels. Based on the results of the results of the survey and productivity analysis, the orientation process was successful for both the company and the employees.

Was the Orientation Process a Success?

1. THE PROBLEM AND THE SOLUTION

In March of 1988, New Wave Weavers, INC. decided to move the operations of the XYZ plant to Oxaca, Mexico. It was also decided that middle and top management personnel would have the option of relocating with the plant. Relocating personnel would have to participate in an orientation process to best prepare them for life in Mexico. The purpose of any orientation program would be to minimize culture shock for these employees.

A proposal was made in late March for a possible program for orientating those employees. The five-stage process was accepted by the Board of Directors and implemented immediately.

The Personnel Department wanted to evaluate the success of the orientation process. Six months after relocated employees had begun working in Oxaca, Mexico, I was asked to research the effectiveness of the process and report my findings. This report addresses the methods used to determine the program effectiveness and the results of those methods.

2. METHODS USED

Two different instruments were used to evaluate the orientation program. The first instrument surveyed personnel that participated in the process, asking them to rate the programs helpfulness, rate what level of culture shock they have experienced in Mexico, and evaluate their confidence about their homelife, job, and future. The second instrument measured the productivity of all employees during the first six months.

There were three parts to the survey. The first part asked the employees to rank each phase of the program on a scale of 1 to 5. A 5 meant that the information gained from that stage was both interesting and very helpful. A 4 meant that the information was very helpful and somewhat interesting. A 3 meant the phase provided information but was not very interesting. If the phase provided little information and was dull, it was ranked a 2; and a 1 meant that no information was provided and it was boring. Employees were also asked to give the process an overall score using the same scale.

The second part of the survey asked the employees to indicate how much culture shock they had experienced. The scale consisted of five possible levels of culture shock. They were complete, high, moderate, low, and none.

The final section of the survey asked employees to evaluate how confident they were about their homelife, job and future. There were only two possible answers, confident or not confident. Confident meant that a category was stable and good, while not confident meant a category was shaky and uncertain.

The second instrument used in evaluating the program measured the productivity levels of all relocated employees. Meta World Business Associates was hired by the Personnel Department to provide an objective evaluation of employees' productivity. Meta World researched the companies overall productivity during the six month period between March 1988 and August 1988. A comparison of individual productivity levels was made against the companies overall performance. Meta World also compared relocated personnel's current productivity levels to their productivity prior to relocation.

3. *THE RESULTS OF THE SURVEY*

There were five parts to the orientation process. They were slide show, pamphlets and reports, guest speakers, culture and language classes, and a visit to Oxaca. The results of the employee evaluation of each phase are charted in Figure 1 [Table A]. Every employee ranked the trip to Oxaca a 5. Every part of the process received a 5 by the majority of employees, except for the slide show. The majority gave the slide show a 4 because it provided some information but was interesting. Every employee rated the overall process a 5.

According to the results of the culture shock and confidence surveys, the relocated employees reexperienced low and moderate levels of culture shock and are basically confident about their jobs and homelife. Most employees are unsure about the future but felt that relocating to Oxaca would positively influence their lives.

The survey results indicate that relocated employees did not experience any emotional set backs. They're morale was high and no adverse emotional effects could be found.

4. *THE RESULTS OF THE PRODUCTIVITY EVALUATION*

The productivity analysis done by Meta World Business Associates had very positive results. Productivity levels were expected to drop 15% because of the move to Mexico. The estimated drop allowed for time needed by relocating employees to adjust to a new environment. Research showed that productivity levels only dropped 5%. In January of 1988, productivity levels for manage-

[TABLE A]   Employee Evaluation of the Orientation Process

	1	2	3	4	5
SLIDE SHOW				10	34	10
PAMPHLETS AND REPORTS			10	14	30
GUEST SPEAKERS				4	50
VISIT TO OXACA					54
OVERALL RATING					54

ment employees were 85%. According to Meta World, in August 1988 our managers are performing at an 80% level.

The comparison between the overall productivity level of New Wave Weavers and productivity levels of individual employees indicates that relocated personnel are not responsible for the companies' decrease in productivity. These results show stable productivity levels within middle and top management. Relocating to Mexico had no adverse effect on management performance on the job.

5. *CONCLUSION: EVALUATING THE RESULTS*

The orientation process was designed to prepare relocating employees for moving to Oxaca, Mexico. In the interest of its employees, the company wanted to minimize possible culture shock and make the move to Mexico as pleasant as possible. The company also wanted to prevent damage to productivity levels and worker morale.

The Personnel Department used two different methods to evaluate the orientation program. The first method surveyed employees that participated in the program, asking them to rate the program. All employ rated the overall process as being very informative and interesting. The employees have reported low and moderate levels of culture shock. The second method, a productivity report, indicates that the relocated employees are performing above expectations.

The results of all research show that the orientation program was a success on two accounts. The employees' have experienced moderate or low culture shock and their job performances are better than anticipated. Both the company and its employees have greatly benefited from the success of the orientation process.

Analysis of Sample Business Paper 1

Perhaps the first impression a reader gets from Karima's paper is that she has read business reports before and knows something about appropriate style and format. Her writing is direct, and she focuses on supplying the information called for.

As it turned out, her solution to the case problem was substantially correct, which figured significantly in her teacher's criteria for success on this assignment. But the way she went about solving the problem is noteworthy. She took the time not only to design an orientation program for relocated employees but to provide a means of measuring whether it worked. This extra effort places her response among the better papers produced for this assignment.

Clearly, Karima has some trouble with surface features. In the first sentence of the executive summary, she uses "weather" rather than "whether." In the last sentence of that same paragraph, she writes "Based on the results <u>of the results</u> of the survey." In the last sentence in the paragraph just before section 4, she writes *"They're* morale was high," when she should have written "Their morale was high." Throughout the paper we see problems with possessives, as well as difficulties with subject/verb agreement.

Overall, the clarity and informativeness of the content isn't seriously compromised by these lapses in mechanics, and on this level the paper is generally successful. But we have to consider the context for this assignment and the training it is designed to provide. There is no question that Karima has mastered part of what it takes to function well in business, but she hasn't mastered another part—correctness of form—that is considered very important. In a different context, with a different audience, the evaluation Karima's paper received might have been more generous. As it stands, we can only say that her work would have benefited significantly from some revising and proofreading.

Guide for Reading

Hal's paper is a slightly below-average response to the assignment. He manages to solve the case problem and displays good reasoning skills in doing so. But his paper is unfocused, containing too much irrelevant information. In addition, Hal, like Karima, lets surface errors seriously distract readers. He doesn't seem to realize (or care) that in business he will be judged repeatedly by how well he communicates with others.

SAMPLE BUSINESS PAPER 2

Canadian Distribution Quarterly Report

Hal R. (a junior)

Introduction

New Wave Weavers is well on its way to becoming a frontrunner in clothing exports. From the outset of our Canadian distribution proposal we set our goals high and put forth our best possible effort. These efforts are now paying off. At the three month point our success can be clearly seen in virtually every aspect of our operation. The only regret we have is that we did not become a part of the Canadian market sooner. Since our efforts began, we have experienced and excellent sales volume and increased new product research and development. We are also experiencing exceptional production levels and are on the verge of tackling our final transportation problems. Our department is thrilled about the immediate success we have achieved. It is with this enthusiasm we present our first report on the Canadian distribution project.

Sales

Once we had determined there was a market for our clothing in Canada the rest was easy. We began interviewing interested retailers and signed contracts until we met our quota. We feel we have established an excellent base for distribution with the following retailers:

   Lacosse Department Stores

   Mackenzie Department Stores

   Canadian Clothing Ltd.

   Fine Clothieers of Montreal

   Draughan and Mendel of Winnipeg

Business Communication   717

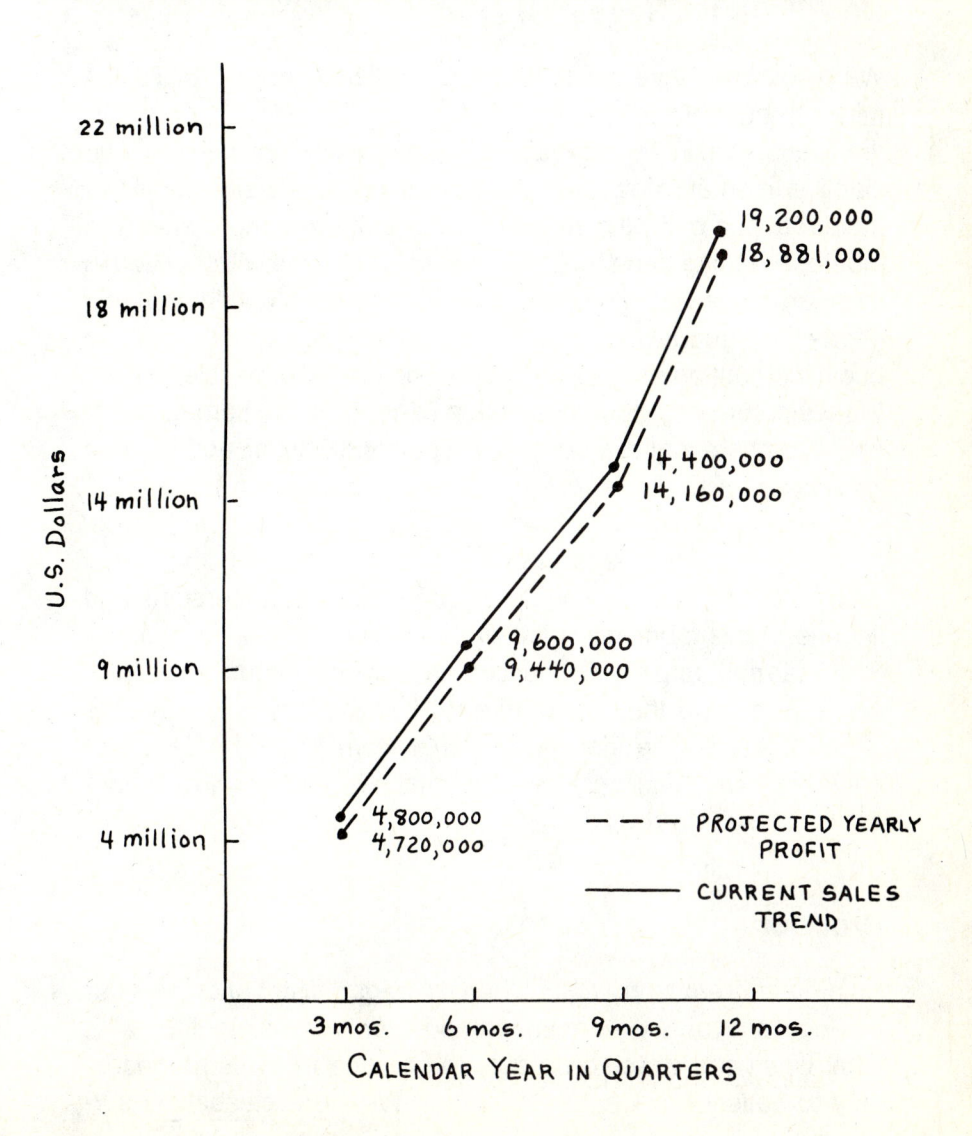

Our spring line was a big success in each of the stores. We filled reorders for each of the contracts within the first month. We anticipate even greater success with our summer line, expected to be shipped later this week. The current sales trends should put us well above our projected yearly profit set forth in our proposal (see graph 1). One major reason for this unforeseen success is the popularity of our lines woven from our innovative Cotlen fabric. These lines have been on back order since their introduction in early March. Other factors that have contributed to our success include: efficient communication between our distribution and production divisions, reliable transportation practices, and cooperative retailers. Aside from bringing in valuable revenues, our current sales rates have spawned research in the area of new product development.

New Product Research

We would not have propose the Canadian move if we did not think we could successfully enter the market with what we currently produce. We soon realized our products fit in well with their clothing market. However, we will never be satisfied until we have reached our full distribution potential. From the mere three months we have been involved, it is apparrent we will succeed in other areas as well. Our market researchers are continuing their efforts throughout Canada and have determined that we need to begin distribution of undergarments and accessories. New Wave Weavers currently doesn't produce either of these commodities. Our designers have produced a complete line of accessories including gloves, handbags, hats, and scarves. We hope to introduce the line this fall in both the U.S. and Canada. Our interest in undergarments stems from the sales success of our Cotlen fabric. We feel that if we begin to produce briefs, undershirts and lingerie of this fabric we will claim a considerable amount of the undergarment market. Production has already begun on each of these items and they should be on the shelf by late May. We never imagined the ideas that would stem from our Canadian endeavors and can only wonder what the future holds for our product research division.

Production

An area of great worry to us when we began distribution was our production level. We were concerned after the closing of the XYZ plant whether we would be able to produce the volume necessary to satisfy our Canadian buyers. We were pleasantlly sur-

Business Writing

prised when we found the Oxaca plant more than capable of producing our desired numbers. In fact, our production levels are higher now than ever and its costing New Wave Weavers less! (see graph 2). Even though we are forced to produce more to satisfy our export needs, the Oxaca plant is operating at a lower budget than the XYZ plant ever did. Our current production cost

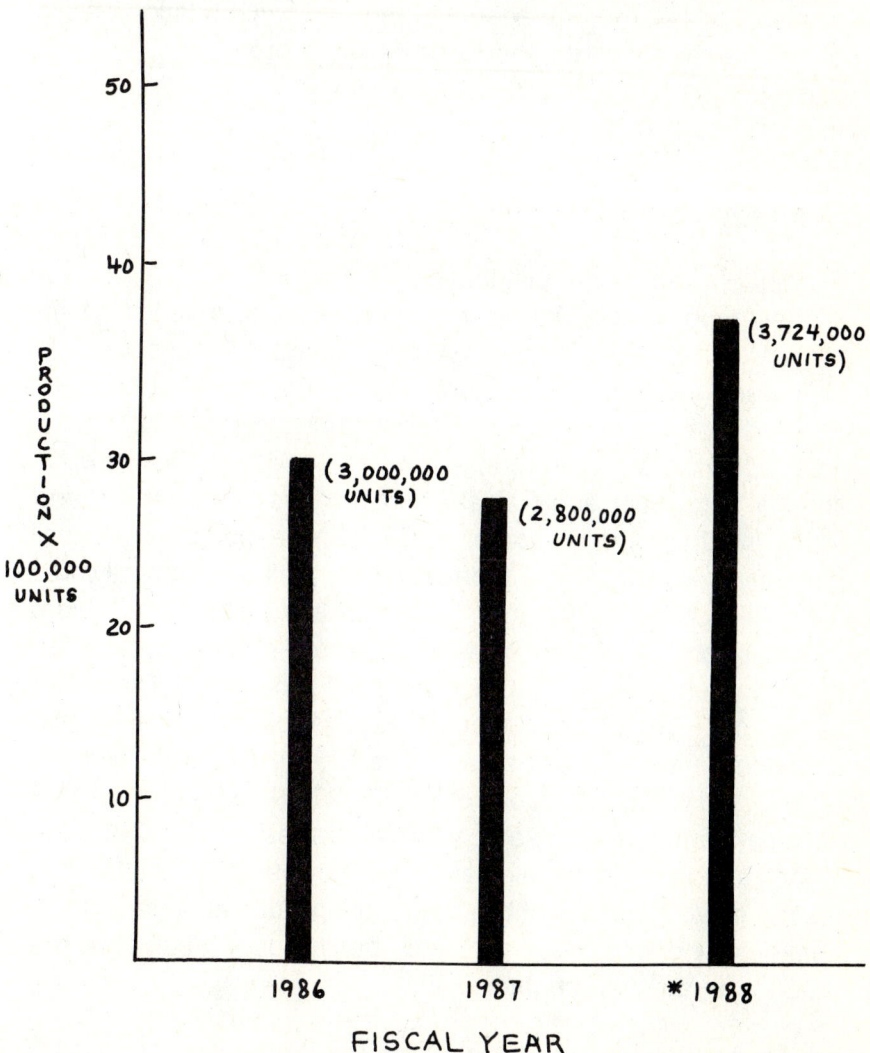

PRODUCTION × 100,000 UNITS

Fiscal Year	Production
1986	(3,000,000 units)
1987	(2,800,000 units)
*1988	(3,724,000 units)

FISCAL YEAR

Production Costs = 1986 — $1,400,000
1987 — $1,300,000
*1988 — $1,100,000

*Projected 1988 Production

is $1,100,000 per year. This number is down from last year's cost of $1,300,000. This doesn't seem to astounding you realize that we now produce one third more per year and have managed to increase revenues 29%, including an increase in profits of 25%. This success is credited to most obviously, the Oxaca plant opening and the Canadian distribution project. And secondarily to the efforts of the management and personnel relations team directly responsible for the Oxaca plant's production. We are confident that current production levels will lead us successfully into the future in the U.S. as well as Canada.

Transportation

From the outset of our distribution plans, transportation was our biggest problem. So big that we changed our distribution objective to reduce costs. Our original yearly anticipated transportation cost was $1,700,000. This figure includes the transportation cost of goods for U.S distribution. After changing our distribution objective, we were able to reduce this cost to $1,400,000. By eliminating Vancouver and Calgary from our five city objective and replacing them with Ottawa and Winnipeg we reduced the transportation cost without compromising revenues. We currently ship by over-night air freight and rail from Oxaca and by road freight and rail from Cleveland. Plans are currently underway for a distribution center near Ottawa, which will replace the Cleveland plant as center for distribution. Construction cost of the distribution center has been determined to be $300,000 with an anticipated yearly operation cost of $75,000. The distribution center has the potential to save New Wave Weavers $100,000 per year and, therefore, should pay for itself by 1993. We feel a great sense of accomplishment in overcoming our transportation dilemmas, and with these problems behind us we can face the future with an even brighter outlook.

Conclusion

With the Canadian project well underway, the marketing division looks forward to monitoring the program's success and solving any problems which may arise. With continued advances in sales, production, new product research, and transportation we are guaranteed progress through the end of this year. At which time, we will reevaluate our Canadian operation and make the necessary alterations to insure maximum profits for the years to come.

Analysis of Sample Business Paper 2

Hal does a good job of solving the distribution problem, and from that perspective, his paper is a success. He understood that it wouldn't be profitable to continue using Atlanta as a distribution point for the Canadian market.

Nevertheless, this paper is not as good as it could have been. Notice that Hal doesn't focus on any details related to setting up the Ottawa facility; instead, he reports on sales, research, and production, as well as on distribution. In other words, he presents quite a bit of information that is not completely relevant to the topic at hand.

On the surface level, there aren't any major problems, just numerous small ones that, taken together, prove quite distracting. For example, Hal frequently neglects to use a comma to set off phrases that introduce sentences. Consider the second sentence in the first paragraph: "From the outset of our Canadian distribution proposal we set our goals high and put forth our best possible effort." The sentence would be easier to read if a comma followed "proposal." Hal doesn't seem to have proofread the paper, because it contains numerous typing errors. Consider this sentence from the middle of the "Production" paragraph that begins: "This doesn't seem to astounding [until] you realize that we now produce one third more per year. . . ."

The tone of the paper doesn't seem entirely appropriate, either. In the next-to-the-last sentence of the very first paragraph, we see that staff members are "thrilled about the immediate success." Reports can be positive without sounding artificially so, and in this instance it appears as though Hal is just trying too hard.

Finally, the paper could have been better if Hal had managed to vary his sentence patterns a little more. When we look carefully at his writing, we note that he rarely uses subordination. That is, most of his sentences repeat a "subject + predicate" pattern again and again, without any use of constructions that begin with such words as *because, although, since, while,* and so forth. As a result, the style of the paper is monotonous.

What can we conclude from this analysis? Hal managed to correctly solve the problem presented in the case study, but his organization, attention to detail, and style do nothing to enhance his solution. In fact, these elements of his paper detract from his successful solution.

Guide for Reading

Chris' paper is an unacceptable response to the assignment for several reasons. He attempts to dramatize the report, which indicates that he has not thought sufficiently about what such a report is supposed to do. Even worse, he misread the case study and got the facts wrong. Such a fundamental error is bad in any class, but in business it is considered disastrous. Finally, pay careful attention to the surface problems in Chris' paper. His teacher found them atrocious. Do you?

SAMPLE BUSINESS PAPER 3

Public Relations Department Report: Counter-Action to Image Damaging Lawsuits of Liebowitz versus New Wave Weavers

Chris P. (a junior)

Introduction

October 21, 1987 marked a day of tragedy for New Wave Weavers when a young lady, Emily Liebowitz, was seriously injured in a machine shop plant in Southern California. The cause of the accident was carelessness and failure of Miss Liebowitz to observe shop safety rules. It was a tragic day for New Wave Weavers because Miss Liebowitz was wearing a company product at the time of her accident, and believed it responsible for the mishap. Consequently, Miss Liebowitz successfully sued New Wave Weavers for design negligence. The lawsuit and the media attention that surrounded the proceedings, created a poor public image resulting in a drastic sales drop in our Southern California retail market.

To rectify the situation, New Wave Weavers embarked on a decisive two part solution. The solution consisted of a pre-trial and a post-trial plan of action directed by the Public Relations Department. The pre-trial plan was three fold: hire a prestigious and successful law firm, attempt to settle out of court with Miss Liebowitz, and hire private investigators to research Miss Liebowitz's social and financial background, in a legal manner.

The post-trial action was also three fold. Perhaps the most important of all action taken, Young and Rubicam of New York, New York was hired to spearhead the rebuilding of New Wave Weavers' Southern California image. Young and Rubicam established a new company theme and directed all media advertising in an effort to reach the majority of the Southern California clothing consumers.

Text

I. Perspective:

Prior to October 21, 1987, New Wave Weavers' major public image problem was the fact that our production occured in, Mexico, giving job opportunities to foreigners. Our competitors realized this and embarked on a major advertising campaign centering around the "made USA" theme. New Wave Weavers simply advertised and offered quality clothing for less money. the advertisements and the cost-effectiveness of purchasing our products, helped to make them a success.

II. Background:

On October 21, 1987, Miss Emily Liebowitz reported to work wearing a New Wave Weavers shirt. The shirt design included shoulder pads and a six inch shirt-tail extension, standard on all "Sports/Action Wear." Miss Liebowitz failed to comply with safety procedures, by not wearing a protective smock, required by her company, Dynamics machinewerk. She leaned to inspect a casting machine and was momentarily caught by the threader arm of the caster. Unable to reach the cut-off switch, a fifteen pound pickwicking bar dropped onto her shoulder severing her clavacle and ultimately parlysing her left side. Miss Liebowitz sued

New Wave Weavers for twenty million dollars charging design negligence had caused her accident.

III. Pre-Trial Action Plan

The pre-trial action consisted of hiring a law firm, attempting to settle the dispute out-of-court, and hiring a private investigation team.

A. New Wave Weavers hired the law firm of Smith, Moore, Smith, Schell, and Hunter to represent our interests and to defend our corporation in a court of law. The law firm based in Greensboro, North Carolina, was chosen because of its prestige, solid reputation, and textile related litigation experience.

B. The first action of Smith, Moore, Smith, Schell, and Hunter was to attempt to settle the dispute out-of-court. An offer of $25,000 was submitted to Miss Liebowitz's counsel. The settlement would include a signed statement by Miss Liebowitz, releasing New Wave Weavers as responsible for the accident. A counter offer of ten million dollars was then submitted by Miss Liebowitz's attorney. The counter-offer was quickly rejected and the pre-trial procedures began

C. Simon and Simon Investigators were hired shortly after Miss Liebowitz's lawsuit filing. The investigation team was hired in an attempt to gain knowledge of Miss Liebowitz's motives for suing New Wave Weavers. Simon and Simon were also hired in an effort to aid New Wave Weavers's councel gain information of Miss Liebowitz's social and financial background. The investigators were instructed to gain their information only in a legal way

IV. Liebowitz versus New Wave Weavers:

The trial began on December 6th, and closing arguments were delivered on January 27th. Smith, Moore, Smith, Schell, and Hunter did an excellent job representing New Wave Weavers while attempting to defend a possible precedent setting case decision. Four days of jury deliberation ended in a decision in favor of the plaintiff, Miss Liebowitz. However, the settlement awarded to Miss Liebowitz was only one dollar. This seemed to characterize the court's true feeling on the accident. The damage to New Wave Weavers's public image had occured regardless of the decision.

V. Post-Trial Action Plan

Young and Rubicam Advertising Agency was hired to rebuild New Wave Weavers's image the moment the trial ended. The agency and the Public Relations Department devised a three part image building plan.

   A. Change the old advertising theme of "Quality for less" to "The Company That Cares What You Wear."

   B. Incorporate a small warning upon existing labels. The label manufacturer, Labelettes Unlimited, will add a thirty-seven character message in small script onto the New Wave Weavers label. The extra message will add a cost of only one cent per label. The advantage of the extra message helps to further New Wave Weavers's image of "The Company That Cares."

   C. Immediately following the trial, bombard the clothing consumer market with advertising.

   1) Prime time television advertisements.

   2) Full page advertisements in Sunday edition of *Los Angeles Times*.

   3) Bus billboard advertisements in San Francisco and San Diego for two weeks.

   4) Promise public to re-inspect all shoulder padded garments in retail stores.

Recommendations

The decisive action taken by the Board of Directors and the Public Relations Division proved to be successful. However, the actions taken were designed to deal with the image problems created for the public. Action has been designed or taken to deal with possible image problems inside the corporation. To deal with this possible problem management should have a meeting with all employees to explain the entire Liebowitz case. It should be stressed that the forty percent sales drop is only momentary and through extensive measures taken by Management sales should rebound. The bad public image will pass and can even be expedited through employee confidence. It should also be stressed at the employee meeting, that at no time during the Liebowitz affair were jobs within the corporation in jeopardy.

Conclusions

The events of October 1987 proved to test New Wave Weavers and its leadership. The test was extremely costly, but it built confidence in management throughout the corporation. The sales drop of forty percent in November and December is projected to rebound by early March due to the investment in a new advertisement campaign. The long run results from the incident of October 21, 1987, may in fact be positive for New Wave Weavers.

Analysis of Sample Business Paper 3

It's interesting that Chris, like Hal in Paper 2, felt compelled to dramatize the report. His reference to "a day of tragedy" in the very first sentence signals immediately that he has not given much thought to the nature of a report or the nature of his audience. Moreover, the first paragraph indicates that Chris hasn't paid much attention to the case study, because he has his facts wrong. Recall that in Case 3 the woman was described as being older, but Chris describes her as a young lady. The case stated that she was wearing a suit with extra-wide shoulder pads, but Chris states that she was wearing a shirt. The case stated that the woman was inspecting an industrial winch, but Chris states that she was inspecting a casting machine.

The first paragraph is so significantly flawed in terms of accuracy that few teachers would be able to avoid mentally assigning a grade to the paper at this point. Nevertheless, some writers, after such an unfortunate beginning, are able to shake off defeat and go on to produce a good paper. Chris isn't one of them. For example, after reading the section title "Perspective," we have to wonder about its entire relevance.

The surface difficulties in this section—the comma in front of "Mexico," starting the last sentence with a lower-case *t*, the comma in front of "helped" in that same sentence—are serious because they hamper readability. But they aren't limited to this one section; they riddle the paper, inclining most readers to withhold any generosity as they struggle to get through the report.

Consider the next-to-last sentence in Section II of "Text": "Unable to reach the cut-off switch, a fifteen pound pickwicking bar dropped onto her shoulder severing her clavacle and ultimately parlysing her left side." In this single sentence, Chris has managed to provide a string of errors: (1) misplacing the introductory clause, such that the "fifteen pound pickwicking bar" was unable to reach the cut-off switch; (2) failing to hyphenate the compound, "fifteen-pound"; (3) failing to use a comma to set off the modifying phrase that begins with "severing"; and (4) misspelling "clavicle" and "paralyzing."

In Section III.C, Chris mentions that a team of detectives was hired to investigate Miss Liebowitz, but he never bothers to say anything about the outcome of the investigation. He does mention that information was obtained "in a legal way," but would readers expect anything different?

Chris' solution to the case problem seems contrived: the plaintiff won but was awarded only $1 in damages. Such events do occur, but in this instance, given the other difficulties in the paper, the decision reinforces the perception that Chris is trying to develop a note of false drama.

A minimal requirement for success on a paper is getting the assignment right. If you misread the assignment, you will have little chance of writing a paper that receives a high grade. In the case of this particular paper, we see several factors working together to guarantee failure: Chris' lack of attention to the details of the case, his formulation of a neat ending to what should have been understood as a nuisance suit to be settled out of court, and the numerous and serious surface errors.

Writing Assignments

The following assignments ask you to assume the role of a business person who must produce a report for company executives. Although actual reports of this nature follow certain conventions that you probably aren't aware of, at this point these conventions aren't as important, ultimately, as the overall tone and informativeness of the report. If you want to make your report more authentic, texts on business writing should be readily available from your college library, and they specify the conventions that characterize such reports.

1. Read seven consecutive issues of your local paper's business section. Select a company that has a problem, whether it be reduced profits, inability to meet environmental regulations, or the need for a curb-side loading zone. Write a 3- to 5-page report that explains what the problem is, what action the company has taken to solve the problem, and what the final outcome is. Successful responses will be informative, detailed, easy to read, and free of surface errors.
2. Over the last couple of decades, campus book stores have expanded

their inventory to include much more than books. Many now stock high-profit items such as computers, clothing, gifts, and so on. Retailers adjacent to college campuses frequently complain that college stores provide unfair competition that robs them of sales, and some states, such as North Carolina, have enacted legislation to prevent campus book stores from selling anything other than textbooks and basic school supplies. Assume that your sportswear company would like to open a store near campus. Conduct some market research that includes interviews with current retailers to assess the level of competition provided by the campus store. Write a 5- to 7-page report that describes the outcome of your research and that states the feasibility of opening the store. Successful responses will be informative, will reflect a thoughtful analysis of the relationship between the campus store and local retailers, and will offer concrete recommendations regarding a course of action.

BUSINESS ASSIGNMENT 2

Course: **Macroeconomics**

Over the course of the semester you will write six short papers on articles dealing with current financial news. Your choice of articles should be guided by what we are covering in class at that time. The length of the papers should be close to one page; a few lines more or less is not that important. The shorter part of your paper should be a summary of the article, focusing on its main points. The rest of the paper should be an explanation of the principle governing the financial situation discussed in the article. You will be graded on 1) relevance of the article to course material; 2) the quality and style of your writing; and 3) your analysis and explanation of the principle(s) involved. A copy of the article must accompany your paper.

Analysis of Business Assignment 2

This assignment demands careful reading and clear, concise writing, because articles addressing finance are sufficiently complex that they will be hard to summarize in one page. Thus the length of the papers forces students to determine the important points of the article and to focus on them closely.

The inherent danger students face in this assignment is the temptation to devote too much space to summary. Many students will mistakenly believe that the aim of their response is to paraphrase the article. But note what the teacher writes concerning the grade; "summary" doesn't figure explicitly into the evaluation. It remains a required part of the task, but it isn't the primary part. More important is the analysis and explanation of the principle governing the financial situation described.

The assignment also emphasizes writing quality and style. In an economics class, teachers rarely have time to offer much in the way of writing instruction. As a result, it can be difficult deciding what constitutes a good style. We would suggest you keep the following ideas in mind when writing papers in response to assignments like the one above. Strive to make your writing flawless with regard to surface features such as spelling, punctuation, sentence structure, and paragraph organization. If you aren't sure about punctuation, buy a handbook or ask your teacher. As for sentence and paragraph construction, get feedback from friends and teachers before handing your papers in. Second, you should not write primarily for your instructor, who is probably aware of the situation and certainly knows the principle involved. Instead, you should write for an intelligent person who has not received formal instruction in economics. This way you will be inclined to explain the principle more carefully, producing a better paper and showing the instructor that you do know what you are writing about.

Class Article 1

As Trade Frictions Rise, Sanyo Joins Japanese Buyers of U.S. Semiconductors

by Jacob M. Schlesinger and Stephen Kreider Yoder

TOKYO—As the U.S. government intensifies its investigations of foreign trade barriers, Japanese manufacturers are rushing to increase their purchases of American computer chips.

"As Trade Frictions Rise, Sanyo Joins Japanese Buyers of U.S. Semiconductors" by Jacob M. Schlesinger and Stephen Kreider Yoder. Reprinted by permission of *The Wall Street Journal*, May 2, 1989. Copyright © 1989 Dow Jones & Company, Inc. All Rights Reserved Worldwide.

In the latest transaction, Sanyo Electric Co. said it will soon stop all in-house production of a certain type of semiconductor and instead buy 36 million of those chips from Motorola Inc. a year. "The underlying reason," a Sanyo spokesman said, "is trade friction."

American access to the Japanese semi-conductor market is one of the most contentious issues in an increasingly tense trade relationship. Last week, a U.S. government report cited Japan for 32 categories of trade barriers, including semiconductors. The Japanese chip market is expected to be included May 30 in a final list of barriers to be investigated for possible retaliation in the next year. That could add to semiconductor sanctions the U.S. government imposed two years ago.

PRESSURE FROM TOKYO

Japanese government officials continue to argue that American chip sales are limited by inferior quality and insufficient marketing and service. But they also are pressuring Japanese companies to buy more. Two weeks ago, the Ministry of International Trade and Industry called together nearly 100 chip buyers and disseminated a 25-page plan aimed at encouraging expanded purchases of foreign semi-conductors.

More and more companies say they are doing just that. Last week, Nissan Motor Co. said it agreed to buy general-purpose memory chips from the Intel Corp. Also, the Japanese press reported that NEC Corp. had decided to buy from foreign suppliers 90% of the semiconductors that will be used in its new series of supercomputers.

To be sure, none of these agreements give U.S. companies a substantial piece of the Japanese market. The Sanyo-Motorola pact involves less than $10 million a year, and the Nissan-Intel agreement less than $1 million a year, according to spokesmen for the Japanese companies. Sanyo says its contract will increase its foreign chip use at most to 12% of the semiconductors it uses from 10% now. A Sanyo official said the two sides will sign a formal agreement, probably later this month.

Cynics dismiss the well-publicized purchases as last-ditch attempts to avoid an official reprimand from the U.S. government later this month. "I'm pleased to see the tendency," said E. David Metz, executive director of the Japan office of the Semiconductor Industry Association, a U.S. trade group. "But, it's not going to make an immediate significant difference in foreign market share."

BREAKS FROM TRADITION

Nonetheless, each of the three agreements mark important breaks from traditional Japanese practices. In deciding to buy general-purpose logic semiconductors—standardized chips that process data—from Motorola, Sanyo is halting production of a product it makes itself. Historically, Japanese companies only have supplemented their own production with foreign purchases. (Sanyo will continue to make more specialized logic chips.)

Furthermore, Sanyo is part of what the U.S. industry considers the second tier of chip companies—mid-sized chip makers that have been more reluctant to buy foreign semiconductors than their larger Japanese competitors. Japanese chip makers also are the country's biggest chip purchasers. But industry officials estimate that while the five largest Japanese semiconductor producers, such as NEC, get 18% of their chips from foreign sources, the next five largest companies, such as Sanyo, average only 8%. The smallest Japanese companies average less than 5%.

Both Sanyo and Nissan also are important contracts because they represent markets that American chip makers have had trouble breaking into. U.S. makers have had the most success in Japan providing chips for computers and telecommunications equipment, but less in consumer electronics and automobiles. Sanyo will use the Motorola chips for televisions, videocassette recorders and other products.

Nissan will use the Intel semiconductors for engine systems in some of its cars. Until recently, Nissan bought virtually no foreign chips. Last year, it agreed to buy chips from Intel, but they were customized chips that could be used for only one car model. In the latest deal, Nissan will buy general-use chips that could be used in all models.

NEC's reported decision to use mainly foreign chips for its supercomputers appears aimed at U.S. concern that Japan's use of domestic chips will help it dominate that emerging market. NEC officials couldn't be reached for comment yesterday.

Guide for Reading

Melissa's paper is slightly below average. She does a competent job of analyzing the magazine article, using quotations to help make her summary more concrete. But she doesn't deal adequately with the second part of the assignment, which asked for an explanation of the principle governing the situation discussed in the article. As you read, ask yourself how Melissa could have better explained this principle.

Untitled

Melissa C. (a junior)

An article in the international section of the *Wall Street Journal* titled "As Trade Frictions Rise, Sanyo Joins Japanese Buyers___U.S. Semiconductors", appeared in this week's paper. This article discusses trade barriers, or restrictions, between the United States and Japan. The biggest issues for these barriers are American computer chips and Japanese semiconductors. The U.S. claims that Japan is placing trade barriers on many of their goods, even the semiconductors, which are "standardized chips that process data." In return, Japanese officials claim that Americans are "limited by inferior quality and insufficient marketing and service." Japanese companies are large quantity purchasers of American computer chips. Japan normally uses American chips for computers and telecommunications equipment, but not in consumer electronics and automobiles.

This article deals with international trade and types of restrictions that may be placed on trade. It also mentions how importing and exporting are good for countries to buy cheap and sell expensive. International trade allows countries to purchase goods which they don't produce themselves. Trade barriers can cause prices to shoot up and cause a great demand for that product due to shortages. International trade is a good thing for all countries.

Business Writing

> ## STUDY QUESTIONS
>
> 1. Melissa's second paragraph should explain the principle governing the situation described in the article but doesn't. What skill do you think her teacher was trying to develop through this part of the assignment?
>
> 2. Reread the assignment carefully and try to visualize the content of the macroeconomics course it comes from. Given your understanding of what this assignment is about and what the teacher was hoping to see in students' responses, what are some specific features missing from Melissa's second paragraph? In other words, what could we reasonably expect to find that she doesn't provide?

Class Article 2

"The Slowdown in Consumer Spending May Be Only a Breather"

by James C. Cooper and Kathleen Madigan

The consumer is still the most important player in this economic expansion. Consumers account for about two-thirds of gross national product, and how they behave this spring will go a long way toward determining the economy's strength and inflation's potential. That, in turn, will decide how much further the Federal Reserve Board will tighten monetary policy—and where interest rates will head.

Right now the economy isn't showing much loss of momentum. The government's final look at real GNP for the fourth quarter produced an upward revision from 2% to 2.4%. Adding back the 1.1 percentage points taken away by the drought puts the growth of the nonfarm economy at a robust 3.5%.

First-quarter growth, even after accounting for the expected post-drought jump in farm output, is shaping up to be strong as well, but quite different in composition. The pace of consumer spending, strong in the

---

"The Slowdown in Consumer Spending May Be Only a Breather" by James C. Cooper and Kathleen Madigan. Reprinted from the April 10, 1989 issue of *Business Week* by special permission. Copyright © 1989 by McGraw-Hill, Inc.

fourth quarter, was much weaker in 1989's first quarter. Capital spending, which dropped at yearend, appears to have rebounded. And the trade deficit, after a huge deterioration, probably improved somewhat.

The Commerce Dept.'s index of 12 leading indicators gives little evidence that any lasting slowdown is on the way. The index did dip 0.3% in February, but its trend remains firmly up (chart) [omitted]. The leading index has risen 3.5% over the past year, up from 2.4% during the previous year.

The best clues to the economy's strength will come from consumer spending—and that's where the Fed most wants to see a slowdown. True, spending cooled off in the first quarter. But will that slowdown last? The stubborn strength of the consumer sector has confounded forecasters throughout this expansion. This latest quarterly lull may well turn out to be as ephemeral as others in the recent past.

The driving forces behind consumer buying are as strong as ever. Unrelenting job growth is generating income at an increasing pace. And consumer confidence remains historically high. So far, all this has more than offset the Fed's yearlong attempt to dampen spending with higher interest rates.

Since last March the Fed has pushed up interest rates using the federal funds rate—the charge on interbank borrowing—as its key policy tool. That rate has soared from 6½% to just under 10% at the end of March, 1989.

Other short-term rates have followed. The yield on three-month Treasury bills, for example, has risen from a bit more than 5½% to a shade below 9½%. Long-term interest rates are also up, but not by as much. As a result, the costs of both fixed- and variable-rate consumer loans are substantially higher than a year ago.

In fact, a few early signs of the impact of past Fed tightening are starting to show. Housing demand is weakening. Sales of new single-family homes tumbled 9.4% in February, to a 626,000 annual rate. That puts sales 4.6% below their year-ago level. Purchases of existing homes also dropped, falling 3.1%, to a yearly pace of 3.44 million. That followed on the heels of a large 9.4% decline in January.

Another possible sign: the persistence of weak car sales in the middle of March, when Detroit's most liberal incentive program in months was in full swing. Sales of domestically made autos rose to only a 6.8 million annual rate from a poor 6.2 million showing early in the month. Sales in both January and February were at 7 million.

When the Fed held its policy meeting on Mar. 28, it undoubtedly took into account these recent signs of slowing in the consumer sector. That may help relieve some of the central bankers' worries about inflation for now, but it's still not clear if that slowdown will last.

In February consumers increased their purchases by a healthy 0.5%, to an annual rate of $3,375.7 billion, following a 0.4% rise in January. Much of the February gain came from increased energy use, which returned to more normal winter levels after January's warm-weather respite. Indeed, after adjustment for prices, real spending rose 0.4% in February, reversing the 0.3% loss posted in January.

February's performance indicates that first-quarter growth in real consumer spending will be the weakest in more than a year. Even if inflation-adjusted buying in March matches the February increase, purchases for the entire quarter will be up by only 1.6% at an annual rate, far below the 3.5% pace in the fourth quarter (chart) [omitted].

Real spending on goods was essentially flat in February, as it was in January. Inflation-adjusted purchases of durable goods fell 0.2% in February, following a 3.8% plunge the month before. Sluggish car sales were the biggest cause.

Real purchases of nondurable goods also fell in February, by 0.1%, but they had jumped 1% in January. Sluggish sales of food and clothing led the February weakness, but the cold weather boosted fuel use by 11.5%.

Services, however, rose a strong 0.9% in February, even after adjusting for prices. One-third of the gain came from a 7.2% jump in electricity use, but spending on education also rose.

Judging by the continued weakness in car sales in March, spending in that month is not off to a good start. And with auto inventories already high, a pickup in car buying in late March will be critical if Detroit is to avoid production cutbacks. Detroit made cars at annual rates of 7.5 million in January and 7.2 million in February.

But excluding autos, sales probably did better in March, if only because Easter fell early this year. That will boost the March numbers on spending, but as usual it will steal some strength from the April sales data.

The slowdown in spending did boost the savings rate in the first quarter, but that usually happens when car sales drop. Still, the rate has been trending higher. In the three months ended in February, personal savings as a percent of aftertax income stood at 5.2%. That's up from 4.2% for all of 1988 and from 3.2% in 1987.

The weakness in consumer spending is likely to be short-lived. For one thing, consumers are still in good spirits. The Conference Board's index of consumer confidence remains very high. Although it fell in March, to 117.7 from 120.7 in February, it was still well above the 115.2 average of the previous year.

For another, consumer purchases of services and nondurable goods—some four-fifths of all spending—are not so sensitive to interest rates. And income growth over the past few months has been too strong for consumers to stop spending for long. Higher interest rates may dampen sales of some durable goods, but strong income gains will keep fueling spending elsewhere.

In February personal income advanced by 1%, to an annual rate of $4,315.3 billion. January's gain was an even sharper 1.7%. An increase in farm subsidies boosted February earnings, but even excluding those payments, income growth was still robust, rising 0.7%.

Wages and salaries—the bulk of personal income—increased a healthy 0.6% in February, following a 1.1% jump in January. Services and the distributive industries, such as wholesale trade and transportation, accounted for the bulk of the February gains. Factory earnings also rose, but not by as much.

So far this year income growth has been impressive. In the first quarter, real nonfarm income, after adjusting for prices, appears to have grown at a 5.3% annual rate (chart) [omitted]. Income growth has been accelerating for three consecutive quarters, and the first-quarter pace is shaping up to be the fastest in five quarters.

Rising interest rates are also benefiting many consumers. Interest income, which accounts for a bigger share of personal income than earnings in manufacturing, continues to lead all income growth. Interest earnings surged 1.4% in both January and February and now stand 13.4% above a year ago. All other income has grown by a slower, but still impressive, 8.7% over the same 12 months.

These solid supports mean that consumer spending is likely to pick up again in the second quarter. If so, look for further Fed tightening—and higher interest rates.

Guide for Reading

Nathan does a good job of summarizing the article, and he also does a good job of explaining the economic principle it illustrates. As a result, his paper is better than average, but it isn't outstanding because of the surface errors throughout. This problem is especially significant because the assignment states specifically that writing quality will be a criterion for success.

SAMPLE BUSINESS PAPER 5

Untitled

Nathan C. (a junior)

The U.S. economy is steadily growing even though the Fed is tightening the money supply. This growth is mainly attributed to the purchasing strength of the consumer sector which is being fueled by steady job and income expansion. The growth in the G.N.P. has seen a moderate jump from a 2% to 2.4% for the fourth quarter. This steady growth has caused the inflation fearing Fed to push the discount rate from 6.5% to just below 10% in late March. The Fed also raised interest rates on three-month treasury bills from 5.5% to around 9.5% in an attempt to slow down consumer spending.

This article from the April 10, 1989 issue of *Business Week* illustrates the monetarist approach to slowing inflation. In this approach to controlling inflation the money supply must be tightened. This tightening is done by the Fed through its three major operations which are <u>controlling the discount buying and selling bonds and setting the reserve requirement</u>. If the Fed wants to try to slow inflation it will raise the discount rate, sell bonds in the open market and if necessary raise the reserve requirement. These three measures tend to slow consumer spending thus slowing inflation.

STUDY QUESTIONS

1. Nathan presents several points in his summary paragraph, but you may have finished it wondering why he didn't provide more. Reread the article from *Business Week*. What details could he have included? Rewrite Nathan's first paragraph, adding these details to make it more informative.

2. Nathan tells us that the article describes the "monetarist approach" to economics. Use your library to learn what this approach is and write a brief paragraph describing it.

BUSINESS ASSIGNMENT 3

Course: **Introduction to Finance**

In the course of the semester you will write six short papers based on articles about situations of current financial interest.

You are limited to one typed page, single-spaced. At the top of the page you must list, in proper bibliographic form, the source for your paper. Under this will be the date, class section number, and your name.

The paper itself will contain three paragraphs. The first is a summary of the article in which you will focus only on those parts of the article relevant to the financial situation. The second paragraph will contain the effect this situation will have on the public. The third paragraph will contain what you have learned from the article. In this last paragraph you are expected to go beyond the information in the article but still stay within the general topic.

You will be graded on your choice of the article, on following the above format, and on the clarity and quality of your writing.

Analysis of Business Assignment 3

This assignment is very similar to the previous one. The teacher states explicitly that grades will be based on the choice of the article, ability to follow the prescribed format, and the clarity of the writing. But if you look closely at the assignment, you begin to understand that the teacher is using it as a more significant learning device. That is, the teacher isn't just interested in discovering whether students can follow directions and write three paragraphs.

Consider the nature of the three paragraphs: The first acts as a summary ("this is what the article said"); the second as interpretation ("this is why it's important"); the third as explanation ("this is what I learned"). Students who can engage in these three activities with any depth will succeed on the assignment.

Some students may reasonably ask why the teacher plans to evaluate one set of criteria while actually being more interested in another. Unfortunately, we have no ready answer to this question. We can only say that it seems fairly common for teachers to address the concerns of their classes—indeed, of their disciplines—indirectly, as though discovering what's important and what isn't is a kind of test designed to differentiate those who will succeed from those who won't. In any event, we encourage students to read their assignments very carefully so they can focus on what their teachers are really trying to accomplish.

Class Article 3

"Wintertime—and the Farmers Aren't Easy"

by Kathleen A. Beholf in Chicago, with Robert D. Hof in San Francisco and Sandra D. Atchison in Denver, and bureau reports

Think of winter on the Great Plains . . . visions of snow-covered fields and white-all-over farmhouses. Think again. It's not white that John Junior Armstrong sees around his Muscotah (Kan.) farm. He's eyeing drought. Laments Armstrong: "I'm in one of the driest counties in the state."

Farmers across Kansas are fretting that their hard, red winter wheat, the state's major crop, may be lying in the soil, dead, the victim of too little moisture and too wild temperatures. Nor is Kansas alone in suffering winter's wrath: There's flooding east of the Mississippi and a big chill in California.

Last summer's drought helped to push long-quiescent food prices up 4% in 1988. This year, with inflation suddenly having become an increasing source of anxiety and folks nationwide wondering what gives with the weather, there's a keen interest in the coming growing season. Do drought, shriveled crops, and sprouting prices lie ahead?

FALSE SUMMER. Not to worry, say the weathermen. Despite the patches of problems in areas beset by weird weather, the Agriculture Dept.'s chief meteorologist, Norton D. Strommen, is optimistic. "The outlook for agricultural production going into the planting season is encouraging," he says, "particularly compared with where we were last fall." One especially good sign: In some areas, there has been a full recharge of soil moisture.

Of course, that's little solace to the farmers in Kansas. There, "winter kill" occurs when the snow cover is so thin that the wheat crop goes unprotected when the "Siberian express" barrels in with subzero temperatures. This year, the weather in parts of Kansas, Oklahoma, and Texas wrought unusual havoc. "On Feb. 1," Armstrong recalls, "we were up to 72 degrees. The wheat was starting to come out. Within 24 hours, it had dropped to seven below zero."

Even if the winter wheat recovers from the frost, continued dryness could doom it. Ed Johannsen, a farmer in Little River, Kan., planted 600 acres of winter wheat. He's anticipating a loss between 30% and 50% if springtime brings little rain. "If it's all gone," Johannsen says, "I will lose between $100 and $200 an acre"—a total of $60,000 to $120,000.

"Wintertime—And the Farmers Aren't Easy" reprinted from the March 6, 1989 issue of *Business Week* by special permission. Copyright © 1989 by Mcgraw-Hill, Inc.

Although only one crop, winter wheat is of no small importance. Planted in October and harvested in June and July, it represents 80% of the nation's wheat crop, a key ingredient in food staples such as bread. Even food companies are worried. Says John Ferris, senior vice-president of finance at the Minneapolis-based Super Valu Stores Inc., a major food distributor: "If we don't get adequate moisture in the spring, there's no question that prices will be affected." Further reflecting the fears is the futures market. The nearby contract for winter wheat now trades around $4.30 a bushel—not far off the $4.32 high hit during the drought last summer.

Winter wheat is not the only concern. Cold weather will likely push up prices on fruits and vegetables, too. Below-zero weather in the Grand Valley farming country of Colorado has done serious damage there. "No apricots, sweet cherries, or peaches," observes Max L. Noland, a farmer in Palisade.

PUMPING COSTS. It's worse yet in California, which is suffering a double whammy of cold and drought. The state's oranges, lemons, and avocados have fallen victim to frigid temperatures. Farmer Donald J. Laux, who supplies Sunkist Growers Inc. with oranges and lemons from his 4,000-acre ranch in the San Joaquin Valley town of Porterville, reckons he lost a quarter of his orange crop and three-fourths of his lemons.

Meanwhile, water levels in the state's reservoirs are 65% of normal. U.S. Bureau of Reclamation officials are warning California farmers that their water allocations may be cut by 50% unless the rains come. That would be the first time in memory that the bureau's Central Valley Project has taken such a step. "This year the drought will have a pretty severe effect," says William I. DuBois, water expert for the California Farm Bureau Federation. That's because pumping groundwater costs a lot more than simply drawing it from government irrigation projects. For example, one Sacramento County farmer now pumps water from 140 feet below the surface, which costs $25 an acre-foot, compared with $3 an acre-foot to get water only 40 feet below ground.

Rain also is the watchword for harvesters of corn, soybeans, and spring wheat. Because last year's drought dramatically lowered crop stockpiles (chart) [omitted] and sucked moisture out of the farmland subsoil, another drought year would be devastating. For example, last year's corn crop of 4.9 billion bushels was 30% lower than the previous year's. That left lower carryover supplies for this season: Current stocks of corn are less than half what they were one year ago. Says Sherman L. Levin, a Chicago agribusiness consultant: "The stocks are sufficient—provided the next growing season has at least a normal crop."

History offers some comfort. "Never have you had two severe

droughts in a row," notes Steve Freed, grain analyst with Dean Witter Reynolds Inc. If history repeats itself and the drought doesn't, inflation watchers will be joining farmers in a huge sigh of relief.

Guide for Reading

Scott meets the minimal requirements for the assignment: he has three paragraphs, and they roughly correspond to the criteria his teacher gave. Nevertheless, his paper is below average. Note that after summarizing the article in paragraph 1, Scott doesn't have much to say in paragraph 2 about how the situation will affect the public. Then, in paragraph 3, he doesn't clearly demonstrate what he learned from the article. He begins by saying that signs are encouraging that another drought won't ravage crops, only to jump to another topic—global warming—that, without more information, will strike most readers as misplaced. What is the relationship here? He goes on to talk about high birthrates, again without making any connections to his topic.

SAMPLE BUSINESS PAPER 6

Untitled

Scott L. (a junior)

Winter wheat, planted in October and harvested in June and July represents 80% of the nation's wheat crop, may be in jeopardy. After last summer's devastating drought pushed food prices up 4%, farmers are concerned that the winter wheat harvest may be lost to "winter kill" which occurs when insufficient snow cover leaves the crop unprotected against sub-zero temperatures. Also radical temperature variations are shocking the crops. On February 1st in Muscotah Kansas, the thermometer fell from 72 degrees to − 7 degrees within 24 hours. The weather has been unpredictable, dynamic, and widespread affecting not only the bread basket of the mid-west but also the San Joaquin Valley in California, thus threatening the prices of fruits and vegetables. If the winter does not devastate the crops another drought could. This could force farmers to pump ground water, at extra costs, from already depleted water tables.

If this happens, the commodities market $4.32 a bushel high, set last summer, may be a memory since a bushel now trades for $4.30. Last years drought depleted corn, soybean, and wheat stocks to such an extent that another drought this year will exhaust the nations reserves. This fear is causing much anxiety and inflationary pressures.

Norton D. Strommen, the chief meteorologist of the Agricultural Department, is optimistic because in some areas a full recovery of soil moisture has occurred. Another encouraging sign is that in our history the U.S. has never had two droughts in a row. However, indications thus far are not all that comforting. If global warming, due to the green house effect, deterioration of the ozone and deforestation causes a trend, the U.S. as well as the world, could be in for a rude awakening. One climatologist said, on T.V. that three droughts in a row could cause small scale famine in the U.S. I believe that the underlying problem is a snow balling birth rate producing more people who are demanding their share of the pie. More people with more environmentally hazardous products is going to take its toll. The pie isn't getting larger; the slices are getting smaller. This article illustrates that in order to keep our fragile and uncertain livelihood we need to incorporate new strategies to continue mankind's success.

STUDY QUESTIONS

1. The assignment specifies that the second paragraph should "contain the effect" the situation described in the article will have on the public. Reread the *Business Week* article and list three possible effects that Nathan fails to mention that the situation could have on the public.

2. What skills do you think the teacher who gave this assignment is trying to develop in each paragraph? Which skill do you believe is the most important? Given this assignment, which paragraph do you think should be the longest of the three?

3. Scott's third paragraph is neither cohesive nor coherent. What changes could you make to improve it?

4. Scott's biggest mechanical problem is perhaps his inability to use commas correctly. What are three other mechanical problems that you see in his paper?

Class Article 4

"Trying Times at Boeing"

by Maria Shao in Seattle, with Seth Payne in Washington, John Templeman in Bonn, Mark Maremont in London, and bureau reports

Is something wrong with Boeing Co.?
 The giant warplane manufacturer keeps getting in the news, and much of the news is bad. On Feb. 24 televisions around the world flashed images of a United Airlines Inc. Boeing 747 jet that had ripped open in flight early that day off Honolulu, killing nine passengers. It was

---

"Trying Times at Boeing" reprinted from the March 13, 1989 issue of *Business Week* by special permission. Copyright © 1989 by McGraw-Hill, Inc.

the fourth fatal accident involving a Boeing jet since December. And the air disasters coincide with problems on the ground: Boeing's management, regarded as one of the best in the aerospace industry, has been badly embarrassed by recent quality-control problems and costly production delays of the brand-new 747-400.

Boeing is a victim of its own success. For 72 years the company has been building high-quality planes, and today, more than 30 years after it introduced its first jetliner, the Seattle-based giant commands 55% of the world's commercial jet market. So the odds are that a major plane accident will involve a Boeing-made aircraft, whether the company is at fault or not. And Boeing's market dominance seems assured through the 1990s, even in the face of fierce competition from McDonnell Douglas Corp. and Airbus Industrie. Just in late February, Boeing landed almost $4 billion in new orders.

But the rush of new orders is leading to production demands the company is struggling to meet. The result: Boeing's sterling reputation for on-time delivery and top-flight quality has been tarnished. Says John Nance, an aviation safety expert based in Tacoma, Wash.: "People expect perfection from Boeing. When Boeing isn't perfect, everyone takes notice."

At the same time the company is feeling the effects of mounting public concern over air safety—even though investigators have not found the company responsible for a major accident since the 1985 crash of a Japan Air Lines 747 was directly linked to faulty repair work done by Boeing.

Boeing argues that it has been a leader in studying aging jets, and that most accidents stem from such factors as human error and weather, not airplane flaws. . . . Nevertheless, the company is the target of intense, often hostile scrutiny around the world. The day after a recent Boeing 707 crash in the Azores, for example, a major Irish newspaper ran the taunting headline: "What has gone wrong this time, Mr. Boeing?"

'OVERCOMMITTED.' While Boeing grapples with the task of explaining its role in air safety, it must also handle some disgruntled customers. The company has piled up a $50 billion backlog stretching into the mid-1990s (chart) [omitted], and 1989 profits should jump 50%, to $918 million, as revenues grow 29%, to $22 billion. Profits should surge further as airlines start replacing aging fleets. Yet with production lines working overtime, Boeing has had to delay delivery of its first batch of 747-400s, the new version of its wide-body, by two to six months.

That's the first time in 20 years Boeing has missed a delivery deadline. "We overcommitted," concedes Dean D. Thornton, president of Boeing's commercial airplane subsidiary. "We violated a covenant with our customers, and I'm pretty damn ashamed of it."

The company will be lucky if it can deliver the 57 new 747s it promised for this year. The push to meet the revised schedule will lower Boeing's profit margins on the 747 to 20%, down from the expected 25%, according to William N. Deatherage, an analyst at Dean Witter Reynolds Inc.

The delays, some announced on short notice, will force airlines such as KLM and Cathay Pacific to reschedule or cut back flights during the peak summer travel season, costing them millions of dollars in revenue. Even concessions that Boeing is now negotiating in an effort to appease its customers are little consolation. "We are angry," says Jürgen Weber, chief operations officer at Lufthansa, which will not receive all six of the 747s it ordered for the year until December. "The whole fleet program will have to be reworked, but we can never fully close all the gaps this year."

Thornton, a 26-year company veteran who managed the successful 767 program, now admits that Boeing underestimated the task of building the 747-400, which has 175 miles of wires and a few million parts. For one thing, the 747 cockpit required a total redesign to incorporate more advanced electronic controls and accommodate two crew members instead of three. To give customers more choices, Boeing also attempted for the first time to win simultaneous Federal Aviation Administration certification for engines from three different manufacturers. And to satisfy unexpectedly heavy demand, the company doubled the production rate in just one year, which caused glitches in parts supplies and forced many planes to be assembled out of sequence.

'STRETCHED THIN.' That quickened pace is taking its toll on workers, too. Although employment at Boeing has jumped 83% since 1983, to 155,000, the increase in manpower has not been enough to relieve the pressure, especially since many of the new workers are unseasoned. Steven R. Huffman, a 747 mechanic, says he has worked 60 hours a week for the past 3½ years. "You're tired. There's no social life, no family," he says. "My wife would like to tell this place where to go." Admits Thornton: "We are stretched thin on resources."

Many in the industry wonder if the stress on workers will lead to quality slips. To counter that possibility, Boeing has stepped up training. At the Everett (Wash.) plant, 5,000 new workers have taken blueprint-reading classes and practiced riveting and drilling before starting assembly-line jobs. Boeing also conducts "pre-employment" training for serious job candidates at local vocational-technical schools.

Straightening out the 747 program is not Thornton's only manufacturing challenge. He also has to detect and correct any quality-control problems that remain. Several reported cases of miswiring on Boeing planes led to an unprecedented directive on Jan. 31 from the FAA ordering the inspection of most Boeing commercial planes produced since 1980. In all, 30 cases of miswiring and incorrectly installed plumbing were discovered. Most of them were in the fire extinguishing systems of cargo compartments.

The miswirings also provoked two sharply worded letters to Boeing from Leroy A. Keith, the FAA's top man in Seattle. Keith accused Boeing of waiting months before it reported miswiring on a Royal Brunei Airlines plane and told the company to review its entire approach to designing and installing components. Boeing's quality-control program is "not as good as it used to be," says Keith.

Boeing feels it violated no rules in reporting the Royal Brunei miswiring, but Thornton admits the company's design made it too easy to switch or incorrectly install the wires. He's already planning steps to make the system "Murphy-proof," and he says Boeing is cooperating fully with the FAA's stepped-up surveillance of Boeing's production, inspection, and installation procedures.

As if all this weren't enough, Thornton and his managers have to worry about their competitors. A resurgent McDonnell Douglas has won an estimated $9 billion in orders for its MD-11 long-range widebody. And Airbus Industrie will begin deliveries in 1990 of widebody A330 and A340 planes. "Boeing can't let its guard down. Both its competitors will continue to challenge it on every front," says Howard Rubel, an analyst at C. J. Lawrence, Morgan Grenfell Inc. In a parry to the MD-11, Boeing expects to begin selling a derivative of its widebody 767, which will feature added seats and possibly a third engine.

Despite all its problems, Boeing enjoys the fundamental trust of its regulators and customers. "We do not question the safety of Boeing aircraft," says Anthony Broderick, the FAA's associate administrator for aviation standards. Even Lufthansa's Weber, annoyed as he is, praises the company: "Boeing has built good aircraft in the past and will in the future." In the months and years to come, Boeing has to make sure it does not betray that trust.

Guide for Reading

Tina's paper is a bit longer than the other two we've looked at, but it isn't necessarily better. She uses too much space summarizing the article, and as a result she has little room left for the other two parts of the assignment. Her paper clearly illustrates what happens when a student fails to consider why teachers give assignments, because she focuses on the easiest part of the task, summarizing, and neglects interpretation and explanation.

Business Writing

SAMPLE BUSINESS PAPER 7

Untitled

Tina Michele F. (a junior)

Boeing Company, a giant manufacturer of airplanes, is receiving all the bad news. Recently, Boeing has been getting complaints about the quality of their planes, including a series of miswirings and concern about the ages of aircraft. There was the older Aloha Airlines 737 incident, where part of its roof was lost in midair. Also, this February, nine passengers died as a massive hole opened up in a United 747, while flying over the Pacific. These and other incidents are the complaints Being Co. keeps hearing about. Is this ruining their image or reputation, as being the builders of high quality planes? Could the causes of these accidents be that the planes are just getting too old? Boeing argues that most of these accidents are from the causes of weather or human error, and not from airplane flaws. Boeing is still receiving 55% of the world's commercial market for jets and recently received new orders totaling $4 billion. However, with this demand for all these new planes, Boeing is facing the problem of not being able to meet deadlines. Their top-flight quality and on-time delivery reputation is becoming tarnished. There is now alot of time spent with the concern of air safety and precautions that have slowed production down. The company is ashamed of delays. Customers are complaining about the delays of their orders. Boeing has had production lines working overtime, but still that is not enough to meet the demand. One employee says that he has been working 60 hours a week for over three years now. Boeing has not missed a delivery deadline in 20 years, until now. Dean D. Thornton, president of Boeing's commercial airline subsidiary, says that they are overcommitted. These delays are hurting airlines and they are having to reschedule flights, while losing millions of dollars. So, is the quality control of Boeing's, "not as good as it used to be"? Some people are saying this, while Boeing feels this is not so. Boeing will make all the attempts necessary to prove their planes are safe.

So, what effect has this had on the public? People are becoming more concerned about the safety of these airplanes and their lives. The competitors are enjoying taking the orders that cannot be met by Boeing. Overall, more safety standards are having to be met to ensure the safety of the passengers.

In this article I learned of all the pressures mounted on Boeing, concerning the newer and safer aircraft. I do hope, however, that these airplane incidents will be eliminated in the near future. No one would like to "Fly the Friendly Skies", to die.

STUDY QUESTIONS

1. Tina devotes most of her paper to summarizing the Boeing article. In addition to slighting the other two parts of the assignment, what problem does this emphasis cause for readers?

2. A certain convention usually governs summaries, and it is that they are supposed to be "value neutral." A writer simply presents the "facts," using another portion of the paper to interpret them and to provide an assessment of their value. Identify words and expressions in Tina's summary that suggest she is not being value neutral. What effect, if any, do these words and expressions have on readers?

3. Does Tina's last paragraph seem appropriate for the assignment? Why or why not?

Writing Assignments

Although the health of the economy affects just about everyone, a surprising number of people have little or no understanding of how it touches their daily lives. The following assignments ask you to address this phenomenon.

1. Find an article in a periodical or newspaper that discusses some aspect of the national economy. In about 2 pages, summarize the content of the article for a group of your peers, then explain the effect

the information has or can have on their lives. Successful responses will focus on explanation, not summary; they will be clear, detailed, and informative.
2. It has become widely accepted that today's young people will not be able to attain a lifestyle above what their parents have, because of the dollar's reduced buying power and because of our reduced earning potential. In a 3- to 5-page paper, describe the changes in prices and incomes that have occurred over the last 20 years and predict what these changes mean for you and your peers. Successful responses will provide detailed descriptions, and their predictions will be well substantiated with facts, trends, and observations.
3. The past several years have marked a period of bank failures. Numerous banks have suffered huge losses as a result of bad loans to Third World countries. More recently, bad loans in the savings and loan industry have forced the federal government to allocate approximately $500 billion to rescue failing S&Ls, a sum that analysts expect will eventually exceed $1 trillion. Drawing on information available in your school library, write a 5- to 7-page paper that traces the history of these financial problems, explains the key factors that led to the current situation, and predicts the effects the situation will have on students over the next 10 years.

INSTRUCTOR'S MANUAL for
The Interdisciplinary Reader

James D. Williams
University of North Carolina—Chapel Hill

David Huntley
Appalachian State University

Christine Hanks
University of North Carolina—Chapel Hill

HarperCollins*Publishers*

ASSIGNMENTS AND PAPERS

The assignments and papers in *The Interdisciplinary Reader* were collected from colleges and universities throughout the United States, so they reflect the broad concerns of faculty who teach undergraduates. Most of the assignments were given to us in written form and are included verbatim. In only a few cases were the assignments conveyed to students orally. For these, we have tried to reproduce, in the form of paragraphs and/or lists, what the teacher remembers saying to the class. We feel that the overall result is a valid representation of the writing tasks that most college students will encounter during their college years.

We have concentrated on assignments written for freshman and sophomore courses, because these are the classes that most students will be taking in addition to freshman composition. For some disciplines, students aren't asked to write much at the introductory level, so some of the assignments come from junior and senior courses. Although most of your students won't have the knowledge to duplicate these assignments, they can write papers that will prepare them for these upper-level courses by responding to the additional assignments we've included.

Our analyses of the assignments are directed to the students and attempt to answer the general question: "How should I respond to this task?" In all cases, we encourage students to recognize the minimal requirements of each assignment and then to go beyond them. We also try to point out what may be implied in an assignment and to explain how to respond to these implications in a way that will produce a better-than-average paper. For example, when an assignment doesn't say anything about style or even dismisses "grammar" as a consideration, we explain that all teachers will respond better to a paper that is well written and pleasing to read, as long as the content is appropriate. In general, we encourage students to become involved in their topic and to write to inform a wide audience. Writing that tries to impress a teacher usually isn't good writing.

In some cases, it is necessary for us to point out what may seem to be shortcomings in an assignment. We do this as a part of our effort to get students to read assignments carefully and critically, not to attack the professor who gave the assignment. Students who can analyze assignments correctly and who can understand the implied requirements will be able to respond more successfully.

The additional assignments included in most sections are designed to imitate the one analyzed without requiring that the students (and teacher) have knowledge of that particular class. Whenever we haven't included additional assignments, we assume that the original one lends itself to enough variety to accommodate the knowledge and interests of the teacher and students.

The sample papers are real student responses and represent a wide range of writing strengths and weaknesses among college students. Whenever possible, we have included a good, an average, and a poor paper to provide models to aspire to and problems to avoid. In a few cases, the good papers are excellent models for the kind of responses most teachers would like to see from their students. Some of the good papers are only partially good, and we have pointed out their strengths and weaknesses. The average responses are those that do what the assignment asks for but that don't engage readers. They are competent but uninspired papers that show students why doing the minimum doesn't deserve an A.

The poor responses vary in the types of problems they represent. Some make a promise that isn't fulfilled; some are the results of the writer misreading the assignment; some are the results of a poorly planned thesis; and some show that the writer put forth no effort beyond writing something to hand in. For a few assignments, the responses differ very little in overall quality (no outstanding or very poor papers). Whenever this is the case, we have pointed out the strengths and weaknesses of each paper and have then explained the necessary ingredients for an excellent paper.

Although having three responses clearly representing good, average, and poor writing for each assignment may seem ideal, we discovered that student writing rarely fits into such neat categories. In fact, such clearly defined models (if they actually exist) don't require much explanation or discussion. The papers that are worth studying are those that show a good idea executed poorly, a weak thesis but some thoughtful insights, a misunderstanding of the assignment, and so forth. If students read and study enough samples, however, they will see characteristics of their own writing from a perspective that isn't provided by viewing their own papers. Seeing in a general way what they tend to do individually should give them the skills to critique their own papers more effectively.

Our "Guide for Reading" paragraphs provide a brief description of each paper's quality, and they ask questions designed to get students involved as they read. We feel that students should know something about the papers in advance so they can look for specific characteristics. Their own response to a paper will be more helpful if they know what to focus on. Our intention is not to force students into identifying the quality of any one paper. Rather, it is to gradually instruct them through numerous examples of good, average, and poor writing.

We have not tried to exhaust all critical comments in the analyses that follow the papers for the first assignment in each chapter. Instead, we have responded to the papers as we would have if our own students had written them. We deal with the most important issue first: content (purpose or thesis, recognition of complexities, the presence of support and evidence). Then we address such features as organization, style, and surface errors. We also point out how well the paper responds to the assignment, making specific references to the assignment when necessary. If the writer's tone is obtrusive, we address this point, because the student's attitude toward the topic can determine the difference between a very good or a poor paper. We have left room for you and your students to go beyond our remarks and to discuss features that you and they feel are important.

One of the most important skills for students to acquire is the ability to assess their own writing critically, so we have not provided full analyses for the sample papers that respond to the second and third assignments in each chapter. The study questions are designed to focus on specific features of the papers as well as to provide practice in rewriting problem sentences and paragraphs. After complete discussions of the analyzed papers and a careful reading of those that aren't analyzed, your students should be able to write an accurate analysis, with practice and the aid of study questions. We feel that this procedure will help students eventually to critique their own writing accurately, an essential skill in good writing.

A few of the papers were submitted to us without grades or comments, and we judged these by how well they responded to the assignment and by what we feel are some universally recognized characteristics of good writing. We didn't ignore grades and comments when they did appear, but for the sake of consistency we judged all the papers by the same standards. In some cases this resulted in our using as poor examples papers that received high grades. We didn't discover any good papers that had received poor grades, leading us to feel that most teachers don't grade papers with the intent to find fault.

SAMPLE UNIT

We have included sample units of chemistry, psychology, and film as proposed methods of using the assignments provided in the text. The nine steps in the units will work for any of the subjects in the text. As you progress through the term, some steps may require less emphasis and time as students acquire analytical and writing skills, and the unit itself can be modified to reflect your objectives and the abilities of your students.

The number of writing tasks you are able to assign will depend on your students and the goals you set for the course. The term can be divided into four sections, with each one focusing on one of the four main sections of the text: the Life and Applied Sciences, the Social Sciences, Humanities, and Business. Assigning one, two, or three papers from each section will familiarize your students with the types of writing they will likely encounter in their undergraduate careers. Of course, as you increase the number of papers students must write, you will have to decrease their length.

Even if you had the time to assign papers from each chapter, your students would still face different assignments in their own course work. We feel, however, that if you emphasize to your class the skill of analyzing assignments and papers, your students will be prepared to respond well to any assignment they may face. The sample unit is designed to teach the process of writing for an assignment as much as it is designed to teach a specific kind of writing.

In the first few assignments for your class, you may want to proceed through each of the nine steps very carefully, placing equal emphasis on the skills of analyzing and writing. By midterm, diligent students should be able to analyze the assignments and sample papers quickly and then move on to their own writing assignment. They should also be able to analyze and respond to an assignment they may be given in any undergraduate class.

The nine steps below are described in general terms so they will apply to any chapter you use. The specific units for chemistry, psychology, and film follow this general description.

Step 1 is designed to familiarize students with the general requirements of writing in the various disciplines. Most students associate writing primarily with English classes, so they need to realize that writing is an important part of all disciplines. Each discipline has its own specific requirements and expectations, but at the same time, all disciplines adhere to similar requirements for what we recognize as good writing.

Our introductions to each chapter were written after examining many assignments from that particular discipline. We have discussed the characteristics of those that appear to be the ones most frequently assigned in undergraduate classes. The introductions, then, cover the basic characteristics of the assignments that your students will most likely be faced with. In addition, if they learn the process of analyzing assignments, they can respond well to a type of assignment not covered in the text.

Step 2 focuses on the skill of analyzing assignments. It is important to stress the necessity of both reading an assignment carefully and then analyzing it completely. Most students read assignments quickly, and as a result they get, at best, a vague idea of what the teacher is asking them to do. They need to realize that the first step in writing a paper is to form a clear and accurate picture of the type of paper their teacher expects them to write. In our analyses of the assignments, we have tried to answer two general questions: "What is this assignment asking me to do, and how can I write a better-than-average paper?" In answering these questions, we have pointed out and explained both the explicit instructions and the implied assumptions often ignored by students.

When working on this step, you will want to help your students see ways to go beyond the minimum requirements while staying within the boundaries of the assignment. In general, we have pointed out that students tend to write good papers when they become involved with their topics and genuinely want to inform their readers. They must recognize that the instructions usually set the minimum standards for a paper; they must search for a topic that will interest readers; and they must sometimes use more resources than those suggested.

We encourage students to write carefully and correctly, even when the assignment states that surface features are of secondary importance. In addition, we believe that most teachers are favorably impressed by papers that contain more relevant information rather than less, even if they go slightly beyond suggested lengths.

Because the next step involves examining the sample papers, your students should first have a clear idea of the type of paper the assignment is asking for. You may want them to write a list of characteristics necessary for an average response and then to add those that the better papers should include. Your students will have a clear standard by which to judge the sample papers.

We believe that students benefit from studying typical responses to specific assignments. Quite often they will recognize characteristics of their own writing (both good and bad) from a perspective that will enable them to understand the effects of these characteristics. When reading their own papers, students are often distracted by what they meant to say and don't see clearly what they actually said. When reading another student's response to an assignment, they are more likely to notice gaps in information, lack of explanation and development, and awkwardly worded passages. Reading a number of responses critically and then analyzing them will enhance students' ability to do the same with their own work.

In our analyses, we have focused on those characteristics of the papers that will affect a reader who knows what the assignments ask for. In most cases this reader is the teacher. We have listed the general criteria we apply to most of the sample papers in **Step 3** of the chemistry unit and a more elaborate list in the same step for the film unit. We do not go through this list for every paper, however, for two reasons: The text would be much too long and cumbersome, and not every paper needs to be discussed in the same way. As an instructional tool early in the term, you may want to have your students respond to a list of criteria for each paper as a starting point for their analyses.

After your students have learned to evaluate papers for content, development, and organization, they can then focus on style and word choice. Too many students think that correct spelling, standard usage, and five paragraphs automatically produce a good paper. By first dealing with the more important issues, you may help dispel this notion, and your students will see that the finer points are to be attended to in the later drafts after they have successfully worked on the substance of the paper.

Step 4 is designed to prepare students to write analyses of sample papers after first analyzing the assignment. All assignments for which we have sample papers are analyzed in the text, so this step will involve more discussion than new analysis. As in **Step 2,** your students should write a list of characteristics necessary for an adequate and a good response before attempting an analysis.

For all of the papers we haven't analyzed, we have included study questions that focus on various strengths and weaknesses of each paper. They require students to read the paper carefully, and in some cases they ask students to make appropriate corrections and revisions. In **Step 5,** working with these questions and any others you add should give your students a good idea of the overall quality of the papers and some of the specific strengths and weaknesses.

Step 6 asks students to complete two tasks: to read carefully and critically and to write. Because they are now engaged in their first writing task (with the exception of making lists), you will want them to be conscious of the same considerations that the assignments ask for (length, audience, tone, language, and so forth). We feel that **Step 6** should be taken as seriously as **Step 8,** even though this isn't the ultimate goal of the unit. Being forced to write well will encourage careful and accurate thinking, and every time students work at writing they are sharpening skills that will help produce better results for the next task.

One skill most students lack is the ability to evaluate their own writing critically. They hand in papers hoping that they have done what the teacher wants but are never sure until the paper is returned with a grade. Many are convinced that the grade is arbitrarily determined by "what the teacher wants" and has very little to do with the accepted standards of good writing. Students who feel this way and want to make good grades are distracted by trying to please the teacher when they should be focusing on the characteristics of their writing. The two are not always the same. **Step 6** gives them practice evaluating a response to a specific assignment (which they have already evaluated), which in turn will help convince them that their own writing can be evaluated by the same standards.

For **Step 7,** you will choose an assignment for your students to respond to. In most cases, we have provided additional assignments that imitate in some way the ones for which there are sample papers. Whenever we haven't included additional assignments, we have assumed that the one in the text can be adapted to your own interests and knowledge. In this step, it's important for your students to describe, in writing, the type of paper the assignment asks for. They may even want to write an analysis as we have in the text. In either case, they need to know what the assignment states, what it implies, what the minimum requirements are, and what they need to do to write a good paper.

The magnitude of **Step 8** depends on the assignment chosen. Some assignments require content work in class or research in the library or both. Others require very little preparation beyond reading an article or attending a concert. If the assignment calls for extensive class discussion, reading, and research, your students should begin working on content as soon as they begin the unit. In fact, you should probably give your students a general idea of the assignment at this time. Form and content can develop together.

Step 9 involves getting students to evaluate their own and their classmates' papers, both the drafts and the final versions. We hope that by the end of the term students will see themselves, the teacher, and classmates as partners in the writing process, and that they will see writing as a collaboration toward a finished product. We recommend using a workshop approach that will facilitate peer interactions.

CHEMISTRY UNIT

The following unit is one possible approach to an assignment in chemistry based on Writing Assignment 1 in Chemistry Assignment 2.

Step 1: Read and study "Introduction to Writing in Chemistry," focusing on the characteristics and demands of undergraduate chemistry assignments. You may want to discuss with your students some of the ways in which writing in chemistry differs from the writing they are familiar with. Most students don't know how to be completely objective in their language, and they have been told to avoid passive voice, which is usually required in lab reports. Because many students feel that scientific subjects often demand an approach completely different from that in writing for English, history, and so forth, you may also want to point out the characteristics that writing in chemistry shares with writing in the humanities and the social sciences. The bulk of a lab report demands an objective approach, but the conclusion needs to be an honest evaluation of the experiment written in a relaxed, objective tone.

Step 2: Read, study, analyze, and discuss Chemistry Assignment 1. The purpose of this exercise is to begin showing students how to read and analyze assignments. In your discussions, you may want to focus on the methods the text uses for analysis, any disagreements your students have with the analysis, and any additional points in the assignment you want to stress. The goal is to get your students to the point where they are reading assignments critically instead of reacting somewhat frantically and blindly to a set of instructions.

They should then write analyses for the three additional assignments that follow the third sample paper. Their analysis should tell students how to respond to the assignments in a way that will produce a good paper. For this particular assignment, you may want to explain how you, as a teacher, respond to topics students select because of apparent ease and then to give some points on how they can pick topics that will interest them as well as you.

It's also important for you to discuss the implications of the last two sentences in the assignment—"The paper will be graded on the basis of content. Style will not be considered unless it is atrocious." Students need to realize that when they are careless with surface features and style, it will seriously affect the readability of the paper.

Step 3: Read and discuss the three sample papers and the analyses provided. In this exercise, you want to stress the skills necessary for reading papers critically: (1) What does the assignment ask for? (2) Does the paper deliver it? (3) Does the paper contain a clear thesis? (4) Does it support the thesis adequately? (5) Does the writer provide relevant and convincing support? (6) What is the intended audience? (7) Is it appropriate for the assignment and topic?

Our analyses in this section deal mainly with reader response. We haven't provided a list of criteria for judging, as some students may expect. Instead, we have responded as readers who want to be informed and entertained (to a degree) and as teachers who are looking for signs that the student responded correctly to the assignment. You may also want to discuss with your students any disagreements they have with the analyses in the text (how do you feel about the double topic in Paper 2?).

Step 4: Read, study, analyze, and discuss Chemistry Assignment 2. It may be necessary for you to explain to your students the purpose of abstracts and the language and length appropriate for them. Showing students how using abstracts can save them time in their own research will impress upon them the value of concise, informative abstracts.

Step 5: Work with the guides for reading that precede the sample papers and the study questions that follow each of the sample papers, adding any questions that you feel are necessary to focus on other important characteristics of the writing.

Step 6: Have your students write analyses of one of the sample papers, using the skills they learned by studying the analyses in the first assignment. Because these papers don't clearly fall into good, average, and poor categories, a good exercise would be to have your class break into small groups and to put together a good paper, using the best parts from the three.

Step 7: Discuss and analyze the first item under "Writing Assignments." You may want your students to write an analysis that imitates the analyses in the text or simply to list the features necessary for a good paper. The object is to get students to produce a specific description of what a good summary will contain and what qualities are necessary to make it suitable for publication in a local newspaper. They will need to define their audience, which will determine the language, length, and technical information appropriate to their summary.

Step 8: Have your students complete Assignment 1; work with them in analyzing their drafts using the guidelines listed in Step 4.

Step 9: When your students hand in their final versions of their paper, you may want to have each one write an analysis of another student's paper and categorize the paper as either good, average, or poor. Emphasizing analysis rather than grading will help students see that a grade indicates how well a paper responds to the assignment and that it isn't something a teacher arbitrarily decides.

PSYCHOLOGY UNIT

The following unit presents one possible approach to teaching the chapter on writing in psychology. The unit leads the student toward writing a paper in response to Writing Assignment 2 in Psychology Assignment 2.

Assignment

Choose another experimental research report published in the *Journal of Abnormal Psychology*. Using the formal structure employed in Psychology Assignment 2, summarize and evaluate the report.

Step 1: Read and discuss the "Introduction to Writing in Psychology." This may be an appropriate time in the course to talk about the different kinds of writing within a discipline. In this chapter, your students will read student papers and one professional sample. One of the assignments asks students to write to an audience of high school students. The other two ask students to write to an audience within the profession, an audience familiar with the conventions and formats that characterize the field.

Encourage your students as they read these works to note how the demands of audience dictate the kind of writing produced. You may want to spend 30 minutes of class time on in-class writing exercises focusing on audience awareness. Have your students write a letter—a form that students easily recognize as audience-oriented—narrating an event to a friend. Then ask them to write a letter narrating the same event to a parent. How did the style and the content of the two letters differ? You may then encourage your students to see that most of the writing they do—in their academic career and outside of it—is directed toward a particular audience for a specific purpose.

The assignments that follow stipulate the audience that students should write to. Remind your students that even when assignments do not prescribe an audience, it is important to ask: "Who will read this writing? What is this audience's needs?"

Step 2: Read, study, analyze, and discuss Psychology Assignment 1. Let your students know that this assignment is quite different from the one they will be given later in the unit: It asks students to write to a high school audience and does not prescribe a formal organization.

At this point, you may want to explain to your students that writing assignments function in one of two ways: they are either integrated within the activities of the class or segregated from them. In other words, many writing assignments are like this one—they ask students to write papers that grow out of class discussion, lectures, and readings. But not all writing assignments do so. To broaden students' knowledge of a field, some teachers ask them to write papers on subjects that are not discussed in class or covered in lectures.

Remind students that an integrated writing assignment like this one requires students to incorporate a variety of course activities into their papers. In essence, their activities in class become part of the writing process. As your students will note in analyzing the three papers for this assignment, the better responses reflect a high level of engagement in class discussion, lectures, and readings.

Step 3: Read and discuss the three sample papers and the analyses that follow. In this step you will want your students to practice "matching" each sample paper to the criteria outlined in the assignment.

Ask your students to find evidence in each paper of the audience addressed in it. How do Angie, Kim, and Heather demonstrate their awareness of audience? How might your students have known, without reading the assignment, that these papers were directed toward high school students?

The teacher who made this assignment will also be looking for evidence within the paper that the student understood class lectures and readings, participated actively in class discussions, and took detailed notes when observing the videotapes. You may want to contrast Angie's and Heather's papers, focusing on the different ways they were developed. Which student has more fully demonstrated her involvement in these various class activities?

Step 4: Read, study, analyze, and discuss Psychology Assignment 2. Ask your students to identify the audience stipulated in this assignment. Also discuss the two parts of the assignment: summary and evaluation. If you have not yet discussed summary, this may be a good time to do so. We discuss summary in some detail in our analysis of Chemistry Assignment 2, so you might want to refer your students to the information found there.

INSTRUCTOR'S MANUAL

The assignment requires students to summarize and evaluate Bouchard's "Comparison of two group brainstorming procedures." Ask your students to read Bouchard's article, included in the text. This professional model offers a good example of the structure and language of formal writing in the social sciences. Ask students to compose a list of characteristics of such writing.

Step 5: Work with the guides for reading that precede the papers and the study questions that follow. Add any questions or points to consider that you think are important.

You might discuss the ratio of summary to evaluation in all these papers. Encourage your students to see evaluation as the real crux of a review paper—summary works in its service. All the papers included here could benefit from more concise summary and more elaborate evaluation.

Step 6: Have your students write analyses of one of the sample papers, using the skills they learned in studying the analyses in the first assignment. You might ask the students to write a letter to one of the student writers with suggestions for revisions.

Step 7: Discuss and analyze the second item under "Writing Assignments." It may be best to have your students review the same journal article. Students can use the details of Sample Assignment 2 as a guide for this paper, but you may need to construct a new set of questions for evaluation. This may be a good exercise for the class workshop.

Step 8: Your students will write their reviews of the journal article. The class workshop could be broken into two sessions: the first session for sharing drafts of the summary section of the paper and the second session for the evaluation section.

Step 9: When your students have completed the assignment, organize a grading workshop. They will be able to evaluate their peers' papers in the same way they evaluated the sample papers for Assignment 2.

FILM UNIT

Writing a critical analysis of a movie will provide students with valuable practice analyzing any art form. Because movies use both visual and verbal techniques and are considered pure entertainment by many students, this assignment will ask students to view a familiar art form from a new perspective with heightened perceptions.

Assignment

Write a 2- to 4-page critical analysis of a movie. Your thesis should deal with theme, character, or technique, and it must be supported by specific references to the film.

Step 1: Read and discuss the "Introduction to Writing in the Arts," focusing on the differences between analyzing a work of fiction and a visual art form. Most of your students will be weak in viewing skills, so you may want to begin developing these skills by having them watch commercials or short film takes on videotape. Looking for details will make them aware of certain techniques (sound, light, camera angles, cuts, framing, and so forth) and will provide practice in being observant.

Step 2: Read, study, analyze, and discuss Film Assignment 1. This step is especially important for this assignment because your students will not be writing a film review. They will probably have read few reviews, so they need to know the characteristics of this form of criticism and how it differs from critical analysis.

This step also gives students practice in analyzing assignments, which can help them understand what type of paper is being asked for. In addition to discussing the textual analysis of this assignment, you will need to discuss what you would expect, successful ways to organize the paper, the typical audience for a movie review, and the audience's expectations regarding language, style, support, and so forth. It would also be helpful to produce a list of the characteristics of what a good review will include, because the assignment doesn't go into much detail on what is expected.

Step 3: Read and discuss the three sample papers and the analyses that follow. In this step, you will want to stress the skills required for reading a paper critically, based on what the assignment asks for and the list produced in the previous step.

The first two papers show a marked difference in the authors' viewing skills and in what they think a review calls for. Mary saw, remembered, and made sense of all elements of the movie *Colors*, whereas Rodney viewed it as most people do—as pure entertainment. George's paper is an example of a personal problem that most students avoid, but one that often influences any evaluative paper to some degree. It will be worth your time to discuss ways your students can be critical in a constructive manner and how they can avoid distracting personal bias in their writing.

In this step, you will want to work on analytical skills as well as on evaluating these three papers.

Step 4: Read, study, analyze, and discuss Film Assignment 2, focusing on the differences in this assignment and the previous one. Your students will need to know how the purpose of a critical analysis differs from that of a review and that the audience of each will have different expectations. Readers of movie reviews expect the movie to be treated primarily as a source of entertainment, whereas the readers of a critical analysis expect to learn that the movie presents a theme or idea that transcends the momentary pleasure of viewing the movie.

In this step, you and your students will want to identify the characteristics of good, average, and poor papers as a guide for analyzing the three that follow. The following criteria will work as a guide for a very good critical analysis. Notice that content is given priority and that surface features are considered last. You can devise a graduated scale by reducing the demands in each category.

> The analysis will contain a clearly stated thesis that is fully explained and supported with relevant references to the movie. It will engage and inform the reader and will invite a second reading.
>
> The analysis will recognize the complexities of the thesis and effectively deal with them.
>
> The organization will be logical and will lead the reader from the beginning to the end in such a way that the argument is clear and convincing.
>
> The paragraphs will be fully developed, and the sentence structure varied and sophisticated.
>
> The analysis will be virtually free of surface errors.

Step 5: Work with the guides for reading that precede the papers and the study questions that follow. Add any questions or points to consider that you think are important.

Sarah's paper is a good model for an excellent analysis, and you may want to pull this one apart to show how she incorporates her thesis with explanation and support. Mike's paper presents a problem because it is initially impressive. He has obviously given some thought to the movie, and his command of sentence structure is more sophisticated than that of most college students. You will want to show how Mike's paper fails to enlighten readers, even though he seems to have discovered a profound message in the movie. This is also a good time to convince your students that an elaborate, self-conscious style isn't nearly as impressive as a reasonable, clear thesis and lucid explanation. Steve's paper is a remarkable example of someone who doesn't know what to say, and Steve ends up chatting about a number of ideas without ever developing any. The fact that he liked the movie and felt that it was relevant to his life is fine for his personal enjoyment, but readers will simply ask, "So what?"

Step 6: Your students will write an analysis of one of the papers following the rubric. You may want to assign grades to each paper and then have your students explain, in essay form with relevant supporting examples, why the paper deserves its grade.

Step 7: Discuss and analyze the additional assignment. This one is very similar to Film Assignment 2, so the step should be completed very quickly.

You will want to decide on which movie to analyze and under what conditions it will be watched. The choice of a movie is very important, because some just don't have enough material that needs discussing, and others are too baffling to be handled by inexperienced viewers. If possible, your class should watch the movie together, discuss it afterwards, and then have the opportunity to watch it at least a second time. Because the purpose of this assignment doesn't include testing students on what they remember from the movie, a full discussion of the story and technique is appropriate.

Step 8: Your students will write their analyses. You will want to work with them on their drafts, using the guidelines in Step 4. Peer evaluation is a productive way for your students to feel that they are writing for an audience broader than their teacher.

Step 9: When your students hand in the final drafts of their analysis, you may want to have them write an analysis of a classmate's paper. Emphasizing analyzing over grading will help them see that a grade really does indicate how well the paper responds to the assignment and isn't something that a teacher arbitrarily assigns.

SAMPLE ANSWERS FOR STUDY QUESTIONS

We have provided answers for all of the study questions for the chemistry, psychology, and English chapters and answers for one assignment in each of the other chapters. We view these answers as suggestions rather than the only correct way to respond to the questions and see them as a way to help define our approach to analyzing and rewriting.

INSTRUCTOR'S MANUAL 17

Chemistry Assignment 2

Sample Chemistry Paper 4

1. Point out the characteristics of Esther's abstract that make it easily understood and complete.
   A. Ester organized her information so readers can understand what was studied, what this study reveals, and what the knowledge gained can be used for. The first sentence identifies the subject of the study, and the second describes, in general terms, the results. The next two sentences briefly describe the first growth phase, and the following two do the same for the second phase.

   In the last sentence, Esther mentions the practical use of the results of the study. Readers are guided through the abstract by the use and/or repetition of key words: *studies, first phase, second phase, clams,* and *mollusks*. As an abstract, this paragraph gives enough information to inform readers about the article that follows, but it eliminates information that would make the abstract confusing and tedious.

2. What information contained in the abstract needs to be more completely explained in the article?
   A. Eshter's article is a disappointment after such a lucid abstract. In the article, she fails to elaborate on using of the information gained from the study. Readers will want to know how this study "makes it possible to determine . . . the evolutional role of algal-molluscan symbiosis" and also why this information is relevant to the human population.

Sample Chemistry Paper 5

1. What specific information does Paul's abstract need before it can provide a good overview of the research?
   A. You may wonder if Paul and Esther are abstracting the same article. He neglected to include the results as well as the use of the study (in general terms), information that is essential to an adequate abstract. Instead, he included specific details ("using stable oxygen and carbon analysis," "10 mm of shell growth") that are confusing and unnecessary at this point. Most readers will have trouble making sense of the details before they have a clear general view of the experiment.

2. At what points in the article do you feel that you need more information to fully appreciate the significance of this research?
   A. In general, Paul's article is well written, explaining the study clearly. In paragraphs 3 and 4, the information concerning ratios, time, seasonal temperatures, and growth rate could be expanded. Readers may want (and need) to know more about these relationships. For example, at what time during the season do the clams grow the fastest?

3. The concluding paragraph of Paul's paper mentions that studying the growth rate of these giant clam shells may provide information about the greenhouse effect. From a rhetorical point of view, what is the strength and weakness inherent in this paragraph?
   A. The strength is that Paul mentions the fact that the study is relevant to most readers. He doesn't develop this point, however, and readers may not be convinced that what he says is true.

Sample Chemistry Paper 6

1. Underline the sentences in Joan's article that explain to readers the purpose and use of this research. Which of these are effective and which need more information?
   A. The purpose and use are explained in paragraph 2, sentences 3–6; paragraph 4, sentences 2 and 3; and the entire last paragraph. The information in paragraphs 2 and 4 is adequate at these points in the article. The last paragraph, as a summation of the experiment, needs to explain more completely how this study is relevant to the human population, or at least how the information gained from the research goes beyond this particular experiment.

2. Throughout this paper, ask Joan questions that would guide her in making this article more interesting and relevant to you.
   A. Paragraph 2: "How will knowing more about changes in the marine environment affect us today?"
   A. Paragraph 4: "What do you mean by 'a potential food source for other experiments'? What other experiments are most likely to follow from this one?"
   A. Final paragraph: "Why is it important for us to know these facts about fossil shells, and how does the sea-level movement affect our lives?"

INSTRUCTOR'S MANUAL

Chemistry Assignment 3

Sample Chemistry Papers, 7, 8, 9

1. Which of the three reports gives you the best picture of the experiment? Identify the characteristics of this report that make it the easiest to understand.
   A. Ricky gives the best picture of the experiment in Paper 9. Although he doesn't separate this report into sections, and although he uses inappropriate language in places (the use of first person in paragraph 4, for example), his description is the clearest. The first paragraph describes the purpose and method of the experiment very simply (and the purpose and method are basically simple), providing readers with enough information to understand and picture what follows. Throughout his paper, Ricky describes each step clearly and separately, letting readers see the experiment at work.

2. Harry is the most careful to separate his report into the necessary sections, yet his conclusion is very weak. What is inappropriate about his conclusion? What could he have said in this section to make it a strong end to his report?
   A. Discussing his enjoyment of the experiment and the apparatus is irrelevant, and the results included here belong in the section headed "Calculations." The conclusion should address such issues as the appropriateness of the methods, how well they were performed, and the validity of the results.

3. Barbara's conclusion is an account of how she handled a mistake. Do you feel that this discussion, even though it indicates a shortcoming in the process of performing the experiment, shows a greater or lesser understanding of the experiment than either Harry's or Ricky's conclusion?
   A. Recognizing a mistake and its consequences is a good sign that Barbara understands the concept of the experiment and the consequences of her lab partner's mistake. Ricky still seems to have the best understanding of the experiment, mainly because he describes each step and the results clearly.

4. In Paper 9, Ricky does not provide subheadings to divide his report. If you were to supply subheadings, where would they go?
   A. Paragraph 1: *Introduction*
      Paragraphs 2–5: *Method*

List (beginning with "Unknown"): *Results* or *Calculations*
Paragraphs 6–7: *Conclusion*
List (beginning with "Settings"): belongs to *Method* section

5. You should notice that each report uses—although inconsistently—the passive voice ("Measurements were made" rather "The investigator measured"). This is an accepted convention in scientific writing, but it sometimes makes sentences hard to read. Examine the reports carefully and find four instances where the writers use passive constructions that are difficult to read and need revising. Rewrite these in a way that will remove the confusion.
   A. Paper 7: sentence 4 under *Procedure:* "The solution was prepared that gave, in unknown sample 1, a concentration of 34.30 mg/L of unknown. In unknown sample 2, the concentration of unknown was 35.90 mg/L."
   A. Paper 8: sentences 2 and 4 under *Principle:* "The amount will be determined by using the method of standard additions. Several standards of copper solution will be prepared, and each solution will contain the same concentration of unknown. For the experiment to work, the solutions must be prepared within a linear range for Atomic Absorption."
   A. Paper 8: sentences 2 and 3 under *Procedure*—removing the parentheses in sentence 2 will eliminate the confusion. Sentence 3 could read: "The unknowns are prepared assuming that they contain 90% copper in the brass solution."
   A. Paper 9: sentence 1 in paragraph 4: "The unknown was weighed out, but not using the method of 'weight by difference.'"
   A. Paper 9: sentence 4 in paragraph 5: "The points that didn't correlate were eliminated from the calculations. The correlation coefficient of the other points was calculated, resulting in a coefficient of 0.9999."

Math Assignment 2

Sample Math Papers 4, 5, 6

1. If all three papers are supposed to convey the same information, which paper is the most informative?
   A. Although it's very short, Andy's paper (#4) gives the best general description of a variable. Ruth's paper (#5) goes into

more detail, but the additional information is confusing to "someone who knows nothing about programming." Joe's paper (#6) doesn't include as much confusing information as Ruth's, but it also doesn't cover the basics as well as Andy's.

2. Which of the three papers answers all of the questions listed in the assignment?
   A. Andy's paper handles all of the questions clearly:

   Q: "What is a variable?"
   A: "A variable can be considered to represent a location in the memory of a computer."
   Q: "Why is it called a variable?"
   A: "The value associated with a given variable can change throughout the program. This is why the term 'variable' is used."
   Q: "What are the things a program can do with a variable?"
   A: "They can be used to store numeric values as well as character strings (other information such as names, addresses, or phone numbers)."
   Q: "What are the important properties of variables that one should know?"
   A: "Important properties of variables include how they are initialized, altered, and used throughout the program. Different languages have different rules regarding these properties. . . ."

3. Ruth's paper is much longer than the other two and longer than specified in the assignment. Does the extra length help make it more informative? Can the information be expressed more concisely? Does it contain any unnecessary information that is distracting? Are the other papers too short?
   A. Even though Ruth's paper may contain more information, it doesn't inform the specific audience as well as Andy's. Paragraphs 2 and 3 are confusing because readers don't know enough to make complete sense of this information. The last two paragraphs are confusing in the same way. This detailed information is more appropriate as instruction to someone who will use variables than it is as general information for someone who knows basically nothing about the topic. Ruth could be more concise in expressing herself, but conciseness would not eliminate the problem.

Andy's paragraph contains 149 words, half again as much as the assignment specifies, so he can't be faulted for brevity.

4. The assignment states that the information should be expressed clearly and pleasantly and that it should not read as a list. In which of the papers (if any) do you feel that the writer is truly trying to communicate information to the reader and not simply showing that he or she has learned something about variables?
   A. Both Andy and Ruth seem to want to inform the reader. Andy does a very good job of answering the questions clearly, and even though Ruth includes too much confusing information, she seems to be trying to teach readers something about the subject. Joe's paragraph is simply a list of separate sentences that contain some of the necessary information, but there seems to be no intent to make this paragraph a pleasurable reading experience.

Biology Assignment 2

Sample Biology Paper 4

1. Read our discussion of subordinate clauses in the guide for reading below. List sentences in which Bobbi uses subordinate clauses to express a causal relationship.
   A. i. "If, for example, a population of animals is drawn close to the edge of extinction, traits which provide resistance to certain diseases might disappear."
   A. ii. "If the new population is exposed to one of those diseases, then it may become extinct despite human effort."

2. Rewrite the first sentence of Bobbi's response, using the exam question in a way that introduces the answer and that avoids the use of *this*.
   A. "Acting to save an endangered species before it becomes too small is important because as a species population becomes very small, the amount of alleles in the gene pool becomes limited."

Sample Paper 5

1. Most of Wandisha's sentences have the reference word *this* as their subject. Mark those sentences where it is difficult to know what *this* refers to and, thus, to know the exact subject of the sentence.

INSTRUCTOR'S MANUAL

    A. "This happens when there is too many homozygous traits for genes." (Does *this* refer to "extinction"?)
    A. "This is caused by inbreeding."
    A. "This can lead to extinction." (Does *this* refer to "fatal"? Or to the entire sentence?)

2. Most of Wandisha's sentences are simple assertions, which means that she doesn't really provide a causal analysis. Using the description of subordinate clauses above, how could you rewrite her answer to make it a causal analysis?
    A. "It is undesirable to let a population of already endangered animals become small, because they will become extinct. If the population of a species becomes too small, inbreeding will occur. If inbreeding does take place, the result will be too many homozygous traits for genes. Because an excess of homozygous genes and a lack of heterozygous genes can be fatal, the ultimate result may be extinction of the species. This process is happening in the cheetah today. Because most of the babies have too many homozygous genes, 70% of cheetah babies die early."

Sample Biology Paper 6

1. Look carefully at Bobbi's response in Sample Paper 4. What details from that paper would you have wanted Skippy to include?
    A. Skippy needs to discuss the "bottleneck" phenomenon and the decline in adaptive abilities that small endangered species may suffer.

2. How would you describe the tone of Skippy's paragraph? Objective and factual or subjective and emotional?
    A. Skippy's paragraph is subjective and emotional: He tells us how he feels about extinction, but does not explain how the process of extinction takes place.

3. Does Skippy's paragraph have a unifying idea? If so, what is it?
    A. Skippy's paragraph has a unifying tone (emotional) but not a unifying idea. Notice how the fourth sentence about natural selection seems especially disconnected from the other sentences in the paragraph.

Physics Assignment 2

Sample Physics Paper 4

1. From time to time, Tonda's paragraphs become so long they are hard to read. Identify which paragraphs cause this difficulty and then show where you would break them up into shorter ones.
    A. The last paragraph of Tonda's Instrumentation and Calibration section could easily be divided into two paragraphs. Tonda could begin a new paragraph when she starts to explain the table of her measurements. The first paragraph of Tonda's Analysis and Conclusions section would also benefit from a paragraph break, most logically when she begins to explain the possible reasons for deviations in her results.

2. Tonda's teacher identified her Error Analysis section as being one of the best parts of her report. There is no question that it works very well with regard to the information it presents, but, stylistically, it has some problems. How would you rewrite these three paragraphs to make them better?
    A. Tonda begins the second and third paragraph in the same way: "Another source of error is . . .". Tonda needs to find a way to relate the three sources of error she discusses, instead of simply listing them. One possibility is: "A second source of error are the assumptions we had to make to convert from luminous to radiant measurements . . . ." "Enclosing the apparatus in a box introduced a third source of error . . . ."

3. Identify places in Tonda's report where she inconsistently uses active and passive voice. If Tonda had asked you for advice on how to use active and passive construction more consistently, what would you have told her?
    A. The Instrumentation and Calibration section of Tonda's paper suffers most from shifting back and forth between active and passive. Tonda might be advised to check for consistency when revising her rough draft. At least in the same paragraph, it would be less disruptive to maintain either an active or passive voice. When writing lab reports, students might find it easier to adhere to the passive voice, which is very hard to avoid when discussing an experiment.

INSTRUCTOR'S MANUAL   25

Sample Physics Paper 5

1. Pretend for a moment you are Eric's physics teacher, and then look carefully at his first paragraph. What additional information would you want Eric to provide there?
    A. You may want Eric to characterize more fully a photovoltaic cell. What materials are used to produce a photovoltaic cell? What is a p-n junction?

2. If you were asked to help edit this report, what changes would you make to paragraph 3?
    A. Eric's first sentence is an example of a "fused sentence." A semicolon before "however" would correct this sentence. The third sentence of the paragraph needs a comma to separate the long introductory phrase from the remainder of the sentence. Also, the final sentence of the paragraph suffers from faulty reference. What does *it* refer to?

3. Look closely at the theory section of the report. What is a theory? What is the difference between theory and experimentation?
    A. Theory is defined as "a system of assumptions, accepted principles, and rules of procedure devised to analyze, predict, or otherwise explain the nature or behavior of a specified set of phenomena" (Webster's II). Theory is in direct opposition to experimentation.

4. Can you identify where Eric describes a theory for solar cells? What has Eric failed to do with regard to theory and application?
    A. Eric has told us what solar cells do, how they function. His discussion is specific, but what is appropriate in this section is a more general discussion of the concepts behind the cell.

Sample Physics Paper 6

1. Although it is usually a mistake to equate the length of a paper to how successfully it addresses the assignment, in the case of David's report the equation seems valid. What information do Tonda and Eric provide in their reports that David fails to provide?
    A. David provides much less detail about the procedures of the experiment than Tonda and Eric. He also chooses not to explain his tables and graphs; he simply refers the reader to them.

2. Identify three places in the report where the language shifts from formal to informal.

A. i. The last sentence of the introduction, "Once all of this is set up, it is time to run the procedure," seems much more casual than the formal writing that precedes it.

A. ii. and iii. The final paragraph has a formal tone with the exception of two sentences: "Another idea was to convert the intensity in footcandle to energy to compare input to output but this also became a mess" and "A less crude method of controlling the intensity could make the experiment run a little smoother."

3. If you were helping David revise this paper, what would you encourage him to do with paragraph 1?
   A. David tries to accomplish too much in one paragraph. The information in this paragraph needs to be divided into at least two paragraphs. Also, his paper would start more smoothly if he introduced his subject gradually, moving more logically from general to specific.

4. David doesn't seem to know how to punctuate correctly. How would you alter the punctuation in his last paragraph?
   A. David needs to learn more about comma usage. The first sentence of this paragraph requires a comma after the introductory phrase. The fourth sentence of the paragraph needs much reworking. It might be revised in the following way: "The reason for the irregular current readings is not known, because they were taken at the same time and thus in the same conditions as the voltage/intensity readings."

Psychology Assignment 2

Sample Psychology Paper 4

1. Read Bouchard's abstract of his report. Are all the sections of the report—Introduction, Method, Results, and Discussion—represented in it? From your reading of this example, what would you say is the purpose of an abstract?
   A. This abstract is complete. The first sentence briefly summarizes the experiment. The second explains a peripheral purpose. The last two sentences summarize the results.

   The purpose of an abstract is twofold. It provides a very brief description of the research performed and then summarizes the results. Someone researching brainstorming would know, after reading Bouchard's abstract, whether this experiment was relevant to his or her research.

2. Read again the Results section of all three student papers. Which paper most exactly reports the results of Bouchard's study? What important piece of information is left out in the other two papers? How does this omission mislead the reader about the actual results of the study?
   A. Mary (Paper 4) gives a more accurate summary of the results because she briefly discusses the three sessions of the experiment separately. She explains that the differences of scores for the second session are insignificant. David and Sonya make synectics sound much more effective than it actually is. In his abstract, Bouchard makes the point that synectics is not significantly superior in all phases of the experiment.

3. What changes in Bouchard's method would the writers of these three papers make? Which student, in your opinion, provides the most practical suggestions?
   A. All three writers question the composition of the groups. Mary suggests that new subjects should have been chosen, because those who had completed a similar task before were able to perform better the second time. David and Sonya suggest that the groups needed to include both males and females. Mary's suggestions seem to be more practical and perceptive, mainly because she explains the flaws in the experiment and how her solutions could make the results more accurate.

4. Point out the information in Mary's paper that you feel is unnecessary. In what way does this information make reading the paper difficult and confusing?
   A. In general, Mary's paper is a complete discussion of the experiment, and most of what she says is necessary for complete understanding. She could have simplified her paper by eliminating the course requirements and hourly wage in the Subjects section. Apparently, requiring students to participate and paying them had no bearing on the results. However, when readers see this in Mary's paper, they tend to think that it is a significant detail that should be remembered.

5. David (Paper 5) asks a valid question: Why weren't any females used in Bouchard's study? Why might Bouchard only include

males in his study? How does this choice affect the significance of his results?

    A. Bouchard might have felt that creativity is gender specific. In this case, mixing genders in his groups would have been equivalent to purposely choosing people who were or were not creative, thus eliminating the randomness of his sample. On the other hand, he could have assumed that creativity *is not* related to gender, in which case the question of using females in the study is irrelevant. Whatever his reasons, Bouchard should have explained why he used only males.

6. Point out the unanswered questions in David's evaluation. What kind of burden do these questions place on readers? How should David treat these concerns?

    A. Unanswered questions make readers do what the writer should do: answer the questions. Unless the writer guides readers to a specific answer, they may answer the question in a way that doesn't support the writer's point of view. In number 3, David could have said, "Because no females were used in the experiment, it can prove only that synectics works for males."

7. What's missing from the response Sonya gives to Question 5 in her evaluation? Why is this paragraph an insufficient response to the question?

    A. Question 5 asks, "Do the experimenter's conclusions follow directly from the results that were reported?" Sonya attempts to answer this (number 3 in her evaluation) with a direct quotation from a later article on Bouchard's experiment. She has not dealt with the question herself. There is nothing wrong with supporting her own answer with a recognized authority, but simply inserting a quotation does not provide an answer.

Psychology Assignment 3

Sample Psychology Paper 7

1. Do you feel that you know Victor Taylor well enough after reading Don's paper? Do you need any more information in sections I–IV to understand sections V–VIII? If so, what facts would you like to know?

    A. Don has given a very good picture of Victor Taylor, covering significant events of his childhood and the present conditions of his adult life. Sections V–VIII are understandable without any additional information. However, it would be interesting, maybe even helpful, to know more about Victor's financial condition. If he is barely making enough money for his living expenses, the stress of such a condition could play a role in his problem.

2. The assignment states that you are to "apply what you are learning in class and your own insights to the individual you encounter in the interview." Mark these two types of information in Don's paper. Are they adequate? In other words, does he seem to know enough from class and is he sufficiently involved in Mr. Taylor's case to explain it convincingly?
   A. Whenever Don uses psychological terms, we can assume that he is exhibiting specific knowledge from the course. His other insights aren't as easy to distinguish, but it is clear that he perceives clearly Victor's personality (the last sentence in section I is one indication of this). Overall, Don shows an adequate knowledge of Victor and psychology to write a convincing report. By avoiding jargon, he has made his report accessible to all intelligent readers.

Sample Psychology Paper 8

1. Compare the Theoretical Perspectives of Don's paper and Jacci's. Which organizes its discussion more successfully? What organizational strategy does the more successful writer use in this section?
   A. Don's Theoretical Perspectives section is well organized and scientifically based. He presents two explanations separately (behavioral/cognitive and psychodynamic) and then explains the strengths and weaknesses of each for this particular case. Readers should sense that Don has evaluated Victor's case objectively, with a strong base of knowledge. Jacci, on the other hand, seems to be randomly tossing out ideas with no plan or scientific support. In her last sentence, she mentions psychodynamic theory, but she doesn't evaluate the appropriateness of this theory in Victor's case.

2. Look at the Disposition section of Jacci's paper. What important aspect of Victor Taylor's case does she ignore in this section?
   A. Jacci doesn't indicate Victor's commitment to psychological treatment. We know from Don's paper that Victor showed

less than satisfactory commitment in the past, an indication that his present treatment isn't the positive sign that Jacci seems to think it is.

Sample Psychology Paper 9

1. Review the Summary and Integration of Findings section of Sheri's paper. How could she have better organized her material? Does she include any observations or interpretations that help the reader integrate these findings? Rewrite this section so the information will seem part of a single topic instead of scattered ideas.
   A. This section reads as if Sheri simply wrote down ideas as they came to her and never went back to organize her thoughts. She does include some observations that help readers see what she means, but basically she places a tremendous burden on readers to make sense of her random observations. Instead of viewing this section as one long paragraph, she should have broken it into several paragraphs, each one dealing with a separate topic followed by supporting facts. The following is an example of how this final section could be revised:

   Victor doesn't have what we would call a normal social life or any close friendships. Even though he claims that he is not a loner, he lives by himself, travels alone, doesn't "hang out" with people, rarely dates, and sees his closest friend only a couple of times a year. On the subject of women, Victor says that he wants to be with cute, decent girls, not cheap, trashy women, but he also indicates that his former therapist didn't turn him on because she was nice and understanding, not trashy. He was engaged for a while in high school, until the girl broke it off. He claims that he is a virgin, getting his sexual excitement just from the thought of exposing himself.

   Victor has few expenses, but his unstable financial situation causes him anxiety and some problems. Even though he's had his present job for two and a half years and his only bill is rent, he doesn't date or go to the doctor because of the expense. Apparently, he frequently bounces checks but claims to always "make them good." In spite of the anxiety caused by his money problems, Victor doesn't really know what his financial situation is.

   Victor is attracted to violent sports and movies, probably as an outlet for his own anger. Playing football did provide a release for his anger; now he watches football (he likes to hear the helmets hit) and wrestling on television. One of his favorite movies is *Friday the 13th,* in which he really likes the main character, Jason. Though he enjoys all of this violence, Victor doesn't fish or hunt because he reportedly doesn't want to kill anything. He claims he doesn't believe in killing someone unless the person is evil.

Church functions seem to be Victor's only type of social activity. He attends church regularly every Sunday morning, Sunday evening, and Wednesday evening when he doesn't have to work. He claims to be a Christian, saved at age 17, and prays every day because it makes him feel good.

Although Victor seems to want to get help controlling his problem, it is clear that part of his reason for therapy is to get a lighter sentence from the judge.

2. Compare each section of Sheri's paper with the same section of Don's (#7). Without listing the specific differences in information, identify what makes Don's report much more informative and complete.
   A. In general, Don describes Victor Taylor in much more detail, providing examples, habits, names, and facts that show readers what he is like. Sheri's rather cursory treatment of Victor Taylor and his problems covers some of the important aspects of the case, but readers only see the results of her interpretation. After reading Don's paper, readers know enough about Victor to see what Don bases his evaluation on and are thus provided with a good basis for either agreement or disagreement. Readers see Don working through this case and are more likely to be convinced that his assessment is valid. Sheri presents readers with an interesting case, but not one that they feel involved with. It's also important to note that Sheri's paper seems more complete than it actually is because it follows two reports that provide necessary information. Readers of this text come to Sheri's paper with the necessary information to fill in the gaps.

Political Science Assignment 2

Sample Political Science Paper 4

1. In a paper containing a summary of someone else's writing, the writer should be very careful to separate the summarized informa-

tion from his or her own information and thoughts. One way to do this is to use such phrases as "According to Church," "He continues by stating," "He says that." Assuming that the first three paragraphs in Jane's paper summarize Church's article, add the necessary cues to make this clear to the reader.

A. "Third World revolutions are primarily nationalistic, not communist. Nationalism, not capitalism or communism, is the dominant political force in the modern world." This excerpt from Church's paper states the focal point the United States must come to grips with while dealing with revolutionary regimes. *He finds* it ironic that the U.S. had its beginnings as a revolutionary force but meets revolutions in other countries with great fear. *For Church,* Vietnam represents a case of American intervention for all the wrong reasons, and as a result the Vietnam war was a huge loss of resources and manpower for the U.S. *According to Church,* the main concern for the U.S. was Central Asia falling into the hands of communist governments, but despite our failure the entire area did not become completely communist.

Church compares the situation in Central America to the Vietnam struggle. *He asks* if we will again waste resources and men in a fight we do not belong in. Church points out that we have learned to live with different degrees of Marxist elements (China, for example) and should not be so afraid of similar governments in Central America.

Church feels that historically our relationship with revolutionary regimes has been so bad that relations between our two countries are permanently scarred when the new revolution proves unsuccessful. The result, *according to Church*, is that the new regime aligns with the Soviet Union instead of the U.S. for assistance.

2. Jane has too many sentences that mention a topic but that don't develop it (for example, the fourth sentence in paragraph 1). Mark all of these and briefly describe the type of information she needs to add.

   A. paragraph 2, sentence 2: It would help if she listed which resources were wasted and how many men were lost.

   A. paragraph 2, sentence 3: Readers need to have an idea of the different degrees of Marxist elements.

INSTRUCTOR'S MANUAL

      A.   paragraph 3, section 1: An example or two of our bad relations with revolutionary regimes would help.

      A.   paragraph 4, sentences 3 and 5: An example of the countries in each sentence would make this more interesting and convincing.

3. Rephrase Jane's second question in paragraph 2 and the rhetorical question (sentence 3) in paragraph 4 into strong convincing statements.
    A. "It's inconsistent for the U.S. to be allies with China and at the same time to be afraid of having a similar government in Central America."
    A. "Although the U.S. is quick to mix in everyone else's problems, we would be angry if someone tried to tell us what kind of government we should have."

Sample Political Science Paper 5

1. Rewrite Daryl's questions, making them strong, convincing statements.
    A. paragraph 1, sentence 1: "The establishment of Marxist revolutionary regimes does not pose a major threat to American security interests."
    A. paragraph 2, sentences 2, 3, 4: "We are likely to repeat the catastrophe of Vietnam in Nicaragua and El Salvador, simply because the Soviet Union and Cuba are involved."
    A. paragraph 3, sentences 4, 5: "El Salvador has also committed itself, and we should honor this commitment."
    A. paragraph 5, sentences 2, 4: "No one country has the right to influence another, for whatever political reason."
    A. paragraph 5, sentences 5, 6, 7: "We don't really know if our nation's security is being threatened by Soviet influence."
    A. paragraph 5, last sentence: leave out *don't*.

2. Point out words that seem inappropriate to the tone that pervades most of the paper. What words would be appropriate in these places?
    A. Possible suggestions: paragraph 2, sentence 1: ". . . we have come unhinged." ". . .we have supported the established government out of unreasonable fear."
    A. paragraph 3, sentence 4: "Why not take them up on their commitments?" "We should honor their commitments."

34 INSTRUCTOR'S MANUAL

    A. paragraph 4, sentence 1: "...with inexorable long-term pull." "... with financial help and respect."

    A. paragraph 4, sentence 2: "We must stop painting countries like Cuba and Nicaragua into a corner." "We must stop labeling countries like Cuba and Nicaragua good or bad simply on the basis of their relationship with communism."

    A. paragraph 5, sentence 14: "... but I think we are overreaching our goals here." "... but I think we are overreacting to an imagined threat to our security."

3. Even though Daryl's critique is thoughtful, it is disorganized. List the different topics covered in this last paragraph and write a comment directing him how to improve this part of his paper.
    A. Topics:
        i. Soviets and U.S. trying to spread their kind of government.
        ii. People must decide for themselves.
        iii. Supporting revolutionary regimes strains the economy.
        iv. Americans are only willing to defend America.
    A. "Treat each of these topics as a separate paragraph and develop each topic enough to convince readers of your position."

Sample Political Science Paper 6

1. Kevin's summary lacks the necessary cues to make it clear what information comes from Church's article. Add these, rewriting sentences if necessary.
    A. Apparently, the first six paragraphs summarize Church's article. Follow the pattern for question 1 on Paper 4.

2. Kevin's critique is much too brief, in part because he doesn't give any specific information to support his statements. Ask him questions that will force him to add the necessary specifics.
    A. "What exactly is the author's point of view?" "What kind of involvement will make more enemies?" "What kind of alliances should we try to make?" "How should we get involved when other countries go against their agreements?"

INSTRUCTOR'S MANUAL 35

Anthropology Assignment 2

Sample Anthropology Paper 4

1. Suppose Susan had asked you to read a draft of this paper and give her some feedback she could use to make it better. You know that if she will focus more on a single feature of the prehistory she can improve the quality of the paper, and you tell her so. Which feature would you ask her to elaborate? How should she go about rewriting that portion of the paper? What should she add?
   A. Susan has several alternatives for focusing her paper. In her introduction, she states that the Nile River "demanded control, thus cooperation, organization and centralization were necessities." Susan might focus her attention on the determining factor played by this great river in the prehistory of the people of Egypt. As is, she mentions it only sporadically within the paper, but it could supply her with an important unifying idea.

2. Without any citations, we have no way of clearly separating Susan's thoughts from those of her sources, nor do we have any way of getting more specific information about individual topics, unless we are willing to go to the bibliography and read through all her sources. Look carefully at any three consecutive paragraphs and indicate those places where you think Susan could have supplied references to help you read her paper. If readers wanted to know more about the Badarian civilization described in paragraphs 5–6, which source would provide this information?
   A. Reading paragraphs 4–6 of Susan's paper, readers may often ask, "How does Susan know this?" For example, in paragraph 4, Susan states that Early Egyptian villages "have to be credited to the farmer because it was he who saw the need for land reclamation and immigration." Is it Susan who credits these early villages to the farmer, or is it experts in Egyptian culture and history? Clearer documentation would help answer this question.
   A. Parenthetical documentation in paragraphs 5 and 6 would help readers know where to go for further details.

3. The teacher's comments on Susan's paper were scathing. For example, in paragraph 3, Susan writes that cereal grains "were part of Late Paleolithic man's diet." The comment in the margin reads,

"Since women aren't doing anything I guess they don't need to eat either." What effect, if any, did Susan's failure to use current conventions regarding gender have on you as you read her paper? Why do you think she might want to be more sensitive to those conventions in the future, aside from the obvious desire to please her teachers?

    A. One result of Susan's failure to use current conventions regarding gender is that female readers of her essay may feel "left out." Some readers may wonder at what points in the paper Susan means "man," designating gender, and at what points she means "man," designating a human being. For these readers, Susan's writing would have been more precise had she avoided the generic use of *man*.

Sample Anthropology Paper 5

1. Titles often tell readers a great deal about a piece of writing, and they sometimes tell readers something about the writer. Look carefully at Mary's title. What does it tell you about her and her work?
    A. In her title, and throughout her paper, Mary misspells "archipelago," which suggests that the work meant so little to her that she couldn't bother to look up the proper spelling in the dictionary.

2. Mary's writing is handicapped by the surface errors throughout the paper. Identify where you found these errors most troublesome. What corrections or changes would you make to improve the readability of that section?
    A. Mary's paragraph 6 suffers from a number of surface errors, including a sentence fragment in the middle of the paragraph. The paragraph might be changed to read in the following way:

    Archaeologists believe that by AD 900–1100, about four to seven centuries after the initial colonization, the population increased and permanent settlements were established. Some of the larger settlements include Kuli'ou'ou and Makaha valleys on O'ahu and Anaeho'omalu on Hawaii island (Kirch, p. 245). Experts believe that, by AD 1400–1500, most of these lowlands were brought under some form of occupation, civilization, and/or exploitation.

3. The final comment Mary's teacher put on the paper was "a little too brief." If you were asked to help Mary revise this paper, what additional information would you ask her to supply?

INSTRUCTOR'S MANUAL

A. Mary mentions in paragraph 3 that the Polynesians brought to the Hawaiian archipelago "their language, customs, rituals, social sanctions, arts, and handicrafts." She never follows up on this statement. Mary might give more details concerning the culture the Polynesians transported to the islands and how that culture changed and developed throughout the prehistory of the archipelago.

Sample Anthropology Paper 6

1. Lack of organization is one of the problems Kim has in this paper. Read it carefully and make an organizational outline of the information she presents. Then revise that outline into a more coherent one.
   A. Students constructing outlines of Kim's paper will notice two main flaws in her organization: (1) she does not arrive at her focus—the Chillon Valley—until the seventh paragraph of the paper and (2) she skips back and forth from the Preceramic period to the Ceramic period. As a result, readers have difficulty ascertaining the chronology of events in the Chillon Valley.

2. Kim's paper has numerous surface errors. It's unlikely that she could be expected to correct all of them on the rewrite that her teacher asked her to do, but she may be able to correct two patterns of error—capitalization, commas, subject/verb agreement, and so forth. Pretend she has asked for your help on the rewrite. What two patterns of error do you think she should concentrate on? Why? How would you help her eliminate these patterns from this and future papers?
   A. Kim will certainly want to eliminate one very glaring error in her paper: her tendency to ignore the conventions of capitalization. Because capitalizing the first word of a sentence is such a rudimentary convention, Kim's failure to do so seems especially careless. Kim's difficulties with comma usage do not fall into a neat pattern: Sometimes she leaves out commas where needed, at other times she places commas where they don't belong. Notice the second sentence of the second paragraph.

3. Many of Kim's paragraphs seem undeveloped. Point out those paragraphs that need more development, and then describe what additional information Kim should have supplied.

A. Paragraph 5 needs more development. Kim states that Wendell C. Bennett and Julio C. Tello "discovered new information on the cultures that were found by Uhle." Kim leaves readers wondering exactly what new information Bennett and Tello discovered and what point she wants to make about their discoveries.

Paragraph 9 also needs elaboration. Kim tells us very little about the discoveries archaeologists made about the food supply available in the Chillon Valley. What other foods besides seeds and root plants were available to the early natives?

Finally, in the next to last paragraph of her paper, Kim refers to two settlements, Plaza Grande and Cerro Culebura, but does not explain why she refers to them. She seems to have little information to recount.

English Assignment 2

Sample English Paper 4

1. Even though Lisa doesn't state her claim, or thesis, in one sentence, she conveys it very clearly to readers. Underline the sentences (in paragraphs 3 and 4) that together form her thesis. In your own words, write a one-sentence thesis for this paper. Why does Lisa gain by not including such a thesis in her introductory paragraphs?

    A. Paragraph 3: sentence 2
    Paragraph 4: the entire paragraph
    "Both Offred and Sam possess a moral power that enables them to prevail in some way over those who possess social power."

    By not limiting her thesis to one sentence, Lisa provides a much more informative background on which to base her analysis. She explains her thesis while she states it, enabling readers to better understand the points she makes throughout the paper.

2. Mark all sentences that contain specific references to the text. Which of these simply remind readers what happens and which are used to support a specific point Lisa is making?

    A. Whenever Lisa refers to the two texts, she supports a specific point in her analysis. She isn't simply trying to prove to her readers that she has read the works by retelling parts of the stories. She also correctly assumes that her readers have read the two works, and so she doesn't need to give long references to them.

3. Has Lisa employed a point-by-point or a subject-by-subject comparison? Is her choice the proper one for this paper? Why or why not?
   A. Lisa employed a subject-by-subject comparison, appropriate for this paper because the two characters, Offred and Sam, share only general similarities. A point-by-point comparison is best employed when the two subjects share characteristics with a one-to-one correspondence. This is not to say that the general similarities are any less significant than those that can be discussed as parallel.

4. Evaluate this paper on the points stated in the last paragraph of the assignment: "clarity, directness, effective organization, and effective, correct use of sources." Give specific examples from the paper to support your evaluation.
   A. *Clarity:* Lisa's language is free of jargon, awkward expressions, and convoluted sentence structure. She works to inform her readers, not to impress them with style or excessive information.

   Directness: This category is similar to the one above. The sentences in paragraph 3 are good examples of the direct manner in which Lisa expresses herself.

   Effective organization: Lisa's choice of a subject-by-subject comparison is effective. Notice also that when Lisa makes the transition from *The Handmaid's Tale* to *"Master Harold"... and the Boys* (paragraphs 9–11), she refers to both works, explaining to readers the parallels and providing a guide for the discussion of Sam.

   Effective, correct use of sources: Lisa uses references to the texts to support her points. These references are complete enough for her readers to understand them, but brief enough not to distract from the analysis.

Sample English Paper 5

1. Point out any information that, although it may be correct, seems irrelevant to Angie's discussion.

>   A. The definition of sexuality and the brief mention of irony in paragraph 4: If these points are relevant, Angie needs to explain the pun and irony of the definition of sexuality.
>
>   The slogan in the next-to-last sentence in paragraph 4: This slogan may be relevant, but Angie must explain its relevance to readers.
>
>   The references to conditions in today's society: This problem is explained below.
>
> 2. Angie includes references both to the real world as she knows it and to the worlds created by the authors. Using "our" world, or common knowledge, as a means of explaining a literary text can be risky and confusing unless it is done skillfully. Are Angie's references enlightening, confusing, and/or irrelevant? Would she have more success in enlightening readers if she focused more on the text? Why or why not?
>
>   A. A major problem with Angie's paper is that her topic and purpose aren't clear. Readers don't know whether she is comparing the works with each other or with our world because she does a little of both. If she wants to read the works as comments on today's society, she needs to give more information on her world view to convince readers that it is accurate. If she is comparing the works with each other, references to the world are irrelevant. Her paper would be less confusing had she not mentioned conditions present in the world today, because the greater focus is on the similarities the works have. Focusing entirely on the texts may have forced her to dwell on the more significant similarities rather than on the superficial ones she wrote about.

Sample English Paper 6

> 1. Do you feel that Nathan has a clear understanding of Jane Austen's satire, or of the concept of satire itself? If so, point out in his essay the information on satire.
>
>   A. Nathan doesn't explain Austen's satire, an omission that prevents his answer from being outstanding. The information that he includes does show some understanding of what is satirical in the novel, especially when he associates ridicule with satire. He has chosen the right examples, so it's clear that he has an idea of how satire is used in the novel.

2. In the last paragraph of his essay, Nathan states that *Pride and Prejudice* attacks both religion and the leisure class. Reread the question and then summarize what he has not included in this part of his essay.
   A. In this paragraph, Nathan is dealing with Austen's satire of professions. He agrees with the question, but he doesn't *explain* how professions are satirized. This is a common reaction to a question—students writing under the pressure of an exam too often feel that they have explained when they have only agreed or disagreed with the question.

Sample English Paper 7

1. Susan begins her first four paragraphs with the following:

   "*Pride and Prejudice* satirized the social customs of marriages and of social classes."
   "Marriage was satirized by Mrs. Bennet."
   "Lady Catherine and Miss Bingley satirized the snobbery of the upper class."
   "Mr. Collins' profession is satirized."

   What is inconsistent and incorrect about these four statements?
   A. The first and fourth statements are accurate. The novel (and the author) are the instruments that satirize. In the second and third statements, Susan states that Mrs. Bennet, Lady Catherine, and Miss Bingley are the instruments of satire, but they are actually the objects of the novel's and Jane Austen's satire. Susan is also inconsistent in her use of tense. When one writes about literature, the present tense is the accepted convention. The events "happen" whenever someone reads the novel, even though the setting is in the past and the novel was obviously written in the past.

2. Mark the paragraphs that have nothing to do with satire. Read the exam question again. Are these paragraphs completely irrelevant to the question? Could these paragraphs be rewritten so they are relevant? In other words, has Susan chosen appropriate examples from the text but simply not explained them in correct terms?
   A. The last three paragraphs, as written, are irrelevant to the question because they don't deal with satire. Paragraphs 5 and 7 could be relevant had Susan explained that Austen used

Jane, Mr. Bingley, and the marriage of Elizabeth and Mr. Darcy as comparisons with the people and marriages she did satirize. Paragraph 6 really belongs in an essay about how the title of the novel is appropriate for its action.

Sample English Paper 8

1. In what way is Amy's opening paragraph not appropriate according to the instructions?
   A. Amy doesn't mention or discuss in this first paragraph, or anywhere else in her essay, the topic of the question: satire. The first sentence is appropriate for a book report or a summary of the novel. The most economical way to handle an essay exam answer is to state the thesis in the first sentence.

2. Based on the references to the text in Amy's essay, what specific social customs and conventions, priorities, lifestyles, and professions do you think Jane Austen is satirizing in *Pride and Prejudice?*
   A. Although she never says so directly, Amy implies that Jane Austen satirizes the institution of marriage and the efforts to marry off one's daughters, gossip, wealth, and the lifestyles of the idle rich. She omits any mention of the professions that are satirized.

3. Pick one of the above categories and write a paragraph explaining how Jane Austen satirizes this particular aspect of the upper-middle class. Use your knowledge of satire and the references to the text in Amy's essay. Treat this one paragraph as the answer to an essay question, following the guidelines on the assignment and the analysis. You will see that Amy knows what Jane Austen is doing in *Pride and Prejudice,* but she hasn't expressed this in her essay.
   A. The paragraphs will certainly vary widely, but after reading all three essays, your students should be able to pull out enough information to focus on one of the categories. The following is an example of what students should be able to write.

In *Pride and Prejudice* Jane Austen satirizes the institution of marriage by showing how anxious Mrs. Bennet is to get her daughters married. The custom was for the oldest daughter of a family to be presented to society in hopes of attracting a suitable husband. Mrs. Bennet, however, is so anxious to find husbands for her daughters that she sends them all out at the same time. The suitability of a husband is based primarily on his wealth—the greater his wealth the more suitable he is. In fact, Mrs. Bennet is so anxious to find a rich husband for her daughters that she immediately likes any man (except Mr. Darcy) who appears to have money and property. Throughout the novel, we see how this desire to find a rich husband causes more problems that it solves.

History Assignment 2

Sample History Paper 3

1. A good introductory paragraph provides readers with a guide for what follows. Make a list of the points covered in Marie's first paragraph, and then compare this list with what follows. Does this introduction do a good job preparing you for the paper? What changes (if any) in the introduction would you as the reader recommend?
    A. This introduction does a very good job of outlining the paper, providing the reader with a guide for the trip. The following is a list of the topics mentioned (in order) and the paragraphs that discuss the topic:
        1. The second Industrial Revolution: paragraphs, 2, 3, 4, and 5
        2. Political and economic effects of the Great Depression: paragraphs 6, 7, 8, 9, and 10
        3. Good Neighbor Policy: paragraph 11
        4. Fear of war and neutrality: paragraphs 12, 13, and 14
        5. World War II: paragraphs 15 and 16
        6. The Cold War: paragraphs 17, 18, and 19
        7. Post-war era and Christmas: paragraph 20

2. Does Marie properly prepare her potential travelers for any hazards or problems that may occur in the course of their journey?
    A. The only real warning is when she mentions that in the Roaring Twenties there are no alcoholic beverages allowed. She mentions some of the conditions of the Depression but doesn't explain how and if these will affect the travelers. She doesn't warn of any danger during the student demonstrations, an omission that could be serious.

3. The main problem with Marie's paper is that it is more solid than creative. Throughout the paper she focuses more on explaining

history than on providing a tour. This focus could easily be altered by changing the wording and choosing events that are visually interesting. Rewrite paragraphs 6, 10, and 16 so readers will feel as if they will be taken somewhere to see something important happen instead of simply being told about the event.

   A. Paragraph 6: "Before leaving New York you will visit the New York Stock Exchange and see the prosperity of the twenties come to an abrupt halt. On October 14, 1929, the day the Stock Market crashed, you will see the frenzy and horror that resulted from plummeting prices as the brokers were ordered to unload vast numbers of shares fast. This day of pandemonium ushered in the Great Depression, which held the country in a tight grip until the outbreak of World War II, ten years later."

       Paragraph 10: "To experience Roosevelt's political genius, you will visit a typical American family as they listen to one of his Fireside Chats. Just like many families, this one is suffering from the Depression, but listening to Roosevelt gives them a sense of purpose and the psychological lift they need to endure and survive."

       Paragraph 16: "On December 7, 1941, you will be taken to a safe spot overlooking Pearl Harbor. Here you will experience the horror of Japan's unannounced attack on the naval base as the Zeroes dropped the bombs that pushed the U.S. into World War II."

4. One final aspect of this paper that needs attention is style. Marie tends to use short sentences that should be connected. A series of these short sentences makes Marie sound as if she is writing down ideas as they come to her. For example, paragraph 13 would read better if revised to something similar to the following: "After touring Latin America, you will visit Princeton University, where you will see student demonstrations against the war. As pacifism swept across the country because of the growing fear of the war, students carried signs reading 'Abolish the R.O.T.C.' and 'Build Schools, Not Battleships.'" Rewrite paragraphs 15 and 20 using clauses, phrases, and adjectives to eliminate the strings of short, simple sentences. Keep the important points in the main clauses and use subordinate parts of the sentence for less important ideas.

   A. Paragraph 15: "Your next stop will be Charlottesville, Virginia, where you will hear Roosevelt invoke a policy of all-out aid to the Allies. In this speech, the President will make a commitment to involve America in the Second World War as he denounces Germany and Italy as 'the gods of force and hate.' "

Paragraph 20: "From East Germany, you will travel to Washington for the inauguration of President Eisenhower, who made the Cold War the primary issue of his presidential campaign. In his inaugural address, you will hear how he wants to end the Cold War and the arms race between America and the Soviet Union by first emphasizing nuclear warfare and then reducing military spending.

"The grand finale of your trip will be spending Christmas with your family of 1955, a year in which family togetherness is emphasized. All the packages under the tree are the result of the prosperity and revival of consumerism that followed World War II and the Korean War. You and your family will find the new kitchen appliances and the television set especially marvelous. Remember to bring your Christmas gifts!"

Sample History Paper 4

1. This is a creative paper with some weaknesses that keep it from being as solid as it should be. Kimberly has caught the essence of the language of advertising, and as a result the paper reads like a travel brochure. Identify specifically what makes the paragraphs, sentences, and focus resemble the language of advertising.

   A. i. The paragraphs are short, averaging 2–3 sentences each.
       ii. The verbs and sentence structure involve the reader in action.
           a. "Journey back to the thrilling . . ." (paragraph 1)
           b. "See first hand the origins . . ." (paragraph 3)
           c. "Dance to 'Hound Dog' . . ." (paragraph 11)
           d. ". . . be there to see it." (paragraph 18)
           There is very little explanation—the emphasis is on doing and seeing. The visual images are often grouped together, coming at the reader at a fast pace.
       iii. The tone is light and upbeat—the tragedies are few and are quickly followed by a cheerful or inspiring scene.
           a. "Hair, even for men, grew longer, skirts rose higher, and bras were discarded." (paragraph 14)
           b. "Witness the tragic and senseless death of an ideal Amer-

ican, Kennedy. Get involved in the still alive racial riots such as the boycotting of segregated busses. Hear 'The King' say, 'I have a dream.' "

2a. Make a list by number of the paragraphs that do not adequately explain the significance of the event that is focused on. (All of the following lists will vary depending on the reader's knowledge of history.) Rewrite one paragraph from each of the three categories to make it appropriate for the assignment.
 A. 3, 5, 9, 12, 13, 15, 16, 18, 19, 20, 22, 25, 26, 27, 28
  Paragraph 20: "Join the excitement as a Southern Christian, Jimmy Carter, becomes President. Experience the frustration as inflation pushes interest rates up as high as 20%, making homes too expensive for all but the wealthy."

2b. Make a list of those paragraphs that need examples so you will know exactly what Kimberly is talking about.
 A. 12, 23, 26, 27, 28
  Paragraph 23: "Women wore whatever they pleased—pants, army fatigues, miniskirts, peasant dresses, bikinis, ragged bell-bottom jeans, overalls, and in some situations, nothing at all."

2c. Make a list of those paragraphs that tell you something about history but do not seem appropriate for a journey.
 A. 4, 16, 19, 20, 27
  Paragraph 16: "Experience a historical moment as Nixon becomes the first U.S. President to resign. Watch as he delivers his tearful farewell speech from the White House on national television."

3a. Throughout the paper, Kimberly has produced some unclear sentences and inaccurate explanations of historical events. Rewrite paragraphs 5 and 15 so the sentences will say clearly what you think Kimberly meant to say.
 A. Paragraph 5: "During the fifties, most Americans adopted the time-honored virtues of home, church, and community. There was a general sense that conforming to established norms was good. Prosperity was exemplified by the husband going to work dressed in a business suit while the wife stayed home to raise the family."
  Paragraph 15: "Demonstrations and marches for peace and love took place on many college campuses. Join in a march

INSTRUCTOR'S MANUAL 47

against the Vietnam War and experience the anger of people who saw no sense in the tragic loss of so many young American soldiers."

3b. Rewrite paragraph 9, expressing more accurately the reaction to Sputnik and the flop of the Edsel. You may want to express the state of America's technology over more than one paragraph.
   A. "Share in America's concern as the Russians launched their Sputnik into space, an event that inspired America to enter the space race with more emphasis on math and science in the schools and millions of dollars spent on creating the technology for exploring outer space. In spite of America's push for advanced technology, you can laugh along with your neighbors at one of the greatest American flops of all time—the Edsel."

3c. Try to make sense of paragraph 27 and express what you think Kimberly meant to say. Here again, you may want to do this in more than one paragraph.
   A. "The American public became outraged at apartheid in South Africa. Join a protest demonstration demanding that companies divest themselves of their South African investments and that the U.S. impose economic sanctions.
   "Heavy metal and hard rock music became popular enough to threaten the conservatives. Attend an Alice Cooper or a Kiss concert and experience for yourself this 'music of a damned group.'"

Philosophy Assignment 2

Sample Philosophy Paper 4

1. Questions can serve as useful prompts to get readers to agree to a particular point of view. They can also inspire readers to disagree with the writer's argument. Which of Ricardo's questions make you want to agree with him, and which make you inclined either to disagree or resent the fact that he hasn't provided an answer?
   A. The questions that Ricardo asks but fails to answer include the following: paragraph 4: "So what is this standard?" Final paragraph: "So what is humanity to do?" A good example of a question that actually works against Ricardo's argument can be found in paragraph 4. Ricardo states, "The entire theory is based upon an absolute moral standard which as of

yet has not been found." He follows this statement with a question, "Therefore, how can ethical absolutism be true?" Readers are apt to disagree with the assumption behind Ricardo's question: That if something is not found, it does not exist and is not "true."

2. When you use sources, it is important to respond to the material you present, to engage in a dialogue with it. How does Ricardo do this in paragraphs 5 and 6?
  A. In paragraph 5, Ricardo introduces Stace's notion about green swans. In paragraph 6, he develops his objections to Stace's "green swan" argument. Ricardo does a good job of engaging in a dialogue with Stace.

3. Ricardo's paper is organized around the problems involved in both ethical relativism and ethical absolutism. Which subject does he reserve for final discussion? Outline this paper in terms of its subject-by-subject approach.
  A. Ricardo discusses the arguments for and against ethical absolutism first and concludes with a discussion of the arguments for and against ethical relativism.

4. In the conclusion, what stance does Ricardo ultimately take? Does he support ethical absolutism, ethical relativism, or both? Do you find his conclusion satisfactory?
  A. Ricardo strives for a moderate position that allows for both ethical relativism and ethical absolutism.

Sample Philosophy Paper 5

1. Chris wisely refers to two authorities in the field of ethics, Walter Stace and Ruth Benedict. But how successful are these references? What does Chris tell us about his sources? What details should be included when one first refers to an outside source? (You may want to refer to the section on documentation in the overview to writing in the humanities.)
  A. Chris gives us only the last names of the two authors he refers to—Stace and Benedict. When first mentioning these authors, Chris needs to give their complete names. Also, he should name the articles by Stace and Benedict from which he received his information.

2. When using outside sources, it is important to clearly mark where reference to a source material ends and your response to the source

material begins. Chris needs to do this in paragraph 3. Revise the paragraph so that it flows smoothly from outside source material to the writer's own argument.

    A. "Stace brings up another problem with ethical absolutism. No one has actually discovered the source of the absolute morality. If we don't know the foundation for absolute morality, Stace argues, how can we be sure that it exists? But Stace has failed to acknowledge that just because we don't know the reasoning behind something does not mean that it does not exist. Stace's argument should not rule out ethical absolutism. For example, humans did not discover gravity until Newton's time, but it always existed. We were affected by it before we understood it."

3. Writers of philosophical arguments often use hypothetical examples to test a theory's validity. In paragraph 6, Chris unwittingly uses a hypothetical example that many would find insensitive to the Chinese. Propose a different hypothetical example that would test the validity of ethical relativism without offending any potential audience.

    A. One could not blame a person of Chinese heritage for dismissing Chris's arguments in paragraph 6! Perhaps Chris could use an example that is more historically based, such as the example of Mormons and polygamy or the example of peyote use in some Indian rituals.

4. Characterize Chris's style in this paper. Does he use effective transitions? Does he use a variety of sentence structures?

    A. Chris does have difficulty making a smooth transition between paragraphs. Look at the two paragraphs that precede his conclusion. His reference to Benedict's statement seems to come out of the blue, with little relation to the information in the preceding paragraph. Also, Chris may want to experiment with sentence structure. Introductory phrases and subordinate clauses could help him connect his thoughts from sentence to sentence and create a more interesting style.

Sample Philosophy Paper 6

1. Throughout this paper, Anthony fails to introduce quotations used from his source. Why is it necessary to provide both parenthetical documentation and introductions to quotations? What are some examples of appropriate introductory phrases?

A. Parenthetical documentation and introductions to quotations work together to make clear where a reference to a source begins and ends. Some useful introductory phrases, or tags, include the following: "According to," "One notable critic argues," "She states."
2. Compare Anthony's documentation format with the *MLA* format in the overview to writing in the humanities. What would you do to Anthony's documentation to make it conform to *MLA* style?
A. Anthony should make use of the format for documenting an essay within an edition.
3. How would you describe the organization of Anthony's paper? Is it entirely a subject-by-subject approach? Are both subjects, ethical absolutism and ethical relativism, discussed in detail?
A. Anthony shifts back and forth between his two subjects. He gives short shrift to ethical absolutism, wedging his discussion of it mainly into two middle paragraphs.
4. In his final paragraph, Anthony refers to the rise of Hitler in Germany as an argument against ethical absolutism. He is wrong in this regard. Fascism was based on moral relativism, on there not being any external absolute value or truth. Can you suggest a better example to use in arguing against ethical absolutism?
A. Anthony's example of Hitler in Germany also lacks originality. More subtle and accurate examples might be garnered from Benedict's essay or other writings on primitive cultures.
5. Does Anthony take into account counterarguments against relativism? What arguments against relativism—some of which we have seen in previous papers—could the writer address?
A. Anthony could address the issue of moral progress and the question of how one defines a moral group.

Business Assignment 2

Sample Business Paper 4

1. Melissa's second paragraph should explain the principle governing the situation described in the article but doesn't. What skill do you think her teacher was trying to develop through this part of the assignment?
A. The second part of the paper should be an analysis. The teacher wants students to recognize, understand, and explain

INSTRUCTOR'S MANUAL

51

a principle relating to the study of macroeconomics that underlies a present economic situation. During class, the teacher explains a certain principle and then gives examples of situations where this principle is at work. To understand the principle for themselves, students need to do the same: make connections between principles and situations. This task requires students to read through appropriate periodicals until they find a situation exemplifying a principle studied in class. As proof of their knowledge, they must explain the connection in the type of paper called for by the assignment. Melissa doesn't explain the connection; she merely identifies the subject (international trade and restrictions).

2. Reread the assignment carefully and try to visualize the contents of the macroeconomics course it comes from. Given your understanding of what this assignment is about and what the teacher was hoping to see in students' responses, what are some specific features missing from Melissa's second paragraph? In other words, what could we reasonably expect to find that she doesn't provide?
   A. i. A clear definition and/or explanation of the principles involving international trade and restrictions.
       ii. An explanation of how these principles apply to this specific case of Japan buying U.S. semiconductors.
       iii. Possibly a brief explanation of how this one situation fits into U.S.-Japanese trade and world trade.

Sample Business Paper 5

1. Nathan presents several points in his summary paragraph, but you may have finished it wondering why he didn't provide more. Reread the article from *Business Week*. What details could he have included? Rewrite Nathan's first paragraph, adding these details to make it more informative.

   A. Additional details that could be included:
      a. Consumer spending has the greatest effect on economic expansion.
      b. The demand for single family homes has dropped, reflecting past federal attempts to tighten the money supply.
      c. Weakened auto sales shows a reaction to tighter money, especially at a time when Detroit was offering some of its most generous incentives.

d. The slowdown in consumer spending is probably temporary, because consumer spirits are high.
e. In some cases, rising interest rates benefit consumers, because interest accounts for a larger part of personal income than profits from manufacturing.

Sample paragraph:
The U.S. economy is steadily growing, even though the Fed is tightening the money supply, mainly because consumer spending has the greatest effect on economic expansion. This growth is mainly attributed to the purchasing strength of the consumer, which is being fueled by steady job and income expansion. The growth in the G.N.P. has seen a moderate jump from 2% to 2.4% for the fourth quarter. This steady growth has caused the inflation-fearing Fed to push the discount rate from 6.5% to just below 10% in late March. The Fed also raised interest rates on three-month treasury bills from 5.5% to around 9.5% in an attempt to slow down consumer spending. Some slowdown has occurred, reflecting past federal attempts to tighten the money supply. The demand for single family houses dropped, and auto sales weakened at a time when Detroit was offering some of its most generous incentives. This slowdown in consumer spending is probably temporary, however: Consumer spirits are high and, in some cases, rising interest rates benefit consumers because interest accounts for a larger part of personal income than profits from manufacturing.

2. Nathan tells us that the article describes the "monetarist approach" to economics. Use your library to learn what this approach is and write a brief paragraph describing it.
    A. Nathan's second paragraph explains this approach fairly well. Your students' paragraphs should go into more detail explaining how inflation can be controlled by raising the discount rate, selling bonds on the open market, and raising the reserve requirement.

3. Nathan's paper has numerous surface errors. Go through the two paragraphs and correct as many as you can find.
    A. The errors involve mainly punctuation problems (commas and hyphens).